THE
unofficial GUIDE®
ᵀᴼ Chicago

8TH EDITION

THE *unofficial* GUIDE®
TO Chicago

8TH EDITION

DAVID HOEKSTRA *with*
ALICE VAN HOUSEN *and* LAURIE LEVY

Please note that prices fluctuate in the course of time and that travel information changes under the impact of many factors that influence the travel industry. We therefore suggest that you write or call ahead for confirmation when making your travel plans. Every effort has been made to ensure the accuracy of information throughout this book, and the contents of this publication are believed to be correct at the time of printing. Nevertheless, the publishers cannot accept responsibility for errors or omissions, for changes in details given in this guide, or for the consequences of any reliance on the information provided by the same. Assessments of attractions and so forth are based upon the authors' own experiences; therefore, descriptions given in this guide necessarily contain an element of subjective opinion, which may not reflect the publisher's opinion or dictate a reader's own experience on another occasion. Readers are invited to write the publisher with ideas, comments, and suggestions for future editions.

Published by:
John Wiley & Sons, Inc.
111 River Street
Hoboken, NJ 07030-5774

Produced by Menasha Ridge Press

Cover design by Michael J. Freeland

Interior design by Vertigo Design

For information on our other products and services or to obtain technical support, please contact our Customer Care Department within the United States at 800-762-2974, outside the United States at 317-572-3993, or by fax at 317-572-4002.

John Wiley & Sons, Inc., also publishes its books in a variety of electronic formats. Some content that appears in print may not be available in electronic formats.

ISBN 978-0-470-37999-8

Manufactured in the United States of America

5 4 3 2 1

CONTENTS

LIST *of* MAPS

ABOUT *the* AUTHORS

LEAD WRITER **David Hoekstra** is a staff writer and columnist at the *Chicago Sun-Times.* He won a 1987 Chicago Newspaper Guild Stick-O-Type Award for Column Writing for outstanding commentary on Chicago nightlife. He has been a contributing writer for *Playboy* and the *Chicago Reader* and a contributing editor for *Chicago* magazine. His anthology of *Sun-Times* travel columns, *Ticket to Everywhere,* was published by Lake Claremont Press in 2000.

FORMER RESTAURANT CONSULTANT **Alice Van Housen** (Part Eight, Dining and Restaurants) is a writer, reviewer, and editor for a variety of food-focused publications and Web sites. She has served as Chicago editor for the print and online editions of *Zagat Survey* since 2001. She has also contributed dining chapters to *Frommer's Chicago* and *Mobil Travel Guides;* served as founding editor of *Local Palate,* a monthly foodie newspaper; and written for numerous local and national publications, including *Fast Company,* the *Los Angeles Times, Wine & Spirits, Plate, Restaurants & Institutions, Restaurant Business,* the *Chicago Tribune*'s Metromix and RedEye supplements, the *Chicago Sun-Times,* the *Chicago Reader, Chicago Social,* and *Front Desk Chicago.* In addition, she has been a contributing Chicago reviewer for the Citysearch online-entertainment and dining guide since its original incarnation as Chicago Sidewalk in 1996.

JOURNALIST–FICTION WRITER **Laurie Levy** (Part Nine, Shopping in Chicago) has written locally for the *Chicago Tribune,* the *Chicago Sun-Times, The Chicago Collection, Chicago* magazine, and *Today's Chicago Woman,* among others, as well as for national publications such as *Business Traveler, Travel Agent,* and *Four Seasons Magazine.* She is the author of three nonfiction books and is an award-winning short-story writer and novelist.

Chicago at a Glance

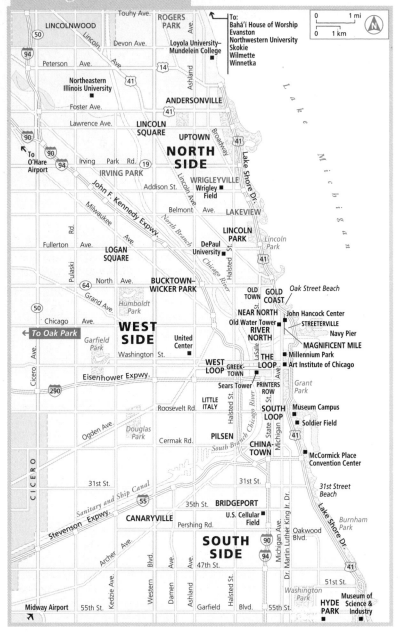

LINCOLNWOOD

Touhy Ave.

ROGERS PARK

To:
Bahá'í House of Worship
Evanston
Northwestern University
Skokie
Wilmette
Winnetka

0   1 mi
0   1 km

Lincoln   Ave.

Devon Ave.

Loyola University–
Mundelein College

Peterson   Ave.

Ashland   Ave.

Northeastern
Illinois University

ANDERSONVILLE

Foster Ave.

Lawrence Ave.

LINCOLN
SQUARE

UPTOWN

NORTH
SIDE

Broadway

To
O'Hare
Airport

Irving   Park   Rd.

IRVING PARK

WRIGLEYVILLE

Lake Shore Dr.

L
a
k
e

M
i
c
h
i
g
a
n

Addison St.

Wrigley
Field

John F. Kennedy Expwy.

Milwaukee

Ave.

North Branch

Lincoln Ave.

Belmont   Ave.

LAKEVIEW

LINCOLN
PARK

Lincoln
Park

Fullerton   Ave.

Pulaski

LOGAN
SQUARE

DePaul
University

Halsted St.

Chicago River

North   Ave.

BUCKTOWN–
WICKER PARK

Grand Ave.

Humboldt
Park

OLD
TOWN

GOLD
COAST

Oak Street Beach

Chicago   Ave.

WEST
SIDE

Garfield
Park

NEAR NORTH

Old Water Tower

RIVER
NORTH

John Hancock Center

STREETERVILLE

Navy Pier

To Oak Park

United
Center

MAGNIFICENT MILE

Washington   St.

WEST
LOOP

GREEK-
TOWN

LaSalle

THE
LOOP

Millennium Park

Art Institute of Chicago

Eisenhower Expwy.

Michigan Ave.

Cicero   Ave.

Sears Tower

PRINTERS
ROW

Grant
Park

LITTLE
ITALY

Halsted St.

Chicago River

SOUTH
LOOP

Museum Campus

Roosevelt Rd.

Soldier Field

Ogden Ave.

Douglas
Park

PILSEN

State

CHINA-
TOWN

Michigan

Cermak Rd.

South Branch Chicago River

McCormick Place
Convention Center

31st St.

31st St.

31st Street
Beach

Sanitary and Ship Canal

35th St.

BRIDGEPORT

Dr. Martin Luther King Jr. Dr.

Burnham
Park

CICERO

CANARYVILLE

U.S. Cellular
Field

Lake Shore Dr.

Stevenson   Expwy.

Pershing Rd.

Oakwood
Blvd.

Archer   Ave.

SOUTH
SIDE

Michigan Ave.

Kedzie Ave.

Western   Ave.

Damen   Ave.

Ashland   Ave.

Halsted St.

Blvd.

47th St.

51st St.

Washington
Park

Midway Airport

55th St.

Garfield   Blvd.   55th St.

HYDE
PARK

Museum of
Science &
Industry

INTRODUCTION

CHICAGO IS THE FRONT PORCH OF AMERICA. Few major American cities are as welcoming. Should you lose your way along North Michigan Avenue, Chicagoans will be happy to help you with directions. They will stop. They will steer the course. And if they have time, they probably will draw a map and buy you a cup of coffee. A majority of the city's residents were born and raised here; others came to Chicago from Michigan, Wisconsin, and northwest Indiana. Whether natives or transplants, they take remarkable ownership in their city.

As with any midwestern front porch, there's room for all kinds of characters. Mayor Richard J. Daley, for instance, likes to act like the crotchety patriarch, but he's really not that bad. (Sometimes he even cries at press conferences.) He's been mayor since 1989, proof that Chicagoans don't like a lot of change. Daley's father was mayor too, from 1955 until his death in 1976.

The city has witnessed tremendous growth under the current Mayor Daley. Downtown is booming after a decade of decline. New dining, shopping, and entertainment choices are enticing young people back downtown to live. Chicago has also become one of the most beautiful cities in America. Flowers and shrubs grow along city sidewalks and in median strips. Tourists consistently comment on how clean the city is.

If New York is "The Big Apple," Chicago is "Green Acres." The mayor has helped create initiatives to increase green roof usage in his goal to make Chicago "the greenest city in America." There's even a rooftop garden with more than 21,000 plants at City Hall downtown. Plus, Chicago has one of the most architecturally recognizable bridge systems in the world. The city has installed a computerized lighting system that at night illuminates 11 bridges along the main branch of the Chicago River—a river that runs backward. Chicago is quirky that way.

Sometimes, though, Mayor Daley and his pals on the front porch get a little carried away with gussying up Chicago. One alderman became famous for his proposed legislation to put diapers on carriage horses. The city council has banned smoking in bars and restaurants. The council also banned foie gras from city restaurants in 2006, then repealed the ban in 2008 to the relief of local gourmands. The city even has its first fashion director. No, you need not wear a coat and tie to gain entrance into Chicago—the city is just trying to enhance its design-and-fashion community.

It took a long time for Chicago to change its image. For many years tourists associated the city with the rat-a-tat-tat of gangster Al Capone, the muscle of the stockyards, and the hardscrabble prose of Nelson Algren, Studs Terkel, and newspaperman Mike Royko. That gritty aura still exists, but now it's a faded tattoo under a new shirt. While leading the Bulls to six NBA titles, Michael Jordan gave Chicago a contemporary global presence. On the flip side, the numbing futility of the Cubs—who haven't won a World Series since 1908—has turned the team's Wrigley Field home into a carnival-like beer garden. Chicago's new face also includes talk-show queen Oprah Winfrey and trash-TV king Jerry Springer. And, along with the Daleys and other legendarily colorful local politicos, we proudly claim Barack Obama, the 44th president of the United States. (No, he's not a native Chicagoan, but why nitpick?)

Visitors should keep in mind that Chicago is not big on nicknames. No one under the age of 90 calls Chicago "Chi-Town" anymore. "The Windy City" is a misnomer: Amarillo, Texas, and Wichita, Kansas, are windier than Chicago; newspaper people coined the term for the city's blustery politicians. And Frank Sinatra's "toddlin' town" is now a world-class city.

It's also America's most livable big city. Where New York is condensed and Los Angeles is spread out, Chicago is easy to get around. Chicago Transit Authority (CTA) buses and trains are generally reliable, and city streets are laid out in an accessible grid system. Michael Jordan still keeps a home in the suburbs, while Chicago-area native Vince Vaughn lives on and off in the area. Rocker Billy Corgan of Smashing Pumpkins never left town, and Mike Ditka remains a Chicago icon, even though it's been more than 20 years since he took "Da Bears" to the Super Bowl. Chicago is a melting pot of diverse personalities, an eclectic abode of ethnic influences. The door is always open, sure to be a portal to memorable adventure.

ABOUT THIS GUIDE

WHY "UNOFFICIAL"?

Most "official" guides to Chicago celebrate the well-known sights, promote local restaurants and hotels indiscriminately, and leave out a lot of good stuff. This book is different. An irreverent city demands an irreverent guide.

Instead of pandering to the tourist industry, we'll tell you if a well-known restaurant's crummy food isn't worth the wait. We'll complain loudly about overpriced hotel rooms that aren't convenient to the Loop (that's the core of downtown) or the airport, and we'll guide you away from the crowds and congestion for a break now and then.

THE PROBLEM WITH GUIDEBOOKS

Most guidebooks are collections of lists. This is true regardless of whether the information is literally presented in list form or artfully distributed through pages of prose. There is insufficient detail in a list, and prose can present tedious helpings of nonessential or marginally useful information. Such guides offer little more than departure points from which readers initiate their own quests.

Many guides are readable and well researched, but they tend to be difficult to use. To select a hotel, for example, a reader must study several pages of descriptions with only the boldfaced hotel names breaking up large blocks of text. Readers generally must work through all the write-ups before beginning to narrow their choices. Recommendations, if any, lack depth and conviction. These guides compound rather than solve problems by failing to narrow the average traveler's choices down to a thoughtfully considered and manageable few.

HOW UNOFFICIAL GUIDES ARE DIFFERENT

Readers care about the author's opinion. The authors care about their city. This, coupled with the fact that the traveler wants quick answers (as opposed to endless alternatives), dictates that authors should be explicit, prescriptive, and above all, direct. The *Unofficial Guide* tries to be just that. It spells out alternatives and recommends specific action. It simplifies complicated destinations and attractions and helps the traveler feel in control in even the most unfamiliar environments. The objective of the *Unofficial Guide* is not to have all the information, but, rather, the most accessible, useful information—unbiased by affiliation with any organization or industry.

Special Features

What you'll get in an *Unofficial Guide*:

- Friendly introductions to Chicago's vast array of ethnic neighborhoods.
- "Best of" listings giving our well-qualified opinions on everything from bagels to pizza, four-star hotels to the best night views of Chicago.
- Listings keyed to your interests, so you can pick and choose.
- Advice on avoiding crowds, traffic, and excess expense.
- Maps that make it easy to find the places you want to visit.
- A hotel chart that helps narrow your choices with expedience.

- Compact listings that include only those restaurants, clubs, and hotels we think are worth considering.

What you *won't* get in an *Unofficial Guide:*

- Long, useless lists where everything looks the same.
- Insufficient information that gets you where you want to go at the worst possible time.
- Information without advice on how to use it.

HOW THIS GUIDE WAS RESEARCHED AND WRITTEN

MANY GUIDEBOOKS HAVE BEEN WRITTEN about Chicago, but few have been evaluative. Some practically regurgitate hotel and tourist promotional material. In preparing this book, nothing was taken for granted. Each museum, monument, art gallery, hotel, restaurant, shop, and attraction was evaluated and rated by trained observers according to formal criteria. Interviews were conducted to determine what tourists of all ages enjoyed most—and least—during their Chicago visit.

The trained evaluator is responsible for much more than observing and cataloging. While the average tourist may be gazing in awe from the observation deck at the Sears Tower, the professional is rating the attraction in terms of how quickly crowds move, the location of restrooms, and how well children can see over the railing in front of the plate-glass windows. The evaluator also checks out nearby attractions, alternatives if the line at a main attraction is too long, and where to find the best lunch. Observers use detailed checklists to analyze hotel rooms, restaurants, nightclubs, and attractions. Finally, evaluator ratings and observations are integrated with tourist reactions and the opinions of patrons for a comprehensive, high-quality profile of each feature and service.

LETTERS, COMMENTS, AND QUESTIONS FROM READERS

WE WANT TO LEARN FROM OUR MISTAKES, as well as from the input of our readers, and to improve with each book and edition. We encourage feedback, both positive and negative. Reader's comments and observations will be incorporated in revised editions of the *Unofficial Guide* and will contribute immeasurably to its improvement.

How to Write the Author

David Hoekstra
The Unofficial Guide to Chicago
P.O. Box 43673
Birmingham, AL 35243
davehoekstra@att.net

Because our work often takes us out of the office for long periods of time, please bear with us if our response is delayed.

Reader Survey

At the back of the guide you'll find a short questionnaire that you can use to express opinions concerning your Chicago visit. Clip the questionnaire along the dotted line and mail it to the above address.

HOW INFORMATION IS ORGANIZED:
By Subject and Geographic Area

TO GIVE YOU FAST ACCESS to information about the best of Chicago, we've organized material in several formats.

HOTELS Because most people visiting Chicago stay in one hotel for the duration of their trip, we've summarized our coverage of hotels in charts, maps, ratings, and rankings that allow you to quickly focus your decision-making process. We concentrate on the variables that differentiate one hotel from another: location, size, room quality, services, amenities, and cost. Comparative and informational hotel charts can be found in Part Three.

RESTAURANTS Chicago is one of the best restaurant cities in the world, and its reputation continues to grow. Because you'll probably eat a dozen or more restaurant meals during your stay, and because you can't even predict what you might be in the mood for on a Saturday night, we provide detailed profiles of the best restaurants in and around Chicago in Part Eight.

ATTRACTIONS To save you time, money, and foot ache, we've organized many of the city's sights into a handy time-saving chart divided by location. Gonna be in the Loop for dinner? Well, see what's in the area and organize your day accordingly.

ENTERTAINMENT AND NIGHTLIFE Visitors frequently try several different clubs during their stay. Because nightspots, like restaurants, are usually selected spontaneously after arriving in Chicago, we believe detailed descriptions are warranted. The best clubs and lounges are profiled in Part Eleven.

GEOGRAPHIC AREA Once you've decided where you're going, getting there becomes the next decision. To help you do that, we've divided Chicago by areas and neighborhoods:

North Side	South Side
North Central–O'Hare Airport	Southern Suburbs
Near North Side	Western Suburbs
The Loop (the core of downtown)	Northwest Suburbs
South Loop	Northern Suburbs
South Central–Midway Airport	

All listings of hotels, attractions, restaurants, and nightspots include location information. For example, if you're staying at a hotel on Chicago's Magnificent Mile (North Michigan Avenue) and want to sample the latest in New American cuisine, scanning the restaurant profiles for those in Near North will get you where you want to go. Remember—in Chicago, each neighborhood is uniquely its own.

PART ONE

UNDERSTANDING *the* CITY

 A **BRIEF HISTORY** *of* **CHICAGO**

THE AMERICAN SPIRIT IS EMBEDDED IN CHICAGO. You hear the sound of rebirth on any given day here. There's the rhythm of electric drills rehabbing old bungalows and the eclectic laughter of children in city parks. Street musicians play steady blues tunes, and around every corner someone is arguing about the Cubs and the White Sox.

Chicago is a true American city, one on the cusp of an eternal spring. It was founded on a suspicious swamp and later rebuilt itself from the ashes of a devastating fire into the nation's third-largest city. With a lakefront skyline recognized around the world, it's a town that owes its verve to generations of big shoulders.

Chicago is going through a renaissance unlike that of any other big city in America. The election of President Barack Obama has brought tremendous pride to residents of all walks of life. (We consider him a Chicagoan, although before he moved to the White House, the magnetic Hawaii-born leader had lived in the city only since 1985.) His election also gives juice to Chicago's bid to host the 2016 Summer Olympics.

Chicago is also a cauldron of bubbling contrasts: shimmering skyscrapers and postindustrial urban decay; a long-suppressed black minority that points with pride to Obama and Oprah. Chicago is Al Capone and Michael Jordan, Jane Addams and Hugh Hefner, Studs Terkel and Saul Bellow.

Muckraking journalist H. L. Mencken was charmed by the place: "I give you Chicago!" he wrote. "It is not London and Harvard. It is not Paris and buttermilk. It is American in every chitling and spare-rib. It is alive from snout to tail."

Chicago is a city of legends, of precious visionaries, and of quite a few scoundrels. Built on swampland at the edge of a prairie, the city has endured cycles of booms and busts. As the nation grew westward,

- Chicago's first nonnative settler was a black man, Jean-Baptiste Pointe du Sable, who established a trading post on the Chicago River in 1779.

- In the first of a long line of innovations, Chicago elevated its street grades more than ten feet just before the Civil War.

- The first Republican president, Abraham Lincoln, was nominated by the new party in Chicago in 1860.

- The nation's first steel railroad rails came out of the North Side in 1865.

- The world's first skyscrapers were built in Chicago following the Great Fire of 1871.

- In 1900, the flow of the Chicago River was reversed, providing safe drinking water from Lake Michigan.

- Chicago's population peaked at 3.6 million in 1950.

- Three of the world's tallest buildings rose in Chicago: Sears Tower, Trump International Hotel & Tower, and the AON Center.

Chicago found itself in a great geographical position to supply raw materials that fed the expansion. The city was incorporated March 4, 1837. "Interesting women are in demand here," a lonely pioneer wrote from Chicago to the *New York Star* in 1837. The women soon arrived—and Chicago began to kick up its heels.

BEGINNINGS

Twelve thousand years ago, Lake Chicago, a larger version of Lake Michigan, covered much of what is now the Midwest. As this great glacial lake receded, it left behind a vast prairie and shoreline swamp that linked North America's two great waterways: the Mississippi River (via the Des Plaines and Illinois rivers) and the Great Lakes. The area's first residents were Native Americans, led by Chief Blackhawk—thus, the name of Chicago's hockey team the Chicago Blackhawks. They named the area *Checago* or *Checaguar*, which likely meant "wild onion" or "swamp gas," probably a reference to the pungent smell of decaying marsh vegetation that permeated the swamp. (After all, deep-dish pizza had yet to be invented.) Either way, the name implied great strength.

FIRST SETTLERS AND A MASSACRE

IN 1673 TWO FRENCH EXPLORERS were the first Europeans to set eyes on what is now Chicago: Louis Jolliet, who was searching for gold, and Father Jacques Marquette, who was searching for souls. When their Native American allies showed them the portage trail linking the Mississippi Valley and the Great Lakes, Jolliet saw Chicago's potential immediately. He predicted to Marquette, "Here some day will be found one of the world's great cities." As a token of appreciation, today the city of Joliet sits along the Illinois–Michigan Canal, 45 miles southwest of Chicago. Joliet is also on the migratory Route 66 from Chicago to Los Angeles.

In the late 18th century, the flat prairies stretching west were as empty and primeval as when the last glacier had retreated a thousand years before. Chicago's first nonnative resident, Jean-Baptiste Pointe du Sable, arrived in 1779 and erected a rough-hewn log house on the north bank of the Chicago River. A tall, French-speaking son of a Quebec merchant and a black slave, du Sable established a trading post at what is now North Michigan Avenue. As the local Native Americans noted, "The first white man to live here was a black man."

After du Sable moved to Missouri in 1800 (leaving a handful of other traders at the mouth of the river), Chicago's first boom began. But first the frontier outpost had to endure a massacre. The Native Americans had been run out in 1795, ceding huge tracts of midwestern land—including "six miles square at the mouth of the Chickago River." The swamp turned into a speculator's dream almost overnight. The wheeling and dealing nature of Chicago was born.

Soldiers of the fledgling United States Republic arrived from Detroit in 1803 and erected Fort Dearborn near what is now the corner of lower Wacker Drive and Michigan Avenue. After evacuating the fort during the War of 1812 against the British, settlers and soldiers fleeing the fort were ambushed by Native Americans in league with the enemy; 52 men, women, and children were slain in the Fort Dearborn Massacre.

BOOM . . .

ILLINOIS BECAME A STATE IN 1818—a time when Chicago was still a struggling backwater far north of southern population centers—and in 1829 the state legislature appointed a commission to plot a canal route between Lake Michigan and the Mississippi River. Chicago was poised for a population explosion. The pace of westward development from bustling eastern seaboard cities was accelerating in the early 19th century, and pioneers roared into the Midwest. The Erie Canal opened in 1825, creating a new water route between Chicago and the East. Pioneer wagons rolled in daily, and Chicago's population swelled from around 50 in 1830 to more than 4,000 in 1837. As waves of Irish and German immigrants arrived, the town's population increased by another 100,000 in the following 30 years.

Speculators swooped in, and lots that sold for $100 in 1830 changed hands for as much as $100,000 in 1837 during a real-estate frenzy fueled by visions of wealth to be made from the planned canal. The first newspaper, the *Chicago Democrat,* was launched in 1833. The editor (and two-time mayor) was "Long John" Wentworth, who liked to carry around a jug of whiskey, allegedly to soothe the blisters on his feet. Naturally, Chicago's first brewery followed in 1836. The first policeman was hired in 1839 and no doubt had his hands full in a town brimming with saloons.

. . . AND BUST

THE BOOM WENT BUST, however, in the Panic of 1837, one of America's first economic depressions. Work on the canal ground to a halt, and many local investors went broke. Slowly, a recovery set in, work on the canal resumed, and Chicago spawned its first ethnic neighborhood.

Originally called Hardscrabble, it was an enclave of Irish laborers digging the waterway. By the time it was annexed in 1863, the South Side neighborhood was known as Bridgeport, later famous as the wellspring for generations of Irish-American politicians—including Mayor Richard J. Daley (aka "Hizzoner") and his son, Mayor Richard M. Daley. The Chicago White Sox are also based in Bridgeport.

A TRANSPORTATION HUB

ALTHOUGH THE WATERWAY WAS A BOON to commerce when it opened in 1848, it was quickly overshadowed by a new form of transportation: railroads. Soon, locomotives were hauling freight along the tracks of the Galena and Chicago Union lines, and the newly opened Chicago Board of Trade brokered commodities in what was to become the world's greatest rail hub. German and Scandinavian immigrants further swelled the city's population, and horse-drawn street railways stimulated the growth of the near suburbs. Also, in 1848, for the first time Chicago was connected with the East by telegraph.

Before growth could proceed much farther, however, the swampbound city had to elevate itself; streets were a quagmire most of the year. Located on the only high spot in the area, Fort Dearborn was torn down in 1868 when the land it stood on was relocated to develop what is now Randolph Street. Street grades were raised as many as a dozen feet, and first floors became basements. It was an impressive technical feat—the first of many to come.

By 1856, Chicago was the hub of ten railroad trunk lines. Lumber from nearby forests, iron ore from Minnesota, and livestock and produce from the fertile Midwest were shipped to the city and manufactured into the products that fueled America's rapid growth. Passenger rail service from New York began in 1857, cutting travel time between the two cities from three weeks to two days. The population of Chicago soared to 28,000 in 1850 and to 110,000 in 1860. Economically, Chicago was the middleman between the East and West, a role it has never ceased to play.

A PRESIDENTIAL NOMINATION AND INNOVATIVE MARKETING

BY 1860 CHICAGO WAS THE NINTH-LARGEST CITY in the United States and hosted the nominating convention of the fledgling Republican Party. "The Wigwam," a jerry-built convention hall with a capacity of 10,000, was erected at Lake and Market streets on the fringe of today's downtown Loop. The Republicans nominated Abraham Lincoln on the third ballot. (Democratic nominee Stephen A. Douglas, incidentally, was a Chicago native.) The city would host another 23 party-nominating conventions, including the controversial 1968 Democratic National Convention. In 1996 the Democrats returned to a city that was more placid and more beautiful.

Just as the city mastered politics and transportation, it shaped marketing geniuses. In 1872 Montgomery Ward opened the world's first mail-order business in the loft of a Chicago barn. Sears, Roebuck & Co. was founded in Chicago, and its influence was felt across America. (The late Roebuck "Pops" Staples of the Chicago-based Staple Singers gospel group had a brother named Sears.) Other legendary names of Chicago merchandising include Marshall Field, Potter Palmer, Samuel Carson, and John Pirie.

One of Chicago's most famous—and odorous—landmarks opened in 1865: the Union Stockyards, Chicago's largest employer for half a century. It was a city within a city, complete with its own newspaper and radio station, from 1865 until it was torn down in 1971. Bubbly Creek ran through the yards. By 1863 the city had earned the moniker "Porkopolis" by processing enough hogs to stretch all the way to New York. Gustavus Swift of meatpacking fame boasted, "We use everything but the squeal." The goat that led lambs up the ramp to the killing floor was called Judas. The darker sides of the yard— poor sanitation problems and horrific working and living conditions for its laborers—were brought to light in 1906 in Upton Sinclair's *The Jungle*. Sinclair later said he aimed at the country's heart and hit its stomach instead.

INDUSTRIAL MIGHT

THE GRITTY CITY CONTINUED TO GROW. In the years following the Civil War, Chicago ranked as the world's largest grain handler and the biggest North American lumber market. The North Side's huge McCormick plant churned out reapers and other farm equipment that were shipped around the globe. George Pullman built his first sleeping car in 1864, the nation's first steel rails came out of the North Side in 1865, and the number of sea vessels docked at Chicago in 1869 exceeded the combined number calling on New York and five other major U.S. ports.

While the swamps were a thing of the past, the city was still seeped in quagmires of different sorts. Cholera and typhoid struck regularly as Chicago fouled its Lake Michigan drinking water via the dangerously polluted Chicago River. Corruption at City Hall became rampant (it still is, in some quarters), and the city was notorious for its gambling, saloons, and 400 brothels. The most famous house of ill repute was Roger Plant's Under the Willow, which covered half a square block near Wells and Monroe streets. Plant painted some of Chicago's first graffiti on the side of his brothel: "Why Not?" Plant, a wealthy Englishman, was married with 20 children. In contrast to the luxury of Plant's bordello, hundreds of thousands of poor Chicagoans were jammed into modest pine cottages on unpaved streets without sewers. Some observers warned of dire consequences unless the city cleaned up its act.

THE GREAT CHICAGO FIRE OF 1871

THOSE WARNINGS PROVED RIGHT. Chicago in 1871 was a densely packed city of 300,000 whose homes were built almost entirely of wood. A lengthy drought had turned the town tinder-dry, setting the stage for the most indelibly mythic event in the city's history: the Great Fire of 1871.

Legend has it that Mrs. Maureen O'Leary's cow kicked over a lantern and started the fire (supposedly, she had gone back inside her house to fetch some salt for an ailing animal). The fire spread rapidly from the O'Leary barn in the West Side, burning its way north and east through the commercial center and residential North Side. More than 17,000 buildings were destroyed, 100,000 people were left homeless, and 250 were killed. The city lay in ashes. The 100-foot-tall Chicago water works, built in 1867, was the only public building to survive and still stands today across the street from the Water Tower Place shopping mall.

Chicago was rebuilt—this time with fireproof brick. Architects, sensing unlimited opportunity, flocked to Chicago. In five years, the city's commercial core was restored with buildings erected to meet stringent fire codes, and a tradition of architectural vision was established. In 1889, the city annexed a ring of suburbs and was crowned America's Second City in the census of 1890.

The city was emerging from an era of cutthroat social Darwinism into an age of social reform. Jane Addams's Hull-House became a model for the nation's settlement-house movement. Addams and her upper-class compatriots provided fresh milk for babies, taught immigrants English, and set up day-care centers for the children of working mothers. Hull House was at ground zero of new immigration to Chicago, in a neighborhood where pathways were made of plank and streets turned to mud in the soggy spring. The crown prince of Belgium once remarked after visiting Hull House, "Such a street—no, not one—existed in Belgium."

The Columbian Exposition of 1893 was a fabulously successful World's Fair that left indelible cultural marks on the city, including the Art Institute of Chicago and the Field Museum. The era ushered in the skyscraper, a distinctly urban form created in Chicago that has reshaped the look of skylines around the world. The University of Chicago, one of the world's great research institutions, was founded in 1892 with funds from the Rockefellers.

In 1900, another architectural feat was performed when the flow of the Chicago River was reversed, much to the relief of a population in desperate need of safe drinking water from Lake Michigan—and to the consternation of populations downstream.

Architect Daniel Burnham left his mark on the city in 1909 by pursuing a plan to preserve Chicago's pristine lakefront through a creation of a series of parks and the acquisition of a green belt of forestlands on the city's periphery. With his partner John Root, Burnham had already built 16-story skyscrapers like the Monadnock Building—the tallest masonry building in Chicago, and possibly the world, still standing at 53 West Jackson Boulevard—on floating "rafts" placed in Chicago's murky earth. "Make no little plans," Burnham urged, and today's Mayor Daley still subscribes to the "Burnham Plan." With the exception of the massive McCormick Place convention center, the lakefront remains an uncluttered recreational mecca . . . and someday they'll probably be planting gardens atop the convention center.

LABOR TROUBLES

AROUND THE TURN OF THE 19TH CENTURY, Chicago seethed with labor unrest and the threat of class warfare. Nascent labor movements argued for better working and living conditions for the city's laborers. Seven policemen were killed in the 1886 Haymarket Riot (on Randolph Street between Des Plaines and Halsted streets), who originally had been called to denounce the police shootings of four workingmen. Four anarchists were subsequently hanged. Later the Pullman Strike of 1894 was crushed by U.S. Army troops after wages were sharply cut by the sleeping-car magnate.

The lowest rung in Chicago's pecking order was reserved for blacks, who started to arrive from the South in substantial numbers, reaching 110,000 by 1920. Most of the families came from Arkansas, Louisiana, Mississippi, and Tennessee, a migration that later gave birth to Chicago blues. Segregation formed a "black belt" ghetto with buildings in poor repair—often without indoor toilets—and substantially higher rents than white housing. A six-day riot in July 1919 left 23 blacks and 15 whites dead; the governor had to send in troops to quell the uprising. But the underlying causes of the unrest weren't addressed.

Carl Sandburg celebrated the city and its tradition of hard work in verse ("Hog Butcher for the World, / Tool Maker, Stacker of Wheat, / Player with Railroads and the Nation's Freight Handler; / Stormy, husky, brawling, / City of the Big Shoulders"). Other pre-Depression literary giants from Chicago include Theodore Dreiser and Ben Hecht; later came James T. Farrell, Nelson Algren, Richard Wright, Saul Bellow, and Pulitzer Prize–winning newspapermen Roger Ebert and Mike Royko.

THE ROARING '20s

FOLLOWING WORLD WAR I, the focus of power shifted from industrialists to politicians; crooked pols and gangsters plundered the city. The smoke-filled room was invented in Chicago at the 1920 Republican National Convention when Warren G. Harding's nomination was dealt and sealed in Suite 804–805 at the Blackstone Hotel.

A baby-faced crook from New York named Alphonse Capone came to Chicago in 1920, right after Prohibition became national law. It was no coincidence: Chicago was soon awash in bootleg hooch, much of it illegally imported by Capone and his mob. If an alderman opposed an item on Capone's agenda, the gangster would wait outside council chambers to smack the alderman around. Capone's younger rival was Dion O'Banion, who ran a flower shop near Holy Name Cathedral. (During the 1970s, there was a Chicago punk-rock club named after the florist-criminal.) But the short, pot-bellied Capone still holds the world record for the highest gross income ever accumulated by a private citizen in a year: $105 million in 1927, when he was 28 years old.

Alas, Capone didn't pay his taxes and was put away by a group of Feds, know as the Untouchables, led by Eliot Ness. The gangster—aka "Scarface," still Chicago's best-known historical figure—served eight years in Alcatraz before dying of syphilis in 1947. During the 1930s Capone's New York compatriot "Big Jim" Colosimo ruled much of Chicago's underworld from his restaurant-showroom, Colosimo's Cafe, on Wabash Avenue. George M. Cohan was a regular guest performer when he visited Chicago. The house favorite was vaudeville singer Dale Winter, whom a newspaper reporter discovered singing in a church choir. Another Colosimo act, Texas Guinan, greeted the audience by saying, "Hello, suckers!"

ANOTHER DEPRESSION . . . AND ANOTHER FAIR

IN THE 1930s, THE GREAT DEPRESSION hit Chicago like the ton of bricks it never had during the Great Chicago Fire. Out-of-work men and women marched down State Street. Businessmen went bust. Nearly 1,400 families were evicted from their homes in the first half of 1931 alone. Hardest hit were Chicago's blacks, whose population then totaled about 250,000.

Yet in 1933 the city hosted another World's Fair: the Century of Progress Exposition, which occupied 47 acres of lakefront south of the Loop. The show attracted about 39 million visitors and actually made money. Texas Guinan appeared at the fair, but the star of the show was fan dancer Sally Rand, who went on stage nude with large props—not only fans but feather boas and large balloons . . . very large balloons. Like Little Egypt at the Columbian Exposition 40 years earlier, Rand drew mobs of men to her shows and further embellished the city's randy reputation.

THE SECOND WORLD WAR

WORLD WAR II AND AN UNPARALLELED SURGE in defense spending lifted Chicago—and the rest of the country—out of the Depression. The $1.3 billion spent to build war plants in the city was unmatched anywhere else in America.

In 1942 a team at the University of Chicago, under the direction of physicist Enrico Fermi, built the world's first nuclear reactor under the stands of Stagg Field, named after the university's football coach, Amos Alonzo Stagg. The school's ability to control the energy of the atom provided critical technology for the development of nuclear power and allowed the nation to embark on the ambitious Manhattan Project, which led to the creation of the atomic bomb. Today the portentous site at Stagg Field is marked by a squat, brooding Henry Moore sculpture.

A NEW ERA

CHICAGO REACHED ITS PEAK POPULATION of 3.6 million in 1950, a year that marked the beginning of a long slide of urban dwellers moving to surrounding suburbs. Following eras of settlement, growth, booms, busts, depression, and war, Chicago moved into one last period: the 21-year rule of Mayor Richard J. Daley, a power-monger who left another indelible mark on the city.

Daley was born in Bridgeport, the only child of immigrant Irish-Catholic parents. He was elected mayor in 1955 with 708,222 votes—a number he used on a vanity license plate for his limousine during his years in office. Under Daley, Chicago's motto was "I Will." And Daley did. He shut down gambling houses and scolded aldermen who talked while city council was in session. He bulldozed neighborhoods, built segregated walls of high-rise public housing, and constructed an elaborate system of freeway exchanges in the heart of the city. Critics said the maze of highways cut the hearts out of flourishing neighborhoods and provided accessible corridors for suburban flight. One way or the other, Daley had earned the nick-name "Da Boss."

In the summer of 1966, Dr. Martin Luther King Jr. and a young preacher named Jesse Jackson confronted the Daley machine when Dr. King tried to encourage racial integration of Chicago's immigrant neighborhoods—including Marquette Park, near the South Side area that Daley grew up in. Daley opposed any power base, black or white, that was not Chicago controlled. King's efforts in Chicago were largely unsuccessful, which became a setback for the civil-rights movement.

Daley was a kingmaker for presidents, delivering the winning—though slim—margin to John F. Kennedy in 1960. In 1968, at the peak of the Vietnam conflict, Daley unleashed his police on antiwar protesters at the Democratic National Convention. Some called it a police riot; Crosby, Stills, Nash, and Young sang about it in "Chicago." Hizzoner pugnaciously scowled at news cameras and growled, "Duh policemen isn't dere to create disorder, duh policemen is dere to *preserve* disorder." The whole world was watching. Not all of it understood.

POSTINDUSTRIAL CHICAGO

DALEY PASSED AWAY IN 1976 WHILE STILL MAYOR. At this point, computer operators outnumbered steel-mill workers, and postindustrial Chicago shuffled along. The Gold Coast and the Magnificent Mile were glitzier than ever, and the Playboy Club was hopping. Chicago's work force—what was left of it—was learning to survive in a service economy. More people fled for greener horizons beyond city limits, trading deteriorating schools and racial strife for safer neighborhoods.

But Chicago hung on. In the 1970s and 1980s, a forest of new skyscrapers shot up on the city's skyline, including the Sears Tower, the world's third-tallest building. The Loop survived an attempt (from 1979 to 1996) to prevent automobiles on State Street's ill-fated outdoor shopping mall. After Daley's death, the city saw its first woman mayor, Jane Byrne, who moved into a housing project for a spell, and its first black mayor, Harold Washington, a grandfatherly figure who died in office in 1987. The city entered the 21st century with Mayor Richard "Richie" Daley, son of Hizzoner, solidly in office with his heart still in the South Side—even though he left Bridgeport for the South Loop. Although the city has been leaking population for decades, 2.84 million people still live in Chicago.

"A REAL CITY"

TODAY, CHICAGO COMPRISES 228 SQUARE MILES, with 30 miles stretching along Lake Michigan's shores. It's 550 parks, eight forest preserves, 29 beaches, 250 good restaurants (many of them world-class), 2,000 average restaurants, and dozens of stands selling the best hot dogs around. It's a city where football is serious business and politics is a game. It's heaven for symphony lovers, nirvana for jazz buffs, and the alternative-rock center of America. Come to Chicago, and within a half hour someone will tell you it's "a city of neighborhoods." Sprinkled with curiosities, the city's ethnic districts offer visitors a flavor of the old world and a chance for discovery.

And the Loop? It's back in a big way. Lines form for theaters and steak houses, a ripple effect from the new Millennium Park. Similarly, the United Center gave rebirth to West Madison Street, where new eateries and hipster taverns stand on the site of a 1970s skid row.

Walk along Michigan Avenue late on a Friday afternoon, and watch the lights wink on in the skyscrapers overhead. Take a carriage ride. Hear the voices that build into a choir of character. There will be a warm moment when you will feel at home—and then you will understand the resilient spirit of Chicago.

SKYSCRAPERS *and* *the* PRAIRIE SCHOOL: *Chicago Architecture*

THOUGH NO ONE SERIOUSLY ARGUES Chicago's status as the Second City—even the most avid boosters concede New York's status as America's leading city in population, culture, and finance—the Windy City lays claim to one superlative title that remains undisputed: the world capital of modern architecture.

And it's not just that the skyscraper was born here. A visit to Chicago is a crash course in the various streams of architecture that have helped shape the direction of 20th-century building design. Even folks with an otherwise casual interest in architecture are bedazzled by the architectural heritage displayed here. Chicago is the world's largest outdoor museum of modern architecture.

A BOVINE BEGINNING

A SUBSTANTIAL AMOUNT OF THE CREDIT for Chicago's status in the world of architecture can be laid at the feet of a cow—if it's true that Mrs. O'Leary's cow kicked over a lantern, starting an inferno of mythic proportions. The Great Chicago Fire of 1871 destroyed four square miles of the central city, and architects from around the world flocked to Chicago—not unlike Sir Christopher Wren, who rushed to London after a great fire leveled much of that city in the late 17th century.

Several other factors figured in Chicago's rise to preeminence in building design in the decades after the fire. The rapidly rising value of real estate in the central business district motivated developers to increase building heights as much as they could. Advances in elevator technology freed designers from vertical constraints; easily rentable space no longer needed to be an easy climb from street level.

But most important was the development of the iron-and-steel skeletal frame, which relieved the walls of the burden of carrying a

Chicago's Best Architecture

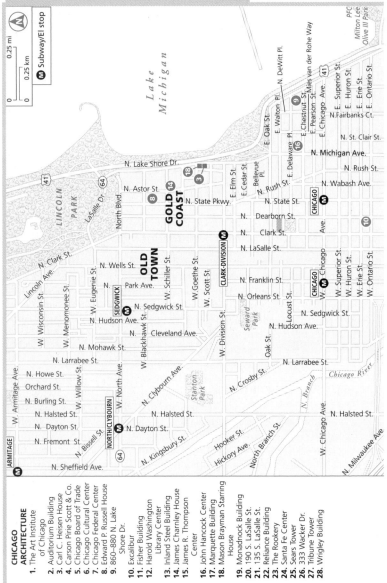

CHICAGO ARCHITECTURE
1. The Art Institute of Chicago
2. Auditorium Building
3. Carl C. Heisen House
4. Carson Pirie Scott & Co.
5. Chicago Board of Trade
6. Chicago Cultural Center
7. Chicago Federal Center
8. Edward P. Russell House
9. 860–880 N. Lake Shore Dr.
10. Excalibur
11. Fisher Building
12. Harold Washington Library Center
13. Inland Steel Building
14. James Charnley House
15. James R. Thompson Center
16. John Hancock Center
17. Marquette Building
18. Mason Brayman Starring House
19. Monadnock Building
20. 190 S. LaSalle St.
21. 135 S. LaSalle St.
22. Reliance Building
23. The Rookery
24. Santa Fe Center
25. Sears Tower
26. 333 Wacker Dr.
27. Tribune Tower
28. Wrigley Building

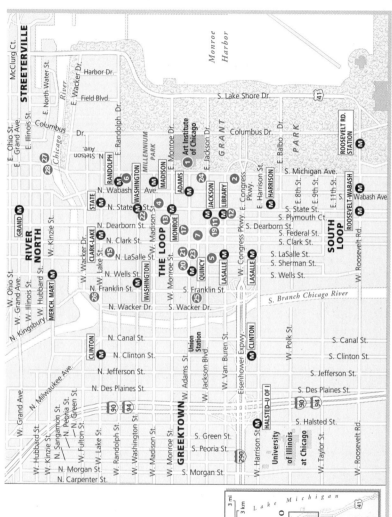

building's weight. For the first time, a structure's exterior walls didn't need to grow thicker as the building grew taller. New technology also allowed for larger windows.

THE CHICAGO SCHOOL

AS NEW TECHNOLOGY TOOK HOLD, many architects felt a building's external form should be equally innovative. The result was a style of architecture with a straightforward expression of structure. A masonry grid covered the steel structure beneath, while projecting bay windows created a lively rhythm on the facade. Any ornamentation was usually subordinated to the overall design and often restricted to the top and bottom thirds of the building, creating a kind of classical column effect. Collectively, the style came to be known as the Chicago School of Architecture.

Early skyscrapers that flaunt the technological innovations that made Chicago famous include the 15-story **Reliance Building** (32 North State Street; Burnham and Root, 1890) and the 12-story structure that until recently housed the **Carson Pirie Scott & Company** department store (1 South State Street; Adler and Sullivan, 1899). These show-off buildings, held up by thin tendons of steel, are close in spirit to the modernist architecture that was to follow.

CLASSICAL DESIGNS BY THE LAKE

DANIEL BURNHAM, WHO DEVELOPED Chicago's urban plan and designed some of its most innovative buildings, also organized the 1893 World's Columbian Exposition. Yet the formal Beaux Arts style used in the major structures that remain were designed by East Coast architects. As a result, cultural institutions such as the **Art Institute** (Michigan Avenue at Adams Street; Shepley, Rutan & Coolidge, 1892) and the **Chicago Cultural Center** (78 East Washington Street; Shepley, Rutan & Coolidge, 1897) have their underlying structures disguised in white, neoclassical historical garb.

THE PRAIRIE SCHOOL

YET NOT ALL OF CHICAGO'S ARCHITECTURAL innovations pushed upward or aped the classical designs of the past. In the early 1900s, Frank Lloyd Wright and his contemporaries were developing a modern style that's now called the Prairie School. The break from historically inspired Victorian house designs is highlighted by low, ground-hugging forms, hovering roofs with deep eaves, and bands of casement windows. Interiors feature open, flowing floor plans, centrally located hearths, natural woodwork, and uniform wall treatments.

Truly shocking in their day, Wright's designs now dot Chicago and its suburbs. The flowing horizontal planes sharply contrast with the upward thrust of skyscrapers in the Loop and convey a feeling of peace and calm. The largest groups of Prairie School houses are found in Oak Park, where Forest Avenue and nearby streets are lined with houses designed by Wright and his disciples.

1920s PROSPERITY AND ART DECO

THE PROSPERITY OF THE 1920s resulted in a building boom; the construction of the Michigan Avenue Bridge encouraged developers to look for sites north of the Chicago River. It was the "heroic age" for the city's skyline, and designers borrowed heavily from European sources. The **Wrigley Building** (400 and 410 North Michigan Avenue; Graham, Anderson, Probst & White, 1922) is a dazzling white terra-cotta–clad lollipop of a building that's strikingly well lighted from the opposite shore of the river; the clock tower remains one of Chicago's most distinctive landmarks.

The **Tribune Tower** (435 North Michigan Avenue; Hood & Howells, 1925) is a neo-Gothic tower (considered "retro" when built) that soars upward like a medieval cathedral. At **333 North Michigan Avenue** stands Chicago's first Art Deco skyscraper, designed by Holabird & Root in 1928. More of the Art Deco impulse is displayed south of the river at the **Chicago Board of Trade Building** (141 West Jackson Boulevard; Holabird & Root, 1930), which anchors LaSalle Street's financial canyon and is topped with a 30-foot aluminum statue of Ceres, the Roman goddess of grain.

THE INTERNATIONAL STYLE

WHEN THE DEPRESSION HIT, most construction ground to a halt and didn't resume until after World War II. But after the postwar economic recovery arrived, German-born Ludwig Mies van der Rohe (who fled Nazi persecution before the war and later taught architecture at the Illinois Institute of Technology) found Chicago a receptive canvas for his daring designs.

Mies's motto was "Less is more," and the result was the sleek and unadorned International Style (often called the Second Chicago School). He was concerned with structural expression and the use of new technology as much as his predecessors in the 1890s, and Chicago boasts some of his most famous designs: the **Illinois Institute of Technology** (State Street between 31st and 35th streets, 1940–1958), the **Federal Center Complex** (Dearborn Street between Jackson Boulevard and Adams Street, 1964–1975), and his last major design, the **IBM Building** (330 North Wabash, 1971).

Mies's signature style is the high-rise with an open colonnaded space around a solid shaft; the glass-and-steel skin is carefully detailed to represent the steel structure within. The designs are macho, strong, and sinewy, with great care given to proportion, play of light, and simplicity. Detractors sniff and call them "glass boxes."

POSTMODERNISM

INEVITABLY, REBELLION BEGAN, and the result was postmodernism, a catchall term describing anything outside the realm of mainstream modernist design. Often the postmodernists overturned modernist beliefs while echoing the Chicago aesthetic of the past in new, often graceful designs. Macho and cold is out; whimsy and colorful are in. The starkness of Mies-inspired architecture gave way to purely decorative elements in designs that are still unmistakably modern.

Arguably the most graceful of the newer buildings in Chicago, **333 North Wacker Drive** (Kohn Pedersen Fox–Perkins and Will, 1983) features a curved facade of glass that reflects the Chicago River in both shape and color. Another stunner is **150 North Michigan Avenue** (A. Epstein & Sons, 1984), whose sloping glass roof slices diagonally through the top ten floors.

Tipping its hat to the past is the **Harold Washington Library Center** (400 South State Street; Hammond, Beeby & Babka, 1991), which references numerous city landmarks. A red-granite base and brick walls pay tribute to the Rookery and Monadnock buildings (two Burnham and Root gems), while the facade and pediments along the roof recall the Art Institute. Even more retro is the **NBC Tower** (455 North Cityfront Plaza; Skidmore, Owings & Merrill, 1989), a 38-story Art Deco tower that successfully mines the architectural past.

One of Chicago's most controversial buildings is the **State of Illinois Center** (100 West Randolph Street; C. F. Murphy–Jahn Associates and Lester B. Knight & Associates, 1983). It's a 17-story glass-and-steel interpretation of the traditional government office building created by the bad boy of Chicago architecture, Helmut Jahn. Inside, 13 floors of balconied offices encircle a 332-foot central rotunda that's topped with a sloping glass skylight 160 feet in diameter. You've got to see it to believe it. The controversy? Some people loathe it—and state employees often endure blistering heat in the summer and freezing cold in the winter.

SCRAPING THE SKY

ANOTHER HARD-TO-IGNORE ELEMENT in recent downtown Chicago designs is height: Chicago claims several of the world's ten tallest buildings, including the 1,454-foot **Sears Tower** (233 South Wacker Drive; Skidmore, Owings & Merrill, 1974). The world's third-tallest building is a set of nine square tubes bundled together to give strength to the whole; seven tubes drop away as the building ascends, and only two go the distance.

Yet the 1,127-foot **John Hancock Center** (875 North Michigan; Skidmore, Owings & Merrill, 1969) usually gets higher marks from critics for its tapered form that's crisscrossed by diagonal wind bracing; locals say the view from the top is better, too. The Hancock

Center is the world's 14th-tallest building, but the world's 13th-tallest is also in Chicago: the 80-story, 1,136-foot **AON Center** (200 East Randolph Street; E. D. Stone–Perkins and Will, 1974). New white-granite cladding on the AON Center replaced a Carrara-marble skin that couldn't stand up to Chicago's wind and temperature extremes.

AN OUTDOOR MUSEUM

MOST OF CHICAGO'S LANDMARK BUILDINGS—and we've only described a few—are located in and around the Loop, making a comfortable walking tour the best way to explore this outdoor museum of modern architecture. If you've got the time and the interest, we strongly recommend taking one of the **Chicago Architecture Foundation**'s two-hour walking tours of the Loop (☎ 312-922-3432; **www.architecture.org**). It's by far the best way to gain a greater appreciation of one of the world's great architectural mosaics.

SCULPTURE *in the* LOOP

CHICAGO, THE WORLD LEADER IN MODERN ARCHITECTURE, also boasts one of the finest collections of public art in the United States. Major pieces by such 20th-century greats as Picasso, Chagall, Calder, Miró, Moore, Oldenburg, Nevelson, and Noguchi are scattered throughout the Loop.

It's a cornucopia of postmodern masterpieces—although some might take a little getting used to. After Picasso's untitled abstract sculpture in the Civic Center plaza was unveiled by Mayor Richard J. Daley in 1967, one Chicago alderman introduced a motion in the city council that it be removed and replaced by a monument to Cubs baseball hero Ernie Banks. Nothing came of the motion, and now the sculpture is a beloved city landmark. Here's an informal tour of some of the Loop's best (see map on following page for these and other works):

1. *Untitled* (1967, Pablo Picasso); Richard J. Daley Plaza (West Washington Street between North Dearborn and North Clark streets); Cor-Ten steel.
2. *Flamingo* (1974, Alexander Calder); Federal Center (219 South Dearborn Street between West Adams Street and West Jackson Boulevard); painted steel.
3. *Chicago* (1967, Joan Miró; installed 1981); Chicago Temple (69 West Washington Street at North Clark Street); bronze, concrete, tile.
4. *The Four Seasons* (1975, Marc Chagall); First National Plaza (West Monroe Street between South Clark and South Dearborn streets); hand-chipped stone, glass fragments, brick.
5. *Monument with Standing Beast* (1985, Jean Dubuffet); State of Illinois Center (100 West Randolph Street at North Clark Street); fiberglass.

Loop Sculpture Tour

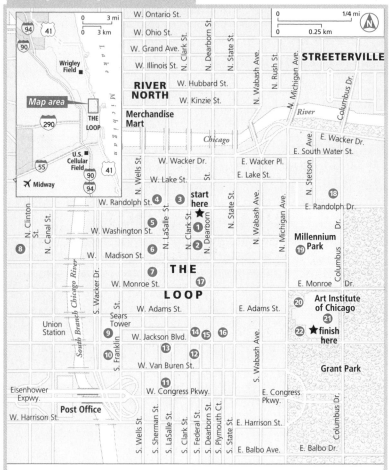

1. *Untitled ("The Picasso")*, Pablo Picasso (1967)
2. *Chicago*, Joan Miró (1981)
3. *Monument with Standing Beast*,
   Jean Dubuffet (1984)
4. *Freeform*, Richard Hunt (1993)
5. *Flight of Daedalus and Icarus*,
   Roger Brown (1990)
6. *Dawn Shadows*, Louise Nevelson (1983)
7. *Loomings* and *Knights and Squires*,
   Frank Stella (1986)
8. *Batcolumn*, Claes Oldenburg (1977)
9. *The Universe*, Alexander Calder (1974)
10. *Gem of the Lakes*, Raymond Kaskey (1990)
11. *San Marco II*, Ludovico de Luigi (1986)

12. *The Town-Ho's Story*, Frank Stella (1993)
13. *Ceres*, John Storrs (1930)
14. *Ruins III*, Nita K. Sutherland (1978)
15. *Flamingo*, Alexander Calder (1974)
16. *Lines in Four Directions*, Sol Lewitt (1985)
17. *The Four Seasons*, Marc Chagall (1974)
18. *Untitled Sounding Sculpture*,
    Harry Bertoia (1975)
19. *Cloud Gate*, Anish Kapoor (2004)
20. *Large Interior Form*, Henry Moore (1983)
21. *Celebration of the 200th Anniversary
    of the Founding of the Republic*,
    Isamu Noguchi (1976)
22. *The Fountain of the Great Lakes*,
    Lorado Taft (1913)

6. *Ceres* (1930, John Storrs); atop Chicago Board of Trade Building (141 West Jackson Boulevard at South LaSalle Street); aluminum.
7. *Batcolumn* (1977, Claes Oldenburg); Social Security Administration Building Plaza (600 West Madison Street at North Clinton Street); painted steel.
8. *Dawn Shadows* (1983, Louise Nevelson); Madison Plaza (200 West Madison Street at North Wells Street); steel.
9. *The Universe* (1974, Alexander Calder); Lobby, Sears Tower (233 South Wacker Drive); painted aluminum.

PART TWO

PLANNING YOUR VISIT

SEASONS *of* CHANGE

CHICAGO IS ONE TOWN THAT WON'T LET YOU DOWN—unless you're talking about the weather, which can change with the snap of a finger. During the mid-1800s, some well-intentioned journalists founded the *Chicago Magazine of Fashion, Music, and Home Reading* in an attempt to introduce Culture to the grizzly midwestern homestead. They wrote, in part: "The uncertainty and inclemency of the spring weather interferes sadly with the permanency of a new toilet, since, if one day is warm enough for a parasol, the next demands a resume of cloak and furs."

These lifestyle pioneers may have meant *toilet* in the sense of grooming and clothes, but their point still holds true today: Chicago's weather is flush with change. In January and February, the climate is often distinguished by a bone-chilling combination of subfreezing temperatures and howling winds. The late singer and Chicago native Lou Rawls sang about these winds as "The Hawk." The average winter snowfall is 40 inches. The less said about that, the better.

The summer months of June, July, and August, on the other hand, are noted for high temperatures (and high humidity) that can approach the triple digits. Though the combination can make for miserably hot and sticky summer afternoons, breezes off of Lake Michigan are often a mitigating factor that can make a stroll through Lincoln Park bearable.

Temperature-wise, spring and fall are the most docile times of year. Many people, in fact, say autumn is their favorite Chicago

unofficial **TIP**
In any season, Chicago's lakefront location and its position in a major west-to-east weather path make atmospheric conditions highly changeable (and, as you'll discover during your stay, difficult to predict). Temperatures in the suburbs often differ from those by the lake. Plan accordingly on all-day outings by bringing along appropriate rain gear and/or extra clothing.

CHICAGO'S AVERAGE TEMPERATURES AND PRECIPITATION

MONTH	AVERAGE DAILY TEMPERATURE (MINIMUM/MAXIMUM, IN DEGREES FAHRENHEIT)	AVERAGE MONTHLY PRECIPITATION
January	18°/34°	1.6"
February	20°/36°	1.3"
March	29°/45°	2.6"
April	40°/58°	3.7"
May	49°/70°	3.2"
June	59°/81°	4.1"
July	65°/86°	3.6"
August	65°/85°	3.5"
September	56°/76°	3.4"
October	45°/65°	2.3"
November	32°/49°	2.1"
December	22°/36°	2.1"

season. Evening temperatures in October and November may dip into the 40s, but the days are usually warm. Starting in mid-October, the fall foliage creates a pastiche of color that tempts thousands of folks to jump in their cars for day trips north of the city along scenic Sheridan Road or longer journeys to Galena, near the Mississippi River in the northwest corner of Illinois.

For visitors enjoying Chicago's museums, galleries, shopping, restaurants, and other attractions, any season is okay—the city goes full blast all year. While winter may be the least desirable time of the year to visit Chicago, it's the cultural season: theater, music, and museum programs are plentiful. In recent years, the city and the convention and tourism bureau have offered considerable hotel discounts to coincide with special winter festivals. It's also fun to check out everyone in their winter gear of wacky hats, scarves, and ear warmers.

AVOIDING CROWDS

THE SUMMER MONTHS—mid-June through mid-August, when school is out—are the busiest times at most tourist attractions. Weekends are busier than weekdays, and Saturdays are busier than Sundays. Most major Chicago attractions offer free admission one day a week; this day is usually the most crowded.

Driving during rush hour should be avoided—whether you're a tourist or native. The traffic will drive you crazy for a number of

unofficial **TIP**
On weekdays during the school year, places such as the Art Institute of Chicago, the Field Museum, and the Lincoln Park Zoo are besieged by scores of school buses. If you'd rather tour when things are a little more mellow, come back in the afternoon. The buses are needed at the end of the school day, so kids are typically whisked back to class by 1:30 p.m.

reasons. For one thing, nearly 3 million people live in Chicago and another 8 million in the surrounding area. For another, Chicago has an antiquated expressway system, not to mention more wide-eyed gapers than Los Angeles or New York. Massive tie-ups are routine on the main arteries leading in and out of the city, as well as major expressways that connect the suburbs. And because that temperamental Chicago weather takes its toll on local streets and highways, there generally is some kind of road construction going on somewhere.

If you must drive, stay off the road before 9 a.m. and after 4 p.m. so you'll miss the worst rush-hour traffic. Likewise, if you're driving to Chicago or planning to get from the airport to downtown by car or cab, avoid arriving during rush hour (especially on Friday afternoon). The drive from O'Hare to the Loop can take up to four hours as all the high-rise office buildings release legions of office workers eager to get home for the weekend. Don't get in their way. And stay off your cell phone—it's illegal to use one while driving within Chicago city limits.

In contrast, getting around by car on weekends and holidays is a breeze, although you may run into an occasional backup on the Eisenhower Expressway (heading west to Naperville) or Kennedy Expressway (heading north to Milwaukee), the two major highways that lead in and out of downtown.

HOW *to* GET MORE INFORMATION *before* YOUR VISIT

FOR INFORMATION ON ENTERTAINMENT, sightseeing, maps, shopping, dining, and lodging in the Chicago area, call or write:

Chicago Office of Tourism, Chicago Cultural Center
78 East Washington Street
Chicago, Illinois 60602
☎ 877-CHICAGO or 312-744-2964 (TDD); **www.877chicago.com**

Also visit the **Chicago Convention and Tourism Bureau** at **www.choose chicago.com.**

In addition, three visitor-information centers are centrally located: in the Historic Water Tower on the Magnificent Mile (on North Michigan Avenue, across from the Water Tower Place shopping mall); in the Chicago Cultural Center (downtown on South Michigan at Washington Street); and in the Explore Chicago kiosk inside the Sears on State store (2 North State Street, in the Loop). All are open daily, offer help planning itineraries, and feature plenty of free information and maps. Chicago's hotels also have some of the best-informed concierges in America.

GETTING *to* CHICAGO

FOLKS PLANNING A TRIP TO CHICAGO have several options: plane, train, bus, or automobile. Your distance from the city—and your ability to tolerate such hassles as traffic congestion and endless waits in holding patterns—will probably determine which mode of transportation you ultimately choose.

FLYING

IF YOU'RE COMING TO CHICAGO from the East, the West, the Gulf Coast, Europe, Asia, South America, or any other place that's more than a 12-hour drive away, you'll likely arrive the way most folks do: by plane into **O'Hare International Airport,** the world's busiest—and often most frustrating—airfield. A 24-hour subway line connects O'Hare with downtown.

unofficial **TIP**
Truly creative travelers take advantage of **Mitchell International Airport,** 75 miles north of Chicago in Milwaukee. An Amtrak station has opened here in an attempt to lure Chicago passengers away from O'Hare. There are seven round-trips daily between Union Station in Chicago and the Milwaukee airport.

But a growing number of domestic fliers avoid the hassles of O'Hare by using less-congested **Midway Airport,** which has been expanded and remodeled in recent years. If you have a choice, fly in here. (See Part Five, Arriving and Getting Oriented, for maps of O'Hare and Midway.) About 15 miles southwest of the Loop, Midway is on a subway line (but the last train out of the airport is 12:55 a.m. daily) and is only about 20 minutes from downtown (longer during rush hour).

TAKING THE TRAIN

JUST AS O'HARE IS A MAJOR HUB between the East and West coasts of the United States, Chicago's **Union Station** is the major rail station between the two coasts. Though long-distance travel by train can be tedious, it enables people who live in the Midwest to come into Chicago without fear of getting stuck in a holding pattern over O'Hare or trapped in a traffic snarl on the Eisenhower Expressway.

Cities closest to Chicago with Amtrak passenger-train service are Milwaukee (1½ hours one-way) and Indianapolis (4½ hours). Other cities offering daily rail service to Union Station include St. Louis (5 hours), Detroit (5 hours), Cincinnati (7 hours, three days a week), Cleveland (6 hours), Kansas City (8½ hours), Omaha (9 hours), and

- To avoid problems booking a room, time your trip to avoid major conventions (see Part Four, pages 72–74).

- Don't drive—parking is a pain, public transportation is good, and cabs are plentiful.

- Fly into Midway (it's closer and easier than O'Hare).

- Chicago's weather is highly changeable—dress accordingly. Depending on the season, take a rain jacket, umbrella, or sweater on outings.

- To avoid busloads of schoolchildren on field trips, plan your weekday museum and zoo outings in the afternoons; the kids head back to school by 1:30 p.m.

Minneapolis (8 hours). For schedules and reservations, call Amtrak at ☎ 800-872-7245 or visit **www.amtrak.com.**

HOP ON THE BUS, GUS

A COMMERCIAL BUS TRIP is always filled with interesting surprises, but the **Greyhound** station in Chicago is not as seedy as it used to be. A station opened in 1991 at 630 West Harrison on the Near South Side, two blocks southwest of the Clinton stop on the El line to O'Hare (☎ 312-408-5800; **www.greyhound.com**). Travelers from Cleveland, Detroit, Indianapolis, and other nearby cities have also used the new no-frills **Megabus** that is popular in Europe (**www.megabus.com**). you plan early enough, you can ride Megabus for $1 using the Internet. There's no station for Megabus passengers—the bus picks people up next to Union Station on the east side of South Canal Street, between Jackson Boulevard and Adams Street—but it's one of the cheapest ways to get to Chicago.

unofficial **TIP**
If you must drive, make sure your hotel offers on-site or nearby off-street parking. Don't arrive during rush hour. Never leave anything of value in your car—hide it in your trunk. It often makes more sense to leave the car parked and take a bus, the El, or a cab.

DRIVING

IF YOU'RE CONSIDERING DRIVING in Chicago, consider again. Not only does the traffic never let up, but parking is tough, too. Convenient, affordable, and/or secure places to leave your car are rare luxuries. Cops are eager to give tickets, and an automated system can issue a ticket that shows up weeks later. Instead of enduring traffic and parking stress, use Chicago's extensive public-transportation system and abundance of taxis. Airport vans also transport visitors to and from downtown hotels. For more information about travel in Chicago without a car, see "Public Transportation" in Part Six, Getting Around.

A CALENDAR *of* FESTIVALS *and* EVENTS

January

CHICAGO BOAT, SPORTS, AND RV SHOW *McCormick Place.* Hands-on displays of sporting goods, boats, motor homes, and recreational vehicles. Admission: $10 adults, $8 seniors, $4 ages 13–15, free for age 12 and under. ☎ 312-946-6200; **www.chicago boatshow.com.**

CHICAGO PARK DISTRICT HOLIDAY FLOWER SHOW *Garfield Park Conservatory.* Through the first week of January. Free. ☎ 312-746-5100; **www.chicagoparkdistrict.com.**

February

CHINESE NEW YEAR PARADE *Chinatown.* Parade complete with fire-crackers and a "dragon" dancing in the streets. Free. ☎ 312-225-0303.

NATIONAL AFRICAN AMERICAN HISTORY MONTH *Various locations.* A month-long city-wide celebration of black Americans' lives, times, and art. Free. ☎ 773-256-0149 (South Shore Cultural Center); **www .chicagoparkdistrict.com.**

March

CHICAGO FLOWER AND GARDEN SHOW *Navy Pier,* 600 East Grand Avenue. Through the second week of March. Displays featuring gardening, demonstrations, tablescapes, and entertainment. Admission: $12 weekdays, $14 weekends, $5 for kids. ☎ 773-435-1250; **www .chicagoflower.com.**

 ST. PATRICK'S DAY PARADE *Columbus Drive from Balbo Drive to Monroe Drive.* Forty pounds of vegetable dye turns the Chicago River green, and everyone is Irish for the day. The parade starts at noon and features floats, marching bands, and hundreds of thousands of spectators. Free. ☎ 312-942-9188; **www .chicagostpatsparade.com.**

April

CHICAGO LATINO FILM FESTIVAL *Various locations.* ☎ 312-431-1330; **www.latinoculturalcenter.org.**

May

ART CHICAGO *Chicago Merchandise Mart.* Art, both past and present, offered for sale by prestigious art galleries. Admission: $20. ☎ 312-527-3701; **www.artchicago.com.**

POLISH CONSTITUTION DAY PARADE *Columbus Drive from Balbo Drive to Monroe Drive.* Free. ☎ 312-745-7799; **www.may3parade.org.**

WRIGHT PLUS *Oak Park.* The only chance to tour the interiors of ten homes designed by Frank Lloyd Wright and his contemporaries. Admission: $95; tickets usually sell out by mid-April. The all-day tour is held on the third Saturday in May. ☎ 708-848-1976; **www.wrightplus.org.**

June

ANDERSONVILLE MIDSUMMER FEST *Neighborhood festival on Clark Street from Foster to Catalpa avenues.* Free. ☎ 773-665-4682.

CHICAGO BLUES FESTIVAL *Petrillo Music Shell, Grant Park.* Fabulous music, food, and dozens of artists from Chicago and beyond. Free. ☎ 312-744-3315; **www.chicagobluesfestival.us.**

GAY AND LESBIAN PRIDE PARADE Starts *at Halsted Street and Belmont Avenue.* Free. ☎ 773-348-8243.

RAVINIA FESTIVAL *Highland Park from early June to mid-August.* A 12-week season of the Chicago Symphony Orchestra; dance, jazz, ballet, folk, and comedy in a picnic setting. For admission prices, call ☎ 847-266-5100 or visit **www.ravinia.org.**

 TASTE OF CHICAGO *Grant Park.* In the week leading up to Independence Day, more than 70 restaurants serve Chicago-style and ethnic cuisine at this alfresco food festival; musical entertainment. ☎ 312-744-3315; **www.tasteofchicago.us.**

WELLS STREET ART FAIR *North Wells Street between North Avenue and Division Street.* Free. ☎ 773-868-3010.

July

CONCERTS IN THE PARKS *Various locations.* More than 80 concerts performed in 64 Chicago parks in July and August. Free. ☎ 312-742-7529; **www.chicagoparkdistrict.com.**

INDEPENDENCE DAY CONCERT AND FIREWORKS *Petrillo Music Shell, Grant Park.* A classical concert kicks off Chicago's traditional Fourth of July celebration. Free. ☎ 312-744-3370.

 IRISH AMERICAN HERITAGE FESTIVAL *Irish American Heritage Center,* 4626 North Knox Avenue. Three days of continuous entertainment, 40 Irish bands, food, Irish step dancing, and museum and art gallery tours. ☎ 773-282-7035; **www.irish festchicago.com.**

SHEFFIELD GARDEN WALK AND FESTIVAL *Corner of Sheffield and Webster avenues at St. Vincent's Church.* Self-guided walking tour of private gardens, garage sales, food, and entertainment. Admission: $6 to $10. ☎ 773-929-9255; **www.sheffieldfestivals.org.**

August

BUD BILLIKEN PARADE *King Drive to Washington Park.* The South

Side African American community's fun-filled event for kids and grown-ups. Free. ☎ 773-536-3710; **www.budbillikenparade.com.**

CHICAGO JAZZ FESTIVAL *Petrillo Music Shell, Grant Park.* A jazz marathon over Labor Day weekend; the world's largest free jazz festival featuring the greats from traditional and swing to bebop, blues, and avant-garde. Free. ☎ 312-744-3370; **www.chicagojazzfestival.us.**

CONCERTS IN THE PARKS *Various locations.* More than 80 concerts performed in 64 Chicago parks in July and August. Free. ☎ 312-742-7529; **www.chicagoparkdistrict.com.**

GINZA HOLIDAY FESTIVAL *Midwest Buddhist Temple,* 435 West Menomonee Street. A celebration of Japanese culture featuring food, dance, mime, martial arts, music, origami, painting, and sculpture. Admission: $4 adults, $3 seniors and students, free for children under age 12. ☎ 312-943-7801; **www.midwestbuddhisttemple.org.**

GOLD COAST RIVER NORTH ART FAIR *Along LaSalle Street at the intersections of Erie, Huron, and Superior streets.* For three days, more than 300 artists display and sell high-quality paintings, photographs, and hand-crafted fine art. Free. ☎ 847-926-4300.

September

 BERGHOFF OKTOBERFEST *Adams Street between State and Dearborn streets.* Long-running street party with beer tents, bands, and dancing. ☎ 312-427-3170.

¡VIVA! CHICAGO LATIN MUSIC FESTIVAL *Petrillo Music Shell, Grant Park.* Free. ☎ 312-744-3315; **www.vivachicago.us.**

October

CHICAGO INTERNATIONAL FILM FESTIVAL *Screenings at various theaters throughout the city.* Exciting new international films, directors, and stars. Admission: $12, $10 seniors, $7 matinees. ☎ 312-332-3456; **www.chicagofilmfestival.org.**

COLUMBUS DAY PARADE *Columbus Drive from Balbo Drive to Monroe Drive.* Free. ☎ 708-450-9050.

HISTORIC PULLMAN DISTRICT'S ANNUAL HOUSE TOUR *Historic Pullman Visitor Center,* 11141 South Cottage Grove Avenue. Annual fall tour of homes and historic buildings. ☎ 773-785-8901; **www .pullmanil.org/housetour.htm.**

November–December

HOLIDAY CANDLELIGHT TOURS OF GLESSNER AND CLARKE HOUSES *South Prairie Avenue, near McCormick Place.* Authentic period Christmas decorations; docents talk about the history of Christmas traditions in Chicago. Admission: $18, $14 kids ages 8 to 12. ☎ 312-326-1480; **www. glessnerhouse.org.**

CHRISTMAS AROUND THE WORLD *Museum of Science and Industry.* A grand ethnic festival, plus entertainment. Admission: $13, $12 seniors, $9 kids ages 3 to 11. ☎ 773-684-1414; **www.msichicago.org.**

MAGNIFICENT MILE LIGHTS FESTIVAL *North Michigan Avenue from the Chicago River to Oak Street.* The kickoff of Chicago's traditional holiday shopping season features stage shows, a parade, fireworks, and 300,000 lights on Michigan Avenue and Oak Street. Free. ☎ 312-642-3570; **www.magnificentmilelightsfestival.com.**

McDONALD'S THANKSGIVING DAY PARADE *State Street from Congress to Randolph.* ☎ 312-235-2217; **www.chicagofestivals.org.**

PART THREE

ACCOMMODATIONS

 ## DECIDING WHERE *to* STAY

THOUGH CHICAGO SPRAWLS FOR MILES NORTH and south along Lake Michigan, and threatens on the West Side to realize some suburban manifest destiny by creeping all the way to the Iowa border, the city is as focused and anchored as Manhattan. Chicago is defined by its city center. Downtown Chicago is not simply the heart of the city, it is the heart of the Midwest. As American as Valley Forge and as foreign as Warsaw, downtown Chicago is a magnet. If you visit Chicago, downtown is where you want to be.

The Chicago hotel scene reflects the dynamism and power of the city's bustling core. By and large, Chicago hotels are big, huge even, soaring 20, 30, and more stories above the lake. Although there are hotels near Midway and O'Hare airports and in smaller towns that have expanded to surround the great city, the majority of Chicago's 67,000 rooms are situated in a narrow strip bordered by Lake Michigan on the east, Clark Street on the west, North Avenue on the north, and Roosevelt Road on the south. All told, the area is about three miles north to south and less than a mile wide.

Though some of the finest hotels in the world are in Chicago, finding comfortable lodging for less than $100 a night is easier here than in New York. Chicago is not cheap, but the quality standards for hotels are generally high. In Chicago, unlike in Boston, Atlanta, or Washington, D.C., the option of booking a less expensive hotel in the suburbs and commuting to downtown is impractical. The commute is long, the suburban hotels few, and the savings insignificant to nonexistent.

Finally, Chicago is the busiest convention city in the United States. If your visit coincides with one or more major conventions or trade shows, hotel rooms will be both scarce and expensive. If, on the other hand, you are able to schedule your visit to avoid big meetings, you will have a good selection of hotels at surprisingly competitive prices.

Central Chicago Accommodations

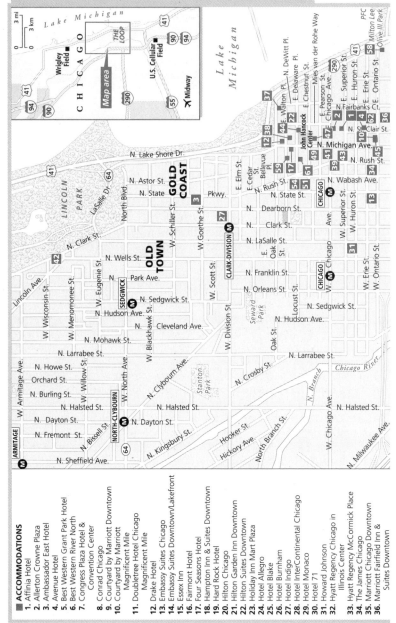

ACCOMMODATIONS
1. Affinia Hotel
2. Allerton Crowne Plaza
3. Ambassador East Hotel
4. Avenue Hotel
5. Best Western Grant Park Hotel
6. Best Western River North
7. Congress Plaza Hotel & Convention Center
8. Conrad Chicago
9. Courtyard by Marriott Downtown
10. Courtyard by Marriott Magnificent Mile
11. Doubletree Hotel Chicago Magnificent Mile
12. Drake Hotel
13. Embassy Suites Chicago
14. Embassy Suites Downtown/Lakefront
15. Essex Inn
16. Fairmont Hotel
17. Four Seasons Hotel
18. Hampton Inn & Suites Downtown
19. Hard Rock Hotel
20. Hilton Chicago
21. Hilton Garden Inn Downtown
22. Hilton Suites Downtown
23. Holiday Inn Mart Plaza
24. Hotel Allegro
25. Hotel Blake
26. Hotel Burnham
27. Hotel Indigo
28. Hotel InterContinental Chicago
29. Hotel Monaco
30. Hotel 71
31. Howard Johnson
32. Hyatt Regency Chicago in Illinois Center
33. Hyatt Regency McCormick Place
34. The James Chicago
35. Marriott Chicago Downtown
36. Marriott Fairfield Inn & Suites Downtown

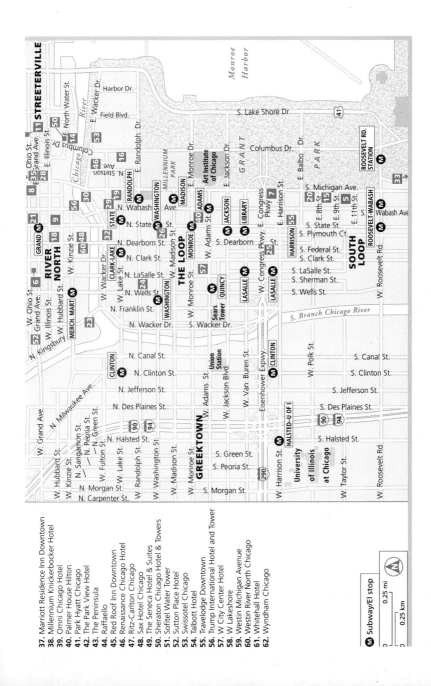

37. Marriott Residence Inn Downtown
38. Millennium Knickerbocker Hotel
39. Omni Chicago Hotel
40. Palmer House Hilton
41. Park Hyatt Chicago
42. The Park View Hotel
43. The Peninsula
44. Raffaello
45. Red Roof Inn Downtown
46. Renaissance Chicago Hotel
47. Ritz-Carlton Chicago
48. Sax Hotel Chicago
49. The Seneca Hotel & Suites
50. Sheraton Chicago Hotel & Towers
51. Sofitel Water Tower
52. Sutton Place Hotel
53. Swissotel Chicago
54. Talbott Hotel
55. Travelodge Downtown
56. Trump International Hotel and Tower
57. W City Center Hotel
58. W Lakeshore
59. Westin Michigan Avenue
60. Westin River North Chicago
61. Whitehall Hotel
62. Wyndham Chicago

Ⓜ Subway/El stop

0.25 mi

0.25 km

If you happen to be attending one of the big conventions, book early and use some of the tips listed below to get a discounted room rate. To assist in timing your visit, we've included a convention and trade-show calendar in Part Four, Visiting on Business (pages 72–74).

SOME CONSIDERATIONS

1. When choosing your Chicago lodging, make sure your hotel is situated in a location convenient to your recreation or business needs, and that it is in a safe and comfortable area. Please note that although it is not practical to walk to McCormick Place (the major convention venue) from any of the downtown hotels, larger conventions and trade shows provide shuttle service.
2. Find out how old the hotel is and when the guest rooms were last renovated. Request that the hotel send you its promotional brochure. Ask if brochure photos of guest rooms are accurate and current.
3. If you plan to take a car, inquire about the parking situation. Some hotels offer no parking at all, some charge dearly for parking, and a few offer free parking.
4. If you're not a city dweller, or perhaps are a light sleeper, try to book a hotel on a more quiet side street. Ask for a room off the street and high up.
5. The Chicago skyline is quite beautiful, as is the lake. If you are on a romantic holiday, ask for a room on a higher floor with a view.
6. If shopping is high on your agenda, try to book a hotel near Michigan Avenue between Oak Street and East Wacker Drive.
7. When you plan your budget, remember that Chicago's combined room and sales tax is a whopping 15.39%.

GETTING *a* GOOD DEAL *on a* ROOM

SPECIAL WEEKEND RATES

ALTHOUGH WELL-LOCATED CHICAGO HOTELS are tough for the budget-conscious, it's not impossible to get a good deal, at least relatively speaking. For starters, most downtown hotels that cater to business, government, and convention travelers offer special weekend discount rates that range from 15% to 40% below normal weekday rates. You can find out about weekend specials by calling individual hotels or your travel agent.

GETTING CORPORATE RATES

MANY HOTELS OFFER DISCOUNTED CORPORATE RATES (5% to 20% off rack rate). Usually you don't need to work for a large company or have a special relationship with the hotel to obtain these rates.

Simply call the hotel of your choice and ask for its corporate rates. Many hotels will guarantee you the discounted rate on the phone when you make your reservation. Others may make the rate conditional on your providing some sort of bona fides, for instance a fax on your company's letterhead requesting the rate, or a company credit card or business card on check-in. Generally, the screening is not rigorous.

HALF-PRICE PROGRAMS

THE LARGER DISCOUNTS ON ROOMS (35% to 60%), in Chicago or anywhere else, are available through half-price hotel programs, often called travel clubs. Program operators contract with an individual hotel to provide rooms at deep discounts, usually 50% off rack rate, on a space-available basis. "Space available" generally means that you can reserve a room at the discounted rate whenever the hotel expects to be at less than 80% occupancy. A little sleuthing to help you avoid citywide conventions and special events (see the calendar on pages 72–74) will increase your chances of choosing a time when the discounts are available.

Most half-price programs charge an annual membership fee or directory subscription charge of $25 to $125. Once enrolled, you are mailed a membership card and a directory listing participating hotels. Examining the directory, you will notice immediately that there are many restrictions and exceptions. Some hotels, for instance, "black out" certain dates or times of year. Others may offer the discount only on certain days of the week, or require you to stay a certain number of nights. Still others may offer a much smaller discount than 50% off rack rate.

Programs specialize in domestic travel, international travel, or both. More established operators offer members between 1,000 and 4,000 hotels to choose from in the United States. All of the programs have a heavy concentration of hotels in California and Florida, and most have a very limited selection of participating properties in New York City or Boston. Offerings in other cities and regions of the United States vary considerably. The programs with the largest selections of Chicago hotels are **Encore, Travel America at Half Price** (Entertainment Publications), **International Travel Card,** and **Quest.** Each of these programs lists between four and 50 hotels in the greater Chicago area.

Encore	☎ 800-638-0930
Entertainment Publications	☎ 888-231-7283
International Travel Card	☎ 800-342-0558
Quest	☎ 800-638-9819

One problem with half-price programs is that not all hotels offer a full 50% discount. Another slippery problem is the base rate against which the discount is applied. Some hotels figure the discount on an exaggerated rack rate that nobody would ever have to pay. A few participating hotels may deduct the discount from a supposed "superior" or "upgraded" room rate, even though the room you get is the hotel's standard accommodation. Though hard to pin down, the majority of participating properties base discounts on the rate published in the *Hotel & Travel Index* (a quarterly reference work used by travel agents) and work within the spirit of their agreement with the program operator. As a rule, if you travel several times a year, your room rate savings will easily compensate for program membership fees.

A noteworthy addendum: deeply discounted rooms through half-price programs are not commissionable to travel agents. In practical terms, this means that you must ordinarily make your own inquiry calls and reservations. If you travel frequently, however, and run a lot of business through your travel agent, he or she will probably do your legwork, lack of commission notwithstanding.

PREFERRED RATES

IF YOU CAN'T BOOK THE HOTEL of your choice through a half-price program, you and your travel agent may have to search for a lesser discount, often called a preferred rate. A preferred rate could be a discount made available to travel agents to stimulate their booking activity, or a discount initiated to attract a certain class of traveler. Most preferred rates are promoted through travel-industry publications and are often accessible only through an agent.

We recommend sounding out your travel agent about possible deals. Be aware, however, that the rates shown on travel agents' computerized reservations systems are not always the lowest rates obtainable. Focus on a couple of hotels that fill your needs in terms of location and quality of accommodations, and then have your travel agent call the hotel for the latest rates and specials. Hotel reps almost always respond to travel agents because travel agents represent a source of additional business. As discussed earlier, there are certain specials that hotel reps will disclose only to travel agents. Travel agents also come in handy when the hotel you want is supposedly booked. A personal appeal from your agent to the hotel's director of sales and marketing will get you a room more than half of the time.

WHOLESALERS, CONSOLIDATORS, AND RESERVATION SERVICES

IF YOU PREFER NOT TO JOIN A PROGRAM or buy a discount directory, you can take advantage of the services of a wholesaler or consolidator. Wholesalers and consolidators buy rooms, or options on rooms (room blocks), from hotels at a low, negotiated rate. They then resell the rooms at a profit through travel agents, tour packagers, or directly to the public. Most wholesalers and consolidators have a provision for returning unsold rooms to participating hotels, but are not inclined to do so. The wholesaler's or consolidator's relationship with any hotel is predicated on volume. If they return rooms unsold, the hotel may not make as many rooms available to them the next time around. Thus wholesalers and consolidators often offer rooms at bargain rates, anywhere from 15% to 50% off rack, occasionally sacrificing their profit margins in the process to avoid returning the rooms to the hotel unsold.

When wholesalers and consolidators deal directly with the public, they frequently represent themselves as "reservation services." When you call, you can ask for a rate quote for a particular hotel, or alternatively ask for their best available deal in the area where you prefer to stay. If there is a maximum amount you are willing to pay, say so. Chances are the service will find something that will work for you, even if they have to shave a dollar or two off their own profit. Sometimes you will have to pay for your room with a credit card when you make your reservation. Other times you will pay as usual, when you check out. Two such services are **Hotel Reservations Network** (☎ 800-964-6835) and **Hot Rooms** (☎ 773-468-7666).

ALTERNATIVE LODGING

B&BS   Chicago Bed & Breakfast Association is a reservation service for guesthouses and furnished apartments primarily in the downtown area. Rates usually range from $95 to $295 for guesthouses and from $185 to $1,000 for furnished apartments. For more information, call ☎ 800-375-7084 or visit **www.chicago-bed-breakfast.com.**

CONDOS If you want to rent a condo for a week in Chicago, you are out of luck. Local law stipulates a minimum rental period of 30 days. If you are planning an extended stay and are interested in a condo, your best bet is to shop realtors in the area where you prefer to stay. If they don't handle rentals, they can refer you to someone who does.

HOW TO EVALUATE A TRAVEL PACKAGE

HUNDREDS OF CHICAGO PACKAGE VACATIONS are offered to the public each year. Packages should be a win-win proposition for both the buyer and the seller. The buyer has to make only one phone call and deal with a single salesperson to set up the whole vacation: transportation, rental car, lodging, meals, attraction admissions, and even golf and tennis. The seller, likewise, has to deal with the buyer only once, eliminating the need for separate sales, confirmations, and billing. In addition to streamlining sales, processing, and administration, some packagers also buy airfares in bulk on contract like a broker playing the commodities market. Buying a large number of airfares in advance allows the packager to buy them at significant savings from posted fares. The same practice is also applied to hotel rooms. Because selling vacation packages is an efficient way of doing business, and because the packager can often buy individual package components (airfare, lodging, and the like) in bulk at discount, savings in operating expenses realized by the seller are sometimes passed on to the buyer, so that, in addition to convenience, the package is also an exceptional value. In any event, that's the way it is supposed to work.

All too often, in practice, the seller cashes in on discounts and passes none on to the buyer. In some instances, packages are loaded additionally with extras that cost the packager next to nothing but inflate the retail price sky-high. As you may expect, the savings to be passed along to customers remain somewhere in Fantasyland.

When considering a package, choose one that includes features you are sure to use. Whether you use all the features or not, you will most certainly pay for them. Second, if cost is of greater concern than convenience, make a few phone calls and see what the package would cost if you booked its individual components (airfare, rental car, lodging, etc.) on your own. If the package price is less than the à la carte cost, the package is a good deal. If the costs are about the same, the package is probably worth buying just for the convenience.

If your package includes a choice of rental car or airport transfers (transportation to and from the airport), take the transfers unless you are visiting Chicago for the weekend. During the weekend, with the exception of some sections of Michigan Avenue, it is relatively easy to get around. During the week, forget it. Also, if you take the car, be sure to ask if the package includes free parking at your hotel.

HELPING YOUR TRAVEL AGENT HELP YOU

WHEN YOU CALL YOUR TRAVEL AGENT, ask if he or she has been to Chicago. If the answer is no, be prepared to give your travel agent some direction. Do not accept any recommendations at face value. Check out the location and rates of any suggested hotel and make certain that the hotel is suited to your itinerary.

Because some travel agents are unfamiliar with Chicago, your agent may try to plug you into a tour operator's or wholesaler's preset package. This essentially allows the travel agent to set up your whole trip with a single phone call and still collect an 8%-to-10% commission. The problem with this scenario is that most agents will place 90% of their Chicago business with only one or two wholesalers or tour operators. In other words, it's the line of least resistance for them, and not much choice for you.

Travel agents will often use wholesalers who run packages in conjunction with airlines. Because of the wholesaler's relationship with the carrier, these trips are very easy for travel agents to book. However, they will probably be more expensive than a package offered by a high-volume wholesaler who works with a number of airlines in a primary Chicago market.

To help your travel agent get you the best possible deal, do the following:

1. Determine where you want to stay in Chicago, and if possible choose a specific hotel. This can be accomplished by reviewing the hotel information provided in this guide, by writing or calling hotels that interest you, and by doing research online.

2. Check out the hotel deals and package vacations advertised in the Sunday travel sections of the *Chicago Tribune* and *Chicago Sun-Times* newspapers. Often you will be able to find deals that beat the socks off anything offered in your local paper. See if you can find specials that fit your plans and include a hotel you like.

3. Call the hotels, wholesalers, or tour operators whose ads you've collected. Ask any questions you have concerning their packages, but do not book your trip with them directly.

4. Tell your travel agent about the deals you find and ask if he or she can get you something better. The deals in the paper will serve as a benchmark against which to compare alternatives proposed by your travel agent.

5. Choose from the options that you and your travel agent uncover. No matter which option you select, have your travel agent book it. Even if you go with one of the packages in the newspaper, it will probably be commissionable (at no additional cost to you) and will provide the agent some return on the time invested on your behalf. Also, as a travel professional, your agent should be able to verify the quality and integrity of the deal.

IF YOU MAKE YOUR OWN RESERVATION

AS YOU POKE AROUND TRYING TO FIND a good deal, there are several things you should know. First, always call the specific hotel as opposed to the hotel chain's national toll-free number. Quite often, the reservationists at the national toll-free number are unaware of local specials. Always ask about specials before you inquire about corporate rates. Do not be reluctant to bargain. If you are buying a hotel's weekend package, for example, and want to extend your stay into the following week, you can often obtain at least the corporate rate for the extra days. Do your bargaining, however, before you check in, preferably when you make reservations.

CHICAGO LODGING *for* BUSINESS TRAVELERS

THE PRIMARY CONSIDERATIONS FOR BUSINESS TRAVELERS are affordability and proximity to the place where you will transact your business. Identify the area(s) where your business will take you, and then use the Chicago Hotels by Location chart later in this chapter (pages 48–49) to find hotels located there. (The Central Chicago Accommodations map, pages 36–37, can also help.) Once

CHAIN-HOTEL TOLL-FREE NUMBERS	
Best Western	☎ 800-780-7234 U.S. and Canada ☎ 800-528-2222 TDD
Comfort Inn	☎ 800-228-5150 U.S.
Courtyard by Marriott	☎ 888-236-2427 U.S.
Days Inn	☎ 800-329-7466 U.S.
Doubletree	☎ 800-222-TREE U.S.
Econo Lodge	☎ 800-424-4777 U.S.
Embassy Suites	☎ 800-362-2779 U.S. and Canada
Fairfield Inn by Marriott	☎ 800-228-2800 U.S. and Canada
Hampton Inn	☎ 800-426-7866 U.S. and Canada
Hilton	☎ 800-445-8667 U.S. ☎ 800-368-1133 TDD
Holiday Inn	☎ 800-465-4329 U.S. and Canada
Howard Johnson	☎ 800-654-2000 U.S. and Canada ☎ 800-654-8442 TDD
Hyatt	☎ 800-233-1234 U.S. and Canada
Loews	☎ 800-23-LOEWS U.S. and Canada
Marriott	☎ 800-228-9290 U.S. and Canada ☎ 800-228-7014 TDD
Quality Inn	☎ 800-228-5151 U.S. and Canada
Radisson	☎ 800-333-3333 U.S. and Canada
Ramada Inn	☎ 800-272-6232 U.S. ☎ 800-228-3232 TDD
Renaissance Hotel	☎ 800-468-3571 U.S. and Canada
Residence Inn by Marriott	☎ 800-331-3131 U.S.
Ritz-Carlton	☎ 800-241-3333 U.S.
Sheraton	☎ 800-325-3535 U.S. and Canada
Wyndham	☎ 877-999-3223 U.S. and Canada

you have developed a short list of possible hotels that are conveniently located, fit your budget, and offer the standard of accommodation you require, you (or your travel agent) can make use of the cost-saving suggestions discussed earlier to obtain the lowest rate.

LODGING CONVENIENT TO McCORMICK PLACE

IF YOU ARE ATTENDING A MEETING or trade show at McCormick Place, the most convenient lodging is downtown Chicago, though none of the hotels, practically speaking, are within walking distance. From most downtown hotels, McCormick Place is a 5- to 14-minute cab or a 10- to 30-minute shuttle ride away. Parking is available at the convention center, but it is expensive and not all that convenient. We recommend that you leave your car at home and use shuttles and cabs. The **Hyatt Regency McCormick Place** has 800 rooms and is connected to McCormick's Grand Concourse.

Commuting to McCormick Place from the suburbs or the airports during rush hour is something to be avoided, if possible. If you want a room downtown, book early . . . *very* early. If you screw up and need a room at the last minute, try a wholesaler or reservation service, or one of the strategies listed in the next section.

CONVENTION RATES:
HOW THEY WORK AND HOW TO DO BETTER

IF YOU'RE ATTENDING A MAJOR CONVENTION or trade show, chances are good that the meeting's sponsoring organization has negotiated "convention rates" with a number of hotels. Under this arrangement, hotels reserve a certain number of rooms at an agreed-on price for conventioneers. Sometimes, as in the case of a small meeting, only one hotel is involved. In the event of a large "city-wide" convention at McCormick Place, however, almost all downtown and airport hotels will participate in the room block.

Because the convention sponsor brings a lot of business to the city and reserves a large number of rooms, it usually can negotiate a volume discount on the room rates, a rate that should be substantially below rack rate. The bottom line, however, is that some conventions and trade shows have more bargaining clout and negotiating skill than others. Hence, your convention sponsor may or may not be able to obtain the lowest possible rate.

Once a convention or trade show sponsor has completed negotiations with participating hotels, it will send its attendees a housing list that includes all the hotels serving the convention, along with the special convention rate for each. When you receive the housing list, you can compare the convention rates with the rates obtainable using the strategies covered in the previous section. If the negotiated convention rate doesn't sound like a good deal, you can try to reserve a room using a half-price club, a consolidator, or a tour operator. Remember, however, that many of the deep discounts are available only when the hotel expects to be at less than 80% occupancy, a condition that rarely prevails when a big convention is in town.

Strategies for Beating Convention Rates

There are several tactics for getting around convention rates:

1. **Reserve early.** Most big conventions and trade shows announce meeting sites one to three years in advance. Get your reservation booked as far in advance as possible using a half-price club. If you book well ahead of the time the convention sponsor sends out the housing list, chances are the hotel will accept your reservation.

2. **Compare your convention's housing list with the list of hotels presented in this guide.** You may be able to find a suitable hotel that is not on the housing list.

3. **Use a local reservations agency or consolidator.** This is also a good strategy to employ if, for some reason, you need to make reservations at the last minute. Local reservations agencies and consolidators almost always control some rooms, even in the midst of a huge convention or trade show.

CHICAGO HOTELS:
Rated and Ranked

WHAT'S IN A ROOM?

EXCEPT FOR CLEANLINESS, state of repair, and decor, most travelers do not pay much attention to hotel rooms. There is, of course, a discernible standard of quality and luxury that differentiates Motel 6 from Holiday Inn, Holiday Inn from Marriott, and so on. In general, however, hotel guests fail to appreciate the fact that some rooms are better engineered than others.

Contrary to what you might suppose, designing a hotel room is (or should be) much more complex than picking a bedspread to match the carpet and drapes. Making the room usable to its occupants is an art, a planning discipline that combines both form and function.

Decor and taste are important, certainly. No one wants to spend several days in a room whose decor is dated, garish, or even ugly. But beyond the decor, several variables determine how "livable" a hotel room is. In Chicago, for example, we have seen some beautifully appointed rooms that are simply not well designed for human habitation. The next time you stay in a hotel, pay attention to the details and design elements of your room. Even more than decor, these will make you feel comfortable and at home.

HOTEL RATINGS

OVERALL QUALITY To distinguish properties according to relative quality, tastefulness, state of repair, cleanliness, and size of standard

★★★★★	Superior	Tasteful and luxurious by any standard
★★★★	Extremely Nice	What you would expect at a Hyatt Regency or Marriott
★★★	Nice	Holiday Inn or comparable quality
★★	Adequate	Clean, comfortable, and functional without frills (like a Motel 6)
★	Budget	Spartan, not aesthetically pleasing, but clean

HOT CHICAGO HOTELS

The big news in the Chicago hotel market is the long-awaited opening of the downtown **Trump International Hotel & Tower** (401 North Wabash Avenue; ☎ 877-458-7867 or 312-588-8000; **www.trumpchicagohotel .com**). The second-tallest building in the city, at 92 stories and nearly 1,400 feet, the Trump comprises a 339-room hotel and 486 condo units. The hotel caters to Chicago travelers with a New York budget—rooms start at $385 a night. Celebrity guests thus far have included Alicia Keys, Diddy, and Patrick Swayze. Sixteen, the critically acclaimed 16th-floor restaurant, is predictably pricey but also offers more-modest fare (a breakfast of two eggs with fries, choice of meat, tomato provençale, and breads costs $17). The second-floor Rebar (yes, a bar) features a resplendent view of the Chicago River that is also somewhat melancholy for literary natives: this same view was once enjoyed by the editorial department of the beloved *Chicago Sun-Times,* whose old building and presses were razed to make way for the stainless-steel-and-glass tower. The hotel is an easy walk to North Michigan Avenue and downtown.

Formerly the House of Blues Hotel, the **Hotel Sax Chicago** (333 North Dearborn Street; ☎ 877-569-3742 or 312-245-0333; **www.hotelsax chicago.com**) opened in 2007. The 353 rooms, remodeled and de-hipped from the House of Blues days, are more practical, albeit a bit gothic. The $25 million renovation did not, however, help the lousy views—most of the rooms on the hotel's south side face the parking garages of the adjacent Marina City complex. The Moroccan castle–like Crimson Lounge is a popular new night-spot. The Hotel Sax is within walking distance to Navy Pier and North Michigan Avenue, and the House of Blues concert hall is still next door.

The **Park View Hotel** (1816 North Clark Street; ☎ 312-664-3040; **www.parkviewhotelchicago.com**) is a completely renovated boutique hotel from the 1920s. The 194-room hotel (formerly the Gold Coast) has a superb view of Lincoln Park and is a 20-minute walk (or short cab or bus ride on the Clark Street bus) north to Wrigley Field. The neighborhood location is a good bet to get away from the hustle and bustle of downtown. Plus, the Park View is pet-friendly and 100% smoke-free.

New is the operative word at the **Fairmont Chicago** (200 North Columbus Drive; ☎ 866-540-4408 or 312-565-8000; **www.fairmont.com/chicago**). Recently renovated to the tune of $50 million, the 692-room hotel boasts a new lobby; a new wine-, cheese-, and chocolate-tasting room called ENO; and a new lifestyle concept called mySpa, along with extensively refurbished guest rooms. The Fairmont offers excellent views of Millennium Park and Lake Michigan.

rooms, we have grouped the hotels and motels into classifications with an overall rating denoted by stars. Star ratings in this guide apply to Chicago-area properties only and do not necessarily correspond to stars awarded by Mobil, AAA, or other travel critics. Because stars carry little weight when awarded in the absence of common standards

Chicago Hotels by Location

NORTH SIDE
Best Western
   Hawthorne Terrace
The Park View Hotel
Willows Hotel

**NORTH CENTRAL–
O'HARE**
aloft (W Hotel)
Best Western O'Hare
Candlewood Suites
   O'Hare
Carleton of Oak Park
Chicago O'Hare Garden
   Hotel
Crowne Plaza Chicago
   O'Hare
Doubletree O'Hare
   Rosemont
Embassy Suites O'Hare
Four Points Sheraton
   O'Hare
Hampton Inn O'Hare
Hilton O'Hare
Holiday Inn Express
   O'Hare
Holiday Inn Select
   O'Hare
Hyatt Regency O'Hare
Hyatt Rosemont
Marriott O'Hare
Marriott Suites O'Hare

Motel 6 O'Hare East
Quality Inn O'Hare
Radisson O'Hare
Residence Inn by
   Marriott O'Hare
Sheraton Gateway
Sofitel Chicago O'Hare
Suites O'Hare
Westin Hotel O'Hare
Wyndham O'Hare

NEAR NORTH
Affinia Hotel
Allerton Crowne Plaza
Ambassador East Hotel
Avenue Hotel
Best Western River
   North
Conrad Chicago
Courtyard by Marriott
   Downtown
Courtyard by Marriott
   Magnificent Mile
Doubletree Hotel
   Chicago Magnificent
   Mile
Drake Hotel
Embassy Suites Chicago
Embassy Suites
   Downtown/Lakefront
Four Seasons Hotel

Hampton Inn & Suites
   Downtown
Hilton Garden Inn
   Downtown
Hilton Suites Downtown
Holiday Inn Mart Plaza
Hotel Indigo
Hotel InterContinental
   Chicago
Howard Johnson
Inn of Chicago
The James Chicago
Marriott Chicago
   Downtown
Marriott Fairfield Inn &
   Suites Downtown
Marriott Residence Inn
   Downtown
Millennium
   Knickerbocker Hotel
Omni Chicago Hotel
Park Hyatt Chicago
The Peninsula
Raffaello
Red Roof Inn Downtown
Ritz-Carlton Chicago
Sax Hotel Chicago
The Seneca Hotel & Suites
Sheraton Chicago Hotel
   & Towers
Sofitel Water Tower

of comparison, we have linked our ratings to expected levels of quality established by specific American hotel corporations.

Star ratings describe the property's standard accommodations. For most hotels, a "standard accommodation" is a room with either one king bed or two queen beds. In an all-suite property, the standard accommodation is either a one- or two-room suite. In addition to standard accommodations, many hotels offer luxury rooms and special suites not rated here. Star ratings are assigned without regard to whether a property has restaurant(s), recreational facilities, entertainment, or other extras.

Sutton Place Hotel
Talbott Hotel
Trump International
   Hotel and Tower
W Lakeshore
Westin Michigan Avenue
Westin River North
   Chicago
Whitehall Hotel
Wyndham Chicago

THE LOOP
Fairmont Hotel
Hard Rock Hotel
Hotel 71
Hotel Allegro
Hotel Burnham
Hotel Monaco
Hyatt Regency Chicago
   in Illinois Center
Palmer House Hilton
Renaissance Chicago
   Hotel
Swissotel Chicago
W City Center Hotel

SOUTH LOOP
Best Western Grant
   Park Hotel
Hotel Blake
Congress Plaza Hotel &
   Convention Center

Essex Inn
Hilton Chicago
Hyatt Regency
   McCormick Place
Travelodge Downtown

SOUTHERN SUBURBS
Hampton Inn Midway
   Bedford Park
Hampton Inn
   Westchester/Chicago
Sleep Inn Midway
   Airport
Wyndham Drake Hotel
   Oak Brook

WESTERN SUBURBS
Comfort Inn
   Downers Grove
Courtyard by Marriott
   Oakbrook Terrace
Doubletree Hotel
   Downers Grove
Doubletree Hotel
   Chicago Oak Brook
Embassy Suites Lombard
Hilton Garden Inn
   Oakbrook Terrace
Hilton Suites Oakbrook
   Terrace
Holiday Inn Express
   Downers Grove

Holiday Inn Oakbrook
   Terrace
La Quinta Inn Oakbrook
   Terrace
Marriott Oak Brook
Marriott Suites
   Downers Grove
Red Roof Inn
   Downers Grove
Renaissance Oak Brook
   Hotel

**NORTHWEST
SUBURBS**
Comfort Inn Elk Grove
   Village
Courtyard by Marriott
   Wood Dale
Holiday Inn Elk Grove
   Village

NORTHERN SUBURBS
Best Western University
   Plaza
Doubletree Hotel
   Chicago North Shore
Hilton Garden Inn
   Evanston
Holiday Inn North Shore
Orrington Hotel
   Evanston

ROOM QUALITY In addition to stars (which delineate broad categories), we also employ a numerical rating system. Our rating scale is 0 to 100, with 100 as the best possible rating, and zero (0) as the worst. Numerical ratings are presented to show the difference we perceive between one property and another. Rooms at the Hotel Allegro, the Sofitel Chicago O'Hare, and the Four Points Sheraton O'Hare are all rated as three and a half stars (★★★½). In the supplemental numerical ratings, the Hotel Allegro is rated an 82, the Sofitel an 81, and the Four Points Sheraton a 79. This means that within the three-and-a-half-star category, the Sofitel is nicer than the Sheraton, and the Allegro has an edge over both.

How the Hotels Compare

HOTEL	OVERALL RATING	QUALITY RATING	COST ($ = $60)	LOCATION
Trump International Hotel and Tower	★★★★★	100	$$$$$$–	Near North
The Peninsula	★★★★★	99	$$$$$$$$+	Near North
Conrad Chicago	★★★★★	96	$$$$$	Near North
Marriott Residence Inn Downtown	★★★★★	96	$$$+	Near North
Park Hyatt Chicago	★★★★★	96	$$$$$$+	Near North
Swissotel Chicago	★★★★★	96	$$$	The Loop
Drake Hotel	★★★★½	95	$$$$$+	Near North
Hilton Chicago	★★★★½	95	$$$$+	South Loop
Ritz-Carlton Chicago	★★★★½	95	$$$$$+	Near North
Westin Michigan Avenue	★★★★½	95	$$$$$$+	Near North
Westin River North Chicago	★★★★½	95	$$+	Near North
Hotel Blake	★★★★½	94	$$$$–	South Loop
Fairmont Hotel	★★★★½	94	$$$–	The Loop
Raffaello	★★★★½	94	$$$$–	Near North
aloft (W Hotel)	★★★★½	93	$+	North Central–O'Hare
Courtyard by Marriott Downtown	★★★★½	93	$$$–	Near North
Hampton Inn & Suites Downtown	★★★★½	93	$$$	Near North
Hotel 71	★★★★½	93	$$$+	The Loop
Hotel InterContinental Chicago	★★★★½	93	$$$$$–	Near North
Hotel Monaco	★★★★½	93	$$$$$$	The Loop
W Lakeshore	★★★★½	93	$$$$+	Near North
Embassy Suites Downtown/Lakefront	★★★★½	92	$$$$$	Near North
Hard Rock Hotel	★★★★½	92	$$$$+	The Loop
Hilton Suites Downtown	★★★★½	92	$$$$$$–	Near North
Omni Chicago Hotel	★★★★½	92	$$$$$–	Near North
Renaissance Chicago Hotel	★★★★½	92	$$$$–	The Loop
Sax Hotel Chicago	★★★★½	92	$$$+	Near North
Sheraton Chicago Hotel & Towers	★★★★½	92	$$	Near North
Sofitel Water Tower	★★★★½	92	$$$$$+	Near North

HOTEL	OVERALL RATING	QUALITY RATING	COST ($ = $60)	LOCATION
Sutton Place Hotel	★★★★½	92	$$$$–	Near North
Affinia Hotel	★★★★½	91	$$$+	Near North
Hotel Burnham	★★★★½	91	$$$$$–	The Loop
Millennium Knickerbocker Hotel	★★★★½	91	$$$–	Near North
Ambassador East Hotel	★★★★½	90	$$$$–	Near North
Congress Plaza Hotel & Convention Center	★★★★½	90	$$$–	South Loop
Hilton Suites Oakbrook Terrace	★★★★½	90	$$–	Western Suburbs
Marriott Suites O'Hare	★★★★½	90	$$+	North Central–O'Hare
Palmer House Hilton	★★★★½	90	$$+	The Loop
Renaissance Oak Brook Hotel	★★★★½	90	$$	Western Suburbs
Talbott Hotel	★★★★½	90	$$$$$+	Near North
Doubletree Hotel Chicago Magnificent Mile	★★★★	89	$$$$+	Near North
Doubletree O'Hare Rosemont	★★★★	89	$$–	North Central–O'Hare
Essex Inn	★★★★	89	$$$$–	South Loop
The James Chicago	★★★★	89	$$$–	Near North
Orrington Hotel Evanston	★★★★	89	$$$+	Northern Suburbs
The Seneca Hotel & Suites	★★★★	89	$$+	Near North
Four Seasons Hotel	★★★★	88	$$$$$$+	Near North
Hilton O'Hare	★★★★	88	$$$–	North Central–O'Hare
Hotel Indigo	★★★★	88	$$$$–	Near North
W City Center Hotel	★★★★	88	$$$$+	The Loop
Wyndham Chicago	★★★★	88	$$$–	Near North
Holiday Inn Select O'Hare	★★★★	87	$$–	North Central–O'Hare
Marriott Oak Brook	★★★★	87	$$	Western Suburbs
Sheraton Gateway Suites O'Hare	★★★★	87	$$	North Central–O'Hare

How the Hotels Compare (continued)

HOTEL	OVERALL RATING	QUALITY RATING	COST ($ = $60)	LOCATION
Westin Hotel O'Hare	★★★★	87	$$+	North Central–O'Hare
Allerton Crowne Plaza	★★★★	86	$$$$–	Near North
Doubletree Hotel Chicago North Shore	★★★★	86	$$$–	Northern Suburbs
Hilton Garden Inn Evanston	★★★★	86	$$$$$–	Northern Suburbs
Hilton Garden Inn Oakbrook Terrace	★★★★	86	$$$–	Western Suburbs
Hyatt Regency Chicago in Illinois Center	★★★★	86	$$$$	The Loop
Hyatt Regency McCormick Place	★★★★	86	$$$$–	South Loop
Residence Inn by Marriott O'Hare	★★★★	86	$$	North Central–O'Hare
Carleton of Oak Park	★★★★	85	$$$	North Central–O'Hare
Courtyard by Marriott Wood Dale	★★★★	85	$+	Northwest Suburbs
Doubletree Downers Grove	★★★★	85	$+	Western Suburbs
Embassy Suites O'Hare	★★★★	85	$$+	North Central–O'Hare
Hampton Inn O'Hare	★★★★	85	$$–	North Central–O'Hare
Hyatt Regency O'Hare	★★★★	85	$$$	North Central–O'Hare
Inn of Chicago	★★★★	85	$$$–	Near North
Marriott O'Hare	★★★★	85	$$+	North Central–O'Hare
Marriott Suites Downers Grove	★★★★	85	$$+	Western Suburbs
Whitehall Hotel	★★★★	85	$$$+	Near North
Avenue Hotel	★★★★	84	$$$$–	Near North
Embassy Suites Lombard	★★★★	84	$$–	Western Suburbs
Hilton Garden Inn Downtown	★★★★	84	$$$$–	Near North
Candlewood Suites O'Hare	★★★★	83	$+	North Central–O'Hare

HOTEL	OVERALL RATING	QUALITY RATING	COST ($ = $60)	LOCATION
Chicago O'Hare Garden Hotel	★★★★	83	$+	North Central–O'Hare
Crowne Plaza Chicago O'Hare	★★★★	83	$$–	North Central–O'Hare
Embassy Suites Chicago	★★★★	83	$$$$+	Near North
Holiday Inn North Shore	★★★★	83	$$+	Northern Suburbs
Hyatt Rosemont	★★★★	83	$$$–	North Central–O'Hare
Radisson O'Hare	★★★★	83	$+	North Central–O'Hare
Courtyard by Marriott Magnificent Mile	★★★½	82	$$$+	Near North
Courtyard by Marriott Oakbrook Terrace	★★★½	82	$+	Western Suburbs
Doubletree Hotel Chicago Oak Brook	★★★½	82	$$–	Western Suburbs
Holiday Inn Elk Grove Village	★★★½	82	$$	Northwest Suburbs
Holiday Inn Mart Plaza	★★★½	82	$$$$$–	Near North
Hotel Allegro	★★★½	82	$$$$+	The Loop
Sofitel Chicago O'Hare	★★★½	81	$$+	North Central–O'Hare
Holiday Inn Express O'Hare	★★★½	80	$$–	North Central–O'Hare
Wyndham Drake Hotel Oak Brook	★★★½	80	$$–	Southern Suburbs
Comfort Inn Elk Grove Village	★★★½	79	$$–	Northwest Suburbs
Four Points Sheraton O'Hare	★★★½	79	$$–	North Central–O'Hare
Hampton Inn Westchester/ Chicago	★★★½	79	$+	Southern Suburbs
Marriott Chicago Downtown	★★★½	79	$$$$$+	Near North
Wyndham O'Hare	★★★½	79	$$$+	North Central–O'Hare
Best Western Grant Park Hotel	★★★½	77	$$$	South Loop
Best Western Hawthorne Terrace	★★★½	77	$$$	North Side

How the Hotels Compare (continued)

HOTEL	OVERALL RATING	QUALITY RATING	COST ($ = $60)	LOCATION
Best Western River North	★★★½	75	$+	Near North
Best Western University Plaza	★★★½	75	$$–	Northern Suburbs
Marriott Fairfield Inn & Suites Downtown	★★★½	75	$$$–	Near North
Holiday Inn Oakbrook Terrace	★★★	74	$$+	Western Suburbs
Best Western O'Hare	★★★	72	$$–	North Central–O'Hare
Hampton Inn Midway Bedford Park	★★★	72	$$	Southern Suburbs
Holiday Inn Express Downers Grove	★★★	72	$$	Western Suburbs
Willows Hotel	★★★	72	$$$+	North Side
Quality Inn O'Hare	★★★	71	$+	North Central–O'Hare

COST Pricing estimates are based on the hotel's published rack rates for standard rooms. Each dollar sign ($) represents $60. Thus, a cost symbol of $$$ means a room (or suite) at that hotel will cost about $180 a night.

LOCATION The location column identifies the neighborhood where you will find a particular property (see chart on pages 48–49).

HOW THE HOTELS COMPARE IN CHICAGO

ON PAGES 58–70 is a hit parade of the nicest rooms in town. We've focused strictly on room quality and excluded any consideration of location, services, recreation, or amenities. In a few instances, a suite can be had for the same price or less than that of a standard hotel room.

If you use subsequent editions of this guide, you will notice that many of the ratings and rankings have changed. In addition to the inclusion of new properties, these changes also consider guest-room renovations or improved maintenance and housekeeping. A failure to properly maintain guest rooms or a lapse in housekeeping standards can negatively affect the ratings.

HOTEL	OVERALL RATING	QUALITY RATING	COST ($ = $60)	LOCATION
Comfort Inn Downers Grove	★★★	70	$	Western Suburbs
Red Roof Inn Downers Grove	★★★	70	$	Western Suburbs
La Quinta Inn Oakbrook Terrace	★★★	67	$+	Western Suburbs
The Park View Hotel	★★★	67	$$$–	North Side
Sleep Inn Midway Airport	★★★	66	$$–	Southern Suburbs
Red Roof Inn Downtown	★★★	65	$$+	Near North
Travelodge Downtown	★★★	65	$$+	South Loop
Howard Johnson	★★½	61	$+	Near North
Motel 6 O'Hare East	★★½	60	$–	North Central–O'Hare

Although unusual, it is certainly possible that the rooms we randomly inspect are not representative of the majority of rooms at a particular hotel. Another possibility is that the rooms we inspect in a given hotel are representative but that by bad luck a reader is assigned a room that is inferior. To avoid disappointment, we recommend that you look on the Web, ask for a photo of a hotel's standard guest room before you book, or at least get a copy of the hotel's promotional brochure. Alas, some hotel chains use the same guest-room photo in their promotional literature for all their properties; a specific guest room may not resemble the brochure photo. Find out how old the property is and when your guest room was last renovated. If you arrive and are assigned an inferior room, demand to be moved.

TOP 30 HOTEL DEALS IN CHICAGO

HAVING LISTED THE NICEST ROOMS in town, let's reorder the list to rank the best combinations of quality and value in a room. The rankings are made without consideration of location or the availability of restaurant(s), recreational facilities, entertainment, or amenities. See the following pages for the full list.

The Top 30 Best Hotel Deals in Chicago

HOTEL	OVERALL RATING	QUALITY RATING	COST ($ = $60)	LOCATION
1. aloft (W Hotel)	★★★★½	93	$+	North Central–O'Hare
2. Courtyard by Marriott Wood Dale	★★★★	85	$+	Northwest Suburbs
3. Doubletree Downers Grove	★★★★	85	$+	Western Suburbs
4. Candlewood Suites O'Hare	★★★★	83	$+	North Central–O'Hare
5. Holiday Inn Select O'Hare	★★★★	87	$$–	North Central–O'Hare
6. Hampton Inn O'Hare	★★★★	85	$$–	North Central–O'Hare
7. Chicago O'Hare Garden Hotel	★★★★	83	$+	North Central–O'Hare
8. Radisson O'Hare	★★★★	83	$+	North Central–O'Hare
9. Hilton Suites Oakbrook Terrace	★★★★½	90	$$–	Western Suburbs
10. Hampton Inn Westchester/Chicago	★★★½	79	$+	Southern Suburbs
11. Doubletree O'Hare Rosemont	★★★★	89	$$–	North Central–O'Hare
12. Crowne Plaza Chicago O'Hare	★★★★	83	$$–	North Central–O'Hare
13. Red Roof Inn Downers Grove	★★★	70	$	Western Suburbs
14. Sheraton Chicago Hotel & Towers	★★★★½	92	$$	Near North
15. Renaissance Oakbrook Hotel	★★★★½	90	$$	Western Suburbs

HOTEL	OVERALL RATING	QUALITY RATING	COST ($ = $60)	LOCATION
16. Embassy Suites Lombard	★★★★	84	$$–	Western Suburbs
17. Comfort Inn Downers Grove	★★★	70	$	Western Suburbs
18. Courtyard by Marriott Oakbrook Terrace	★★★½	82	$+	Western Suburbs
19. Marriott Suites O'Hare	★★★★½	90	$$+	North Central–O'Hare
20. Holiday Inn Express O'Hare	★★★½	80	$$–	North Central–O'Hare
21. Motel 6 O'Hare East	★★½	60	$–	North Central–O'Hare
22. Quality Inn O'Hare	★★★	71	$+	North Central–O'Hare
23. Residence Inn by Marriott O'Hare	★★★★	86	$$	North Central–O'Hare
24. Best Western River North	★★★½	75	$+	Near North
25. Marriott Oak Brook	★★★★	87	$$	Western Suburbs
26. Sheraton Gateway Suites O'Hare	★★★★	87	$$	North Central–O'Hare
27. Wyndham Drake Hotel Oak Brook	★★★½	80	$$–	Southern Suburbs
28. Palmer House Hilton	★★★★½	90	$$+	The Loop
29. Four Points Sheraton O'Hare	★★★½	79	$$–	North Central–O'Hare
30. Westin River North Chicago	★★★★½	95	$$+	Near North

Hotel Information Chart

aloft (W Hotel) ★★★★½		Affinia Hotel ★★★★½		Allerton Crowne Plaza ★★★★	
9700 Balmoral Ave.		166 East Superior Street		701 North Michigan Avenue	
Rosemont 60018		Chicago 60611		Chicago 60611	
☎ 847-671-4444		☎ 312-787-6000		☎ 312-440-1500	
TOLL-FREE ☎ 877-462-5638		TOLL-FREE ☎ 800-367-7701		TOLL-FREE ☎ 800-227-6963	
www.alofthotels.com		www.affinia.com		www.theallertonhotel.com	
ROOM QUALITY	93	ROOM QUALITY	91		
COST ($ = $60)	$+	COST ($ = $60)	$$$+	ROOM QUALITY	86
LOCATION	N. Central–O'Hare	LOCATION	Near North	COST ($ = $60)	$$$$–
NO. OF ROOMS	251	NO. OF ROOMS	140	LOCATION	Near North
PARKING	Self, $22; valet, $25	PARKING	Valet, $48	NO. OF ROOMS	443
		ROOM SERVICE	•	PARKING	Valet, $40
ROOM SERVICE	—	BREAKFAST	—	ROOM SERVICE	•
BREAKFAST	—	ON-SITE DINING	•	BREAKFAST	—
ON-SITE DINING	•	POOL	•	ON-SITE DINING	•
POOL	—	SAUNA	—	POOL	—
SAUNA	—	EXERCISE FACILITIES	•	SAUNA	—
EXERCISE FACILITIES	—			EXERCISE FACILITIES	•

Best Western Hawthorne Terrace ★★★½		Best Western O'Hare ★★★		Best Western River North ★★★½	
3434 North Broadway Street		10300 West Higgins Road		125 West Ohio Street	
Chicago 60657		Rosemont 60018		Chicago 60610	
☎ 773-244-3434		☎ 847-296-4471		☎ 312-467-0800	
TOLL-FREE ☎ 888-860-3400		TOLL-FREE ☎ 800-528-1234		TOLL-FREE ☎ 800-704-6941	
www.hawthorneterrace.com		www.bestwesternohare.com		www.rivernorthhotel.com	
ROOM QUALITY	77	ROOM QUALITY	72	ROOM QUALITY	75
COST ($ = $60)	$$$	COST ($ = $60)	$$–	COST ($ = $60)	$+
LOCATION	North Side	LOCATION	N. Central–O'Hare	LOCATION	Near North
NO. OF ROOMS	59			NO. OF ROOMS	150
PARKING	Valet, $22	NO. OF ROOMS	143	PARKING	Lot, free
ROOM SERVICE	• (limited)	PARKING	Lot, free	ROOM SERVICE	•
BREAKFAST	Continental	ROOM SERVICE	•	BREAKFAST	—
ON-SITE DINING	—	BREAKFAST	—	ON-SITE DINING	•
POOL	—	ON-SITE DINING	•	POOL	•
SAUNA	—	POOL	•	SAUNA	•
EXERCISE FACILITIES	•	SAUNA	—	EXERCISE FACILITIES	•
		EXERCISE FACILITIES	•		

Chicago O'Hare Garden Hotel ★★★★		Comfort Inn Downers Grove ★★★		Comfort Inn Elk Grove Village ★★★½	
8201 West Higgins Road		3010 Finley Road		2550 Landmeier Road	
Chicago 60631		Downers Grove 60515		Wood Dale 60191	
☎ 773-693-2323		☎ 630-515-1500		☎ 847-364-6200	
TOLL-FREE ☎ 877-999-3223		TOLL-FREE ☎ 800-228-5150		TOLL-FREE ☎ 877-424-6423	
www.hotelchicagooharegarden.com		www.comfortinn.com		www.comfortinnchicago.com	
ROOM QUALITY	83	ROOM QUALITY	70	ROOM QUALITY	79
COST ($ = $60)	$+	COST ($ = $60)	$	COST ($ = $60)	$$–
LOCATION	N. Central–O'Hare	LOCATION	Western Suburbs	LOCATION	Northwest Suburbs
NO. OF ROOMS	117	NO. OF ROOMS	120	NO. OF ROOMS	100
PARKING	Lot, free	PARKING	Lot, free	PARKING	Lot, free
ROOM SERVICE	•	ROOM SERVICE	—	ROOM SERVICE	—
BREAKFAST	—	BREAKFAST	Continental	BREAKFAST	Continental
ON-SITE DINING	•	ON-SITE DINING	—	ON-SITE DINING	•
POOL	•	POOL	•	POOL	—
SAUNA	•	SAUNA	—	SAUNA	—
EXERCISE FACILITIES	•	EXERCISE FACILITIES	•	EXERCISE FACILITIES	•

Ambassador East Hotel ★★★★½

1301 North State Parkway
Chicago 60610
☎ 312-787-7200
TOLL-FREE ☎ 888-506-3471
www.theambassadoreasthotel.com

ROOM QUALITY	90
COST ($ = $60)	$$$$–
LOCATION	Near North
NO. OF ROOMS	285
PARKING	Valet, $36
ROOM SERVICE	•
BREAKFAST	—
ON-SITE DINING	•
POOL	—
SAUNA	—
EXERCISE FACILITIES	•

Avenue Hotel ★★★★

160 East Huron Street
Chicago 60611
☎ 847-283-5110
TOLL-FREE ☎ 800-333-3333
www.avenuehotelchicago.com

ROOM QUALITY	84
COST ($ = $60)	$$$$–
LOCATION	Near North
NO. OF ROOMS	350
PARKING	Valet, $39
ROOM SERVICE	•
BREAKFAST	—
ON-SITE DINING	•
POOL	•
SAUNA	—
EXERCISE FACILITIES	-

Best Western Grant Park Hotel ★★★½

1100 South Michigan Avenue
Chicago 60605
☎ 312-922-2900
TOLL-FREE ☎ 800-472-6875
www.bestwestern.com

ROOM QUALITY	77
COST ($ = $60)	$$$
LOCATION	South Loop
NO. OF ROOMS	172
PARKING	Valet, $24 (cars only)
ROOM SERVICE	•
BREAKFAST	—
ON-SITE DINING	•
POOL	•
SAUNA	—
EXERCISE FACILITIES	•

Best Western University Plaza ★★★½

1501 Sherman Avenue
Evanston 60201
☎ 847-491-6400
TOLL-FREE ☎ 800-381-2830
www.bestwestern.com

ROOM QUALITY	75
COST ($ = $60)	$$–
LOCATION	Northern Suburbs
NO. OF ROOMS	159
PARKING	Self, $10
ROOM SERVICE	—
BREAKFAST	—
ON-SITE DINING	•
POOL	•
SAUNA	—
EXERCISE FACILITIES	•

Candlewood Suites O'Hare ★★★★

4021 North Mannheim Road
Schiller Park 60176
☎ 847-671-4663
TOLL-FREE ☎ 888-CANDLEWOOD
www.candlewoodsuites.com

ROOM QUALITY	83
COST ($ = $60)	$+
LOCATION	N. Central–O'Hare
NO. OF ROOMS	160
PARKING	Self, $8
ROOM SERVICE	—
BREAKFAST	—
ON-SITE DINING	—
POOL	—
SAUNA	—
EXERCISE FACILITIES	•

Carleton of Oak Park ★★★★

1110 Pleasant Street
Oak Park 60302
☎ 708-848-5000
TOLL-FREE ☎ 888-227-5386
www.carletonhotel.com

ROOM QUALITY	85
COST ($ = $60)	$$$
LOCATION	N. Central–O'Hare
NO. OF ROOMS	150
PARKING	Lot, free
ROOM SERVICE	•
BREAKFAST	—
ON-SITE DINING	•
POOL	—
SAUNA	—
EXERCISE FACILITIES	—

Congress Plaza Hotel & Convention Center ★★★★½

520 South Michigan Avenue
Chicago 60605
☎ 312-427-3800
TOLL-FREE ☎ 800-635-1666
www.congressplazahotel.com

ROOM QUALITY	90
COST ($ = $60)	$$$–
LOCATION	South Loop
NO. OF ROOMS	870
PARKING	Self, $27; valet, $32
ROOM SERVICE	•
BREAKFAST	—
ON-SITE DINING	•
POOL	—
SAUNA	—
EXERCISE FACILITIES	•

Conrad Chicago ★★★★★

521 North Rush Street
Chicago 60611
☎ 312-645-1500
TOLL-FREE ☎ 800-266-7237
www.conradhotels.com

ROOM QUALITY	96
COST ($ = $60)	$$$$$
LOCATION	Near North
NO. OF ROOMS	311
PARKING	Self, $29; valet, $48
ROOM SERVICE	•
BREAKFAST	—
ON-SITE DINING	•
POOL	—
SAUNA	—
EXERCISE FACILITIES	•

Courtyard by Marriott Downtown ★★★★½

30 East Hubbard Street
Chicago 60611
☎ 312-329-2500
TOLL-FREE ☎ 800-321-2211
www.marriott.com

ROOM QUALITY	93
COST ($ = $60)	$$$–
LOCATION	Near North
NO. OF ROOMS	337
PARKING	Valet, $45
ROOM SERVICE	•
BREAKFAST	—
ON-SITE DINING	•
POOL	•
SAUNA	•
EXERCISE FACILITIES	•

Hotel Information Chart (continued)

Courtyard by Marriott Magnificent Mile ★★★½		
165 East Ontario Street		
Chicago 60611		
☎ 312-573-0800		
TOLL-FREE ☎ 800-321-2211		
www.marriott.com		

ROOM QUALITY		82
COST ($ = $60)		$$$+
LOCATION		Near North
NO. OF ROOMS		306
PARKING		Self, $28; valet, $42
ROOM SERVICE		—
BREAKFAST		—
ON-SITE DINING		•
POOL		—
SAUNA		—
EXERCISE FACILITIES		•

Courtyard by Marriott Oakbrook Terrace ★★★½
6 Transam Plaza Drive
Oakbrook Terrace 60181
☎ 630-691-1500
TOLL-FREE ☎ 800-321-2211
www.marriott.com

ROOM QUALITY	82
COST ($ = $60)	$+
LOCATION	Western Suburbs
NO. OF ROOMS	147
PARKING	Lot, free
ROOM SERVICE	—
BREAKFAST	—
ON-SITE DINING	•
POOL	•
SAUNA	—
EXERCISE FACILITIES	•

Courtyard by Marriott Wood Dale ★★★★
900 North Wood Dale Road
Wood Dale 60191
☎ 630-766-7775
TOLL-FREE ☎ 800-321-2211
www.marriott.com

ROOM QUALITY	85
COST ($ = $60)	$+
LOCATION	Northwest Suburbs
NO. OF ROOMS	149
PARKING	Lot, free
ROOM SERVICE	—
BREAKFAST	—
ON-SITE DINING	•
POOL	•
SAUNA	—
EXERCISE FACILITIES	•

Doubletree Hotel Chicago North Shore ★★★★
9599 Skokie Boulevard
Skokie 60077
☎ 847-679-7000
TOLL-FREE ☎ 800-222-TREE
www.skokieillinoishotel.com

ROOM QUALITY	86
COST ($ = $60)	$$$–
LOCATION	Northern Suburbs
NO. OF ROOMS	367
PARKING	Lot, free
ROOM SERVICE	•
BREAKFAST	—
ON-SITE DINING	•
POOL	•
SAUNA	—
EXERCISE FACILITIES	•

Doubletree Hotel Chicago Oak Brook ★★★½
1909 Spring Road
Oak Brook 60523
☎ 630-472-6000
TOLL-FREE ☎ 800-222-TREE
www.doubletree.com

ROOM QUALITY	82
COST ($ = $60)	$$–
LOCATION	Western Suburbs
NO. OF ROOMS	427
PARKING	Garage, free
ROOM SERVICE	•
BREAKFAST	—
ON-SITE DINING	•
POOL	•
SAUNA	—
EXERCISE FACILITIES	•

Doubletree O'Hare Rosemont ★★★★
5460 North River Road
Rosemont 60018
☎ 847-292-3538
TOLL-FREE ☎ 800-222-TREE
www.doubletree.com

ROOM QUALITY	89
COST ($ = $60)	$$–
LOCATION	N. Central– O'Hare
NO. OF ROOMS	369
PARKING	Self, $11; valet, $24
ROOM SERVICE	•
BREAKFAST	—
ON-SITE DINING	•
POOL	•
SAUNA	—
EXERCISE FACILITIES	•

Embassy Suites Lombard ★★★★
707 East Butterfield Road
Lombard 60148
☎ 630-969-7500
TOLL-FREE ☎ 800-EMBASSY
www.embassysuites.com

ROOM QUALITY	84
COST ($ = $60)	$$–
LOCATION	Western Suburbs
NO. OF ROOMS	262
PARKING	Lot, free
ROOM SERVICE	•
BREAKFAST	Cooked to order
ON-SITE DINING	•
POOL	•
SAUNA	—
EXERCISE FACILITIES	•

Embassy Suites O'Hare ★★★★
5500 North River Road
Rosemont 60018
☎ 847-678-4000
TOLL-FREE ☎ 800-EMBASSY
www.embassysuites.com

ROOM QUALITY	85
COST ($ = $60)	$$+
LOCATION	N. Central– O'Hare
NO. OF ROOMS	294
PARKING	Self, $20
ROOM SERVICE	•
BREAKFAST	Continental
ON-SITE DINING	•
POOL	•
SAUNA	—
EXERCISE FACILITIES	•

Essex Inn ★★★★
800 South Michigan Avenue
Chicago 60605
☎ 312-939-2800
TOLL-FREE ☎ 800-621-6909
www.essexinn.com

ROOM QUALITY	89
COST ($ = $60)	$$$$–
LOCATION	South Loop
NO. OF ROOMS	254
PARKING	Valet, $36
ROOM SERVICE	•
BREAKFAST	•
ON-SITE DINING	•
POOL	•
SAUNA	•
EXERCISE FACILITIES	•

Crowne Plaza Chicago O'Hare ★★★★
5440 North River Road
Rosemont 60018
☎ 847-671-6350
TOLL-FREE ☎ 888-642-7344
chi-ohare.crowneplaza.com

ROOM QUALITY	83
COST ($ = $60)	$$–
LOCATION	N. Central–O'Hare
NO. OF ROOMS	505
PARKING	Self, $18
ROOM SERVICE	•
BREAKFAST	—
ON-SITE DINING	•
POOL	•
SAUNA	•
EXERCISE FACILITIES	•

Doubletree Downers Grove ★★★★
2111 Butterfield Road
Downers Grove 60515
☎ 630-971-2000
TOLL-FREE ☎ 800-222-TREE
www.doubletree.com

ROOM QUALITY	85
COST ($ = $60)	$+
LOCATION	Western Suburbs
NO. OF ROOMS	247
PARKING	Lot, free
ROOM SERVICE	•
BREAKFAST	—
ON-SITE DINING	•
POOL	•
SAUNA	—
EXERCISE FACILITIES	•

Doubletree Hotel Chicago Magnificent Mile ★★★★
300 East Ohio Street
Chicago 60611
☎ 312-787-6100
TOLL-FREE ☎ 800-HOLIDAY
www.chicc.com

ROOM QUALITY	89
COST ($ = $60)	$$$$+
LOCATION	Near North
NO. OF ROOMS	500
PARKING	Self, $38
ROOM SERVICE	•
BREAKFAST	—
ON-SITE DINING	•
POOL	•
SAUNA	•
EXERCISE FACILITIES	•

Drake Hotel ★★★★½
140 East Walton Place
Chicago 60611
☎ 312-787-2200
TOLL-FREE ☎ 800-55-DRAKE
www.thedrakehotel.com

ROOM QUALITY	95
COST ($ = $60)	$$$$$+
LOCATION	Near North
NO. OF ROOMS	535
PARKING	Valet, $41
ROOM SERVICE	•
BREAKFAST	—
ON-SITE DINING	•
POOL	—
SAUNA	—
EXERCISE FACILITIES	•

Embassy Suites Chicago ★★★★
600 North State Street
Chicago 60610
☎ 312-943-3800
TOLL-FREE ☎ 800-EMBASSY
www.embassysuites.com

ROOM QUALITY	83
COST ($ = $60)	$$$$+
LOCATION	Near North
NO. OF ROOMS	367
PARKING	Valet, $44
ROOM SERVICE	•
BREAKFAST	Full
ON-SITE DINING	•
POOL	•
SAUNA	—
EXERCISE FACILITIES	•

Embassy Suites Downtown/Lakefront ★★★★½
511 North Columbus Drive
Chicago 60611
☎ 312-836-5900
TOLL-FREE ☎ 800-EMBASSY
www.embassysuites.com

ROOM QUALITY	92
COST ($ = $60)	$$$$$
LOCATION	Near North
NO. OF ROOMS	455
PARKING	Self, $41; valet, 48
ROOM SERVICE	•
BREAKFAST	Full
ON-SITE DINING	•
POOL	•
SAUNA	•
EXERCISE FACILITIES	•

Fairmont Hotel ★★★★½
200 North Columbus Drive
Chicago 60601
☎ 312-565-8000
TOLL-FREE ☎ 800-257-7544
www.fairmont.com

ROOM QUALITY	94
COST ($ = $60)	$$$–
LOCATION	The Loop
NO. OF ROOMS	692
PARKING	Valet, $49
ROOM SERVICE	•
BREAKFAST	—
ON-SITE DINING	•
POOL	—
SAUNA	•
EXERCISE FACILITIES	•

Four Points Sheraton O'Hare ★★★½
10249 West Irving Park Road
Schiller Park 60176
☎ 847-671-6000
TOLL-FREE ☎ 800-323-1239
www.starwoodhotels.com

ROOM QUALITY	79
COST ($ = $60)	$$–
LOCATION	N. Central–O'Hare
NO. OF ROOMS	295
PARKING	Lot, free
ROOM SERVICE	•
BREAKFAST	—
ON-SITE DINING	•
POOL	•
SAUNA	•
EXERCISE FACILITIES	•

Four Seasons Hotel ★★★★
120 East Delaware Place
Chicago 60611
☎ 312-280-8800
TOLL-FREE ☎ 800-819-5053
www.fourseasons.com

ROOM QUALITY	88
COST ($ = $60)	$$$$$$+
LOCATION	Near North
NO. OF ROOMS	343
PARKING	Self, $26; valet $36
ROOM SERVICE	•
BREAKFAST	—
ON-SITE DINING	•
POOL	•
SAUNA	•
EXERCISE FACILITIES	•

Hotel Information Chart (continued)

Hampton Inn & Suites Downtown ★★★★½
33 West Illinois Street
Chicago 60610
☎ 312-832-0330
TOLL-FREE ☎ 800-HAMPTON
www.hamptoninn.com

ROOM QUALITY	93
COST ($ = $60)	$$$
LOCATION	Near North
NO. OF ROOMS	230
PARKING	Valet, $38
ROOM SERVICE	•
BREAKFAST	Full
ON-SITE DINING	—
POOL	•
SAUNA	—
EXERCISE FACILITIES	•

Hampton Inn Midway Bedford Park ★★★
6540 South Cicero Avenue
Bedford Park 60638
☎ 708-496-1900
TOLL-FREE ☎ 800-HAMPTON
www.hamptoninn.com

ROOM QUALITY	72
COST ($ = $60)	$$
LOCATION	Southern Suburbs
NO. OF ROOMS	170
PARKING	Self, $10
ROOM SERVICE	•
BREAKFAST	Full
ON-SITE DINING	•
POOL	—
SAUNA	—
EXERCISE FACILITIES	•

Hampton Inn O'Hare ★★★★
3939 North Mannheim Road
Schiller Park 60176
☎ 847-671-1700
TOLL-FREE ☎ 800-446-4656
www.hamptoninnohare.com

ROOM QUALITY	85
COST ($ = $60)	$$–
LOCATION	N. Central–O'Hare
NO. OF ROOMS	150
PARKING	Lot, free
ROOM SERVICE	•
BREAKFAST	Continental
ON-SITE DINING	•
POOL	•
SAUNA	—
EXERCISE FACILITIES	•

Hilton Garden Inn Downtown ★★★★
10 East Grand Avenue
Chicago 60611
☎ 312-595-0000
TOLL-FREE ☎ 877-STAY-HGI
www.hiltongardenchicago.com

ROOM QUALITY	84
COST ($ = $60)	$$$$–
LOCATION	Near North
NO. OF ROOMS	357
PARKING	Self, $26; valet, $44
ROOM SERVICE	•
BREAKFAST	Full
ON-SITE DINING	•
POOL	•
SAUNA	—
EXERCISE FACILITIES	•

Hilton Garden Inn Evanston ★★★★
1818 Maple Avenue
Evanston 60201
☎ 847-475-6400
TOLL-FREE ☎ 877-782-9444
www.hiltongardeninn.com

ROOM QUALITY	86
COST ($ = $60)	$$$$$–
LOCATION	Northern Suburbs
NO. OF ROOMS	178
PARKING	Self, $10
ROOM SERVICE	•
BREAKFAST	—
ON-SITE DINING	•
POOL	•
SAUNA	—
EXERCISE FACILITIES	•

Hilton Garden Inn Oakbrook Terrace ★★★★
1000 Drury Lane
Oakbrook Terrace 60181
☎ 630-941-1177
TOLL-FREE ☎ 877-STAY-HGI
www.hilton.com

ROOM QUALITY	86
COST ($ = $60)	$$$–
LOCATION	Western Suburbs
NO. OF ROOMS	128
PARKING	Garage, free
ROOM SERVICE	•
BREAKFAST	•
ON-SITE DINING	•
POOL	•
SAUNA	—
EXERCISE FACILITIES	•

Holiday Inn Elk Grove Village ★★★½
1000 Busse Road
Elk Grove Village 60007
☎ 847-434-1142
TOLL-FREE ☎ 800-972-2494
www.ichotelsgroup.com

ROOM QUALITY	82
COST ($ = $60)	$$
LOCATION	Northwest Suburbs
NO. OF ROOMS	160
PARKING	Lot, free
ROOM SERVICE	•
BREAKFAST	—
ON-SITE DINING	•
POOL	•
SAUNA	•
EXERCISE FACILITIES	•

Holiday Inn Express Downers Grove ★★★
3031 Finley Road
Downers Grove 60515
☎ 630-810-9500
TOLL-FREE ☎ 800-HOLIDAY
www.ichotelsgroup.com

ROOM QUALITY	72
COST ($ = $60)	$$
LOCATION	Western Suburbs
NO. OF ROOMS	133
PARKING	Lot, free
ROOM SERVICE	—
BREAKFAST	Continental
ON-SITE DINING	—
POOL	—
SAUNA	—
EXERCISE FACILITIES	—

Holiday Inn Express O'Hare ★★★½
6600 North Mannheim Road
Rosemont 60018
☎ 847-544-7500
TOLL-FREE ☎ 800-972-2494
www.ichotelsgroup.com

ROOM QUALITY	80
COST ($ = $60)	$$–
LOCATION	N. Central–O'Hare
NO. OF ROOMS	274
PARKING	Self, $14
ROOM SERVICE	—
BREAKFAST	Full
ON-SITE DINING	—
POOL	—
SAUNA	—
EXERCISE FACILITIES	•

Hampton Inn Westchester/Chicago ★★★½
2222 Enterprise Drive
Westchester 60154
☎ 708-409-1000
TOLL-FREE ☎ 800-HAMPTON
www.hamptoninn.com

ROOM QUALITY	79
COST ($ = $60)	$+
LOCATION	Southern Suburbs
NO. OF ROOMS	112
PARKING	Lot, free
ROOM SERVICE	—
BREAKFAST	Full
ON-SITE DINING	—
POOL	—
SAUNA	—
EXERCISE FACILITIES	•

Hard Rock Hotel ★★★★½
230 North Michigan Avenue
Chicago 60601
☎ 312-345-1000
TOLL-FREE ☎ 866-966-5166
www.hardrockhotelchicago.com

ROOM QUALITY	92
COST ($ = $60)	$$$$+
LOCATION	The Loop
NO. OF ROOMS	381
PARKING	Valet, $38
ROOM SERVICE	•
BREAKFAST	—
ON-SITE DINING	•
POOL	—
SAUNA	—
EXERCISE FACILITIES	•

Hilton Chicago ★★★★½
720 South Michigan Avenue
Chicago 60605
☎ 312-922-4400
TOLL-FREE ☎ 800-HILTONS
www.hilton.com

ROOM QUALITY	95
COST ($ = $60)	$$$$+
LOCATION	South Loop
NO. OF ROOMS	1,544
PARKING	Self, $41; valet, $49
ROOM SERVICE	•
BREAKFAST	—
ON-SITE DINING	•
POOL	•
SAUNA	—
EXERCISE FACILITIES	•

Hilton O'Hare ★★★★
O'Hare International Airport
Chicago 60666
☎ 773-686-8000
TOLL-FREE ☎ 800-HILTONS
www.hilton.com

ROOM QUALITY	88
COST ($ = $60)	$$$–
LOCATION	N. Central–O'Hare
NO. OF ROOMS	858
PARKING	Self, $45
ROOM SERVICE	•
BREAKFAST	—
ON-SITE DINING	•
POOL	•
SAUNA	—
EXERCISE FACILITIES	•

Hilton Suites Downtown ★★★★½
198 East Delaware Place
Chicago 60611
☎ 312-664-1100
TOLL-FREE ☎ 800-222-TREE
www.hilton.com

ROOM QUALITY	92
COST ($ = $60)	$$$$$$–
LOCATION	Near North
NO. OF ROOMS	345
PARKING	Valet, $50
ROOM SERVICE	•
BREAKFAST	—
ON-SITE DINING	•
POOL	•
SAUNA	•
EXERCISE FACILITIES	•

Hilton Suites Oakbrook Terrace ★★★★½
10 Drury Lane
Oakbrook Terrace 60181
☎ 630-941-0100
TOLL-FREE ☎ 800-HILTONS
www.hilton.com

ROOM QUALITY	90
COST ($ = $60)	$$–
LOCATION	Western Suburbs
NO. OF ROOMS	211
PARKING	Lot, free
ROOM SERVICE	•
BREAKFAST	—
ON-SITE DINING	•
POOL	•
SAUNA	—
EXERCISE FACILITIES	•

Holiday Inn Mart Plaza ★★★½
350 West Mart Center Drive
Chicago 60654
☎ 312-836-5000
TOLL-FREE ☎ 800-HOLIDAY
www.ichotelsgroup.com

ROOM QUALITY	82
COST ($ = $60)	$$$$$–
LOCATION	Near North
NO. OF ROOMS	521
PARKING	Self, $31; valet, $41
ROOM SERVICE	•
BREAKFAST	—
ON-SITE DINING	•
POOL	•
SAUNA	•
EXERCISE FACILITIES	•

Holiday Inn North Shore ★★★★
5300 West Touhy Avenue
Skokie 60077
☎ 847-679-8900
TOLL-FREE ☎ 888-221-1298
www.holiday-inn.com

ROOM QUALITY	83
COST ($ = $60)	$$+
LOCATION	Northern Suburbs
NO. OF ROOMS	244
PARKING	Lot, free
ROOM SERVICE	•
BREAKFAST	—
ON-SITE DINING	•
POOL	•
SAUNA	•
EXERCISE FACILITIES	•

Holiday Inn Oakbrook Terrace ★★★
17 West 350 22nd Street
Oakbrook Terrace 60181
☎ 630-833-3600
TOLL-FREE ☎ 800-325-3535
www.ichotelsgroup.com

ROOM QUALITY	74
COST ($ = $60)	$$+
LOCATION	Western Suburbs
NO. OF ROOMS	222
PARKING	Lot, free
ROOM SERVICE	•
BREAKFAST	—
ON-SITE DINING	•
POOL	•
SAUNA	—
EXERCISE FACILITIES	—

Hotel Information Chart (continued)

Holiday Inn Select O'Hare ★★★★
10233 West Higgins Road
Rosemont 60018
☎ 847-954-8600
TOLL-FREE ☎ 800-HOLIDAY
www.holiday-inn.com

ROOM QUALITY	87
COST ($ = $60)	$$–
LOCATION	N. Central–O'Hare
NO. OF ROOMS	300
PARKING	Lot, free
ROOM SERVICE	•
BREAKFAST	—
ON-SITE DINING	•
POOL	—
SAUNA	—
EXERCISE FACILITIES	•

Hotel Allegro ★★★½
171 West Randolph Street
Chicago 60601
☎ 312-236-0123
TOLL-FREE ☎ 866-672-6143
www.allegrochicago.com

ROOM QUALITY	82
COST ($ = $60)	$$$$+
LOCATION	The Loop
NO. OF ROOMS	483
PARKING	Self, $16–$25; valet $36
ROOM SERVICE	•
BREAKFAST	—
ON-SITE DINING	•
POOL	—
SAUNA	—
EXERCISE FACILITIES	•

Hotel Blake ★★★★½
500 South Dearborn Street
Chicago 60605
☎ 312-344-4966
TOLL-FREE ☎ 800-233-1234
www.hotelblake.com

ROOM QUALITY	94
COST ($ = $60)	$$$$–
LOCATION	South Loop
NO. OF ROOMS	162
PARKING	Valet, $36
ROOM SERVICE	•
BREAKFAST	—
ON-SITE DINING	•
POOL	—
SAUNA	—
EXERCISE FACILITIES	•

Hotel Monaco ★★★★½
225 North Wabash Avenue
Chicago 60601
☎ 312-960-8500
TOLL-FREE ☎ 866-610-0081
www.monaco-chicago.com

ROOM QUALITY	93
COST ($ = $60)	$$$$$$
LOCATION	The Loop
NO. OF ROOMS	192
PARKING	Valet, $36
ROOM SERVICE	•
BREAKFAST	—
ON-SITE DINING	•
POOL	—
SAUNA	—
EXERCISE FACILITIES	•

Hotel 71 ★★★★½
71 East Wacker Drive
Chicago 60601
☎ 312-346-7100
TOLL-FREE ☎ 800-621-4005
www.hotel71.com

ROOM QUALITY	93
COST ($ = $60)	$$$+
LOCATION	The Loop
NO. OF ROOMS	454
PARKING	Valet, $39
ROOM SERVICE	•
BREAKFAST	—
ON-SITE DINING	• (undergoing renovations)
POOL	—
SAUNA	—
EXERCISE FACILITIES	•

Howard Johnson ★★½
720 North LaSalle Street
Chicago 60610
☎ 312-664-8100
TOLL-FREE ☎ 800-446-4656
www.hojo.com

ROOM QUALITY	61
COST ($ = $60)	$+
LOCATION	Near North
NO. OF ROOMS	71
PARKING	Lot, free
ROOM SERVICE	—
BREAKFAST	—
ON-SITE DINING	•
POOL	—
SAUNA	—
EXERCISE FACILITIES	—

Hyatt Rosemont ★★★★
6350 North River Road
Rosemont 60018
☎ 847-518-1234
TOLL-FREE ☎ 800-233-1234
rosemont.hyatt.com

ROOM QUALITY	83
COST ($ = $60)	$$$–
LOCATION	N. Central–O'Hare
NO. OF ROOMS	206
PARKING	Garage, free
ROOM SERVICE	•
BREAKFAST	—
ON-SITE DINING	•
POOL	—
SAUNA	—
EXERCISE FACILITIES	•

Inn of Chicago ★★★★
162 East Ohio Street
Chicago 60611
☎ 312-787-3100
TOLL-FREE ☎ 800-557-2378
www.innofchicago.com

ROOM QUALITY	85
COST ($ = $60)	$$$–
LOCATION	Near North
NO. OF ROOMS	357
PARKING	Self, $36; valet, $41
ROOM SERVICE	—
BREAKFAST	—
ON-SITE DINING	—
POOL	—
SAUNA	—
EXERCISE FACILITIES	•

The James Chicago ★★★★
55 East Ontario Street
Chicago 60611
☎ 312-337-1000
TOLL-FREE ☎ 877-526-3755
www.jameshotels.com

ROOM QUALITY	89
COST ($ = $60)	$$$–
LOCATION	Near North
NO. OF ROOMS	297
PARKING	Self, $32; valet, $42
ROOM SERVICE	•
BREAKFAST	—
ON-SITE DINING	•
POOL	•
SAUNA	•
EXERCISE FACILITIES	•

Hotel Burnham ★★★★½
1 West Washington Street
Chicago 60602
☎ 312-782-1111
TOLL-FREE ☎ 866-690-1986
www.burnhamhotel.com

ROOM QUALITY	91
COST ($ = $60)	$$$$$–
LOCATION	The Loop
NO. OF ROOMS	122
PARKING	Valet, $35
ROOM SERVICE	•
BREAKFAST	—
ON-SITE DINING	—
POOL	—
SAUNA	—
EXERCISE FACILITIES	•

Hotel Indigo ★★★★
1244 North Dearborn Parkway
Chicago 60610
☎ 312-787-4980
TOLL-FREE ☎ 866-521-6950
www.goldcoastchicagohotel.com

ROOM QUALITY	88
COST ($ = $60)	$$$$–
LOCATION	Near North
NO. OF ROOMS	167
PARKING	Self and valet, $35
ROOM SERVICE	•
BREAKFAST	—
ON-SITE DINING	•
POOL	—
SAUNA	—
EXERCISE FACILITIES	•

Hotel InterContinental Chicago ★★★★½
505 North Michigan Avenue
Chicago 60611
☎ 312-944-4100
TOLL-FREE ☎ 800-628-2112
www.intercontinental.com

ROOM QUALITY	93
COST ($ = $60)	$$$$$–
LOCATION	Near North
NO. OF ROOMS	863
PARKING	Valet, $49
ROOM SERVICE	•
BREAKFAST	—
ON-SITE DINING	—
POOL	•
SAUNA	•
EXERCISE FACILITIES	•

Hyatt Regency Chicago in Illinois Center ★★★★
151 East Wacker Drive
Chicago 60601
☎ 312-565-1234
TOLL-FREE ☎ 800-233-1234
www.hyatt.com

ROOM QUALITY	86
COST ($ = $60)	$$$$
LOCATION	The Loop
NO. OF ROOMS	2,019
PARKING	Valet, $41
ROOM SERVICE	•
BREAKFAST	—
ON-SITE DINING	•
POOL	—
SAUNA	—
EXERCISE FACILITIES	•

Hyatt Regency McCormick Place ★★★★
2233 Martin Luther King Drive
Chicago 60616
☎ 312-567-1234
TOLL-FREE ☎ 800-233-1234
www.hyatt.com

ROOM QUALITY	86
COST ($ = $60)	$$$$–
LOCATION	South Loop
NO. OF ROOMS	800
PARKING	Self, $25; valet, $36
ROOM SERVICE	•
BREAKFAST	—
ON-SITE DINING	•
POOL	•
SAUNA	•
EXERCISE FACILITIES	•

Hyatt Regency O'Hare ★★★★
9300 West Bryn Mawr Avenue
Chicago 60018
☎ 847-696-1234
TOLL-FREE ☎ 800-233-1234
ohare.hyatt.com

ROOM QUALITY	85
COST ($ = $60)	$$$
LOCATION	N. Central–O'Hare
NO. OF ROOMS	1,100
PARKING	Self, $25; valet, $28
ROOM SERVICE	•
BREAKFAST	—
ON-SITE DINING	•
POOL	•
SAUNA	•
EXERCISE FACILITIES	•

La Quinta Inn Oakbrook Terrace ★★★
1 South 666 Midwest Road
Oakbrook Terrace 60181
☎ 630-495-4600
TOLL-FREE ☎ 800-531-5900
www.lq.com

ROOM QUALITY	67
COST ($ = $60)	$+
LOCATION	Western Suburbs
NO. OF ROOMS	152
PARKING	Lot, free
ROOM SERVICE	—
BREAKFAST	Continental
ON-SITE DINING	—
POOL	•
SAUNA	—
EXERCISE FACILITIES	•

Marriott Chicago Downtown ★★★½
540 North Michigan Avenue
Chicago 60611
☎ 312-836-0100
TOLL-FREE ☎ 800-228-9290
www.marriott.com

ROOM QUALITY	79
COST ($ = $60)	$$$$$+
LOCATION	Near North
NO. OF ROOMS	1,198
PARKING	Valet $45
ROOM SERVICE	—
BREAKFAST	—
ON-SITE DINING	•
POOL	•
SAUNA	•
EXERCISE FACILITIES	•

Marriott Fairfield Inn & Suites Downtown ★★★½
216 East Ontario Street
Chicago 60611
☎ 312-787-3777
TOLL-FREE ☎ 800-228-2800
www.marriott.com

ROOM QUALITY	75
COST ($ = $60)	$$$–
LOCATION	Near North
NO. OF ROOMS	185
PARKING	Valet, $38
ROOM SERVICE	—
BREAKFAST	Continental
ON-SITE DINING	—
POOL	—
SAUNA	—
EXERCISE FACILITIES	•

Hotel Information Chart (continued)

Marriott Oak Brook ★★★★
1401West 22nd Street
Oak Brook 60523
☎ 630-573-8555
TOLL-FREE ☎ 800-228-9290
www.marriott.com

ROOM QUALITY	87
COST ($ = $60)	$$
LOCATION	Western Suburbs
NO. OF ROOMS	347
PARKING	Lot, free
ROOM SERVICE	—
BREAKFAST	Pastries
ON-SITE DINING	•
POOL	•
SAUNA	—
EXERCISE FACILITIES	•

Marriott O'Hare ★★★★
8535 West Higgins Road
Chicago 60631
☎ 773-693-4444
TOLL-FREE ☎ 800-228-9290
www.marriott.com

ROOM QUALITY	85
COST ($ = $60)	$$+
LOCATION	N. Central–O'Hare
NO. OF ROOMS	703
PARKING	Self, $22; valet, $25
ROOM SERVICE	—
BREAKFAST	—
ON-SITE DINING	•
POOL	•
SAUNA	—
EXERCISE FACILITIES	•

Marriott Residence Inn Downtown ★★★★★
201 East Walton Place
Chicago 60611
☎ 312-943-9800
TOLL-FREE ☎ 800-331-3131
www.marriott.com

ROOM QUALITY	96
COST ($ = $60)	$$$+
LOCATION	Near North
NO. OF ROOMS	221
PARKING	Valet, $45
ROOM SERVICE	—
BREAKFAST	Buffet
ON-SITE DINING	—
POOL	—
SAUNA	—
EXERCISE FACILITIES	•

Motel 6 O'Hare East ★★½
9408 West Lawrence Avenue
Schiller Park 60176
☎ 847-671-4282
TOLL-FREE ☎ 800-4-MOTEL6
www.motel6.com

ROOM QUALITY	60
COST ($ = $60)	$–
LOCATION	N. Central–O'Hare
NO. OF ROOMS	143
PARKING	Lot, free
ROOM SERVICE	—
BREAKFAST	—
ON-SITE DINING	—
POOL	—
SAUNA	—
EXERCISE FACILITIES	—

Omni Chicago Hotel ★★★★½
676 North Michigan Avenue
Chicago 60611
☎ 312-944-6664
TOLL-FREE ☎ 800-843-6664
www.omnihotels.com

ROOM QUALITY	92
COST ($ = $60)	$$$$$–
LOCATION	Near North
NO. OF ROOMS	347
PARKING	Valet, $40
ROOM SERVICE	•
BREAKFAST	—
ON-SITE DINING	•
POOL	•
SAUNA	—
EXERCISE FACILITIES	•

Orrington Hotel Evanston ★★★★
1710 Orrington Avenue
Evanston 60201
☎ 847-866-8700
TOLL-FREE ☎ 888-677-4648
www.hotelorrington.com

ROOM QUALITY	89
COST ($ = $60)	$$$+
LOCATION	Northern Suburbs
NO. OF ROOMS	269
PARKING	Valet, $20
ROOM SERVICE	•
BREAKFAST	—
ON-SITE DINING	•
POOL	—
SAUNA	•
EXERCISE FACILITIES	•

The Peninsula ★★★★★
108 East Superior Street
Chicago 60611
☎ 312-337-2888
TOLL-FREE ☎ 866-288-8889
www.peninsula.com

ROOM QUALITY	99
COST ($ = $60)	$$$$$$$$+
LOCATION	Near North
NO. OF ROOMS	339
PARKING	Valet, $26
ROOM SERVICE	•
BREAKFAST	—
ON-SITE DINING	•
POOL	•
SAUNA	—
EXERCISE FACILITIES	•

Quality Inn O'Hare ★★★
3801 North Mannheim Road
Schiller Park 60176
☎ 847-678-0670
TOLL-FREE ☎ 877-424-6423
www.choicehotels.com

ROOM QUALITY	71
COST ($ = $60)	$+
LOCATION	N. Central–O'Hare
NO. OF ROOMS	144
PARKING	Lot, free
ROOM SERVICE	•
BREAKFAST	Continental
ON-SITE DINING	•
POOL	•
SAUNA	—
EXERCISE FACILITIES	•

Radisson O'Hare ★★★★
1450 East Touhy Avenue
Des Plaines 60018
☎ 847-296-8866
TOLL-FREE ☎ 800-333-3333
www.radisson.com

ROOM QUALITY	83
COST ($ = $60)	$+
LOCATION	N. Central–O'Hare
NO. OF ROOMS	246
PARKING	Lot, free
ROOM SERVICE	•
BREAKFAST	—
ON-SITE DINING	•
POOL	•
SAUNA	—
EXERCISE FACILITIES	•

Marriott Suites Downers Grove ★★★★
1500 Opus Place
Downers Grove 60515
☎ 630-852-1500
TOLL-FREE ☎ 800-228-9290
www.marriott.com

ROOM QUALITY	85
COST ($ = $60)	$$+
LOCATION	Western Suburbs
NO. OF ROOMS	254
PARKING	Lot, free
ROOM SERVICE	—
BREAKFAST	—
ON-SITE DINING	•
POOL	•
SAUNA	•
EXERCISE FACILITIES	•

Marriott Suites O'Hare ★★★★½
6155 North River Road
Chicago 60018
☎ 847-696-4400
TOLL-FREE ☎ 800-228-9290
www.marriott.com

ROOM QUALITY	90
COST ($ = $60)	$$+
LOCATION	N. Central–O'Hare
NO. OF ROOMS	256
PARKING	Self, $22
ROOM SERVICE	•
BREAKFAST	—
ON-SITE DINING	•
POOL	•
SAUNA	•
EXERCISE FACILITIES	•

Millennium Knickerbocker Hotel ★★★★½
163 East Walton Place
Chicago 60611
☎ 312-751-8100
TOLL-FREE ☎ 866-866-8086
www.millenniumhotels.com

ROOM QUALITY	91
COST ($ = $60)	$$$–
LOCATION	Near North
NO. OF ROOMS	305
PARKING	Valet, $39
ROOM SERVICE	•
BREAKFAST	•
ON-SITE DINING	•
POOL	—
SAUNA	—
EXERCISE FACILITIES	•

Palmer House Hilton ★★★★½
17 East Monroe Street
Chicago 60603
☎ 312-726-7500
TOLL-FREE ☎ 800-HILTONS
www.hilton.com

ROOM QUALITY	90
COST ($ = $60)	$$+
LOCATION	The Loop
NO. OF ROOMS	1,639
PARKING	Self, $35
ROOM SERVICE	•
BREAKFAST	—
ON-SITE DINING	•
POOL	•
SAUNA	—
EXERCISE FACILITIES	•

Park Hyatt Chicago ★★★★★
800 North Michigan Avenue
Chicago 60611
☎ 312-335-1234
TOLL-FREE ☎ 800-233-1234
www.hyatt.com

ROOM QUALITY	96
COST ($ = $60)	$$$$$$+
LOCATION	Near North
NO. OF ROOMS	198
PARKING	Valet, $44
ROOM SERVICE	•
BREAKFAST	—
ON-SITE DINING	•
POOL	•
SAUNA	—
EXERCISE FACILITIES	•

The Park View Hotel ★★★
1816 North Clark Street
Chicago 60614
☎ 312-664-3040
TOLL-FREE ☎ 800-637-7200
www.sterlinghotels.com

ROOM QUALITY	67
COST ($ = $60)	$$$–
LOCATION	North Side
NO. OF ROOMS	124
PARKING	Valet, $22
ROOM SERVICE	—
BREAKFAST	Continental
ON-SITE DINING	—
POOL	—
SAUNA	—
EXERCISE FACILITIES	—

Raffaello ★★★★½
201 East Delaware Place
Chicago 60611
☎ 312-943-5000
TOLL-FREE ☎ 800-983-7870
www.raffaellochicago.com

ROOM QUALITY	94
COST ($ = $60)	$$$$–
LOCATION	Near North
NO. OF ROOMS	175
PARKING	Valet, $41
ROOM SERVICE	•
BREAKFAST	—
ON-SITE DINING	•
POOL	—
SAUNA	—
EXERCISE FACILITIES	•

Red Roof Inn Downers Grove ★★★
1113 Butterfield Road
Downers Grove 60515
☎ 630-963-4205
TOLL-FREE ☎ 800-RED-ROOF
www.redroof.com

ROOM QUALITY	70
COST ($ = $60)	$
LOCATION	Western Suburbs
NO. OF ROOMS	135
PARKING	Lot, free
ROOM SERVICE	—
BREAKFAST	—
ON-SITE DINING	—
POOL	—
SAUNA	—
EXERCISE FACILITIES	—

Red Roof Inn Downtown ★★★
162 East Ontario Street
Chicago 60611
☎ 312-787-3580
TOLL-FREE ☎ 800-RED-ROOF
www.redroof.com

ROOM QUALITY	65
COST ($ = $60)	$$+
LOCATION	Near North
NO. OF ROOMS	195
PARKING	Off-site, $36
ROOM SERVICE	—
BREAKFAST	—
ON-SITE DINING	•
POOL	—
SAUNA	—
EXERCISE FACILITIES	—

Hotel Information Chart (continued)

Renaissance Chicago Hotel ★★★½
1 West Wacker Drive
Chicago 60601
☎ 312-372-7200
TOLL-FREE ☎ 800-228-9290
www.marriott.com

ROOM QUALITY	92
COST ($ = $60)	$$$$–
LOCATION	The Loop
NO. OF ROOMS	553
PARKING	Valet $45
ROOM SERVICE	•
BREAKFAST	—
ON-SITE DINING	•
POOL	•
SAUNA	•
EXERCISE FACILITIES	•

Renaissance Oak Brook Hotel ★★★½
2100 Spring Road
Oak Brook 60523
☎ 630-573-2800
TOLL-FREE ☎ 800-228-9290
www.renaissancehotels.com

ROOM QUALITY	90
COST ($ = $60)	$$
LOCATION	Western Suburbs
NO. OF ROOMS	168
PARKING	Self, free; valet, $5
ROOM SERVICE	—
BREAKFAST	—
ON-SITE DINING	•
POOL	—
SAUNA	—
EXERCISE FACILITIES	•

Residence Inn by Marriott O'Hare ★★★★
7101 Chestnut Street
Rosemont 60018
☎ 847-375-9000
TOLL-FREE ☎ 800-331-3131
www.marriott.com

ROOM QUALITY	86
COST ($ = $60)	$$
LOCATION	N. Central–O'Hare
NO. OF ROOMS	192
PARKING	Lot, free
ROOM SERVICE	—
BREAKFAST	Buffet
ON-SITE DINING	—
POOL	•
SAUNA	—
EXERCISE FACILITIES	•

Sheraton Chicago Hotel & Towers ★★★★½
301 East North Water Street
Chicago 60611
☎ 312-464-1000
TOLL-FREE ☎ 877-242-2558
www.sheratonchicago.com

ROOM QUALITY	92
COST ($ = $60)	$$
LOCATION	Near North
NO. OF ROOMS	1,209
PARKING	Self, $48
ROOM SERVICE	—
BREAKFAST	—
ON-SITE DINING	•
POOL	•
SAUNA	•
EXERCISE FACILITIES	•

Sheraton Gateway Suites O'Hare ★★★★
6501 North Mannheim Road
Rosemont 60018
☎ 847-699-6300
TOLL-FREE ☎ 800-325-3535
www.sheraton.com

ROOM QUALITY	87
COST ($ = $60)	$$
LOCATION	N. Central–O'Hare
NO. OF ROOMS	296
PARKING	Self, $12
ROOM SERVICE	•
BREAKFAST	—
ON-SITE DINING	•
POOL	•
SAUNA	•
EXERCISE FACILITIES	•

Sleep Inn Midway Airport ★★★
6650 South Cicero Avenue
Bedford Park 60638
☎ 708-594-0001
TOLL-FREE ☎ 877-424-6423
www.choicehotels.com

ROOM QUALITY	66
COST ($ = $60)	$$–
LOCATION	Southern Suburbs
NO. OF ROOMS	120
PARKING	Self, $10
ROOM SERVICE	—
BREAKFAST	Continental
ON-SITE DINING	—
POOL	—
SAUNA	—
EXERCISE FACILITIES	•

Swissotel Chicago ★★★★★
323 East Wacker Drive
Chicago 60601
☎ 312-565-0565
TOLL-FREE ☎ 800-637-9477
www.swissotelchicago.com

ROOM QUALITY	96
COST ($ = $60)	$$$
LOCATION	The Loop
NO. OF ROOMS	632
PARKING	Valet, $49
ROOM SERVICE	•
BREAKFAST	—
ON-SITE DINING	•
POOL	•
SAUNA	• (fee)
EXERCISE FACILITIES	• (fee)

Talbott Hotel ★★★★½
20 East Delaware Place
Chicago 60611
☎ 312-944-4970
TOLL-FREE ☎ 800-TALBOTT
www.talbotthotel.com

ROOM QUALITY	90
COST ($ = $60)	$$$$$+
LOCATION	Near North
NO. OF ROOMS	130
PARKING	Valet, $32
ROOM SERVICE	•
BREAKFAST	—
ON-SITE DINING	•
POOL	—
SAUNA	—
EXERCISE FACILITIES	free access

Travelodge Downtown ★★★
65 East Harrison Street
Chicago 60605
☎ 312-427-8000
TOLL-FREE ☎ 800-578-7878
www.travelodge.com

ROOM QUALITY	65
COST ($ = $60)	$$+
LOCATION	South Loop
NO. OF ROOMS	250
PARKING	Self, $32
ROOM SERVICE	•
BREAKFAST	—
ON-SITE DINING	•
POOL	—
SAUNA	—
EXERCISE FACILITIES	—

Ritz-Carlton Chicago ★ ★ ★ ★ ½
160 East Pearson Street
Chicago 60611
☎ 312-266-1000
TOLL-FREE ☎ 800-621-6906
www.fourseasons.com

ROOM QUALITY	95
COST ($ = $60)	$$$$$+
LOCATION	Near North
NO. OF ROOMS	435
PARKING	Self, $25; valet, $36
ROOM SERVICE	•
BREAKFAST	—
ON-SITE DINING	•
POOL	•
SAUNA	•
EXERCISE FACILITIES	•

Sax Hotel Chicago ★ ★ ★ ★ ½
333 North Dearborn Street
Chicago 60610
☎ 312-245-0333
TOLL-FREE ☎ 877-569-3742
www.hotelsaxchicago.com

ROOM QUALITY	92
COST ($ = $60)	$$$+
LOCATION	Near North
NO. OF ROOMS	367
PARKING	Valet, $42
ROOM SERVICE	•
BREAKFAST	—
ON-SITE DINING	•
POOL	—
SAUNA	—
EXERCISE FACILITIES	•

The Seneca Hotel & Suites ★ ★ ★ ★
200 East Chestnut Street
Chicago 60611
☎ 312-787-8900
TOLL-FREE ☎ 800-800-6261
www.senecahotel.com

ROOM QUALITY	89
COST ($ = $60)	$$+
LOCATION	Near North
NO. OF ROOMS	268
PARKING	Valet, $48
ROOM SERVICE	—
BREAKFAST	—
ON-SITE DINING	•
POOL	—
SAUNA	—
EXERCISE FACILITIES	•

Sofitel Chicago O'Hare ★ ★ ★ ½
5550 North River Road
Rosemont 60018
☎ 847-678-4488
TOLL-FREE ☎ 800-763-4835
www.sofitel.com

ROOM QUALITY	81
COST ($ = $60)	$$+
LOCATION	N. Central–O'Hare
NO. OF ROOMS	300
PARKING	Self, $18; valet, $28
ROOM SERVICE	•
BREAKFAST	—
ON-SITE DINING	•
POOL	•
SAUNA	•
EXERCISE FACILITIES	•

Sofitel Water Tower ★ ★ ★ ★ ½
20 East Chestnut Street
Chicago 60611
☎ 312-324-4000
TOLL-FREE ☎ 800-763-4835
www.sofitel.com

ROOM QUALITY	92
COST ($ = $60)	$$$$$+
LOCATION	Near North
NO. OF ROOMS	415
PARKING	Self, $36; valet, $44
ROOM SERVICE	•
BREAKFAST	—
ON-SITE DINING	•
POOL	—
SAUNA	—
EXERCISE FACILITIES	•

Sutton Place Hotel ★ ★ ★ ★ ½
21 East Bellevue Place
Chicago 60611
☎ 312-266-2100
TOLL-FREE ☎ 800-606-8188
www.suttonplace.com

ROOM QUALITY	92
COST ($ = $60)	$$$$–
LOCATION	Near North
NO. OF ROOMS	246
PARKING	Valet, $29–$39
ROOM SERVICE	•
BREAKFAST	—
ON-SITE DINING	•
POOL	—
SAUNA	—
EXERCISE FACILITIES	•

Trump International Hotel and Tower ★ ★ ★ ★ ★
401 North Wabash Avenue
Chicago 60611
☎ 312-588-8000
TOLL-FREE ☎ 877-458-7867
www.trumpchicagohotel.com

ROOM QUALITY	100
COST ($ = $60)	$$$$$–
LOCATION	Near North
NO. OF ROOMS	339
PARKING	Self, $42; valet, $48
ROOM SERVICE	•
BREAKFAST	—
ON-SITE DINING	•
POOL	•
SAUNA	•
EXERCISE FACILITIES	•

W City Center Hotel ★ ★ ★ ★
172 West Adams Street
Chicago 60603
☎ 312-332-1200
TOLL-FREE ☎ 888-625-5144
www.whotels.com

ROOM QUALITY	88
COST ($ = $60)	$$$$+
LOCATION	The Loop
NO. OF ROOMS	369
PARKING	Valet, $48
ROOM SERVICE	•
BREAKFAST	—
ON-SITE DINING	•
POOL	—
SAUNA	—
EXERCISE FACILITIES	•

W Lakeshore ★ ★ ★ ★ ½
644 North Lakeshore Drive
Chicago 60611
☎ 312-943-9200
TOLL-FREE ☎ 888-625-5144
www.starwoodhotels.com

ROOM QUALITY	93
COST ($ = $60)	$$$$+
LOCATION	Near North
NO. OF ROOMS	520
PARKING	Valet, $41
ROOM SERVICE	•
BREAKFAST	—
ON-SITE DINING	•
POOL	•
SAUNA	—
EXERCISE FACILITIES	•

Hotel Information Chart (continued)

Westin Hotel O'Hare ★★★★
6100 River Road
Rosemont 60018
☎ 847-698-6000
TOLL-FREE ☎ 800-228-3000
www.westinohare.com

ROOM QUALITY	87
COST ($ = $60)	$$+
LOCATION	N. Central–O'Hare
NO. OF ROOMS	525
PARKING	Self, $18; valet, $27
ROOM SERVICE	•
BREAKFAST	—
ON-SITE DINING	•
POOL	•
SAUNA	•
EXERCISE FACILITIES	•

Westin Michigan Avenue ★★★★½
909 North Michigan Avenue
Chicago 60611
☎ 312-943-7200
TOLL-FREE ☎ 800-228-3000
www.westinmichiganave.com

ROOM QUALITY	95
COST ($ = $60)	$$$$$$+
LOCATION	Near North
NO. OF ROOMS	752
PARKING	Valet, $38
ROOM SERVICE	•
BREAKFAST	
ON-SITE DINING	•
POOL	—
SAUNA	—
EXERCISE FACILITIES	•

Westin River North Chicago ★★★★½
320 North Dearborn Street
Chicago 60610
☎ 312-744-1900
TOLL-FREE ☎ 800-WESTIN-1
www.westinchicago.com

ROOM QUALITY	95
COST ($ = $60)	$$+
LOCATION	Near North
NO. OF ROOMS	424
PARKING	Valet, $36–$45
ROOM SERVICE	•
BREAKFAST	
ON-SITE DINING	•
POOL	•
SAUNA	•
EXERCISE FACILITIES	•

Whitehall Hotel ★★★★
105 East Delaware Place
Chicago 60611
☎ 312-944-6300
TOLL-FREE ☎ 800-948-4255
www.thewhitehallhotel.com

ROOM QUALITY	85
COST ($ = $60)	$$$+
LOCATION	Near North
NO. OF ROOMS	230
PARKING	Valet, $34–$50
ROOM SERVICE	•
BREAKFAST	—
ON-SITE DINING	•
POOL	—
SAUNA	•
EXERCISE FACILITIES	•

Willows Hotel ★★★
555 West Surf Street
Chicago 60657
☎ 773-528-8400
TOLL-FREE ☎ 800-787-3108
www.cityinns.com

ROOM QUALITY	72
COST ($ = $60)	$$$+
LOCATION	North Side
NO. OF ROOMS	55
PARKING	Self, $22
ROOM SERVICE	—
BREAKFAST	Continental
ON-SITE DINING	—
POOL	—
SAUNA	—
EXERCISE FACILITIES	—

Wyndham Chicago ★★★★
633 North St. Clair Street
Chicago 60611
☎ 312-573-0300
TOLL-FREE ☎ 800-WYNDHAM
www.wyndham.com

ROOM QUALITY	88
COST ($ = $60)	$$$–
LOCATION	Near North
NO. OF ROOMS	417
PARKING	Valet, $49
ROOM SERVICE	•
BREAKFAST	—
ON-SITE DINING	•
POOL	•
SAUNA	•
EXERCISE FACILITIES	•

Wyndham Drake Hotel Oak Brook ★★★½
2301 York Road
Oak Brook 60523
☎ 630-574-5700
TOLL-FREE ☎ 800-996-3426
www.wyndham.com

ROOM QUALITY	80
COST ($ = $60)	$$–
LOCATION	Southern Suburbs
NO. OF ROOMS	160
PARKING	Self and valet, free
ROOM SERVICE	•
BREAKFAST	Continental
ON-SITE DINING	•
POOL	•
SAUNA	—
EXERCISE FACILITIES	•

Wyndham O'Hare ★★★½
6810 North Mannheim Road
Rosemont 60018
☎ 847-297-1234
TOLL-FREE ☎ 800-333-3333
www.wyndham.com

ROOM QUALITY	79
COST ($ = $60)	$$$+
LOCATION	N. Central–O'Hare
NO. OF ROOMS	466
PARKING	Self, $16
ROOM SERVICE	•
BREAKFAST	Continental and buffet
ON-SITE DINING	•
POOL	•
SAUNA	•
EXERCISE FACILITIES	•

PART FOUR

VISITING *on* BUSINESS

CONVENTION CENTRAL, U.S.A.

CHICAGO, THE HEART OF THE MIDWEST and the third-largest city in the United States, attracts more than 7 million overnight pleasure visitors a year. Tourists from all over the world come to experience the city's fabled attractions, take in the legendary skyline, and enjoy the endless summer season's free lakefront festivals. Summer is short in Chicago, but the summer spirit is long.

In 2007, the **Shedd Aquarium** and the **Museum of Science and Industry,** Chicago's most popular fee-charging attractions, drew 2.1 million visitors and 1.7 million visitors, respectively, and **Taste of Chicago** attracts 3.6 million outdoor-fun seekers annually around the Fourth of July weekend. **Navy Pier** is Chicago's top attraction, with a mind-boggling 7 million visitors per year.

Yet not everyone visiting Chicago arrives with a tourist agenda. Because of its central location, Chicago bills itself as the Convention Capital of the World, hosting more top trade shows than any other city in the country. In 2007 Chicago attracted 12.3 million business travelers. There are 8,000 restaurants and 67,000 hotel rooms to accommodate nearly 5 million trade-show and convention visitors annually.

The Windy City also boasts an unparalleled location to house all those exhibitions: **McCormick Place Convention Center,** the largest convention hall in North America. On the shores of Lake Michigan a mile or so south of downtown, McCormick Place is a sprawling 27-acre venue with 2.6 million square feet of exhibit space, a 4,000-seat theater, and ceilings up to 50 feet high. A $987 million expansion of McCormick Place in the 1990s included the construction of the 840,000-square-foot South Building (near the intersection of the

Calendar of Conventions and Special Events

2009

DATE FEB 13–22
EVENT Chicago Auto Show
LOCATION McCormick Place
ATTENDANCE –*

DATE FEB 27–MAR 1
EVENT Chicago Dental Society's
Midwinter Meeting
LOCATION McCormick Place
ATTENDANCE 33,000

DATE MAR 15–19
EVENT Assoc. of periOperative
Registered Nurses Annual
Congress
LOCATION McCormick Place
ATTENDANCE 13,000

DATE APR 21–24
EVENT Coverings 2009: The
Ultimate Tile + Stone
Experience
LOCATION McCormick Place
ATTENDANCE 35,000

DATE APR 25–30
EVENT American Urological
Assoc. Annual Meeting
LOCATION McCormick Place
ATTENDANCE 15,000

DATE MAY 2
EVENT Mayor Daley's 11th
Annual Kids and Kites
Festival
LOCATION Lincoln Park
ATTENDANCE –*

DATE MAY 4–6
EVENT American College of
Obstetricians and
Gynecologists
LOCATION McCormick Place
ATTENDANCE 15,000

DATE MAY 4–7
EVENT WINDPOWER Conference &
Exhibition
LOCATION McCormick Place
ATTENDANCE 14,000

DATE MAY 16–19
EVENT Nat. Restaurant Assoc.
Restaurant Hotel-Motel
Show
LOCATION McCormick Place
ATTENDANCE 74,000

DATE MAY 19–21
EVENT The All-Candy Sweets &
Snack Show (Nat.
Confectioners Assoc.)
LOCATION McCormick Place
ATTENDANCE 15,000

DATE MAY 20–28
EVENT Loyal Order of Moose
Annual North American
Convention
LOCATION Hyatt Regency
ATTENDANCE 10,000

DATE MAY 23
EVENT Chicago Memorial Day
Parade
LOCATION Downtown
ATTENDANCE –*

DATE MAY 30–JUN 2
EVENT Digestive Disease Week
LOCATION McCormick Place
ATTENDANCE 22,500

DATE JUN 6–7
EVENT 25th Annual Chicago
Gospel Music Festival
LOCATION Millennium Park
ATTENDANCE –*

DATE JUN 9–11
EVENT SUPERCOMM 2009
LOCATION McCormick Place
ATTENDANCE 20,000

DATE JUN 12–14
EVENT 26th Annual Chicago Blues
Festival
LOCATION Grant Park
ATTENDANCE –*

DATE JUN 12–16
EVENT ASICS Junior National
Volleyball Championship
LOCATION Navy Pier
ATTENDANCE 40,000

DATE JUN 15–17
EVENT NeoCon World's Trade
Fair 2009
LOCATION Merchandise Mart
ATTENDANCE 50,000

DATE JUN 16–18
EVENT All Things Organic
LOCATION McCormick Place
ATTENDANCE –*

DATE JUN 22–26
EVENT Society of the Plastics
Industry Expo
LOCATION McCormick Place
ATTENDANCE 91,000

DATE JUN 26–JUL 5
EVENT 29th Annual Taste of
Chicago
LOCATION Grant Park
ATTENDANCE –*

DATE JUN 28
EVENT 17th Annual Race to the
Taste
LOCATION Grant Park–South
Loop
ATTENDANCE –*

DATE JUL 9–15
EVENT 2009 American Library
Assoc. Annual Conference
LOCATION McCormick Place
ATTENDANCE 25,000

DATE JUL 14–AUG 25 (Tuesday
nights)
EVENT 10th Annual Chicago
Outdoor Film Festival
LOCATION Grant Park
ATTENDANCE –*

DATE JUL 20–23
EVENT American Assoc. for
Clinical Chemistry
LOCATION McCormick Place
ATTENDANCE 20,000

DATE JUL 21–23
EVENT Advertising Specialty
Institute–ASI Show
LOCATION McCormick Place
ATTENDANCE 10,000

DATE JUL 25
EVENT 52nd Annual Venetian
Night
LOCATION Lake Michigan
Waterfront
ATTENDANCE –*

DATE JUL 25–28
EVENT Nat. Council of La Raza
LOCATION McCormick Place
ATTENDANCE 18,000

Attendance figures not available.

DATE JUL 26
EVENT 2nd Annual Chicago
Criterium
LOCATION Grant Park
ATTENDANCE–*

DATE AUG 15–16
EVENT 51st Annual Chicago Air
and Water Show
LOCATION North Avenue Beach
ATTENDANCE –*

DATE SEP 3–6
EVENT 31st Annual Chicago
Jazz Festival
LOCATION Grant Park
ATTENDANCE–*

DATE SEP 11–16
EVENT PRINT 09
LOCATION McCormick Place
ATTENDANCE 75,000

DATE OCT 7–9
EVENT ISSA/INTERCLEAN
LOCATION McCormick Place
ATTENDANCE 18,000

DATE OCT 9–10
EVENT Bank of America Health &
Fitness Expo
LOCATION McCormick Place
ATTENDANCE 18,000

DATE OCT 11
EVENT Bank of America Chicago
Marathon
LOCATION Grant Park
ATTENDANCE 40,000

DATE OCT 17–21
EVENT Neuroscience 2009
LOCATION McCormick Place
ATTENDANCE 30,000

DATE OCT 23–31
EVENT Halloween Franken Plaza
LOCATION Daley Plaza
ATTENDANCE–*

DATE OCT 24
EVENT Halloween Happening
Parade
LOCATION State Street
ATTENDANCE –*

DATE NOV 1–5
EVENT ASRO 51st Annual
Meeting
LOCATION McCormick Place
ATTENDANCE –*

DATE NOV 15–18
EVENT FABTECH International
LOCATION McCormick Place
ATTENDANCE 30,000

DATE NOV 26–DEC 24
EVENT Santa's House
LOCATION Daley Plaza
(Washington &
Dearborn)
ATTENDANCE –*

DATE NOV 27
EVENT 96th Annual Christmas
Tree Lighting Ceremony
LOCATION Daley Plaza
ATTENDANCE –*

DATE NOV 29–DEC 4
EVENT Radiological Society of
North America 95th
Scientific Assembly and
Annual Meeting
LOCATION McCormick Place
ATTENDANCE 60,000

DATE DEC 27–28
EVENT Mayor Daley's 10th
Annual Holiday Sports
Festival
LOCATION McCormick Place
ATTENDANCE –*

2010

DATE FEB 25–27
EVENT Chicago Dental Society
Midwinter Meeting
LOCATION McCormick Place
ATTENDANCE 30,000

DATE MAR 14–16
EVENT Int'l. Home and
Housewares Show
LOCATION McCormick Place
ATTENDANCE 59,000

DATE APR 10–12
EVENT Nat. School Boards
Association
LOCATION McCormick Place
ATTENDANCE 13,000

DATE MAY 3–6
EVENT Biotechnology Industry
Organization
LOCATION McCormick Place
ATTENDANCE 20,000

DATE MAY 17–19
EVENT American Society for
Training and Development
LOCATION McCormick Place
ATTENDANCE 10,000

DATE MAY 22–25
EVENT 2010 National Restaurant
Association Restaurant,
Hotel-Motel Show
LOCATION McCormick Place
ATTENDANCE 73,500

DATE JUN 4–8
EVENT American Society of
Clinical Oncology
LOCATION McCormick Place
ATTENDANCE 35,000

DATE JUN 8–10
EVENT The All-Candy Sweets &
Snack Show
LOCATION McCormick Place
ATTENDANCE 18,000

DATE JUN 14–16
EVENT NeoCon World's Trade
Fair 2010
LOCATION Merchandise Mart
ATTENDANCE 40,000

DATE JUN 20–23
EVENT American Water Works
Assoc.
LOCATION McCormick Place
ATTENDANCE 18,000

DATE JUN 22–24
EVENT NXTcomm Show 2010
LOCATION McCormick Place
ATTENDANCE 20,000

DATE JUL 3–5
EVENT Islamic Society of North
America
LOCATION Hyatt Regency O'Hare
ATTENDANCE 10,000

DATE JUL 14–15
EVENT ASI Show
LOCATION McCormick Place
ATTENDANCE 10,000

DATE JUL 18–21
EVENT Institute of Food
Technologists
LOCATION McCormick Place
ATTENDANCE 25,000

*Attendance figures not available.

Calendar of Conventions and Special Events (continued)

2010 (continued)

DATE AUG 12–14
EVENT Fall Dealer Markets
         Meeting
LOCATION McCormick Place
ATTENDANCE 10,000

DATE SEP 13–18
EVENT Int'l. Manufacturing
         Technology Show
LOCATION McCormick Place
ATTENDANCE 185,000

DATE OCT 12–14
EVENT The 2010 Motivation
         Show
LOCATION McCormick Place
ATTENDANCE 20,000

DATE OCT 16–19
EVENT American Academy of
         Ophthalmology
LOCATION McCormick Place
ATTENDANCE 26,000

DATE NOV 14–17
EVENT American Heart Assoc.
         Scientific Sessions
LOCATION McCormick Place
ATTENDANCE 35,000

DATE NOV 28–DEC 3
EVENT RSNA 96th Scientific
         Assembly and Annual
         Meeting
LOCATION McCormick Place
ATTENDANCE 55,000

Stevenson Expressway and Lake Shore Drive), a glass-enclosed Grand Concourse linking three of the four buildings that make up the convention center, a five-acre landscaped park, and renovations to existing facilities.

In 2007, the newest addition to McCormick Place—the West Building—opened, adding about 460,000 square feet of exhibit space and 250,000 square feet of meeting space (including a 100,000-square-foot ballroom).

OTHER BUSINESS VISITORS

IN ADDITION TO CONVENTIONEERS and trade-show attendees who are bound for McCormick Place or another convention hall, other people come to conduct business at the city's wide array of manufacturing and financial firms (many of which are located in Chicago's suburbs). In addition to Chicago's four major financial exchanges (**Chicago Mercantile Exchange, Chicago Stock Exchange, Chicago Board of Trade,** and **Chicago Board Options Exchange**), the Windy City is also home to such corporations as Sears, Allstate, Amoco, Caterpillar, Motorola, and Sara Lee.

The city's large number of higher-learning institutions (including the **University of Chicago, Northwestern University,** the **University of Illinois at Chicago, DePaul University,** the **Illinois Institute of Technology,** and **Loyola University**) attract visiting academics, college administrators, and students and their families.

HOW THE *UNOFFICIAL GUIDE* CAN HELP

IN MANY WAYS, THE PROBLEMS FACING business visitors and conventioneers on their first trip to Chicago don't differ much from the problems of tourists intent on seeing Chicago's best-known attractions.

Business visitors need to locate a convenient hotel, want to avoid the worst of the city's traffic, face the same problems of navigating a huge city, must figure out the public transportation system, and want to pinpoint Chicago's best restaurants. This book can help.

For the most part, though, business visitors aren't nearly as flexible about the timing of their visit as people who pick Chicago as a vacation destination. While we advise that the best times for visiting the city are spring and fall, the necessities of business may dictate that you pull into the Windy City in hot and humid August—or even worse, January, a month when cold temperatures and stiff winds off Lake Michigan often create double-digit negative windchill readings.

Yet much of the advice and information presented in the *Unofficial Guide* is as valuable to business visitors as it is to tourists. As for our recommendations on seeing the city's many sights . . . who knows? Maybe you'll be able to squeeze a morning or an afternoon out of your busy schedule, grab this book, and spend a few hours exploring some of the attractions that draw more than 6 million tourists each year.

CONVENTION OVERLOAD

BUSINESS VISITORS HAVE A HUGE IMPACT on Chicago when, say, 70,000 exhibitors and trade-show attendees come into town and snatch up literally every hotel room within a 100-mile radius of the Loop. Finding a place to sleep can be nearly impossible when all the radiologists in the United States converge on Chicago for their national convention.

The good news: the large trade shows register no discernible effect on the availability of cabs and restaurant tables, or on traffic congestion; it seems that only hotel rooms and rental cars become scarce when a big convention hits town. Consult our Calendar of Conventions and Special Events on pages 72–74 when you're planning your trip to Chicago.

McCORMICK PLACE CONVENTION CENTER

IT'S BIG . . .

THE LARGEST EXHIBITION AND MEETING FACILITY in North America is Chicago's **McCormick Place** (2301 South Lake Shore Drive; ☎ 312-791-7000; fax 312-791-6543; **www.mccormickplace.com**). With 2.6 million square feet of exposition space (1.2 million on one level) and nearly 600,000 square feet of meeting, banquet, and ballroom space, as well as three theaters (including the 4,249-seat **Arie Crown Theater**), McCormick Place is the 800-pound gorilla of Chicago convention venues.

McCormick Place Convention Center

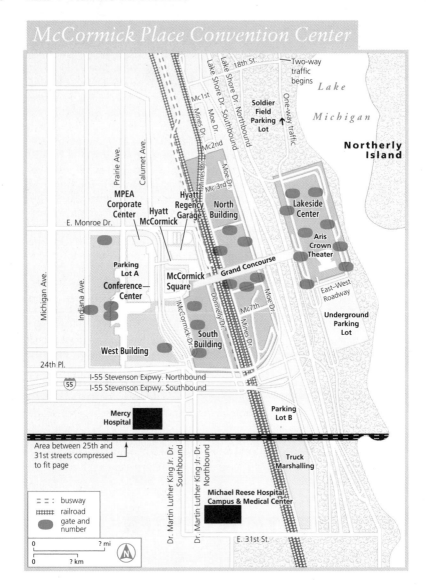

The original McCormick Place was the brainchild of Col. Robert R. McCormick, a former owner of the *Chicago Tribune*. It opened in 1960 and enjoyed seven years of success before being destroyed by fire in 1967. A more comprehensive structure, the **Lakeside Center,** replaced it in 1971 and, along with the **North Building** (added in 1986), the **South Building** (completed in 1996), and the **West Building** (completed in 2007), composes today's McCormick Place.

. . . AND IT HAS ITS DRAWBACKS

McCORMICK PLACE IS HUGE and its drawbacks varied. The convention center's location on Lake Michigan destroys any vestiges of an open, uncluttered Chicago lakefront; a formidable tangle of ramps and viaducts connects the Stevenson Expressway (Interstate 55) to Lake Shore Drive. For weary conventioneers looking for a respite from crowded exhibition halls, there's nothing—repeat, nothing— within walking distance of the huge complex that can provide distractions, with the possible exception of a stroll along the bike path that follows the shoreline of placid Lake Michigan.

As one spokesman for the giant hall once commented, McCormick Place is "totally business-oriented. There is no lounge area in the lobby. There aren't even any clocks in this place. The reason this place is popular with exhibitors is once a guy is here, he's stuck." Though we've spotted a few clocks in Lakeside Center, the rest of the statement remains essentially true: the closest hotels and restaurants (with the exception of eating places inside the center) are a $5 cab ride away. Even the food court in the South Building offers relatively few dining options—and with $7 hamburgers and $3 fries, it's overpriced.

THE LAYOUT

THREE OF McCORMICK PLACE'S FOUR CONVENTION VENUES— Lakeside Center, the North Building, and the South Building—are connected by the Grand Concourse, which serves as a unified entrance to McCormick Place and a link among the three. (A sky-bridge connects the West and South buildings.) The spectacular 100-foot-high, 900-foot-long pedestrian walkway includes visitor lobbies, a business center, cafes, coffee shops, specialty shops, and fountains. The glass-enclosed multilevel concourse also crosses Lake Shore Drive to provide a seamless connection with the Lakeside Center and allows the South and North buildings' exhibit halls to be combined for a total of 1.2 million square feet of exhibition space on one level.

Finding Your Way

EXHIBIT HALLS ARE NAMED BY CONSECUTIVE LETTERS. The South Building contains Exhibit Hall A; the North Building houses Exhibit Halls B (level 3) and C (level 1); the Lakeside Center contains Exhibit Halls D (level 3) and E (level 2); and the West Building houses

Exhibit Hall F (level 3). Sometimes halls may be divided: D1 and D2, for example.

All meeting-room numbers begin with *E, N, S,* or *W* and stand for Lakeside Center (formerly the East Building), North Building, South Building, and West Building, respectively. The next numeral (1, 2, 3, or 4) indicates the level, and the last two digits specify the exact room. Some meeting rooms with divider walls can create several smaller meeting rooms; these will have an *a, b, c,* or *d* suffix following the number. Thus, meeting room N126b is located on the first level of the North Building, room 26.

Lakeside Center

EAST OF SOUTH LAKE SHORE DRIVE on the shores of Lake Michigan, the Lakeside Center has a business center, cafe-bar, and gift shop. It handles small and midsized events, in contrast with the huge shows that take place at the other three buildings. The building contains more than a half-million square feet of exhibit areas and a 2,100-space underground parking garage.

Level 2, the lobby and mezzanine level, features the 283,000-square-foot **Hall E1,** the building's second-largest major exhibit area (which has its own loading docks). Also on this level is the **Arie Crown Theater,** a site for major entertainment productions, corporate meetings, and convention keynote addresses; it's the largest theater in Chicago.

The 75,000-square-foot lobby on Level 2 accommodates registration and includes private show-management offices and a press facility. The **McCormick Place Business Center** (☎ 312-791-6400; fax 312-791-6501) offers a wide array of services, including faxing, photocopying, equipment rentals, shipping, secretarial services, office supplies, foreign-currency exchange, and more. There's also an additional 10,000 square feet of meeting rooms on this level.

Level 3 contains a 45,000-square-foot **Grand Ballroom and Lobby** that's divisible into two 22,500-square-foot rooms. **Hall D,** with a north–south divider wall, can be divided into two 150,000-square-foot exhibition spaces for midsized shows. Two meeting rooms add another 58,000 square feet of space. The Grand Concourse connects Lakeside Center with the North and South buildings across Lake Shore Drive. Loading docks are located at the north end of the building.

Level 1 houses the McCormick Place administrative offices and the offices of the **Chicago Convention and Tourism Bureau,** the **Professional Convention Management Association,** and the **Trade Show Exhibitors Association,** along with snack and beverage machines. Level 4, the small upper level, contains three meeting rooms totaling 35,000 square feet.

The North Building

THE NORTH BUILDING BOASTS 188,000 square feet of exhibit space, additional escalators, a business center, and a gift shop. Level

1, the lower level, contains **Hall C1,** a 148,500-square-foot exhibition space that can be used independently or in conjunction with the larger upper level hall; and **Hall C2,** a 61,000-square-foot extension area that can be used for additional exhibit space or crate storage. The lower-level lobby has dedicated taxi space and areas for bus loading and unloading, 15 meeting rooms, and direct access to 4,000 outside parking spaces.

Level 3, the upper level, contains **Hall B1,** a 369,000-square-foot exhibition hall with an adjoining 127,000 square feet of space (**Hall B2**) that can be used for exhibits or crate storage; both halls can be combined with exhibition space in the South Building for a total of 1.2 million square feet of space on one level. A suspended-roof design provides virtually column-free exhibition space and allows for clear ceiling heights of up to 40 feet. Loading docks are at the north end of the building. The Grand Concourse connects the North Building with the South Building and the Lakeside Center.

Level 2, the mezzanine level, provides easy access to both the upper- and lower-level exhibition halls, as well as eight meeting rooms, two restaurants, and service areas. More than 50,000 square feet of lobby space is available for registration. Level 4 has two meeting rooms totaling 14,555 square feet.

The South Building

THE SOUTH BUILDING PROVIDES 840,000 square feet of exhibition space and 45 meeting rooms totaling another 170,000 square feet. It also boasts the 22,000-square-foot **Vista Room** and the 33,000-square-foot **Grand Ballroom.** Behind the scenes, the building has 170,000 square feet of indoor crate storage and full in-floor utilities. The South Building has 65 concealed truck docks and a special ramp for oversized exhibits. The weather-protected west entrance faces five-acre **McCormick Square,** featuring lighted 75-foot pylons, fountains, and landscaping.

Level 3 contains **Hall A1** and **Hall A2,** which, when combined, total 840,000 square feet. Loading docks are located on the east and south ends of the building. Across the Grand Concourse is Level 3 of the North Building and another half-million square feet of exhibition space.

Level 1 features the main entrance and lobby, the Grand Ballroom, and six meeting rooms; Level 2.5 contains a food court, a restaurant, a business center, a first-aid station, access to Metra commuter trains, and retail stores; Level 4 has five meeting rooms totaling about 24,000 square feet and the two-story, 22,000-square-foot **Vista Room;** Level 5 contains five meeting rooms with nearly 19,000 square feet of space.

The West Building

THE NEW WEST BUILDING offers 470,000 square feet of exhibition space and 61 meeting rooms totaling another 250,000 square feet. One highlight is the **Skyline Ballroom,** one of the largest in the world at 100,000 square feet. You could easily fit Soldier Field's football field inside the ballroom, which features theater-style seating for 11,500 guests.

Built at a cost of $882 million, the West Building looks more futuristic than the North and South buildings across the expressway. A rooftop garden can accommodate 800 guests for receptions and up to 300 for a sit-down event. It is LEED (Leadership in Energy and Environmental Design) Certified—the largest new construction in the United States to receive this certification. Indoor-dining options include a 200-plus-seat fine-dining restaurant with table service, a 400-plus-seat food court, and a 600-plus-seat Overlook Cafe connected to the exhibition floor.

A skybridge connects the ballroom and main entrance of the South Building with the Central Concourse area of the West Building. The West Building also showcases approximately 50 commissioned pieces of art by 30 Chicago and Illinois artists.

PARKING AT McCORMICK PLACE

OUR ADVICE TO CHICAGO VISITORS is the same whether you're vacationing or attending a convention at McCormick Place: don't drive. Not only is the traffic congestion of epic proportions, but finding a place to put your car is equally frustrating—and expensive. While McCormick Place has 6,000 adjacent parking spaces and an underground parking garage ($12 a day for private cars), save yourself the expense and bother of fighting the traffic, and leave the car at home.

In fact, so many people fly into Chicago for conventions that McCormick Place officials claim parking is a major problem (read: nearly impossible) only during large public shows that attract local residents. Example: the world's largest car show, held at McCormick Place each February, draws 1.1 million auto buffs.

EXHIBITOR MOVE-IN AND MOVE-OUT

THOUGH IT'S EXPENSIVE, we recommend shipping your display as opposed to hauling it yourself. McCormick Place is not really set up to accommodate smaller exhibitors who want to bring in their own displays. If you elect to move yourself in and out, the easiest way is to arrive at McCormick Place in a cab. If you have too much stuff to fit in a cab, you can try to fight your way into one of the tunnels servicing the loading docks. (Access to the 65 loading docks serving the South Building should be easier—they're above ground and accessible from Martin Luther King Jr. Drive.) Because move-in and set-up usually take place over two- to three-day periods, getting in is less of a problem than getting out (when everyone wants to leave at the same time). In any event, be prepared to drag your exhibit a long way. Try to pack everything into cases with wheels or bring along some sort of handcart or dolly.

GETTING TO AND FROM McCORMICK PLACE

LARGE CONVENTIONS PROVIDE BUS SHUTTLE service from major downtown hotels to McCormick Place. On weekends, the shuttle service operates pretty smoothly. On weekdays, however, when the buses must contend with Chicago traffic, schedules break down and meeting attendees must wait a long time. To compound the problem, neither police nor convention authorities seem able to control the taxicabs that constantly block the buses from getting to their convention-center loading zones. The predictable result of this transportation anarchy is gridlock.

A preferable option to shuttle buses and cabs is to take the commuter train, accessible from the Grand Concourse. Each train can accommodate several thousand conventioneers at once. At most shows, we recommend using the shuttle buses in the morning to go to the convention center and returning in the evening by train. To commute to downtown hotels from McCormick Place, take the northbound train three stops to the Randolph Station at the end of the line. You will emerge from the station in the Loop area, a reasonably safe part of Chicago just south of the Chicago River. From here you can take a cab or walk to most downtown hotels in about 15 minutes. On weekdays, the trains run frequently enough that you don't really need to consult a schedule. On weekends, however, the trains run up to 45 minutes apart.

unofficial **TIP**
If you depend on shuttle buses or cabs to get to and from McCormick Place, prepare for long queues. Give yourself an hour to arrive in the morning and two hours to get back to your hotel at night. If you want to take a cab to an outside restaurant for lunch, go before noon or after 1:30 p.m.

In 2002 a dedicated busway was created that allows charter buses to bypass local traffic on an exclusive two-lane, 2.5-mile roadway. This decreases travel times, and subsequently busing costs, for transporting attendees between their hotels and the convention center. The free busway runs from Randolph Street (downtown) to 25th Street at Martin Luther King Jr. Drive, parallel to Michigan Avenue. Entrance and exits are on Lower Randolph, just east of Columbus, and just south of McCormick Place at 25th Street. For a map and more information, visit **www.choosechicago.com/meetingplanners/why_choose_chicago/pages/busway.aspx**.

GETTING TO AND FROM THE AIRPORT

FOR VAN SERVICE to and from McCormick Place and O'Hare and Midway airports, call **Airport Express** (☎ 888-284-3826). The vans depart from the main entrance at the new Grand Concourse. The fare to O'Hare is $25 one-way; the ride to Midway is $27.

Cab fare to O'Hare is about $30, and $35 to Midway; actual fares vary depending on traffic conditions and don't include a tip. However, the cost will be the same regardless of the number of passengers.

LUNCH ALTERNATIVES AT McCORMICK PLACE

EATING AT McCORMICK PLACE is a real hassle. There are too few food-service vendors for the size of the facility, and even fewer table areas where you can sit and eat your hard-won victuals. Almost without exception, you must wait in one queue to obtain your food and in another to pay for it.

If you're an exhibitor, a small cooler should be an integral part of your booth. Ice frozen in a gallon milk jug lasts for days to keep drinks cold. Both exhibitors and nonexhibitors should eat breakfast before going to the show. After breakfast but before you catch your shuttle, stop at one of the many downtown delis and pick up a sandwich, chips, fruit, and some drinks for lunch as well as for snacking throughout the day. If you want to leave campus for lunch, get in the cab queue before 11:30 a.m. or after 1:30 p.m. Getting back to McCormick Place by cab after lunch will not be a problem. If you're looking for a more upscale place to enjoy a business lunch, see Part Eight, Dining and Restaurants.

NAVY PIER

IN THE SUMMER OF 1995, **Navy Pier** (600 East Grand Avenue; ☎ 800-595-PIER or 312-595-PIER; **www.navypier.com**), a Chicago landmark jutting out nearly a mile into Lake Michigan, was reopened after a $200-million face-lift. (The pier first opened in 1916.) Today, it's a year-round tourist attraction and convention center for exhibitions, meetings, and special events. **Festival Hall,** near the east end of the pier, contains 170,000 square feet of exhibit space and 65,000 square feet of meeting rooms designed for small- and medium-sized shows. The hall is surrounded by dining spots, cruise boats, a 150-foot Ferris wheel, a shopping mall, and a drop-dead view of Chicago's skyline.

Unlike visitors to McCormick Place, conventioneers and trade-show attendees at Festival Hall have access to 13,000 hotel rooms located within a few blocks, enclosed parking for 1,900 cars (which still isn't enough—we recommend either walking, public transportation, or cabs to reach Festival Hall), and on-the-pier restaurants and catering providing choices ranging from fast food to elegant dining with skyline and waterfront views. Plus, Chicago's best hotels, shopping, and restaurants are only a few blocks away. Navy Pier is within walking distance of the Magnificent Mile and the Loop. For more information on Navy Pier, see its profile in Part Seven, Sightseeing, Tours, and Attractions (page 183).

NAVY PIER CONVENTION FACILITIES

FESTIVAL HALL FEATURES MORE THAN 170,000 square feet of exhibit space divisible into two areas of 113,000 square feet (**Hall A**) and 56,000 square feet (**Hall B**). Taking maximum advantage of the pier's lakefront setting, the halls boast ceiling heights of up to 60 feet (30 feet minimum) and a full range of electrical and telecommunication amenities for exhibitors' needs.

The main halls are on the second level; small exhibitors can carry or roll show material from the public parking area on the first level. Loading docks are on the second (main hall) level at the west end of Festival Hall. The ramp to the loading docks is reached from the drive along the north side of Navy Pier.

Meeting rooms divisible into as many as 36 separate areas total more than 48,000 square feet and are located on a mezzanine overlooking the exhibition floor and on the exhibition level. The 18,000-square-foot **Grand Ballroom,** featuring an 80-foot domed ceiling and panoramic water views, continues to serve banquet, performance, and special exhibit functions as it has since the pier first opened in 1916.

DONALD E. STEPHENS CONVENTION CENTER

NORTHWEST OF DOWNTOWN CHICAGO and five minutes from O'Hare International Airport, the **Donald E. Stephens Convention Center** (5555 North River Road, Rosemont; ☎ 847-692-2220; fax 847-696-9700; **www.rosemont.com**) is an exhibition venue offering convenience for fly-in exhibitors and trade-show attendees—but not much else. Unfortunately, the suburban location west of Chicago is nowheresville in terms of easy access to the attractions, restaurants, nightlife, and ethnic diversity that make the Windy City a world-class travel destination.

Stephens is, however, a clean, modern facility, offering 840,000 square feet of flexible convention space that can accommodate a continuous 250,000-square-foot space containing up to 1,150 booths. A 5,000-space parking garage and more than 3,000 nearby hotel rooms (in the **Sofitel Chicago O'Hare** and **Hyatt Regency O'Hare**) are connected by a 7,000-linear-foot enclosed pedestrian Skybridge Network. Heated in the winter and air-conditioned in the summer, it's very nice when the weather is nasty outside and you want to get to your car or one of the nearby hotels.

Stephens handles a wide variety of both public and trade shows, ranging from the Chicago Midwest Bicycle Show (trade) to public ski shows. The center's six halls feature ceiling heights ranging from 16 to 26 feet and five drive-in freight doors. The conference center offers an additional 52,000 square feet of floor space in 34 meeting rooms located on two levels.

Other hotels close to Stephens include the **Westin Hotel O'Hare** (525 rooms), **Holiday Inn Select O'Hare** (300 rooms), and **Sheraton**

Gateway Suites O'Hare (325 suites). For places to eat that rise above standard hotel dining rooms, see Part Eight, Dining and Restaurants.

Getting to downtown Chicago from Stephens takes about 20 minutes by car (except during rush hours) and about 45 minutes by train. To drive, take I-90 (the Kennedy Expressway) east. You can board the CTA O'Hare Line train to downtown at either O'Hare or River Road in Rosemont (which has parking).

PART FIVE

ARRIVING *and* GETTING ORIENTED

COMING *into* CHICAGO *by* CAR

ONE WORD OF ADVICE: *relax.*

The major north–south route into Chicago is **Interstate 90/94** (better known as the **Dan Ryan Expressway** south of downtown and the **Kennedy Expressway** to the north). Make sure your camera is nearby. Each expressway has magnificent views of the downtown skyline, and you'll have ample time to take a snapshot. These expressways are usually backed up—the Dan Ryan is in the midst of a two-year construction project, the largest road rehabilitation in the city's history. People are cryin' on the Ryan, and we aren't lyin'.

South of the city, I-90/94 links with **I-80,** a major east–west route that connects Chicago to South Bend, Indiana; Toledo and Cleveland, Ohio; and New York City to the east and Davenport and Des Moines, Iowa; Omaha, Nebraska; and other points to the west. I-90/94 also joins I-57, which continues south through Illinois to Kankakee, Champaign, and eventually Memphis, Tennessee, on a historic migratory path.

 unofficial **TIP**
The Dan Ryan Expressway is the Chicago area's busiest and most accident-plagued highway. About 320,000 vehicles travel it every day. Interstate 90/94, which runs roughly north to south through Chicago (paralleling Lake Michigan), features express lanes (without exits) and local lanes (with exits). All in all, it's a helter-skelter system guaranteed to exasperate first-time visitors.

North of downtown, I-90/94 changes names to become the Kennedy Expressway; it veers northwest toward O'Hare International Airport before splitting. I-90 (now called the **Northwest Tollway**) continues northwest past the airport to Madison, Wisconsin, where it meets I-94. Got it?

The **Stevenson Expressway** (I-55) enters Chicago near McCormick Place from the southwest; this interstate begins in New Orleans and goes north through Memphis and St. Louis before crossing I-80 and passing Midway Airport to its terminus in the city at Lake Shore Drive. From the west, the **Eisenhower Expressway** (I-290) comes into the Loop from **I-88** (the East–West Tollway) and De Kalb.

West of the city limits, two highways run north and south through Chicago's suburbs to link the major roads coming into Chicago from the south, west, and north; the highways serve as "beltways" in otherwise beltway-less Chicago. **I-294** (the Tri-State Tollway) starts at I-80 south of the city and crosses the Stevenson Expressway, the Eisenhower Expressway, and the Kennedy Expressway near O'Hare. North of Chicago it merges with I-94 en route to Milwaukee.

A few miles west of I-294, the newer **US 355** (the North–South Tollway) connects I-55 and I-88 to I-290 west of O'Hare; I-290 goes north to I-90, the Northwest Tollway that links Madison and Chicago.

US 41, a popular route also known as the **Edens Expressway,** links I-90/94 on Chicago's North Side (north of the Chicago River) with the densely populated northern suburbs of Skokie and Highland Park before merging with I-94 south of the Wisconsin state line. As if all this isn't goofy enough, the Edens Expressway is named after William G. Edens, a local banker . . . who never drove a car. Farther south into the city, US 41 becomes **Lake Shore Drive,** which follows Lake Michigan south past downtown and into Indiana.

unofficial **TIP**
Don't discount US 41 South as an option when the Dan Ryan Expressway is backed up.

COMING *into* CHICAGO *by* PLANE

OVER THE PAST FEW YEARS, the title of world's busiest airport has gone back and forth between **O'Hare International Airport** and Hartsfield-Jackson Atlanta International Airport. These statistical flip-flops are easier to take than the holding pattern that folks often experience in the air at O'Hare, which in 2007 served 76 million passengers—nearly 12 million of them international visitors. The airport is 17 miles northwest of downtown Chicago. That means there are usually enough travelers on hand to turn the huge facility into its own city when lousy weather snarls air traffic and strands travelers by the thousands.

Yet O'Hare isn't the only game in town. **Midway Airport,** a long 15 miles southwest of downtown, handles about one-tenth the passenger traffic of its big brother to the north, making it a more hassle-free point of arrival and departure for many visitors to Chicago.

O'HARE INTERNATIONAL AIRPORT

OPENED IN 1955 AND NAMED FOR Congressional Medal of Honor winner Edward O'Hare, a Navy pilot killed in the Battle of Midway, this sprawling airport includes four terminals connected by passenger walkways, moving sidewalks, and a "people mover," an automated transit system that covers 2.7 miles of airport property. Statistics at O'Hare are impressive. For decades, it has been the commercial-aviation capital of the world, providing service to all 50 states and many foreign countries. The mammoth airport alternates with its Atlanta rival for the greater number of passengers and flights served (in 2007 O'Hare handled 935,000 flights, Hartsfield-Jackson about 994,000). More than 200,000 passengers pass through O'Hare each day, and an average of 100 aircraft arrive or depart each hour. Covering 7,700 acres, the airport regularly serves about 60 commercial, commuter, and cargo airlines.

The airport is connected to Chicago's subway system—albeit a long walk—and is close to I-90 (the Kennedy Expressway), which goes downtown to the Loop. Although O'Hare is renowned for its holding patterns in the air, on the ground it boasts a modern international terminal, is easy to get around, and is still growing. More than $700 million in improvements (including new runways and a new Terminal 6) are planned over the next few years.

The Layout

The "core" of O'Hare contains Terminals 1, 2, and 3, where most domestic flights come and go. Terminal 2 lies in the center of the horseshoe-shaped arrangement and faces the O'Hare Hilton, a parking garage, and parking lots. Don't look for Terminal 4—there is none. Terminal 5 handles international flights. Located south of the core, it is reached via the Airport Transit System (or "people mover"). In the three main terminals, the second-floor departure level features fast-food eateries, bars, shops, newsstands, and a "restaurant rotunda" between Terminals 2 and 3. From the gate, arriving passengers follow signs to the baggage-claim area on the lower level.

The People Mover

If you need to get from, say, Terminal 1 to Terminal 3 or your destination is the long-term parking area, take the "people mover" train. Escalators and elevators in front of the ticket counters take you over the roadway, where departing passengers are dropped off. The people mover is free, and a train comes every few minutes.

unofficial **TIP**
If you've got some time to kill before your flight, explore the people mover. This mini-El of a transportation system is fun to ride, and you'll be treated to nice views of the airfield.

Getting Downtown

CABS AND SHUTTLES Visitors who fly into Chicago have to make a choice when it comes

O'Hare International Airport

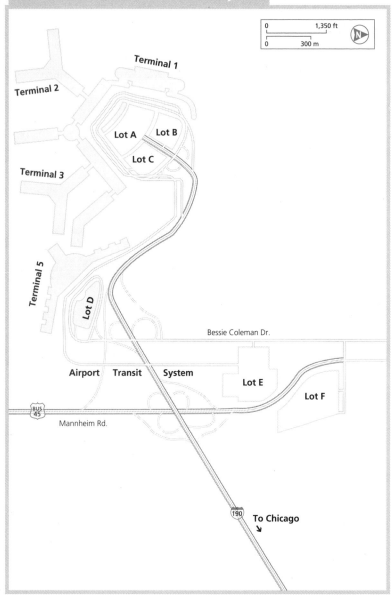

Terminal 1

Terminal 2

Lot A   Lot B

Lot C

Terminal 3

Terminal 5

Lot D

Bessie Coleman Dr.

Airport   Transit   System

Lot E

BUS 45

Lot F

Mannheim Rd.

190   To Chicago

0   1,350 ft
0   300 m

to getting downtown. If your final destination is a major hotel near the Loop or the Magnificent Mile (which is where most of them are), **Airport Express** (☎ 888-284-3826) is the cheapest and easiest way to go—unless you're not schlepping luggage (take the train) or in a group (take a cab). Just inquire at the Airport Express desk in the baggage-claim areas of O'Hare or Midway, and ask if the van goes to your hotel. It's also a good idea to ask if your hotel is one of the first or last stops the van makes.

The service operates vans to major downtown hotels from 5:15 a.m. to 11:30 p.m. daily that leave about every 10 to 15 minutes. Ticket counters are in the baggage-claim areas of all four O'Hare terminals. One-way fares are $25; round-trip fares are $46. Figure on a 45-minute ride to your hotel during non-rush-hour traffic. Call to make reservations for a pickup from your downtown hotel, or for a guaranteed seat, on the day before you leave; last-minute reservations can be made up to an hour before departure on a space-available basis.

If your hotel isn't served by Airport Express, taxis, buses, hotel vans, and rental-car pickups are located outside the lower-level baggage areas. Cab fares to downtown run about $35 to $40 one-way for the normal travel time of 30 minutes; share-the-ride cabs cost $20 per person for a taxi shared by two to four passengers headed downtown. Allow at least an hour and a half during rush hour, and expect to pay a higher fare for the longer cab ride.

PUBLIC TRANSPORTATION If you're traveling light, the Chicago Transit Authority (CTA) **Blue Line** train terminal is located in front of and beneath Terminal 2 (follow the signs that read TRAINS TO DOWNTOWN); it's about a 40-minute trip to the Loop that costs $1.75 one-way. Trains leave about every 10 minutes weekdays and about every 15 minutes early evenings and weekends. Unfortunately, there's no place to store luggage on the rapid-transit trains (although one piece of luggage is usually manageable, as many airline employees attest). For more information, call the CTA at ☎ 312-836-7000.

DRIVING If you're renting a car and driving, getting to the Loop is pretty easy. Follow signs out of the airport to I-90 east, which puts you on the Kennedy Expressway; it's a straight 18-mile ride to downtown that takes about a half hour (longer during rush hour; Friday afternoons are the worst). As you approach the city, Chicago's distinctive skyline, anchored by the John Hancock Center on the left and the Sears Tower on the right, comes into view—if it's not raining.

If you're headed for the Loop, move into the right lane as you approach the tunnel (just before the city center) and get ready to exit as you come out of the tunnel. Take the Ohio Street exit to get to the north-downtown area. The last of four exits to downtown is the Congress Parkway (where I-290 west, aka the Eisenhower Expressway, meets the Kennedy Expressway) to South Loop; miss it and you're on your way to Indiana. Taking the Congress Parkway exit scoots you

HANGING OUT AT O'HARE

Unbeknownst even to natives, O'Hare is now a city unto itself. Additions in recent years have included, for example, a satellite of Chicago's landmark **Berghoff Café** on Concourse C in Terminal 1 and **Wolfgang Puck's** in Terminal 3. If you're stuck overnight in O'Hareland, here's a tip: international Terminal 5 has the airport's only 24-hour restaurants. O'Hare orphans can get hot dogs, frozen yogurt, and assorted snacks there. In addition, Terminal 5's food court has cheaper prices and is usually less crowded overall than food courts in other terminals.

The **O'Hare Hilton** hotel is connected to the airport through an underground tunnel and outdoor walkway. The underground passage includes a bookstore, clothing shop, currency exchange, and dentist (with limited hours). The Hilton features a sports-themed restaurant and bar and a basement athletic club with a dry sauna and pool. Even Traveler's Aid will suggest that if you need to freshen up, buy a one-day membership at the club for $10 and take a quick shower there.

If you have time to explore, wander through the hotel lobby, at the west end of which sits the last **Gaslight Club** in America. The Gaslight started in 1953 as a private club on Chicago's Gold Coast. Cofounder Burton Browne set out to re-create a 1920s speakeasy with Dixieland jazz and servers dressed in skimpy flapper outfits. Browne's concept was a prototype for Hugh Hefner's Playboy Clubs. The dimly lit O'Hare Gaslight Club, which opened in 1973, is a separate operation from the Hilton.

through the U.S. Post Office building to the south edge of the Loop; South Michigan Avenue and South Lake Shore Drive lie straight ahead. For more information on getting around Chicago, see Part Six, Getting Around.

Visitor Services

Twenty-six multilingual information specialists are on hand to provide information and translation assistance to travelers. Five information booths are located throughout the airport on the lower levels of Terminals 1, 2, and 3 and on the lower and upper levels of Terminal 5. The booths are open daily from 8:15 a.m. to 8 p.m. For more information, call the main airport number (☎ 773-686-2200).

The **U.S. Postal Service** operates an office in Terminal 2 on the upper level. Hours are 7 a.m. to 7 p.m. weekdays. Teletext phones for the hearing impaired can be found next to the information booths in the three domestic terminals (lower level) and outside the customs area in the international terminal. More teletext phones are located in phone banks throughout the airport; ☎ 773-601-8333.

Foreign-currency exchanges are located in Terminals 1, 3, and 5. Hours are 8 a.m. to 8 p.m. daily.

A duty-free shop, in Terminal 5 in the center court on the upper level, offers a wide range of merchandise. Hours vary; the shop frequently stays open later than normal to serve international flights. Satellite shops are also located in Terminal 1 near gate C18 and in Terminal 3 across from gate K11; hours vary according to flight times.

ATMs are located on the upper levels of Terminals 1, 2, and 3 near the concourse entrances (airside) and on the upper and lower levels of Terminal 5.

Lost stuff? For items lost near a ticket counter, in a gate area, or on a plane, contact the airline. For items lost in the public areas of the terminals, contact Chicago Police at ☎ 773-686-2385. For items lost in a food-service location, call ☎ 773-686-6148. Don't lose these numbers.

Kids on the Fly is an exhibit for youngsters operated by the Chicago Children's Museum. Centrally located in Terminal 2 (near the security checkpoint), the 2,205-square-foot interactive playground lets children ages 1 to 12 burn off excess energy as they explore a kid-sized air-traffic-control tower, a ceiling-high model of the Sears Tower, a cargo plane, a luggage station (enjoy the fun of waiting!), and a fantasy helicopter. It's free and open to all visitors during regular flight hours and to ticketed passengers after 10 p.m.

unofficial **TIP**
Be aware that O'Hare is a no-smoking airport. At Hartsfield-Jackson in Atlanta, five of the six concourses have at least one smoking lounge. At O'Hare, smoking is permitted only in certain airlines' members-only lounges. So plan accordingly. For example, if you're at Concourse C in Terminal 1, it can take as long as 20 minutes to walk outside for a smoke.

Parking

O'Hare provides more than 12,000 spaces in short- and long-term parking lots and a garage (☎ 773-686-7530; for maps and detailed information, visit **www.ohare.com/ohare/parking**). There's even valet parking; $10 for the first hour, then $32 a day. Short-term parking in the first level of the garage is $3 for the first hour, $21 for the next four hours (and another $21 after that), and finally $50 for 9 to 24 hours. Parking on Levels 2 to 6 of the parking garage and inside lots B and C costs $3 for an hour or less, with a maximum fee of $26 for 24 hours. Rates in short-term Lot D (next to the international terminal) are $3 for an hour or less and $30 for 13 to 24 hours. Long-term parking in the faraway Lot E (served by the "people mover") is $13 per day.

MIDWAY AIRPORT

TUCKED AWAY IN A CLASSIC CHICAGO BUNGALOW community 15 miles southwest of downtown Chicago, this airport is everything O'Hare isn't: small, convenient, and relatively uncongested. If you can get a direct flight into Midway, take it. Why fight the hassles of O' Hare?

Midway Airport

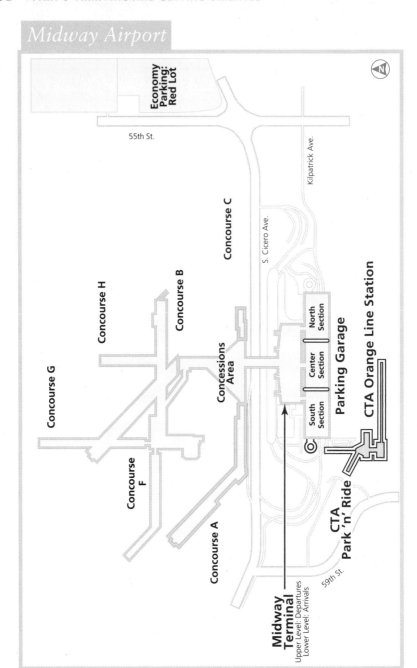

Economy Parking: Red Lot

55th St.

Kilpatrick Ave.

Concourse C

S. Cicero Ave.

Concourse H

Concourse B

Concourse G

North Section

Concessions Area

Center Section

Parking Garage

South Section

CTA Orange Line Station

Concourse F

CTA Park 'n' Ride

Concourse A

59th St.

Midway Terminal
Upper Level: Departures
Lower Level: Arrivals

The homespun airport was once owned by the Chicago Board of Education. In fact, until 1955 an elementary school was on the property, just 100 yards from an active runway of what was then the world's busiest airport.

Southwest Airlines is the most popular carrier at Midway (American and United ended all scheduled service here in 2006). The new terminal at Midway has six concourses. From your gate, follow signs to the baggage area to pick up your luggage. Passenger pickup and drop-off, taxis, buses, car rental, and the CTA **Orange Line** train station are right outside the door. (The last train out is at 12:55 a.m.) Free shuttles to the long-term economy-parking lot arrive every 15 minutes.

Cab fares from Midway to downtown run about $40, and the ride doesn't show the best side of Chicago (it's not dangerous, just ugly). The trip takes between 20 minutes and a half hour; figure on a higher fare during heavy traffic and/or bad weather.

Share-the-ride cabs let you split the trip with up to three other passengers going downtown; the cost is $10 per person.

Airport Express (☎ 888-284-3826) offers van service to and from downtown hotels; the fare is $18 one-way for adults and $8.50 for children under age 12 with an adult. The trip takes about 30 minutes, and vans depart every 15 to 20 minutes. Round-trip fare for adults is $30. For a return reservation, call a day in advance. Last-minute reservations can be made up to an hour before departure as space allows.

CTA's **Orange Line** connects Midway to downtown, and its trains offer plenty of room for luggage. The fare is $1.75 one-way; the ride lasts 35 minutes. Trains run every day from 5 a.m. to 11 p.m. weekdays and Saturdays, and 7:30 a.m. to 11 p.m. Sundays and holidays. Trains run every six to eight minutes during rush hour and every ten minutes the rest of the time. Weekday-morning rush-hour bus service to downtown is via the **#99M Midway Express** (avoid this bus in the evening). Pick it up at the airport's center entrance. The **#62 Archer bus** provides 24-hour service to downtown. Fares are $1.75 for both buses.

If you're renting a car and driving downtown, take South Cicero Avenue north a few miles to I-55 (the Stevenson Expressway) east. The highway ends at Lake Shore Drive and the McCormick Place complex; take Lake Shore Drive north to get downtown or places farther north.

As you bear left onto Lake Shore Drive, you're treated to a great view of the Chicago skyline and Lake Michigan. After passing the Field Museum on the right, turn left onto Balbo Avenue to reach Michigan Avenue, the Loop, and I-290 (the Eisenhower Expressway). Or continue straight along the lake across the Chicago River to reach the Magnificent Mile, Navy Pier, and other points north. From Midway, the 15-mile drive to downtown takes about 20 minutes (longer during rush hour).

COMING *into* CHICAGO *by* TRAIN

CHICAGO'S HISTORIC **Union Station** (210 South Canal, across the Chicago River) is a hub for **Amtrak** rail service and **Metra** commuter trains. Unfortunately, the train station's location makes it rather inconvenient, unless you're connecting to the Chicago suburbs. If you have time, take a close look at this grand old dame. Union Station was built between 1913 and 1925 as a palace commemorating Chicago's status as a transportation center. Today, the only part of the original station that remains is the so-called Great Hall (the rest was razed and remodeled in 1969). The Great Hall waiting room, which covers a city block, is aglow with a 90-foot-high skylighted ceiling, pink Tennessee-marble floors, and bronze torches. The barreled and vaulted ceiling is said to be patterned after an ancient Roman bath. This main waiting room harks back to the golden days of railroading. The only drawback is that napping is difficult on the Great Hall's uncomfortable wooden benches.

Union Station is not particularly close to anything such as major hotels or subway stations (the John Hancock Center is a couple of blocks east), and its layout is confusing. Amtrak trains arrive on the concourse level of the station. After picking up your baggage, head for the taxi stand near the north concourse (Adams Street exit). The "El" train is several blocks to the east—too far to walk if you're carrying luggage. The only public-transportation option is the **#151 bus**—also not a good idea if you're lugging a suitcase or two—which you can catch outside Canal Street. The bus goes through the Loop and up North Michigan Avenue. To sum up: if you're not being picked up by someone in a car, a cab is your best option for getting out of Union Station.

GETTING ORIENTED

THE OPERATIVE WORD FOR CHICAGO, the nation's third-largest city, is *big*.

New York City is bigger, Los Angeles more spread out. Chicago is midwestern muscle. Located a third of the way between the East and West coasts, Chicago covers 227 square miles and stretches 33 miles along the southwestern coastline of Lake Michigan (the second largest of the five Great Lakes, after Lake Superior). With a population of just under 3 million—in a metropolitan area of over 6 million—Chicago is not only the largest city in Illinois, it's the de facto economic and cultural capital of the Midwest. (But it's not the capital of the state: that distinction belongs to Springfield, 200 miles south.)

A GEOGRAPHY LESSON

CHICAGO IS IN THE NORTHEAST CORNER of Illinois, a very large midwestern state bordered by (starting clockwise southeast of the city), Indiana, a bit of Kentucky, Missouri, Iowa, and Wisconsin; Michigan is to the east and north across the lake. Most of the land that surrounds the city is flat—like most of the Midwest—a fact, theorists say, that may explain the city's passion for tall buildings and the easily recognizable skyline.

To the southeast, just past the city line on the southern tip of Lake Michigan, lies the gritty industrial town of **Gary, Indiana** (birthplace of Michael, Janet, and various other Jacksons). North along the lake, the city merges with the comfortable suburban enclave of **Evanston** (home of Northwestern University); farther north, but still within commuting range of Chicago, are **Highland Park** (near where Michael Jordan still keeps a home) and **Waukegan.** The Wisconsin state line lies about 40 miles north of the **Loop,** the heart of downtown Chicago.

The closest major city is **Milwaukee,** a blue-collar beer-drinking town on Lake Michigan, 90 miles to the north. Other midwestern cities arrayed around Chicago are **Detroit** (290 miles to the east), **Indianapolis** (180 miles to the southeast), **St. Louis** (300 miles to the southwest), **Des Moines** (360 miles to the west), and **Minneapolis–St. Paul** (410 miles to the northwest).

CHICAGO'S LAYOUT

River and Lake

The other major geographic feature of Chicago is the narrow **Chicago River,** which meets **Lake Michigan** downtown along the carefully pre-served lakefront (which is lined with parks and a wildly popular bike and jogging trail, not factories and wharves). The direction of the river was reversed in 1900. Today it flows away from Lake Michigan downstate to the Illinois River, which connects with the Mississippi River, forming a major shipping route to the Gulf of Mexico. Boat tours on the Chicago offer some of the best views of the city's fabled architecture.

The Loop and Grant Park

Tucked south and east of a bend in the river is the **Loop,** Chicago's downtown core of government buildings, financial and trading insti-tutions, office buildings, hotels, and retail establishments.

A couple of blocks east of the Loop and hugging Lake Michigan is **Grant Park,** a barrier of green where millions of Chicagoans and visitors flock each summer to enjoy outdoor events and music festi-vals, including concerts at the **Jay Pritzker Pavilion** in the new **Millennium Park.** Grant Park also provides a campuslike setting for some of the city's largest museums, colorful **Buckingham Fountain,** and many softball fields. The view of the Chicago skyline from the park is spectacular.

WHAT IS THE LOOP?

You'll see the Loop mentioned a lot in this book. So what exactly is it? The Loop is what locals call downtown Chicago. It gets its name from the elevated train tracks ("the El") that circle the central business district—the second largest downtown in the United States after Midtown Manhattan.

Over the years, the Loop's definition has expanded beyond the El tracks. Some say the Loop goes as far west as the Chicago River and as far south as Roosevelt Road—an area that only recently has become known as the South Loop. But real Chicagoans know that the real Loop is downtown, surrounded by the El.

And that's the scoop on the Loop.

Lake Shore Drive

Running north and south through Grant Park and along Lake Michigan is **Lake Shore Drive.** "LSD," as locals call it, opened in 1937 as Leif Erickson Drive, which sounds more like a Minneapolis byway than a Chicago highway. Although the multilane road's high speeds and congestion usually result in a scary driving experience for first-time visitors, a cruise along the highway provides cool vistas of the Chicago skyline, yacht basins, parks full of trees and greenery, beaches, and oceanlike Lake Michigan stretching east to the horizon. (The views at night are even more mind-boggling. In 1971 the nocturnal sights were the subject of a regional pop hit, "Lake Shore Drive," by Alliota, Haynes, and Jeremiah.) Lake Shore Drive is also a major north–south corridor through the city, which is longer than it is wide.

In late 1996 Lake Shore Drive was relocated to the west of the **Field Museum** and **Soldier Field.** In 1997 the old lanes to the east were demolished and transformed into ten acres of new parkland, creating a traffic-free "Museum Campus" for the Field Museum, the **Adler Planetarium,** and the **Shedd Aquarium.** With its paths, bikeways, a pedestrian concourse under Lake Shore Drive that serves as a gateway to the Museum Campus, and extensive landscaping, this new lakefront park provides Chicagoans and visitors with another place to stroll, bike, run, and relax as they take in the views. For drivers, an extensive system of new directional signs was installed.

Near North

North of the Chicago River are two areas popular with out-of-town visitors: the **Magnificent Mile,** a glitzy strip of North Michigan Avenue full of the city's toniest shops and galleries (Oprah Winfrey has an apartment in this neighborhood), and **River North** (one of Chicago's premier nightclub and restaurant districts). Renovated and reopened in 1995 and jutting out into Lake Michigan is **Navy Pier,** featuring amusement rides, a shopping mall, clubs, a theater, restaurants, and convention space. The pier is popular with tourists; locals don't go there except for special events. Farther north are the **Gold Coast,** an enclave of exclusive homes (and a great walking destination), and **Lincoln Park.** Surrounded by a residential neighborhood of young urban professionals and high-rises, the park is the site of the most visited zoo in the United States.

South and West of the Loop

South of the Loop along the lake is the sprawling **McCormick Place,** North America's largest convention venue. Farther south are the **Museum of Science and Industry** and **Hyde Park,** home of the regal **University of Chicago** campus (and more museums). The West Loop is booming, thanks in part to Oprah Winfrey opening **Harpo Studios,** her TV-production house, at 1058 West Washington Boulevard in 1988. In the late 1960s and early 1970s, West Washington was off skid row; today it has several good restaurants and a few boutiques. Move farther west, past such landmarks as the **United Center,** and things get a little iffy. Still, there are some not-to-be-missed attractions west of the Loop, including **Hull-House** (where Nobel Prize winner Jane Addams gave turn-of-the-19th-century immigrants a leg up on the American dream), ethnic restaurants in **Greektown** and **Little Italy,** the beautiful **Garfield Park Conservatory,** and, just west of the city line, **Oak Park** (hometown of famed architect Frank Lloyd Wright and equally famous Nobel-laureate novelist Ernest Hemingway).

Scattered throughout the city to the north, west, and south of downtown are a wide array of urban neighborhoods featuring shops, museums, and dining that honor the ethnic diversity of Chicago; see "Exploring Chicago's Neighborhoods" in Part Seven, Sightseeing, Tours, and Attractions, for descriptions and locations. Beyond the city limits are more attractions worth the drive: the **Brookfield Zoo, Chicago Botanic Garden,** and **Morton Arboretum** are all less than an hour from downtown Chicago (allow more time in rush-hour traffic).

THE MAJOR HIGHWAYS

THE MAJOR INTERSTATE ROUTES to Chicago's Loop are **I-90/94** (better known to Chicagoans as the **Dan Ryan Expressway** south of downtown and the **Kennedy Expressway** to the north and west), **I-290** (the **Eisenhower Expressway**), and **I-55** (the **Stevenson Expressway,** which ends about a mile south of downtown at McCormick Place).

West of the city, **I-294** (the **Tri-State Tollway**) parallels Lake Michigan through Chicago's suburbs as it heads north and links I-80 (a major transcontinental route south of the city) to I-90 (which goes to Milwaukee). I-294 also skirts **O'Hare International Airport,** where it intersects with I-90 (which links Chicago to Madison, Wisconsin).

A Word about Driving: Don't

With four major interstates converging downtown at or near the Loop, entering the city makes for a very interesting driving experience, especially if it's your first visit to Chicago . . . and it's rush hour.

unofficial **TIP**
Our advice: if you're staying at a downtown hotel, don't drive.

The congestion in America's third-largest city is unrelenting: morning and evening rush-hour traffic reports endlessly list backups, accidents, and delays occurring throughout the metropolitan area. And parking? Forget it. Chicago is notorious for its lack of convenient and affordable places to park.

Whether you're in town for business or pleasure, spare yourself the frustration of battling traffic, lanes that change direction depending on the time of day, and a tangle of highways. Instead, ride Chicago's extensive public-transportation systems, take airport vans to and from downtown hotels, and take advantage of an abundance of taxis to get around town. (For more information on how to negotiate Chicago without a car, see "Public Transportation" in Part Six, Getting Around, page 109.)

FINDING YOUR WAY AROUND CHICAGO

CHICAGO'S SHEER SIZE CAN BE OVERWHELMING, but here's a tip for visitors: the city is a "right angle" town, a characteristic that's invaluable in finding your way around. Except for the rare diagonal street, Chicago is laid out numerically on a grid, with **State** and **Madison streets** (in the Loop) intersecting at the zero point. This is another reason Chicago is called "The City That Works."

And it works like this: North Side Chicago is north of Madison Street, and South Side is south of it. The West Side, logically enough, is west of State Street. And the East Side? It hardly exists; most of what could be termed "East Side" is Lake Michigan, since State Street is only a few blocks west of the lakefront.

Street numbers run in increments of 100 per block, with eight blocks to the mile. (Folks can spend their spare time figuring distances using street addresses.) Generally speaking, North Side streets and north–south streets on the South Side have names (Michigan Avenue, Erie Street, Chicago Avenue), while east–west streets on the South Side are usually numbered (for example, the popular Museum of Science and Industry is on 57th Street at Lake Shore Drive; Chicago blues legends migrated to East 43rd Street in the 1940s and 1950s).

unofficial **TIP**
To stay oriented when exploring Chicago, just remember this: if the street numbers are going up, you're headed away from downtown. If they're going down, you're moving to the center of the city.

After you've tried it a few times, navigating Chicago's grid can be fun—at least on weekends, when the traffic is relatively light. Locating, say, the **Balzekas Museum of Lithuanian Culture** is a snap. The address,

6500 South Pulaski Road, tells you the museum is at the corner of South Pulaski and 65th Street. It also helps that many (but not all) major avenues traverse the entire city from north to south. Like old friends, names such as Western, Cermak, Halsted, and Clark crop up over and over as you explore the city.

WHERE TO FIND TOURIST INFORMATION IN CHICAGO

IF YOU'RE SHORT ON MAPS or you need more information on sight-seeing, hotels, shopping, and other activities in and around Chicago, there are several places to pick up maps and brochures:

- In downtown Chicago, the **Visitor Information Center** in the Randolph Lobby of the Chicago Cultural Center (78 East Washington Street at Michigan Avenue; ☎ 312-744-2400) dispenses literature and advice to tourists. Orientations with videos and displays are provided just off the lobby. Open Monday through Friday, 10 a.m. to 6 p.m.; Saturday, 10 a.m. to 5 p.m.; and Sunday, 11 a.m. to 5 p.m. Closed on major holidays.

- On the Magnificent Mile north of the Loop, the **Chicago Water Works Visitor Center** at Pearson Street and Michigan Avenue (you can't miss it—the tower is one of two structures that survived the Great Fire of 1871) provides tourist information, maps, hotel reservations, and advice. In addition, the center stocks plentiful info on tourist attractions throughout Illinois. Open daily, 7:30 a.m. to 7 p.m.; closed Thanksgiving and Christmas; ☎ 312-744-8783.

- In the Loop, the **Explore Chicago** kiosk inside the Sears on State store (2 North State Street) is open Monday through Saturday, 10 a.m. to 6 p.m.; and Sunday, noon to 5 p.m.

- In suburban Oak Park, visitors interested in touring the former residences of Frank Lloyd Wright and Ernest Hemingway should make their first stop at the **Oak Park Visitors Bureau** (158 Forest Avenue; ☎ 888-OAK-PARK or 708-848-1500). Visitors can park free in the adjacent parking garage on weekends, and can purchase tickets and pick up free maps in the visitor center. Open daily, 10 a.m. to 5 p.m.

THINGS *the* NATIVES ALREADY KNOW

CHICAGO CUSTOMS AND PROTOCOL

CHICAGOANS HAVE EARNED A well-deserved reputation for friendliness yet often display a degree of forwardness that can put off foreigners and visitors from more formal parts of our country. (Do ya got a problem with dat?) Sometimes the locals come off as brash or blunt, since many value getting directly to the point:

unofficial **TIP**
If you're not sure how to dress before you go out to eat, call ahead—or dress "chic casual": relaxed but put together, not sloppy (no T-shirts or running shoes).

Chicagoans don't have time to waste. In this respect, Chicago can be a Puritan city. And that's mostly good news for tourists, who can count on plenty of help finding a destination when riding a crowded rush-hour bus, for example. The moral is, don't hesitate to ask a native for assistance. Even if he's wearing a Bears sweatshirt—and Bears stocking cap—and Bears warm-up jacket . . .

Eating in Restaurants

By and large, *casual* is the byword when dining in Chicago. Only the most chichi eateries require men to wear a jacket or prohibit ladies from wearing shorts or tank tops. Even swank spots such as the Ritz-Carlton downtown have stopped requiring men to wear ties at dinner. Although people tend to dress up more for dinner downtown, you'll still find plenty of casual restaurants (the ones at Navy Pier, for example). Just about all ethnic restaurants beyond downtown have nonexistent dress codes.

Tipping

Is the tip you normally leave at home appropriate in Chicago? Yes. Just bear in mind that a tip is a reward for efficient service. Here are some guidelines.

PORTERS AND SKYCAPS A dollar a bag, more if the bags are cumbersome.

CAB DRIVERS Almost everything depends on service and courtesy. If the fare is less than $8, give the driver the change and a dollar. Example: if the fare is $4.50, give the cabbie 50¢ and a buck. If the fare is more than $8, give the driver the change and $2. If you ask the cabbie to take you only a block or two, the fare will be small, but you should tip large ($3 to $5) to make up for his or her wait in line and to partially compensate him or her for missing a better-paying fare. Add an extra dollar to your tip if the driver handles a lot of luggage.

PARKING For a valet, $2 is correct if he or she is courteous and demonstrates some hustle. A dollar will do if the service is just okay. Pay only when you check your car out, not when you leave it. Especially around the Gold Coast area, valets have been under scrutiny in recent years.

BELLHOPS AND DOORMEN When a bellhop greets you at your car with a rolling luggage cart and handles all your bags, $6 is about right. The more luggage you carry yourself, the less you should tip. Add $1 or $2 if the bellhop opens your room. For calling a taxi, tip the doorman $1.

WAITERS Whether you eat at a coffee shop, dine at an upscale eatery, or order room service from the hotel kitchen, the standard gratuity hovers around 20% of the tab before sales tax. At buffets or brunches where your serve yourself, leave $1 per diner for the bussers. Some restaurants, however, have adopted the European custom of automatically adding gratuity to the bill, so check before leaving a cash tip. Thousands of Chicago coffee shops now have a tip cup near the register. Staff often don't expect a tip, but leave $1 or more if the service is extraordinary.

unofficial **TIP**
Veteran Chicago bartenders and cocktail waiters frown on loose change. They're often pressed for time and don't like picking up three quarters, two dimes, and a nickel off the bar.

SOMMELIER Tips aren't required, but if the sommelier has excelled, Chicagoans often leave 15% of the cost of the first bottle of wine.

COCKTAIL WAITERS AND BARTENDERS Here you tip by the round: for two people, $1 a round; for more than two, $2 a round. For a large group, use your judgment. Is everyone drinking beer, or is the order long and complicated? Tip accordingly.

HOTEL MAIDS On checking out, leave a dollar or two per day for each day of your stay, provided the service was good.

How to Look and Sound Like a Native

Chicagoans are tough. They're mostly down-to-earth realists who take a sort of pride in their city's legendarily crooked politicians, horrible winters, and screwy traffic jams. Because the city shuns phoniness, visitors who want to blend in need only be themselves. But if it's important to you not to look like a tourist, we offer the following advice.

1. Don't call Chicago the "Windy City." Natives don't do that. That would be like San Franciscans calling their elegant city "San Fran."

2. Don't crash-diet. Except for razor-thin fashion victims haunting the boutiques along the Magnificent Mile, Chicagoans disdain the froufrou svelteness that's the norm in New York or Los Angeles. Being overweight in Chicago isn't a social faux pas—this is, after all, a town known for its pizza, steaks, Italian beef and sausage sandwiches, and many other kinds of artery-clogging, waistband-expanding delicacies. And when Chicagoans are feeling too fat, they just head 90 miles north to Milwaukee, where they always fit in.

3. Be obsessive about the Bears. Pick either the Cubs or White Sox in baseball—you can't root for both. (By the way, never, ever call the Cubs the "Cubbies." They're a sad enough operation without sounding like something rescued from an animal shelter.) Talk about Jerry Sloan, Norm Van Lier, and Chet Walker in the days before the Bulls had Michael Jordan. No one talks about the Blackhawks anymore.

4. Talk through your nose. Master the flat phonetics of the Midwest: give the letter *A* a harsh sound and throw in a few *dems* and *doses* when attempting to converse with natives.

5. Occasionally, for no apparent reason, erupt in your best attempt at a Chicago accent: "Yah, but the city works." Or "Da Bears."

6. Do not, under any circumstances, put ketchup on a Chicago-style hot dog.

7. Read the *Sun-Times* on a bus or the El. Read the *Tribune* on a train to the suburbs.

PUBLICATIONS FOR VISITORS

CHICAGO HAS TWO MAJOR DAILY NEWSPAPERS, the *Chicago Sun-Times* and the *Chicago Tribune*. Both are morning papers that cover local, national, and international news; both also have Friday editions with up-to-the-minute information on entertainment for the weekend. A more comprehensive source for entertainment and arts listings is in the weekly *Chicago Reader*, a free alternative newspaper that shows up on downtown newsstands (as well as at a variety of clubs, bars, bookstores, cafes, and shops) on Thursday afternoons.

The weekly *Time Out Chicago* magazine is also popular with tourists. It's published by the same folks who created *Time Out New York* and *Time Out London*. The Chicago edition has gobs of bar, restaurant, and entertainment recommendations. *Chicago* is a slightly stuffy monthly magazine (owned by the *Tribune*) that's strong on lists (top 20 restaurants, and so on) and provides a calendar of events, dining information, and feature articles.

Windy City Sports is a free monthly guide to fitness and outdoor recreation that highlights seasonal sports such as skiing, bicycling, running, inline skating, and sailboarding. Look for it at bike shops and outdoors outfitters.

Chicago Scene highlights Chicago's beautiful people and visiting celebs as they nibble canapés at the town's top social events; the free monthly also contains articles on dining and fashion. Pick up a copy at swank shops, hair salons, and cafes up and down the Gold Coast. At the other end of the social spectrum, *Street Wise*, published twice monthly, is sold by homeless and formerly homeless men and women for $1 (look for identifying vendor badges). The newspaper includes features, a calendar of events, sports, poetry, and film reviews.

CHICAGO ON THE AIR

ASIDE FROM THE USUAL BABBLE of format rock, talk, easy listening, and country music, Chicago is home to a few radio stations that really stand out for high-quality broadcasting. Tune in to what hip Chicagoans listen to, as listed at top right.

ACCESS FOR THE DISABLED

LIKE MOST LARGE AMERICAN CITIES, Chicago tries to make itself accessible to people with physical disabilities. Most museums and restaurants, for example, feature wheelchair access. At the **Art**

CHICAGO'S BEST RADIO STATIONS		
FORMAT	FREQUENCY	STATION
NPR, News	91.5 FM	WBEZ
Progressive Rock	93.1 FM	WXRT
Jazz	95.5 FM	WNUA
Classic Rock	97.1 FM	WDRV
Classical	98.7 FM	WFMT

Institute of Chicago, wheelchair access is through the Columbus Drive (east) entrance, and a limited number of wheelchairs and strollers are available free at both main entrances. Most public areas associated with the **Chicago History Museum** are accessible to the disabled, and a limited number of wheelchairs are also available. Parking for disabled visitors is provided in the parking lot adjacent to the building.

The **Field Museum** has wheelchairs available on the ground level near the West Entrance and first-floor North Door, and the **Adler Planetarium** has wheelchair-accessible restrooms on the first floor (down the vending machine hallway). Elevators are available for folks in wheelchairs, parents with strollers, and those with other special needs.

The **Chicago Botanic Garden** has wheelchairs available at the Information Desks in the Gateway and Education centers. Accessible parking is located in parking lots 1, 2, and 3. The garden's Orientation Center is equipped with assistive-listening devices, closed-caption monitors, and signs in Braille. The **Brookfield Zoo** provides assistive-listening devices in the Administration Building near the South Gate and in the Discovery Center near the North Gate. A telecommunications device for the deaf (TDD and TTY) is also available in the Administration Building.

Services for the Disabled

THE **City of Chicago Department on Disability** offers information and reference: ☎ 312-744-6673 or 312-744-4964 (TDD).

Handicapped visitors can arrange door-to-door transportation from the airport or train station to their hotel, as well as transportation anywhere in the city in special vans; the rate is $1.50 each time you board. Call the **Chicago Transportation Authority Special Services Division** at ☎ 312-432-7025 or 312-432-7116 (TDD) for more information.

The **Chicago Transit Authority (CTA)** operates 112 routes with lift-equipped buses; look for the blue wheelchair symbol displayed on the first bus–last bus chart on the CTA map. For routes, fares, schedules, and a copy of the latest transit map, call ☎ 312-836-7000 from 5 a.m. to 1 a.m. The TDD number is ☎ 888-282-8891. Some (but not all) train stations are wheelchair-accessible. Here's the list; call ☎ 312-836-7000 for hours of operation:

- **Blue Line** (O'Hare-Congress-Douglas): O'Hare, Rosemont, Cumberland, Harlem-Higgins, Jefferson Park, Logan Square, Western, Clark-Lake (Lake transfer), Jackson, UIC–Halsted-Morgan, Polk, 18th, Cicero-Cermak, Medical Center (Damen entrance), Kedzie-Homan, and Forest Park.
- **Brown Line** (Ravenswood): Kimball, Western, Clark-Lake, Washington-Wells, and Merchandise Mart.
- **Green Line** (Lake Street–Jackson Park): Ashland-63rd, Halsted, East 63rd–Cottage Grove, 51st, 47th, 43rd, 35th-Bronzeville-ITT, King Drive, Roosevelt, Clark-Lake, Clinton, Ashland-Lake, California, Kedzie, Conservatory–Central Park Drive, Pulaski, Cicero, Laramie, Harlem-Lake (Marion entrance), and Central.
- **Orange Line** (Midway): All stations between Midway Airport and Roosevelt; also Clark-Lake and Washington-Wells.
- **Pink Line** (54th-Loop): 54th-Cermak, Cicero, Kostner, Pulaski, Central Park, Kedzie, California, Western, Damen, 18th, Polk, Clark-Lake, Library-State–Van Buren, and Washington-Wells.
- **Purple Line** (Evanston): Linden, Davis, Merchandise Mart, Clark-Lake, Library-State–Van Buren, and Washington-Wells.
- **Red Line** (Howard–Dan Ryan): Loyola, Granville, Addison, Chicago, Lake, Washington, Jackson, Roosevelt, and Sox-35th, 79th, 95th–Dan Ryan.
- **Yellow Line** (Skokie).

TIME ZONE

CHICAGO IS IN THE CENTRAL TIME ZONE, which puts the city one hour behind New York, two hours ahead of the West Coast, an hour ahead of the Rocky Mountains, and six hours behind Greenwich Mean Time.

PHONES

THE CHICAGO AREA IS SERVED BY FIVE AREA CODES: ☎ **312** for the Loop and downtown, ☎ **773** for the rest of the city, ☎ **630** for the far-western suburbs, ☎ **708** for the near-western and southern suburbs, and ☎ **847** for the northern suburbs. Calls from pay phones are 50¢. To dial out of Chicago to the suburbs, dial 1, then the appropriate area code, then the phone number you want to reach. While the initial call to the suburbs costs the same as an intracity call, keep some change handy. On longer calls, you may have to plug in more coins or get disconnected. If you're calling into the city from the suburbs, dial 1, then ☎ 312 or ☎ 773, then the phone number.

LIQUOR, TAXES, SMOKING, AND PIGEONS

IN CHICAGO THE LEGAL DRINKING AGE IS 21, and no store may sell alcoholic beverages before noon on Sundays. The local sales tax is

9%; the combined sales and hotel-room tax is 15.39%. Chicago now bans smoking in public places, including nightclubs and restaurants; in addition, smoking is prohibited on public transportation. Chicago is also the only major American city that has banned racing pigeons.

CRIME IN CHICAGO

FOR MOST OBSERVERS, Chicago and crime go together like Bonnie and Clyde. The image is mostly left over from the Prohibition era, when bootlegger Al Capone and arch-gangster John Dillinger earned the city worldwide notoriety. Mention Chicago almost anyplace in the world, and the response is likely to be a pantomimed machine gun with a "rat-a-tat-tat" flourish.

The truth is, Chicago wasn't all that dangerous for John Q. Public in the 1920s. Only 75 hoodlums went down in gang warfare in 1926—about 10% of today's annual murder count. Sadly, although metropolitan Chicago has about the same population that it did in the Roaring '20s, the average person today is more likely to become a crime statistic.

Places to Avoid

Like virtually all large U.S. cities, Chicago has its low-income, high-crime areas. Until recently, one of the most infamous was **Cabrini-Green,** a high-rise public-housing complex that came to be a national symbol of the failure of mid-20th-century urban planning. Over the last couple of years, the Near North neighborhood in which Cabrini-Green once stood has undergone dramatic changes because of the real-estate boom. There's even a farmer's market at the once-dangerous corner of Division Street and Clybourn Avenue.

While this area is becoming gentrified, much of the South and Near West sides contain areas that most visitors should avoid (exceptions include **Chinatown, Hyde Park,** and **Pullman** on the Far Southeast Side). On the North Side,

unofficial **TIP**
Often in Chicago, relative safety is a question of day or night. The lakefront, public parks, the Loop, and River North are active during the day but are deserted at night except around restaurants and clubs. Take a cab or drive to nighttime destinations in these areas.

glitzy neighborhoods are often next door to dicier areas, so don't wander too far afield. Here's some more advice: the city has been installing cameras on light posts in high-crime neighborhoods, so if you see a box with a blinking blue light, it's best to vamoose. (For more information on crime in the city, visit **www.chicagocrime.org.**)

Safe areas at virtually any time of day or night include the Magnificent Mile and Oak, Rush, and Division streets in the Gold Coast community. Just stay within well-lighted areas, and keep your eyes peeled for shady-looking characters who may have sinister designs on your purse or billfold. Never look tentative. Pickpockets, by the way, are especially active in downtown shopping crowds during

unofficial **TIP**
If you need to catch a cab at the train station or one of the airports, always choose one from the official queue. These taxis are properly licensed and regulated. Never accept an offer for a cab or limo from a stranger in the terminal or baggage-claim area. At best, you'll be significantly overcharged for the ride; at worst, you could be abducted.

the holiday season and on subway trains to and from O'Hare airport.

Even with these recommendations, though, keep in mind that crime can happen anywhere. Chicago, unfortunately, is an innovator when it comes to new ways of victimizing people; this is where carjacking and "smash and grab"—that is, breaking a car window and snatching a purse off the seat— first gained national notoriety.

Taxicab Safety

When hailing a cab, you are somewhat vulnerable. Particularly after dusk, call a reliable taxi company and wait for your cab inside. When it arrives, check out the driver's certificate, which by law must be posted on the dashboard. Address the cabbie by his or her last name, or mention the cab number. If your driver knows you've made a point of remembering him or her, not only will you be safer, but the cabbie will think twice about running up the fare.

If you are comfortable reading maps, familiarize yourself with the most direct route to your destination ahead of time, or go over it with the concierge at your hotel. If you can say "Piper's Alley movie theater on North Wells via State Street," the driver is less likely to take a longer—and more expensive—route.

Carjackings

Special precautions are also in order when you're the one doing the driving. Stay alert in traffic. Keep doors locked and windows rolled up. Watch out for people offering to wash your windshield on the Near West and South sides. Leave enough space in front of your car that you can make a U-turn in case someone approaches and starts beating on your windows or otherwise acts threatening. Store your purse or briefcase under your knees or your seat rather than on the seat beside you.

PART SIX

GETTING AROUND

DRIVING YOUR CAR:
A Really Bad Idea

FOUR MAJOR INTERSTATES, road construction, unpredictable weather, and rush-hour traffic jams of mythic proportions are some of the sober realities faced by drivers who venture into downtown Chicago on any day but Sunday. Throw in a shortage of on-street parking, astronomical rates at most parking garages, and the in-your-face driving style of most Chicago drivers, and you've got a recipe for meltdown.

Yet as the traffic congestion attests, lots of people continue to brave the streets of Chicago by car every day—and that includes visitors. What if you're one of them?

TIME OF DAY

FIRST-TIME CHICAGO DRIVERS who are staying downtown should map out their routes in advance, avoid arriving or departing during rush hour (7 to 9:30 a.m. and 3 to 7 p.m. weekdays), and then plan on leaving the car parked in their hotel garage during most of their stay. Exceptions to the don't-drive rule are weekday evenings, weekends, and holidays.

PARKING

CHICAGO'S DEARTH OF ON-STREET PARKING is legendary. And watch for towing signage in certain lots. The Lincoln Park Pirates are a towing company that was popularized in song by the late folk artist Steve Goodman. They are expensive. Moreover, they are not friendly. If you decide to try your luck at finding a space, however, bring lots of quarters—most meters demand 50¢ for 15 minutes, with a two-hour limit (which isn't much time for sightseeing or attending a business meeting). Some metered spots are now taking credit cards. The fine for parking at an expired meter, by the way, is $50. Within 15 feet of a fire hydrant? That's $100, and the police *will* measure the 15 feet. (Chicago traffic cops are notoriously efficient at handing out tickets and towing illegally parked cars.)

While the chances of finding an on-street spot in the Loop on weekdays are virtually nil, you'll have better luck east of the **Loop** on **Congress Parkway** between **Lake Shore Drive** and **South Michigan Avenue** (behind the Art Institute, facing the lake). Be patient, and be prepared to do a lot of circling before snagging a space. A better idea: head south of the Loop for one of the many outside commercial parking lots along **State** and **Wabash** streets south of Congress Parkway. After about 9:30 a.m., you can park for about $6 a day. On weekends, finding on-street parking in and around the Loop is a bit easier—but more young people are moving downtown to live.

Parking near the Magnificent Mile is another magnificent headache. Street parking is virtually impossible—and that includes evenings and weekends. Most major area hotels have under- or above-ground parking garages; be sure to check when making a hotel reservation. Spaces can be tight, so leave your SUV at home.

The farther you go from downtown, the easier it generally is to find a parking spot, although exceptions abound. For example, in popular and hip Old Town near Second City, forget about finding street parking on a Friday or Saturday night; even the garages fill up.

unofficial **TIP**
Some out-of-the-way museums offer convenient parking. The **Museum of Science and Industry** in Hyde Park is one example, and there's a secret lot just north of the **Chicago History Museum** on Clark Street.

Same thing goes for the nightlife area around Wrigley Field. It doesn't matter if the Cubs are in town or it's the middle of November— Wrigleyville, as locals call it, is the new Rush Street. In addition, the most popular neighborhoods have resident-only parking rules that prohibit visitors from grabbing scarce spaces in the evenings. During snowstorms, locals observe a storied Chicago tradition: placing lawn furniture and assorted household items on the street to mark their parking spots. Don't mess with this stuff, either.

A final note: when you do find a space, don't leave your valuables in your car or trunk.

INSIDER TIPS FOR DRIVERS

MANY NATIVE CHICAGOANS who own cars routinely use public transportation or taxis to get downtown. The hassle and expense of parking just aren't worth it. This is especially true during the holidays, when out-of-towners and suburbanites converge on the city to shop—and parking the car for a long evening of shopping and enjoying the lights can cost $15. Yet because Chicago is fairly easy to navigate and traffic levels drop off significantly after rush hour and on weekends, sometimes driving makes sense, at least if you've already got a car. For example, if you're going out to dinner, call ahead and see if the restaurant offers valet parking or is close to a commercial lot.

SUBTERRANEAN CHICAGO

ADVENTUROUS DRIVERS CAN EXPLORE subterranean **Lower Wacker Drive** and **Lower Michigan Avenue** (actually, they're at lake level; Chicago's downtown streets were elevated before the Civil War). They're generally less congested than their surface counterparts, but they are a bit scary for drivers making the descent for the first time. You'll pass the legendary **Billy Goat Tavern,** which is 40 feet below ground level despite its aboveground address of 430 North Michigan. Drawbacks include lots of truck traffic, poor signage, and underground murkiness. Pluses include quick access to the Eisenhower Expressway, nice scenes of the river, and views of locations used in popular films such as *The Untouchables* and *Code of Silence*. The city has also cleared out most of the homeless population that used to reside on Lower Wacker.

PUBLIC TRANSPORTATION

THE CTA

WHILE NATIVES MOAN ABOUT BUS, subway, and train service, out-of-towners are usually impressed by the extensive public-transportation system operated by the **Chicago Transit Authority.** It's so cool, in fact, it was the original name of the rock band Chicago. True, much of the system's infrastructure is aging, but many CTA routes run 24 hours a day, crisscrossing the city and providing service to a number of bordering suburbs. And consider the alternative: battling Chicago's endless traffic jams in a car. For the most part, CTA service is clean and dependable, even though it's an uneven mix of the sleek and the seedy as some routes get upgraded while others are bypassed. Most routes take visitors to places they want to be—or at least within a few blocks. (A notable exception is the lack of train service to McCormick Place, although charter buses can now get there nonstop on a dedicated busway.) CTA ridership in 2007—nearly 500 million rides—reached its highest point since 1992.

unofficial **TIP**
Warning: After 10 p.m., don't take a chance with public transportation in any form. Either drive or take a cab.

THE EL

FOR VISITORS, THE MOST IMPORTANT and easiest-to-master segment of the CTA service is rapid transit, usually called the subway in other cities. But in Chicago, it's called **"the El"** (for "elevated"), although large parts of the train system do run underground or down the middle of expressways. Never mind: the entire train system is known as the El, and you'll have an 'ell of a good time. You might even make a new friend!

Chicago currently boasts eight train routes that run north, northeast, east, southeast, west, and south from downtown. The newest of these is the **Pink Line (54th-Loop),** a name that beefy, brawny Chicagoans have had a hard time getting used to. Opened in 2006, it runs from the Loop elevated and on the surface to the West Side and Near West suburbs, and comprises the Lake branch, Paulina connector, and Cermak (Douglas) branch. The **Red (Howard–Dan Ryan), Blue (O'Hare-Congress-Douglas),** and **Yellow (Skokie)** trains run underground or on the surface. The **Brown (Ravenswood), Purple (Evanston),** and **Orange (Midway Airport)** lines are elevated. The **Green Line** is an elevated line linking Jackson Park (south), the Loop, and Lake Street (east).

unofficial **TIP**
Enjoy riding the CTA? Take some of it home with you. A merchandise Web site, **www.ctagifts.com,** carries items such as old CTA tokens set in sterling silver and made into cufflinks and a wooden replica of a Red Line train car.

Downtown, the El defines the Loop as it circles Chicago's core financial and retail district, and it's obvious that this part of the system is more than 100 years old as the trains rattle, shake, and roar overhead. The aging, peeling structures that hold the trains up don't inspire much confidence in most first-time visitors. Just think of the rickety setup as Chicago's answer to Coney Island.

Fares

You must pay your fare for the train with a CTA fare card or pass—cash is not accepted. Prices are $2 with a Transit Card or $1.75 with the premium Chicago Card or Chicago Card Plus. Transfers (25¢) allow you two additional rides within two hours—but not on the route you started on. You can also transfer from a bus to a train (and vice versa). Kids ages 7 to 11 ride for 85¢ (transfers 15¢); kids age 6 and younger ride free.

unofficial **TIP**
It's very wise to visit **www.transitchicago.com** before you plan to brave the El or bus system. It will save you lots of hassles.

You can load your Transit Card with $1.75 to $100 worth of rides on the system's trains and buses; the Chicago Card and Chicago Card Plus give you a bonus $2 worth of rides for every $20 purchased. The cards are available at machines installed in the train stations as well as from select grocery stores, currency-exchange centers, drugstores, and the CTA Web site (**www.transitchicago.com**), which also maintains a full list of sales locations.

If you plan to use the El or buses a lot during your stay, consider purchasing a one-, two-, three-, or five-day Visitor Pass for unlimited rides. The passes range in price from $5 (one day) to $18 (five days) and are sold at O'Hare and Midway airports, Union Station, visitor-information centers, grocery stores, currency-exchange centers, some attractions, and the CTA Web site.

Train-line Names

The eight El lines are color-coded, such as the Red Line. Watch out, though—some signs at stations and on the trains themselves were never changed to show the color names. So it's good to know that the Red Line is also called the Howard–Dan Ryan line (the names identify the two ends of the line).

The Red Line travel time is also the slowest of all CTA rail lines. On a good day, trains run every 3 to 12 minutes during rush hour; every 6 to 15 minutes midday, early evenings, and weekends; and every 6 to 20 minutes in the later evening. From 1:30 to 4:30 a.m., only four lines operate: the Red Line (every 15 minutes), the Purple Line (every 30 to 45 minutes), and the Blue and Green lines (every 30 to 60 minutes). There is 24-hour service out of O'Hare International Airport, but Midway Airport passengers should know that the last train leaves there at 12:55 a.m.

Riding the El

In the Loop, finding the stations is easy: just look up. Then climb the stairs up to the platform, pay the fare, and enjoy the weather and sights as you await the next train—the elevated stations are partially covered but not enclosed. To determine the direction of the train you want, use the maps displayed and the signs posted overhead and on columns.

Taking the Plunge in the Loop

Figuring out which lines are elevated and which ones are under-ground—and how they all interconnect—is a headache-inducing experience in the Loop, where all the El lines converge. Here's a tip: on the elevated lines circling the Loop, as you face north, the Orange Line to Midway runs counterclockwise and the Brown Line to Ravenswood runs clockwise; at the Clark-Lake, State-Lake, Adams-Wabash, and LaSalle–Van Buren stations, riders can transfer free to other lines, including the underground Blue Line to O'Hare and the Red Line to the North Side. Sounds complicated, but it's not as bad as Tokyo.

Our advice: to get familiar with the system, take the plunge and board the elevated Brown (Ravenswood) El in the Loop. The views as you circle the downtown area are spectacular. Next, the train passes the Merchandise Mart near the river and continues northwest.

If it's a nice day, continue north to the Diversey station; get off the train and reboard the next one south. The postcard view of the approaching skyline that unfolds as you return downtown should not be missed. At $1.75 to $2, the ride is one of the best tourist bargains in town. If you haven't had your fill of aerial views of Chicago, board

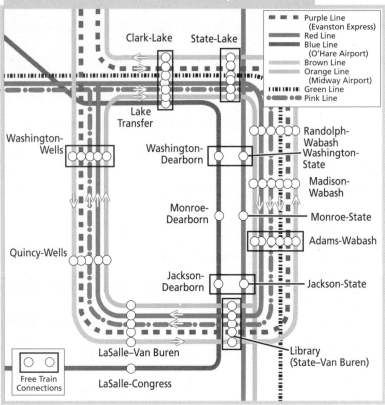

Downtown El and Subway Stations

the Orange Line and take the elevated train to Midway Airport and back (a half-hour ride one-way).

To reach the platform at underground stations, riders descend a set of narrow stairs to the (often-seedy) stations. After paying the fare, descend to the next level and the platform, which is usually narrow, not climate-controlled, and noisy when a train comes through. No one makes eye contact down here. The trains themselves, however, are usually clean and free of litter and graffiti.

BUSES

BUS FARES ARE $2 CASH or $1.75 with a fare card or pass; transfers cost 25¢ (cash not accepted). Kids' fares are the same as for the El. If you pay in cash, you'll need exact change. Chicago bus drivers are friendly and will answer any questions you have about reaching your intended destination.

Depending on the route and the time of day, fellow passengers are another matter. It's usually best to steer clear. Two more warnings about riding Chicago's buses: first, rush-hour crowds, especially along hectic Michigan Avenue, are mind-boggling, and you'll often have to wait for a bus that's not packed full. Second, after the evening rush hour, you should either drive or take a cab for safety's sake.

Chicago's bus system is massive and complicated . . . and ultimately best left to commuters. Buses are also much slower than trains, especially in Chicago's dense traffic. Yet a few bus lines that follow relatively unconvoluted routes are invaluable to visitors staying downtown—particularly those lodging in hotels along the subway-less Magnificent Mile. We don't recommend that visitors on vacation use the bus system exclusively when in town, but we do think using it judiciously can save tourists, business travelers, and conventioneers a lot of walking, not to mention cab fares and/or parking fees.

unofficial **TIP**
Though it's not a long walk to the below-ground Red Line train station at State Street and Chicago Avenue from hotels on North Michigan Avenue, it's often more convenient to grab one of the buses going up and down the Magnificent Mile. This is especially true on days when it's cold, raining, windy, snowing, or any combination of brazen Chicago weather.

Buses **#145, #146,** and **#151** (among others) provide quick, easy access south to the Loop and attractions such as the Field Museum along Lake Michigan. The **#36** bus that goes north along State and Clark streets provides easy access to Lincoln Park, the Lincoln Park Zoo, and Old Town. The **#6** express bus, which can be boarded at State and Lake streets in the Loop, quickly traverses the South Side to the Museum of Science and Industry (which does not have an El station). The **#56** bus heads out Milwaukee Avenue through Chicago's extensive Polish neighborhoods. It's a measured look at Old Chicago. Buses **#29, #56, #65,** and **#66** stop at Navy Pier, Chicago's most popular tourist attraction.

Which Bus?

To get exact, efficient directions for the bus and El routes, check with your hotel concierge or call ☎ 312-836-7000 from anywhere in the Chicago area between 5 a.m. and 1 a.m. daily. CTA personnel who answer the phones are generally polite and helpful; just tell them where you are and where you want to go, and they'll give you precise directions on routes and transfers (if needed). Make sure you have a pen and paper handy to write down the directions. If you have more lead time, you can get extensive route maps and directions from the CTA's Web site, **www.transitchicago.com.**

TAXIS

IN CHICAGO, CABS ARE PLENTIFUL and constitute one of the primary modes of transportation in this spread-out city. Along major

MAJOR CAB AND LIMOUSINE COMPANIES

American-United Taxi	☎ 773-248-7600
Blue Diamond Taxi	☎ 312-881-3188
Checker Taxi	☎ 312-225-5411
Crown Cars and Limousines	☎ 800-876-7725
Limousine of Chicago	☎ 800-460-6090
Mercury Limousine Service	☎ 866-987-0088
Yellow Cab	☎ 312-829-4222

thoroughfares it's easy to hail a taxi, with the possible exception of rush hour and when the weather has turned nasty (and everyone needs one). You'll also find cab stands in front of major hotels.

Chicago's taxi-fare system is straightforward and similar to New York City's. It's based on both distance and time—which means a $5 fare during non–rush hours can double when traffic is slow and heavy. The basic charge is $2.25 for the first mile and $1.80 for each mile after. A three-mile jaunt downtown from a hotel along the Magnificent Mile or from McCormick typically will run about $8 (non–rush hour). If you need a cab, ask your hotel doorman or call a taxi company that offers 24-hour service. Tips for all involved are virtually mandatory.

WALKING *in* CHICAGO

WHILE CHICAGO IS A HUGE PRAIRIE CITY stretching about 30 miles north and south along Lake Michigan and 15 miles to the west, the major areas of interest to visitors are concentrated in a few fairly compact areas: the Loop, the Magnificent Mile along North Michigan Avenue (also called Streeterville), Grant Park (a campuslike setting that's home to some of the city's best museums), and the Near North Side (which offers a wide range of shopping, dining, and nightlife options). There isn't a hill for miles around. Given good weather and a relaxed schedule, walking is the best mode of discovering the city.

unofficial **TIP**
Here's a secret: find the block-long **Alta Vista Terrace,** between Grace and Byron streets, a block north of Wrigley Field. It's an easy walk, and the early-1900s row houses—replicas of those found in London's Mayfair district—make this street unlike any other in Chicago.

Great places to take a walk or a stroll include the **Loop; Grant Park** (great views of the skyline and the lake); nearby **Millennium Park;** the **Gold Coast** (where Chicago's richest citizens have lived since the 1890s); and, just west of the city limits, **Oak Park** (with 25 homes, churches, and fountains designed by Frank Lloyd Wright). Chicago's varied ethnic neighborhoods, such as **Andersonville** on the Far North Side (a charming mix of Swedish and Middle Eastern), are also fine walking destinations.

PEDWAYS

IN ADDITION, DOWNTOWN IS HONEYCOMBED with an underground system of pedestrian walkways that make Chicago a lot easier to negotiate when the weather is bad. The "pedways" link train stations and major buildings (such as the State of Illinois Center, Macy's, the Chicago Cultural Center, and the Hyatt Regency in Illinois Center). Visitors seeking a mole's-eye view of the city will even find shops and cafes as they explore the still-growing pedway system.

PART SEVEN

SIGHTSEEING, TOURS *and* ATTRACTIONS

TOURING CHICAGO

A VISIT TO CHICAGO WILL KEEP you on your toes—no one is a passive participant. Not only does Chicago offer a wide selection of world-class museums, but the city itself is a museum. The Loop and the lakefront, for example, encompass the world's largest collection of outdoor modern architecture. Turn any corner, and you're confronted with yet another aesthetic or technical innovation in building design.

There's more. Tourists, professionals, and residents jam Chicago's downtown streets year-round to absorb its muscular skyline, lakefront, art, history, shopping, cultural attractions, and festivals—which run every weekend during the summer. Inevitably, out-of-towners rub big shoulders with the city's outspoken (and often-humorous) natives, most of whom are remarkably friendly to visitors and take pride in their city. Here are some tips to assist first-time visitors in discovering this sprawling, dynamic place.

TAKING AN ORIENTATION TOUR

VISITORS CAN'T MISS THE REGULAR PROCESSION of open-air tour buses—"motorized trolleys" might be a more accurate term—that prowl Michigan Avenue, the Loop, and the museums and attractions along the lakeshore. The **Chicago Trolley and Double Decker Company** (☎ 773-648-5000; **www.coachusa .com/chicagotrolley**) runs regularly scheduled shuttle buses that drop off and pick up paying customers along a route that incorporates the town's most popular attractions. Between stops, passengers listen to a tour guide talk about the city's cataclysmic fire of 1871, machine-gun-toting gangsters, and spectacular architecture.

The guides also suggest places to eat and drop tidbits of interesting information—such as the best places to go for an Oprah sighting (her studio on the Near West Side and the Crate & Barrel on North

Michigan Avenue). You'll be riding amid Chicago tradition. Dating back to the horseless carriages of the late 1800s, Chicago's level topography has created a fertile landscape for streetcars, buses, and trolleys.

If this is your first visit to Chicago, take one of the tours early in your trip. Here's why: Chicago is on a plot of land 228 miles square. Seen from the air, the city is surprisingly contained. Its towers rise up from the lakeside with a stunning vertical thrust but then give way to the prairie flatness that characterizes the Midwest. Yet once on the ground, visitors discover that the city is too vast to take in—and that includes its downtown. Although it's possible to embark on a walking tour that includes River North, the Magnificent Mile, the Loop, Grant Park, and Chicago's major museums, you'll murder your feet—and your enthusiasm for touring—in the process.

Chicago Trolley tickets are $29 for adults ($26 online), $24 for seniors age 65 and over ($21 online), and $17 for children ages 3 to 11 ($15 online). Youngsters can use their ticket to ride the trolley free for three consecutive days; a three-day ticket for adults and seniors is $45 ($41.50 online). Approach these narrated tours as a basic educational system that not only gets you to the most well-known attractions but also provides a timely education on the city's history and scope. (One quibble: the references to Roaring '20s gangsters are clichéd.)

Tour buses run every 10 to 15 minutes, and boarding locations include the city's most popular downtown attractions. You can board at any stop on the route and pay the driver. The complete tour lasts about two hours. Heated in the winter and open air in the summer, the trolleys operate rain or shine, from 9 a.m. to 5 p.m. daily, November 3 through March 8 and until 6:30 p.m. March 9 through November 2.

The tour buses make 13 stops: **Wacker Drive South,** the **Art Institute,** the **Field Museum, Millennium Park,** the **Theater District,** the **Chicago Hilton and Towers, Sears Tower,** the **John Hancock Center,** the historic **Water Tower, North Pier–Sheraton Chicago Hotel & Towers, Navy Pier, Wacker Drive North,** the **Magnificent Mile,** and the **River North** shopping district.

ARCHITECTURE AND BOAT TOURS

IT'S OFTEN SAID THAT IN CHICAGO, architecture is a spectator sport. While an introductory bus tour of downtown Chicago gives first-time visitors a sense of the city's layout and a glimpse of Chicago architecture, things look different from the Chicago River. Don't miss it. During the warmer months, riverboats glide down the river for a dockside view of downtown architecture and historical sites. And the Loop takes on a new perspective after embarking on a walking tour with a docent pointing out and explaining the modern architectural trends on display in Chicago's ever-changing downtown.

Boat Tours

Not so long ago, everyone made fun of the first Mayor Daley's dream of people someday fishing in the Chicago River, which he loved inordinately. Every St. Patrick's Day he had it dyed green, a tradition that continues today. Once scorned as a sewage canal, the Chicago has been cleaned up. The now-resplendent river offers outstanding views of the city's best buildings, including the Sears Tower, the Civic Opera Building on Wacker Drive, the IBM Building (Mies van der Rohe's last major Chicago structure), and the NBC Tower, built in 1989.

unofficial **TIP**
Tours offered by the Chicago Architecture Foundation emphasize the city's buildings and its role as a leader in modern urban architecture. If you're not that big of a culture vulture and you don't need to hear another word about Louis Sullivan, you'll probably get more out of a generalist tour from an operator such as Mercury or Wendella. Can't make up your mind? Pick the cruise that best fits your schedule.

On downtown boat tours, guides weave history and technology as they tell the story of the Great Chicago Fire of 1871 and the role of the structural iron frame in rebuilding the city. The result was the skyscraper and a truly modern style unencumbered by any allegiance to the past.

CHOOSING A BOAT TOUR Visitors can choose from several boat-touring companies that sail on 90-minute narrated cruises up the Chicago River or out on Lake Michigan for a view of the city's fabled skyline. All the modern, motorized ships are enclosed and air-conditioned, and they offer beverage services while en route; the cruises are offered spring through fall.

Chicago Architecture Foundation Tours

The **Chicago Architecture Foundation** (CAF) offers 86 different tours by foot, bus, and boat. Each tour is led by a volunteer from a fleet of about 450 docents (tour guides). The tour leaders are witty, incredibly informed, and enthusiastic about Chicago architecture. Go on at least one Foundation tour during your visit. Better yet, take a walking tour of the Loop *and* an architectural boat tour. You won't regret it.

BY BOAT *Chicago's First Lady, Chicago's Fair Lady,* and *Chicago's Little Lady* depart from Riverside Gardens at the southwest corner of Michigan Avenue and Wacker Drive for the **CAF Architecture River Cruise.** The yachts, which offer outdoor seating on the upper deck and air-conditioned interior seating, depart 3 to 9 times daily from late April until mid-November, 7 to 13 times daily on weekends and holidays; tickets are $28 on weekdays, $32 on weekends and holidays. Cruises board 15 minutes before departure; advance reservations are highly recommended.

In addition to the unique river perspective on Chicago architecture, you'll see Chicago's newly built Trump International Hotel & Tower, on the site of the former *Chicago Sun-Times* building. In the summer of 2004, the *Little Lady* scored a notch in Chicago lore when a bus driver for the Dave Matthews Band illegally dumped 800 pounds of raw sewage onto unsuspecting upper-deck passengers enjoying the scenery near the Merchandise Mart. Even though that was a once-in-a-lifetime glitch, it's a good idea to bring headgear, as cruises depart rain or shine. For more information, visit **www.cruisechicago.com;** for reservations, call Ticketmaster at ☎ 312-902-1500 or visit **www .ticketmaster.com.**

BY FOOT Two-hour walking tours of the Loop and bus excursions to Chicago's neighborhoods start at the CAF's headquarters and gift shop at 224 South Michigan Avenue (across from the Art Institute of Chicago). The walking tours complement the boat tour, allowing you to observe the buildings from street level as well as catch some lobbies that are every bit as spectacular as the buildings' exteriors. Tours are $10 per person and are offered daily on a varying schedule throughout the year. For more information, visit **www.architecture.org;** for reservations, call Ticketmaster at ☎ 312-902-1500 or visit **www.ticket master.com.**

MORE CAF TOURS In addition to Loop walking tours and boat cruises, CAF offers the three-and-a-half-hour **Chicago Architecture Highlights by Bus** tour (Wednesday and Saturday at 9:30 a.m through March 2009; $40 per person) and the four-hour **Frank Lloyd Wright Neighborhoods by Bus** and **Frank Lloyd Wright by Bus** tours ($40 and $52 per person, respectively; 2009 dates to be determined). For more information, visit **www.architecture.org;** for reservations, call ☎ 312-922-3432.

Historical and Architectural Lake and River Cruises from North Pier

Chicago Line boat tours on the Chicago River and Lake Michigan are different from the CAF's in that they are a little less formal in their approach to architecture, and refreshments are served during cruises. On the historical cruise, visitors pass the spot where du Sable first established a trading post among the local Native Americans and where Fort Dearborn stood to protect the community. The tour also passes through the heart of the city, where the fire of 1871 reduced buildings to ash at a rate of 65 acres an hour.

On Lake Michigan, the boat passes **Buckingham Fountain,** where the Columbian Exposition of 1893 left its legacy of the **Field Museum, Shedd Aquarium, Adler Planetarium,** and the **Museum of Science and Industry.** When you hear someone talk about the "Museum Campus," this is it. But the highlight of the cruise is a view of the magnificent skyline of Chicago, a profile recognized around the world.

Architectural cruises take visitors downtown for up-close views of Chicago's most recognized buildings, including the **Tribune Tower,** the **Merchandise Mart, Lake Point Tower** (where Sammy Sosa once lived), and of course, the **Sears Tower,** the third-tallest office building in the world. Visitors also see the spot near the **Kinzie Street Bridge** where the Chicago River flooded an old railroad freight tunnel in April 1991, shutting down the Loop and causing hundreds of millions of dollars in damage. The 90-minute cruises leave North Pier daily on the hour, 9 a.m. to 4 p.m. from May to September and on a reduced schedule in April and October; there's also a 6 p.m. cocktail cruise. Prices are $34 for adults, $30 for seniors, and $20 for children and students ages 7 to 18. For more information and reservations (highly recommended), call ☎ 312-527-1977 or visit **www.chicagoline.com.**

Other Boat Cruises

Mercury, The Skyline Cruiseline (☎ 312-332-1353; **www.mercurysky linecruiseline.com**) offers architectural, maritime, and canine (yes, canine) tours May through September from the lower level and southeast corner of the Michigan Avenue Bridge over the Chicago River (at Wacker Drive). Cruises range from 90 minutes to 2 hours in length, each with continuous commentary. Tours depart throughout the day from morning to late evening; prices are $22 to $24 for adults, $10 to $13 for children ages 3 to 11, and $7 for dogs; kids under age 3 are admitted free. Tickets go on sale an hour before the cruise (no reservations necessary).

   Wendella (☎ 312-337-1446; **www.wendellaboats.com**) operates the city's throwback boat tour, dating back to 1935. The company was founded by Albert "Bo" Borgstrom, a Swedish immigrant who refurbished a 65-foot-long wooden yacht named **Wendela** (it was spelled with one *L* until the 1950s) and began offering 30-minute guided boat tours from Navy Pier. Today a beautiful fleet hosts cruises on the Chicago River and along the lakefront from mid-April to mid-October. Combined lake and river tours (which go through the Chicago Lock) last 90 minutes and cost $22 for adults, $20 for seniors age 65 and older, and $10 for children age 11 and under (free for kids under age 3). Tours leave throughout the day and evening from the base of the Wrigley Building, at the northwest corner of the Michigan Avenue Bridge over the Chicago River. During the spring and summer, commuters also take the popular **Chicago Water Taxi** from stops near Union Station to Michigan Avenue. Tickets are $2 one-way and $15 for ten rides.

Bridgehouse Tours

The nonprofit **Friends of the Chicago River** has been a force in cleaning up and revitalizing the waterway since 1979. The organization also developed the **McCormick Tribune Bridgehouse & Chicago River Museum** (376 North Michigan Avenue; ☎ 312-977-0227; **www.bridge housemuseum.org**). After viewing the historic bridgeworks, visitors can climb to the top of the tower to see river views. Exhibits detail the history of bridges in Chicago, the styles and designs that were created in Chicago, and how the Michigan Avenue Bridge works. The museum is open May through October, Thursday through Monday, 10 a.m. to 5 p.m. Tickets are $3 per person; kids under age 5 are admitted free.

The Fish Hotel

Swimming with the fishes has always been part of Chicago's mob lexicon, but this is a new day.

The Friends of the Chicago River has opened the **Fish Hotel**—a beautiful aquatic structure that floats year-round along the south bank of the Chicago River on the downtown Chicago Riverwalk between State and Dearborn streets. The project is an effort to help restore the river to a fish-friendly place. Depending on the season, you can see green sunfish, baby bluegills, carp, and sometimes Lake Michigan trout and salmon that have wandered into the joint.

The structure is made of aquatic plant beds and fish cribs, all encased by a perimeter of buoys extending 10 feet out into the river along 42 feet of riverwalk. More than 20 different Illinois native plant species are represented, and there's ample housing for fish. Free tours from the nearby Bridgehouse Museum (see lower right) are offered May 1 through November 1, Thursday through Monday at 12:30 p.m. For more information, call ☎ 312-939-0490 or visit **www.chicago river.org/projects/fish_hotel**.

SPECIALIZED TOURS

Gray Line (☎ 800-621-4153 or 312-251-3100; **www.grayline.com**) offers general-interest tours (as opposed to the CAF tours, which focus on architecture) around the city, plus special tours on architectural highlights and Chicago neighborhoods (such as the two-hour **North Side Tour**, $25 for adults and $12.50 for children ages 5 to 14). **Inside Chicago: The Grand Tour** takes visitors to Chicago's parks and most scenic spots as well as the Loop, the Magnificent Mile, Wrigley Field, Lincoln Park Conservatory, the Adler Planetarium, the University of Chicago campus, and the Museum of Science and Industry. The tour also makes periodic stops at sites such as the Botanic Gardens on the North Side, where visitors can briefly debark and explore on their own. The cost of the four-hour tour is $40 for adults and $20 for children ages 5 to 14. Gray Line bus tours start at the **Palmer House Hilton** hotel in the Loop (17 East Monroe Street). Unlike the hard benches on the "trolley" tours, the buses feature comfortable reclining seats, overhead lights, and air-conditioning.

Gangsters and Ghosts

Chicago has scores of spooky sights (not including the haunted grounds of Wrigley Field), and **Supernatural Tours** (☎ 708-499-0300; **www.ghosttours.com**) does a super job with the supernatural. Even locals take in owner Richard Crowe's 70-passenger coach and bus tours, which highlight the city's heritage of ghost stories and folklore, bizarre tales, murder sites, cemeteries, gangsters, pubs, and restaurants. In 1973 Crowe became the Midwest's first full-time ghost hunter. You'll see and learn about Al Capone's grave site, the John Dillinger death site near the Biograph Theatre, and the "Hanged Man Ghost of the Water Tower." You'll learn why the alley next to the Gene Siskel Film Center downtown is known as "Death Alley" (125 people jumped to their deaths there during the 1903 Iroquois Theater fire). Tours are scheduled on select weekends from 7 to 11 p.m.; the cost is $44 per person, and reservations are required. Don't even think about going on Halloween night unless you book weeks ahead. The trips depart from the **Goose Island Brewery,** 1800 North Clybourn Avenue (not the Goose Island by Wrigley Field—too scary).

The folks at **Untouchable Tours** (☎ 773-881-1195; **www.gangster tour.com**) go directly for the jugular: Chicago's gangster history. Friendly actors in pinstripe suits and fedoras escort visitors on a two-hour bus tour of Chicago's creepy past, including the site of Al Capone's former headquarters, the Biograph Theatre, and the site of the St. Valentine's Day Massacre on Clark Street. The tour is historically correct and a crowd-pleaser, appealing to youngsters. It begins at the **Rock 'n' Roll McDonald's** on North Clark Street (look for the black bus). Guns not permitted. In addition to daily tours at 10 a.m., tours are scheduled on Thursday at noon; Friday at noon, 2 p.m., and 7:30 p.m.; Saturday at noon, 3 p.m., and 5 p.m.; and Sunday at noon. The cost is $27 for adults and $20 for children; reservations are recommended. Guests get free gangster gags as a souvenir.

Dining on Lake Michigan

While not guided tours, Lake Michigan cruises on the **Odyssey** feature fine dining, live music, dancing, and memorable views of Chicago's skyline. Cruising on the elegant 850-passenger ship is a great way to see the city, and the operation is top-notch. (No *Gilligan's Island*/ Jimmy Buffett shenanigans allowed.) There's a dress code; men should wear jackets. Best bet: a sunset dinner cruise. Second-best bet: the Moonlight Lounge Cruise. There's also a two-hour lunch cruise, along with various holiday and special-occasion cruises. (Prices and schedules for 2009 were forthcoming at press time, so call or check online as information becomes available.) The **Odyssey** departs from Navy Pier throughout the year. (There are also **Odysseys** in Washington, D.C., and Boston.) For more information and reservations, call ☎ 866-305-2469 or visit **www.odysseycruises.com.**

CARRIAGE RIDES

AN EASY AND ROMANTIC WAY to see downtown Chicago is by horse and buggy. **Noble Horse Carriages** (☎ 312-266-7878; **www.noble horsechicago.com**), at the southwest corner of Michigan and Chicago avenues, provides horse-drawn carriage rides weekdays from 10 a.m.

to 4:30 p.m. and 6 p.m. to midnight, and weekends from 10 a.m. to 1 a.m. The cost is $35 per half hour or $70 per hour for up to four adults (maximum) and $5 extra for each additional adult. Reservations are not necessary.

The **Antique Coach & Carriage Company** (☎ 773-735-9400; **www.antiquecoach-carriage.com**) offers rides daily from the southeast corner of Michigan Avenue and Huron Street. Hours are 6:30 p.m. to 1 a.m. Monday through Thursday, 6:30 p.m. to 2 a.m. Friday, 1 p.m. to 2 a.m. Saturday, and 1 p.m. to 1 a.m. Sunday. The cost is $40 per half hour or $80 per hour.

TOURING ON YOUR OWN: OUR FAVORITE ITINERARIES

IF YOUR TIME IS LIMITED and you want to experience the best of Chicago in a day or two, here are some game plans. The schedules assume you're staying downtown, have already eaten breakfast, and are ready to hit the streets around 9 a.m.

Day One

1. Tour downtown on one of the open-air shuttle-bus services with unlimited reboarding privileges for the day. If the weather's clear, get off at the **Sears Tower** and check out the view. Then catch the next shuttle.
2. Pick one: explore the **Shedd Aquarium** or the **Adler Planetarium** (they're close together on the "Museum Campus"). Then get back on the bus.
3. Next stop: **Navy Pier** and lunch at the **Navy Pier Beer Garden** or **Charlie's Ale House,** featuring 38 different types of beer.
4. Take a deep breath of cool Chicago air, and climb aboard for a scenic 30-minute **skyline cruise on Lake Michigan** that leaves Navy Pier every half hour in warm weather.
5. After the boat ride, take the shuttle bus to the **Historic Water Tower** on North Michigan Avenue. Explore the shops along Michigan, one of the world's great shopping streets, and check out the **Museum of Contemporary Art** (with one of the city's most eclectic gift shops).
6. Grab dinner at a restaurant in **River North.** Afterward, catch some live music and shake your moneymaker at **Blue Chicago** (736 North Clark Street; ☎ 312-642-6261; **www.bluechicago.com**), a blues bar with a dignified roster of Chicago musicians.
7. Finish the evening with a visit to the **John Hancock Observatory** for an excellent view of the city and beyond.

Day Two

1. Sleep in—but not too late. You don't want to miss the 10 a.m. **Chicago Architecture Foundation** walking tour of the Loop.
2. Wander over for lunch at the **Billy Goat Tavern,** a longtime Chicago journalists' hangout that was popularized by John Belushi on *Saturday*

Night Live ("cheezburger, cheezburger"). You know what to order. Then jump on the **Ravenswood El** for a ride around the Loop; take it north past the huge **Merchandise Mart,** and catch the next train back (south) for some terrific views of the city.

3. Explore the **Art Institute of Chicago**. Try to catch the free tour that begins daily at 1 p.m. near the Grand Staircase.

4. Reward the kids with a trip to the **Chicago Children's Museum** at Navy Pier. Or explore the other Navy Pier attractions, including multiple views of the skyline. Take a ride on the pier's Ferris wheel for one of the most intimate views of the city.

5. Take in an evening of improvisational comedy at **The Second City** (1616 North Wells Street; ☎ 312-664-4032; **www.secondcity.com**).

6. Dump the kids and have a postcomedy coffee at the 24-hour **Starbucks** on North Wells, directly south of The Second City. The coffee shop is one of the most kinetic spots on the North Side. If you want something a little more authentic and moody, head across the street to the **Old Town Ale House** (219 West North Avenue; ☎ 312-944-7020; **www.oldtownalehouse.net**), which is open until 5 a.m. on Saturday and 4 a.m. Sunday and weekdays.

If You've Got More Time . . .

If you're spending more than two days in town, or if you're a return visitor, consider some of these options for an in-depth Chicago experience:

1. Explore one of Chicago's many neighborhoods beyond downtown. Suggestions: **Hyde Park** (South Side) has the **University of Chicago** and several museums; shop and eat lunch in **Chinatown** (Near South Side). **Andersonville** (North Side) features an eclectic mix of Swedish and Middle Eastern shops and inexpensive ethnic restaurants.

2. **Oak Park,** just west of the city line, boasts two famous native sons: architect Frank Lloyd Wright and Nobel Prize–winning novelist Ernest Hemingway. Spend a morning or afternoon learning about them. There's also the **Lake Theatre,** a grand old movie house that shows first-run flicks in downtown Oak Park (1022 Lake Street; ☎ 708-848-9088).

3. Hit two Chicago museums that are so large, each requires a full day: the **Field Museum** and the **Museum of Science and Industry.**

4. Stretch your legs along the **Gold Coast,** where Chicago's wealthiest residents have made their homes for more than a century; it's just north of the Magnificent Mile. Or rent a bike and ride the path along **Lake Michigan.**

5. **Go to a play.** Chicago boasts well more than 100 active theater companies.

6. Kick back and enjoy a festival in **Grant Park** or a concert in **Millennium Park.**

7. Spend a few hours browsing the art galleries in **River North**.

8. Check out **Macy's** on State Street. This used to be **Marshall Field's,** and the name change rankled most longtime Chicagoans. (For more info, see Part Nine, Shopping in Chicago.)

9. Attend a concert by the **Chicago Symphony Orchestra,** consistently rated as one of the best orchestras in the world.

10. Hop on a train or rent a car to west-suburban **Naperville,** named by *Money* magazine as the third-best place to live in America in 2008 and the second-best in 2006. Several Chicago chefs have opened restaurants in downtown Naperville, and the Riverwalk is reminiscent of San Antonio's.

11. Root for the **Cubs** at **Wrigley Field,** the **White Sox** at **U.S. Cellular Field** (locals call it "The Cell"), or the **Bulls** or **Blackhawks** at the **United Center.** Minor-league hockey is also huge in Chicago: the **Wolves** play at **Allstate Arena** in Rosemont, near O'Hare International Airport.

EXPLORING CHICAGO'S NEIGHBORHOODS

NEIGHBORHOODS FORM THE PERSONAL SCALE that makes a city work. The nearly 3 million people of Chicago form a quilt of nearly 3 million colorful threads, and you will find vitality and warmth within this quilt. Chicago's rich architectural history and cultural diversity are embraced in the city's many communities, some ethnically mixed and some not.

What follows is not a comprehensive guide to Chicago's neighborhoods, since the city officially claims 77 in all, but our suggestions for dipping in and sampling the remarkably vibrant array of individualistic architecture, cuisine, history, and culture that defines Chicago. In so many ways, Chicago is 77 little cities wrapped into one. An extended ride on the **Ravenswood El** lets you survey the spectacle of Chicago's neighborhoods (and back porches and rooftop graffiti) without getting your feet wet. (For route and fare information on CTA and Metra, call ☎ 312-836-7000.)

unofficial **TIP**
Apart from a bike ride along the lakefront, Chicago is a city best explored on foot. You can use the El, the bus system, or a car to get around, but in most cases we recommend stepping out for a stroll to get the feel and flavor of these neighborhoods.

Our sampling tour of Chicago neighborhoods starts in the north and generally flows south along the lake, with several excursions to the northwest and southwest.

ANDERSONVILLE

YOU MAY BE SURPRISED AT THE NOTION of "Swede Town" in Chicago, but amble north along Clark Street from Foster and you'll see Swedish flags flying; you might even hear a little ABBA. Check out the **Swedish American Museum** (5211 North Clark Street; ☎ 773-728-8111; **www.samac.org;** see attraction profile on page 187), and savor excellent coffeecakes and pastries at the **Swedish Bakery** (5348 North Clark; ☎ 773-561-8919; **www.swedishbakery.com**) or Swedish pancakes and *limpa* bread at **Svea Restaurant** (5236 North Clark; ☎ 772-275-7768). The cinnamon rolls from **Ann Sather** (5207 North Clark; ☎ 773-271-6677; **www.annsather.com**) are known across Chicago. Buy a dozen to take home—if they last that long.

In spite of its Scandinavian influence, Andersonville, like most Chicago neighborhoods, is a mixing and melting pot. The well-kept redbrick "two-flats" (long, narrow buildings with one apartment stacked atop another) on the streets fanning east from Clark have become the city's newest mecca for gays and lesbians. The Clark Street strip features a number of feminist stores and shops, such as **Women & Children First** (5233 North Clark; ☎ 773-769-9299; **www.womenand childrenfirst.com**), with its wide selection of progressive books by women. Along Clark, you'll also find some cool thrift shops. Gays and straights alike flock to **Reza's Restaurant** (5255 North Clark; ☎ 773-561-1898; **www.rezasrestaurant.com**), a Persian-Mediterranean eatery with huge portions. The **Hopleaf Bar** (5148 North Clark; ☎ 773-334-9851; **www.hopleaf.com**) carries more than 200 beers, many of them from Belgium. Chicago isn't known for its delis, but you'll find one of the best here: **Erickson's Delicatessen** (5250 North Clark; ☎ 773-561-5634) has great flatbread and the only frozen lingonberries in Chicago, along with food from Denmark and Norway. Open seven days a week (but not at night), Erickson's ships anywhere in the country.

TO GET THERE Take the CTA Red Line (Howard) to the Berwyn station, and then walk west on Foster about four blocks. Or transfer to the #92 Foster bus at the station.

By car from the Loop, drive north on Lake Shore Drive to the Foster exit, and head west to Clark Street. There's metered parking along Clark and free parking on side streets.

DEVON AVENUE

ON A FRIDAY NIGHT ALONG DEVON AVENUE, you're likely to see Orthodox Jews in dark suits and black hats heading home from synagogue on the same sidewalks as Indians in bright, flowing saris. Mixed among the kosher butchers, Bangladeshi vendors, and Pakistani groceries on the stretch from Western Avenue (2400 West Devon Avenue) to the north branch of the Chicago River (3200 West Devon) is a newer sprinkling of Thai and Korean shops and restaurants. This makes for one of the most colorful neighborhoods on the North Side of Chicago.

*un*official **TIP**
Don't ask how to get to "DEE-von Avenue." Locals pronounce it "duh-VON."

You can pick up a yarmulke at **Rosenblum's World of Judaica** (2906 West Devon; ☎ 800-626-6536 or 773-262-1700; **www.alljudaica.com**) or check out the colorful saris at **Taj Sari Palace** (2553 West Devon; ☎ 773-338-0177). **Gitel's Kosher Pastry Shop** (2745 West Devon; ☎ 773-262-3700) and **Tel-Aviv Kosher Bakery** (2944 West Devon; ☎ 773-764-8877) sell traditional Sabbath challah bread. **Viceroy of India** (2518 West Devon; ☎ 773-743-4100; **www.viceroy ofindia.com**) is highly rated for its curries and breads. **Ebner's Kosher Meat Market** (2649 West Devon; ☎ 773-764-1446) has been a staple of the neighborhood since 1966. Everything is kosher in this authentic Chicago butcher shop, even the attitude. Chicago hipsters check out **Atlantic Video Rentals** (2541 West Devon; ☎ 773-338-3600), which carries hard-to-find Indian and Pakistani CDs. The video shop is also known for its wide selection of ethnic soap operas and cricket matches.

TO GET THERE Take the CTA Red Line (Howard) north to Loyola, and then transfer to a westbound #155 Devon Avenue bus.

By car from the Loop, drive north on Lake Shore Drive. At its northern end, take Ridge (west) to Devon and turn left (west); or take the Kennedy Expressway (I-90/94) north, then merge onto the Edens Expressway (I-94), exit at Petersen heading east, and turn north (left) on Kedzie to Devon.

> **unofficial TIP**
> Note that many stores on Devon Avenue close early on Friday night and remain closed on Saturday for the Jewish Sabbath.

UPTOWN

HANDS-DOWN, UPTOWN IS ONE OF CHICAGO'S most interesting neighborhoods.

After World War II, Uptown attracted European immigrants, laborers from the Deep South, and Midwest transplants. This was one of the only Chicago neighborhoods where landlords did not require long-term leases or security deposits, which was attractive to the thrifty urban pioneers. During the mid-1960s, Uptown had the largest concentration of Southern whites in the northern United States.

At one time Uptown had two major movie palaces within one block of each other—the **Uptown** and the **Riviera**—and a grand dance hall, the **Aragon.** The Uptown is shuttered, but the Riviera (4746 North Racine Avenue; ☎ 773-275-6800; **www.jamusa.com/ venues/riviera**) is still used for rock concerts, and the Aragon (1106 West Lawrence Avenue; ☎ 773-561-9500; **www.aragon.com**) is vital with live rock and salsa concerts, live boxing, and other events.

Uptown is coming back after a long period of seedy transition. Pockets of elegance have been restored in the huge homes that line **Hutchinson Street** and **Castlewood Terrace,** and a Borders bookstore would have been unheard of a few years ago. The community near

unofficial **TIP**
If you stray from the Broadway–Argyle axis, you'll quickly see the funkier parts of Uptown: don't try it alone or on foot after dark.

Broadway and Argyle, often called **New Chinatown,** is in fact, a brimming mix of Vietnamese, Laotian, Chinese, Cambodian, and Thai immigrants. You'll find Asian groceries, bakeries, gift shops, and restaurants; some of Chicago's top chefs buy ingredients here. Try **Furama Restaurant** (4936 North Broadway; ☎ 773-271-1161; **www.furama chicago.net**) for dim sum.

Former rock musician Ric Addy is the unofficial mayor of Uptown. Check out his used-book store, **Shake Rattle & Read** (4812 North Broadway; ☎ 773-334-5311), a local treasure in the shadow of the old Uptown Theater. The shop has been in the same location for 20 years, and the large inventory reflects its sedentary nature: 15,000 paperbacks; 10,000 hardcover books; 10,000 magazines; and 5,000 jazz, soul, and country albums. He's obviously not moving anytime soon. A few doors down, the **Green Mill Jazz Club** (4802 North Broadway; ☎ 773-878-5552; **www.greenmilljazz.com**) offers jazz and Sunday-night poetry slams of national renown each week.

TO GET THERE The CTA Red Line (Howard) stops at Argyle Street, where there's a $100,000 pagoda over the station.

By car from the Loop, drive north along Lake Shore Drive, exit at Lawrence (4800 North), head west to Broadway, and then go north to Argyle.

LINCOLN SQUARE

IN 1998 THE LEGENDARY **Old Town School of Folk Music** (students included Steve Goodman, John Prine, and Roger McGuinn of the Byrds) moved into an old library at 4544 North Lincoln Avenue in the heart of Lincoln Square (☎ 773-728-6000; **www.oldtown school.org**). A statue of Abraham Lincoln presides over the intersection of Lincoln, Lawrence, and Western avenues.

unofficial **TIP**
Don't confine yourself to just the square area: it's safe to walk around here.

The centerpiece of Lincoln Square is the small shopping area—virtually a pedestrian mall—along the 4700 block of Lincoln Avenue. Stop by **Merz Apothecary** (4716 North Lincoln Avenue; ☎ 773-989-0900; **www.merzapothecary.com**), in the neighborhood for more than a century, for imported soaps or any homeopathic remedies you might need. If you have kids or are a repressed kid yourself, don't miss **Quake Collectibles** (4628 North Lincoln; ☎ 773-878-4288), packed to the walls with action figures, vintage board games, and old lunch boxes. It's like walking into Pee Wee's Playhouse.

Check out the glorious Louis Sullivan facade of the **Kelmscott Building** (4611 North Lincoln Avenue) and the periodicals section—and modern design—of the **Conrad Sulzer Library** (4455 North

Lincoln; ☎ 773-728-2062). A large **wall mural** at 4662 North Lincoln depicts scenes from the German countryside.

Some of the best Thai food on the North Side is found at **Siam Country** (4637 North Damen; ☎ 773-271-0700; **www.siamcountry chicago.com**), under the El's Damen Brown Line stop. The spring rolls (not fried) are a must.

Lincoln Square's German residents are nestled against **Greektown** west of the mall along Lawrence Avenue between Talman and Maplewood. **St. Demetrios Orthodox Greek Church,** a 1928 basilica-style structure at 2727 West Winona Street (☎ 773-561-5992), serves the Greek community. **St. Matthias,** an 1887 German church, is at 2310 West Ainslie (☎ 773-506-2191).

TO GET THERE Take the CTA Brown Line (Ravenswood) to the Western Avenue stop (Monday through Saturday until midevening; on Sunday, take the Red Line to Belmont and transfer to the Brown Line there) or the #11 bus, which connects the Loop with Lincoln Square, though it is a very long ride.

By car, take Lake Shore Drive north, exit at Lawrence Avenue (4800 North), and head west to Western Avenue (2400 West). There's metered parking on Lincoln Avenue and a lot at Leland next to the El station.

LAKEVIEW-WRIGLEYVILLE

THE LEGENDARY **Wrigley Field** (☎ 773-404-CUBS; **chicago .cubs.mlb.com**) is the centerpiece of this neighborhood, which has replaced Rush Street and Division Street as Chicago's top night-life district. Wrigley Field—home of baseball's hapless Cubs—opened in 1914 on the grounds that formerly housed the Chicago Lutheran Theological Seminary. Cubs fans are devout, but generations of them have never seen a world championship in this ballpark.

So very sad.

That's why this neighborhood parties hard.

There is a bar and/or restaurant in just about every storefront south of Wrigley Field (at the corner of Addison and Clark streets). The most storied stops are **Murphy's Bleachers** (3655 North Sheffield Avenue, across from the bleacher entrance; ☎ 773-281-5356; **www .murphysbleachers.com**), **The Cubby Bear** (1059 West Addison Street; ☎ 773-327-1662; **www.cubbybear.com/wrigleyville**), and **Bernie's Tavern** (3644 North Clark Street; ☎ 773-525-1898), and they all have dozens of TVs for watching sports year-round. The city's most popular reggae bar is the **Wild Hare,** just a block south of the ballpark (3530 North Clark; ☎ 773-327-0868; **www.wildharemusic.com**).

Wrigley Field is a real neighborhood ballpark where fans stream in from the Addison El stop and others pay premium prices to watch from the roofs of nearby three-flats. (Don't be afraid to try for day-of-game tickets at the window.) It's common to see tourists wandering by Wrigley in the dead of winter just to take a picture of this landmark.

A 2005 ballpark renovation also incorporated a sidewalk peephole in the right-field corner so pedestrians can look in and check out the team's annual rebuilding plans.

So very sad.

The mansions along **Hawthorne Place** (a one-way street heading east between Broadway and Sheridan Road) exude a stately lakeside grandeur. The facing rows of townhouses on **Alta Vista Terrace** (1054 West between Byron and Grace streets north of Wrigley Field) are mirror images.

Locals flock to **Ann Sather** (929 West Belmont Avenue, a branch of the Andersonville store; ☎ 773-348-2378; **www.annsather.com**), drawn by the irresistible lure of addictive cinnamon rolls and well-prepared, moderately priced food. You'll find thrift shops, hip shops, bookstores, and espresso on nearly every corner, including the pungent smell of beans roasting at the **Coffee and Tea Exchange** (3311 North Broadway; ☎ 773-528-2241; **www.coffeeandtea.com**), one of the city's finest purveyors of coffee and equipment for making it. Now 28 years old, **Unabridged Books** (3251 North Broadway; ☎ 773-883-9119; www.**unabridgedbookstore.com**) is one of the staunch independents holding out against the invasion of Borders and Barnes & Noble. You'll find the city's largest cluster of gay bars along Halsted and Broadway between Belmont and Addison and an eclectic variety of stores selling things antique to antic along the commercial strips of Belmont, Diversey, Broadway, Halsted, and Clark.

TO GET THERE From the Loop, take the CTA Red Line (Howard) or Brown Line (Ravenswood) to Belmont or the #151 bus along Michigan Avenue north to Belmont, and then walk west. The #22 Clark Street bus, a quicker option, will put you in the heart of Lakeview-Wrigleyville.

By car, drive north on Lake Shore Drive to the Belmont Avenue exit, and head west on Belmont. Wrigley Field is about five blocks north of Belmont. (There's a CTA Red Line stop at Addison, near the ballpark.)

MILWAUKEE AVENUE

CHICAGO IS KNOWN AS AMERICA'S SECOND CITY, but it is also a City of Second Chances due to its influx of immigrants during the early 20th century. Nowhere is this more apparent than the long and winding road that is Milwaukee Avenue.

The heart of the city's Polish community was once at Milwaukee and Division but has since angled north to the neighborhood called **Avondale,** although Milwaukee Avenue, especially between Central Park and Pulaski, remains a primary Polish corridor. On weekend afternoons, this section teems with shoppers and diners, all gossiping—in Polish—and talking about the Pope.

Your best bet is to stroll along the avenue, taking in the sights and sounds. Step into **Andy's Deli** (5442 North Milwaukee Avenue; ☎ 773-631-7304; **www.andysdeli.com**) to gape at the 25 varieties of sausage lining the back wall and choose among packaged pierogi, *gulasz,* and Polish comic books. At the Polish department store **Syrena** (3044 North Milwaukee; ☎ 773-489-4435), you can snap up that missing tuxedo for your children in white or black.

For a sit-down meal from which you'll struggle to rise, consider the buffet at **Red Apple** (3123 North Milwaukee, ☎ 773-588-5781; 6474 North Milwaukee, ☎ 773-763.3407; **www.redapplebuffet.com**). Owner Czerwone Jabluszko is known across the Northwest Side for his huge portions of Wiener schnitzel, cheese blintzes, and gonzo potato pancakes.

St. Hyacinth Basilica (3636 West Wolfram Street; ☎ 773-342-3636; **www.sthyacinthbasilica.org**) looms over the tidy bungalows and two-flats wedged on the side streets angling off Milwaukee. The Catholic church, built in ornate Renaissance Revival style, draws up to 1,000 people at a time for Polish-language masses.

TO GET THERE The CTA #56 Milwaukee Avenue bus takes the *s-l-o-w* scenic route through some of Chicago's oldest—and now graying—immigrant communities. Yet it is one of the most compelling bus rides in the city. You'll see Polish, Serbian, German, and Hispanic residents. Board at Randolph and Michigan or along Madison in the Loop. For a quicker (but not as interesting) ride, take the CTA Blue Line (O'Hare) to Logan Square, and transfer to a northbound #56 Milwaukee Avenue bus.

By car from the Loop, take the Kennedy Expressway (I-90/94) north to the Kimball (Belmont) or Addison exits, and head west (left) to Milwaukee Avenue.

WICKER PARK AND BUCKTOWN

IF YOU WANT TO SEE HIPSTER CHICAGO and hang out where slacker attitude prevails, head for Wicker Park and Bucktown. Adjoining neighborhoods stretching from Division on the south to Fullerton on the north, between the Kennedy Expressway and Western Avenue, these formerly Polish, currently Puerto Rican communities have seen significant incursions by artists and yuppies of all stripes. Near **Wicker Park** itself, a small triangle at Schiller and Damen, are the late-1800s stone mansions of beer barons lining Pierce, Hoyne, Oakley, and Damen. Chicago author Nelson Algren once lived along here, which is why Evergreen Avenue is also called Nelson Algren Avenue. Note the gingerbread house at **2137 West Pierce Street.**

The cradle of the flourishing arts scene is the **Coyote Building** at 1600 North Milwaukee Avenue and its across-the-street landmark counterpart, the **Flatiron Arts Building** (1579 North Milwaukee). Each year in September, the galleries and studios hold a celebratory open house called **Around the Coyote** (☎ 773-342-6777; **www.aroundthe coyote.org**). Nearby is **Pentimento** (1629 North Milwaukee; ☎ 773-227-0576), featuring clothes by local designers.

Damen Avenue has become a mecca for small bistros, such as chef-owned **Le Bouchon** (1958 North Damen Avenue; ☎ 773-862-6600; **www.lebouchonofchicago.com**). Neighborhood stalwart **Northside Bar and Grill** (1635 North Damen; ☎ 773-384-3555; **www.northside chicago.com**) has an outdoor patio and a lively crowd. Steep yourself in the late-night music scene at the **Double Door** (1572 North Milwaukee; ☎ 773-489-3160; **www.doubledoor.com**).

TO GET THERE From the Loop, take the CTA Blue Line (O'Hare) to the Damen Avenue stop, which places you right at the confluence of Damen, North, and Milwaukee avenues in the heart of Bucktown. The #56 Milwaukee Avenue bus also takes you through Wicker Park and Bucktown.

By car from the Loop, drive north on the Kennedy Expressway (I-90/94) to the Division Street or North Avenue exits, and head west.

UKRAINIAN VILLAGE

UKRAINIAN VILLAGE IS MORE AUTHENTIC than Wicker Park, its gentrified neighbor to the north. On any given morning, you can still see old-world Ukrainians sweeping their sidewalks in front of the gingerbread cutouts and stained glass on their homes in this cozy neighborhood. (During the same morning in Wicker Park, you'll see trust-fund kids staggering home after a night on the town.)

Ukrainian Village stretches west along Chicago Avenue between Ashland and Western and north to Division. Locals now call it "East Village" (east of Damen Avenue) and "West Town," which runs from Damen Avenue west to California Avenue.

The neighborhood's spiritual center is the **St. Nicholas Ukrainian Catholic Cathedral** (2238 West Rice Street at Oakley Avenue; ☎ 773-276-4537; **www.stnicholascathedralukrcath.org**). The 13 copper-clad domes are modeled after those of the Basilica of St. Sophia in Kiev. But the real jewel is the much-smaller **Holy Trinity Cathedral** (1121 North Leavitt Street at Haddon Street; ☎ 773-486-6064; **www .holytrinitycathedral.net**), a Russian Orthodox church designed by Louis Sullivan in 1901 and bearing his characteristic stenciling and ornamentation.

The hipster Wicker Park influence is evident in many new bars and restaurants that have opened up along Chicago Avenue. Younger people congregate at the **High Dive** (1938 West Chicago Avenue; ☎ 773-235-3483), where old-school soul plays loudly over the juke-box. Down the street, **The Continental** (2801 West Chicago Avenue; ☎ 773-292-1200) has a 4 a.m.-weekday-to-5 a.m.-Saturday liquor license, plus some of the city's best DJs. Next door to The Continental is **Feed** (2803 West Chicago Avenue; ☎ 773-489-4600), which serves Southern-style rotisserie chicken and catfish at affordable prices. At **Tommy's Rock & Roll Cafe** (2548 West Chicago Avenue; ☎ 773-486-6768; **www.tommysguitars.com**), you can buy one of more than 300 hundred electric guitars hanging on the wall while waiting for breakfast or lunch. Rocker Tom Petty did.

Thursday through Sunday, stop in at the **Ukrainian National Museum of Chicago** (2249 West Superior Street; ☎ 312-421-8020; **www.ukrainiannationalmuseum.org**), featuring exhibits of traditional folk art, a rare-book library, and an archive chronicling the history of the city's Ukrainian community (see full profile on page 188). **RR #1 Chicago** (814 North Ashland Avenue at Chicago Avenue; ☎ 312-421-9079) carries handmade soaps, herbal teas, and all manner of kitschy gifts. The shop is housed in a 1940s drugstore with more than 100 evenly cut oak medicine drawers and faded pharmaceutical-art prints.

TO GET THERE By public transportation, take the CTA Blue Line (O'Hare) northbound to Chicago Avenue, transfer to a westbound #66 bus, and travel to Damen or Ashland. Or get on the #66 bus westbound near Water Tower Place at Chicago and Michigan.

By car from the Loop, drive north on Michigan Avenue to Chicago Avenue. Turn left (west) and continue to Ukrainian Village. This is one of the closest working-class neighborhoods to the Loop.

GOLD COAST AND OLD TOWN

BEHIND THE HIGH-RISES STRETCHING NORTH of Michigan Avenue along Lake Shore Drive are some of the most elegant townhouses and stately mansions in Chicago. It costs a fortune to live here, thus the name "Gold Coast," but it costs nothing to stroll along Astor Street or its neighbors from Division to North Avenue. Along the way, imagine urbane life in the former **Patterson-McCormick Mansion** (20 East Burton), which has since been divided into condominiums, or count the chimneys at **1555 North State Parkway,** the official residence of Chicago's Catholic archbishop.

Consider treating yourself to lunch at the **Pump Room** (1301 North State Parkway; ☎ 312-266-0360; **www.pumproom.com**), in the **Ambassador East Hotel,** which was Frank Sinatra's home away from home when he visited Chicago.

Old Town, which stretches west along North Avenue, was once a bohemian haven for artists, folkies, jazz clubs, and strip joints. Now the rehabbed town homes and coach houses have made it quieter (and costlier), with upscale boutiques and trendy shops along Wells. Many children of the city's blue-blood families enroll at the private **Latin School of Chicago** (59 West North Boulevard; ☎ 312-582-6000; **www.latinschool.org**).

Conversely, you'll find a young, beery crowd at some of the bars along Division. When the young ones get old and bitter, they graduate to the legendary **Old Town Ale House** (219 West North Avenue; ☎ 312-944-7020; **www.oldtownalehouse.net**), which raised eyebrows during the 2008 election season by displaying a nude portrait of GOP vice-presidential candidate Sarah Palin, painted by co-owner Bruce Elliott (he later created a companion nude of ousted Illinois governor Rod Blagojevich). The most authentic place to eat in Old Town is **Twin Anchors,** established in 1932 (1655 North Sedgwick Street; ☎ 312-266-1616; **www.twinanchorsribs.net**). It's known for its ribs, lots of Sinatra on the jukebox, and long waits. (See full profile on page 268.)

TO GET THERE Street parking is at a premium on the Gold Coast, so consider walking north from Michigan Avenue or taking the #151 bus and getting off anywhere between Oak Street and North Avenue. Walk west one block. For Old Town, there's a large parking garage next to the Piper's Alley theaters on North Avenue; you can also take the #22 or #36 buses heading north (board downtown along Dearborn) into the heart of the area.

CHINATOWN

CHICAGO'S TRADITIONAL CHINATOWN is a crowded, bustling area along the Wentworth Avenue corridor, its formal entrance marked by the ornate **Oriental arch** at Wentworth and Cermak Road. Walk south along Wentworth and note the templelike **Pui Tak Center** (2216 South Wentworth Avenue), the cornerstone of the commercial district, where immigrant bachelors in years past rented space in apartments on the second floor. (The building now serves as a Christian community center.) Wentworth offers a lively, teeming mix of restaurants, shops, groceries, even a wholesale-noodle company. The Chinatown branch of the **Chicago Public Library** (2353 South Wentworth Avenue; ☎ 312-747-8013) circulates more books and cassettes (many in Chinese) than any other in the city. Newer shopping areas have spilled out across Cermak Road and Archer Avenue, and newer Chinese and Asian neighborhoods have evolved on the Far North Side near Argyle Street, but for the sights and smells most of us expect in Chinatown, this is where you'll find them.

TO GET THERE From the Loop, take the CTA southbound Red Line (Dan Ryan) from State Street to the Cermak-Chinatown stop. The #24 Wentworth bus heads south from Clark and Randolph in the Loop, and the #62 Archer Avenue bus travels south along State Street (get off at Cermak and Archer, and walk one block east).

By car from the Loop, drive south on Michigan Avenue to 22nd Street (Cermak Road), turn right, and drive five blocks to a public parking lot at Wentworth and Cermak. Or drive south on the Dan Ryan Expressway and take the 22nd Street–Canalport turnoff, which leads to Chinatown.

TAYLOR STREET AND LITTLE ITALY

ONCE THE HEART OF ITALIAN CHICAGO, **Taylor Street** was severely altered by the construction of the University of Illinois at Chicago campus in the early 1960s, which displaced thousands of residents. Still, the Taylor Street area has undergone a renaissance, with new townhouses being built and coffeehouses and fern bars offering proximity to the Loop with the lure of the university. Combine a tour of the area with a visit to the **Jane Addams Hull-House Museum** (800 South Halsted Street; ☎ 312-413-5353; **www.hull housemuseum.org;** see full profile on page 173) as well as the celebrated **Robert J. Quinn Fire Academy** (558 West DeKoven Street; ☎ 312-747-7239), built on the spot where the Great Chicago Fire allegedly started.

For a taste of Taylor Street, try **Al's #1 Italian Beef** (1079 West Taylor Street; ☎ 312-226-4017; **www.alsbeef.com**)—so famous that tour buses stop here—followed by an Italian ice at **Mario's Lemonade Stand** on Taylor between Aberdeen and Carpenter streets (no phone, open only in summer; you'll have to wait in line or wend your way through cars parked three abreast). For Italian provisions, don't miss the **Conte Di Savoia** deli (1438 West Taylor; ☎ 312-666-3471; **www .contedisavoia.com**) or the **Original Ferrara Bakery** (2210 West Taylor; ☎ 312-666-2200; **www.ferrarabakery.com**). A classic neighborhood stop is **Tufano's Vernon Park Tap** (1073 West Vernon Park Place, across from the park; ☎ 312-733-3393). Opened in 1931 as a social club, the restaurant was discovered in the 1960s by author Nelson Algren, who would stop in on his way to White Sox games at Old Comiskey Park.

One of the city's best-kept secrets—even some locals don't know about it—is the **Little Italy** strip, on Oakley Avenue south of Taylor. Residents here don't like to be compared to Taylor Street: many Little Italy families have roots in northern Italy, while Taylor Street residents are mostly of Sicilian descent.

Taylor Street is roughly surrounded by 16th Street, Western Avenue, the Stevenson Expressway, and the south branch of the Chicago River. There are several storefront restaurants and delis; one of the best is **Bruna's Ristorante** (2424 South Oakley Avenue; ☎ 773-254-5550), which has been in the quiet neighborhood since the 1930s. Little Italy, meanwhile, has opened its big arms to **Mila's European Pastry and Cafe** (2401 South Oakley; ☎ 773-579-0800), a popular Polish stomping ground that also serves Italian cannoli and tiramisù.

North on Polk Street, between Laflin and Loomis, you can see some turn-of-the-19th-century homes built in the style prevalent before the Great Fire of 1871. **Bishop Street** between Taylor and Polk and **Ada Street** between Flournoy Street and Columbus Park also give a great feel to the neighborhood. **St. Basil Greek Orthodox Church** (733 Ashland Avenue at Polk Street; ☎ 312-243-3738; **stbasil.il.goarch.org**) bears witness to the neighborhood's ethnic evolution from Jewish to Greek to Italian—the church was once a synagogue, and a Hebrew inscription is still visible on the exterior.

TO GET THERE Take any CTA Blue Line train heading west to the UIC-Halsted stop or the Racine stop. During the week you can take the #37 bus southbound on Wells through the Loop.

By car from the Loop, drive west on the Eisenhower Expressway (I-290) to the Ashland exit, and head south to Taylor Street. To get to Little Italy, take the Western exit until the 2400 block, and turn left on Oakley.

PILSEN–LITTLE VILLAGE

CALL THESE CHICAGO'S BARRIOS—home to the largest population of Mexican Americans in the Midwest—where the signs are in Spanish and the smells are enticing. **Pilsen** lies principally along 18th Street between Canal Street and Damen Avenue. **Little Village,** considered somewhat more prosperous and stable, opens with its own pink-stucco gateway arch at 26th Street and Albany and unwinds in boisterous fashion west along 26th to Kostner.

Once the province of Bohemians and Poles, Pilsen is now home to thousands of Mexicans. It also has a thriving artist's colony and is home to the **National Museum of Mexican Art** (1852 West 19th Street; ☎ 312-738-1503; **www.nationalmuseumofmexican.org;** see full profile on page 181). The museum, which opened in 1987 in the converted Harrison Park Boat Craft Shop, strives to showcase the wealth and breadth of Mexican art in its exhibitions. Works from legends such as Diego Rivera and David Siquieros are part of the museum's permanent collection. Find time to survey some of the 20 **hand-painted murals** depicting various cultural, religious, and political themes; they're scattered throughout Pilsen (at 1305 West 18th Street, 18th and Racine, 18th and Wood, and lining the concrete wall along the tracks at 16th and Allport). When you visit, notice the elaborate cornices and roofs of some of the 19th-century storefronts and two-flats along 18th Street west of Halsted. The **Providence of God Church** (717 West 18th Street; ☎ 312-226-2929) is the focal point for many celebrations, including a powerful Via Crucis (Way of the Cross) procession on Good Friday.

A favorite gathering place is the **Cafe Jumping Bean** (1439 West 18th Street; ☎ 312-455-0019), where you're sure to run into neighborhood artists and teachers drinking coffee or enjoying a hot focaccia sandwich. Local art is also featured on the walls. "The Bean," as locals call the cafe, is on the first floor of the most breathtaking structure on 18th Street, a three-story building constructed in 1907. An aqua dome sits on top, creating a castlelike ambience.

Plenty of taquerias, bakeries, and taverns line the strip. Check out **Panaderia Nuevo Leon** (1634 West 18th Street; ☎ 312-243-5977) for sweets or **Carnitas Uruapan** (1725 West 18th Street; ☎ 312-226-2654) for chunks of slow-cooked pork (*carnitas*), fried pork rinds (*chicharrones*), and spicy salsa.

The neighborhood's favorite (and safest) tavern is **Skylark** (2149 South Halsted; ☎ 312-948-5275), where a fine selection of beer is accented by Southern-style comfort food. The atmosphere is deep 1960s, with green-leather couches and groovy lighting. Chicago foodies are also flocking to the new **Mundial Cocina Mestiza** (1640 West 18th Street; ☎ 312-491-9908; **www.mundialcocinamestiza.com**) for its made-to-order tortillas and made-from-scratch tamales. Don't miss the grilled salmon with caramelized papaya and mango.

Little Village has its own colorful wall murals, such as the **Broken Wall** mural in the back of Los Comales Restaurant next to McDonald's (26th and Kedzie). You'll find others at 26th and Homan, 25th and St. Louis, and 25th and Pulaski. Here, too, the neighborhood pulses along the commercial strip of 26th. Consider selecting a piñata from the many styles found at **La Justicia Grocery** (3644 West 26th Street at Millard Avenue; ☎ 773-522-5240), and try the dependable Mexican fare at **Lalo's** (4126 West 26th Street; ☎ 773-762-1505; **www.lalos.com**).

TO GET THERE For Pilsen: by public transportation, board the westbound CTA Blue Line at Dearborn in the Loop, and get off at the 18th Street stop in the heart of Pilsen. By car, drive south on the Dan Ryan Expressway (I-90/94), exit at 18th Street, and head west.

For Little Village: by public transportation, board the #60 Blue Island–26th Street bus westbound on Adams in the Loop. By car from Pilsen, continue west along 18th Street to Western, go south (left) to 26th Street, and proceed west past the Cook County Courthouse and the turrets marking the perimeter of the Cook County Jail to the arch at Albany.

BRIDGEPORT

IF YOU REALLY WANT TO KNOW CHICAGO, get to know Bridgeport. Just south of Chinatown, it's the home of the White Sox and the bar with the oldest liquor license in town (now that the original **Berghoff** has closed). Bridgeport has also supplied the city with its bodacious mayors, except for a brief respite between 1979 and 1989. In a city where politics is played at Super Bowl level (with the occasional quarterback sneak), the shrines to Chicago's leaders are what you would expect: the family home, the neighborhood pub, and the ward organization office—or, in an earlier era, what might have irreverently been called "the machine shop."

First stop on the pilgrimage, then, is **3536 South Lowe,** the former home of the late Mayor Richard J. and Eleanor "Sis" Daley, parents of the current mayor, Richard M. Daley. The modest redbrick bungalow is distinguished from its neighbors only by a flagpole. At the end of the block is a police station whose handy placement was arranged by Hizzoner. A few years ago, when the younger Mayor Daley left the neighborhood for the South Loop, it made front-page news locally.

A few blocks to the west and south, you'll find the other two neighborhood shrines right across the street from each other, at 37th and Halsted streets: the **11th Ward Democratic Organization** and **Schaller's Pump** (3714 South Halsted; ☎ 773-376-6332), licensed to sell liquor longer than any other tavern in Chicago: 125 years. The Pump's dim lights and tin ceiling warmed many of the elder Mayor Daley's victory celebrations. During the 1940s and 1950s, workers from the nearby Union Stockyards lunched here. Today Schaller's is a popular postgame hangout for White Sox fans, but it retains its sense of history. The Schaller family might even tell you how Bridgeport got its name: a port was built because a low bridge at Ashland Avenue and the Chicago River forced the unloading and reloading of barges in order to pass.

The walk around Bridgeport is remarkable. You'll see longtime residents sitting on their bungalow stoops and families playing boccie in the park. Have a meal at the **Polo Cafe** (3322 South Morgan Street; ☎ 773-927-7656; **www.polocafe.com**), where pasta, salads, and fish are served in the Old Eagle Room, a converted 1914 nickelodeon that, in its former incarnation as the Eagle Theater, was popular with Lithuanian immigrants.

Stroll north along Halsted to sample the changing flavor of Bridgeport. You'll see Chinese, Mexican, Italian, and Lithuanian establishments all within a few blocks. Above all, don't miss **Healthy Food Restaurant** (3236 South Halsted; ☎ 312-326-2724; **www.healthy foodlithuanian-chicago.com**), where slim waitresses in flowing skirts dish out ample portions of hearty Lithuanian *kugelis* and mushroom soup to the music of Tchaikovsky.

TO GET THERE Take the CTA Red Line (Dan Ryan) to the new 35th Street stop at U.S. Cellular Field (from there it's a bit of a hike to Halsted, or you can transfer to a #35 bus westbound). Or board a #44 bus southbound on State Street in the Loop.

By car, drive south on Lake Shore Drive to the 31st Street exit and then west on Halsted, or drive south on the Dan Ryan Expressway to the 35th Street exit and then west to Halsted.

HYDE PARK-KENWOOD

THIS IS THE PLACE FOR BIG HOMES, big ideas, and a great cluster of cultural institutions. Drive along Ellis, Greenwood, and Woodlawn between 47th and East Hyde Park Boulevard (5100 South) in **Kenwood,** and you'll marvel at the number of grand mansions on large lots. Years ago, these were homes of titans of industry; today they more than likely harbor faculty from the nearby **University of Chicago,** a hotbed of Nobel laureates that anchors **Hyde Park** with its cerebral gray presence between 57th Street and the Midway Plaisance, a wide, grassy boulevard created for the 1893 Columbian Exposition. Descend the stairs to the **Seminary Co-op Bookstore** (5757 South University Avenue; ☎ 800-777-1456 or 773-752-4381; **semcoop.book sense.com**), and you can't help but feel like a scholar yourself. At the **Reynolds Club** (57th Street and University; ☎ 773-834-0858), you can survey the eternal student scene at Hutchinson Commons from behind one of the nouveau 'zines free for the taking.

Hyde Park is also one of the city's better integrated communities. The late Mayor Harold Washington used to live here, and the Fifth Ward is considered one of the city's most liberal. **KAM Isaiah Israel** (1100 East Hyde Park Boulevard; ☎ 773-924-1234; **www.kamil.org**), the Midwest's oldest Jewish congregation, is here as well. Good shopping can be found at the bustling commercial strips along 53rd and 57th streets. You'll certainly shed the tourist label if you tip back a brew at **Woodlawn Tap** (1172 East 55th Street; ☎ 773-643-5516) or eat at **Valois** (1518 East 53rd Street; ☎ 773-667-0647), a cafeteria hangout for cops, cabbies, and students of urban life where the motto is "See Your Food."

TO GET THERE Be prepared for a lot of walking (not recommended after dark), or plan to tour the avenues by car. If you want to use public transportation, take the #6 Jeffery Express bus (30¢ surcharge) southbound from State Street to 57th, and walk to the University of Chicago. Or take the slower #1 Indiana–Hyde Park bus east on Jackson from Union Station, then south on Michigan to East Hyde Park Boulevard for a tour of Kenwood.

Metra electric trains also serve Hyde Park. Board underground at Randolph and Michigan or at Van Buren and Michigan, and exit at the 53rd and Lake Park stop, the combined 55th-56th-57th Street stop, or the University of Chicago stop at 59th Street and Harper. (The fare is $2.35 one-way.)

> *unofficial* **TIP**
> The **Chicago Architecture Foundation** (☎ 312-922-3432) offers two-hour walking tours of Kenwood in May, June, September, and October.

By car from the Loop, drive south on Lake Shore Drive to the 57th Street exit. Pass in front of the Museum of Science and Industry, and follow the signs for the University of Chicago. Or take the 47th Street exit, drive west, and then turn south on Woodlawn or Greenwood for a look at the mansions.

BRONZEVILLE

KNOWN AS "THE BLACK METROPOLIS" in the early 20th century (and immortalized in poet Gwendolyn Brooks's *A Street in Bronzeville*), this South Side community is on the rebound in the early 21st century. Luminaries such as Louis Armstrong, Nat "King" Cole, and boxer Joe Louis lived in Bronzeville in its heyday; the neighborhood is coming back in their spirit. The boundaries of Bronzeville are roughly 22nd Street (just south of McCormick Place) south to 51st

Chicagoans can be so myopically proud of their city, many claim President Barack Obama as a native. Wrong.

Obama was born and raised in Honolulu, Hawaii. Chicago is a lot colder than Hawaii.

The president did, however, come of age in Chicago after his arrival in June 1985. Here are a few key places in "Obamaland":

During the 2008 presidential election, tourists from across the world flocked to Obama's house at **5046 South Greenwood Avenue** in the South Side neighborhood of Kenwood. Obama and his wife, Michelle, bought the mansion in 2005 for $1.65 million and plan to keep the property as their "Western White House." Not surprisingly, you can no longer get close to the house—blocks around the home are surrounded by Secret Service agents and Chicago police. In keeping with Chicago's big-town–small-town nature, even Obama's neighbors have become celebrities.

Obama's work as a community organizer was a hot topic during the 2008 presidential campaign. In the late 1980s, he began that work in the **Altgeld Gardens** public-housing development at the corner of 131st Street and Ellis Avenue on the Far South Side. Here he spearheaded a campaign for asbestos removal.

The president likes to work out at the upscale **East Bank Club** (500 North Kingsbury Street; ☎ 312-527-5800; **www.eastbankclub.com**). For years he's played basketball and tennis in the sprawling health club along the east bank of the Chicago River. (If he shows up now, of course, he'll be shooting hoops one-on-ten with his Secret Service agents.) The gym is still a regular hangout for Chicago Mayor Richard M. Daley, civil-rights leader Jesse Jackson, and editors and columnists for the *Chicago Sun-Times,* who work in the Merchandise Mart across the street.

Any good workout creates a good appetite. Don't be surprised to see Obama sneaking into **MacArthur's Restaurant** (5412 West Madison Street; ☎ 773-261-2316; **www.macarthursrestaurant.com**), on the Far West Side. His

Street, east to the lake, and west to the Dan Ryan Expressway. The **Bronzeville Walk of Fame,** along the eastern sidewalk of King Drive near 22nd Street, features markers honoring past residents such as singers Sam Cooke and Howlin' Wolf.

The hub of activity is near the **Harold Washington Cultural Center** (4701 South King Drive; ☎ 773-373-1900), which presents concerts in a 1,000-seat theater and features rotating exhibits. Across the street from the cultural center, residents gather for coffee at the **Spoken Word Cafe** (4655 South King Drive; ☎ 773-373-2233). Enjoy live jazz and remarkable soul food at the **Negro League Café** (301 East 43rd Street; ☎ 773-536-7000; **www.thenegroleaguecafe.info**) or stand-up comedy at a club called **Jokes and Notes** (4641 South King Drive;

picture is on the wall, along with those of Shaquille O'Neal and other celebrity diners. Obama named the soul-food restaurant as one of his favorites in his 2006 best seller, *The Audacity of Hope.* Try the candied yams, the meat loaf, or the President's rumored favorite, the turkey legs and dressing. On the North Side, the First Couple favor the iconic **RJ Grunts,** established in 1971 (2056 Lincoln Park West; ☎ 773-929-5363; **www.rjgruntschicago.com**), for casual fare (soups, salads, burgers, and such). And Michelle Obama enjoys the American cuisine at **Sepia,** housed in a converted 1890 print shop just west of downtown (123 North Jefferson Street; ☎ 312-441-1920; **www.sepiachicago.com**).

The huge **Trinity United Church of Christ,** just off the Dan Ryan Expressway (400 West 95th Street; ☎ 773-962-5650; **www.tucc.org**), is where Obama worshiped for two decades. It is also the home church of Chicago gospel-soul vocalist Mavis Staples and her family. Obama and his family left the church in May 2008 following inflammatory comments from former senior pastor Jeremiah Wright Jr., who officiated at the Obamas' wedding.

Finally, the Hyde Park neighborhood vibe was essential to the embryonic Obama. It's only an empty storefront now, but the original **Hyde Park Hair Salon and Barber Shop,** at 1464 East 53rd Street, was where Obama got his hair cut on Sunday mornings when he arrived in the city in the mid-1980s. In 2007 the shop moved to 5324 South Blackstone Avenue (☎ 773-493-6028; **www.hydeparkhairsalon.net**) because of a University of Chicago redevelopment project. The president's Chicago barber, Zariff, has also become a local celebrity and is planning to open his own shop in Washington, D.C. (if he becomes First Barber, of course, he'll have to make house calls). In his 1995 book, *Dreams from My Father,* Obama wrote that Chicago was where "I discovered I was black," and he learned about the role race plays in the city's politics by talking to the regulars at the barber shop, which he called "Smitty's" in the book to protect its privacy.

And privacy is a rare premium for the new president, in Obamaland or elsewhere.

☎ 773-373-3390; **www.jokesandnotes.com**). And you haven't been to the South Side until you've tried spicy **Harold's Chicken.** Harold's #7 (108 East 47th Street; ☎ 773-285-8362) has been in Bronzeville forever. The **Bronzeville Visitor Information Center,** in the Supreme Life Building (East 35th Street and King Drive; ☎ 773-373-2842), offers tours, exhibits, and a small gift shop.

Over the years, Bronzeville has had its share of notable residents. **Louis Armstrong** lived at 421 East 44th Street until 1931, when the trumpet legend relocated to California. Bluesman **Muddy Waters** built a small studio in the basement of his house near Lake Michigan at 4339 South Lake Park, where he lived from 1954 to 1974. Crooner **Nat "King" Cole** once called 4023 South Vincennes home. Even the

Marx Brothers lived in the neighborhood around 1910 (at 4512 South King Drive) while playing the Chicago vaudeville circuit. They cooked up some story about being farmers on the South Side, but in truth Groucho, Chico, Harpo, Zeppo, and Gummo slacked off while watching baseball at nearby Comiskey Park.

TO GET THERE The CTA Green Line Stop at 47th Street is still funky and dangerous, so it's best to drive or take a taxi. Take the Dan Ryan Expressway south to 47th Street, and turn left (east) to King Drive.

SOUTH SHORE

LOCATED BETWEEN EAST 67TH and 79th streets and reaching from Lake Michigan on the east to Stony Island Avenue on the west, South Shore has been home to Chicagoans for more than 100 years. Today, many affluent African Americans dwell in some of the large, elegant homes lining South Euclid, Constance, and Bennett streets between East 67th and East 71st at South Jeffery Boulevard. Though the commercial strip along East 71st has suffered, **ShoreBank** (East 71st and Jeffery; ☎ 773-288-1000; **www.sbk.com**) has become a national leader in innovative financing for community-development projects.

The **South Shore Cultural Center** (☎ 773-256-0149), at the intersection of East 71st Street and South Shore Drive, remains a gem. A onetime country club, the stucco Spanish-style structure fell on hard times until the Chicago Park District purchased it 20 years ago. Now restored and open to the public (Barack and Michelle Obama held their wedding reception here in 1992), the center has a golf course, stables for Chicago Police Department horses, and up-close lakefront views. In the winter you'll see a few solitary cross-country skiers; in the summer, there's picnicking and lakeside play.

The massive **Church of St. Philip Neri** (2132 East 72nd Street; ☎ 773-363-1700), one of Chicago's largest, has an exquisite sequence of mosaics depicting the Stations of the Cross. Another impressive house of worship is **Mosque Maryam** (7351 South Stony Island Avenue; ☎ 773-324-6000), headquarters of the Nation of Islam. The mosque occupies what once was the largest Greek Orthodox church in North America.

To experience some local cuisine, try **Army & Lou's** for soul food (422 East 75th Street; ☎ 773-483-3100; **www.armyandlous.com**) or **Alexander's Steak House and Cocktail Lounge** (3010 East 79th Street; ☎ 773-768-6555), where they've been dishing out prime rib and jazz at night for more than 50 years. **Salaam Restaurant & Bakery,** (700 West 79th Street; ☎ 773-874-8300) is a showcase community investment by the Nation of Islam.

TO GET THERE The CTA #14 Jeffery Express bus goes southbound on State Street to 71st Street and Jeffery. A quicker option is the Metra electric train from Randolph and Michigan—the station is underground—which stops at Bryn Mawr (71st Street and Jeffery; the fare is $2.35 one-way).

By car from the Loop, drive south along Lake Shore Drive through Jackson Park to South Shore.

OTHER NEIGHBORHOODS OF INTEREST

Rogers Park

The city's northernmost conglomeration of cultures and lifestyles, Rogers Park mixes well-preserved lakeside condos with 1960s hippie holdovers and ethnic groups ranging from Russian to Jamaican to Pakistani. Visit the **Heartland Cafe** (7000 North Glenwood Avenue;

unofficial **TIP**
Rogers Park sprawls pretty far, and it's probably best not to wander alone or travel on foot after dark.

☎ 773-465-8005; **www.heartlandcafe.com**) for vegetarian food served with radical politics. Sip espresso at **No Exit Cafe** (6970 North Glenwood; ☎ 773-743-3355) or **Ennui Cafe** (6981 North Sheridan Road; ☎ 773-973-2233).

Lincoln Park–DePaul

This section, sandwiched between Old Town and Lakeview, may have the city's largest concentration of young white urban professionals (aka "Trixies" and "Todds")—or at least the loudest and most visible. Students at **DePaul University,** the large Catholic institution renowned for its Blue Demons basketball team, probably can't afford to live here after graduation unless they double up in one of the two- or three-flats along Bissel or Sheffield whose back porches face the El tracks.

It's fun to roam the pleasant, tree-lined streets and check out the gentrified town homes. Lincoln Park was one of the first North Side neighborhoods to turn over a new leaf in the 1960s and 1970s. The most majestic homes line Fullerton Parkway as you head west from the lake, but a walk along any of the side streets, such as Hudson, Cleveland, Belden, and Fremont, will provide ample viewing pleasure.

Oz Park (2021 North Burling Street; ☎ 312-742-7898) is a favorite playground for kids and adults. Nearby **Glascott's Groggery** (2158 North Halsted Street; ☎ 773-281-1205) is a favorite playground for adults acting like kids. The shops, galleries, boutiques, and restaurants clustered along Halsted, Armitage, and Clark are fun for browsing and spending. With the closing of Demon Dogs underneath the El tracks, the most venerable restaurant in the neighborhood is now **Geja's Cafe** (340 West Armitage Avenue; ☎ 773-281-9101; **www.gejascafe.com**), a romantic fondue hideaway that opened in Old Town in 1965 and moved to Lincoln Park a few years later. Live classical and flamenco guitarists accompany the best fondue in the Midwest. It is, however, pricier than Demon Dogs.

TO GET THERE The CTA Brown Line (Ravenswood) stops at Armitage or Fullerton; the Red Line (Howard) also goes to Fullerton (the stop closest to DePaul, where Demon Dogs was). The #151 bus is a beautiful ride through Lincoln Park, while the #22 or #36 buses (board north along Dearborn) put you closer to the shopping district.

By car, drive north on Lake Shore Drive to the Fullerton exit, and then head west. Or take the North Avenue exit to Stockton, and drive through Lincoln Park.

Humboldt Park–Logan Square

Originally settled by Polish and Russian Jews, then by Scandinavians, Ukrainians, and Eastern Europeans, Humboldt Park and Logan Square are now home to a large number of Hispanic residents, along with young artists and musicians getting bargains on spacious apartments and condos.

A tour here opens the door to an earlier era of residential gentility. Many elegant graystones line the grand boulevards of Humboldt, Palmer, Kedzie, and Logan (one of the city's widest). **Logan Square** was the northwesternmost point of Daniel Burnham's 1909 Chicago Plan, which mixed dense green landscaping with affordable housing for immigrants. The hot dining spot here is **Lula** (2537 North Kedzie Boulevard; ☎ 773-489-9554), known for fabulous breakfasts with natural ingredients (see profile in Part Eight, Dining and Restaurants). Sometimes, though, you can cut the hipness with a knife. In addition, Logan Square has Chicago's most unusual intersection—a traffic circle with a massive marble column commemorating the centennial of Illinois statehood. Some of the areas off the boulevards are dicey but improving. Still, be careful.

TO GET THERE The CTA Blue Line (O'Hare) stops at Logan Square. By car, drive west along North Avenue to Humboldt Boulevard and then north to Palmer Square.

Pullman

Originally a company town built by George Pullman to house workers at his railroad-car factory, this area is now a historic district, with more than 80% of the original 1,800 buildings still standing. Start your tour at the **Historic Pullman Foundation,** housed in the Florence Hotel (named for Pullman's daughter) at 11141 South Cottage Grove Avenue (☎ 773-785-8901; **www.pullmanil.org**). The neighborhood harbors architecturally unique mansions—once the executives' houses—and far more modest two-story attached row houses in muted Queen Anne style.

TO GET THERE Pullman is on the Far Southwest Side, almost at the city's southern boundary. By public transportation, take the Metra Electric train ($2.75 one-way) from the station under Randolph and Michigan to the Pullman stop at 111th and Cottage Grove (it's one block to the Florence Hotel) or to the Kensington stop at 115th, which has more frequent service.

By car, drive south on the Dan Ryan Expressway (I-90/94); continue south on the Calumet Expressway (I-94), and exit at 111th Street. Head west a few blocks to South Forrestville.

FINAL NOTE

AS RICH AS CHICAGO IS in architecture, history, culture, and ethnic diversity, it is a major American city—which is to say, it is grappling with problems of unemployment, decaying infrastructure (especially the so-called expressways), crime, and besieged public schools. Many areas of the city's West Side never recovered from the fires and looting that followed the assassination of Martin Luther King Jr. in 1968. You need only drive west on 47th Street after touring the mansions of Kenwood to see the once-stately buildings on Drexel Boulevard now boarded up and barren, or glance across the Dan Ryan Expressway from U.S. Cellular Field to the forlorn hulks of Stateway Gardens and the Robert Taylor Homes (the largest public-housing complex in the world). In such juxtapositions of wealth and poverty, you will recognize the challenges facing Chicago. But as you get to know Chicago, you will know the city can stand up to the task.

CHICAGO *for* CHILDREN

kids QUESTION: Besides the requisite trip to the top of the Sears Tower, what else is there to entertain kids on a Chicago vacation?

Answer: A lot. Chicago offers plenty of fun-filled places to visit and things to do that will satisfy the most curious—and fidgety—kids. Their folks will have fun, too.

The *Unofficial Guide* rating system for attractions includes an Appeal by Age Group category ranging from one star (★), meaning don't bother, to five stars (★★★★★), meaning not to be missed. To get you started, we've provided a list of the attractions in and around Chicago that are most likely to appeal to children. (Also look for the "Kids" icon next to kid-friendly listings in our main attraction profiles, starting on page 150.)

MORE THINGS TO DO WITH CHILDREN

CHICAGO HAS MORE FOR KIDS to enjoy than museums, zoos, and tall buildings. Some ideas: swimming in Lake Michigan at **Oak Street Beach** and **North Avenue Beach** or browsing at **NikeTown,** a high-tech shoe store (669 North Michigan Avenue; ☎ 312-642-6363), or the hugely popular three-level **American Girl Place** (835 North Michigan Avenue; ☎ 877-247-5223; **www.americangirl.com**), with a cafe, a photo salon, and even a beauty shop for dolls. Another hit is *That's Weird, Grandma,* a collection of skits written by Chicago public-school children and performed by Barrel of Monkeys, a theater ensemble dedicated to arts education. The popular show is staged every Monday night at the **Neo-Futurarium** (5153 North Ashland Avenue; tickets: ☎ 312-409-1954; **www.barrelofmonkeys .org/performances/tickets**).

PRO SPORTS AND A REALLY BIG AMUSEMENT PARK

DEPENDING ON THE SEASON and ticket availability, take the gang to a **Bears, Blackhawks, Bulls, Cubs,** or **White Sox** game. In the summer, don't forget **Buckingham Fountain** in Grant Park: computer-controlled water displays send 14,000 gallons of water a minute through 133 jets. Colorful displays can be seen nightly from dusk to 11 p.m.

unofficial **TIP**
Six Flags Great America gets packed—go early in the day during the week, and avoid weekends.

Farther afield (if you've got a car), take a drive to **Six Flags Great America,** a monster amusement park north of Chicago with more than 100 rides (including 13 roller coasters), shops, stage shows, and special theme sections representing different eras in American history. The park is open from May through October with varying hours; admission is $54.99 for adults, $34.99 for children. With prices like these, plan on spending the day. For more information and directions, call ☎ 847-249-4636 or visit **www.sixflags .com/greatamerica.**

Other neat activities kids will enjoy: bicycling or Rollerblading on the bike path along Lake Michigan or taking an **Untouchable Tour** and exploring the old haunts of Chicago's gangsters (for more information, call ☎ 800-660-8824 or 773-881-1195).

HELPFUL HINTS *for* VISITORS

HOW TO GET INTO MUSEUMS FOR HALF PRICE

SAVE MORE THAN $30 when you visit Chicago's most popular museums and attractions with a **CityPass,** a book of tickets that cuts the price of admission in half at the Field Museum, Adler Planetarium and Astronomy Museum, Shedd Aquarium, and either the John Hancock Observatory or Sears Tower Skydeck.

The passes cost $59 for adults and $49 for children ages 3 to 11. Ticket books are sold at participating attractions and are good for nine days, beginning with the first day you use them. Don't remove the individual tickets from the booklet; just present the CityPass at each attraction. The clerk at the site removes the ticket, and you walk on in (usually without waiting in line to buy a ticket). For more information, call ☎ 888-330-5008 or visit **www.citypass.com.**

WHEN ADMISSION IS FREE

MANY CHICAGO MUSEUMS that usually charge admission open their doors at no charge one day a week. If you'd like to save a few bucks during your visit, use our list when planning your touring itinerary.

In addition, a few worthy attractions around town are free to the public year-round. Here's the list:

- Chicago Botanic Garden ($15 parking)
- Chicago Cultural Center
- Garfield Park Conservatory (donation requested during flower shows)
- Harold Washington Library Center
- Jane Addams Hull-House Museum
- Lincoln Park Conservatory
- Lincoln Park Zoo
- National Museum of Mexican Art (admission charged for performing-arts events)
- The Oriental Institute Museum ($5 donation suggested)
- The Polish Museum of America ($5 donation requested)
- Smart Museum of Art

Other Free-admission Days

DAILY
Art Institute of Chicago (February 1–21)

VARIOUS
Adler Planetarium (visit **www.adlerplanetarium.org/plan** for details)
Museum of Science and Industry (visit **www.msichicago.org** for details)

MONDAY
Chicago Children's Museum (first Monday of the month; age 15 and under only)
Chicago History Museum

TUESDAY
Brookfield Zoo (October–March; $8 parking)

International Museum of Surgical Science
Museum of Contemporary Art

THURSDAY
Art Institute of Chicago (evenings)
Brookfield Zoo (October–March; $8 parking)

FRIDAY
Chicago Children's Museum (evenings)

SUNDAY
DuSable Museum of African American History

SCENIC DRIVES

THOUGH WE RECOMMEND that visitors to Chicago forgo driving and rely on airport vans, taxis, and public transportation, not everyone will heed our advice. In addition, rental cars are plentiful in Chicago, and traffic gets downright manageable on weekends. If you've got access to a set of wheels and you feel the urge to roam, here are a few ideas.

Around Town

The best views of the city unfold anywhere along **Lake Shore Drive.** For an urban exploration beyond the lakefront, tour Chicago's boulevards and greenways, a series of wide streets laid out in the 19th century that link seven parks along what once was the city's western border.

Heading North

For a quick and scenic escape from the city, head north on Lake Shore Drive until it becomes **Sheridan Road.** This pleasant drive meanders along the lakeshore and passes through affluent neighborhoods full of gorgeous homes and mansions. In Evanston, Sheridan skirts the beautiful campus of **Northwestern University** and, in Wilmette, the breathtaking **Bahá'í House of Worship.**

Farther north along Sheridan Road in Glencoe is the **Chicago Botanic Garden**—worth a stop in any season—and, in Highland Park, the **Ravinia Festival,** where evening summertime performances range from Joan Baez to the Chicago Symphony Orchestra.

unofficial **TIP**
A drive along Sheridan Road is especially popular with Chicagoans in the fall when the leaves change. To avoid the worst of the traffic, go early in the day.

GREAT VIEWS

Nobody comes to the Midwest for the views, right? Wrong—at least in Chicago. Here's a list of ten great spots that offer breathtaking vistas of skyline, Lake Michigan, and the city stretching toward the horizon.

1. The observation decks atop **Sears Tower** and the **John Hancock Center** offer stupendous vistas from vantage points over 1,000 feet high. Go on a clear day; better yet, go at night. We prefer the Hancock Center, which is closer to the lake and usually not very crowded.

2. **Lake Shore Drive** offers dramatic views of the Chicago skyline and the lake all along its length. We especially like the vantage point looking north where the Stevenson Expressway joins Lake Shore Drive (at McCormick Place).

3. **Grant Park** is a great place to walk and look up at Chicago's downtown. *Note:* Unless there is a summer festival going on, consider the park unsafe at night.

4. The view of downtown from the **Shedd Aquarium** is a knockout, especially at dusk as the lights begin to wink on.

5. The **Michigan Avenue Bridge** over the Chicago River offers a heart-stopping view of downtown buildings, especially at night, when the Wrigley Building and Tribune Tower are both illuminated.

6. Starting around Thanksgiving, the **Festival of Lights** along North Michigan Avenue features over 300,000 white lights for the holidays.

unofficial **TIP**
Enjoy the scenery along Lake Shore Drive, but for safety's sake, don't get too distracted by the sights as you navigate this busy highway.

7. The **Ravenswood El** has surprises around every corner as it encircles the Loop. Don't get off—take it north, then grab the next train toward downtown for more views of the city.

8. **Montrose Harbor** offers a spectacular view of the Chicago skyline, especially at night. You'll need a car: the harbor is near the northern end of Lincoln Park on a finger of land jutting out into Lake Michigan; get there from Lake Shore Drive.

9. As a lot of Chicago runners and bicyclists know, a stunning sunrise is a frequent reward on an early morning jaunt on the **Lakefront Trail** along Lake Michigan.

10. Or try this not-to-be-forgotten scene from anywhere on the lakefront (if the heavens cooperate on your trip): moonrise over **Lake Michigan.**

OPRAH'S ON!

The Unofficial Guide to Chicago is written by natives. And these natives are restless that more people ask about getting into **The Oprah Winfrey Show**—the number-one talk show in America—than getting into the Art Institute of Chicago. Still, lots of people visit the city just to see Oprah. If you're one of them, here's what to do:

For audience reservations, call ☎ 312-591-9222 at least one month before your visit. A better bet is to visit **www.oprah.com** for last-minute e-mail reservations. There's no charge, and reservations are accepted for up to four people (who must be age 18 or older). **Harpo Studios** (*Harpo* is *Oprah* spelled backward), where the shows are taped twice daily (early and late morning; days vary) is a couple of blocks west of the Loop at 1058 West Washington Boulevard. The show goes on hiatus from late June to late August and again from mid-December through mid-January, when Oprah usually takes her staff on a highfalutin vacation. The reservations line is also closed during this time.

Jer-RY! Jer-RY! Jer-RY!

Can't get a ticket to *Oprah*? There's always the classy consolation prize of **The Jerry Springer Show.** Call at least one month in advance. Tickets are free, and parties are (sensibly) limited to four people; shows are usually taped at 10 a.m. and 1 p.m. on Mondays, Tuesdays, and Wednesdays, and on Tuesday evenings at 6 and 8 p.m. (No shows are taped in July—there are enough fireworks as it is.) The studios are located at the NBC Tower (454 North Columbus Drive, north of the Loop and just east of Michigan Avenue; ☎ 312-321-5365). Jerry's Web site (**www.jerryspringertv.com**) also has reservation forms and lists of tasteful upcoming topics. If you strike out here, you could move on to *Judge Mathis.* The reality-based court show tapes on Thursdays and Fridays from April through mid-July, also at the NBC Tower (☎ 866-362-8447 or 866-837-3428).

CHICAGO ATTRACTIONS

THE FOLLOWING PROFILES PROVIDE you with a comprehensive guide to Chicago's top attractions. We give you enough information so that you can choose the places you want to see, based on your own interests. Each attraction includes a location description so you can plan your visit logically without spending a lot of valuable time criss-crossing the city.

ATTRACTIONS BY TYPE AND LOCATION

BECAUSE OF THE WIDE RANGE OF ATTRACTIONS in and around Chicago—from an unparalleled collection of French Impressionist paintings in the Art Institute to America's tallest building—we provide the following charts to help you prioritize your touring at a glance. You'll find attractions organized by type and neighborhood, complete with authors' ratings from one star (skip it) to five stars (not to be missed). Individual attraction profiles follow the charts, organized alphabetically by attraction name.

ATTRACTION PROFILES

Adler Planetarium and Astronomy Museum   ★★½

APPEAL BY AGE	PRESCHOOL ★	GRADE SCHOOL ★★★★	TEENS ★★★
YOUNG ADULTS ★★★		OVER 30 ★★★	SENIORS ★★★

1300 South Lake Shore Drive, South Loop; ☎ 312-922-STAR; www.adlerplanetarium.org

Type of attraction Narrative sky shows in a domed theater, a slide presentation, and exhibits on astronomy and space exploration; a self-guided tour. **Admission** *Daily:* $19 adults, $15 children ages 3–14 for 1 show and audio tour; 2 shows, add $4; unlimited shows, add $5. *Far Out Fridays:* $20 adults, $17 kids ages 4–17 and seniors age 65 and over. Free general admission on select days year-round except July (check Web site for details); show admission costs still apply. **Hours** Daily, 9:30 a.m.–4:30 p.m. (summer, late December, and early January until 6 p.m.); first Friday of each month, 9:30 a.m.–10 p.m.; closed Thanksgiving and Christmas. **When to go** Anytime. **Special comments** The comfortable, high-backed seats in the theater almost guarantee you won't get a stiff neck from watching the show on the domed ceiling. Some fascinating stuff on display, but the low-key planetarium show is geared to younger viewers and hard-core space cadets. **How much time to allow** 40 minutes for the show and at least half an hour to view the exhibits.

DESCRIPTION AND COMMENTS The Adler Planetarium was the first in the country when it opened in 1930. The 12-sided pink-granite building that houses the Sky Theater was funded by a Sears, Roebuck & Company executive who had the Zeiss projector imported from Germany. In addition to the narrated sky shows (which change throughout the year), visitors can explore a wide range of exhibits on topics that include telescopes, the planets, man-made satellites, the moon, optics, and navigation. It's a modern, informative place that will delight youngsters and adults who read Carl Sagan. In early 1997, the Adler embarked on a $40-million expansion and renovation program that added 60,000 square feet of new space.

TOURING TIPS Enter the planetarium through the glass building that faces the planetarium, not via the granite steps. On Friday nights (when the planetarium is open until 10 p.m.), visitors can tour the Doane Observatory and see its 20-inch telescope. Visit the planetarium late in a day of hard sightseeing; relaxing in a comfortable, high-backed chair for 40 minutes is nirvana even if you don't give a hoot about the cosmos. The view of the city skyline on the promontory leading to the building is spectacular, especially at sunset when the skyscrapers begin to light up.

OTHER THINGS TO DO NEARBY The John G. Shedd Aquarium and the Field Museum of Natural History are both within easy walking distance on the traffic-free Museum Campus. Bad news if you're hungry: getting something to eat beyond a hot dog requires flagging a cab or grabbing a bus downtown.

Art Institute of Chicago ★★★★★

APPEAL BY AGE	PRESCHOOL ★	GRADE SCHOOL ★★★	TEENS ★★★
YOUNG ADULTS ★★★★	OVER 30 ★★★★★		SENIORS ★★★★★

111 South Michigan Avenue, The Loop; ☎ 312-443-3600; www.artic.edu

Type of attraction Internationally acclaimed collections of paintings and sculptures housed in a complex of neoclassical buildings erected for the World's Columbian Exposition of 1893; guided and self-guided tours. **Admission** $12 adults, $7 students and seniors; children age 12 and under free. Free admission daily, February 1–February 21; Thursday and Friday evenings, 5–9 p.m., May 31–August 31; and Thursday evenings, 5–8 p.m., throughout the rest of the year. Checkroom, $1 per item. **Hours** *May 31–August 31:* Monday–Wednesday, 10:30 a.m.–5 p.m.; Thursday and Friday, 10:30 a.m.–9 p.m.; Saturday and Sunday, 10 a.m.–5 p.m. *Rest of year:* Monday–Wednesday and Friday, 10:30 a.m.–5 p.m.; Thursday, 10:30 a.m.–8 p.m.; Saturday and Sunday, 10 a.m.–5 p.m. Closed Christmas, New Year's Day, and Thanksgiving. **When to go** During the school year, the museum is often besieged by groups of schoolchildren on field trips in the mornings; afternoons are usually less crowded. **Special comments** The first floor is the only level that connects the three buildings that compose the Art Institute. It also provides access to Michigan Avenue (west) and Columbus Drive (east), food, restrooms, and water fountains. Disabled access is at the Columbus Drive entrance. The best of a handful of attractions that elevate Chicago to world-class status. Not to be missed. **How much time to allow** At least 2 hours for a brief run-through, all day for art lovers. Better yet, try to visit the Art Institute more than once—the place is huge.

DESCRIPTION AND COMMENTS The massive classical-Renaissance–style home of the Art Institute of Chicago was completed in 1892, just in time for

Chicago Attractions by Type

ATTRACTION | ZONE | AUTHOR'S RATING

GARDENS, PARKS, AND ZOOS

Brookfield Zoo | Southern Suburbs | ★★★★
Chicago Botanic Garden | Northern Suburbs | ★★★★
Garfield Park Conservatory | North Central–O'Hare Airport | ★★★
Lincoln Park Zoo | North Side | ★★★
The Morton Arboretum | Western Suburbs | ★★★½

MUSEUMS

Art Institute of Chicago | The Loop | ★★★★★
Balzekas Museum of Lithuanian Culture | South Central–Midway Airport | ★★
Chicago Children's Museum | Near North Side | ★★
Chicago History Museum | North Side | ★★★
DANK-Haus German Cultural Center | North Side | ★★★
David and Alfred Smart Museum of Art | South Side | ★★★
DuSable Museum of African American History | South Side | ★★★½
Ernest Hemingway Museum | North Central–O'Hare Airport | ★★
Field Museum of Natural History | South Loop | ★★★★★
International Museum of Surgical Science | Near North Side | ★★½
Intuit: The Center for Intuitive and Outsider Art | Near North Side | ★★★★
Jane Addams Hull-House Museum | South Central–Midway Airport | ★★½
Museum of Contemporary Art | Near North Side | ★★★★½
Museum of Holography | North Central–O'Hare Airport | ★★½

the 1893 World's Columbian Exposition. Located on the edge of Grant Park near the Loop, the museum is easily identified by the two bronze lions standing guard on Michigan Avenue.

It's a world-class museum especially renowned for its Impressionist collection, which includes five of the paintings in Monet's haystack series; Caillebotte's *Paris Street, a Rainy Day;* and perhaps the museum's best-known painting, Seurat's pointillist masterpiece *Sunday Afternoon on the Island of La Grande Jatte.* The new Modern Wing, designed by architect Renzo Piano, houses the museum's collection of contemporary art. The Nichols Bridgeway provides a direct link from Millennium Park to the third floor of the Modern Wing, where visitors can enjoy free access to the museum's new sculpture terrace and dining facilities. The large

ATTRACTION | ZONE | AUTHOR'S RATING

MUSEUMS (CONTINUED)

Museum of Science and Industry | South Side | ★★★★★

National Museum of Mexican Art | South Central–
  Midway Airport | ★★★½

National Vietnam Veterans Art Museum | South Loop | ★★★

The Oriental Institute Museum | South Side | ★★★★

The Peggy Notebaert Nature Museum | North Side | ★★★

The Polish Museum of America | North Central–O'Hare Airport | ★★½

Swedish American Museum Center | North Side | ★★½

Ukrainian National Museum of Chicago | North Central–
  O'Hare Airport | ★

SKYSCRAPERS

John Hancock Observatory | Near North Side | ★★★★★

Sears Tower Skydeck | The Loop | ★★★★★

TOURIST LANDMARKS

Adler Planetarium and Astronomy Museum | South Loop | ★★½

Chicago Cultural Center | The Loop | ★★★½

Ernest Hemingway Birthplace Home | North Central–O'Hare Airport | ★½

Frank Lloyd Wright Home and Studio | North Central–
  O'Hare Airport | ★★★★

Harold Washington Library Center | The Loop | ★★★

John G. Shedd Aquarium | South Loop | ★★★★★

Navy Pier | Near North Side | ★★★★

museum shop features calendars, books, cards, gifts (mugs, scarves, posters, CDs), and a huge collection of art books (some at reduced prices).

TOURING TIPS The second-floor gallery of European art is arranged chronologically from late medieval to post-Impressionist, with paintings and sculptures arranged in skylight-brightened rooms; prints and drawings are hung in corridor galleries.

OTHER THINGS TO DO NEARBY The Loop is a block west; Grant Park and Lake Michigan are behind the Art Institute. Walking tours of downtown Chicago start across the street at the Chicago Architecture Foundation; no visit to the Windy City is complete until you've taken at least one. Culture vultures in search of more art (but with a modern slant) can cross Michigan Avenue to the Museum of Contemporary Photography,

Chicago Attractions by Location

ATTRACTION | DESCRIPTION | AUTHOR'S RATING

NORTH SIDE

Chicago History Museum | Chicago, U.S. history | ★★★

DANK-Haus German Cultural Center | All things *Deutsch* | ★★★

Lincoln Park Zoo | Urban animal park | ★★★

Peggy Notebaert Nature Museum | Interactive kids' museum | ★★★

Swedish American Museum Center | Swedish-immigrant story | ★★½

NORTH CENTRAL–O'HARE AIRPORT

Frank Lloyd Wright Home and Studio | Famous architect's home | ★★★★

Garfield Park Conservatory | Botanical gardens | ★★★

Ernest Hemingway Birthplace Home | Victorian house | ★½

Ernest Hemingway Museum | Writer's memorabilia | ★★

Museum of Holography | 3D photo gallery | ★★½

The Polish Museum of America | Ethnic art and history | ★★½

Ukrainian National Museum of Chicago | Folk art | ★

NEAR NORTH SIDE

Chicago Children's Museum | High-tech playground | ★★

International Museum of | History of surgery | ★★½
  Surgical Science

Intuit: The Center for Intuitive and Outsider Art |
  Nontraditional art | ★★★★

John Hancock | 94th-floor view | ★★★★★ | Observatory

Museum of Contemporary Art | Avant-garde art | ★★★★½

Navy Pier | All-purpose tourist mecca | ★★★★

THE LOOP

Art Institute of Chicago | Highbrow art palace | ★★★★★

Chicago Cultural Center | Art, architecture, tourist info | ★★★½

Harold Washington Library Center | Largest library in U.S., art | ★★★

on the grand floor of Columbia College, 600 North Michigan Avenue. It's the only museum of its kind in the Midwest and features rotating exhibits of modern photography. It's free and open weekdays 10 a.m. until 5 p.m. (until 8 p.m. on Thursdays) and Saturdays noon to 5 p.m.; ☎ 312-663-5554; **www.mocp.org.** For lunch, Michigan Avenue has several fast-food places nearby, or try the Euro-deli next to the Chicago Architecture Foundation shop.

ATTRACTION | DESCRIPTION | AUTHOR'S RATING

THE LOOP (CONTINUED)

Sears Tower Skydeck | View from America's tallest building | ★★★★★

SOUTH LOOP

Adler Planetarium and Astronomy Museum | Star show and space exhibits | ★★½

Field Museum of Natural History | Nine acres of natural history | ★★★★★

John G. Shedd Aquarium | Largest indoor fish emporium | ★★★★★

National Vietnam Veterans Art Museum | Emotionally powerful art | ★★★

SOUTH CENTRAL–MIDWAY AIRPORT

Balzekas Museum of Lithuanian Culture | Lithuanian culture and history repository | ★★

Jane Addams Hull-House Museum | Birthplace of social work | ★★½

National Museum of Mexican Art | Mexican art and culture | ★★★½

SOUTH SIDE

David and Alfred Smart Museum of Art | Highbrow art gallery | ★★★

DuSable Museum of African American History | African American art and culture | ★★★½

Museum of Science and Industry | Technology, hands-on exhibits ★★★★★

Oriental Institute Museum | Near East archaeology | ★★★★

SOUTHERN SUBURBS

Brookfield Zoo | Campuslike animal park | ★★★★

WESTERN SUBURBS

The Morton Arboretum | 1,500 acres of trees, shrubs | ★★★½

NORTHERN SUBURBS

Chicago Botanic Garden | Formal, elegant gardens | ★★★★

Balzekas Museum of Lithuanian Culture ★★

| APPEAL BY AGE | GROUP PRESCHOOL ★★ | | GRADE SCHOOL ★★ | TEENS ★★ |
| YOUNG ADULTS ★★ | | OVER 30 ★★ | | SENIORS ★★★ |

6500 South Pulaski Road, South Central–Midway Airport;
☎ **773-582-6500; www.balzekasmuseum.org**

Type of attraction An eclectic collection of exhibits on Lithuanian history and

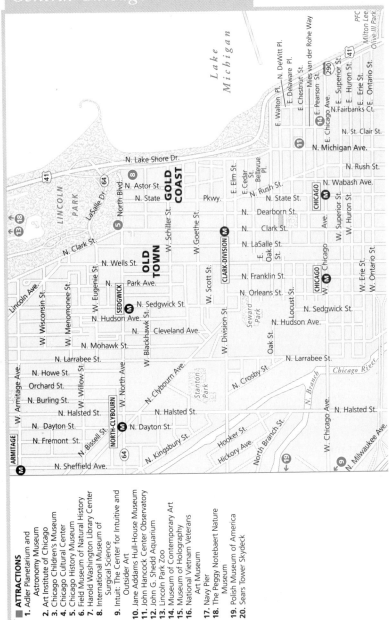

Central Chicago Attractions

ATTRACTIONS
1. Adler Planetarium and Astronomy Museum
2. Art Institute of Chicago
3. Chicago Children's Museum
4. Chicago Cultural Center
5. Chicago History Museum
6. Field Museum of Natural History
7. Harold Washington Library Center
8. International Museum of Surgical Science
9. Intuit: The Center for Intuitive and Outsider Art
10. Jane Addams Hull-House Museum
11. John Hancock Center Observatory
12. John G. Shedd Aquarium
13. Lincoln Park Zoo
14. Museum of Contemporary Art
15. Museum of Holography
16. National Vietnam Veterans Art Museum
17. Navy Pier
18. The Peggy Notebaert Nature Museum
19. Polish Museum of America
20. Sears Tower Skydeck

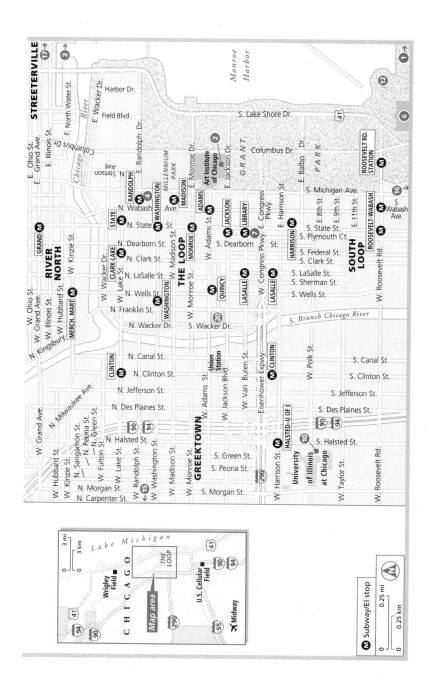

culture; a self-guided tour. **Admission** $5 adults, $4 seniors and students, $2 children; half-price admission during December. **Hours** Daily, 10 a.m.–4 p.m.; closed Easter, Christmas, and New Year's Day. **When to go** Anytime. **Special comments** Call in advance for information on special exhibits and programs. All exhibits are located on the ground floor. Although there's some interesting stuff here, it's a small museum that lacks coherence. **How much time to allow** 30 minutes–1 hour.

DESCRIPTION AND COMMENTS Inside this small museum you'll find items ranging from a suit of armor to press clippings from World War II and everything in between: old photos of immigrants, folk art (including dolls, toys, leather items, wooden household utensils), photos of rural Lithuania, genealogical information, a playroom for children (with a poster depicting the ancient kings of Lithuania), glass cases full of old prayer books, swords, rare books, jewelry, native costumes, coins, stamps. . .

TOURING TIPS Visitors can watch a short video about Lithuania that primes them for a tour of the museum.

OTHER THINGS TO DO NEARBY Not much. If you're flying in or out of Midway, it's only a few blocks away. Oak Park, the hometown of Frank Lloyd Wright and Ernest Hemingway, is about five miles to the north, just off the Eisenhower Expressway (I-290).

kids Brookfield Zoo ★★★★

APPEAL BY AGE	PRESCHOOL ★★★★★	GRADE SCHOOL ★★★★★	TEENS ★★★★
YOUNG ADULTS ★★★★	OVER 30 ★★★★		SENIORS ★★★★

First Avenue and 31st Street, Brookfield (14 miles west of the Loop), Southern Suburbs. By car, take I-55 (Stevenson Expressway), I-290 (Eisenhower Expressway), or I-294 (Tri-State Tollway) and watch for signs. By train, take the Burlington/Metra Northern Line to the Zoo Stop at the Hollywood Station. For information on reaching the zoo by bus, call ☎ 312-836-7000 (city) or 800-972-7000 (suburbs); ☎ 800-201-0784; www.brookfieldzoo.org

Type of attraction A zoo featuring 2,500 animals and more than 400 species spread throughout 215 acres of naturalistic habitat; a self-guided tour. **Admission** $11 adults, $7 seniors age 65 and older and children ages 3–11; free admission on Tuesdays and Thursdays October–December (good only during normal zoo hours). **Hours** *Memorial Day–Labor Day:* daily, 9:30 a.m.–6 p.m. (until 7:30 p.m. Sunday); *rest of year:* daily, 10 a.m.–5 p.m (until 6 p.m. weekends April–May and September–October, until 9 p.m. weekends in December). **When to go** On weekdays in the spring and fall; go after 1:30 p.m. to avoid large school groups. **Special comments** Electronic convenience vehicles, wheelchairs, assistive listening devices, and strollers available. Widely separated buildings, well-landscaped grounds, and a campuslike setting make for a pleasant (not spectacular) zoo. **How much time to allow** 2 hours to half a day.

DESCRIPTION AND COMMENTS Attractions at this lush wooded park include bottlenosed dolphins, stingrays, and re-creations of steamy rain forests featuring exotic animals. More-traditional sights include lions, tigers, snow leopards, reptiles, and elephants. The Australia House features a variety of unusual animals from Down Under.

Although the zoo is spread out, visitors don't necessarily have to hoof it from exhibit to exhibit. Motor Safari, an open-air tram that operates from late spring to early fall, lets you get off and reboard four times along its route; the trams run every 5 to 15 minutes. The fee is $3 for adults and $2 for seniors and children ages 3 to 11.

TOURING TIPS The most popular exhibits at Brookfield Zoo are the dolphin show at the 2,000-seat Seven Seas Panorama ($3 for adults, $2.50 for seniors and kids ages 3 to 11; for showtimes, check at the Web site, zoo kiosks, or the Seven Seas ticket booth; it's free anytime to watch the sea mammals under water through plate-glass windows), Tropic World (a huge indoor rain forest containing gorillas, monkeys, free-flying tropical birds, waterfalls, rocky streams, and big trees), Habitat Africa, "The Swamp" (a replica of a Southern cypress swamp), and summertime elephant demos. The zoo's Wolf Woods features a pack of five male gray wolves on a 2.1-acre site.

First-time visitors can catch a free slide presentation at the Discovery Center that runs every 15 minutes (longer intervals in the winter). Finally, when planning a visit to the zoo, keep in mind that the most pleasant weather occurs in the spring and fall, animals are most active in the mornings and late afternoons, and the zoo is least crowded on rainy, chilly days.

OTHER THINGS TO DO NEARBY Oak Park, hometown of Ernest Hemingway and Frank Lloyd Wright, is a few miles east of the Brookfield Zoo on the Eisenhower Expressway. Take I-290 east to Harlem Avenue (Route 43 north), then turn right on Lake Avenue to Forest Avenue and the visitor center. In addition to snack bars in the zoo, there's fast food on the road linking the zoo and the Eisenhower Expressway.

Chicago Botanic Garden ★★★★

| APPEAL BY AGE | PRESCHOOL ★★★ | GRADE SCHOOL ★★★ | TEENS ★★★ |
| YOUNG ADULTS ★★★★ | OVER 30 ★★★★ | | SENIORS ★★★★★ |

1000 Lake Cook Road, Glencoe, Northern Suburbs. From Chicago, take Sheridan Road north along Lake Michigan, or I-94 (the Edens Expressway) to Lake-Cook Road. The gardens are about 15 miles north of the Loop; ☎ 847-835-5440; www.chicagobotanic.org

Type of attraction 23 formal gardens that feature collections showcasing plants of the Midwest (including plants being tested for their performance in the Chicago area) and native and endangered flora of Illinois; guided and self-guided tours. Admission Free. Parking is $15, $7 for seniors on Tuesday. Hours Daily, 8 a.m.–sunset; closed Christmas. When to go June through August to see the most plants in bloom. Yet staffers say the gardens are gorgeous year-round—and especially after a heavy snowfall. Avoid summer afternoons on weekends, when crowds are at their heaviest; come in the morning and leave by 1 p.m. to miss the worst crowds. Special comments Prohibited activities include bicycling (except on designated bike routes), inline skating, or other sports activities such as Frisbee throwing, skiing, fishing, or skating; collecting plants and flowers; climbing on trees and shrubs; standing or walking in garden beds; and feeding wildlife. No pets are allowed except service animals. A stunning collection of beautifully designed gardens, pathways, ponds and pools, and outdoor sculpture. **How much time to allow** Half a day.

DESCRIPTION AND COMMENTS This living museum is a 385-acre park of gently rolling terrain and water that contains 23 garden areas brimming with plants. Other collections include an herbarium of 12,000 dried plants, rare books, and an art collection of plant-related prints, drawings, sculpture, and decorative objects.

Among the most popular areas are the Japanese, English Walled, Naturalistic, Prairie, and Rose gardens. Linking the formal gardens are paths that wander past lakes, ponds, and greens that are meticulously groomed and provide impressive views. The Orientation Center near the parking lots features an audiovisual presentation, exhibit panels, computers, and a wall map to help visitors plan their visit. Food is available in the Gateway Center, and a picnic area is located between parking lots 1 and 2.

TOURING TIPS Narrated tram tours lasting 45 minutes are offered from April through October; the tours depart every 30 minutes from 10 a.m. to 3:30 p.m. Tickets are $5 for adults, $4 for seniors, and $3 for children ages 3 to 15.

If you're short on time and want to see the garden's highlights, cross the footbridge from the Gateway Center and turn left at the Heritage Garden. Then visit the Rose, English Walled, Waterfall, and Japanese gardens.

Combine a visit with a workout: the North Branch Bicycle Trail starts at Caldwell and Devon avenues in Chicago and continues north 20 miles along the North Branch of the Chicago River to the Chicago Botanic Garden. Bring a lunch and eat it at the picnic area between parking lots 1 and 2.

OTHER THINGS TO DO NEARBY Ravinia, the summer home of the Chicago Symphony Orchestra, is only a few minutes away on Sheridan Road, which follows Lake Michigan and is one of the best scenic drives around Chicago. Take a left onto Lake Cook Road; it becomes Sheridan Road at the third traffic light.

kids Chicago Children's Museum ★★

APPEAL BY AGE	PRESCHOOL ★★★★★	GRADE SCHOOL ★★★★★	TEENS ★
YOUNG ADULTS ★		OVER 30 ★	SENIORS ★

Navy Pier, 600 East Grand Avenue (just north of the Chicago River on the lakefront), Near North Side; ☎ 312-527-1000; www.chicagochildrensmuseum.org

Type of attraction A high-tech playground and engaging interactive exhibits for children up to age 12; a self-guided tour. **Admission** $9 adults and children, $8 seniors, free for infants under age 1; free first Monday of every month (age 15 and under); free family night, Thursday, 5–8 p.m. (all ages); closed Thanksgiving and Christmas. **Hours** Sunday–Wednesday and Friday, 10 a.m.–5 p.m.; Thursday and Saturday, 10 a.m.–8 p.m. **When to go** During the summer, on weekends, and on school holidays, arrive when the museum opens at 10 a.m. During the school year, come in the afternoon to avoid school groups that arrive in the morning. **Special comments** This isn't a babysitting service. While activities are supervised by the museum staff, all children must be accompanied by someone age 16 or older. Nirvana for youngsters through age 12, for other age groups not so much. **How much time to allow** Half a day.

DESCRIPTION AND COMMENTS This $14.5-million, 60,000-square-foot "museum"—really a high-tech playground for ankle biters and kids through the fifth grade—provides an active play and learning environment spread across three levels of Navy Pier. A dozen exhibits provide a range of age-appropriate activities that captivate toddlers as well as older children. One of the most popular attractions is WaterWays, where kids don raincoats (provided) and pump, squirt, and manipulate water (they can shoot a stream 50 feet into the air). In the Inventing Lab, children can build and launch gliders from a 50-foot tower. In Treehouse Trails and Kids Town, youngsters can explore an indoor "nature park" (with a hiking trail, pond, waterfall, trees, log cabin, and animal homes) and shop in a realistic grocery store, change a tire, or "drive" a CTA bus. The Play It Safe exhibit teaches safety at home and in the environment. *Note:* The museum will move to a new location in Daley Plaza in 2010 or 2011.

TOURING TIPS Start a visit with the Climbing Schooner, a three-story replica of a sailing ship that lets kids burn off energy by climbing the rigging up 35 feet to the crow's nest and then sliding down a ladder. Then explore the rest of the museum.

OTHER THINGS TO DO NEARBY Make a day of it by exploring Navy Pier. Take a scenic cruise on Lake Michigan, relax in the IMAX theater, ride the Ferris wheel and carousel, eat lunch in the food court, or simply take a stroll to enjoy the Chicago skyline and Lake Michigan stretching out to the horizon.

Chicago Cultural Center   ★★★½

APPEAL BY AGE	PRESCHOOL ★★	GRADE SCHOOL ★★	TEENS ★★★
YOUNG ADULTS ★★★		OVER 30 ★★★★	SENIORS ★★★★

78 East Washington Street, The Loop; ☎ 312-346-3278; www.chicagoculturalcenter.org

Type of attraction A huge neoclassical structure containing eclectic art and a free visitor-information center; a downtown refuge for weary tourists; a self-guided tour. **Admission** Free. **Hours** Monday–Thursday, 8 a.m.–7 p.m.; Friday, 8 a.m.–6 p.m.; Saturday, 9 a.m.–6 p.m.; closed Columbus Day, Veterans Day, Thanksgiving, Christmas, and New Year's Day. **When to go** Anytime. **Special comments** Free building tours are offered on Wednesday, Friday, and Saturday at 1:15 p.m. An impressive building with a little bit of everything. **How much**

time to allow An hour for a quick run-through. Because of its convenient location and free admission, plan to stop here throughout your visit.

DESCRIPTION AND COMMENTS The nation's first free municipal cultural center served as Chicago's central library for nearly 100 years. Today it dispenses culture the way it once loaned books. Highlights of the building are spectacular stained-glass domes located in the north and south wings, which originally served as skylights. They were later enclosed in copper and backlighted to fully reveal and protect their beauty; the 38-foot dome in Preston Hall is thought to be the world's largest Tiffany dome, with a value estimated at $38 million. Preston Bradley Hall was renovated in the 1970s into a performance hall and hosts free weekly classical music concerts; the G.A.R. Rotunda and Memorial Hall will intrigue Civil War buffs.

First-time visitors to Chicago should take advantage of the Visitor Information Center in the main lobby and the Welcome Center, which provides orientation to the city and downtown. The Randolph Café serves beverages and snacks and provides a respite for weary feet. A number of nearby corridors serve as art galleries showcasing established and emerging artists. The Grand Staircase features multicolored mosaics set in the balustrades, while the fourth floor of the Cultural Center boasts nearly 13,000 square feet of art-exhibition space.

TOURING TIPS Plan to stop at this prime example of 19th-century Beaux Arts architecture early in your visit; the Visitor Information Center in the lobby dispenses free information and touring advice. Then head up the Grand Staircase to view the Tiffany stained-glass dome on the third floor. From there, walk to the fourth-floor exhibition hall to see what's on display. Then take a peek into the beautiful Preston Bradley Hall.

OTHER THINGS TO DO NEARBY The Art Institute of Chicago is two blocks south on Michigan Avenue; the Loop is a block to the west. Directly across from the Art Institute on South Michigan Avenue is the Chicago Architecture Foundation, the starting point of not-to-be-missed daily walking tours of the Loop. For a great view, walk three blocks north to the Michigan Avenue Bridge and look up.

Chicago History Museum ★★★

APPEAL BY AGE	PRESCHOOL ★	GRADE SCHOOL ★★★	TEENS ★★★
YOUNG ADULTS ★★★★		OVER 30 ★★★★	SENIORS ★★★

1601 Clark Street, North Side; ☎ 312-642-4600; www.chicagohistory.org

Type of attraction A spacious 20,000-square-foot museum highlighting Chicago history, from early frontier days to the present; a self-guided tour. Recently rehabbed and renamed to get with the 21st century. Admission $14 adults, $12 seniors age 65 and older and students age 13–22; free for children age 12 and under. General admission free on Monday. Hours Monday–Wednesday, Friday, and Saturday, 9:30 a.m.–4:30 p.m.; Thursday, 9:30 a.m.–8 p.m.; Sunday, noon–5 p.m. When to go Weekdays during the school year; plan your visit in the afternoon after the school field trips are over. Special comments In the past a visit here was as stuffy as the former name. Known for years as the Chicago Historical Society, the museum was closed for nearly a year to reconfigure with a more contemporary vibe. It is now a better museum. Parking spaces for disabled visitors provided in the adjacent lot. There's also a parking garage at Clark and LaSalle that charges $9; enter on Stockton Drive. **How much time to allow** 2 hours.

DESCRIPTION AND COMMENTS Visitors enter off Clark Street, walking through expanses of gridded glass. The clean and modern interior features high ceilings and plenty of elbow room for perusing the many exhibits. The revamped museum includes a new five-sensory gallery devoted to children and a temporary space featuring the work of contemporary Chicago artists.

There are also galleries hung with paintings, glass cases filled with artifacts (in the tradition of Victorian collecting), and a seemingly endless procession of static displays explaining the city's past. The new museum even includes artifacts from the Chicago White Sox 2005 World Series championship. (Winning baseball championships are truly historic events in Chicago: the White Sox broke an 88-year drought in 2005, and the Cubs haven't won a World Series since 1908.) Other exhibitions include a real steam locomotive and miniature scenes depicting Chicago's rapid growth in the 19th century.

TOURING TIPS The centerpiece of the $27.5-million renovation is the new permanent exhibit *Chicago: Crossroads of America,* which dissects the city's defining moments. Visitors can see the city's first elevated train car, purchased in 1892 in order to take tourists to the World's Columbian Exposition of 1893, and items from Riverview Park, which was Chicago's version of Coney Island. There's also *City in Crisis,* which uses artifacts from events such as the 1871 Chicago Fire and *My Kind of Town,* which celebrates the city as a cultural and entertainment center. Chicago blues legend Buddy Guy even performed at the museum's grand reopening.

The museum's critically acclaimed American-history galleries, with artifacts from the Revolutionary and Civil wars, reopened to the public in 2008 after being moved, reconfigured, and enlarged. Hungry? The Big Shoulders Cafe on the first floor gets rave reviews from local diners. The museum also features an excellent Chicago-centric gift shop.

OTHER THINGS TO DO NEARBY The Lincoln Park Zoo is within easy walking distance. Head west on North Avenue to find a selection of fine restaurants and fast-food restaurants. Or take the pedestrian bridge over Lake Shore Drive to take a look at Lake Michigan.

DANK-Haus German Cultural Center ★★★

APPEAL BY AGE	PRESCHOOL –	GRADE SCHOOL ★	TEENS ★
YOUNG ADULTS ★★★★	OVER 30 ★★★★★	SENIORS ★★★★★	

4740 North Western Avenue, North Side; ☎ 773-561-9181; www.dankhaus.com

Type of attraction Cultural and social space. **Admission** Varies. **Hours** 8:30 a.m.–4:30 p.m.; Wednesday, 11 a.m.–7:30 p.m; open later for concerts and special events. **When to go** On an evening when a concert is being held. **Special comments** The center is part museum, part lounge, making a unique atmosphere. **How much time to allow** As much as you want—time drifts away here.

DESCRIPTION AND COMMENTS The DANK-Haus German Cultural Center was founded in 1959 as a chapter of the German American National Congress, a national organization for Americans of German descent (*DANK* is an acronym for the group's name in German). You get an authentic feel of ethnic Chicago at DANK-Haus, located in the heart of the bustling Lincoln Square neighborhood. At noon on Saturdays, old-school Germans gather on the center's second floor for "Kaffee, Kuchen, und Kino": coffee (*Kaffee*), pastries (*Kuchen*), and classic German films (*Kino*) that date back to the 1940s. You need not speak German to hang out.

North Side hipsters flock to the cultural center in the summer and fall for concerts that range from tiki tributes to punk polka in the sixth-floor Skyline Lounge. The adjacent outdoor patio affords one of the most panoramic views of Chicago. Jazz nights are held starting at 8:30 p.m. every first Friday except in December and January. The brick-and-limestone building dates back to 1927, when it opened as the Three Links Association lodge, meeting hall, and hotel. Most of the building was a residential hotel until the late 1960s.

TOURING TIPS The DANK-Haus also has a library with many German and German-American volumes, including works no longer available in Germany, and a fourth-floor museum that is used for rotating exhibits.

OTHER THINGS TO DO NEARBY There's lots of shopping and strolling in Lincoln Square, and the Old Town School of Folk Music (see page 352) is just a few blocks away. The DANK-Haus is a mere half-block from the Western Avenue station on the CTA Brown Line.

David and Alfred Smart Museum of Art ★★★

APPEAL BY AGE	PRESCHOOL ★	GRADE SCHOOL ★★	TEENS ★★★
YOUNG ADULTS ★★★		OVER 30 ★★★	SENIORS ★★★

5550 South Greenwood Avenue (on the University of Chicago campus), South Side; ☎ **312-702-0200; smartmuseum.uchicago.edu**

Type of attraction A collection of art objects spanning five millennia, including works by Albrecht Dürer, Auguste Rodin, Frank Lloyd Wright, Walker Evans, and Mark Rothko; a self-guided tour. **Admission** Free. **Hours** Tuesday, Wednesday, and Friday, 10 a.m.–4 p.m.; Thursday, 10 a.m.–8 p.m.; Saturday and Sunday, 11 a.m.–5 p.m.; closed Monday and holidays. **When to go** Anytime. **Special comments** All the galleries are on 1 level and are wheelchair-accessible. Free parking is available in the lot on the corner of 55th Street and Greenwood Avenue on weekends. A sparkling white series of rooms featuring an eclectic array of art; you're sure to find something you like. **How much time to allow** 1–2 hours.

DESCRIPTION AND COMMENTS The art on display ranges from ancient Greek to outrageous modern works culled from a permanent collection of more than 7,000 objects. In addition, the museum schedules eight special exhibitions each year. The feel of the place, like the campus around it, is serious, cerebral, and highbrow.

TOURING TIPS Don't miss the furniture on display designed by Frank Lloyd Wright. In particular, *Dining Table and Six Side Chairs* (1907–1910) is a prime example of the Chicago architect's spare, modern style. (And you thought the Wizard of Oak Park only designed houses you can't afford.) The Smart, a museum named for the founders of *Esquire* magazine, is a compact and easy gallery to explore. The bookstore features art books, posters, cards, children's books, and jewelry. A cafe offers sandwiches, salads, pastas, and other goodies.

OTHER THINGS TO DO NEARBY The Oriental Institute Museum and the DuSable Museum are close. If the weather is nice, stroll the beautiful University of Chicago campus; look for the Henry Moore sculpture (placed on the site of the first self-sustaining nuclear reaction on December 2, 1942) across from the Enrico Fermi Institute. The massive Museum of Science and Industry (see page 179) is on 57th Street. Join the locals for lunch at Valois, at 1518 East 53rd Street (☎ 773-667-0647).

DuSable Museum of African American History ★★★½

APPEAL BY AGE	PRESCHOOL ★★	GRADE SCHOOL ★★★	TEENS ★★★
YOUNG ADULTS ★★★	OVER 30 ★★★★		SENIORS ★★★★

740 East 56th Place (57th Street and Cottage Avenue near the eastern edge of the University of Chicago), South Side; ☎ 773-947-0600; www.dusablemuseum.org

Type of attraction A collection of artifacts, paintings, and photos that trace the black experience in the United States; a self-guided tour. Admission $3 adults, $2 students, $1 children ages 6–13; free for children under age 6 and for everyone on Sunday. Hours Monday–Saturday, 10 a.m.–5 p.m.; Sunday, noon–5 p.m.; closed Monday, June through December; the third Saturday and Sunday in February; and most major holidays. When to go Anytime. Special comments The large main-floor gallery hosts permanent exhibits; check the *Chicago Reader* or call before visiting to find out what's on display in the museum's temporary exhibits on the upper levels. Fascinating stuff, including, on our visit, an eye-opening show on the everyday lives of slaves in the antebellum South. How much time to allow 1–2 hours.

DESCRIPTION AND COMMENTS This museum, which once served as a park-administration building and a police lockup, is named after Jean-Baptiste Pointe du Sable, a Haitian of mixed African and European descent who was Chicago's first permanent settler in the late 18th century. Exhibits include paintings by African Americans, displays that vividly portray the lives of blacks in pre–Civil War days, and a room dedicated to black hero Joe Louis.

TOURING TIPS Avoid weekday mornings, when large school groups schedule visits; Sundays, when admission is free, are also crowded. The gift shop features jewelry, fabrics, and arts and crafts created by African Americans.

OTHER THINGS TO DO NEARBY Outside the DuSable Museum, the beautiful lawns of Washington Park beckon in nice weather. The nearby University of Chicago campus is a great place to stroll; other places to visit include the Oriental Institute Museum and the Smart Museum of Art. The immense Museum of Science and Industry is on 57th Street. Valois. Don't venture too far from the campus, though; the neighborhood is only marginally safe.

Ernest Hemingway Birthplace Home ★½

APPEAL BY AGE	PRESCHOOL ★	GRADE SCHOOL ★	TEENS ★★
YOUNG ADULTS ★★	OVER 30 ★★		SENIORS ★★

339 North Oak Park Avenue, Oak Park, North Central–O'Hare Airport; ☎ 708-848-2222

Type of attraction The restored Victorian house where Ernest Hemingway was born in 1899; a guided tour. **Admission** $8 adults, $6 seniors and students, free for children age 5 and under; fee covers admission to both museum (see following profile) and birthplace. **Hours** Sunday–Friday, 1–5 p.m.; Saturday, 10 a.m.–5 p.m. **When to go** Anytime. **Special comments** One short but rather steep flight of stairs leads to the second floor. Strictly for die-hard Hemingway fans. **How much time to allow** 45 minutes.

DESCRIPTION AND COMMENTS Despite a nearly complete restoration, this fine Victorian house (opened to the public in 1993) will only interest folks seeking a glimpse of upper-middle-class life in turn-of-the-19th-century Oak Park. Hemingway lived here for a mere five years as a child, and only a few of the items on display are original. Upstairs, visitors can look into (but can't enter) the lavishly restored room where the writer was born.

TOURING TIPS Look for the embalmed muskrats (at least, that's what we and the docent guessed they are) that Hemingway and his doctor father stuffed when the great writer was a boy. Unfortunately, visitors are subjected to a much-too-long video (15 minutes, actually) that tells them more than they'll ever want to know about the Nobel Prize winner's grandparents.

OTHER THINGS TO DO NEARBY The Ernest Hemingway Museum is down the street; the Frank Lloyd Wright Home and Studio is only a few blocks away (see profiles below and on page 169). Unity Temple, a National Historic Landmark designed by Wright in 1905, is located at 951 Chicago Avenue; it's considered a masterpiece and is open weekdays 10:30 a.m. to 3:30 p.m. for self-guided tours ($12 for adults and $10 for seniors and children under age 18). Downtown Oak Park offers several dining and fast-food options. Brookfield Zoo is a few miles west, off I-290.

Ernest Hemingway Museum ★★

APPEAL BY AGE	PRESCHOOL ★	GRADE SCHOOL ★	TEENS ★★
YOUNG ADULTS ★★	OVER 30 ★★		SENIORS ★★

Oak Park Arts Center, 200 North Oak Park Avenue, Oak Park, North Central–O'Hare Airport; ☎ 708-848-2222; www.ehfop.org

Type of attraction A small collection of exhibits featuring rare photos of the Nobel laureate, his childhood diary, letters, early writing, and other memorabilia focusing on the writer's Oak Park years; a self-guided tour. **Admission** $8 adults, $6 seniors and students, free for children age 5 and under; fee covers admission to both museum and birthplace (see previous profile). **Hours** Sunday–Friday, 1–5 p.m.; Saturday, 10 a.m.–5 p.m. **When to go** Anytime. **Special comments** Hemingway's Birthplace is about a block and a half away on the other side of Oak Park Avenue. A *very* narrow slice of the great writer's life that will be best appreciated by hard-core fans. **How much time to allow** 30 minutes.

DESCRIPTION AND COMMENTS A handful of display cases in the basement of a former church house this small collection of Hemingway memorabilia. Artifacts on view range from photos, diaries, and family items to a violin and typewriter once owned by the writer, whom many critics consider the greatest American author. A six-minute video recalls Hemingway's upper-middle-class high-school years . . . but doesn't mention that he left town for good at age 20 and, unlike most famous writers from Chicago, wrote very little about his hometown.

TOURING TIPS There's one gem to be found in this smallish collection: the "Dear John" letter Hemingway received from Agnes von Kurowsky, the nurse who tended his wounds in Italy after he was injured while serving as a volunteer ambulance driver during World War I. "For the rest of his life Hemingway was marked by his scars from battle and by an abiding distrust of women," the exhibit notes. Hem got his revenge, though; check out the ending of *A Farewell to Arms*—the beautiful nurse who tended the wounded hero croaks in the last chapter. What you *won't* find is any reference to his alleged remark that Oak Park is a town of "broad lawns and narrow minds."

OTHER THINGS TO DO NEARBY The Frank Lloyd Wright Home and Studio (see page 169) is only a few blocks away. Unity Temple, a National Historic Landmark designed by Wright in 1905, is located at 875 Lake Street; it's considered a masterpiece and is open weekdays 10:30 a.m. to 4:30 p.m. for self-guided and group tours ($8 for adults, $6 for groups, seniors, and students age 22 and under, free for children age 5 and under), and on weekends for guided tours at 1, 2, and 3 p.m.; call ☎ 708-383-8873 or visit **www.unitytemple-utrf.org** for more information. Downtown Oak Park has a selection of dining and fast-food options. Brookfield Zoo (see page 158) is a few miles west off the Eisenhower Expressway (take Route 171 south).

kids **Field Museum of Natural History** ★★★★★

| APPEAL BY AGE | PRESCHOOL ★★★★★ | GRADE SCHOOL ★★★★★ | TEENS ★★★★★ |
| YOUNG ADULTS ★★★★★ | | OVER 30 ★★★★★ | SENIORS ★★★★ |

1400 South Lake Shore Drive (in Grant Park), South Loop;
☎ **312-922-9410; www.fieldmuseum.org**

Type of attraction One of the largest public museums in the United States, with more than 9 acres of exhibits; a self-guided tour. **Admission** $14 adults,

$11 seniors and students, $9 children ages 4–11; $15 parking (north garage). Free admission to all exhibits the second Monday of each month; free general admission on other select dates (check Web site for details). **Hours** Daily, 9 a.m.–5 p.m.; closed Christmas. **When to go** Anytime. **Special comments** If someone in your party needs to make a pit stop while touring the special exhibits, go to the Dinosaur Hall exit and speak to a Visitor Services Representative (in a red jacket). This world-renowned institution draws on more than 20 million artifacts and specimens to fill its exhibits. If you can't find something you like here, it's time to get out of Chicago. **How much time to allow** 2 hours for a brief run-through; all day for a more leisurely exploration (but even then you won't see it all).

DESCRIPTION AND COMMENTS Founded in 1893 to create a permanent home for the natural-history collections gathered in Chicago for the World's Columbian Exposition, the Field Museum today is one of the great institutions of its kind in the world, focusing on public learning and scientific study of the world's environments and cultures. For visitors, it's a chance to explore a mind-boggling assortment of the world's wonders.

While much of the museum reflects the Victorian mania for specimen collecting—aisle after aisle of wood-and-glass display cases and dioramas are filled with items from around the world—much of what you find here includes newer, more dynamic exhibits. Many emphasize hands-on fun and thematic exhibits, such as *Africa, Underground Adventure, Inside Ancient Egypt, Traveling the Pacific,* and *Evolving Planet,* a high-tech journey that takes visitors through 4 billion years of the history of life.

TOURING TIPS Folks with youngsters in tow or with a strong interest in dinosaurs should make their way to the second level to explore *Evolving Planet.* It's a kid-oriented exhibit that's heavy on education, hands-on science stuff, and TV monitors showing "newscasts" by suit-clad anchors "reporting" on the beginning of life a billion years ago. It all ends up in a huge hall filled with dinosaur fossils and reconstructed skeletons. It's pure bliss for the Barney crowd.

After exploring the world of dinosaurs and mammoths (including Sue, the largest, most complete fossil of *T. rex* yet discovered), check your map and pick something of interest. Here's some help: Tots will enjoy the play area on the second floor, while older folks can check out exhibits of gems and jades also on the second floor. The popular Egyptian tomb (complete with mummies) is on the first floor, as are exhibits on Native Americans, Africa, birds, reptiles, a re-creation of a wilderness, and a "nature" walk. The ground floor features places to grab a bite to eat and exhibits on bushmen, sea mammals, prehistoric people, and ancient Egypt. Finally, an indoor parking garage provides spaces for 2,500 cars (across McFetridge Drive); $15 per day.

OTHER THINGS TO DO NEARBY The Shedd Aquarium and Adler Planetarium are both within easy walking distance on the new, traffic-free Museum Campus. Fast food is available inside the museum, but anything else requires taking a cab or bus downtown.

Frank Lloyd Wright Home and Studio ★★★★

| APPEAL BY AGE | PRESCHOOL ★ | GRADE SCHOOL ★★ | TEENS ★★ |
| YOUNG ADULTS ★★★ | OVER 30 ★★★★ | | SENIORS ★★★★ |

951 Chicago Avenue, Oak Park, North Central–O'Hare Airport. If you drive, park in the garage next to the Oak Park Visitor Center at 158 Forest Avenue. The center is open daily (except Thanksgiving, Christmas, and New Year's Day) from 10 a.m. to 5 p.m. and centrally located, within easy walking distance to all the Wright and Hemingway attractions in town; purchase your tickets and pick up a map and more information inside. Parking in the garage is free on weekends; ☎ 708-848-1976; www.wrightplus.org

Type of attraction The Oak Park home of famed architect Frank Lloyd Wright and the birthplace of the Prairie School of architecture; guided and self-guided tours. **Admission** *Guided home and studio tours, guided and self-guided historic-district walking tours:* $12 adults, $10 seniors age 65 and over and children ages 11–18, $5 children ages 4–10, free for children age 3 and under. **Hours** 45-minute guided home and studio tours begin at 11 a.m., 1 p.m., and 3 p.m. Monday–Friday and about every 20 minutes 11 a.m.–3:30 p.m. on weekends; closed Thanksgiving, Christmas, and New Year's Day. Self-guided hourlong tours of the exteriors of 13 Wright-designed houses along nearby Forest Avenue are available 10 a.m.–3:30 p.m. daily. Guided walking tours of the neighborhood take place at 11 a.m. and 4 p.m. weekends, March–October; tours begin at noon, 1 p.m., and 2 p.m., November–February. **When to go** Anytime. For the walking tours, bring an umbrella if it looks like rain. **Special comments** The house tour involves climbing and descending a flight of stairs. A fascinating glimpse into the life of America's greatest architect. **How much time to allow** 1 hour.

DESCRIPTION AND COMMENTS Between 1889 and 1909, this house with prominent gables, window bays, and dark, shingled surfaces served as home, studio, and architectural laboratory for young Chicago architect Frank Lloyd Wright. Today it offers a permanent visual record of the beginnings of his continuous exploration of the relationship of light, form, and space. This is where Wright established the principles that guided his life work and launched a revolution that changed the architectural landscape of the 20th century. Yet this house that Wright built with $5,000 borrowed from his employer doesn't reflect his Prairie School of design, the first distinctly American style of architecture featuring low, earth-hugging dwellings. That would come later.

TOURING TIPS What's fascinating about the tour—and what you should watch out for—are glimpses of early examples of elements that would become hallmarks of a Wright-designed home: large rooms that flow together, unity of design, minimal form, functionality, and the fusion of art and design elements. The tour guides do a good job of pointing them out.

The studio, which ends the tour and was added to the house by Wright in 1898, is a stunner, with walls supported by chains and a two-story octagonal drafting room. Here, working with 15 apprentices,

Wright completed about 150 commissions and refined his Prairie School principles.

OTHER THINGS TO DO NEARBY The Ernest Hemingway Birthplace Home and Museum (see page 166) are only a few blocks away; both destinations are pleasant walks when the weather is nice. Unity Temple, a National Historic Landmark designed by Wright in 1905, is located at 875 Lake Street; it's considered a masterpiece and is open weekdays 10:30 a.m. to 4:30 p.m. for self-guided and group tours ($8 for adults, $6 for groups, seniors, and students age 22 and under, free for children age 5 and under), and on weekends for guided tours at 1, 2, and 3 p.m.; call ☎ 708-383-8873 or visit **www.unitytemple-utrf.org** for more information.

Garfield Park Conservatory ★★★

APPEAL BY AGE	PRESCHOOL ★★★	GRADE SCHOOL ★★★	TEENS ★★★
YOUNG ADULTS ★★★	OVER 30 ★★★		SENIORS ★★★

300 North Central Park Avenue, North Central–O'Hare Airport;
☎ **312-746-5100; www.garfield-conservatory.org**

Type of attraction Four and a half acres of grounds and 5,000 species and varieties of plants, most of them housed under the glass of a landmark 1907 structure; self-guided tours. Admission Free; donations (generally $1 or $2) suggested for flower shows. Hours Daily, 9 a.m.–5 p.m. (until 8 p.m. Thursday). When to go Anytime. Special comments Garfield Park is in a high-crime area, although the park itself is quite safe; the free parking lot is only a few steps away from the conservatory entrance. Some really big plants (many dating from 1907) and plenty of interior space promote a feeling of serenity. How much time to allow 1 hour (or longer if you've got a green thumb).

DESCRIPTION AND COMMENTS Four times as large as the conservatory in Lincoln Park, the Garfield Park Conservatory offers a world-class collection of botanical gardens for visitors to enjoy. The Palm House displays a variety of graceful palms, while the Desert House encloses one of the nation's finest cactus displays (including giant saguaros) arranged in a typical Southwestern desert motif.

TOURING TIPS Horticulture hounds and home gardeners can quiz the trained personnel that staff the conservatory about house plants and gardening in general. If you can't make it in person, call in your questions at ☎ 312-746-5100. The conservatory hosts major flower shows throughout the year; see "A Calendar of Festivals and Events" in Part Two, Planning Your Visit to Chicago (page 31).

OTHER THINGS TO DO NEARBY Garfield Park, one of the areas of green linked by the city's network of boulevards, has outdoor gardens and sculpture, miles of walking trails, and more. It's best, though, not to venture into the neighborhood surrounding the park.

Harold Washington Library Center ★★★

APPEAL BY AGE	GROUP PRESCHOOL ★	GRADE SCHOOL ★★	TEENS ★★
YOUNG ADULTS ★★★	OVER 30 ★★★		SENIORS ★★★

400 South State Street, The Loop; ☎ 312-747-4300;
www.chipublib.org/branch/details/library/harold-washington

Type of attraction The world's second-largest public library (after the British Library in London); guided and self-guided tours. **Admission** Free. **Hours** Monday–Thursday, 9 a.m.–9 p.m.; Friday and Saturday, 9 a.m.–5 p.m.; Sunday, 1–5 p.m. **When to go** Anytime. **Special comments** The library isn't very visitor-friendly: From the enclosed lobby on the 1st floor, take the escalators to the 3rd floor, which serves as the main entrance to the library proper. From there, elevators and escalators provide access to the other 7 levels. Conversely, to leave the building, you must return to the 3rd floor and take the escalators down to the exit level (elevators are available for disabled folks). What a pain. Though a trip to the library isn't on most travel itineraries, consider making an exception in Chicago. It's definitely worth a stop. **How much time to allow** An hour; consider joining a free public tour beginning at 2 p.m., Monday through Sunday. The guided tour lasts an hour and starts in the 3rd-floor Orientation Theater.

DESCRIPTION AND COMMENTS This neoclassical building with elements of Beaux Arts, classical, and modern ornamentation opened in 1991 and cost $144 million. Named after the late Chicago mayor (a notorious bookworm), the 750,000-square-foot Harold Washington Library Center serves as the Loop's southern gateway.

Inside are housed more than 2 million volumes; an electronic directory system that displays floor layouts, book locations, and upcoming events; a computerized reference system; more than 70 miles of shelving; a permanent collection of art spread over ten floors.

TOURING TIPS Several not-to-be-missed attractions include the ninth-floor glass-enclosed Winter Garden; the Harold Washington Collection (an exhibit located next to the Winter Garden); and the Chicago Blues Archives (eighth floor).

Folks with time and interest should visit the eighth-floor Listening/Viewing Center, where patrons can watch videos and listen to music from the collection's 100,000 78-rpm records, LPs, and CDs. Selections are particularly plentiful in popular music, jazz, and blues. Hours are Tuesday through Thursday, 1 until 6 p.m.; Friday and Saturday, 1 to 4:30 p.m.; closed Sunday. You don't have to be a Chicago resident to take advantage of the free service, although all patrons are limited to one session per day; there is a one-hour time limit if other people are waiting. Because the Center relies on a large array of electronics, it's often closed for maintenance; call ☎ 312-747-4850 before going.

In addition, the library presents a wide range of special events throughout the year, including films, dance programs, lectures, story-telling sessions for children, concerts, special programs for children, art exhibits, and more. See the *Chicago Reader* (a free alternative paper) to find out what's happening during your visit.

OTHER THINGS TO DO NEARBY The Loop is a block to the north; hang a right to head toward Grant Park and the Art Institute of Chicago. Turn left at the elevated tracks to reach the Chicago Board of Trade and the

Sears Tower. Eating and shopping establishments abound throughout the heart of downtown.

International Museum of Surgical Science ★★½

APPEAL BY AGE	PRESCHOOL ★	GRADE SCHOOL ★★	TEENS ★★
YOUNG ADULTS ★★★	OVER 30 ★★★		SENIORS ★★★

1524 North Lake Shore Drive, Near North Side; ☎ 312-642-6502; www.imss.org

Type of attraction Exhibits from around the world trace the history of surgery and related sciences; a self-guided tour. **Admission** $10 adults, $6 seniors and students; free on Tuesday with a suggested donation of the regular admission; guided tours on Saturday ($3; reservation required). **Hours** *October–April:* Tuesday–Saturday, 10 a.m.–4 p.m.; *May–September:* Tuesday–Sunday, 10 a.m–4 p.m. **When to go** Anytime. **Special comments** Though the truly squeamish should avoid this place like the plague, there's actually very little on display that's overtly gory or upsetting. The museum is located on the #151 bus route, and limited parking is available in a small lot behind the building; additional parking is located in Lincoln Park and at North Avenue Beach. It's a short, pleasant stroll away from North Michigan Avenue. A must-see for folks in the medical field; otherwise, it's a nice fill-in spot when exploring the Gold Coast on foot. **How much time to allow** 1 hour for most folks; half a day for those with a keen interest in medical science.

DESCRIPTION AND COMMENTS The mysteries, breakthroughs, failures, and historic milestones of surgical science are on display in this unusual museum housed in an elegant mansion facing Lake Michigan. Implements on display range from the truly horrifying (2,000-year-old skulls with holes bored into them and tin-and-wood enema syringes from the 1800s) to the quaint (such as an X-ray shoe fitter from the early 1950s). The first floor features a re-creation of a 19th-century pharmacy and an early-20th-century dentist's office.

TOURING TIPS Start on the first floor and explore displays of antique medical instruments, then work your way up to the fourth floor. The second floor's Hall of Immortals features 12 eight-foot statues representing great medical figures in history, while the third floor includes an exhibit of antique microscopes and early X-ray equipment. Look for Napoleon's original death mask and more ancient medical instruments on the fourth floor. A guided tour is offered on Saturdays at 2 p.m.; call ☎ 312-642-6502, ext. 3130, for a reservation.

OTHER THINGS TO DO NEARBY Explore Chicago's opulent Gold Coast neighborhood on foot. It's only a few blocks south to the Magnificent Mile, which features expensive shops, malls, department stores, and a knock-your-socks-off view from the 94th-floor observatory in the John Hancock Center (when it's not raining).

Intuit: The Center for Intuitive and Outsider Art) ★★★★

APPEAL BY AGE	PRESCHOOL –	GRADE SCHOOL ★	TEENS ★★★
YOUNG ADULTS ★★★★	OVER 30 ★★★★★		SENIORS ★★★★★

756 North Milwaukee Avenue, Near North Side; ☎ 312-243-9088; www.art.org

Type of attraction Repository of works by quirky self-taught artists. **Admission** Free. **Hours** Tuesday–Saturday, 11 a.m.–5 p.m.; until 7:30 p.m. Thursday. **When to go** Thursday night and Saturday (when parking tends to be easier). **Special comments** If you're looking for something affordable and outside the norm in Chicago, this is your place. **How much time to allow** 30 minutes.

DESCRIPTION AND COMMENTS Founded in 1991, Intuit has grown to become one of America's focal points of the outsider-art movement. The loftlike street-level space promotes understanding of the work of artists who demonstrate little or no influence from the mainstream art world. Intuit's permanent collection includes the works of William Dawson, Minnie Evans, Howard Finster, Wesley Willis, and many others.

In 2008, the museum's crowning jewel was set with the permanent installation of the Henry Darger Room, featuring the artist's furnishings (including his chair and work table) and architectural components (including a fireplace and mantel) from his original one-room Chicago apartment. Darger, a church janitor and eccentric who lived a largely solitary life, was most prolific in the 1930s and '40s. He produced a large quantity of watercolored and collaged drawings to illustrate his self-penned, 15,000-page epic fantasy (*In the Realms of the Unreal*); wrote a multivolume autobiography and kept various journals; and collected diverse objects such as eyeglasses and balls of string. The exhibit offers a compelling window into Darger's kinetic world.

TOURING TIPS Allow a half hour to see the collection, but be sure to check out the nifty gift shop and the new Robert A. Roth Study Center. The cozy library features a noncirculating collection with an emphasis on the fields of outsider and contemporary self-taught art. Intuit's holdings include books, catalogs, periodicals, slides, photographs, and videotapes, many of them dating back to the 1960s and '70s, when the outsider-art movement began to take form in Chicago. Access to the collection is dependent on staff availability; to schedule an appointment, e-mail **studycenter@art.org** with your request.

OTHER THINGS TO DO NEARBY Intuit staff and visitors often can be seen having a burger and a beer next door at The Matchbox (see nightlife profile on page 351), and the gallery is less than a five-minute ride from the Loop and downtown.

Jane Addams Hull-House Museum ★★½

APPEAL BY AGE	PRESCHOOL ★	GRADE SCHOOL ★★	TEENS ★★★
YOUNG ADULTS ★★★		OVER 30 ★★★	SENIORS ★★★

800 South Halsted Street, on the campus of the University of Illinois at Chicago, South Central–Midway Airport; ☎ 312-413-5353; www.hullhousemuseum.org

Type of attraction The restored 1856 country home that became the nucleus of the world-famous settlement-house complex founded by Jane Addams (a Nobel

Peace Prize winner) at the end of the 19th century; a self-guided tour. **Admission** Free; parking $2.75–$11. **Hours** Tuesday–Friday, 10 a.m.–4 p.m.; Sunday, noon– 4 p.m.; closed Monday and Saturday. **When to go** Anytime. **Special comments** Park across the street in the University of Illinois parking lot. An oasis of dignity, this restored museum is all that remains of a once-vibrant ethnic melting pot served by the Nobel laureate. **How much time to allow** 1 hour.

DESCRIPTION AND COMMENTS This square brick 19th-century house in the shadow of the University of Illinois at Chicago is where Jane Addams and Ellen Gates Starr began the settlement work that helped give immigrants a better shot at the American dream. The lush Victorian interior includes Addams's desk, an old Oliver typewriter, photos of the staff, and several rooms of rich furnishings.

TOURING TIPS Start your tour upstairs in the residents' dining hall with the 15-minute slide show on the settlement-house movement. The tour ends in the restored mansion.

OTHER THINGS TO DO NEARBY Sample some pasta in Little Italy, southwest of the University of Illinois campus. Greektown and more great ethnic dining are north on Halsted, just past the Eisenhower Expressway. The Loop is a few blocks to the northeast.

kids John G. Shedd Aquarium ★★★★★

APPEAL BY AGE	PRESCHOOL ★★★★★	GRADE SCHOOL ★★★★★	TEENS ★★★★★
YOUNG ADULTS ★★★★★		OVER 30 ★★★★★	SENIORS ★★★★★

1200 South Lake Shore Drive, South Loop; ☎ 312-939-2438; www.sheddaquarium.org

Type of attraction The world's largest indoor aquarium; the Oceanarium, the world's largest indoor marine-mammal facility, which re-creates a Pacific Northwest coastline; a self-guided tour. **Admission** *Aquarium only:* $11 adults, $9 seniors age 65 and over and children ages 3–11; free for kids age 2 and under, and for everyone Monday and Tuesday. *Total Experience Pass (includes general admission plus all exhibits, dog show, and one 4-D presentation):* $17.95 adults, $13.95 kids and seniors. **Hours** Monday–Friday, 9 a.m.–5 p.m. (until 6 p.m. weekends and in summer), closed Christmas. The Oceanarium is closed for renovations until June 2009. **When to go** Before noon during the summer and on major holidays. Try to time your visit to coincide with the aquarium's Caribbean Reef feedings—a diver enters the circular 90,000-gallon exhibit and hand-feeds an assortment of tropical fish; kids love it. Feeding times are 9:30 a.m., 11 a.m., 12:30 p.m., 1:30 p.m., 3 p.m., and 3:30 p.m. daily. **Special comments** Invest in one of the all-access passes—they give you a lot for the money. **How much time to allow** 2 hours.

DESCRIPTION AND COMMENTS Not only does the Shedd Aquarium house more than 22,000 aquatic animals, the building itself is an architectural marvel, featuring majestic doorways, colorful mosaics, and wave and shell patterns on the walls. The Oceanarium, which treats visitors to a wide array of sea mammals through glass windows, is currently closed while habitats and life-support systems are being renovated and new interactive exhibits created. It's scheduled to reopen in June 2009; the aquarium's Web site features blogs and photos that chronicle the progress of the renovation. A new dog show in Phelps Auditorium demonstrates the adaptability of whale- and dolphin-training techniques to man's best friend.

In the aquarium, cool and dark rooms are lined with tanks filled with a wide assortment of creatures, including a huge alligator, snapping turtle, electric eels, piranhas, and an especially creepy-looking green moray eel (which, we're sad to report, is actually blue; its skin appears green because it's coated with thick yellow mucus—yuck). The *Amazon Rising* exhibit features 250 species in a re-creation of the Amazon River Basin.

TOURING TIPS   Check out one of the 4-D theater presentations in Phelps Auditorium. They combine high-definition digital 3-D video, high-tech audio, and "special FX" seats with various sensory surprises. And don't forget about the feedings in the coral reef (see previous page for times).

OTHER THINGS TO DO NEARBY   The Adler Planetarium and the Field Museum of Natural History are both within walking distance on the traffic-free Museum Campus. If it's late in the afternoon and the sun's about to set, stick around; the Chicago skyline is about to do its nighttime thing. It's a view you won't soon forget.

  John Hancock Observatory ★★★★★

APPEAL BY AGE	PRESCHOOL ★★★★★	GRADE SCHOOL ★★★★★	TEENS ★★★★★
YOUNG ADULTS ★★★★★		OVER 30 ★★★★★	SENIORS ★★★★★

875 North Michigan Avenue, Near North Side; ☎ 888-875-VIEW** or ☎ 312-751-3681; www.hancock-observatory.com**

Type of attraction A 39-second elevator ride leading to a spectacular 94th-floor view of Chicago; a self-guided tour. **Admission** $15 adults, $13 seniors, $9 children ages 4–11, free for children under age 4; prices include self-guided multimedia Sky Tour. **Hours** Daily, 9 a.m.–11 p.m. (no tickets sold after 10:45 p.m.). **When to go** Anytime. **Special comments** This is an excellent alternative to the Sears Tower Skydeck, where the lines can be very long. In fact, most Chicagoans say the view is better. If the top of the building is hidden in clouds, come back another day. A stunning view, especially at sunset or at night. **How much time to allow** 30 minutes.

DESCRIPTION AND COMMENTS   This distinctive building with the X-shaped exterior crossbracing is the 16th-tallest structure in the world. Although the 94th-floor observatory is nine floors lower than the Sears Tower Skydeck, some folks say the view is better here, perhaps due to its proximity to Lake Michigan.

TOURING TIPS   The ideal way to enjoy the vista (you're 1,030 feet above Michigan Avenue) is to arrive just before sunset. As the sun sinks lower in the west, slowly the city lights blink on—and a whole new view appears.

OTHER THINGS TO DO NEARBY The 95th and 96th floors of the John Hancock Center house the highest restaurant and lounge in the city. (You can relax with a drink for about the same cost as visiting the observatory, but there's no guarantee you'll get a seat with a view.) Or return to street level and shop till you drop along chichi North Michigan Avenue; the Water Tower Place shopping mall is next door.

kids Lincoln Park Zoo ★★★

APPEAL BY AGE	PRESCHOOL ★★★★	GRADE SCHOOL ★★★★★	TEENS ★★★★★
YOUNG ADULTS ★★★★		OVER 30 ★★★	SENIORS ★★★★

2200 North Cannon Drive (Lincoln Park, off Lake Shore Drive at Fullerton Avenue north of the Magnificent Mile), North Side; ☎ 312-742-2000; www.lpzoo.com

Type of attraction The most visited zoo in the nation, featuring more than 1,600 animals, birds, and reptiles; a self-guided tour. **Admission** Free; parking $14–$24. **Hours** Daily, 9 a.m.–6 p.m. (until 5 p.m. November 1–March 31 and until 7 p.m. Memorial Day–Labor Day); buildings open at 10 a.m. **When to go** Anytime, except weekday mornings from mid-April to mid-June, when as many as 100 school buses converge on the zoo; by 1:30 p.m., the hordes of youngsters are gone. Weekend afternoons during the summer also attract big crowds. **Special comments** Don't rule out a visit on a rainy or cold day: a lot of the animals are housed indoors. Interestingly enough, neighbors residing in nearby high-rises report they can hear wolves howling on warm summer nights. Alas, this stately, old-fashioned zoo isn't in the same league as newer animal parks springing up around the nation. But it's still a refreshing oasis in the heart of bustling Chicago. **How much time to allow** 2 hours.

DESCRIPTION AND COMMENTS Beautifully landscaped grounds, Lake Michigan, nearby high-rises, and the Chicago skyline in the distance are the hallmarks of this venerable but smallish park. Plus, the stately old buildings that house many of the zoo's inhabitants lend a Victorian elegance. Adults and especially children won't want to miss the Farm-in-the-Zoo (a farm featuring chickens, horses, and cows) and a children's zoo where the kids can enjoy a collection of small animals at eye level.

TOURING TIPS If you're pressed for time, the most popular exhibits at the zoo are the polar bears, the elephants, and (hold your nose) the Regenstein Center for African Apes, where chimps and gorillas cavort behind thick panes of glass. Before or after your visit, stop by the Lincoln Park Conservatory, three acres of Victorian greenhouses built in 1891 that provide a lush rain-forest setting for flora and fauna from around the world. Seasonally, the Christmas poinsettias and Easter lilies draw huge crowds.

The conservatory is just outside the zoo's northwest entrance (near the elephants), and it's free. The restored Café Brauer serves salads, sandwiches, and ice cream.

OTHER THINGS TO DO NEARBY The Chicago History Museum (and its acclaimed cafe) is an easy stroll from the zoo. A walk west for a block or two leads to a number of fast-food restaurants. Or take the pedestrian bridge across Lake Shore Drive and watch the waves crash against the Lake Michigan shoreline.

The Morton Arboretum   ★★★½

APPEAL BY AGE	PRESCHOOL ★★★	GRADE SCHOOL ★★★	TEENS ★★★
YOUNG ADULTS ★★★★	OVER 30 ★★★★		SENIORS ★★★★

Route 53 (just off I-88) in Lisle (25 miles west of the Loop), Western Suburbs; ☎ 630-719-2400 or 630-968-0074; www.mortonarb.org

Type of attraction A 1,700-acre landscaped outdoor "museum" featuring more than 4,000 kinds of trees, shrubs, and vines from around the world; guided and self-guided tours. **Admission** $9 adults, $8 seniors, $6 children ages 2–17; Wednesdays: $6 adults, $5 seniors, $4 children ages 2–17; free for kids under age 2; admission includes free parking. **Hours** Daily, 7 a.m.–7 p.m. or sunset (whichever comes first). On major holidays, the grounds are open but the buildings are closed. **When to go** Spring and fall are the most beautiful seasons to visit, although the arboretum is worth a look year-round. May and October weekends are the busiest; come in the morning to avoid the heaviest crowds. **Special comments** If throngs are packing the arboretum during your visit, head for the trails in Maple Woods at the east side of the park; most visitors don't venture far from the visitor center. You don't have to be a tree hugger to appreciate this unusual and beautiful park. **How much time to allow** An hour for a scenic drive; half a day to explore by foot.

DESCRIPTION AND COMMENTS   In 1922, Joy Morton, the man who started the Morton Salt Company, founded this arboretum, a large park honeycombed with 25 miles of trails and 12 miles of one-way roads for car touring. Terrains here include native woodlands, wetlands, and prairie. The Visitor Center provides information on tours, trails, and places of special interest, such as the Plant Clinic, and houses a free library with books and magazines on trees, gardening, landscaping, nature, and other plant-related subjects.

The park, approximately four miles long and a mile wide, is divided into two segments bisected by Route 53; the visitor center is located on the east side. By car or on foot, visitors can explore a wide range of woodlands ranging from Northern Illinois and Western North American forests to collections of trees from Japan, China, the Balkans, and Northeast Asia. Interspersed between the woods are gently rolling hills and lakes.

TOURING TIPS   Driving the 12 miles of roadway takes about 45 minutes without stopping. Good places to park the car and stretch your legs include Lake Marmo on the west side (park in lot P23) and the Maple Woods on the east side (lot P15). Foot trails range from pavement to wood chips, mowed paths, and gravel.

Daily open-air tram tours of the grounds are offered April through October from the Visitor Center. Tickets are $6 adults, $5 children ages 3 to 17; call ☎ 630-968-0074 for departure times.

OTHER THINGS TO DO NEARBY Argonne National Laboratory, one of the nation's largest centers of energy research, is about five miles south of the arboretum. Saturday tours are available and advanced reservations are required; call ☎ 630-252-5562. If you're heading back to Chicago on I-88 to I-290 (the Eisenhower Expressway), both the Brookfield Zoo and Oak Park are convenient stopping-off points.

Museum of Contemporary Art ★★★★½

APPEAL BY AGE	PRESCHOOL ★★★	GRADE SCHOOL ★★★	TEENS ★★★
YOUNG ADULTS ★★★★	OVER 30 ★★★★★		SENIORS ★★★★

220 East Chicago Avenue, Near North Side; ☎ 312-280-2660; www.mcachicago.org

Type of attraction An art museum dedicated to the avant-garde in all media; a self-guided tour. Admission $10 adults, $6 students and seniors; free for children age 12 and under, and for all on Tuesday. Hours Wednesday–Sunday, 10 a.m.–5 p.m.; Tuesday, 10 a.m.–8 p.m.; closed on Monday, Thanksgiving, Christmas, and New Year's Day. When to go Anytime. Special comments Paid parking ($6–$29) is available in the museum garage; the MCA has wheelchair-accessible entrances, elevators, and restrooms. Bright, cheerful, and filled with paintings and sculpture, as well as some other difficult-to-categorize artwork. A not-to-be-missed destination for anyone who enjoys art that's both beautiful and challenging. How much time to allow 1–2 hours; dyed-in-the-wool art mavens should figure on at least half a day.

DESCRIPTION AND COMMENTS This five-story art museum opened in 1996 and provides a major world-class showcase for the MCA's permanent collection of late-20th-century art. Bright and airy on the inside, the building doesn't overwhelm visitors as, say, the huge Art Institute might. Most of the art is displayed on the fourth floor, with two smaller galleries on the second floor dedicated to special and traveling exhibitions. With lots of seating, carpeting, and sunlight streaming in through large windows, the MCA is an easy place to visit.

The permanent exhibit shows off paintings, sculpture, prints, and a wide variety of art utilizing a mind-boggling range of materials: acrylics, video, sound, neon, an inflatable raft, flashing lights. . . . Kids, perhaps unsaddled with preconceptions of what defines art, seem to especially enjoy the MCA's eclectic offerings. The artists represented include Andy Warhol, Roy Lichtenstein, Robert Rauschenberg, Alexander Calder, Marcel Duchamp, Franz Kline, René Magritte, and Willem de Kooning.

TOURING TIPS From either the ground-floor entrance or the second-floor entrance at the top of the stairs facing Michigan Avenue, take the elevator to the fourth floor. Free 45-minute tours depart from the second floor at 1 p.m., 2 p.m., and 6 p.m. on Tuesday; 1 p.m. Wednesday through Friday; and noon and 2 p.m. on weekends. The bilevel book and gift shop features a wide selection of art books and kids' stuff. Puck's at the MCA, a Wolfgang Puck–owned restaurant overlooking the outdoor sculpture garden and Lake Michigan, features casual fare (soups, salads, sandwiches, pizza, and such).

OTHER THINGS TO DO NEARBY The MCA is only a block off the Magnificent Mile, Chicago's shopping mecca; the Water Tower Place shopping mall (and its huge food court) is only a stone's throw away. The John Hancock Observatory and a wide array of restaurants are within easy walking distance. Children will enjoy NikeTown (669 North Michigan Avenue; ☎ 312-642-6363), which features an actual basketball court on the fifth floor.

Museum of Holography ★★½

APPEAL BY AGE	PRESCHOOL ★★	GRADE SCHOOL ★★	TEENS ★★★
YOUNG ADULTS ★★★		OVER 30 ★★★	SENIORS ★★★

1134 West Washington Boulevard, North Central–O'Hare Airport; ☎ 312-226-1007; www.holographiccenter.com

Type of attraction A small gallery exhibiting holograms, laser-produced photographic images that are three-dimensional and often feature movement, color change, and image layering; a self-guided tour. **Admission** $4 adults, $3 children ages 6–12, free for children under age 6. **Hours** Wednesday–Sunday, 12:30–5 p.m.; closed Monday and Tuesday. **When to go** Anytime. **Special comments** Located just west of the Loop in an otherwise-drab neighborhood of warehouses; 1 flight of stairs. Images are at adult eye level, so small fry will need a lift to get the full effect. Not high art, but fascinating—sometimes startling—images. **How much time to allow** 30 minutes–1 hour.

DESCRIPTION AND COMMENTS It would probably take a physics degree to really understand how holograms are created, but the results are fascinating just the same. The museum, the only one of its kind in the United States (and perhaps the world), features stunning 3-D images, such as a microscope that leaps off the surface; when you look into the "eye piece," you're rewarded with the sight of a bug frozen in amber!

Other holograms produce a motion-picture effect as you move your head from left to right in front of the image. Though the museum is small—it's essentially four small galleries (150 holograms) and a gift shop—the stuff on display is unusual, to say the least.

TOURING TIPS The gift shop offers a wide array of holograms for sale, ranging from bookmarks and cards to framed images. Prices range from a few bucks to several hundred dollars for large, framed holograms. *Note:* Before purchasing a hologram, keep in mind that to get the full effect at home, it needs to be illuminated by an unfrosted incandescent bulb mounted at a 45-degree angle to the image.

OTHER THINGS TO DO NEARBY Nothing within walking distance, but the Loop is only a few blocks to the east.

 kids Museum of Science and Industry ★★★★★

APPEAL BY AGE	PRESCHOOL ★★★★★	GRADE SCHOOL ★★★★★	TEENS ★★★★★
YOUNG ADULTS ★★★★★		OVER 30 ★★★★★	SENIORS ★★★★★

57th Street and Lake Shore Drive, South Side; ☎ 800-GO-TO-MSI or 773-684-1414; www.msichicago.org

Type of attraction 14 acres of museum space housing more than 2,000 wide-ranging exhibits (many of them hands-on), an Omnimax theater, the Henry Crown Space Center, and a replica of a coal mine; a self-guided tour. Admission Museum: $13 adults, $12 seniors, $9 children ages 3–11; combination tickets for museum and Omnimax Theater: $20 adults, $19 seniors, $14 kids. Free admission on select days in January, June, September, November, and December; call or check Web site for an exact schedule. Hours Monday–Saturday, 9:30 a.m.–4 p.m.; Sunday, 11 a.m.–4 p.m.; closed Christmas Day. *June–August:* daily, 9:30 a.m.–5:30 p.m.; Sunday, 11 a.m.–5:30 p.m. (Summer hours also apply on other select days throughout the year; call or check Web site for details.) When to go Monday–Wednesday is least crowded, except on free-admission days. Weekends are usually packed, but Sundays are generally less crowded than Saturdays. Special comments Expect to get lost (well, disoriented) while exploring this immense—and often bewildering—museum. The public-address system, by the way, is reserved for summoning the parents of lost children. Can there be too much of a good thing? Probably not, but this huge place comes close. Anyway, you'll find one full-sized wonder after another, plus plenty of hands-on fun that makes other museums seem boring by comparison. How much time to allow Even a full day isn't enough to explore the museum in depth. First-time visitors should figure on spending at least half a day and plan to come back.

DESCRIPTION AND COMMENTS It might be easier to catalog what you *won't* find in this megamuseum, which once held the distinction of being the second-most-visited museum in the world (after the National Air and Space Museum in Washington, D.C.) before it started charging admission in 1991. Even with its rather steep admission price, the place still attracts nearly 2 million visitors a year.

Full-size exhibits include a real Boeing 727 jetliner, a Coast Guard helicopter, World War II German fighter planes—all suspended from the ceiling; the Apollo 8 command module that circled the moon in 1968; a mock-up of a human heart you can walk through; exhibits on basic science and, of all things, plumbing; and re-creations of 19th-century living rooms. Visitors can also thrill to a film in the domed Omnimax Theater, which boasts a five-story, 72-foot-diameter screen and a 72-speaker, 20,000-watt sound system.

TOURING TIPS Unless you've got all day and feet of steel, do some home-work. Grab a map at the entrance and make a short list of must-see attractions. Just make sure you walk past the information booth to the rotunda and the eye-popping view of that 727 docked at the balcony overlooking the main floor.

To get to the Henry Crown Space Center and the Omnimax Theater, walk through the *Farm Tech* exhibit near the main entrance and descend to the ground floor near the U.S. Navy exhibit. The space exhibit features lunar modules, moon rocks, and a mock-up of a space shuttle. Nearby is U-505, a German submarine captured on June 4, 1944; on busy days, the wait to tour the interior can last an hour.

At *Navy: Technology at Sea,* kids can man the helm of a warship. Other exhibits include *Petroleum Planet,* antique cars, bicycles, historic locomotives, computers, an energy lab, dolls, architecture—the list goes on and on and on.

OTHER THINGS TO DO NEARBY The University of Chicago campus is full of beautiful buildings and interesting museums that offer a nice contrast to the hectic—and sometimes confusing—Museum of Science and Industry. It's a short walk from the museum. For a bite to eat, join the locals at Valois (1518 East 53rd Street), a cafeteria frequented by cops, cab drivers, and students.

National Museum of Mexican Art   ★★★½

APPEAL BY AGE	PRESCHOOL ★	GRADE SCHOOL ★	TEENS ★★★
YOUNG ADULTS ★★★★	OVER 30 ★★★★		SENIORS ★★★★

1852 West 19th Street, South Central–Midway Airport;
☎ **312-738-1503; www.nationalmuseumofmexicanart.org**

Type of attraction The only Mexican museum in the Midwest features permanent and temporary exhibits by local, national, and international artists; a self-guided tour. **Admission** Free. **Hours** Tuesday–Sunday, 10 a.m.–5 p.m.; closed Monday and major holidays. **When to go** Anytime. **Special comments** All the exhibition space is on 1 level. The galleries are attractive and well lit; the Day of the Dead exhibit shown during our visit was an entertaining collection of colorful, funny, and bizarre folk art. **How much time to allow** 1 hour.

DESCRIPTION AND COMMENTS As you approach Harrison Park in the Pilsen neighborhood, there is no doubt about which building is the National Museum of Mexican Art (there's an Aztec design in the brickwork along the top of the structure). There are five different areas inside the museum: the permanent collection, the interactive room, the temporary art exhibits, the museum store, and the performing-arts theater. The permanent collection offers a walk-through tour of Mexican history. Starting in ancient Mexico, you then visit colonial Mexico, the Mexican Revolution, and the Mexican experience in the United States. Each exhibit displays artifacts, social structures, and significant developments along with the people that brought them about. An abundance of information accompanies each display (written in both English and Spanish). At the end, a large-screen display runs a short movie about the Mexican experience. After leaving the permanent collection, the interactive room offers touchscreen computers that provide a look into other Mexican traditions as well as the opportunity to hear indigenous music. Most computers are set up for standing interaction, but there are a few terminals on a small desk for children. The temporary collection displays artwork from local, national, and international artists in a spacious gallery. Call ahead for a schedule of upcoming exhibits and performances, or visit the museum's Web site.

TOURING TIPS The large gift shop offers an extensive selection of Mexican items, such as handicrafts, posters, toys, and books. Free guided tours in English, Spanish, or both are offered Tuesday through Sunday (reservations and schedules: ☎ 312-738-1503, ext. 3842). In addition to changing exhibits by Hispanic artists, the National Museum of Mexican Art presents an ongoing series of readings, performances, and lectures.

OTHER THINGS TO DO NEARBY Pilsen, located along 18th Street between Canal Street and Damen Avenue, is a thriving Hispanic neighborhood with signs in Spanish and lots of spicy smells (good ethnic eateries, too). The Jane Addams Hull-House Museum is about two miles northeast of the museum on Halsted Street (at the University of Illinois at Chicago). On weekends and holidays, the Blue Line does not stop at the museum; however, the city has provided a free trolley service to the museum that runs every 20 minutes on these off-days. For more information on the other locations visited by the free trolley, call ☎ 877-CHICAGO or visit **www.choosechicago.com.**

National Vietnam Veterans Art Museum   ★★★

APPEAL BY AGE	PRESCHOOL ★	GRADE SCHOOL ★	TEENS ★★
YOUNG ADULTS ★★	OVER 30 ★★★		SENIORS ★★★

1801 South Indiana Avenue (in the Prairie Avenue Historic District), South Loop; ☎ 312-326-0270; www.nvvam.org

Type of attraction Museum featuring more than 500 works of art (paintings, sculpture, and photographs) created by combat veterans from all nations that fought in the Vietnam War; a self-guided tour. **Admission** $10 adults, $7 students. **Hours** Tuesday–Friday, 11 a.m.–6 p.m.; Saturday, 10 a.m.–5 p.m.; closed Sunday, Monday, and major holidays. **When to go** Anytime. **Special comments** The museum is off the beaten tourist path; if you don't have a car, consider public transportation. From Michigan Avenue, take the bus south to 18th Street, then walk a block east (toward Lake Michigan) to the museum. Spartan and grim—and a potentially wrenching experience for anyone who served in Vietnam, lost a friend or relative in the war, or is old enough to remember the conflict. **How much time to allow** 1–2 hours.

DESCRIPTION AND COMMENTS Opened in a renovated industrial space in August 1996, this museum—the only one of its kind—is filled with disturbing images of a conflict many Americans would rather forget. But the 130 artists who created the 1,000 works on display can't forget; they all pulled combat duty in Vietnam, and their work is visceral and gut-wrenching. Images of death and dying are a recurrent theme, as are shredded American flags, bombs with dollar bills as fins, a painting of LBJ with an American-flag shirt and tie, a GI strung to a post by barbed wire (titled *Waiting for Kissinger*), and a wide array of weapons and artillery displayed as works of art (including a 122-millimeter Viet Cong rocket launcher sitting in front of a painting titled *Rocket Attack*). The bare concrete floors and exposed piping and air ducts add to the no-nonsense, serious tenor of the gallery.

TOURING TIPS Be warned: a visit to this museum is no stroll in the park—it's relentlessly grim and powerful. A good way to start a tour is in the small multimedia theater on the first floor, which continuously shows slide images of the war through the eyes of the soldiers. Many of the images reappear later in the art on display.

OTHER THINGS TO DO NEARBY Next door is the Glessner House Museum, encompassing two historic houses that provide visitors a glimpse into Chicago's prairie heritage and later Victorian splendor. Docent-guided tours are offered Wednesday through Sunday, noon and 2 p.m. (Glessner House) and 1 p.m. and 3 p.m. (Clarke House); the cost for a tour of either house is $10 for adults, $9 for students and seniors, and $6 for children ages 5 to 12; a combo tour is $15 for adults, $12 for students and seniors, and $8 for kids ages 5 to 12 (kids under age 5 admitted free to all tours). For more information, call ☎ 312-326-1480 or visit **www.glessnerhouse.org.**

  Navy Pier ★★★★

| APPEAL BY AGE | PRESCHOOL ★★★★★ | GRADE SCHOOL ★★★★★ | TEENS ★★★★★ |
| YOUNG ADULTS ★★★★ | | OVER 30 ★★★★ | SENIORS ★★★★ |

600 East Grand Avenue (just north of the Chicago River on the lakefront), Near North Side; ☎ 800-595-PIER (outside the 312 area code), ☎ 312-595-PIER, and ☎ 312-595-5100 (administrative offices); www.navypier.com

Type of attraction A renovated landmark on Lake Michigan with more than 50 acres of parks, gardens, shops, restaurants, a 150-foot Ferris wheel, an IMAX theater, a convention center, a children's museum, and other attractions; a self-guided tour. Admission Free; some attractions such as the Chicago Children's Museum, the Ferris wheel, cruise boats, the Wave Swinger (a 40-foot-high thrill ride), Transporter FX (a high-speed thrill ride to Antarctic, the moon, Africa, and other exotic destinations), and the IMAX theater have separate admission charges. Hours *November 1–March 31:* Monday–Thursday, 10 a.m.–8 p.m., Friday and Saturday, 10 a.m.–10 p.m., Sunday, 10 a.m.–7 p.m.; *April 1–Thursday before Memorial Day, Tuesday after Labor Day–October:* Sunday–Thursday, 10 a.m.–8 p.m., Friday and Saturday, 10 a.m.–10 p.m.; *Friday before Memorial Day–Labor Day:* Sunday–Thursday, 10 a.m.–10 p.m., Friday and Saturday, 10 a.m.–midnight. Restaurants are open later throughout the year. Closed Thanksgiving and Christmas. When to go Attracting 5 million visitors a year, Navy Pier has catapulted past the Lincoln Park Zoo to become Chicago's #1 attraction—and during warm weather, the place is jammed. Try to arrive before 11 a.m., especially if you're driving and on weekends. Special comments Although 3 on-site parking garages handle more than 1,700 cars, finding a place to put the family car remains a problem at this very popular attraction. Arrive early—or, better yet, take public transportation (the #29, #56, #65, #66, #120, and #121 buses stop at the entrance) or a cab. The view of Chicago's skyline alone makes this a must-see destination. The ultimate is dinner at a window table at Riva or an evening dinner cruise on the *Odyssey*. How much time to allow Depending on the weather, anywhere from an hour to half a day—or longer if a festival or concert is taking place during your visit.

DESCRIPTION AND COMMENTS A former U.S. Navy training facility and a campus of the University of Illinois, Navy Pier reopened in 1995 after a $196 million face-lift as Chicago's premier visitor attraction. There's something for everyone: a children's museum; a shopping mall and food court; a huge Ferris wheel and a carousel; a six-story-high, 80-foot-wide IMAX theater screen; scenic and dinner cruises on Lake Michigan; a convention center; a beer garden; a concert venue; and ice skating in the winter.

Here's the scoop on Navy Pier's most popular attractions: The Ferris wheel is open year-round (weather permitting) and costs $6 for all ages; it's a 7½-minute ride. Long waits in line aren't a problem because it rotates nonstop at a slow speed that lets visitors load and unload almost continuously. The IMAX theater is located near the entrance of the Family Pavilion shopping mall; tickets for the shows start at $11 for adults, $10 for seniors, and $9 for children.

Crystal Gardens (a one-acre indoor tropical garden with fountains and public seating), Festival Hall, Pepsi Skyline Stage, and the Grand Ballroom feature performances of jazz, blues, rock, theater, and dance, as well as special events such as consumer trade shows, art festivals, miniature golf, and ethnic festivals; most charge admission. The Chicago Shakespeare Theater opened in October 1999. For tickets, call ☎ 312-595-5600. For more information on the popular Chicago Children's Museum, see its attraction profile on page 160. Cruise boats depart from Navy Pier's south dock, as does the Shoreline Shuttle, a sightseeing boat that departs every 30 minutes for the Shedd Aquarium.

TOURING TIPS Unless your visit to Navy Pier is midweek during the winter, avoid the hassles and expense of parking (a $19 flat rate on weekdays, $23 on weekends and holidays) by arriving via bus or cab. And try to pick a nice day: the Ferris wheel shuts down in the rain, and the view of Chicago's magnificent skyline is what separates this shopping, restaurant, and festival venue from all the others. If you're taking the kids to the Chicago Children's Museum, either arrive when it opens in the morning (when school is out) or in the afternoon during the school year (to avoid school groups that often arrive in the mornings). Before leaving home, call Navy Pier for a schedule of special events taking place during your visit.

OTHER THINGS TO DO NEARBY Stroll the Lakefront Trail or, better yet, rent a bike or inline skates at Bike Chicago (in Navy Pier).

The Oriental Institute Museum ★★★★

APPEAL BY AGE	PRESCHOOL ★★	GRADE SCHOOL ★★★	TEENS ★★★★
OVER 30 ★★★★	YOUNG ADULTS ★★★★		SENIORS ★★★★

1155 East 58th Street (on the campus of the University of Chicago), South Side; ☎ 773-702-9520; oi.uchicago.edu/museum

Type of attraction A showcase for the history, art, and archaeology of the ancient Near East; a self-guided tour. Admission Free; suggested donation $5 adults, $2 children under age 12. Hours Tuesday and Thursday–Saturday,

10 a.m.–6 p.m.; Wednesday, 10 a.m.–8:30 p.m.; Sunday, noon–6 p.m.; closed Monday, Independence Day, Thanksgiving, Christmas, and New Year's Day. **When to go** Anytime. **Special comments** With galleries devoted to seven ancient Near Eastern civilizations, from Egypt to Mesopotamia (a region encompassing modern-day Iraq and parts of Iran, Syria, and Turkey), this is an often-overlooked gem that shouldn't be missed. **How much time to allow** 1–2 hours.

DESCRIPTION AND COMMENTS   Most of the artifacts displayed in this stunning collection are treasures recovered from expeditions to Iraq (Meso-potamia), Iran (Persia), Turkey, Syria, and Palestine. The University of Chicago's Oriental Institute has conducted research and archaeological digs in the Near East since 1919, and since 1931 has displayed much of its collection in this impressive building. Items date from 9000 BC to the tenth century AD and include papyrus scrolls, mummies, everyday items from the ancient past, and gigantic stone edifices.

TOURING TIPS   Not-to-be-missed artifacts on display include a cast of the Rosetta Stone (195 BC, which provided the key for unlocking the mean-ing of Egyptian hieroglyphics; wall-sized Assyrian reliefs; a striding lion from ancient Babylon that once decorated a gateway; a colossal ten-ton bull's head from Persepolis (a Persian city destroyed by Alexander the Great in 331 BC); and a 17-foot-high statue of King Tut. The museum is a real find for archaeology buffs and anyone interested in ancient history.

OTHER THINGS TO DO NEARBY   The DuSable Museum, the Smart Museum of Art, and the rest of the University of Chicago campus are all close—and well worth exploring. The huge Museum of Science and Industry is on 57th Street. For lunch, try Valois, a cafeteria hangout for local gen-darmes and residents located at 1518 East 53rd Street.

kids The Peggy Notebaert Nature Museum   ★★★

APPEAL BY AGE	PRESCHOOL ★★★★★		GRADE SCHOOL ★★★★★	TEENS ★★
YOUNG ADULTS ★★		OVER 30 ★★		SENIORS ★★

2430 North Cannon Drive in Lincoln Park (on the northwest corner of Fullerton Parkway and Cannon Drive), North Side; ☎ 773-755-5100; ☎ 773-871-2668 for 24-hour line with recorded message, including information on bus routes; www.chias.org

Type of attraction An interactive museum dedicated to nature, from microcosms to wilderness walks, and a children's play gallery with puppets and a beaver lodge. Admission $9 adults, $7 seniors (age 60 and older) and students, $6 children ages 3–12; free for children under age 3. Some exhibits may require an additional charge. Hours Monday–Friday, 9 a.m.–4:30 p.m.; Saturday and Sunday, 10 a.m.–5 p.m. When to go Anytime. Special comments The museum runs special public programs for adult and child education alike. If traveling by car, park on the east side of Cannon Drive only; move your car by 4 p.m. Wheelchair- and stroller-accessible. Bike lockup is available. Educational for the young and refreshing for adults. How much time to allow A good 2 hours for adults, teenagers, and young adults. For families or groups with children, allow at least 3 hours.

DESCRIPTION AND COMMENTS A mellow, kid-centric museum with a beautiful array of photographs and fun, interesting exhibits—including a live haven of butterflies, a wilderness walk, an active water lab, and children's gallery. It's a pleasant visit that is full of interesting scientific information. A small, comfortable cafeteria sells slightly pricey but healthy sandwiches and snacks. In the summer, a patio provides a pleasant dining area overlooking the river.

TOURING TIPS Visit the butterfly haven first and enjoy the spectacular beauty of these graceful and docile creatures in their natural environment. Please be sure to respect the do's and don'ts video at the entrance. There is a nature museum shop for souvenir hunters.

OTHER THINGS TO DO NEARBY Head south on Cannon Drive to Chicago's Lincoln Park Zoo or east to Lake Michigan for a bike ride, stroll, or skate. During the summer months, call the museum for trolley tour information.

The Polish Museum of America ★★½

APPEAL BY AGE	PRESCHOOL ★★	GRADE SCHOOL ★★	TEENS ★★★
YOUNG ADULTS ★★★		OVER 30 ★★★	SENIORS ★★★

984 North Milwaukee Avenue, North Central–O'Hare Airport;
☎ **773-384-3352; www.polishmuseumofamerica.org**

Type of attraction One of the largest and oldest ethnic museums in the United States, featuring Polish and Polish American paintings, sculptures, drawings, and lithographs; a self-guided tour. Admission Free; requested donation $5 per adult; $4 for seniors and students; $3 children under age 12. Hours Friday–Wednesday, 11 a.m.–4 p.m.; closed Thursday and on major holidays. When to go Anytime. Special comments The museum is on the 2nd and 3rd floors; visitors must climb 2 flights of stairs. An eclectic collection of high-quality art, colorful crafts, and historical items ranging from 17th-century armor to modern paintings. How much time to allow 1 hour.

DESCRIPTION AND COMMENTS Located in the heart of Chicago's first Polish neighborhood, the Polish Museum emphasizes the art and history of an ethnic group that maintains a strong national identity; famous Poles include Paderewski, Pulaski, Kosciuszko, Copernicus, Sienkiewicz, Madame Curie, and Chopin. Interesting items on display include a one-horse open sleigh carved from a single log in 1703 that a Polish king gave to his daughter, Princess Maria, who married Louis XV of France.

Other stuff on display here—much of it colorful and reflecting a high degree of craftsmanship—include Polish folk costumes, exquisite hand-decorated Easter eggs, wood sculpture, prints, and paintings. It's not a very large place, but there's a lot to see.

TOURING TIPS The third floor contains an attractive, well-lit art gallery featuring modern graphic art, paintings, and busts. Check out the stairwell and you'll find a Picasso lithograph and a Chagall etching.

OTHER THINGS TO DO NEARBY Walk a few blocks north on Milwaukee Avenue to explore the old Polish neighborhood, which still has a few shops and restaurants with signs written in Polish; there's an El station at Ashland and Milwaukee avenues.

kids Sears Tower Skydeck ★★★★★

| APPEAL BY AGE | PRESCHOOL ★★★★★ | GRADE SCHOOL ★★★★★ | TEENS ★★★★★ |
| YOUNG ADULTS ★★★★★ | | OVER 30 ★★★★★ | SENIORS ★★★★★ |

233 South Wacker Drive (enter at Jackson Boulevard), The Loop; ☎ 312-875-9696; www.the-skydeck.com

Type of attraction Spectacular views into four states from the world's third-tallest building; a self-guided tour. **Admission** $12.95 adults, $9.50 children ages 3–11, free for kids under age 3. **Hours** *April–September:* daily, 10 a.m.–10 p.m.; *October–March:* daily, 10 a.m.–8 p.m. **When to go** Early or late on weekends and holidays March–November; waits in line for the elevator ride to the top can exceed 2 hours on busy afternoons. On hot days, go after 6:30 p.m. to avoid the heat and to see the city at sunset or at night. Skip it in inclement weather or when clouds obscure the top of the building. **Special comments** Incredible. Part of the fun is looking down on all those other skyscrapers. Don't enter the main lobby of the building facing South Wacker Drive–go to the Skydeck entrance on Jackson Boulevard. If the line is long, consider as an alternative the John Hancock Observatory on North Michigan Avenue (see page 175). Though not quite as high (it's only the 16th-highest building in the world), it offers a better view, some say, and long waits are rare. **How much time to allow** At least 30 minutes once you reach the viewing deck; signs posted at various points in the waiting area in the basement tell you how long you'll stand in line before boarding an elevator.

DESCRIPTION AND COMMENTS The distinctive 110-story Sears Tower (easily identified by its black aluminum skin, towering height, and twin antenna towers) reaches 1,454 feet; the Skydeck on the 103rd floor is 1,353 feet above the ground. It's a 70-second elevator ride to the broad, wide-windowed viewing area, where you're treated to a magnificent 360-degree view of Chicago, Lake Michigan, and the distant horizon.

TOURING TIPS Enter the building at the Skydeck entrance on Jackson Boulevard; take the elevator *down* to purchase a ticket. Try to visit the tower on a clear day; or go at night when the crowds are thinner and a carpet of sparkling lights spreads into the distance.

OTHER THINGS TO DO NEARBY The Chicago Mercantile Exchange is around the corner on Wacker Drive; go downstairs for something to eat from a wide array of eateries. To view more unrestrained capitalism in action, head south toward the Sears Tower, then east on Jackson Boulevard to the Chicago Board of Trade.

Swedish American Museum Center ★★½

| APPEAL BY AGE | PRESCHOOL ★ | GRADE SCHOOL ★★ | TEENS ★★★ |
| YOUNG ADULTS ★★★ | | OVER 30 ★★★ | SENIORS ★★★★ |

5211 North Clark Street, North Side; ☎ 773-728-8111; www.samac.org

Type of attraction An attractive storefront museum highlighting Swedish culture and the Swedish immigrant experience; a self-guided tour. **Admission** $10 families, $4 adults, $3 seniors and children, free for kids under age 1. **Hours** Tuesday–Friday, 10 a.m.–4 p.m.; Saturday and Sunday, 11 a.m.–4 p.m.; closed Monday and major holidays. **When to go** Anytime. **Special comments** All the exhibits are located on the ground floor. Small, but attractive and interesting—and located in a great ethnic neighborhood. **How much time to allow** 30 minutes to 1 hour.

DESCRIPTION AND COMMENTS Swedes were a major immigrant group in 19th-century Chicago, and this museum provides insight into Swedish history and culture and the life of early immigrants. Items on display include jewelry from Lapland, old family Bibles, 19th-century hand tools, and a re-creation of a typical Swedish American home from the early 20th century.

The gallery also exhibits fascinating black-and-white photos, including old pictures of the departed laid out in their coffins before burial: "Death was present everywhere, in a different way than it is today, and the local photographer would often be asked to immortalize deceased persons, both old and young." How things change.

TOURING TIPS The well-stocked and attractive museum shop features a wide range of items such as Swedish videos (including several films directed by Ingmar Bergman), books, road maps of Scandinavia, audio crash courses in Swedish, and traditional handicrafts from the Old Country. The Children's Museum of Immigration tells the story of immigration for youngsters ages 3 to 12.

OTHER THINGS TO DO NEARBY Explore Andersonville, the last ethnic stronghold of Swedes in Chicago. It's a fascinating neighborhood—an unusual mix of Swedish and Middle Eastern—full of interesting shops and inexpensive ethnic restaurants. (See "Exploring Chicago's Neighborhoods," page 125.)

Ukrainian National Museum of Chicago ★

APPEAL BY AGE	PRESCHOOL ★	GRADE SCHOOL ★★	TEENS ★★
YOUNG ADULTS ★★		OVER 30 ★★	SENIORS ★★

2249 West Superior Street, North Central–O'Hare Airport;
☎ **312-421-8020; www.ukrainiannationalmuseum.org**

Type of attraction A collection of Ukrainian folk art, embroidery, wood carvings, ceramics, beadwork, and painted Easter eggs; a self-guided tour. **Admission** Free; suggested donation $5. **Hours** Thursday–Sunday, 11 a.m.–4 p.m.; Monday–Wednesday, by appointment only. **When to go** Anytime. **Special comments** Visitors must climb a set of stairs to reach the entrance. Though some beautiful objects are on display here, this museum is too small and out of the way to recommend for a special trip. **How much time to allow** 30 minutes–1 hour.

DESCRIPTION AND COMMENTS Ukraine, a nation of 52 million people that was once part of the former Soviet Union and an independent state since 1991, is the second-largest country in Europe. Crammed into this tiny but bright museum is a wide variety of folk art, including linens, colorful costumes, exquisitely detailed painted Easter eggs, musical instruments, wood models of native Ukrainian houses, swords, and paintings.

TOURING TIPS Make this a stop on an ethnic exploration of Chicago; see our description of the Ukrainian Village in "Exploring Chicago's Neighborhoods" earlier in this chapter.

OTHER THINGS TO DO NEARBY Next door is Sts. Volodymyr and Olha Ukrainian Catholic Church (2245 West Superior Street; ☎ 312-829-5209), topped by three gold domes and decorated by rich mosaics over the door. On nearby Chicago Avenue are several Ukrainian eateries and bakeries.

PART EIGHT

DINING *and* RESTAURANTS

By Alice Van Housen

DINING *in* CHICAGO

CHICAGO'S DINING SCENE IS PERPETUALLY SHAPE-SHIFTING, refusing ready labels. Our 20-year boom in restaurant quality, variety, inventiveness, and celebrity defies the decades-old characterization of the "third coast" as foodie flyover country. You can still get great steak, gooey deep-dish pizza, or red-sauce Italian by the trough, but the culinary alternatives rival those of any major dining city in the world—from comfort food at neighborhood ethnics to perhaps the most memorable meal of your life.

Smoking is history in Chicago restaurants, defying the old Big Shoulders image of the smoke-filled rooms where things *really* got done. Somehow the original **Morton's** (see profile, page 244) just isn't the same. But don't worry; the stockyards are long gone too, and our steaks are still the best.

NOTEWORTHY DEBUTS

BUCKTOWN'S **mado** (1647 North Milwaukee Avenue; ☎ 773-342-2340; **www.madorestaurantchicago.com**), a husband-and-wife labor of love, serves affordable Italian-Mediterranean fare in a rustic-chic setting with a communal farmhouse table. Wicker Park's **MANA** food bar does great artisanal vegetarian minus the fake meat (1742 West Division Street; ☎ 773-342-1742; **www.manafoodbar.com**). Takashi Yagihashi returned to Chicago to open his eponymous, Asian-inspired contemporary-American restaurant, **Takashi** (1952 North Damen Avenue; ☎ 773-772-6170; **www.takashichicago.com**), in Bucktown's former Scylla space. (Scylla chef Stephanie Izard took some time off to go win TV's *Top Chef* competition.) And Oprah's private chef, Art Smith, opened his upscale Gold Coast American comfort-food cottage, **Table Fifty-Two,** which is almost as hard to get into as O's show (52 West Elm Street; ☎ 312-573-4000; **www.tablefifty-two.com**).

HAUTE HOTEL DINING

WITH THE HUSHED, FORMAL HOTEL RESTAURANT on the verge of extinction, Chicago has experienced a rush on modern destination dining that happens to be housed in hotels.

New American newcomers include **Lockwood,** in the Loop's venerable Palmer House Hilton (17 East Monroe Street; ☎ 312-917-3404; **www.lockwoodrestaurant.com**); **Perennial,** in Lincoln Park's new Park View Hotel (1800 North Lincoln Avenue; ☎ 312-981-7070; **www .perennialchicago.com**); and **Sixteen** (see profile, page 260), in the swanky new Trump International Hotel & Tower. Superlative seafood has settled into the Belden-Stratford's former Ambria space with Laurent Gras's **L2O** (see profile, page 239), and at River North's new Affinia Hotel with **C-House,** courtesy of Marcus Samuelsson (166 East Superior Street; ☎ 312-523-0923; **www.c-houserestaurant.com**). Asian steak house **ajasteak** has taken up residence in the new Dana Hotel & Spa (660 North State Street; ☎ 312-202-6050; **www.danahotelandspa .com**), and Catalan tapas specialist **Mercat a la Planxa** (see profile, page 242) has brought Barcelona to the historic Blackstone Hotel.

CHEF MOVES

MARTIAL NOGUIER DEPARTED **one sixtyblue** (see profile, page 250) for **Café des Architectes** (see profile, page 220). Tony Priolo, longtime chef at **Coco Pazzo** (see profile, page 224), realized his own little dream with **Piccolo Sogno** (464 North Halsted Street; ☎ 312-421-0077; **www .piccolosognorestaurant.com**), reviving one of the city's best outdoor-dining escapes. Graham Elliot Bowles broke away from formal dining with his whimsical River North entry, **graham elliot** (217 West Huron Street; ☎ 312-624-9975; **www.grahamelliot.com**), Curtis Duffy having ably taken the baton at Bowles's former outpost, **Avenues** (108 East Superior Street, in the Peninsula Chicago hotel; ☎ 312-573-6754; **chicago.peninsula.com**). **Le Francais** has closed for good, and Randy Zweiban headed from **Nacional 27** (see profile, page 246) to an LEED-certified (read: environmentally friendly) building in the South Loop to open his Latin-influenced New American establishment, **Province** (161 North Jefferson Street; ☎ 312-669-9900; **www.province restaurant.com**).

SURPRISES

FOIE GRAS WAS BANNED IN A BOISTEROUS BROUHAHA involving chefs and foodies versus aldermen and animal-rights activists, only to return to menus with a vengeance months later. Upscale Thai debuted in the Ogilvie train station (**Thai Urban Kitchen,** 500 West Madison Street; ☎ 888-955-5885; **www.thaiurbankitchen.com**); there's gambling in River North at **Stretch Run** (544 North LaSalle Street; ☎ 312-644-4477; **www.stretchrunchicago.com**); and, at long last, dining with full bar in the Merchandise Mart at **Bluprint** (222 Merchandise Mart Plaza; ☎ 312-410-9800; **www.bluprintchicago.com**). Sample scaloppine

Newcomers and Other Recommendations

AMERICAN

Big Jones (Southern) 5347 North Clark Street; ☎ 773-275-5725; Andersonville

RL 115 East Chicago Avenue; ☎ 312-475-1100; Gold Coast

Table Fifty-Two 52 West Elm Street; ☎ 312-573-4000; Gold Coast

CHINESE

Emperor's Choice 2238 South Wentworth Avenue; ☎ 312-225-8800; Chinatown

Lao Sze Chuan 2172 South Archer Avenue; ☎ 312-326-5040; Chinatown

CONTEMPORARY ASIAN

Red Light 820 West Randolph Street; ☎ 312-733-8880; Near West

Shanghai Terrace The Peninsula hotel, 108 East Superior Street; ☎ 312-573-6744; River North

urbanbelly 3053 North California Avenue; ☎ 773-583-0500; Logan Square

FRENCH

Brasserie Ruhlmann 500 West Superior Street; ☎ 312-494-1900; River North

Old Town Brasserie Market 1209 North Wells Street; ☎ 312-943-3000; Old Town

INDIAN

Hema's Kitchen 2411 North Clark Street; ☎ 773-529-1705; Lincoln Park; 6406 North Oakley Avenue; ☎ 773-338-1627; Northwest Side

India House 59 West Grand Avenue; ☎ 312-645-9500; River North

Marigold 4832 North Broadway; ☎ 773-293-4653; Uptown

ITALIAN

Anteprima 5316 North Clark Street; ☎ 773-506-9990; Andersonville

mado 1647 North Milwaukee Avenue; ☎ 773-342-2340; Bucktown

Merlo 2638 North Lincoln Avenue; ☎ 773-529-0747; Lincoln Park; 16 West Maple Street; ☎ 312-335-8200; Gold Coast

RoSal's 1154 West Taylor Street; ☎ 312-243-2357; Little Italy

312 Chicago 136 North LaSalle Street; ☎ 312-696-2420; Loop

MEXICAN

Maiz 1041 North California Avenue; ☎ 773-276-3149; Humboldt Park

Dorado 2301 West Foster Avenue; ☎ 773-561-3780; Lincoln Square

Real Tenochtitlán 2451 North Milwaukee Avenue; ☎ 773-227-1050; Logan Square

MIDDLE EASTERN

Maza 2748 North Lincoln Avenue; ☎ 773-929-9600; Lincoln Park

Tizi Melloul 531 North Wells Street; ☎ 312-670-4338; River North

NEW AMERICAN

HB Home Bistro 3404 North Halsted Street; ☎ 773-661-0299; Lakeview
Perennial 1800 North Lincoln Avenue; ☎ 312-981-7070; Lincoln Park
Schwa 1466 North Ashland Avenue; ☎ 773-252-1466; Bucktown–Wicker Park
Sepia 123 North Jefferson Street; ☎ 312-441-1920; Market District
Sola 3868 North Lincoln Avenue; ☎ 773-327-3868; Lakeview
Takashi 1952 North Damen Avenue; ☎ 773-772-6170; Bucktown

PIZZA

The Art of Pizza 3033 North Ashland Avenue; ☎ 773-327-5600; Lakeview
Coalfire 1321 West Grand Avenue; ☎ 312-226-2625; West Loop
Pizza D.O.C. 2251 West Lawrence Avenue; ☎ 773-784-8777; Lincoln Square
Pizzeria Due 619 North Wabash Avenue; ☎ 312-943-2400; River North

SEAFOOD

Fulton's on the River 315 North LaSalle Street; ☎ 312-822-0100; River North
Half Shell 676 West Diversey Parkway; ☎ 773-549-1773; Lakeview
Oceanique (French) 505 Main Street, Evanston; ☎ 847-864-3435;
          Northern Suburbs

STEAK HOUSES

Custom House Hotel Blake, 500 South Dearborn Street; ☎ 312-523-0200;
          Printer's Row
David Burke's Primehouse The James Chicago Hotel, 616 North Rush Street;
          312-660-6000; River North
Gene & Georgetti 500 North Franklin Street; ☎ 312-527-3718; River North
Tango Sur (Argentinean) 3763 North Southport Avenue; ☎ 773-477-5466;
          Wrigleyville

SUSHI

Ai 358 West Ontario Street; ☎ 312-335-9888; River North
Meiji 623 West Randolph Street; ☎ 312-887-9999; Near West
sushi wabi 842 West Randolph Street; ☎ 312-563-1224; West Loop

THAI

Spoon Thai 4608 North Western Avenue; ☎ 773-769-1173; Lincoln Square
Thai Pastry 4925 North Broadway; ☎ 773-784-5399; Uptown
Thai Urban Kitchen 500 West Madison Street; ☎ 888-955-5885; Loop

TURKISH

Turquoise 2147 West Roscoe Street; ☎ 773-549-3523; Roscoe Village

VEGETARIAN

MANA Food Bar 1742 West Division Street; ☎ 773-342-1742; Wicker Park

everything in the Bloomingdale's building at **Frankie's Scaloppine** (900 North Michigan Avenue; ☎ 312-266-2500; **www.leye.com/restaurants**), or haute nightcaps and nibbles at the seductive **Drawing Room at Le Passage** (937 North Rush Street; ☎ 312-255-0022; **www.lepassage.com**). Wolfgang Puck cooks kosher in the **Spertus Museum** (610 South Michigan Avenue; ☎ 312-322-1701; **www.spertus.edu**); the Midwest's only active certified blowfish chef is at River North's **Ai** (358 West Ontario Street; ☎ 312-335-9888; **www.aichicago.us**); and multicourse chef's tasting menus at BYO prices can be had at Logan Square's funky New American **Bonsoirée** (2728 West Armitage Avenue; 773-486-7511; **www.bon-soiree.com**). Youth-oriented **HUB 51** debuted from restaurant magnate Rich Melman's kids (51 West Hubbard Street; ☎ 312-828-0051; **www.hub51chicago.com**), and deli hell froze over when sentimental favorite **Manny's Coffee Shop & Deli** (see profile, page 241) added both alcohol and dinner service.

TOURIST TRADE-OFFS

CHICAGO HAS BRAGGING RIGHTS to some distinctive destinations. We have our own junk food (the Chicago dog; see **Superdawg Drive-In** profile, page 264) and our own pizza style (see **Lou Malnati's** profile, page 238). Clubby **RL** (115 East Chicago Avenue; ☎ 312-475-1100; **www.rlrestaurant.com**) is Ralph Lauren's only restaurant in the world; dining there is like living in one of his ads. We are proud to claim such champions of cultural cuisines as Rick Bayless (**Frontera Grill,** profile on page 229; **Topolobampo,** profile on page 266; and a new fresh-casual Mex next door—think churros, chocolate, and *tortas*—in the works for spring 2009) and Arun Sampanthavivat (**Arun's Thai Restaurant;** see profile, page 210). Oh, and let's not forget *Gourmet* magazine's best restaurant in the nation for 2006, **Alinea** (see profile, page 207).

You're not likely to find them there, but you can enjoy a meal at one of Barack and Michelle Obama's favorite restaurants, including **Blackbird** (see profile, page 217); **avec** (see profile, page 210), which spawned Sam Kass, the Obamas' personal chef in Chicago and now part of the White House culinary team; and **Spiaggia** (see profile, page 262).

On the other hand, unless you consider yourself a card-carrying tourist, some of the touted attractions aren't always worth the price in dollars, quality, hassle, or all of the above. Instead of an overpriced view at tired and touristy **Cité** or the **Signature Room at the 95th,** try a new view from Donald Trump's posh **Sixteen,** or the rooftop lounges at **C-View** (166 East Superior Street; ☎ 312-523-0923; **www.c-houserestaurant.com**) and the River North meat-eater's mecca **ZED451** (739 North Clark Street; ☎ 888-493-3451 or 312-266-6691; **www.zed451.com**).

The Keefer's crew's **Tavern at the Park** (130 East Randolph Street; ☎ 312-552-0070; **www.tavernatthepark.com**) was met with less than raves considering the culinary pedigree and the panoramic promise of Millennium Park—partly because the main dining room doesn't have a view (ask to eat upstairs if you want to see trees). Or, for a bite or beverage in the area, check out Park Grill (see profile, page 252) or The Gage (see profile, page 230).

Navy Pier is wildly popular—and thus a dining nightmare for all but the most party-hardy or stout-hearted. There are restaurants, yes, but the gimmicky ones cater to big, noisy crowds, and the fine dining is uninspired. Plan to eat elsewhere—somewhere with more Chicago character, be it old or new.

RESTAURANTS:
Rated and Ranked

OUR FAVORITE CHICAGO RESTAURANTS: EXPLAINING THE RATINGS

WE'VE DEVELOPED DETAILED PROFILES for what we consider the best restaurants in town. Each profile features an easy-to-scan heading that allows you to check out the restaurant's name, cuisine, star rating, cost, quality rating, and value rating very quickly.

OVERALL RATING The overall rating encompasses the entire dining experience, including style, service, and ambience in addition to the taste, presentation, and quality of the food. Five stars is the highest rating possible and connotes the best of everything. Four-star restaurants are exceptional, and three-star restaurants are well above average. Two-star restaurants are good. One star is used to connote an average restaurant that demonstrates an unusual capability in some area of specialization—for example, an otherwise unmemorable place that has great barbecued chicken.

COST Under the star rating is an expense description, which provides a comparative sense of how much a complete meal will cost. A complete meal for our purposes consists of an entree with vegetable or side dish and a choice of soup or salad. Appetizers, desserts, drinks, tips, and tax are excluded.

Inexpensive	$20 or less per person
Moderate	$21–$35 per person
Expensive	$36–$75 per person
Very expensive	More than $75 per person

A NOTE ON MENUS AND PRICES The better restaurants in Chicago change their menus at least seasonally. Others change them monthly or weekly or even daily. Or with what's available at the market, or at the chef's whim. Anything we tell you is on the menu today might not be there tomorrow. Of course, prices will fluctuate with the menu

The Best Chicago Restaurants

NAME	OVERALL RATING	PRICE RATING	QUALITY RATING	VALUE RATING
AMERICAN				
Prairie Grass Cafe	★★★	Mod	★★★★	★★★★
Park Grill	★★★	Mod	★★★	★★★
Bongo Room	★★½	Inexp	★★★	★★★
Twin Anchors	★★½	Mod	★★½	★★★
Lou Mitchell's Restaurant	★★	Inexp	★★★	★★★★
ASIAN				
Japonais	★★★	Exp	★★★	★★
Opera	★★½	Mod	★★★½	★★
BELGIAN				
The Publican	★★★½	Mod	★★★★	★★★
BREAKFAST				
Orange	★★	Inexp	★★★	★★★★
BREW PUB				
Piece	★★	Inexp	★★★	★★★★
CAJUN				
Wishbone	★★½	Inexp	★★★	★★★★★
CHINESE				
Three Happiness	★★½	Inexp	★★★½	★★★★★
Phoenix	★★	Inexp	★★	★★★
COSTA RICAN				
Irazu	★★★	Inexp	★★★★	★★★★★
DELI				
Manny's Coffee Shop & Deli	★★	Inexp	★★★★	★★★
ECLECTIC				
Lula	★★★½	Mod	★★★½	★★★★
FAST FOOD				
Superdawg Drive-In	★★	Inexp	★★½	★★

NAME	OVERALL RATING	PRICE RATING	QUALITY RATING	VALUE RATING
FRENCH				
Everest	★★★★★	Very exp	★★★★★	★★★
Le Colonial	★★★½	Mod	★★★★	★★★
Bistro Campagne	★★★	Mod	★★★½	★★★★
GERMAN				
Berghoff Restaurant and Café	★★½	Mod	★★½	★★★
GREEK				
Santorini	★★★	Mod	★★★	★★★
Artopolis	★★½	Inexp	★★★★	★★★★
HOT DOGS				
Hot Doug's	★★★	Inexp	★★★★★	★★★★★
IRISH				
Chief O'Neill's and Restaurant Pub	★★	Mod	★★	★★★
ITALIAN				
Spiaggia	★★★★★	Very exp	★★★★★	★★★
Spacca Napoli	★★★★	Inexp	★★★★	★★★★
Coco Pazzo	★★★★	Exp	★★★★	★★
Follia	★★★	Mod	★★★½	★★★
JAPANESE				
Mirai Sushi	★★★½	Mod	★★★★½	★★★
KOREAN				
Jin Ju	★★★	Mod	★★★	★★★½
MEDITERRANEAN				
NAHA	★★★★	Exp	★★★★	★★★
avec	★★★	Mod	★★★★	★★★
MEXICAN				
Topolobampo	★★★★½	Exp	★★★★★	★★★

The Best Chicago Restaurants (cont'd)

NAME	OVERALL RATING	PRICE RATING	QUALITY RATING	VALUE RATING
MEXICAN (CONTINUED)				
Frontera Grill	★★★★	Mod	★★★★½	★★★
Salpicón	★★★	Mod	★★★★½	★★★
de cero	★★½	Mod	★★½	★★★½
NEW AMERICAN				
Alinea	★★★★★	Very exp	★★★★★	★★★
Charlie Trotter's	★★★★★	Very exp	★★★★★	★★★
Green Zebra	★★★★	Mod	★★★★	★★★★
L2O	★★★★★	Very exp	★★★★★	★★★
TRU	★★★★★	Very exp	★★★★★	★★★
Spring	★★★★½	Exp	★★★★	★★
Blackbird	★★★★	Exp	★★★★½	★★★
mk	★★★★	Exp	★★★★½	★★★
moto	★★★	Very exp	★★★	★★
NAHA	★★★★	Exp	★★★★	★★★
NoMI	★★★★	Exp	★★★★½	★★★
North Pond	★★★★	Exp	★★★★½	★★★
one sixtyblue	★★★★	Exp	★★★★½	★★★
BOKA	★★★★	Exp	★★★★	★★★★
Sixteen	★★★★	Very exp	★★★★	★★★
Seasons	★★★★	Very exp	★★★★	★★
Bin 36	★★★	Mod	★★★½	★★★
The Gage	★★★	Mod	★★★	★★★
NEW FRENCH				
Café des Architectes	★★★½	Exp	★★★★	★★½
NUEVO LATINO				
Nacional 27	★★★★	Mod	★★★★	★★★
Cuatro	★★★	Mod	★★★	★★★
Carnivale	★★★	Exp	★★★	★★
PIZZERIA				
Lou Malnati's	★★½	Inexp	★★½	★★★★
Piece	★★	Inexp	★★★	★★★★

NAME	OVERALL RATING	PRICE RATING	QUALITY RATING	VALUE RATING
SEAFOOD				
Spring	★★★★½	Exp	★★★★	★★
Shaw's Crab House	★★★½	Exp	★★★½	★★
Santorini	★★★	Exp	★★★	★★★
Joe's Seafood, Prime Steak & Stone Crab	★★★	Exp	★★★½	★★
SOUTHERN				
Wishbone	★★½	Inexp	★★★	★★★★★
SPANISH/TAPAS				
Mercat a la Planxa	★★★★	Mod	★★★★	★★★
Café Iberico	★★★	Inexp	★★★	★★★★
STEAK				
Morton's	★★★½	Exp	★★★★½	★★
Gibsons Bar & Steakhouse	★★★½	Exp	★★★★	★★½
N9NE Steakhouse	★★★½	Exp	★★★★	★★
Smith & Wollensky	★★★½	Exp	★★★★	★★
Joe's Seafood, Prime Steak & Stone Crab	★★★	Exp	★★★½	★★
Chicago Chop House	★★★	Exp	★★★	★★
SUSHI				
Mirai Sushi	★★★½	Mod	★★★★½	★★★
SUSHISAMBA rio	★★½	Exp	★★★	★★
THAI				
Arun's Thai Restaurant	★★★★½	Very exp	★★★★★	★★
VEGETARIAN				
Green Zebra	★★★★	Mod	★★★★	★★★★
VIETNAMESE				
Le Lan	★★★★	Mod	★★★★	★★★
Le Colonial	★★★½	Mod	★★★★	★★★
WINE BARS				
Bin 36	★★★	Mod	★★★½	★★★

Chicago Restaurants by Location

SOUTH LOOP–CHINATOWN

Bongo Room

Cuatro

The Gage

Manny's Coffee Shop & Deli

Mercat a la Planxa

Opera

Orange

Phoenix

Three Happiness

THE LOOP

Berghoff Restaurant and Café

Everest

Lou Mitchell's

Morton's

Park Grill

WEST LOOP–NEAR WEST–GREEKTOWN

Artopolis

avec

Blackbird

Carnivale

de cero

Follia

Japonais

moto

N9NE Steakhouse

one sixtyblue

Santorini

The Publican

Wishbone

RIVER NORTH

Bin 36

Café Iberico

Chicago Chop House

Coco Pazzo

Frontera Grill

Joe's Seafood, Prime Steak & Stone Crab

Le Lan

Lou Malnati's

mk

Nacional 27

NAHA

Shaw's Crab House

Sixteen

Smith & Wollensky

SUSHISAMBA rio

Topolobampo

changes, but not a lot, and they go down as well as up. Just don't be surprised if things aren't quite the same when you get there.

QUALITY RATING The food quality is rated on a scale of one to five stars, with five stars being the best rating attainable. The rating is based expressly on the taste, freshness of ingredients, preparation, presentation, and creativity of food served. There is no consideration of price. If you want the best food available and cost is not an issue, you need look no further than the quality ratings.

VALUE RATING If, on the other hand, you are looking for both quality

GOLD COAST–STREETERVILLE

Café des Architectes

Gibsons Bar & Steakhouse

Le Colonial

Morton's

NoMI

Seasons

Spiaggia

TRU

OLD TOWN–LINCOLN PARK

Alinea

BOKA

Charlie Trotter's

Lou Malnati's

L2O

North Pond

Salpicón

Twin Anchors

BUCKTOWN–WEST TOWN– WICKER PARK

Bongo Room

Green Zebra

Irazu

Mirai Sushi

Piece

Spring

LAKEVIEW-WRIGLEYVILLE

Orange

Wishbone

ANDERSONVILLE–LINCOLN SQUARE–RAVENSWOOD

Bistro Campagne

Jin Ju

Spacca Napoli

LOGAN SQUARE–ROSCOE VILLAGE

Hot Doug's

Lula

NORTH CENTRAL–O'HARE AIRPORT

Arun's Thai Restaurant

Chief O'Neill's

Lou Mitchell's

Morton's

Superdawg Drive-In

NORTHERN SUBURBS

Lou Malnati's

Morton's

Prairie Grass Cafe

Shaw's Crab House

and value, then you should check the value rating. The value ratings, expressed in stars, are defined as follows:

★★★★★	Exceptional value, a real bargain
★★★★	Good value
★★★	Fair value, you get exactly what you pay for
★★	Somewhat overpriced
★	Significantly overpriced

PAYMENT We've listed the type of payment accepted at each restaurant, using the following codes: AE equals American Express (Optima), CB equals Carte Blanche, D equals Discover, DC equals Diners Club, JCB equals JCB (originally Japan Credit Bureau), MC equals MasterCard, and V equals Visa.

WHO'S INCLUDED Restaurants in Chicago open and close at an alarming rate. So for the most part we've tried to confine our list to establishments with a proven track record over a fairly long period of time. The exceptions are the newer offspring of the demigods of the culinary world—these places are destined to last, at least until our next update. Newer or changed establishments that demonstrate staying power and consistency will be profiled in subsequent editions. Also, the list is highly selective. Exclusion of a particular place does not necessarily indicate that the restaurant is not good, only that it was not ranked among the best in its genre. Detailed profiles of individual restaurants follow in alphabetical order at the end of this chapter.

THE BEST . . .

Best Beer

- **Bistro Campagne** (see profile, page 217)
- **Chicago Brauhaus** 4732 North Lincoln Avenue, Lincoln Square; ☎ 773-784-4444
- **Chief O'Neill's** (see profile, page 224)
- **Clark Street Ale House** 743 North Clark Street, River North; ☎ 312-642-9253
- **Goose Island Brewpub** 3535 North Clark Street, Wrigleyville; ☎ 773-832-9040
- **Hopleaf** 5148 North Clark Street, Andersonville; ☎ 773-334-9851
- **Map Room** 1949 North Hoyne Avenue, Bucktown; ☎ 773-252-7636
- **Piece** (see profile, page 254)
- **The Publican** (see profile, page 256)
- **The Red Lion Pub** 2446 North Lincoln Avenue, Lincoln Park; ☎ 773-348-2695
- **Resi's Bierstube** 2034 West Irving Park Road, North Central; ☎ 773-472-1749
- **Sheffield's Beer and Wine Garden** 3258 North Sheffield Avenue, Lakeview; ☎ 773-281-4989
- **Village Tap** 2055 West Roscoe Street, Roscoe Village; ☎ 773-883-0817

Best Bistros

- **Bistro Campagne** (see profile, page 217)
- **Bistrot Margot** 1437 North Wells Street, Old Town; ☎ 312-587-3660
- **Brasserie JO** 59 West Hubbard Street, River North; ☎ 312-595-0800
- **Chez Joël** 1119 West Taylor Street, Little Italy; ☎ 312-226-6479

- **Cyrano's Bistrot & Wine Bar** 546 North Wells Street, River North; ☎ 312-467-0546
- **Kiki's Bistro** 900 North Franklin Street, River North; ☎ 312-335-5454
- **La Sardine** 111 North Carpenter Street, West Loop; ☎ 312-421-2800
- **Le Bouchon** 1958 North Damen Avenue, Bucktown; ☎ 773-862-6600

Best Brunch

- **Bongo Room** (see profile, page 219)
- **Café Selmarie** 4729 North Lincoln Avenue, Lincoln Square; ☎ 773-989-5595
- **David Burke's Primehouse** 616 North Rush Street, River North; ☎ 312-660-6000
- **erwin** 2925 North Halsted Street, Lakeview; ☎ 773-528-7200
- **Feast** 1616 North Damen Avenue, Bucktown; ☎ 773-772-7100
- **Frontera Grill** (Saturday only) (see profile, page 229)
- **Green Zebra** (see profile, page 232)
- **Ina's** 1235 West Randolph Street, Near West; ☎ 312-226-8227
- **Jane's** 1655 West Cortland Street, Bucktown; ☎ 773-862-5263
- **m. henry** 5707 North Clark Street, Andersonville; ☎ 773-561-1600
- **North Pond** (see profile, page 250)
- **Orange** (see profile, page 252)
- **Phoenix** (see profile, page 253)
- **Toast** 2046 North Damen Avenue, Bucktown; ☎ 773-772-5600; 746 West Webster Avenue, Lincoln Park; ☎ 773-935-5600
- **Wishbone** (see profile, page 269)

Best Delis

- **The Bagel** 3107 North Broadway, Lakeview; ☎ 773-477-0300
- **Eleven City Diner** 1112 South Wabash Avenue, South Loop; ☎ 312-212-1112
- **Manny's Coffee Shop & Deli** (see profile, page 241)
- **N.Y.C. Bagel Deli** 1001 West North Avenue, Lincoln Park; ☎ 312-274-1278
- **Steve's Deli** 354 West Hubbard Street, River North; ☎ 312-467-6868

Best Fast Food

- **Billy Goat Tavern** 430 North Lower Michigan Avenue, Loop; ☎ 312-222-1525
- **Byron's Hot Dogs** 1017 West Irving Park Road, Uptown; ☎ 773-281-7474; 1701 West Lawrence Avenue, Lincoln Square; ☎ 773-271-0900
- **Hot Doug's** (see profile, page 233)
- **Mr. Beef** 666 North Orleans Street, River North; ☎ 312-337-8500
- **Muskie's** 2878 North Lincoln Avenue, Lakeview; ☎ 773-883-1633
- **Superdawg Drive-In** (see profile, page 264)

- **The Wieners Circle** 2622 North Clark Street, Lincoln Park; ☎ 773-477-7444
- **Yats** 955 West Randolph Street, West Loop; ☎ 312-829-7930

Best Late-night Eateries

- **avec** (see profile, page 210)
- **Beat Kitchen** 2100 West Belmont Avenue, Roscoe Village; ☎ 773-281-4444
- **Bijan's Bistro** 663 North State Street, River North; ☎ 312-202-1904
- **The Bluebird** 1749 North Damen Avenue, Bucktown; ☎ 773-486-2473
- **The Bristol** 2152 North Damen Avenue, Bucktown; ☎ 773-862-5555
- **Cru Café & Wine Bar** 25 East Delaware Place, Gold Coast; ☎ 312-337-4001
- **Gibsons Bar & Steakhouse** (see profile, page 231)
- **Landmark** 1633 North Halsted Street, Lincoln Park; ☎ 312-587-1600
- **LuxBar** 18 East Bellevue Place, Gold Coast; ☎ 312-642-3400
- **Quartino** 626 North State Street, River North; ☎ 312-698-5000
- **San Soo Gab San** 5247 North Western Avenue, Northwest Side; ☎ 773-334-1589
- **Tavern on Rush** 1031 North Rush Street, Gold Coast; ☎ 312-664-9600
- **Tempo** 6 East Chestnut Street, Gold Coast; ☎ 312-943-4373
- **Three Happiness** (see profile, page 265)
- **Twisted Spoke** 501 North Ogden Avenue, Near West; ☎ 312-666-1500
- **The Wieners Circle** 2622 North Clark Street, Lincoln Park; ☎ 773-477-7444

Best Outdoor Dining

- **Athena** 212 South Halsted Street, Greektown; ☎ 312-655-0000
- **Bistro Campagne** (see profile, page 217)
- **BOKA** (see profile, page 218)
- **Café Ba-Ba-Reeba!** 2024 North Halsted Street, Lincoln Park; ☎ 773-935-5000
- **Japonais** (see profile, page 234)
- **Le Colonial** (see profile, page 236)
- **Park Grill** (see profile, page 252)
- **Pegasus** 130 South Halsted Street, Greektown; ☎ 888-558-2637 or 312-226-3377
- **Piccolo Sogno** 464 North Halsted Street, Near West; ☎ 312-421-0077
- **Puck's at the MCA** 220 East Chicago Avenue, Streeterville; ☎ 312-397-4034
- **Smith & Wollensky** (see profile, page 261)
- **SUSHISAMBA rio** (see profile, page 264)
- **Topo Gigio** 1516 North Wells Street, Old Town; ☎ 312-266-9355

Best Pizza

- **Art of Pizza** 3033 North Ashland Avenue, Lakeview; ☎ 773-327-5600

- **Bricks** 1909 North Lincoln Avenue, Lincoln Park; ☎ 312-255-0851
- **Coalfire** 1321 West Grand Avenue, Near West; ☎ 312-226-2625
- **Frasca** 3358 North Paulina Street, Lakeview; ☎ 773-248-5222
- **Lou Malnati's** (see profile, page 238)
- **Piece** (see profile, page 254)
- **Pizza D.O.C.** 2251 West Lawrence Avenue, Lincoln Square; ☎ 773-784-8777
- **Pizzeria Due** 619 North Wabash Avenue, River North; ☎ 312-943-2400
- **Pizzeria Uno** 29 East Ohio Street, River North; ☎ 312-321-1000
- **Spacca Napoli** (see profile, page 261)
- **Trattoria D.O.C.** 706 Main Street, Evanston; ☎ 847-475-1111

Best Places with Music

- **Bite/The Empty Bottle** *Alternative rock* 1039 North Western Avenue, Ukrainian Village; ☎ 773-395-2483
- **Chicago Chop House** *Piano bar* (see profile, page 223)
- **Chief O'Neill's** *Irish* (see profile, page 224)
- **Cyrano's Bistrot** *Cabaret* 546 North Wells Street, River North; ☎ 312-467-0546
- **Green Dolphin Street** *Jazz* 2200 North Ashland Avenue, Lincoln Park; ☎ 773-395-0066
- **House of Blues** *Blues, rock* 329 North Dearborn Street, River North; ☎ 312-527-2583
- **Joe's Be-Bop Cafe and Jazz Emporium** *Jazz* Navy Pier, 600 East Grand Avenue, Streeterville; ☎ 312-595-5299
- **Pete Miller's Seafood & Prime Steak** *Jazz* 1557 Sherman Avenue, Evanston; ☎ 847-328-0399
- **Philander's** *Jazz* Carleton Hotel, 1110 Pleasant Street, Oak Park; ☎ 708-848-4250
- **Smoke Daddy** *Blues, jazz* 1804 West Division Street, Wicker Park; ☎ 773-772-6656

Best Ribs

- **Hecky's BBQ** 1902 Green Bay Road, Evanston; ☎ 847-492-1182
- **Lem's BBQ** 311 East 75th Street, South Side; ☎ 773-994-2428
- **Leon's Bar-B-Q** 8249 South Cottage Grove Avenue, South Side; ☎ 773-488-4556; 1200 West 59th Street, South Side; ☎ 773-778-7828; 1640 East 79th Street, South Side; ☎ 773-731-1454
- **Merle's #1 Barbecue** 1727 Benson Avenue, Evanston; ☎ 847-475-7766
- **The Rib Joint** 432 East 87th Street, South Side; ☎ 773-651-4108
- **Ribs 'n' Bibs** 5300 South Dorchester Avenue, South Side; ☎ 773-493-0400
- **Robinson's No. 1 Ribs** 655 West Armitage Avenue, Lincoln Park; ☎ 312-337-1399
- **Smoke Daddy** 1804 West Division Street, Wicker Park; ☎ 773-772-6656

- **Twin Anchors** (see profile, page 268)
- **Weber Grill Restaurant** 539 North State Street, River North; ☎ 312-467-9696

Best Soul Food

- **Army & Lou's** 422 East 75th Street, South Side; ☎ 773-483-3100
- **BJ's Market and Bakery** 8734 South Stony Island Avenue, South Side; ☎ 773-374-4700
- **Dixie Kitchen & Bait Shop** 825 Church Street, Evanston; ☎ 847-733-9030; 5225 South Harper Avenue, Hyde Park; ☎ 773-363-4943
- **MacArthur's** 5412 West Madison Street, West Side; ☎ 773-261-2316
- **Wishbone** (see profile, page 269)

Elegant Prix-fixe Menus

- **Alinea** (see profile, right)
- **Arun's Thai Restaurant** (see profile, page 210)
- **Carlos'** 429 Temple Avenue, Highland Park; ☎ 847-432-0770
- **Charlie Trotter's** (see profile, page 222)
- **Everest** (see profile, page 227)
- **Green Zebra** (see profile, page 232)
- **Les Nomades** 222 East Ontario Street, Streeterville; ☎ 312-649-9010
- **L2O** (see profile, page 239)
- **mk** (see profile, page 243)
- **moto** (see profile, page 245)
- **NoMI** (see profile, page 249)
- **Seasons** (see profile, page 258)
- **Spiaggia** (see profile, page 262)
- **Spring** (see profile, page 263)
- **Tallgrass** 1006 South State Street, Lockport; ☎ 815-838-5566
- **Topolobampo** (see profile, page 266)
- **TRU** (see profile, page 267)
- **Zealous** 419 West Superior Street, River North; ☎ 312-475-9112

Trendy Scene Places

- **avec** (see profile, page 210)
- **Bin 36** (see profile, page 216)
- **Blackbird** (see profile, page 217)
- **BOKA** (see profile, page 218)
- **Cuatro** (see profile, page 225)
- **Drawing Room at Le Passage** 937 North Rush Street, Gold Coast
- **Follia** (see profile, page 228)
- **Gibsons Bar & Steakhouse** (see profile, page 231)
- **Japonais** (see profile, page 234)
- **Mercat a la Planxa** (see profile, page 242)

- **N9NE Steakhouse** (see profile, page 248)
- **Otom** 951 West Fulton Market, West Loop; ☎ 312-491-5804
- **Rockit Bar & Grill** 22 West Hubbard Street, River North; ☎ 312-645-6000
- **Sixteen** (see profile, page 260)

RESTAURANT PROFILES

Alinea ★★★★★

NEW AMERICAN	VERY EXPENSIVE	QUALITY ★★★★★	VALUE ★★★

1723 North Halsted Street, Lincoln Park; ☎ 312-867-0110;
www.alinearestaurant.com

Reservations Highly recommended. **When to go** Midweek, special occasions (reserve early). **Entree range** Degustations only; "tasting," $145 (12 courses); "tour," $225 (20-plus courses). **Payment** AE, D, DC, MC, V. **Service rating** ★★★★. **Friendliness rating** ★★★. **Parking** Valet, $10. **Bar** Limited. **Wine selection** Vast, world-class, well organized, with a strength in old-world gems; $30–$2,700 bottle, $7–$28 glass. **Dress** Jacket suggested. **Disabled access** Yes. **Customers** Foodies, CEOs, well-heeled couples. **Hours** Wednesday–Friday, 5:30–9:30 p.m.; Saturday and Sunday, 5–9:30 p.m.

SETTING AND ATMOSPHERE If James Bond opened a restaurant, it might have an entrance like the narrowing hallway that intentionally disorients diners approaching Alinea. Suddenly, an automatic door opens to usher you into another world, one of spare sophistication with Zen touches and reverent service—without the hushed, walking-on-eggshells feel of some haute-cuisine temples. Bilevel rooms are all chic modernity, but seating and tables are comfortable and spacious enough for these marathon meals.

> *unofficial* **TIP**
> If you don't comply with Alinea's 48-hour cancellation policy, your credit card will be charged $100 per reserved guest if your table can't be rebooked.

HOUSE SPECIALTIES Never one to rest on his laurels (or apparently to rest at all—even during his highly publicized recent cancer treatment to save his tongue), Grant Achatz perpetually changes his ultracontemporary American menu of deadly serious whimsies—and the outré serving pieces they ride in on. Things are served on space-age hatpins, grated over your food, and smoked on hot rocks at the table just for the aroma. Humble ingredients such as peanut butter and broccoli stem take on whole new identities. It's culinary performance art at its finest, meaning nearly everything tastes out of this world, and the entire sensory experience is as exhilarating as a carnival ride—without seeming silly or overly experimental.

OTHER RECOMMENDATIONS The tasting-only menus maintain the mystery, teasing with succinct ingredient groupings (the marquee ingredient in caps, the complements in lowercase—for example, LOBSTER popcorn, butter, curry; COBIA tobacco, radish, cedarwood. If you don't know your mastic from your yuba or your *verjus* from your *umebashi*, ask lots of questions, or just let it all wash over you.

River North Dining and Nightlife

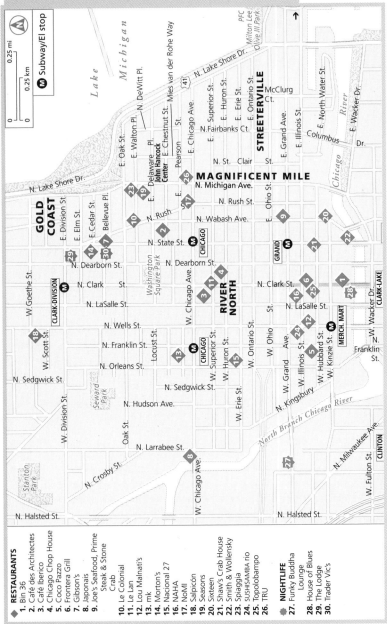

Ⓐ

Ⓜ Subway/El stop

0.25 mi
0.25 km

Lake Michigan

GOLD COAST

STREETERVILLE

McClurg Ct.

MAGNIFICENT MILE

N. Michigan Ave.

RIVER NORTH

Chicago River

North Branch Chicago River

Washington Square Park

Seward Park

Stanton Park

Streets labeled: N. Lake Shore Dr., E. Oak St., E. Walton Pl., N. DeWitt Pl., Mies van der Rohe Way, E. Superior St., E. Huron St., E. Erie St., E. Ontario St., E. North Water St., E. Wacker Dr., E. Chestnut St., Pearson St., E. Chicago Ave., N. Fairbanks Ct., E. Grand Ave., E. Illinois St., Columbus Dr., Delaware Pl., John Hancock Center, N. St. Clair St., E. Ohio St., N. Rush St., N. Wabash Ave., N. State St., N. Dearborn St., N. Clark St., N. LaSalle St., N. Wells St., N. Franklin St., Locust St., N. Orleans St., N. Sedgwick St., N. Hudson Ave., W. Erie St., W. Ontario St., W. Ohio St., W. Grand Ave., W. Illinois St., W. Hubbard St., W. Kinzie St., N. Kingsbury, N. Wacker Dr., W. Goethe St., E. Division St., E. Elm St., E. Cedar St., Bellevue Pl., W. Scott St., N. Clark St., N. LaSalle St., W. Division St., Oak St., N. Larrabee St., N. Crosby St., W. Chicago Ave., N. Halsted St., W. Fulton St., N. Milwaukee Ave., Franklin St.

Subway stops: CLARK-DIVISION, CHICAGO, GRAND, CLARK-LAKE, MERCH. MART, CLINTON

SUMMARY AND COMMENTS This master chef has taken the culinary world by storm with his unique blend of skill and daring—earning Alinea the 2006 designation as *Gourmet* magazine's best restaurant in the nation. Achatz is a protégé of Thomas Keller (French Laundry) and an alum of Charlie Trotter's and the now-closed, highly revered Trio, but his star now blazes with no need for reflected glory. There's mastery in his art and a world-class dining experience in store here—if you can stomach the tariff. If you can, go with sommelier Joe Catterson's wine pairings for the complete experience (they generally add 60% to 70% to the meal cost, with higher-end choices available by request). And plan to spend five hours–plus if you opt for the "tour" (20-plus courses), with a few minutes afterward for a brief glimpse into the clockwork kitchen humming with young chefs cooking their hearts out.

Artopolis ★★½

GREEK	INEXPENSIVE	QUALITY ★★★★	VALUE ★★★★

306 South Halsted Street, Greektown; ☎ 312-559-9000; www.artopolischicago.com

Reservations Not accepted. **When to go** Weekday lunch. **Entree range** $7–$17. **Payment** AE, DC, MC, V. **Service rating** ★★. **Friendliness rating** ★★★. **Parking** Pay lot, $5; street. **Bar** Full service. **Wine selection** Mostly Greek; $7–$35 bottle, $5–$6 glass. **Dress** Casual. **Disabled access** Yes. **Customers** Urban workers. **Hours** Monday–Thursday, 9 a.m.–midnight; Friday and Saturday, 9 a.m.–1 a.m.; Sunday, 10 a.m.–11 p.m.

SETTING AND ATMOSPHERE The French doors at this Greek cafe and bakery (in the heart of Greektown) spill onto bustling Halsted Street. A small balcony perches over the cafe tables in the front, and a spacious, dark-oak, copper-trimmed, marble-topped bar in the center divides the back retail area from the dining room. Terra-cotta tile floors are handsomely set off by the rich cherry tables and chairs arranged closely in the cafe area.

HOUSE SPECIALTIES Mediterranean fest appetizer (a sampling of hummus, fava beans, baba ghanoush, tzatziki, tabbouleh, and olives); smoky harvest sandwich with oven-roasted vegetables; smoked turkey, tomato, romaine, provolone, and eggplant-garlic spread on Kalamata-olive bread; *artopitas* (signature flaky, calzonelike stuffed pockets with a variety of fillings, such as spinach and Feta; ham and Kasseri cheese; crumbled Feta, Kasseri, and fresh mint; and portobello mushroom and Emmentaler cheese).

OTHER RECOMMENDATIONS *Frutti di mare* salad with rock shrimp, octopus, and calamari; *kotosalata* sandwich (mesclun greens topped with chicken salad, walnuts, Granny Smith apple, celery, and pesto on walnut bread); roasted lamb with mint aioli sauce; seasonal fresh-fruit tart; all fresh breads.

SUMMARY AND COMMENTS This Greektown staple brings a French pastry chef's exquisite rustic breads and pastries together with innovative, casual Greek fare. The ambitious staff is eager to please, although lunch is self-service. Wood-fired pizzas and *artopitas* (cheese-, meat-, and vegetable-stuffed pastries) make a nice light lunch, while other special-ties are heartier. During nice weather, French doors open for inviting sidewalk dining.

Arun's Thai Restaurant ★★★★½

THAI	VERY EXPENSIVE	QUALITY ★★★★★	VALUE ★★

4156 North Kedzie Avenue, North Central–O'Hare Airport;
☎ 773-539-1909; www.arunsthai.com

Reservations Required. **When to go** Reservations for weekend dinner can be difficult to get, but this is the best time to go. **Entree range** $85 for a 12-course tasting menu. **Payment** AE, D, DC, MC, V. **Service rating** ★★★★. **Friendliness rating** ★★★½. **Parking** Valet, $12 (Fridays and Saturdays only). **Bar** Full service with several Asian beers. **Wine selection** Massive list covering the globe, with several by the glass, $7–$15; by the bottle, $45–$330. **Dress** Dressy. **Disabled access** Yes. **Customers** Mature patrons, some professionals. **Hours** Sunday and Tuesday–Thursday, 5–10 p.m.; Friday and Saturday, 5–11 p.m.; closed Monday.

SETTING AND ATMOSPHERE The nondescript exterior is no indication of the exquisite interior at this upscale Thai restaurant. The tranquil, narrow room is clean and simple, with several semiprivate alcoves and a raised gallery seating area. The mustard-colored walls are trimmed in deep mahogany wood and adorned with Thai artifacts, paintings, and silk panels.

HOUSE SPECIALTIES Crab spring rolls; Thai-style sweet-and-sour striped bass with shiitake mushrooms and crispy egg noodles; garlic prawns and sea scallops; musman beef curry.

OTHER RECOMMENDATIONS Steamed assorted mini–rice dumplings filled with chicken or pork; lychee sorbet.

SUMMARY AND COMMENTS The Chef's Design Menu leaves the ordering up to chef Arun Sampanthavivat, a master of creative and innovative Thai cooking. Servers inquire about patrons' likes, dislikes, and spice tolerance; then a dozen small tasting courses come streaming out. Arun has received accolades since he opened in 1985 for his exquisite balance of flavors, intricate and artistic garnishes, and ability to raise Thai food to new heights of elegance. Some find it pricey, but most revel in the luxury.

avec ★★★

MEDITERRANEAN	MODERATE	QUALITY ★★★★	VALUE ★★★

615 West Randolph Street, West Loop; ☎ 312-377-2002;
www.avecrestaurant.com

Reservations Not accepted. **When to go** Early evening, late night. **Entree range** $14.50–$20.50. **Payment** AE, D, DC, MC, V. **Service rating** ★★★½. **Friendliness rating** ★★★. **Parking** Valet, $10. **Bar** Full service. **Wine selection** Esoteric Southern Italian, French, Spanish, Portuguese, $19–$157 bottle, $10–$18 glass. **Dress** Casual, downscale chic. **Disabled access** Yes. **Customers** Food-industry locals, hipsters, foodies, well-dressed theatergoers. **Hours** Monday–Thursday, 3:30 p.m.–midnight; Friday–Saturday, 3:30 p.m.–1 a.m.; Sunday, 3:30 p.m.–10 p.m.

Loop Dining and Nightlife

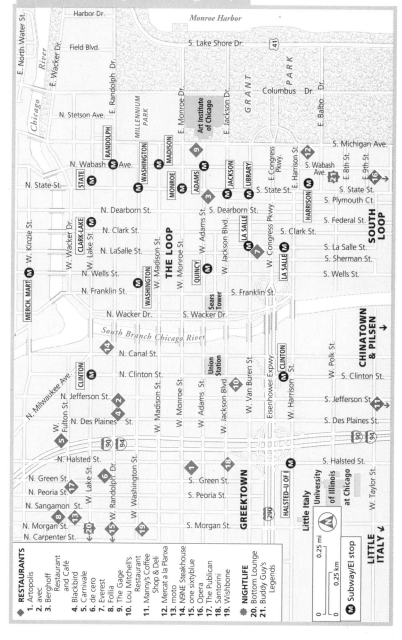

RESTAURANTS
1. Artopolis
2. avec
3. Berghoff Restaurant and Café
4. Blackbird
5. Carnivale
6. de cero
7. Everest
8. Follia
9. The Gage
10. Lou Mitchell's Restaurant
11. Manny's Coffee Shop & Deli
12. Mercat a la Planxa
13. moto
14. N9NE Steakhouse
15. one sixtyblue
16. Opera
17. The Publican
18. Santorini
19. Wishbone

NIGHTLIFE
20. Bottom Lounge
21. Buddy Guy's Legends

Ⓜ Subway/El stop

Lincoln Park and Wrigleyville Dining and Nightlife

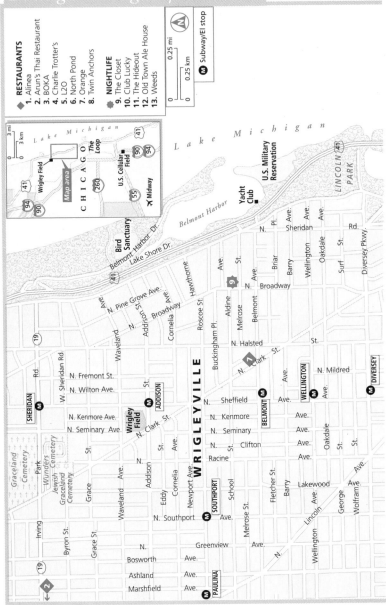

RESTAURANTS
1. Alinea
2. Arun's Thai Restaurant
3. BOKA
4. Charlie Trotter's
5. L2O
6. North Pond
7. Orange
8. Twin Anchors

NIGHTLIFE
9. The Closet
10. Club Lucky
11. The Hideout
12. Old Town Ale House
13. Weeds

0   0.25 mi
0   0.25 km

Ⓜ Subway/El stop

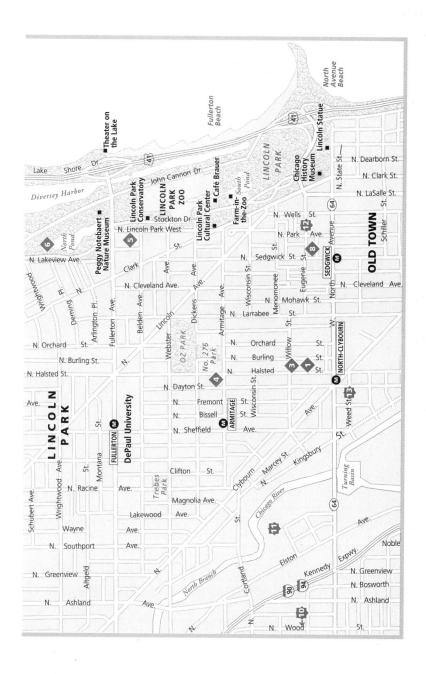

North Avenue Beach

Fullerton Beach

Lincoln Statue

N. Dearborn St.

N. Clark St.

N. LaSalle St.

Chicago History Museum

N. State St.

Schiller

LINCOLN PARK

OLD TOWN

Theater on the Lake

Lake Shore Dr.

Diversey Harbor

John Cannon Dr.

Café Brauer

Lincoln Park Conservatory

LINCOLN PARK ZOO

Lincoln Park Cultural Center

Farm-in-the-Zoo

South Pond

N. Wells St.

N. Park Ave.

N. Sedgwick St.

Eugenie St.

Mohawk St.

Menomonee

Wisconsin St.

N. Cleveland Ave.

Peggy Notebaert Nature Museum

Stockton Dr.

N. Lincoln Park West

N. Lakeview Ave.

North Pond

Clark Ave.

Deming Pl.

N. Cleveland Ave.

Belden Ave.

Lincoln Ave.

Dickens Ave.

Armitage Ave.

N. Larrabee St.

N. Orchard St.

N. Burling St.

N. Halsted St.

Arlington Pl.

Fullerton Ave.

Webster Ave.

OZ PARK

No. 276 Park

N. Orchard St.

N. Burling St.

N. Halsted St.

Willow St.

NORTH-CLYBOURN

W.

N. Dayton St.

N. Fremont St.

N. Bissell St.

N. Sheffield Ave.

ARMITAGE

Wisconsin St.

Weed St.

Wrightwood Ave.

LINCOLN PARK

DePaul University

FULLERTON

Montana St.

Clifton St.

Trebes Park

Clybourn

Marcey St.

Kingsbury St.

Turning Basin

N. Racine Ave.

Magnolia Ave.

Lakewood Ave.

Wayne Ave.

N. Southport Ave.

Schubert Ave.

Chicago River

Ave.

Noble

Elston Ave.

Kennedy Expwy.

N. Greenview

N. Bosworth

N. Ashland

N. Greenview

Altgeld St.

N. Ashland Ave.

North Branch

Cortland St.

N. Wood St.

Wicker Park and Bucktown Dining and Nightlife

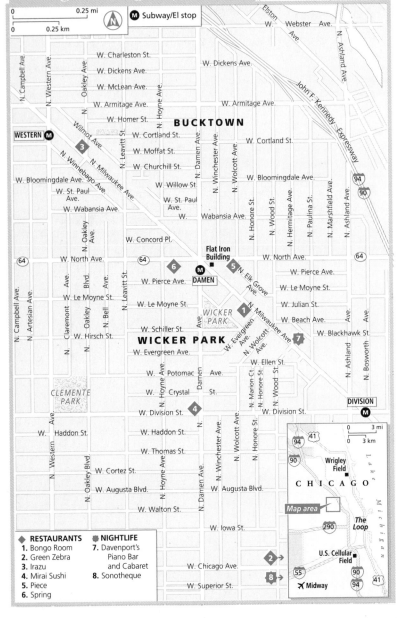

0   0.25 mi

0   0.25 km

Ⓜ Subway/El stop

RESTAURANTS
1. Bongo Room
2. Green Zebra
3. Irazu
4. Mirai Sushi
5. Piece
6. Spring

NIGHTLIFE
7. Davenport's
   Piano Bar
   and Cabaret
8. Sonotheque

SETTING AND ATMOSPHERE Communal seating at one of the five eight-person tables makes the room tight, cozy, and extremely social. It's not a quiet destination for a romantic date but a place to meet fellow diners. The light cedar walls, hickory floors, and ceiling are striking in their simplicity, although the hard bench seating can be uncomfortable.

HOUSE SPECIALTIES Whole roasted fish with wilted cabbage, oysters, and pecan vinaigrette; crispy duck leg with plums, tarragon, grilled onions, and savory streusel.

OTHER RECOMMENDATIONS House-marinated olives; chorizo-stuffed madjool dates with smoked bacon and piquillo pepper–tomato sauce; wood-roasted chicken thigh with toasted farro, swiss chard, roasted shallots, confit fingerlings, and toasted pumpkin seeds.

SUMMARY AND COMMENTS The medley of rustic Mediterranean dishes comes out of a wood-burning stove that's visible from any seat in the dining room. The well-selected and unusual wine offerings are top-notch, and the waitstaff makes useful suggestions for food pairings. This sibling to neighboring Blackbird brings in crowds that snake out the door until the wee hours of the night, when food-industry veterans flock in. The late-night scene is something to behold, making it one of the best stops in town for a midnight snack.

 Berghoff Restaurant and Café   ★ ★ ½

GERMAN/NEW AMERICAN	MODERATE	QUALITY ★ ★	VALUE ★ ★ ★

17 West Adams Street, The Loop; ☎ 312-408-0200 (Berghoff Restaurant), ☎ 312-427-7399 (Berghoff Café); www.theberghoff.com

Reservations Accepted at restaurant only. **When to go** Weekday lunch, after work. **Entree range** Restaurant, $10–$20; Café, $4–$13. **Payment** AE, D, MC, V. **Service rating** ★ ★ ★. **Friendliness rating** ★ ★ ★. **Parking** Lot at 17 East Adams, discount with validation. **Bar** Full service, house beers. **Wine selection** Bargain-priced, California focus; $20–$35 bottle, $5–$10 glass. **Dress** Business/travel casual. **Disabled access** Yes. **Customers** Loopers, tourists, families, and seniors. **Hours** *Restaurant:* Monday–Thursday, 11 a.m.–9 p.m.; Friday, 11 a.m.–10 p.m.; Saturday, 11:30 a.m.–10 p.m.; closed Sunday. *Café:* Monday–Friday, 11 a.m.–2:30 p.m.; closed Saturday–Sunday.

SETTING AND ATMOSPHERE After a brief closing and ownership change (within the family), the beloved Berghoff is once again serving lunch to grateful Loopers, with the same cafeteria-style service and ambience and many of the old German-American favorites still on the menu. The legendary bar, now expanded, keeps the heritage alive with wood and more wood, stained glass, marquetry murals, castle-worthy light fixtures—and now plush leather barstools.

HOUSE SPECIALTIES Cafe signatures include Wiener schnitzel, sauerbraten, hand-carved sandwiches (corned or roast beef, roast turkey, turkey meatloaf); Cobb salad; German potato salad; beet salad; apple strudel;

unofficial **TIP**

Carry-out at Berghoff Restaurant and Café for parties of 5 or more requires a one-hour advance notice; for 15 or more, give at least two hours' notice.

root-beer float. Updated fare includes a selection of panini (such as Black Forest ham, grilled portobello–asparagus, corned beef or turkey Reuben); Asian chicken salad; thin-crust pizzas (four-cheese, pepperoni).

OTHER RECOMMENDATIONS Berghoff Restaurant offers such classics as a sausage trio; the famous creamed spinach; and spaetzles, plus such updated items as mushroom–goat cheese strudel "cigars."

SUMMARY AND COMMENTS The reformed Berghoff valiantly straddles competing demands for the nostalgic and the new. Lunch or dinner, you can still pack on pounds of heavy German classics or opt for lighter fare. A short-lived effort at "European tapas" in the bar gave way to more traditional menu items by popular demand. And they're still pourin' those Berghoff brews (lager, dark, amber, hefeweizen, or seasonal, from Berghoff Brewery of Wisconsin).

Bin 36 ★★★

| NEW AMERICAN/WINE BAR | MODERATE | QUALITY ★★★ | VALUE ★★★ |

339 North Dearborn Street, River North; ☎ 312-755-9463; www.bin36.com

Reservations Accepted. **When to go** Weekday lunch or dinner. **Entree range** Lunch, $10–$15; dinner, $17–$25. **Payment** AE, D, DC, MC, V. **Service rating** ★★½. **Friendliness rating** ★★★. **Parking** Valet, $11 for up to 3 hours, $16 for longer stays. **Bar** Full service. **Wine selection** From all wine-producing nations; flights of 4 (2.5-ounce) pours, $13.20–$18; 49 by the glass, $6–$16.50. **Dress** Casual to chic. **Disabled access** Yes. **Customers** Suburbanites, well-dressed yuppies, showgoers. **Hours** Monday–Thursday, 6:30–10 a.m., 11 a.m.–2 p.m., and 5–10 p.m.; Friday, 7 a.m.–2 p.m., and 5–11 p.m.; Saturday, 7 a.m.–noon and 5–11 p.m.; Sunday, 7 a.m.–2 p.m. and 5–9 p.m.

SETTING AND ATMOSPHERE This spacious room has a wall of 30-foot windows draped with rich velvet floor-to-ceiling curtains, a zinc-topped oval bar at center, and a dining room tucked under an overhanging mezzanine used for private parties. The minimalist decor features stark white walls, high ceilings, and lots of glass, lending the feeling of a *Jetsons* space station.

HOUSE SPECIALTIES Peppercorn-crusted blue marlin, mashed potatoes, onion rings, *sauce bordelaise;* slow-roasted veal shoulder, pumpkin polenta, grapefruit-and-shallot *agrodolce;* roast pork tenderloin and braised pork belly with roasted apples, parsnip pancakes, and apple-Cognac sauce.

OTHER RECOMMENDATIONS Lobster club with house-made tomato soup; charcuterie plate for two (prosciutto di Parma, country pork pâté, house-cured duck prosciutto with pickled pearl onions, house-marinated olives, herb salad, and whole-grain mustard).

SUMMARY AND COMMENTS There are two dining areas in this ultraswanky Marina City restaurant—the full-service Cellar dining room and the Tavern tasting area—along with a small wine retail corner and breakfast coffee bar. Though the fare can be hit or miss, the cheese selection is top-notch, as is the diverse selection of wine and tasting flights.

Bistro Campagne ★★★

FRENCH	MODERATE	QUALITY ★★★	VALUE ★★★★

4518 North Lincoln Avenue, Lincoln Square; ☎ 773-271-6100; www.bistrocampagne.com

Reservations Accepted. When to go Weekday dinner; in warm weather for outdoor dining. Entree range $12–$26. Payment AE, MC, V. Service rating ★★★. Friendliness rating ★★★★. Parking Coin lot across the street; $1 per hour. Bar Full service with unique microbrews. Wine selection Limited but well selected, mostly French, $30–$78; $7–$16 glass. Dress Casual. Disabled access Yes. Customers Young to middle-aged locals, musicians from neighboring music school. Hours Monday–Thursday, 5:30–9:30 p.m.; Friday and Saturday, 5:30–10:30 p.m.; Sunday, 11 a.m.–2 p.m. and 5–9:30 p.m.

SETTING AND ATMOSPHERE The slender room is homey and smart with simple white walls, dark oak trim, and modern works of local art. The garden surrounding the outdoor patio is second to none, with the same number of tables as the dining room.

HOUSE SPECIALTIES Onion soup; *croque monsieur*; Gunthorp Farms pork shoulder braised in apple cider, roasted loin, semolina cake, and apple-celery salad; warm goat-cheese-and-field-greens salad with a Dijon vinaigrette; steak frites; creamed spinach; profiteroles; crème brûlée.

OTHER RECOMMENDATIONS Mussels steamed in Belgian ale; caramelized onion strudel; grilled trout with fennel, pea tendrils, and lemon vinaigrette; chocolate soufflé.

SUMMARY AND COMMENTS Casual and comfortable, this Lincoln Square French bistro draws a steady crowd for a limited but solid menu of classic bistro fare. The outdoor patio is one of the best in town, and the wine list is well selected. Even the beer offerings were compiled with utmost attention to detail. Don't let the low prices fool you—the expertly prepared organic ingredients make this one of the best values in town.

Blackbird ★★★★

NEW AMERICAN	EXPENSIVE	QUALITY ★★★★	VALUE ★★★

619 West Randolph Street, West Loop; ☎ 312-715-0708; www.blackbirdrestaurant.com

Reservations Recommended. When to go Weekend evenings. Entree range Lunch, $8–$19; dinner, $25–$38. Payment AE, D, DC, MC, V. Service rating ★★★★. Friendliness rating ★★★★. Parking Valet, $8. Bar Full service. Wine selection Mostly French and Californian, some German and Oregonian, $24–$419 bottle; ample by-the-glass options, $9–$18. Dress Stylish, chic. Disabled

access Yes. **Customers** Hip urban dwellers, professionals by day. **Hours** Monday–Thursday, 11:30 a.m.–2 p.m. and 5:30–10:30 p.m.; Friday, 11:30 a.m.–2 p.m. and 5:30–11:30 p.m.; Saturday, 5:30–11:30 p.m.

SETTING AND ATMOSPHERE This minimalist, stark white West Loop hot spot exudes a New York attitude. A diverse and always well-dressed crowd flocks here weekdays through the weekend, making reservations necessary. An exposed kitchen at back is the main visual attraction in the otherwise sparsely decorated space. Tables are extremely close and the noise level often high.

HOUSE SPECIALTIES The ever-changing seasonal menu might feature roasted Hudson Valley foie gras with preserved grapefruit, sherry-braised radishes, sea beans, and lychee espresso; a charcuterie plate of duck mole country pâté and smoked-eel rillette with green almonds, cucumber, haricots verts, and sesame brittle; and braised rack of lamb with fresh chickpeas, spring radishes, pickled feta, and lovage.

OTHER RECOMMENDATIONS Braised organic pork belly; veal sweetbreads.

SUMMARY AND COMMENTS Stylish patrons fill this hip eatery on an offbeat stretch of west Randolph Street. Executive chef Paul Kahan and chef de cuisine Mike Sheerin consistently dazzle diners with French-rooted contemporary American fare, which takes full advantage of peak ingredients. The seasonal menu has its share of classic combinations along with just enough innovative dishes to keep it interesting. Pastry chef Tim Dahl is fond of experimental combinations of sweet and savory, not to everyone's taste. The wine list is one of the best in town, with hard-to-find selections in a range of prices.

BOKA ★★★★

NEW AMERICAN	EXPENSIVE	QUALITY ★★★★	VALUE ★★★

1729 North Halsted Street, Lincoln Park; ☎ 312-337-6070; www.bokachicago.com

Reservations Accepted. **When to go** Weekday or weekend evenings. **Entree range** $25–$38. **Payment** AE, D, DC, MC, V. **Service rating** ★★★. **Friendliness rating** ★★★★. **Parking** Valet, $10. **Bar** Full service. **Wine selection** Californian, French, Australian, Italian, Spanish, South African; $32–$500 bottle, $10–$14 glass. **Dress** Modern chic. **Disabled access** Yes. **Customers** Hip young locals, professionals, couples, pretheater. **Hours** Sunday–Friday, 5–9 p.m.; Friday–Saturday, 5–10 p.m.; bar open until midnight Sunday–Friday, until 1 a.m. Saturday.

SETTING AND ATMOSPHERE Chic and trendy, the room is done in gunmetal and black but for a huge white-mesh tarp that stretches across the ceiling. A front lounge doubles as dining space, with a bar separating it from the main dining room. There's even a cell phone booth for your privacy, and everyone else's relief.

HOUSE SPECIALTIES Charlie Trotter's veteran Giuseppe Tentori breathed new life into the menu here with such dishes as wild-mushroom broth with stinging nettle, organic egg ravioli, and onion-porcini ragout; crisp veal sweetbreads with maitake mushrooms, fava beans, and oregano mole;

chamomile-dusted quail with caramelized fennel, Swiss chard, and semolina–goat cheese croquette; stuffed squid with baby spinach, spicy pineapple, and black tapioca; Angus strip loin and short ribs with mushroom spaetzle, grilled-elephant-garlic sauce, and spinach flan; and trout with grilled salsify, braised leeks, watercress, and truffle emulsion.

OTHER RECOMMENDATIONS You can make a meal from the appetizer and raw-bar selections, which include innovative combinations such as Japanese hamachi with young coconut–Buddha's hand vinaigrette, kombu, and cilantro sauce or marinated bigeye tuna with Asian pear, jicama, jalapeño gelée, and mâche. Desserts are equally intriguing, along the lines of sesame macaroon with dark-chocolate ice cream, roasted pineapple, and sweet soy, or coconut tapioca with banana fritters, passion-fruit sorbet, and aged rum.

SUMMARY AND COMMENTS The Lincoln Park neighborhood and pretheater crowds populate this combination of swanky ambience, well-executed foodie fare, and amicable staff. The seasonal menu has something to suit most tastes and Tentori's appetizers and raw items make a memorable light meal.

Bongo Room   ★★½

AMERICAN	INEXPENSIVE	QUALITY ★★★	VALUE ★★★

1470 North Milwaukee Avenue, Wicker Park; ☎ 773-489-0690
1152 South Wabash Avenue, South Loop; ☎ 312-291-0100

Reservations Not accepted. **When to go** Early weekend, weekday breakfast, lunch. **Entree range** Breakfast, $5–$11; lunch, $9–$13. **Payment** AE, D, MC, V. **Service rating** ★★. **Friendliness rating** ★★★. **Parking** Street. **Bar** Brunch drinks, beer. **Wine selection** None. **Dress** Come as you are. **Disabled access** Yes. **Customers** Hipsters, families, gal pals, hung-overs. **Hours** Monday–Friday, 8 a.m.–2:30 p.m.; Saturday and Sunday, 9 a.m.–2 p.m.

SETTING AND ATMOSPHERE Funky-chic surroundings welcome bedheads and stroller-pushers alike—anyone willing to wait a while in crowded surroundings at peak hours. Popularity and a no-reservations policy may play havoc with your plans, and even lunch can be surprisingly busy (the Bongo Room does not serve dinner).

HOUSE SPECIALTIES Regulars return for the seasonally shifting pancake (for example, banana–Heath bar, Key lime cheesecake) and Benedict (such as lobster, lump crab, or roasted red pepper–feta) specialties; ultrafluffy custom omelets from a massive ingredient list; croissant sandwiches; and a hunky breakfast burrito. Lunch sees such sandwiches as sliced tenderloin tarted up with Saint Andre cheese, watercress-apple relish, and horseradish aioli; a chicken-pear club; and nice vegetarian options, including a portobello burger.

OTHER RECOMMENDATIONS Try one of the tantalizing eye-openers, such as a passion fruit–raspberry sorbet or black raspberry–grapefruit mimosa, or a chewy caraway Bloody Mary.

SUMMARY AND COMMENTS Brunch is the house specialty, and the Wicker Park location is notoriously frenetic at peak times. Service humps when it has to, slacks when it can. The prevailing wisdom for impatient would-be brunchers who've just gotta have their chocolate-tower-French-toast fix is to head to the South Loop location, where the wait is usually shorter (and the menu the same).

Café des Architectes ★★★½

NEW FRENCH	EXPENSIVE	QUALITY ★★★★	VALUE ★★

**Sofitel Chicago Water Tower hotel, 20 East Chestnut Street, Gold Coast;
☎ 312-324-4000; www.cafedesarchitectes.com**

Reservations Accepted. **When to go** Weekday lunch. **Entree range** Lunch, $13–$23; dinner, $27–$34. **Payment** AE, D, DC, MC, V. **Service rating** ★★★. **Friendliness rating** ★★. **Parking** Pay lot, $22; valet, lunch $10, dinner complimentary. **Bar** Full service. **Wine selection** Mostly French and Californian; $38–$220 bottle, $8–$19 glass. **Dress** Business attire, upscale. **Disabled access** Yes. **Customers** Fashion executives, other worker bees, and hotel guests. **Hours** Daily, 6 a.m.–11 p.m. sigh tea served Friday and Saturday, 2–4:30 p.m.

SETTING AND ATMOSPHERE The dramatically appointed room, situated inside the Sofitel Chicago Water Tower hotel and designed by Pierre-Yves Rochon, is stunning. White walls are highlighted by bright-purple high-backed banquettes and brilliant crimson carpeting, with 6-foot-long satin light fixtures affixed to the 30-foot ceilings.

HOUSE SPECIALTIES Five-hour-braised short ribs with star-anise reduction; hamachi carpaccio with tangerine, artichoke puree, and orange vinaigrette; peekytoe-crab salad with piquillo-pepper puree, apple gelée, and watermelon radish; port-marinated foie gras with pineapple chutney, balsamic reduction, and brioche; pink-peppercorn-crusted ahi tuna with crispy wild mushrooms and spicy curry caramel; venison strip loin with parsley-root puree, poached pears, and Balinese-long-pepper reduction.

OTHER RECOMMENDATIONS The seasonal specialties of new chef Martial Noguier (longtime chef of one sixtyblue) include such dishes as scallop carpaccio with mango vinaigrette, passion-fruit seeds, papaya, and avocado tian; spiced marinated duck confit with glazed quince, fennel puree, and black-olive sauce; seared dorade with zucchini aioli, calamari, and Chardonnay sauce. At brunch, savor pan-seared spicy salmon salad with grapefruit, avocado, greens, and citrus vinaigrette; tagliatelle pasta with pesto cream, tomatoes, and grilled shrimp.

SUMMARY AND COMMENTS The first branch of this ultraluxurious hotel company to hit Chicago, the spectacular structure jets into the Gold Coast sky. On entering, the cafe evokes a true Parisian feel; windows overlook the street for a view to the action. Service can be stern, but it makes the place feel more European.

Café Iberico ★★★

SPANISH/TAPAS	INEXPENSIVE	QUALITY ★★★	VALUE ★★★★

**739 North LaSalle Street, River North; ☎ 312-573-1510;
www.cafeiberico.com**

Reservations For parties of 6 or more only, Sunday–Thursday and noon–3 p.m. Friday–Saturday. **When to go** Weekday evenings for no waits and a quieter room. **Entree range** Tapas, $5–$8; entrees, $9–$11. **Payment** D, DC, MC, V. **Service rating** ★★. **Friendliness rating** ★½. **Parking** Valet, $10. **Bar** Full service. **Wine selection** Sangria, $13.95 per pitcher; several sherries, $3.50–$12 per glass; Spanish wines, $16–$50 bottle, $3.50–$6 glass. **Dress** Casual to trendy. **Disabled access** Yes. **Customers** Loop workers, young and lively diners. **Hours** Monday–Thursday, 11 a.m.–11:30 p.m.; Friday, 11 a.m.–1:30 a.m.; Saturday, noon–1:30 a.m.; Sunday, 11 a.m.–11 p.m.

SETTING AND ATMOSPHERE The two rooms at this casual, fun tapas bar (plus the basement on busy Wednesday through Saturday nights) get more character from the crowds than from the decor. There are only a few Spanish artifacts along with a tile border to add a splash of color to the otherwise underwhelming space. The food is the main attraction; always fresh, intriguing, and plentiful.

HOUSE SPECIALTIES Roasted veal served cold with raspberry vinaigrette; Spanish cured ham with manchego cheese and tomato bread; grilled squid in olive oil, garlic, and lemon juice; grilled mushrooms; *croquetas* (chicken-and-ham puffs with an aioli sauce); paella Iberico with sea-food, chicken, pork, and saffron rice.

OTHER RECOMMENDATIONS Spanish potato salad with carrots, tuna, and peas; *tortilla española* (vegetarian Spanish omelet); grilled salmon with green-peppercorn sauce; grilled Spanish sausages; Galician white-bean-and-rapini soup.

SUMMARY AND COMMENTS The atmosphere is lively—even rowdy when packed—and the food just right at this River North tapas bar. The menu has a dozen or more each of hot and cold tapas along with a few entrees, the paella Iberico being the best pick. Large parties are com-mon and work best with the tasting menu, meant to be shared. Service can be slow at times and even forgetful, but pitchers of sangria help pass the time painlessly.

Carnivale ★★★

NUEVO LATINO	MODERATE	QUALITY ★★★	VALUE ★★

702 West Fulton Street, Near West; ☎ 312-850-5005; www.carnivalechicago.com

Reservations Accepted. **When to go** Drinks, night on the town, group dining. **Entree range** Lunch, $8–$16; dinner, $16–$35. **Payment** AE, D, DC, MC, V. **Service rating** ★★. **Friendliness rating** ★★. **Parking** Valet, $5. **Bar** Full service, specialty cocktails. **Wine selection** Moderately priced, mostly Californian, Spanish, and South American; $29–$275 bottle, $7–$35 glass. **Dress** Trendy. **Disabled access** Yes. **Customers** Singles, 20- and 30-something dates, clubbers. **Hours** Monday–Thursday, 11:30 a.m.–2:30 p.m. and 5–10 p.m.; Friday, 11:30 a.m.–2:30 p.m. and 5–11 p.m.; Saturday, 5–11 p.m.; Sunday, 5–10 p.m.

SETTING AND ATMOSPHERE Life is a carnival at Carnivale, a Latin-tinged, salsa-soundtracked one with owner Jerry Kleiner's (Marché, Red Light,

Opera) unique design and nightclub sensibilities. The cavernous former Drink space retains its multiple environments, a variety of wildly colorful, trippy settings (some bright, some dim) for dining or debauchery (with four bars). Design highlights include modern paintings and photography, oversized furnishings, Kleiner's signature piles of wine, a secluded area with a fireplace, and a catwalk over the dining area.

HOUSE SPECIALTIES *Pernil* (rum-glazed pork shoulder, Puerto Rican rice and beans, fried plantain); *arrachera* (grilled skirt steak with chimichurri sauce, rice, beans, and sweet red onions); fried-whitefish tacos with citrus tartar sauce and tart slaw; seviche sampler (choices include shrimp, yellowtail, arctic char, and tuna); Farmer's Market Mojito with seasonal locally grown fruit.

OTHER RECOMMENDATIONS *Ropa vieja* (Cuban braised beef with sweet plantains and spicy mayo); sofrito rice with shrimp, mussels, clams, squid, chorizo, peas, chicken, and lobster broth.

SUMMARY AND COMMENTS Carnivale is sizzling fun for a youthful (or at least young-at-heart) audience. Seclusion-seekers be warned: this bustling be-seener can be loud (in decibel level, decor, and staff characters), though there are a few dark corners, some private dining areas, and seasonal outdoor dining.

Charlie Trotter's ★★★★★

NEW AMERICAN	VERY EXPENSIVE	QUALITY ★★★★★	VALUE ★★★

816 West Armitage Avenue, Lincoln Park; ☎ 773-248-6228; www.charlietrotters.com

Reservations Required weeks in advance. **When to go** Any day you can get in; reserve several months in advance. **Entree range** Vegetable degustation menu, $135; grand degustation menu, $165; chef's table, $225. **Payment** AE, D, DC, MC, V. **Service rating** ★★★★½. **Friendliness rating** ★★★. **Parking** Valet, $10. **Bar** Wine only. **Wine selection** Award-winning wine list with more than 1,800 French, Italian, Californian, Australian, German, South African, and other bottles, $30–$19,000; about 20 by the glass, $12–$45. **Dress** Jackets required; formal attire. **Disabled access** Yes, first floor. **Customers** Tourists, suburbanites, and food aficionados. **Hours** Seatings Tuesday–Thursday, 6–9:30 p.m.; Friday and Saturday, 5:30–9:30 p.m.; closed Sunday–Monday.

SETTING AND ATMOSPHERE This attractive Lincoln Park two-flat is easy to miss, tucked behind a billowing trellis of greenery. The three small dining rooms, with a subdued decor in rich tones of burgundy and green (each seating 30), are quite formal yet intimate, with white linens and exquisite stemware and silverware. There's even a kitchen table for four to six guests, allowing a behind-the-scenes view of the masterful kitchen.

HOUSE SPECIALTIES The menu, which changes daily, might include roasted-beet risotto with wild asparagus, porcini mushrooms, and toasted almonds; Tasmanian sea trout with radish; rabbit with collard greens and turnip; Millbrook venison loin with rice beans, cumin-infused roasted eggplant, and sage; rhubarb sorbet with spring-onion marmalade and

Manni olive oil; olive-oil-poached hamachi, wild watercress, and tamarind-orange vinaigrette; buttermilk-poached poularde breast with salsify, chanterelle mushrooms, and thyme-infused consommé; whole roasted squab with cippollini onion and black truffles.

OTHER RECOMMENDATIONS Ragout of fire beans and dragon-tongue beans with fingerling potatoes and garlic-infused mushroom sauce; monkfish liver with lemongrass and ginger root; poached breast of *poussin* (chicken) with zucchini and hen-of-the-woods-mushroom sauce.

SUMMARY AND COMMENTS Early planning is required for a table at the world-renowned eatery where award-winning chef Charlie Trotter consistently turns out culinary masterpieces. Trotter's degustation menus, grand and vegetable, are each like a symphony—one petite course (too petite for big-shoulders Chicago types) lays the foundation for the next. All dishes involve impeccably fresh ingredients in innovative preparations and presentations. For a real splurge, the table in the kitchen is the way to go for an exquisite menu, fine entertainment, and brushing shoulders with the man himself. Service is top-notch and the wine list unparalleled, with selections from all wine-producing regions of the world at a range of prices. The selection of large-format wines (such as magnums) is remarkable.

 ## Chicago Chop House ★★★

STEAK	EXPENSIVE	QUALITY ★★★	VALUE ★★

60 West Ontario Street, River North; ☎ 312-787-7100; www.chicagochophouse.com

Reservations Highly recommended. **When to go** Lunch or early dinner. **Entree range** Lunch, $9–$24; dinner, $21–$105. **Payment** AE, D, MC, V. **Service rating** ★★★. **Friendliness rating** ★★★. **Parking** Valet ($8 lunch, $12 dinner). **Bar** Full service. **Wine selection** More than 650 selections, from affordable to heavy hitters with specialty in American Cabernet verticals; $24–$1,950 bottle, $6–$15 glass. **Dress** Upscale casual. **Disabled access** No. **Customers** Businessmen, politicos, tourists, cigar smokers. **Hours** Monday–Thursday, 11:30 a.m.–11 p.m.; Friday, 11:30 a.m.–11:30 p.m.; Saturday, 4–11:30 p.m.; Sunday, 4–11 p.m.

SETTING AND ATMOSPHERE Though it's been around for less than 25 years, this non-chain, old-boy-network clubhouse in a restored Victorian brownstone is a well-established institution for swaggering carnivores, steak-seeking visitors, politicians, and other people who get things done around here. Quaint, dark, and noisy wood-paneled environs are decorated with more than 1,400 vintage Chicago photographs from the era when, as the restaurant puts it, "meat-packers, politicians, and gangsters vied for control." Many regulars prefer the even more boisterous bar scene on the lower level, where a nightly piano bar (5 p.m. weeknights, 6 p.m. weekends) adds nostalgic conviviality (and cigar smoke in the back).

unofficial **TIP**
If you want a bargain at the Chicago Chop House, try going at lunch, when entrees run less than $25.

HOUSE SPECIALTIES Hand-cut prime steaks (such as 16- or 24-ounce New York strip or 64-ounce porterhouse); roasted 24-ounce bone-in prime rib; broiled Alaskan king crab legs; seafood platter (broiled lobster tail, salmon, and French-fried shrimp); potato pancakes; Caesar salad.

OTHER RECOMMENDATIONS Sautéed lake perch with lemon butter; shrimp De Jonghe; clams Casino; crab cakes with mustard sauce; broiled lamb chop, veal chop, and filet mignon; roast rack of lamb; carrot or chocolate cake.

SUMMARY AND COMMENTS Don't come here looking for innovation. This is all about classic meat, potatoes, and martinis. Service can be friendly or cavalier, and while tightwads love that dinner includes salad and potatoes (most top-end competitors are all à la carte), it's still an expensive meal.

Chief O'Neill's Pub and Restaurant ★★

IRISH	MODERATE	QUALITY ★★	VALUE ★★★

3471 North Elston Avenue, North Central–O'Hare Airport;
☎ **773-473-5263; www.chiefoneillspub.com**

Reservations Accepted. **When to go** Tuesday during music jam sessions; Sunday, Irish brunch. **Entree range** $9–$27. **Payment** AE, D, DC, MC, V. **Service rating** ★★★. **Friendliness rating** ★★★★. **Parking** Small lot, free on street. **Bar** Full service, with an excellent array of imported and tap beers, $4–$6. **Wine selection** Limited; $24–$50 bottle, $6–$12 glass. **Dress** Casual. **Disabled access** Yes. **Customers** Locals, Irish Chicagoans, police, music fans. **Hours** Monday–Thursday, 4 p.m.–2 a.m.; Friday, 3 p.m.–3 a.m.; Saturday, 9 a.m.–3 a.m.; Sunday, 10 a.m.–2 a.m. (brunch 10 a.m.–2 p.m.); food service ends at 10 p.m. weeknights, 11 p.m. Saturday–Sunday.

SETTING AND ATMOSPHERE It's all things Irish at this traditional pub, from the Celtic knots on the tin ceiling to the instruments mounted in glass cases around the room. Most of the staff have thick accents. The dark, wood-trimmed space is mammoth, especially when the outdoor picnic tables are available.

HOUSE SPECIALTIES Beer-battered North Atlantic cod fish-and-chips; shepherd's pie; braised lamb shank; Irish breakfast.

OTHER RECOMMENDATIONS Mussels in white wine–garlic sauce; wild Atlantic salmon; Cheddar cheese–Guinness soup; corned beef and cabbage.

SUMMARY AND COMMENTS Irish food and music fans are regulars at this huge but homey pub. Live music and jam sessions are staged Tuesdays and Sundays, and pints of beer are the norm. The fare is the real Irish deal; the Sunday brunch features American standards (waffles, bacon, omelets, French toast, and such) and eye-opening Bloody Marys. The mostly Irish staff adds to the ambience with cheerful greetings and friendly service.

Coco Pazzo ★★★★

ITALIAN	EXPENSIVE	QUALITY ★★★★	VALUE ★★

300 West Hubbard Street, River North; ☎ 312-836-0900; www.cocopazzochicago.com

Reservations Highly recommended. **When to go** Lunch; client and date dinners. **Entree range** Lunch, $10–$24; dinner, $15–$39. **Payment** AE, D, DC, MC, V. **Service rating** ★★★★. **Friendliness rating** ★★. **Parking** Valet, $12 (lunch and dinner). **Bar** Full service. **Wine selection** All Italian, both mainstream and small producers, $38–$790 bottle, $8–$24 glass. **Dress** Jacket suggested. **Disabled access** Yes. **Customers** Businessmen, well-heeled couples. **Hours** Monday–Thursday, 11:30 a.m.–2:30 p.m. and 5:30–10:30 p.m.; Friday, 11:30 a.m.–2:30 p.m. and 5:30–11 p.m.; Saturday, 5:30–11 p.m.; Sunday, 5–10 p.m.

SETTING AND ATMOSPHERE This upscale River North haven is at once polished and rustic-chic. The loftlike white-tablecloth setting, done in warm wood and Mediterranean blue, is as simply sophisticated as the food, with polished service worthy of a big deal or momentous rendezvous.

> *unofficial* **TIP**
> Those on tight budgets can head to Coco Pazzo's cheaper, more casual spin-off, **Coco Pazzo Cafe** (Red Roof Inn, 636 North Saint Clair Street, Near North Side; ☎ 312-664-2777; **www.cocopazzocafe.com**).

HOUSE SPECIALTIES The menu changes seasonally, but typical dishes might include shaved raw artichokes and baby arugula with lemon oil and Pecorino Toscano; thinly sliced octopus with French beans, new potatoes, and Ligurian olives; cauliflower-filled dumplings with smoked prosciutto, pine nuts, and sage; handmade wide noodles with wild-boar *ragù;* braised rabbit with tomato and olives over baked polenta; herb-crusted half lamb rack with stewed baby artichokes, roasted tomato, and great northern beans; breaded veal chop with arugula, tomato, and red onion; and handmade black-squid-ink pasta with shrimp, zucchini, chiles, and basil.

OTHER RECOMMENDATIONS Lunch creations include wood-roasted duck breast with radicchio, pancetta, oyster mushrooms, and balsamic vinegar; and such sophisticated wood-burning oven pizzas selections as Robiola cheese and truffle oil or speck, stracchino, and arugula.

SUMMARY AND COMMENTS Coco Pazzo is a reliable source for a civilized adult meal reminiscent of the home country's modern fine dining. Regulars of this refined Northern Italian should note the departure of longtime chef Tony Priolo, with new chef Chris Macchia migrating from Coco Pazzo Cafe. The menu philosophy of simple Tuscan cuisine using locally sourced seasonal ingredients, a wood-burning oven, and fresh pastas (with widely acclaimed risotto and gnocchi preparations) remains the same.

Cuatro ★★★

NUEVO LATINO	MODERATE	QUALITY ★★★	VALUE ★★★

2030 South Wabash Avenue, South Loop; ☎ 312-842-8856; www.cuatro-chicago.com

Reservations Accepted. **When to go** Dates, late, Sunday brunch. **Entree range** $13–$31. **Payment** AE, D, DC, MC, V. **Service rating** ★★★. **Friendliness rating**

★★★. **Parking** Street, valet $10. **Bar** Full service, specialty cocktails. **Wine selection** Limited wine list, $24–$450; about 15 by the glass, $6–$16; BYO corkage, $15. **Dress** Hip casual. **Disabled access** Yes. **Customers** South Loop mix of artsy, business, and hip. **Hours** Monday–Thursday, 5–10 p.m.; Friday–Saturday, 5 p.m.–2 a.m.; Sunday, 10 a.m.–3 p.m. and 5–10 p.m.

SETTING AND ATMOSPHERE   The mod hacienda building is faced with a wall of garage doors for an airy feel with daytime natural light and night city views when the lighting is low. Saltwater fish tanks add an escapist feel to the clubby environs of exposed brick, open ductwork, urban artwork, and ceiling fans, with a mix of tables, banquettes, and high-tops. Live music Thursday through Saturday and at Sunday brunch introduces that Latin beat.

HOUSE SPECIALTIES   Signature dishes include Brazilian *moqueca do mar* (tilapia, shrimp, sea scallops, squid, and littleneck clams in a spicy tomato–coconut milk broth with coconut rice and fried plantains) and a Caribbean-Latin fusion called *chuleta en mole de platano macho* (a moist, monolithic double pork chop cured in sugarcane juice and served with plantain mole). For dessert, don't miss the Oaxacan chocolate-mousse cake filled with tequila cream and plated with sweet-corn ice cream.

OTHER RECOMMENDATIONS   Chicken brochettes with tamarind jerk sauce and *moros y cristianos* (black beans and rice) represent limited Caribbean menu accents. Brunchers can design an omelet, swoosh tortillas through a variety of egg dishes, or indulge in extra-thick French toast stuffed with vanilla-roasted plantains and farmer's cheese, then drizzled with fresh berries and Vermont maple syrup. The drinks menu lists several intriguing cane-rum cocktails. But if you're of drinking age, we urge you toward the fresh blood-orange margarita—a strong contender for the best cocktail in history.

SUMMARY AND COMMENTS   Hip and high-quality, the family-run Cuatro is among a growing breed of swanky (or at least interesting) South Loop adopters. Good-neighbor benefits include online ordering and payment for quicker carry-out, and a night-owl-friendly light menu offered Thursday through Saturday till 2 a.m. Oh, and did we mention the blood-orange margarita?

de cero   ★★½

MEXICAN	MODERATE	QUALITY ★★	VALUE ★★★

814 West Randolph Street, West Loop; ☎ **312-455-8114;**
www.decerotaqueria.com

Reservations Accepted. **When to go** Weekend dinner. **Entree range** $11–$17. **Payment** AE, D, DC, MC, V. **Service rating** ★★★★. **Friendliness rating** ★★★★. **Parking** Valet, $10. **Bar** Full service with extensive fruit and herb margaritas and daiquiris. **Wine selection** Very limited Chilean, Spanish, French, Portuguese, Argentinean, American; $22–$45 bottle, $7.50–$12 glass. **Dress** Casual, chic. **Disabled access** Yes. **Customers** Fun, lively, big groups. **Hours** Monday–

Thursday, 11:30 a.m.–2 p.m. and 5–10 p.m.; Friday, 11:30 a.m.–2 p.m. and 5–11 p.m.; Saturday, 5–11 p.m.; Sunday, 5–10 p.m.

SETTING AND ATMOSPHERE It's a modern-day taqueria with a hacienda-style room that's sparse but for a few colorful works of Mexican folk art on rustic terra-cotta walls. Wood tables and chairs are generously spaced, except for those lined up against the walls. Noise rebounds off the hard surfaces, making it extremely loud.

HOUSE SPECIALTIES *Tres salsas* (pickled jalapeño, verde, and picante) with house-made chips; duck nachos (five house-made tortilla chips served with duck, queso, pico de gallo, mashed pinto beans, and crema); *carne asada* (skirt steak marinated in pickled jalapeños, cumin, and garlic, served with mashed pinto beans, white basmati rice, and tortillas); grilled chicken mole (boneless half chicken grilled and served with *mole poblano* sauce, basmati white rice, and sautéed greens).

OTHER RECOMMENDATIONS Seviche of rock shrimp and baby scallops with citrus, jalapeño, tomato, and cilantro with house-made chips; cumin-rubbed rib-eye skewers served with avocado crema and smoky tomato salsa; grilled pork chop marinated in tequila served with garlic mojo, mashed pinto beans, and basmati white rice; shrimp fajita sautéed with garlic, white onions, and red and poblano peppers.

SUMMARY AND COMMENTS The casual Mexican dining room fits right into the industrial-chic neighborhood, and the enormous space can accommodate crowds well. One room is strictly devoted to a bar—just right for waiting or lounging over one of the sprightly fruit and herb–blended cocktails. The main dining room has great energy, and the fresh coastal Mexican fare is made with heart and soul, down to the chips and tortillas, both of which are house-made.

Everest ★★★★★

FRENCH   VERY EXPENSIVE   QUALITY ★★★★★   VALUE ★★★

One Financial Place, 440 South LaSalle Street, 40th Floor, The Loop;
☎ **312-663-8920; www.everestrestaurant.com**

Reservations Recommended. When to go Special occasions. Entree range Pretheater menu, $54; 3-course prix-fixe menu, $89; 4-course prix-fixe menu, $98; evening tasting menu, $120. Payment All major credit cards. Service rating ★★★★. Friendliness rating ★★★★. Parking Complimentary valet parking in building. Bar Full service. Wine selection Extensive award-winning list with more than 1,700 international wines, mostly French, Alsatian, and American; $39 and up per bottle; 20–25 selections by the glass, $14–$34. Dress Jacket strongly recommended; tie optional. Disabled access Wheelchair-accessible; call ahead for special accommodations. Customers Upscale professionals, couples. Hours Tuesday–Thursday, 5:30–9 p.m.; Friday, 5:30–9:30 p.m.; Saturday, 5–10 p.m.; closed Sunday and Monday.

SETTING AND ATMOSPHERE Everest offers a luxurious, softly lit setting for spectacular dining with a view to match; the twinkling city lights far below your posh perch add a wonderful, far-from-the-madding-crowd element to dining here. The decor blends traditional elegance with modern flash; the table appointments are stunning, with lots of great specialty-serving gewgaws.

HOUSE SPECIALTIES The menu changes frequently, but representative dishes include foie gras terrine with apple and Alsace Tokay gelée; salmon soufflé attributed to Paul Haeberlin of L'Auberge de L'Ill (chef Jean Joho's mentor); roasted Maine lobster in Alsatian Gewürztraminer, butter, and ginger; fillet of halibut wrapped and roasted in potato; poached tenderloin of beef, pot-au-feu style, with horseradish cream.

OTHER RECOMMENDATIONS Standouts from the ever-changing menu have included cream of Alsace cabbage soup with home-smoked sturgeon and caviar; cold bouillabaisse terrine of seafood and shellfish; mosaic of guinea hen and duck with *petite salade;* filet of venison with wild huckleberries, braised pear, and Alsatian *knepfla* (dumplings); lemon-soufflé parfait with tapioca-almond milk; caramelized banana tart with maple–cap mushroom ice cream; warm almond nougatine and roasted figs with cardamom ice milk.

SUMMARY AND COMMENTS Everest rides high atop the Chicago Stock Exchange, continuing to enjoy a superlative reputation as one of Chicago's finest. In partnership with Lettuce Entertain You Enterprises, Chef Jean Joho's culinary vision is the true heart of this excellent restaurant as he weaves authentic Alsatian touches into his artful French fare. Joho's pedigree includes an early entry into the business at the age of 13, many subsequent years of European training, and a position as sous chef at a Michelin two-star restaurant at the age of 23. Service is carried out seamlessly by a tuxedoed team.

Follia ★★★

ITALIAN	MODERATE	QUALITY ★★★	VALUE ★★★

953 West Fulton Market, West Loop; ☎ 312-243-2888; www.folliachicago.com

Reservations Accepted. When to go Weekend dinner. Entree range $12–$30. Payment AE, D, DC, MC, V. Service rating ★★★. Friendliness rating ★★★. Parking Valet, $8; street. Bar Full service. Wine selection Italian, $32–$280 bottle, $8–$14 glass. Dress Chic, all black. Disabled access Yes. Customers Fashionable, stylish, well-heeled. Hours Tuesday–Thursday, 5–11 p.m.; Friday and Saturday, 5 p.m.–midnight; closed Sunday and Monday.

SETTING AND ATMOSPHERE The front windows of the market district storefront have mannequins in haute couture, giving just a hint at the well-appointed room. Walls and countertops are finished in cool blues and greens with tiny Italian glass tiles and a single work of art—a canvas covered in grass.

HOUSE SPECIALTIES The menu changes every couple of weeks, but representative dishes include flat pizza from a wood-burning oven in such varieties as *quattro formaggi* (Gorgonzola, Taleggio, mozzarella, and Parmigiano-Reggiano cheeses); veal scaloppine with green peppercorns; New York strip steak with rosemary-infused olive oil; and steamed sole with shrimp, tomatoes, and capers.

OTHER RECOMMENDATIONS Selections from the changing menu might include antipasti, including caprese salad with fresh mozzarella; *tagliolini* with shrimp and zucchini; ziti with tomato sauce and ricotta cheese; risotto specials such as porcini mushroom and asparagus; and veal in lemon sauce with fresh parsley and potatoes.

SUMMARY AND COMMENTS Sandwiched between meat markets on a little-traveled stretch of Fulton Market, the clandestine location makes this chic little eatery even more alluring. The mostly model waitstaff struts the floor, greeting customers and serving with sex appeal. The simple food is made from ingredients of the utmost freshness, but there are not too many of them on a given plate.

Frontera Grill ★★★★

REGIONAL MEXICAN   MODERATE   QUALITY ★★★★   VALUE ★★★

445 North Clark Street, River North; ☎ 312-661-1434; www.rickbayless.com

Reservations Limited number, parties up to 10 only. When to go Lunch, early weeknight dinner, Saturday brunch. Entree range $10.50–$36. Payment All major credit cards. Service rating ★★★½. Friendliness rating ★★★. Parking Valet, $12; pay lots; street. Bar Beer, tequilas, and margaritas. Wine selection Extensive global, 120 selections, $30–$260 per bottle; 10 by the glass, $11. Dress Casual. Disabled access Wheelchair-accessible. Customers A mixed bag. Hours Tuesday, 11:30 a.m.–2:30 p.m. and 5:20–10 p.m.; Wednesday–Thursday, 11:30 a.m.–2:30 p.m. and 5–10 p.m.; Friday, 11:30 a.m.–2:30 p.m. and 5–11 p.m.; Saturday, 10:30 a.m.–2:30 p.m. and 5–11 p.m.; closed Sunday and Monday.

SETTING AND ATMOSPHERE With vibrantly colored walls and scene-setting Mexican artwork, Frontera Grill is casual, even boisterous, while still managing to convey an almost reverent sense of commitment to authenticity and quality. This is not your neighborhood chips-and-salsa, refried-beans Mexican joint—not by a long shot.

HOUSE SPECIALTIES Menus evolve constantly. Some evergreen items include: daily tamale specials; *ensalada de jicama* (crunchy jicama salad with oranges, grapefruit, and pineapple, tossed with orange-lime vinaigrette); *sopa de tortilla* (rich tortilla soup with pasilla chiles, avocado, Jack cheese, and thick cream); Ceviche Fronterizo (crisp little tortillas piled with lime-marinated marlin, manzanillo olives, tomato, serrano chile, and cilantro); *carne asada* (naturally raised Black Angus rib eye, marinated in spicy red chiles and wood-grilled, served with black beans, fried plantains, sour cream, and guacamole); *tacos al carbon* (wood-grilled meat, poultry, fish, or mushrooms, sliced and served with roasted-pepper *rajas,* two salsas, *frijoles charros,* guacamole, and house-made tortillas); *pollo à la Yucateca* (achiote-marinated Gunthorp Farms chicken in roasted tomato–habanero sauce with orange-dressed pea shoots, avocado-leaf-flavored black beans, crispy ham, grilled orange, and zucchini).

unofficial **TIP**
Frontera Grill chef-owner Rick Bayless's newest venture is **Frontera Fresco**, a quick-service restaurant on the seventh floor of Macy's (formerly Marshall Field's) at 111 North State Street (☎ 312-781-4884; **www .rickbayless.com**). It's open Monday–Saturday, 11 a.m.–4 p.m.; closed Sunday.

OTHER RECOMMENDATIONS Examples of changing seasonal dishes include *sopa de espinacas* (spicy spinach-potato soup with grilled chicken, poblano chiles, roasted carrots, and cilantro); *cazuela de pato y hongos* (Gunthorp Farms duck braised with tomatillos, shiitake mushrooms, and roasted vegetables, over white rice and served with onions and tortillas for making soft tacos); and *lobina criolla* (grilled Atlantic striped bass in roasted tomato sauce with chipotle chiles, bacon, pineapple, jicama relish, and plantain-studded red-chile rice).

SUMMARY AND COMMENTS Serving a seductive menu of grilled dishes, moles, and chile-thick braises, Frontera Grill ups the ante on casual Mexican cuisine. The fare here is informed by the world-renowned commitment and talents of chef-owner Rick Bayless; there's a lot to explore in the exciting universe of Mexican regional cooking, and Bayless is one of the world's foremost guides through this taste-bud-tantalizing terrain. The adjacent, more formal Topolobampo (see page 266) takes things to an even higher plane. If you've had your fill of omelets and pancakes, try the Saturday-only brunch.

The Gage ★★★

| NEW AMERICAN | MODERATE | QUALITY ★★★ | VALUE ★★★ |

24 South Michigan Avenue, South Loop; ☎ **312-372-4243; www.thegagechicago.com**

Reservations Recommended. **When to go** After work; before or after museum or park visits or Loop shopping. **Entree range** $10–$42. **Payment** AE, D, DC, MC, V. **Service rating** ★★★. **Friendliness rating** ★★★★. **Parking** Valet (at University Club on Monroe Street); garage (see Unofficial Tip). **Bar** Full service, emphasis on beers, whiskeys, and signature cocktails. **Wine selection** Well-rounded selection by the 8-ounce glass ($12–$21) or bottle ($38–$125); reserve list, $80–$300. **Dress** Casual. **Disabled access** Yes. **Customers** Loop workers and residents, sightseers, after-work crowd. **Hours** Monday–Friday, 11–2 a.m.; Saturday, 10–3 a.m.; Sunday, 10 a.m.–midnight.

SETTING AND ATMOSPHERE From the grand, vintage-inspired exterior light fixtures to the green subway tiles, classic Chicago tin ceiling (expect high decibels at peak hours), and imposing, 50-foot mahogany bar, this 300-seat gastropub has the gravitas to go with the somewhat pricey "upscale comfort food" menu. Easiest approached by foot, by public transportation, or maybe by parachute, the primo location across from Millennium Park (and near the Art Institute) has limited accessibility.

HOUSE SPECIALTIES Beyond-your-basic bar foods such as Scotch eggs, fried chicken livers with spicy mustard, and fries with curry gravy are one way to go; for a full meal, creative seasonal dishes might include basil-marinated escargots with melted-red-onion and goat-cheese soup;

venison tartare with fava and egg yolk; peppered Angus hanger steak with shaved pears, blue cheese, endive, and walnuts; peach-wood-smoked Kona Kampachi on lobster potato salad with chive and yuzu; or a salad of braised rabbit with greens, crisp rice, Langhe Robiola cheese, and horseradish vinaigrette.

OTHER RECOMMENDATIONS More-casual selections include a USDA prime burger with local Camembert and melted-onion marmalade on a toasted malt roll; fish-and-chips in Guinness batter with malt tartar sauce; roasted Amish chicken with goat-cheese-tossed green beans; and local sausages with crisp Brie potato. At lunch, try potato soup with smoked bacon and clams or the peppered salmon club with caper aioli on focaccia. At Saturday and Sunday brunch, look for the traditional Irish breakfast of eggs, rashers, black and white puddings, Irish sausages, tomato with beans, and toast on the side; crab and asparagus omelet; steel-cut Irish oatmeal brûlée; or chocolate-pistachio-ricotta French toast.

> *unofficial* **TIP**
> Parking for The Gage is a gouge at Grant Park North Garage; if you insist on garage parking, the far southwest entrance (look for the Saturn icon) is the closest.

SUMMARY AND COMMENTS This nabe needed a spot like this, and The Gage feels long-established, despite having opened in spring of 2007. Situated in three architecturally significant, beautiful old millinery buildings on Michigan Avenue, The Gage has used its heritage wisely in a very inviting, classy tavern setting serving thinking-man's tavern cuisine.

Gibsons Bar & Steakhouse ★★★½

| STEAK | EXPENSIVE | QUALITY ★★★★ | VALUE ★★ |

1028 North Rush Street, Gold Coast; ☎ 312-266-8999; www.gibsonssteakhouse.com

Reservations Recommended. **When to go** Weekends for the scene. **Entree range** $9–$135 (the latter for surf and turf). **Payment** AE, D, DC, JCB, MC, V. **Service rating** ★★★½. **Friendliness rating** ★★. **Parking** Valet, $11. **Bar** Full service. **Wine selection** American, Italian, New Zealand; $22–$621 bottle, $7–$37 glass. **Dress** Trendy to dressy. **Disabled access** Yes. **Customers** Mature, showy locals; middle-aged singles. **Hours** Daily, 11 a.m.–midnight.

SETTING AND ATMOSPHERE The 1940s men's-club decor, with dark-wood wainscoting and trim plus tile floors, continues to draw fans who pack the front bar. There's usually a wait, but patrons don't seem to mind; mingling before dinner is part of the allure. A favorite of the midlife-to-senior social set, Gibsons is one of three Rush Street nightspots collectively known as the "Viagra Triangle" (see Part 11, Entertainment and Nightlife). The crowd is a central-casting mix of "dese and dose" Chicagoans, singles and preeners, pinky-ring aficionados and politicos.

HOUSE SPECIALTIES Caesar salad; bone-in sirloin; veal chop; New York sirloin; double-baked potato; sautéed spinach and broccoli with olive oil and garlic; asparagus with hollandaise sauce.

OTHER RECOMMENDATIONS Spicy lobster cocktail; baby back ribs; double-cut lamb chops; Australian and colossal lobster tails; London broil.

SUMMARY AND COMMENTS High-quality steaks and land-of-the-giants desserts are served in obscene quantities, usually in straightforward preparations, at this popular Gold Coast steak house. There's also a limited selection of fish and chicken offered along with classic sides, but fans rave most about the prime, dry-aged beef. It's a happening scene on most nights, with live piano and a bounty of singles with eyes wide open.

Green Zebra ★★★★

CONTEMPORARY NEW AMERICAN/VEGETARIAN	MODERATE
QUALITY ★★★★	VALUE ★★★★

**1460 West Chicago Avenue, West Town; ☎ 312-243-7100;
www.greenzebrachicago.com**

Reservations Recommended. **When to go** Weekday or weekend dinner. **Entree range** $11–$16. **Payment** AE, D, DC, MC, V. **Service rating** ★★★★. **Friendliness rating** ★★★★. **Parking** Street. **Bar** Full service. **Wine selection** French, Italian, Spanish, Californian; $28–$78 bottle, $8–$17 glass. **Dress** Casual. **Disabled access** Yes. **Customers** Hip vegetarians and vegans, foodies. **Hours** Monday–Thursday, 5:30–10 p.m.; Friday and Saturday, 5–11 p.m.; Sunday, 10:30 a.m.–2 p.m., 5:30–9 p.m.

SETTING AND ATMOSPHERE The sleek, upscale room is done in neutral tones with cool recessed lighting, a stairway on one wall that leads to nowhere, and textured tabletops that resemble reed grass. There are a limited number of tables, so waiting can get crowded at the slender bar up front.

HOUSE SPECIALTIES The seasonally changing menu might include crispy sweet-potato dumplings with water chestnuts and dandelion miso broth; crimson-lentil cake spiced with shallot-and-red-pepper jam; chicken breast with new potatoes, crisp skin, and wild honey; roasted halibut with fiddlehead ferns, yellow wax beans, and creamed watercress.

OTHER RECOMMENDATIONS Seasonal offerings might include roasted baby beets with fennel flan and candied beets; buckwheat crepe with escarole, sugar snap peas, and morel mushrooms; grilled trumpet royale mushrooms, roasted white corn, and herb vinaigrette; curry-spiced eggplant soup.

SUMMARY AND COMMENTS This widely acclaimed venture by well-known local chef Shawn McClain (named 2006's Best Midwest Chef by the James Beard Foundation) offers an innovative take on meatless fare. Sharing-size dishes (you'll need more than one) have so much flavor and texture that you don't miss the meat, although there are a very few nonvegetarian options with chicken or fish. The global and reasonable wine list marries well with the menu for a most tantalizing tasting experience. Green Zebra has recently added Sunday brunch, a great option for jaded palates.

Hot Doug's   ★★★

FAST FOOD   INEXPENSIVE   QUALITY ★★★★★   VALUE ★★★★★

**3324 North California Avenue, Roscoe Village; ☎ 773-279-9550;
www.hotdougs.com**

Reservations Not accepted. **When to go** Lunch, afternoon, or early dinner, as it closes at 4 p.m. **Entree range** $1.50–$8. **Payment** Cash only. **Service rating** ★★★. **Friendliness rating** ★★★★★. **Parking** Street. **Bar** BYOB. **Wine selection** BYOB. **Dress** Casual. **Disabled access** No. **Customers** Foodies, students, blue-and white-collars. **Hours** Monday–Saturday, 10:30 a.m.–4 p.m.; closed Sunday.

SETTING AND ATMOSPHERE Brightly colored and casual, this come-as-you-are "Sausage Superstore and Encased Meat Emporium" has a cultish following that prompts ever-longer lines out the door (friendly, efficient service keeps things moving). There's plenty of Elvis and wiener kitsch, wild music, a larger seating area than the original (prefire) location, and easy street parking—but still those frustrating funky hours.

HOUSE SPECIALTIES Daily specials are the highlight and might include venison, rattlesnake, or alligator. Examples include bacon-Cheddar elk sausage with Guinness stout mustard and sage derby cheese, and Cognac-infused pheasant sausage with black truffle mustard and foie gras "butter" (yes, foie is back on the menu after Chicago's absurd flap over the formerly felonious lobes). Even the condiments are special, with four styles of mustard (yellow, spicy brown, honey, and Dijon) and onions raw or caramelized. The French fries are cooked in duck fat on Fridays and Saturdays.

unofficial **TIP**
Hot Doug's takes its leisure seriously, so if you're headed there on even a minor holiday, it pays to call in advance.

OTHER RECOMMENDATIONS Classic Chicago dog with all the fixin's (steamed, grilled, deep-fried, or deep-fried *and* grilled); bratwurst soaked in beer; vegetarian dog; corn dog; bagel dogs and potato nuggets for kids.

SUMMARY AND COMMENTS "Gourmet encased meats" may sound like a joke, but in the hands of Doug Sohn, the dog has its day in forms familiar and fantastic. Hot Doug's is a category killer with national recognition and a crazed, beloved genius at the helm. Menu items get silly celeb names (which change on a whim).

kids Irazu   ★★★

COSTA RICAN/VEGETARIAN   INEXPENSIVE   QUALITY ★★★★   VALUE ★★★★★

**1865 North Milwaukee Avenue, Bucktown; ☎ 773-252-5687;
www.irazuchicago.com**

Reservations Not accepted. **When to go** Breakfast, lunch, early weeknight dinner. **Entree range** $5–$13.50. **Payment** Cash only. **Service rating** ★★. **Friendliness rating** ★★★★. **Parking** Lot, street. **Bar** BYOB. **Wine selection** BYOB. **Dress** Neighborhood casual. **Disabled access** Yes. **Customers** Locals, students, Central Americans. **Hours** Monday–Saturday, 11:30 a.m.–9:30 p.m.; closed Sunday.

SETTING AND ATMOSPHERE This cozy little Costa Rican joint is a family-run Bucktown favorite with a warm, if no-frills, ambience. Service is friendly (and kid-friendly), and the counter and small dining room are usually buzzing with grateful neighborhood denizens and bargain hunters. There's a bit of sidewalk dining to help with the crowd overflow.

HOUSE SPECIALTIES Traditional *casado* (thin rib-eye steak, chicken breast, tilapia, or vegetable of the day, white rice, black beans, sweet plantains, an over-easy egg, and cabbage salad); vegetarian burrito; *gallo pinto* (breakfast dish of white rice, whole black beans, and eggs or plantains); milk or water "shakes" (such as oatmeal, blackberry, tamarind, or cornmeal).

OTHER RECOMMENDATIONS Mashed-potato tacos; hearts of palm salad; fried or boiled yuca (cassava) with garlic oil; *pepito* sandwich (rib-eye steak, sautéed onions, cheese, and pinto beans); French toast with sour cream; homemade flan; fresh carrot juice.

SUMMARY AND COMMENTS A few Mexican and American items dot a menu of Costa Rican cooking, including lots of interesting vegetarian items for breakfast, lunch, and dinner. Since the place is very popular—not just for the big portions of oh-so-fresh food but also for the el-cheapo prices—and is walk-in only, try early weeknights for dinner, or call ahead for takeout. Expect slow service from the small kitchen when the place is busy.

Japonais ★★★

ASIAN FUSION	EXPENSIVE	QUALITY ★★★	VALUE ★★

600 West Chicago Avenue, Near West; ☎ 312-822-9600; www.japonaischicago.com

Reservations Accepted. **When to go** Weekday dinner. **Entree range** Lunch, $11–$19; dinner, $19–$72. **Payment** AE, DC, MC, V. **Service rating** ★★½. **Friendliness rating** ★★★. **Parking** Valet, $6 at lunch, $12 at dinner. **Bar** Full service with extensive martinis and sake. **Wine selection** Californian, French, New Zealand, and German; $38–$680 bottle, $10–$28 glass. **Dress** Casual chic or business casual during day. **Disabled access** Yes. **Customers** Trendy, young; suburbanites on weekends. **Hours** Monday–Thursday, 11:30 a.m.–2:30 p.m. and 5–11 p.m.; Friday, 11:30 a.m.–2:30 p.m. and 5–11:30 p.m.; Saturday, 5–11:30 p.m.; Sunday, 5–10 p.m.

SETTING AND ATMOSPHERE Two distinct dining areas are separated by a limestone waterfall. Step down on the lounge side into a sunken dining room with black granite tables and a large fireplace, or dine in the opposing raised dining area flanked by a sushi bar and banquettes around the room's perimeter. The dreamlike downstairs lounge opens to an outdoor patio overlooking the river, attracting a late-night see-and-be-seen crowd.

HOUSE SPECIALTIES Spicy octopus roll topped with spicy tuna and sweet *unagi* sauce; crab cakes; lobster spring rolls with mango relish and blood-orange vinaigrette; shrimp tempura with a brie fondue sauce; Kobe beef carpaccio; *kani nigiri* (king crab); stir-fried soba noodles with tofu and seasonal vegetables; "Le Quack Japonais" (whole-maple-leaf-smoked duck with hoisin sauce, mango chutney, and mu shu wraps).

OTHER RECOMMENDATIONS *Bin cho* (marinated sashimi of baby tuna with arugula and shaved daikon in a citrus-sake vinaigrette); fried calamari tossed in a sweet-and-sour sauce with wasabi vinaigrette; Japonais fried rice with chicken, beef, or shrimp; yuzu-almond crème brûlée (homemade creamy citrus custard served with almond tuile cookie).

SUMMARY AND COMMENTS Some of the same stylish team that created the popular Mirai Sushi (see page 243) has expanded on its concept with similar painstaking attention to the decor. The food gets almost as much focus, with intriguing combinations of flavors and textures, along with appealing presentations.

Jin Ju ★★★

KOREAN	MODERATE	QUALITY ★★★	VALUE ★★★

5203 North Clark Street, Andersonville; ☎ 773-334-6377; www.jinjuchicago.com

Reservations Accepted. **When to go** Any day for dinner. **Entree range** $9–$18. **Payment** AE, MC, V. **Service rating** ★★★. **Friendliness rating** ★★★. **Parking** Street only. **Bar** Full service. **Wine selection** Ordinary and limited Californian, European, Korean; $14–$64 bottle, $5–$7 glass. **Dress** Casual. **Disabled access** No. **Customers** Young locals. **Hours** Tuesday–Wednesday, 5–9:30 p.m.; Thursday, 5–10 p.m.; Friday–Saturday, 5–11 p.m.; Sunday, 5–9:30 p.m.; closed Monday.

SETTING AND ATMOSPHERE The dining room at this Korean establishment feels more like a sushi bar, with clean lines, dark oak floors, and black spinning fans overhead. Original tin ceilings remain, but the overall feeling is contemporary—mimicking the style of the food, which puts a new spin on traditional Korean fare.

HOUSE SPECIALTIES *Pajun* (lightly fried scallion pancake served with a soy dipping sauce); *mandoo* (Korean dumplings filled with beef, onions, scallions, bean sprouts, and tofu); *te gim* (tempura-style fried shrimp, squid, and vegetables); crab and cucumber salad; *chap chae* (vermicelli noodles with beef sirloin, spinach, roasted red peppers, shiitake mushrooms, carrots, onions, and scallions); *kim chee chigae* (kim chee soup with pork, tofu, scallions, and green chiles); *kalbi* (beef short ribs marinated in a sweet soy sauce then grilled and served with lettuce and bean paste).

OTHER RECOMMENDATIONS *Myuk* (mild seaweed soup with scallions in a mussel broth); *kim bap* (seaweed roll filled with rice, *bulgolgi* [grilled marinated beef], spinach, carrots, fish cake, egg, and yellow pickled radish); *dol sut bi bim bap* (rice bowl with beef, bean sprouts, spinach, carrots, red leaf lettuce, mushrooms, fried egg, and spicy red-pepper paste served in a hot stone pot); *o jinga bokum* (sautéed squid with green chile peppers, onions, and carrots in a red-pepper sauce).

SUMMARY AND COMMENTS It's the first of its kind to bring traditional Korean fare into the mainstream—with killer *soju*-tinis. The hip room makes tasting this unusual cuisine more palatable, although after an initial introduction it's not all that intimidating. Flavorful dishes are spiced just hot enough for the American palate, but many still have kick. It's a charming addition to the Asian restaurant scene, situated conveniently in Andersonville.

Joe's Seafood, Prime Steak & Stone Crab ★★★

STEAK/SEAFOOD	EXPENSIVE	QUALITY ★★★	VALUE ★★

60 East Grand Avenue, River North; ☎ 312-379-5637;
www.joesstonecrabchicago.com

Reservations Highly recommended. **When to go** Power lunch, early or late dinner. **Entree range** $14–$45. **Payment** AE, D, DC, MC, V. **Service rating** ★★★. **Friendliness rating** ★★★. **Parking** Valet, $12 for up to 3 hours, $16 for longer. **Bar** Full service. **Wine selection** Broad price range, strength in California Cabs; $28–$1,745 bottle, $7–$14 glass. **Dress** Business casual. **Disabled access** Yes. **Customers** Expense accounters, tourists, groups. **Hours** Monday–Thursday, 11:30 a.m.–10 p.m.; Friday, 11:30 a.m.–11 p.m.; Saturday, 11 a.m.–11 p.m.; Sunday, 11 a.m.–9:30 p.m. (lounge serves food a half hour later than dining room).

SETTING AND ATMOSPHERE Spun from the Miami Beach mainstay Joe's Stone Crab, this Lettuce Entertain You Enterprises concept is more clubby urban steak house than seaside getaway; it does have that Lettuce "instant history" in the old-guard masculine decor (dark wood, plush booths, moody vintage photography), but at least it avoids some of that corporate group's over-the-top decorative indulgences—and takes reservations. And this is Chicago—so while stone crab has a season, prime beef does not. Expect an upscale but unstuffy atmosphere with polished, professional service (some tableside) in tuxes and a crowded, boisterous scene.

HOUSE SPECIALTIES Florida stone-crab claws (fresh in season mid-October to mid-May, frozen off-season) with mustard sauce; Alaskan king-crab legs; bone-in prime filet mignon or New York strip; hash browns; fried green tomatoes; cole slaw mixed with relish; pies (Key lime, peanut butter, coconut, or banana cream).

OTHER RECOMMENDATIONS Oysters Rockefeller; fried chicken; jumbo lump crab cakes; Parmesan-crusted halibut; grilled swordfish; crab-stuffed sole with lobster sauce; calf's liver with bacon and onions; chopped salad; beef tenderloin salad (lunch only); fried asparagus.

SUMMARY AND COMMENTS Okay, so you're paying the airfare per crab. We may have a lake, but we don't have an ocean—and sometimes nothing but the "sea" in seafood will do. Lunch is calmer and cheaper (but still pricey), and you may experience a long wait, even with reservations.

Le Colonial ★★★½

VIETNAMESE/FRENCH	MODERATE	QUALITY ★★★★	VALUE ★★★

937 North Rush Street, Gold Coast; ☎ 312-255-0088;
www.lecolonialchicago.com

Reservations Recommended. **When to go** Weekend evenings, during warm weather. **Entree range** Lunch, $17–$25; dinner, $18–$31. **Payment** AE, DC, MC, V. **Service rating** ★★½. **Friendliness rating** ★★★. **Parking** Valet, $15 (no valet for Sunday or Monday lunch). **Bar** Full service. **Wine selection** French and Californian, $40–$300 bottle; 30 by the glass, $8.50–$13; Champagne, $9–$18 glass. **Dress** Stylish to dressy. **Disabled access** Yes. **Customers** Older local crowd, well dressed. **Hours** *Lunch:* daily, 11:30 a.m.–2:30 p.m. *Dinner:* Monday–Wednesday, 5–11 p.m.; Thursday–Saturday, 5 p.m.–midnight; Sunday, 5–10 p.m.

SETTING AND ATMOSPHERE Sultry, French colonial–style room with spinning ceiling fans, live palm plants, bamboo shutters, and sepia-toned vintage photos of Vietnam. There's an intimate upstairs lounge that's a real find, and balcony seating in warm weather.

HOUSE SPECIALTIES *Goi bo* (spicy marinated-beef salad); *bo bia* (soft salad rolls with julienne vegetables and a spicy-sweet peanut-plum dipping sauce); *ca chien Saigon* (crisp Vietnamese whole red snapper); *vit quay* (ginger-marinated roast duck with a tamarind sauce); *banh uot* (grilled sesame beef rolls with lettuce, cucumber, and fresh herbs).

OTHER RECOMMENDATIONS *Ca tim nuong* (spicy basil-lime grilled eggplant); *com tho ga* (ginger chicken with vegetables and rice in a clay pot); *com chien* (house fried rice with chicken and vegetables); *bahn cuon* (steamed Vietnamese ravioli with chicken and mushrooms).

SUMMARY AND COMMENTS The appealing, film-set-like dining room at this Rush Street Vietnamese restaurant draws crowds regularly, as does the sultry upstairs lounge. The flavors are quite authentic, and the combinations of warm and cold, sweet and spicy, and soft and crunchy make the fare tasty and sensuous. The food here is approachable enough for a timid American palate.

unofficial **TIP**
For a convenient Gold Coast night on the town, dine at Le Colonial and head downstairs to **The Drawing Room at Le Passage**, a stylish, revamped lounge.

Le Lan ★★★★

VIETNAMESE	MODERATE	QUALITY ★★★★	VALUE ★★★

749 North Clark Street, River North; ☎ 312-280-9100; www.lelanrestaurant.com

Reservations Recommended. **When to go** Weekend dinner. **Entree range** $21–$35. **Payment** ae, dc, jcb, mc, v. **Service rating** ★★★★. **Friendliness rating** ★★★. **Parking** Valet, $10. **Bar** Full service. **Wine selection** French, Californian, Australian, New Zealand, and Alsatian; $30–$375 bottle, $8–$16 glass. **Dress** Upscale. **Disabled access** Yes. **Customers** Food fans, suburbanites, visitors. **Hours** Monday–Thursday, 5–9:30 p.m.; Friday, 5–10 p.m.; Saturday, 5:30–10:30 p.m.; closed Sunday.

SETTING AND ATMOSPHERE Designed by one of the owners, the room is rich with dark walnut walls, jade-green tile floors, and Vietnamese artifacts. There's an ominous mural of a Chinese dragon painted on the back wall, subtly lit from above and below.

HOUSE SPECIALTIES Tea-smoked duck breast with savory bread pudding and star-anise reduction; Asian bouillabaisse with curried fingerling potatoes; banana-leaf-wrapped red fish with red Thai curry; Colorado lamb loin and rack with hen-of-the-woods mushrooms and green curry sauce.

OTHER RECOMMENDATIONS Young Thai coconut soup with olive-oil-poached shrimp, galangal root, and lemongrass; Asian-style stuffed crab claw with caper rémoulade and oranges; wagyu beef carpaccio with rosemary brioche crouton, marinated jicama, and pink peppercorns; golden pineapple-mango financier with coconut-lime tapioca sauce.

SUMMARY AND COMMENTS This stylish French-Asian fine-diner brings executive chef Chad Starling's delicate, rich flavors of France together with spicy and tangy pan-Asian flavors in a unique take on traditional dishes. The room is almost a museum of textiles and art, enhancing the elegance of the dining experience. A well-selected wine list rounds out the nicely executed menu.

Lou Malnati's ★★½

PIZZA/ITALIAN	INEXPENSIVE	QUALITY ★★	VALUE ★★★★

439 North Wells Street, River North; ☎ 312-828-9800; www.loumalnatis.com
958 West Wrightwood Avenue, Lincoln Park; ☎ 773-832-4030
6649 North Lincoln Avenue, Lincolnwood; ☎ 847-673-0800
1520 North Damen Avenue, Bucktown–Wicker Park; ☎ 773-395-2400
1850 Sherman Avenue, Evanston; ☎ 847-328-5400; plus
numerous additional suburban locations

Reservations Not accepted. When to go Anytime. Entree range $5.50–$8 (individual); more for pizza. Payment AE, D, DC, MC, V. Service rating ★★. Friendliness rating ★★★. Parking Varies by location. Bar Full service. Wine selection Generic, limited; $18–$25 bottle, $5–$6 glass. Dress Casual. Disabled access Varies by location. Customers One and all. Hours Vary by location.

SETTING AND ATMOSPHERE Settings vary widely, from the quaint, freestanding Lincolnwood original to the ho-hum frat-dining-room setting of the River North location. Hardly the point, however—you just need a place to sit and someone to cook and bring you your pizza.

HOUSE SPECIALTIES Butter-crust deep-dish pizza; thin-crust pizza; stuffed spinach bread; meatball sandwich; antipasto salad; chocolate-chip "pizza" dessert.

OTHER RECOMMENDATIONS Low-fat cheese pizza; gluten-free, low-carb "crustless" pizza; mostaccioli; chicken club salad; Granny Smith apple pie. There's a kids' menu with chicken nuggets, corn dogs, and such.

SUMMARY AND COMMENTS In a city of fight-to-the-death pizza partisanship, Lou's perpetually rises to the top with its long-standing consistency and just plain addictive 'za (the house sausage and chunky tomato sauce are noteworthy). You come here for the pizza and perhaps a frosty brew, and everything else—including the other food—is window dressing. You can take home frozen pies for later or to share the sinful goodness of this hometown favorite with others. Or if you get hooked on it while in town, you can have it shipped nationwide for the price of a haute-cuisine meal (visit **www.tastesofchicago.com**).

Lou Mitchell's Restaurant ★★

AMERICAN   INEXPENSIVE   QUALITY ★★★   VALUE ★★★★

565 West Jackson Boulevard, The Loop; ☎ 312-939-3111;
www.loumitchellsrestaurant.com
Lou Mitchell's Express, O'Hare Airport, Terminal 5,
5600 North Mannheim Road; ☎ 773-601-8989

Reservations Accepted for parties of 6 or more, Monday–Thursday only. **When to go** Breakfast, lunch. **Entree range** $6–$15. **Payment** Cash only. **Service rating** ★★. **Friendliness rating** ★★½. **Parking** Public lots, street. **Bar** None. **Wine selection** None. **Dress** Casual. **Disabled access** No. **Customers** Loop workers, die-hard fans. **Hours** Monday–Saturday, 5:30 a.m.–3 p.m.; Sunday, 7 a.m.–3 p.m.

SETTING AND ATMOSPHERE Lou Mitchell's celebrates the technological break-throughs of Naugahyde, Formica, and fake plants. This is lowbrow, high-camp, retro-diner authenticity at its finest, complete with Rat Pack background music.

HOUSE SPECIALTIES Eggs and fluffy, in-the-skillet omelets made with double-yolk eggs (including Greek sausage, tomato, green pepper, and onion, or Michigan sweet apples with old English Cheddar cheese); Belgian malted waffles; grilled French toast; homemade pie. Extensive daily specials run the gamut from corned beef hash to chicken potpie, baked short ribs, and "creamed baked macaroni au gratin."

OTHER RECOMMENDATIONS Club sandwich; baked meat loaf; grilled patty melt; fresh banana pancakes; milk shakes.

SUMMARY AND COMMENTS Head back in time at this legendary diner-restaurant, opened in 1923. Lou Mitchell's is famous for its gruff anti-service, free doughnut holes for those standing in line and Milk Duds for the ladies and kids, and classic diner schtick. A commitment to freshness is evident in the fresh-squeezed juice, fresh breads and pastries, and homemade marmalade.

L2O ★★★★★

SEAFOOD, NEW AMERICAN   VERY EXPENSIVE   QUALITY ★★★★★   VALUE ★★★

2300 North Lincoln Park West; ☎ 773-868-0002;
www.l2orestaurant.com

Reservations Highly recommended. **When to go** Splurges and special occasions. **Entree range** Tasting only; 4-course, $110; 12-course, $165 (pricey à la carte courses can be ordered off the menu). **Payment** ae, d, dc, mc, v. **Service rating** ★★★★. **Friendliness rating** ★★★. **Parking** Valet, $10. **Bar** Lounge area, full bar service. **Wine selection** Vast, world class, with strengths in highly allocated, rare vintage Champagnes and Burgundies, bottles from the $30s to down-payment-on-a-house territory; $11–$24 glass. **Dress** Jackets suggested. **Disabled access**

Yes. **Customers** Power money, well-heeled foodies, milestone celebrants. **Hours** Monday, Wednesday, and Thursday, 6–10 p.m.; Friday and Saturday, 5–11 p.m.; Sunday, 5–9 p.m.; closed Tuesday.

SETTING AND ATMOSPHERE A clandestine entrance swallows you up into stunning, subdued modern surroundings in the former Ambria space. The minimal dining room is done in dark and light woods, frosted glass, and sophisticated neutrals, with ivory leather seats, a gold-painted "reef" showcase, and a "rain" effect created by floor-to-ceiling, zen-dustrial steel tension wires. Tatami rooms for two or eight are an intimate way to stage a memorable business or romantic meal.

HOUSE SPECIALTIES Laurent Gras conjures artful creations using global artisanal ingredients in a changing menu of seasonal shellfish in raw, warm, and main dishes. Examples include yellowtail with yuzu, soy sauce, olive oil, and micro chives; mackerel with red miso, breakfast radishes and daikon flowers, and soy salt; gold egg yolk with amberjack, Kurobuta pork, sake, and green apple granite; black bass with smoked shellfish bouillon, saffron, Rhode Island mussels, and sorrel leaves.

unofficial **TIP**
At L2O, a glossary is provided to help you sort out the seafood without feeling like an idiot.

OTHER RECOMMENDATIONS Shellfish platters (two sizes); skate wing with bordelaise and asparagus; scallop with sassafras, hibiscus and tomato; butterfish shabu-shabu, cooked in the kitchen, not at the table, then returned to diners in a soup format with scallions, noodles, and yuzu; dessert soufflés; coffee (the restaurant has a rare specialty Clover coffeemaker that produces world-class java).

SUMMARY AND COMMENTS As the contrived name implies, chef Laurent Gras does have a unique formula for transforming the denizens of the sea into tiny, beautifully composed cups, plates, bowls, and glasses. His inventive, ultramodern delicacies roll out of the kitchen, borne by poised and professional servers who are ably abetted by passionate, knowledgeable sommeliers. It's over-the-top expensive, but really special—especially if you can appreciate the wine list, both literally and figuratively.

Lula ★★★½

ECLECTIC/VEGETARIAN	MODERATE	QUALITY ★★★	VALUE ★★★★

2537 North Kedzie Boulevard, Logan Square; ☎ 773-489-9554; www.lulacafe.com

Reservations Not accepted. **When to go** Early. **Entree range** $7–$27; 3-course "Monday Night Farm Dinner," $28. **Payment** AE, MC, V. **Service rating** ★★. **Friendliness rating** ★★★. **Parking** Street. **Bar** Full service. **Wine selection** Value-priced eclectic; $21–$65 bottle; $7–$14 glass. **Dress** Funky-casual. **Disabled access** Yes. **Customers** Hipsters, locals, vegetarians. **Hours** Sunday, Monday, Wednesday, and Thursday, 9 a.m.–10 p.m.; Friday and Saturday, 9 a.m.–11 p.m.; closed Tuesday.

SETTING AND ATMOSPHERE It's a laid-back scene at funky-chic Lula, unless it's packed (which it often is). Lucky Logan Square locals don't seem to mind sardining into the small, cafe-style dining room with worn wood floors and local artwork, or waiting in the cozy adjoining bar. Off-hours find neighbors grabbing a barista coffee drink or chilling over a moderately priced meal.

HOUSE SPECIALTIES Bucatini pasta with Moroccan cinnamon, feta, garlic, and brown butter; olive-oil-marinated beet bruschetta with arugula and goat cheese; chilled peanut-satay sesame noodles with gomae and marinated tofu; three-egg frittata with your choice of ingredients; breakfast burrito; brioche French toast.

OTHER RECOMMENDATIONS Daily specials are a key element in the of-the-moment seasonal cooking here. Examples include mascarpone-stuffed brioche French toast with farm cherries, figs, vanilla anglaise, and graham-cracker strudel; prosciutto omelet with arugula, pecorino, sweet onion, and peach preserves; Nova Scotia lobster soup with new potatoes, watercress, and quail egg; grilled Gunthorp Farms pork loin with shiso-juniper cabbage, glazed carrots, and sweet plum jus.

unofficial TIP
A South Loop sequel to Lula is in the works at an undisclosed location.

SUMMARY AND COMMENTS Wonderful organic and vegetarian-vegan options abound on Amalea Tshilds and Jason Hammel's intelligent, eclectic menu. It's a welcoming spot with "hipster hangout" written all over it, but not to the extreme— plenty of black and tattoos are in evidence, but neither is required to feel at home here. Especially after a rhubarb gimlet or passion-fruit daiquiri.

Manny's Coffee Shop & Deli ★★

| DELI/CAFETERIA | INEXPENSIVE | QUALITY ★★★★ | VALUE ★★★ |

1141 South Jefferson Street, South Loop; ☎ **312-939-2855;**
www.mannysdeli.com
Concourse A, Midway Airport, ☎ **773-948-6300**

Reservations Not accepted. **When to go** Breakfast, lunch, dinner. **Entree range** $6–$16. **Payment** AE, D, MC, V. **Service rating** ★★. **Friendliness rating** ★★★. **Parking** Free valet, street, small lot. **Bar** Limited beer and wine. **Dress** Shirt and shoes required. **Disabled access** Yes. **Customers** Blue- and white-collar melting pot, South Loop denizens. **Hours** Monday–Saturday, 5 a.m.–8 p.m.; closed Sunday.

SETTING AND ATMOSPHERE This beloved cafeteria-style deli, dishing it up since 1942, oozes authenticity with the fast-paced counter service, no-frills furnishings, water served in paper cones, and cashier station–candy counter selling sweet treats and cheap cigars. Down-to-earth, City of Big Shoulders patrons are here to tie on a serious feedbag—and now they can do it at night thanks to a shocking development: the addition of night hours and alcohol service.

HOUSE SPECIALTIES Mile-high corned beef and pastrami sandwiches; Reubens; beef brisket; meat loaf; beef stew; liver and onions; short ribs; knishes; borscht and matzo-ball soup.

unofficial **TIP**
Manny's, once a cash-only institution, now accepts credit cards.

OTHER RECOMMENDATIONS Corned-beef omelets; lox breakfast; chopped liver. Daily specials include chop suey and fried smelts with mushrooms.

SUMMARY AND COMMENTS This place is a Chicago institution, and deservedly so. To quote Manny's Web site, "At Manny's you don't diet. You don't snack. You don't nosh. You come to this landmark lunchroom to pile your tray high and eat like there's no tomorrow." Gruff, old-timey counter staff in paper hats sling heavenly, hearty fare; at the end of the line is a time-warp sweets section featuring stewed prunes, Jell-O, rice pudding, and German chocolate cake.

Mercat a la Planxa ★★★★

SPANISH/TAPAS	MODERATE	QUALITY ★★★★	VALUE ★★★

Blackstone Hotel, 638 South Michigan Avenue, South Loop;
☎ **312-765-0524; www.mercatchicago.com**

Reservations Accepted. **When to go** After work or sightseeing, seeking variety for breakfast, lunch, or dinner. **Entree range** Tapas, $5–$28; entrees, $9–$54. 7-75 **Payment** AE, D, DC, MC, V. **Service rating** ★★★★. **Friendliness rating** ★★★. **Parking** Pay lot; validated valet, $14. **Bar** Seasonal sangrias, signature cocktails, ports, and sherries. **Wine selection** Generous selection of Spanish and New World still and sparkling wines, most by the bottle ($28–$275) or glass ($6–$17). **Dress** Upscale casual. **Disabled access** Yes. **Customers** Dates, groups sharing, business travelers, sightseers. **Hours** Monday–Thursday, 6:30 a.m.–3 p.m. and 5–11 p.m.; Friday-Saturday, 6:30 a.m.–3 p.m. and 5–midnight; Sunday, 6:30 a.m.–3 p.m. and 5–10 p.m.

SETTING AND ATMOSPHERE Mercat's hip, Barcelona-style scene is as modern as The Blackstone (the hotel that houses it) is traditional. Above a winding staircase, Gaudi-inspired decorative elements, bright colors, clashing curves, two communal tables, and multilevel dining add up to a chic space that's vibrant with energy. Giant illustrations imply the bustling markets of Spain. In nice weather, you can dine outdoors.

HOUSE SPECIALTIES The name refers to the 20 or so choices of grilled meats and seafood, including prawns, American prime rib eye, and Uruguayan filet mignon. Contemporary and classic tapas include cut-to-order charcuterie and cheeses. You can opt for a chef's tapas tasting, or, for parties of four or more, a whole-roasted suckling pig is prepared with grilled green onions, herb-roasted fingerling potatoes, Catalan spinach, and rosemary white beans (72 hours' notice required).

OTHER RECOMMENDATIONS Spanish octopus with confit potato and smoked paprika; slow-cooked short ribs and diver scallops with shaved Parmesan and artichokes; slow-cooked pork belly with cider glaze, green apples, and truffle.

SUMMARY AND COMMENTS Chef Jose Garces's (Philly's Amada and Tinto) Catalan specialties of all sizes issue from an open kitchen. Mercat is sexy for a date, while great for families with teens, who'll dig the hip, worldly scene and a menu with something for even the pickiest of eaters.

Mirai Sushi   ★★★½

JAPANESE/SUSHI	MODERATE	QUALITY ★★★★	VALUE ★★★

2020 West Division Street, Wicker Park; ☎ 773-862-8500; www.miraisushi.com

Reservations Recommended. **When to go** Dinner (weeknights for less crowding). **Entree range** $6–$23. **Payment** AE, D, MC, V. **Service rating** ★★★. **Friendliness rating** ★★★. **Parking** Valet, $10; street. **Bar** Full service, emphasis on sake. **Wine selection** 54 global, $34–$106; 13 by the glass, $8–$12. **Dress** Casual. **Disabled access** Wheelchair-accessible first floor only. **Customers** Hip urbanites of all ages. **Hours** Monday–Wednesday, 5–10 p.m.; Thursday–Saturday, 5–11 p.m.; upstairs lounge open 5:30 p.m.–1 a.m.; closed Sunday.

SETTING AND ATMOSPHERE This bustling, bilevel Wicker Park place is a sushi scene, with a bright first-floor restaurant and sushi bar and a dark, sensuous sake lounge upstairs with living-room furniture, dining tables, and bar. Try the house cocktail, a "Red One," composed of vodka, cranberry juice, fresh passion fruit, and orange and lime juices.

HOUSE SPECIALTIES Daily sushi selection based on season and market (usually several varieties of tuna, salmon, shrimp, and roe); *sakana carpaccio moriawase* (tuna, salmon, and whitefish carpaccio with cilantro, capers, and sesame oil); *hirame usuzukuri* (sashimi of fluke with spicy radish and house ponzu).

OTHER RECOMMENDATIONS Seared scallops with sautéed arugula in a sweet soy-mustard sauce; *ebi su* (shrimp tempura wrapped in cucumber and served with vinegary *tozasu* sauce).

SUMMARY AND COMMENTS Fresh fish and funky patrons are the allure at this fashionable sushi hot spot. The cut-above Japanese fare is creative and well executed, the sake menu extensive and informative, and the ambience decidedly Wicker Park artsy chic (with a live DJ on Fridays and Saturdays). Focus on the extensive nightly specials for the most intriguing dishes, both sushi and otherwise. Consider reserving a dining spot among the lounge furniture and low tables on the second floor.

mk   ★★★★

NEW AMERICAN	EXPENSIVE	QUALITY ★★★★	VALUE ★★★

868 North Franklin Street, River North; ☎ 312-482-9179; www.mkchicago.com

Reservations Highly recommended. **When to go** Stylish dinner. **Entree range** $25–$52; 4-course degustation menu, $74. **Payment** AE, D, DC, MC, V. **Service rating** ★★★½. **Friendliness rating** ★★★. **Parking** Valet, $10. **Bar** Full service. **Wine selection** 550 well-chosen international bottles, $29–$1,200; 21 by the glass, $10–$25. **Dress** Upscale casual to business. **Disabled access** Wheelchair-accessible. **Customers** Trendies and power money, nice age mix. **Hours** Sunday–Thursday, 5:30–10 p.m.; Friday and Saturday, 5:30–11 p.m.

SETTING AND ATMOSPHERE Stylish and contemporary without being severe, mk's architectural dining room is spacious and airy, with a pleasantly sophisticated neutral color palette. Plush lounge furniture in the entry area is a great stop for a glass of bubbly before or after.

HOUSE SPECIALTIES Belgian endive salad with French beans, apple, watercress, Roquefort cheese, and pecans; lobster soup; prime New York sirloin grilled over hardwood charcoal with red-wine syrup; roasted Amish chicken with creamy polenta, braised kale, chanterelle mushrooms, and roasted-tomato vinaigrette.

OTHER RECOMMENDATIONS Sliced calf's liver with stone-ground mustard, burnt onions, smoked bacon, and aged balsamic vinegar; wood-grilled veal porterhouse with French green beans, trumpet royale mushrooms, and balsamic brown butter.

SUMMARY AND COMMENTS mk, named for owner and renowned chef Michael Kornick (though who's in the kitchen changes every few years), is a mainstay of Chicago's foodie faithful, a restaurant of both style and substance. Expect clean flavor combinations and plate presentations—gratifying without contrivance, handsome without pretense. In the dining room, the staff reaches a fine balance between personable and efficient.

 Morton's ★★★½

STEAK	EXPENSIVE	QUALITY ★★★★	VALUE ★★

1050 North State Street, Gold Coast; ☎ 312-266-4820 (original);
www.mortons.com
9525 West Bryn Mawr Avenue, Rosemont; ☎ 847-678-5155
65 East Wacker Place, The Loop; ☎ 312-201-0410
1470 McConnor Parkway, Schaumburg; ☎ 847-413-8771
699 Skokie Boulevard, Northbrook; ☎ 847-205-5111

Reservations Recommended. When to go Anytime. Entree range $26.50–$57. Payment AE, D, DC, MC, V. Service rating ★★★. Friendliness rating ★★★. Parking On-site garage (validated). Bar Full service. Wine selection 275 wines, primarily Californian, French, and German with a good selection from other countries, $30–$3,200; 30 by the glass, $8.50–$39. Dress Business casual. Disabled access Yes, all locations. Customers Business diners, couples. Hours Monday–Saturday, 5:30–11 p.m.; Sunday, 5–10 p.m. Lunch at Wacker Place only, Monday-Friday, 11:30 a.m.–5:30 p.m.; Saturday, noon–5:30 p.m.

SETTING AND ATMOSPHERE Morton's is renowned for its clubby, masculine decor; the State Street original is quintessential Chicago steak-house territory, complete with photo-lined walls and a discreet entrance reminiscent of a speakeasy. While handsome (and newer), the other locations smack of upscale chain, but the quality is remarkably consistent throughout Chicago—and everywhere else in the world, making it a reliable choice for business travelers.

HOUSE SPECIALTIES Jumbo lump crabmeat or shrimp cocktail; Caesar salad; lobster bisque; double filet mignon, *sauce béarnaise;* 24-ounce porterhouse steak, also available as a 48-ounce double; whole baked Maine lobster; farm-raised salmon; hash browns; steamed asparagus with hollandaise.

OTHER RECOMMENDATIONS Blue-point oysters on the half shell; broiled sea scallops wrapped in bacon with apricot chutney; shrimp Alexander with *sauce beurre blanc;* domestic double-rib lamb chops; Godiva hot-chocolate cake; soufflé for two (chocolate, Grand Marnier, lemon, or raspberry).

SUMMARY AND COMMENTS Founded by the late, lamented Chicago restaurateur Arnie Morton, the Gold Coast location of this steak lover's sanctuary has spawned a thriving national chain of near-legendary status. This is the original, a real bastion of old-guard, carnivorous dining delights; steady as she goes, Morton's delivers quality and consistency (the beef is the same all over the world) without a hint of highfalutin fussiness—unless you consider the visual "menu" of football-sized foods over the top.

unofficial **TIP**
Morton's newer Loop locale serves lunch Monday–Saturday (convenient and easier on the wallet), and that its bar, 12•21 (also at the Schaumburg and Northbrook locations), serves a "Bar Bites" menu that's discounted from 5 to 6:30 p.m. and 9:30 to 11 p.m. weeknights.

moto ★★★

NEW AMERICAN	VERY EXPENSIVE	QUALITY ★★★	VALUE ★★

945 West Fulton Market, West Loop; ☎ 312-491-0058; www.motorestaurant.com

Reservations Accepted. **When to go** Weekend nights, special occasions. **Entree range** $115–$175 for 10- or 20-course tasting menus. **Payment** AE, DC, MC, V. **Service rating** ★★★. **Friendliness rating** ★★. **Parking** Valet, $8. **Bar** Full service. **Wine selection** Californian, French, Italian, Austrian, Spanish; 10-course ($70) and 20-course ($90) flights, $48–$1,400 bottle, $8–$20 glass. **Dress** All black, ultramodern. **Disabled access** Yes. **Customers** Curious foodies, serious diners. **Hours** Tuesday–Thursday, 5–10 p.m.; Friday–Saturday, 5–11 p.m.; closed Sunday and Monday.

SETTING AND ATMOSPHERE Sleek, minimalist decor with no clutter in the entire dining room. There are white walls with subtle accents of cinnamon and cocoa in the banquettes and floor covering, plus dim lighting and a waitstaff dressed in black lab coats. "Aromatherapy flatware" is threaded with sprigs of fresh herbs.

HOUSE SPECIALTIES Ten- and twenty-course meals might include bass steamed tableside with heart of palm; rice balls injected with sweet-and-sour sauce; fillet of black bass steamed tableside in Pacific oceanic products; sashimi of hamachi or East Coast bluefin with sesame-milk soup; white-truffle ice-cream spaghetti; smoked-watermelon soup; scallop-jalapeño-lime sorbet.

OTHER RECOMMENDATIONS The ever-changing offerings also might include pear broth with gherkin ice cubes and ham-flavored cotton candy; brown-butter-basted bobwhite quail with Swiss chard broth and porcini oil; citrus togarashi sprinkled on lime sorbet; deconstructed egg roll with pull-apart duck; *sous vide* tenderloin of beef with braised oxtail.

SUMMARY AND COMMENTS There's nothing conventional about this far-flung concept, where chef Homaro Cantu holds numerous patents for serving pieces and edible menus, and custom-made silverware threaded with herbs is considered a "course." In his favor, he focuses his ever-changing menu on farm-raised meats and organic or artisanal ingredients. Despite the pristine ingredients, dinner here feels more like you're inside an experimental laboratory than in a dining room. If nothing else, the unique experience is a riot of conflicting flavors and textures, along with such drama as food injections and savory ice cream and candy. This is Chicago's true representative of the "molecular gastronomy" trend to the nth degree.

Nacional 27 ★★★★

| NUEVO LATINO | MODERATE | QUALITY ★★★★ | VALUE ★★★ |

325 West Huron Street, River North; ☎ 312-664-2727; www.nacional27.net

Reservations Accepted. When to go After-work cocktails, hot dates. Entree range $16–$28. Payment AE, D, DC, MC, V. Service rating ★★★. Friendliness rating ★★★. Parking Nearby lots; valet, $10 (cheaper than the lots). Bar Full bar, Latin and culinary cocktails, Latin beers. Wine selection Affordable Old and New World, including Spanish and South American; $18–$195 bottle, $9–$17 glass. Dress Business, trendy. Disabled access Yes. Customers After-work, dates, and dancers. Hours Monday–Thursday, 5:30–9:30 p.m.; Friday and Saturday, 5:30 p.m.–11 p.m. Lounge open until 11 p.m. on Thursday, until 2 a.m. on Friday, and until 3 a.m. on Saturday; closed Sunday. *Note:* Parties of 8 or more are restricted to a set menu.

SETTING AND ATMOSPHERE Despite being a Lettuce Entertain You Enterprises operation, the place offers swanky space that's mercifully lacking in decorative overkill. Sophisticated urban ambience, with earth tones, tiles, massive pillars, and sensuous draping, makes a smart setting for a promising date or deal. The modern fine-dining mood heats up with salsa dancing on weekends (starting at 11 p.m.).

HOUSE SPECIALTIES Longtime chef de cuisine Francisco "Chico" Vilchez has taken over for Randy Zweiban (who's moved on to open his own spot, Province), maintaining the balanced blend of 27 national cuisines that make up the menu at this Nuevo Latino hot spot. Seasonal dishes might include numerous seviches (shrimp-scallop, hamachi-apple, ahi tuna–watermelon); combination platter with smoked-chicken empanada, boniato-and-plantain *croquetas,* barbecued-lamb taco, and shrimp skewer; slow-roasted Gunthorp Farms pork with sweet plantains, black beans, coconut rice, and an orange mojo;

unofficial **TIP**
Nacional 27 is known for offering a variety of great specials and deals for different day-parts and days of the week. Bargain hunters can consult the Web site for the latest offerings.

truffle-crusted filet mignon with three-potato–chorizo hash and Malbec reduction.

OTHER RECOMMENDATIONS Light bites might include tiny tacos (grouper with olives, barbecued lamb with avocado salsa, beef tenderloin with spicy tomatillo salsa); croquetas (boniato-plantain, blue crab–purple potato); and bamboo skewers (chicken with cilantro sofrito, beef tenderloin with adobo–three-chile salsa, shrimp adobado with pineapple-vanilla salsa).

SUMMARY AND COMMENTS In addition to being one of the few dine-and-dance date options, the place also offers a sexy destination bar and lounge with small bites (such as tiny barbecued-lamb tacos with avocado salsa, and boniato-and-plantain croquetas with black-bean salsa and roasted-garlic aioli) and cocktails so clever (for example, pomegranate-ginger-chile mojito, spicy ginger beer–muddled lime–Goslings rum) they warrant their own award-winning "bar chef," Adam Seger.

NAHA ★★★★

MEDITERRANEAN/NEW AMERICAN   EXPENSIVE   QUALITY ★★★★   VALUE ★★★

500 North Clark Street, River North; ☎ 312-321-6242; www.naha-chicago.com

Reservations Accepted. **When to go** Weekday lunch, weekend dinner. **Entree range** Lunch, $14–$28; dinner, $22–$48. **Payment** AE, D, DC, MC, V. **Service rating** ★★★½. **Friendliness rating** ★★★★. **Parking** Valet, $10. **Bar** Full service. **Wine selection** Global with emphasis on French, Californian, and other U.S. wines; $30–$600 bottle, $9–$30 glass. **Dress** Upscale casual. **Disabled access** Yes. **Customers** Professional, older crowd, with locals by day. **Hours** Monday–Thursday, 11:30 a.m.–2 p.m. and 5:30–9:30 p.m.; Friday, 11:30 a.m.–2 p.m. and 5:30–10 p.m.; Saturday, 5:30–10 p.m.; closed Sunday.

SETTING AND ATMOSPHERE The contemporary, Zen-like space features walls of windows on two sides, low-backed chrome-and-leather chairs, and works of abstract modern art on the cool gray walls. The front bar area is spacious for waiting.

HOUSE SPECIALTIES Menus change seasonally and may include Mediterranean Greek salad with warm feta; salmon with white asparagus, black trumpet mushrooms, and Jerusalem artichokes; pink snapper with red-rib dandelion, baba ghanoush, fennel, ratatouille, olive tapenade, saffron-aioli toast, and bouillabaisse broth; lacquered and aged duck breast with baby turnips, broccoli rabe, huckleberries, celery-root puree, and port; wood-grilled rib-eye steak with glazed Dutch yellow shallots and spring ramps, macaroni–goat cheese gratin, oxtail–red-wine sauce, and *fleur de sel;* wood-grilled Swiss chard and ragout of applewood slab bacon, red pearl onions, artichokes, cured tomatoes, and marjoram.

OTHER RECOMMENDATIONS Tartare of Hawaiian yellowfin tuna, cured Tasmanian ocean trout, and hard-cooked quail egg with mosaic vegetables, niçoise garnishes, and aigrelette sauce; sea scallops, caramelized Belgian endive and Bosc pears, and candied rind scented with apple mint.

SUMMARY AND COMMENTS The ever-changing seasonal menu never ceases to dazzle diners at this Mediterranean-inflected New American restaurant, former home to the venerable Gordon. Service is ultraprofessional without being intimidating. Wonderful harder-to-find bottles grace the wine list, and the beautifully presented fare tastes as good as it looks.

N9NE Steakhouse ★★★½

| STEAK | EXPENSIVE | QUALITY ★★★★ | VALUE ★★ |

440 West Randolph Street, West Loop; ☎ 312-575-9900; www.n9ne.com

Reservations Highly recommended. **When to go** Early evening for quieter dining, later and weekends for scene. **Entree range** Lunch, $12–$43; dinner, $20–$115. **Payment** AE, DC, MC, V. **Service rating** ★★★★. **Friendliness rating** ★★★½. **Parking** Valet, $10; street. **Bar** Three full-service bars; emphasis on specialty martinis, Champagne cocktails, and sake. **Wine selection** Well-chosen, well-rounded list of 150-plus selections; emphasis on France and California; large Champagne selection and several magnums; $38–$1,200 by the bottle, a dozen or so wines by the glass, $10–$22. **Dress** Officially "casual chic"; unofficially the greatest fashion show in town. **Disabled access** Wheelchair-accessible. **Customers** Celebs and beautiful people; all-ages diners and bar denizens. **Hours** Monday–Thursday, 11:30 a.m.–2 p.m. and 5:30–10 p.m.; Friday, 11:30 a.m.–2 p.m. and 5 p.m.–midnight; Saturday, 5 p.m.–midnight; closed Sunday.

SETTING AND ATMOSPHERE *Grand, sizzling, spectacular.* N9NE calls out the adjectives with its tastefully Vegas-tinged ambience, soaring, silver-leaf domed ceiling, waterfall wall, mirrored pillars, light show, and plushy Ultrasuede booths. Pose in the cushy lounge; imbibe at the main bar; indulge at the central Champagne-and-caviar bar; dine in the vast dining room with ultrasocial sightlines; hold a private party with state-of-the-art audiovisual capabilities; or climb the stairs to the ethereal Ghostbar, one of the hippest hangouts in town.

HOUSE SPECIALTIES American caviar parfaits (black tobiko, salmon, and whitefish) with crisp potato pancakes; crispy Carolina rock shrimp with two dipping sauces; shellfish platters; 12-ounce filet mignon with béarnaise sauce; 16-ounce New York strip steak; 22-ounce porterhouse; grilled salmon with Chinese-mustard glaze, bok choy, shiitake mushrooms, and ginger vinaigrette.

OTHER RECOMMENDATIONS Cold or steamed Alaskan king crab legs; 24-ounce bone-in rib eye.

SUMMARY AND COMMENTS When it opened in April 2000, N9NE wowed Chicago with its luxurious ambience and contemporary-decadent menu and bar offerings. This place is a great scene—with great steakhouse-and-beyond food—the perfect place for an evening of well-earned indulgence. The fashionable, often eye-popping crowd is a big part of the action here, but the food assures that N9NE goes beyond the "now you're hot, now you're not" fate of many trendy restaurants. Make an evening of it—make a reservation for the

Champagne-and-caviar bar before dinner, and head up to Ghostbar afterward. Thanks to the Loop location, N9NE also does a busy business lunch.

NoMI ★★★★

NEW AMERICAN	EXPENSIVE	QUALITY ★★★★	VALUE ★★★

Park Hyatt hotel, 800 North Michigan Avenue, Gold Coast;
☎ **312-239-4030; www.nomirestaurant.com**

Reservations Recommended. **When to go** Weekend evenings. **Entree range** Lunch, $27–$34; dinner, $34–$52. **Payment** AE, D, DC, MC, V. **Service rating** ★★★½. **Friendliness rating** ★★★★. **Parking** Valet, $13. **Bar** Full service with sake selection. **Wine selection** American, French, Australian, New Zealand, Italian, and Spanish, $42–$6,900 per bottle; 42 wines by the glass, $9–$50. **Dress** Chic to dressy; jacket recommended. **Disabled access** Yes. **Customers** Tourists, mature patrons. **Hours** *Breakfast:* Monday–Friday, 6:30–10:30 a.m; Saturday and Sunday, 7–10:30 a.m. *Brunch:* Sunday, 11 a.m.–2:30 p.m. *Lunch:* Monday–Saturday, 11:30 a.m.–2:30 p.m. *Dinner:* Daily, 5:30–10 p.m.

SETTING AND ATMOSPHERE   The spectacular room, designed by Tony Chi and perched on the seventh floor of the Park Hyatt hotel, has fabulous views of North Michigan Avenue (hence the name). The entryway alone is worth a visit; it's a temperature-controlled wine cellar that opens into a handsome adjoining lounge. The white-linen-topped tables in the dining room are nicely spaced, there's a small sushi bar with a few tables (an add-on demanded by the owners), and the exposed kitchen is finished in eye-catching, iridescent aqua tile. Dale Chihuly–designed light fixtures are suspended above the top tables, those in the "prow" of the restaurant with the massive windows overlooking the historic Water Tower.

HOUSE SPECIALTIES   Sushi platters of tuna, salmon, eel, prawns, and yellowtail; butter-poached Maine lobster with sunchokes, *jamón ibérico,* and Burgundy truffles; Jamison Farms lamb with braised-lamb *pastilla,* eggplant marmalade, and pistachio.

OTHER RECOMMENDATIONS   Catch of the day with Yukon Gold potato puree, wilted spinach, and *sauce vierge;* steak sandwich with béarnaise aioli, caramelized onions, arugula, and smoked-paprika chips.

SUMMARY AND COMMENTS   Classically trained French chef Christophe David executes straightforward fare, highlighting the intrinsic flavors of ingredients in a most artistic and refined manner. The wine list offers affordable gems along with slightly pricier options. Top-shelf tea offerings include rare and limited leaves such as Royal Ceylon Platinum Tips (grown in the mountains of Sri Lanka), as well as pairings of teas and spirits that range from $14 to $700. It's an experience best reserved for a special occasion.

unofficial **TIP**
In warm weather, NoMI's landscaped roof deck offers some of the best upscale outdoor dining in the Gold Coast.

North Pond ★★★★

| NEW AMERICAN | EXPENSIVE | QUALITY ★★★★ | VALUE ★★★ |

2610 North Cannon Drive, Lincoln Park; ☎ 773-477-5845; www.northpondrestaurant.com

Reservations Recommended. **When to go** Weekday evenings. **Entree range** $32–$39; brunch $32. **Payment** AE, D, DC, MC, V. **Service rating** ★★★★. **Friendliness rating** ★★★★. **Parking** Street; valet, $8 (dinner and Sunday). **Bar** Full service with a nice selection of local microbrews and spirits. **Wine selection** Well-appointed list featuring ample American wines from California, Oregon, and Washington, along with a wide selection of French wines; $30–$450 bottle, $7–$20 glass. **Dress** Casual to upscale. **Disabled access** Yes. **Customers** Mix of suburban diners and young neighborhood patrons. **Hours** *Lunch:* June–September, Tuesday–Friday, 11:30 a.m.–1:30 p.m. *Brunch:* Sunday, 10:30 a.m.–1:30 p.m. *Dinner:* Tuesday–Sunday, 5:30–10 p.m.; closed Monday; January through April, also closed Tuesday.

SETTING AND ATMOSPHERE This renovated warming house is perched on the edge of a serene pond in Lincoln Park, with wood-trimmed windows spanning three walls. The Prairie-style room harmonizes nicely with the park; the ceiling frescoes depict wild prairie grass, and Arts and Crafts light fixtures illuminate the Frank Lloyd Wright–style tables and chairs. It's sophisticated but still lively and energetic, with a bustling exposed kitchen running the length of one wall.

HOUSE SPECIALTIES The menu changes often; representative dishes have included pancetta-wrapped salmon with white grits, glazed knob onions, and pea puree; candied gold, red, white, and Chiogga beets with grape-leaf-enrobed goat cheese; grilled honey-glazed pork chop with suckling pig–potato cake, Italian greens, and tart-cherry reduction; and sautéed soft-shell crab with English pea–almond bulgur, minted tomato broth, and Bordeaux spinach.

OTHER RECOMMENDATIONS Grilled white sea bass, cornmeal waffle, lemon–French bean timbale, and sweet-corn reduction; roasted eggplant–Parmesan ravioli, grilled fennel, and Provençale vegetables in broth; red butterhead lettuce with citrus and green-shallot vinaigrettes.

SUMMARY AND COMMENTS This charming Craftsman-style room is inconveniently located in the heart of Lincoln Park, and parking can be tricky. There's room to wait at the bar, and a few dozen additional tables overlook the pond. The American fare is skillfully executed, incorporating seasonal ingredients in intriguing combinations. The Sunday brunch is a great option. The American and French wine list is well selected and reasonable. Service has its missteps, but the food and ambience more than make up for it.

one sixtyblue ★★★★

| NEW AMERICAN | EXPENSIVE | QUALITY ★★★★ | VALUE ★★★ |

160 North Loomis Street, West Loop (restaurant); 1400 West Randolph Street (parking lot); ☎ 312-850-0303; www.onesixtyblue.com

Reservations Recommended. **When to go** Dinner anytime; special occasions and with favored visitors. **Entree range** $19–$35; pretheater, $38 per person. **Payment** AE, DC, MC, V. **Service rating** ★★★★. **Friendliness rating** ★★★. **Parking** Valet, $7. **Bar** Full service. **Wine selection** Eclectic international list organized by varietals; about 325 selections, from $35 up; 20 or so by the glass, $8–$26. **Dress** Chic casual. **Disabled access** Complete. **Customers** Stylish diners of all ages, neighborhood regulars. **Hours** Monday–Thursday, 5–9:30 p.m.; Friday and Saturday, 5–10:30 p.m.; closed Sunday.

SETTING AND ATMOSPHERE Designed by Adam Tihany, one sixtyblue is a remarkably chic, high-concept restaurant. The color scheme of black, neutrals, and citrus hues manages to be crisp and clean without sterility; table dividers with light boxes provide the illusion of privacy while allowing for discreet spying on fellow diners.

HOUSE SPECIALTIES House-cured king salmon with citron, crispy hash browns, and lemon curd; leek gnocchi with leek emulsion and truffle; Maine diver sea scallop with cauliflower puree and pickled cauliflower; Alaskan halibut with veal cheek, celery root, and braised celery; wagyu short rib with creamy grits, marrow crouton, and fresh horseradish.

OTHER RECOMMENDATIONS Bobwhite quail with wild-mushroom risotto and quail jus; slow-cooked pork belly with orange-fennel salad and tangerine reduction; Berkshire pork chop with homemade sauerkraut, crisp potato noodle, and mustard seed; house hash browns with caramelized shallot and duck-fat powder.

SUMMARY AND COMMENTS One sixtyblue enjoys an excellent reputation as one of Chicago's best—among many—contemporary American culinary destinations. Michael Jordan, His Airness himself, is a partner in this gem of a restaurant, anchoring the west end of the Randolph Street restaurant row. After the departure of longtime chef Martial Noguier, the appointment of new chef Michael McDonald—veteran of two of Charlie Trotter's restaurants, Everest, Gray Kunz's Café Gray in New York, and more—boded well at press time (dishes reflect his opening menu).

Opera ★★½

CONTEMPORARY ASIAN   MODERATE   QUALITY ★★★   VALUE ★★

1301 South Wabash Avenue, South Loop; ☎ 312-461-0161; www.opera-chicago.com

Reservations Recommended. **When to go** Early evening or late night on busy weekends. **Entree range** $16–$33. **Payment** AE, D, DC, MC, V. **Service rating** ★★½. **Friendliness rating** ★★★. **Parking** $10. **Bar** Full service. **Wine selection** Austrian, Californian, Australian, Alsatian; $32–$157 bottle, $19–$69 half bottles, $8–$14 glass. **Dress** Urban chic. **Disabled access** Yes. **Customers** Hip, loud, young. **Hours** Sunday–Thursday, 5–10 p.m.; Friday and Saturday, 5 p.m.–11:30 p.m.

SETTING AND ATMOSPHERE The room is eye candy for the trendy, with oddly shaped light fixtures, colorful silk drapes, jewel-toned velvet pincushion chairs, and opulent room dividers covered in Japanese newsprint. The clientele is equally colorful.

HOUSE SPECIALTIES Crisp Maine lobster spring roll with tropical fruit–chile relish and mango sauce; mussels with lotus, bamboo, cilantro, and chile-coconut broth; Peking duck service (three presentations); "beef and broccoli" (grilled filet mignon, Chinese broccoli, shiitake mushrooms, and Burgundy red wine sauce; Szechuan dry-cooked green beans with ground pork.

OTHER RECOMMENDATIONS Mahogany-grilled quail with Chinese sausage–brown rice stuffing, edamame, pearl onions, and rock sugar–soy glaze; slow-roasted, bacon-wrapped pork tenderloin with carrots, corn, coconut fried rice, and kiln-dried blueberry hoisin sauce; and a brief vegan menu with such offerings as twice-cooked, ginger-scented rice, stir-fried choi sum, white flower mushrooms, and sweet peas, all wrapped and steamed in a lotus leaf.

SUMMARY AND COMMENTS This spot is brimming with action from an energetic crowd and lively staff. The social aspect almost overshadows the food, which the restaurant considers modern Chinese and we consider suited for the American palate—large portions and intense flavors.

Orange ★★

GLOBAL/BREAKFAST	INEXPENSIVE	QUALITY ★★★	VALUE ★★★★

3231 North Clark Street, Lakeview; ☎ 773-549-4400
75 West Harrison Street, South Loop; ☎ 312-447-1000

Reservations Not accepted. **When to go** Weekend breakfast or brunch. **Entree range** $5–$12. **Payment** AE, D, MC, V. **Service rating** ★★. **Friendliness rating** ★★★. **Parking** Street. **Bar** Juice only. **Wine selection** None. **Dress** Casual. **Disabled access** Yes. **Customers** Young locals, hungover late-night club hoppers. **Hours** Monday–Friday, 8 a.m.–1:30 p.m.; Saturday–Sunday, 8 a.m.–2:30 p.m.

SETTING AND ATMOSPHERE The Lakeview original is a homey, cheerful storefront with orange crates as art, exposed-brick walls, natural floors, and an eye-appealing fresh juice bar.

HOUSE SPECIALTIES "Frushi" specialty (rice rolled with fresh fruit in fruit leather); cinnamon-roll pancakes; green eggs and ham (scrambled eggs with basil pesto, roasted tomatoes, buffalo mozzarella, and diced pancetta); jelly-doughnut pancakes with lingonberries.

OTHER RECOMMENDATIONS French-toast kebabs (coconut-infused French toast skewered and grilled with fresh strawberries and pineapple).

SUMMARY AND COMMENTS For a funky, lively early-morning spot, these Lakeview and South Loop gems are just the place. Fresh ingredients are the keys to clever and creative dishes and drinks. Even the coffee gets infused with orange zest. It's one of the most neighborly breakfast haunts in town.

Park Grill ★★★

AMERICAN	MODERATE	QUALITY ★★★	VALUE ★★★

11 North Michigan Avenue, The Loop; ☎ 312-521-7275;
www.parkgrillchicago.com

Reservations Accepted. **When to go** Weekend lunch or dinner. **Entree range** Lunch, $11–$19; dinner, $18–$42; pretheater menu, $35 per person; child's menu, $6. **Payment** AE, D, DC, MC, V. **Service rating** ★★. **Friendliness rating** ★★★. **Parking** Underground garage, $16 with validation at dinner, otherwise $8 an hour. **Bar** Full service. **Wine selection** Californian, French, Italian; $26–$275 bottle, $7–$14 glass. **Dress** Casual or business attire. **Disabled access** Yes. **Customers** Tourist, business-lunch crowd. **Hours** Sunday–Thursday, 11 a.m.– 9:30 p.m.; Friday and Saturday, 11 a.m.–10:30 p.m.

HOUSE SPECIALTIES The seasonally changing menu has included roasted Atlantic salmon with sweet corn, trumpet mushrooms, and garlic gloves; summer-tomato rigatoni pasta with broccolini, stewed tomatoes, olives, and goat cheese; calamari with roasted goat-horn peppers, caper berries, and Italian parsley; jumbo crab cakes with yellow curry sauce and snow pea–apple salad; chocolate–peanut butter tart with roasted banana and peanut brittle.

OTHER RECOMMENDATIONS Park Grill salad (chopped salad with French green beans, radishes, cucumbers, sweet peppers, onions, potatoes, tomatoes, bacon, artichoke hearts, hearts of palm, and crumbled blue cheese, with Thousand Island dressing and topped with garlic croutons); pizzas topped with tomato and basil, barbecue chicken, spinach, grilled balsamic onions, and fontina cheese, or oven-roasted tomatoes, arugula, and Parmesan cheese; sautéed whitefish with assorted squash and basil-tomato vinaigrette; veal chop with radishes, hedgehog mushrooms, and aged sherry vinaigrette.

SUMMARY AND COMMENTS The best thing about this restaurant is the spectacular view of the Chicago skyline, fronted by the ice rink at Millennium Park. The American fare is somewhat predictable but well prepared and presented with a menu offering something for everyone. Elegant fish dishes can be had alongside a decent burger or a simple appetizer. The materials—floors, wood bar, and furniture—are strikingly beautiful, crafted of such natural materials as marble, slate, and Brazilian oak.

Phoenix ★★

CHINESE	INEXPENSIVE	QUALITY ★★	VALUE ★★★

2131 South Archer Avenue, Chinatown; ☎ 312-328-0848; www.chinatownphoenix.com

Reservations Accepted for breakfast-lunch dim sum only. **When to go** Dinner, Saturday dim sum. **Entree range** $11–$80. **Payment** AE, D, DC, MC, V. **Service rating** ★★. **Friendliness rating** ★★. **Parking** Pay lot (discounted with validation). **Bar** Full service. **Wine selection** Limited, moderately priced; $25–$50 bottle, $6 glass. **Dress** Casual. **Disabled access** Yes. **Customers** Groups, families, tourists, students, couples. **Hours** Monday–Thursday, 9 a.m.–3 p.m. and 5–9:30 p.m.; Friday, 9 a.m.–3 p.m. and 5–10:30 p.m.; Saturday, 8 a.m.–3 p.m. and 5–10:30 p.m.; Sunday, 8 a.m.–3 p.m. and 5–9:30 p.m.

SETTING AND ATMOSPHERE Somewhat upscale and plain (low-kitsch) for Chinatown, this clean and spacious Mandarin and dim sum house is a perennial favorite for families, tourists, students, dates—in other words, everyone. Big communal tables are covered with white tablecloths and lazy Susans, and second-floor windows offer panoramic city views. Expect a language barrier with the waitstaff (just point to what you want).

HOUSE SPECIALTIES Dim sum dishes include steamed shrimp dumplings, steamed pork buns, taro "bird's nests," deep-fried seaweed wrap, silky tofu with sweet syrup, fried crab-claw dumplings, octopus in curry, fried cuttlefish, fried bean curd, sticky rice in lotus leaf, fried sesame balls with lotus-bean paste, custard tarts, and steamed yellow cake.

OTHER RECOMMENDATIONS Main menu dishes include Peking duck, steamed whole sea bass, spicy jellyfish, baked shrimp with spiced salt, steamed minced pork with squid, crispy orange chicken, fresh lobster steamed in Chinese wine, Dungeness crab fried with beer, and mango pudding.

SUMMARY AND COMMENTS While not up to the standards of some world-traveled dim sum purists, Phoenix aims to please with a big selection and less-grotty surroundings than many of its counterparts (perhaps one reason regulars don't mind the slightly higher prices). Especially popular for its daily carts-and-communal-tables dim sum, the 500-seat space is hectic at peak hours, so if you're not into crowds (or waits), go at off-times (but be prepared for a more limited selection; on slow weekdays you might order from a dim sum menu).

Piece ★★

PIZZERIA/BREW PUB   INEXPENSIVE   QUALITY ★★★   VALUE ★★★★

1927 West North Avenue, Wicker Park; ☎ 773-772-4422; www.piecechicago.com

Reservations Accepted only for parties of 10 or more. When to go Weekdays, late night, quick lunch. Entree range $11–$17. Payment AE, D, MC, V. Service rating ★★. Friendliness rating ★★★★. Parking Valet after 5 p.m., $10. Bar Full bar notable for 8 house-made, award-winning beers, plus 10 regional microbrews. Wine selection Limited Italian and American; $22–$36 bottle, $6–$9 glass. Dress Casual. Disabled access Yes. Customers Young, urban locals, actors, and athletes. Hours Monday–Thursday, 11:30 a.m.–1:30 a.m. (kitchen closes 10:30 p.m. Monday–Wednesday and 11 p.m. Thursday); Friday, 11:30 a.m.–2 a.m. (kitchen closes 12:30 a.m.); Saturday, 11 a.m.–3 a.m. (kitchen closes 12:30 a.m.); Sunday, 11 a.m.–1 a.m. (kitchen closes 10 p.m.)

SETTING AND ATMOSPHERE Formerly a truck garage, this lofted space still has an industrial feel with poured concrete floors and high ceilings with a long glass skylight running the length. That's not to say there aren't any stylish details—a sunken lounge area up front sports comfy blue and green couches and floor-to-ceiling windows which open onto bustling North Avenue. Piece is famous for having played a role as a *Real World* cast hangout.

HOUSE SPECIALTIES East Coast (New Haven, Connecticut)–style pizza pies topped with traditional ingredients, along with some more adventurous toppings such as meatballs, clams, and broccoli. Choose your base: plain (tomato with Parmesan, garlic, and olive oil), white (olive oil with garlic and mozzarella), or red (tomato with mozzarella; barbecue sauce also available).

OTHER RECOMMENDATIONS Salad with candied pecans, pears, and Gorgonzola.

SUMMARY AND COMMENTS It's a natural location for this pizzeria and microbrewery, right in the heart of the young and happening Wicker Park neighborhood. Not only does the original East Coast–crust recipe come straight from the source, but a former Sierra Nevada brewmaster was installed to supervise the microbrewery attached to this 5,800-square-foot dining room. It all works like a well-oiled machine, and there's space for crowds—even on a major game night when the many TVs are all tuned in.

Prairie Grass Cafe ★★★

AMERICAN	MODERATE	QUALITY ★★★★	VALUE ★★★★

**601 Skokie Boulevard, Northbrook; ☎ 847-205-4433;
www.prairiegrasscafe.com**

Reservations Accepted. **When to go** Anytime but prime-time weekend dinner. **Entree range** Lunch, $8.50–$23; dinner, $13.50–$29. **Payment** AE, D, DC, MC, V. **Service rating** ★★. **Friendliness rating** ★★★. **Parking** Lot. **Bar** Full service. **Wine selection** Moderately priced mix with American focus, $30–$330 bottle, $7–$12 glass. **Dress** Casual chic. **Disabled access** Yes. **Customers** Couples from the north suburbs, work groups, families. **Hours** Monday, 11 a.m.–2 p.m. and 5–9 p.m.; Tuesday–Thursday, 11 a.m.–2 p.m. and 5–9:30 p.m.; Friday, 11 a.m.–2 p.m. and 5–10:30 p.m.; Saturday, 10 a.m.–2 p.m. (brunch) and 5–10:30 p.m.; Sunday, 9:30 a.m.–2 p.m. (brunch) and 5–9 p.m.

SETTING AND ATMOSPHERE Open dining amid a modernized Prairie School milieu sets a casually sophisticated tone that bustles when the place is busy. The room is chic yet warm in stone and wood, with giant, hovering light fixtures, and a dividing line between bar and dining of plasma TVs that slow-pulse random images, including amber waves of grain.

HOUSE SPECIALTIES Salad featuring a slice of Amish blue cheese and grapes rolled in candied walnuts; homemade pâté in a crock with apples and port wine–balsamic reduction; baked feta cheese, spicy banana peppers, and tomatoes; moussaka; crispy half boneless chicken; Mom's seasonal pie.

OTHER RECOMMENDATIONS Lunch includes a generous selection of entree salads, burgers, and crepes; brunch favorites include smoked-salmon Benedict and large French-style crepes with raspberry cream cheese and fresh berries.

SUMMARY AND COMMENTS When top-ranked Ritz-Carlton chefs Sarah Stegner and George Bumbaris headed for the 'burbs to cook comfort food, most of Chicago had culinary whiplash. The results are a solid success showcasing their super-satisfying American cooking (and Sarah's mom's lovely pies)—if you can overlook the sometimes suburban-quality service. Kids can make their own pizzas on Friday nights.

The Publican ★★★½

| BELGIAN/ECLECTIC | MODERATE | QUALITY ★★★★ | VALUE ★★★ |

837 West Fulton Market, West Loop; ☎ 312-733-9555; www.thepublicanrestaurant.com

Reservations Accepted. **When to go** Late afternoon or early evening to avoid crowds. **Entree range** $11–$38. **Payment** AE, MC, V. **Service rating** ★★★. **Friendliness rating** ★★★. **Parking** Limited street; valet, $10. **Bar** Full service; esoteric 100-plus beer list with heavy Belgian emphasis. **Wine selection** Well-chosen, value-priced ($24–$99, most less than $50); 250-milliliter carafina, $9–$14. **Dress** Hip casual. **Disabled access** Yes. **Customers** Hipsters and foodies. **Hours** Monday–Thursday, 3:30–10:30 p.m.; Friday–Saturday, 3:30–11:30 p.m.; Sunday, 5–10 p.m.

SETTING AND ATMOSPHERE An über-chic yet earthy spot along the lines of avec (another restaurant from the team behind fine-dining Blackbird), this stylized take on a European beer hall–brasserie draws hip crowds to an eclectic environment of walnut wood; raised-relief wall treatments in butter and brown; and funky, vintage-inspired globe lighting. Seating options include a wraparound, 90-seat communal table, central standing tables for light bites and drinks, and semisecluded alcoves with low swinging doors. Vintage beer steins and other beer antiques add decorative interest.

HOUSE SPECIALTIES The menu changes daily but has included fresh pork rinds with malt vinegar; various regional oysters; potted pork rillettes with fig, grilled red onion, balsamic vinegar, and bread; buchot mussels with gueuze beer, bay, celery butter, and baguette; whole roasted Dover sole from Brittany with pan vinaigrette and baby carrots; charcuterie plate (game bird terrine, morteau sausage, and head cheese), served with pickles and mustard; poté of pork shank, bacon, and tenderloin with chanterelle mushrooms, root vegetables, and horseradish aioli; grilled country ribs with watermelon, cherry tomatoes, cilantro, and green coriander.

OTHER RECOMMENDATIONS Wood-oven sardines with preserved lemon, olives, and almond relish; steak tartare with fried egg and frites; fish stew with salt cod, loup de mer, mussels, spot prawns, littleneck clams, octopus, tomatoes, orange, and rouille; wood-roasted half chicken with frites and summer sausage; *boudin blanc* with marinated beets, truffles, frisée, and hash browns.

*un*official **TIP**
Sunday at The Publican is family-style 4-course-dinner night (reservations encouraged; $45).

SUMMARY AND COMMENTS It's all about pork, seafood, and beer at this contemporary American version of a Belgian pub. Chef-driven takes on rustic pub fare feature sustainable ingredients and a fair share of offal (it will be interesting to see if this catches on with Chicago diners). The exceptional beer list is an education in itself—a fun one, of course. Though new at press time, this long-awaited spot, with its primo pedigree, is destined to become one of Chicago's hottest dining destinations.

Salpicón ★★★

REGIONAL MEXICAN	MODERATE	QUALITY ★★★★	VALUE ★★★

1252 North Wells Street, Old Town; ☎ 312-988-7811; www.salpicon.com

Reservations Recommended. **When to go** Lively weekend dinner. **Entree range** $17–$28. **Payment** AE, D, MC, V. **Service rating** ★★★. **Friendliness rating** ★★½. **Parking** Valet, $8. **Bar** Beer, wine, and tequila drinks only. **Wine selection** French, American, Australian, Chilean, Austrian, Italian, Spanish, Argentinian, and German, $29–$1,250 bottle; several by the glass, $7–$19. **Dress** Chic to casual. **Disabled access** Yes. **Customers** Urban workers, mature locals. **Hours** Sunday–Thursday, 5–10 p.m.; Friday and Saturday, 5–11 p.m.; Sunday brunch, 11 a.m.–2:30 p.m.

SETTING AND ATMOSPHERE The lively, two-room storefront space is splashed with color, from the brightly painted walls to the large Mexican canvases and artifacts. Tables are tightly spaced, making it feel inordinately crowded at times.

HOUSE SPECIALTIES Jalapeños rellenos de queso *capeados* (jalapeños stuffed with Chihuahua cheese, dipped in light egg batter, sautéed, and served with black-bean sauce); three corn tamales: one with queso fresco, serrano chiles, mocajete salsa, and crema; another with black beans, rajas, Chihuahua cheese, and black-bean puree; and another with zucchini and chipotles.

OTHER RECOMMENDATIONS *Pescado al carbón* (fillet of seasonal fish, charcoal-grilled and served with salsa and white rice); chef's seven-course tasting menu ($65; subject to availability, so check when reserving).

SUMMARY AND COMMENTS Chef Priscila Satkoff prepares the Mexican cuisine of her homeland in an elegant, upscale manner. Dishes can be spicy, so it's best to inquire before ordering. The menu features clean, authentic flavors from the indigenous ingredients, such as chipotle chiles, mangos, tomatillos, and her fabulous homemade mole. An on-site wine cellar houses more than 800 bottles of wine for an outstanding selection, not to mention a killer premium-tequila list.

Santorini ★★★

GREEK, SEAFOOD	MODERATE	QUALITY ★★★	VALUE ★★★

800 West Adams Street, Greektown; ☎ 312-829-8820; www.santorinichicago.com

Reservations Accepted. **When to go** Before United Center events. **Entree range** $10–$48. **Payment** AE, D, DC, MC, V. **Service rating** ★★★½. **Friendliness rating** ★★★. **Parking** Valet, free. **Bar** Full service. **Wine selection** Greek, French,

Californian, Italian, and Australian; $17–$250 bottle, $6–$12 glass. **Dress** Casual to dressy. **Disabled access** Yes. **Customers** Mixed crowd; professionals by day, families and suburbanites by evening. **Hours** Sunday–Thursday, 11 a.m.–midnight; Friday and Saturday, 11 a.m.–1 a.m.

SETTING AND ATMOSPHERE This upscale Greektown eatery has a wood-burning fireplace in the center of the dining room, with various Mediterranean artifacts and baskets scattered about. It's rustic, homey, and comfortable.

HOUSE SPECIALTIES Roasted whole fish (red snapper or black sea bass), prepared simply with olive oil and lemon juice; Kamari beach calamari char-grilled with garlic, lemon juice, and olive oil; lemon sole; seafood platter (lobster, shrimp, oysters, and fish).

OTHER RECOMMENDATIONS Char-grilled octopus; tzatziki; *kolokithakia* (fried zucchini with garlic sauce); Florida grouper.

SUMMARY AND COMMENTS This cozy yet bustling addition to Greektown specializes in seafood, with Mediterranean-style whole fish that's a standout. Service is professional and attentive, accommodating sports fans on their way to a game. Family-style multicourse dinners are offered for large parties at a rate of $20 to $41 per person.

Seasons ★★★★

NEW AMERICAN   VERY EXPENSIVE   QUALITY ★★★★   VALUE ★★

Four Seasons Hotel Chicago, 120 East Delaware Place, Gold Coast; ☎ 312-649-2349; www.fourseasons.com/chicagofs/dining.html

Reservations Highly recommended. **When to go** Big moments, big business. **Entree range** $32–$48; 5-course tasting menu $95 ($149 with wine); 8-course grand tasting menu $115 ($166 with wine). **Payment** AE, D, DC, JCB, MC, V. **Service rating** ★★★★. **Friendliness rating** ★★. **Parking** Lot ($14 first hour or $30 for 24 hours); valet ($22 hourly or $40 for 24 hours). **Bar** Full service. **Wine selection** Fine, extensive, California-centric; $32–$670 bottle, $9–$24 glass. **Dress** Jacket suggested. **Disabled access** Yes. **Customers** Business travelers, sedate couples, celebrants. **Hours** Monday, 6:30–10 a.m. and 11:30 a.m.–1:30 p.m.; Tuesday–Saturday, 6:30–10 a.m., 11:30 a.m.–2 p.m., and 6–10 p.m.; Sunday, 6:30–9 a.m., 10:30 a.m.–1:30 p.m. (brunch).

SETTING AND ATMOSPHERE This civilized aerie seven floors above the Gold Coast offers a traditional, tasteful setting of plush carpets, mahogany walls, chandeliers, and oversized upholstered chairs—all enhanced by views of Michigan Avenue and Gold Coast goings-on. It's a grand, classy setting for a deal, be it business or romance.

unofficial **TIP**
The top-dollar brunch at Seasons is best for hotel guests who don't feel like leaving the property.

HOUSE SPECIALTIES Representative seasonal dishes have included organic carnaroli risotto with green garlic and Burgundy hazelnut snails; surf-and-turf tartare of American Kobe beef with violet-mustard ahi tuna, wasabi sorbet, and tamari soy gelée; Alaskan halibut cooked in a clay pot with Kaffir lime–scented broth, Chinese sausage, forbidden black rice, and Thai basil; farmer's egg ravioli with celeriac and white-truffle sauce; smoked-paprika-crusted duck with persimmon gastrique, duck confit agnolotti, and creamed Brussels sprouts.

OTHER RECOMMENDATIONS The buffet lunch and high tea in Seasons Lounge and Conservatory are both delightful and a better value than Seasons, though hardly the caliber of dining, of course. Depends on what you're looking for.

SUMMARY AND COMMENTS While chefs come and go here and the resulting output hovers between three and a half and five stars, Seasons delivers a quality New American dining experience with formal pampering on the side. There's a time for this sort of dining—and Seasons is a good place for it. Expense accounters should take advantage of the great wine list.

Shaw's Crab House ★★★½

| SEAFOOD | EXPENSIVE | QUALITY ★★★ | VALUE ★★ |

21 East Hubbard Street, River North; ☎ 312-527-2722; www.shawscrabhouse.com

1900 East Higgins Road, Schaumburg, Northern Suburbs; ☎ 847-517-2722

Reservations Recommended. **When to go** Anytime. **Entree range** $16–$60. **Payment** All major credit cards. **Service rating** ★★★½. **Friendliness rating** ★★★½. **Parking** Valet, $10. **Bar** Full service. **Wine selection** 200+ selections from around the world, $25–$1,200; 20 by the glass, $6–$25. **Dress** Business casual, dressy. **Disabled access** Wheelchair-accessible. **Customers** Professionals, tourists, and seafood lovers. **Hours** *Downtown:* Monday–Thursday, 11:30 a.m.–2 p.m. and 5:30–10 p.m.; Friday, 11:30 a.m.–2 p.m. and 5–11 p.m.; Saturday, 5–11 p.m.; Sunday, 10:30 a.m.–2 p.m. (brunch) and 5–10 p.m. *Schaumburg:* Monday–Thursday, 11:30 a.m.–2 p.m. and 5:30–9 p.m.; Friday, 11:30 a.m.–2 p.m. and 5:30–10 p.m.; Saturday, 5:30–10 p.m.; Sunday, 5–9 p.m.

SETTING AND ATMOSPHERE Upscale and clubby, with rich woods and all the accoutrements of fine dining.

HOUSE SPECIALTIES Fresh oysters, generally a half-dozen regional selections plus a sampler plate; seasonal crab (for example, chilled Florida stone-crab claws, Alaskan "red" king-crab legs, Alaskan Dungeness); Shaw's crab cakes; fresh Maine lobster, whole or stuffed.

OTHER RECOMMENDATIONS Sautéed yellow perch with lemon butter.

SUMMARY AND COMMENTS Though the tariff is high, this is the price we pay for fresh seafood in the Midwest. The quality and selection are there for lovers of the bounties of the sea, and the clubby atmosphere is suitably tony. Service is polished and professional. The adjoining Oyster Bar is more casual, with a great East Coast oyster bar feel and occasional live music.

unofficial **TIP**
Shaw's city location has added Sunday brunch service with classic breakfast fare; house specialties; a seafood bar; omelet, carving, and dessert stations; and a make-your-own Bloody Mary and mimosa bar.

Sixteen ★★★★

Trump International Hotel & Tower, 401 North Wabash Avenue, River North; ☎ 312-588-8030; www.trumpchicagohotel.com

Reservations Recommended. **When to go** Extravagant celebrations, business, romance. **Entree range** Lunch, $22–$34; dinner, $39–$54; 6-course tasting, $95; chef's blind tasting, $130. **Payment** AE, D, DC, JCB, MC, V. **Service Rating** ★★★★. **Friendliness Rating** ★★★. **Parking** Restaurant-validated self-park is $15 (a bargain for this neighborhood). **Bar** Full bar with specialty cocktails. **Wine selection** Vast, global, emphasis on Champagne, $14–$38 by the glass, $40–$6,500 by the bottle (more down-to-earth than you might expect); nice half-bottle selection; supplement for pairings with tasting menus. **Dress** Fashionable, business casual. **Disabled access** Yes. **Customers** Flashy dates, doyennes and silver foxes, power shoppers, international business travelers. **Hours** Monday–Wednesday, 6:30–10:30 a.m., 11:30 a.m.–2:30 p.m., and 5:30–10 p.m.; Thursday and Friday, 6:30 a.m.–10:30 a.m., 11:30 a.m.–2:30 p.m., and 5:30–10:30 p.m.; Saturday, 6:30 a.m.–noon and 5:30–10:30 p.m.; Sunday 6:30–10:30 a.m., 11 a.m.–3 p.m. (brunch), and 5:30–10 p.m.

SETTING AND ATMOSPHERE   On the 16th floor of The Donald's spiffy new sky-scraping hotel, walk through a wine alley into a stunning, futuristic-chic room with an equally stunning vista of sky, lake, and Chicago architecture (lucky diners face the Wrigley and Tribune buildings rather than aging condos). The main dining room has a soaring ceiling, 30-foot windows, a Swarovski chandelier, rich zebrawood paneling echoed in the abstract carpeting, creamy leather seating, and art-glass accents everywhere (including on the tables). There's lots of natural light by day, and when the city lights come up, ooh, baby.

unofficial **TIP**
If you use the Trump's self-parking, you'll be funneled out into the unglamorous bowels of the Loop. Just head for the light.

HOUSE SPECIALTIES   Changing seasonal menu of such dishes as crab salad in pink-peppercorn-laced rock melon with pineapple dressing; trio of duck (foie gras, duck ham, duck confit), Sauternes jelly, and orange tuile; diver scallop with horseradish, smoked bacon, cucumber chutney, and beets; Gunthorp Farms pork loin with pepper puree, apricot chutney, and potato fondant; study of strawberry with parfait, sorbet, and tuile bound with vanilla oil; killer cheese plate.

OTHER RECOMMENDATIONS   For lunch, try the classic Cobb salad with chicken, blue cheese, tomato, egg, bacon, and avocado, or the Mar-a-Lago tur-key burger with pear compote and tamarind glaze. Power lunch could be time for a creative nonalcoholic cocktail. Both the hotel breakfast standards and such creative dishes as lobster tostada with poached eggs and béarnaise or scrambled eggs with smoked bacon, fresh mint, and caviar on brioche are expense-account priced.

SUMMARY AND COMMENTS   Super-swanky with surprising restraint, super-expensive, and really, really good. If you can afford it, the setting and food are worthy of a special occasion. Sharp servers wear designer black and butcher aprons; some of the secondary servers are a little green. When the outdoor dining opens in 2009, most likely with a lighter (cheaper) menu, it's going to be a high-demand destination. This is modern amuse-bouche-and-petit-fours dining, but not a great destination cocktail spot; there's a bar-lounge for gathering, but the real bar scene is down on the mezzanine at Rebar.

Smith & Wollensky ★★★½

STEAK	EXPENSIVE	QUALITY ★★★★	VALUE ★★

318 North State Street, River North; ☎ 312-670-9900; www.smithandwollensky.com

Reservations Suggested. **When to go** Deals and dates. **Entree range** Lunch, $11–$35; dinner, $19.50–$49. **Payment** All major credit cards. **Service rating** ★★★. **Friendliness rating** ★★★. **Parking** Valet, $12. **Bar** Full service. **Wine selection** 200+ selections, mostly American, French, Italian, and Spanish, $40–$5,000; 20 by the glass, $12–$20. **Dress** Casual, business. **Disabled access** Yes. **Customers** Older power money, professionals, and upscale diners. **Hours** Daily, 11:30 a.m.–11 p.m.; grill open until 1:30 a.m.

SETTING AND ATMOSPHERE Smith & Wollensky has one of the most beautiful, inviting buildings and locations in town, with a grand entrance and clubby steak-house atmosphere of dark wood, marble, creamy walls, and globe light fixtures. The pomp is punctuated with a whimsical collection of American folk art, including a group of antique carved bears commemorating Chicago Bears football greats. Great outdoor dining on the Chicago River in warm weather.

unofficial **TIP**
Wollensky's Grill, below Smith & Wollensky's main dining room, has lower prices on dishes that are comparable to those at the main restaurant.

HOUSE SPECIALTIES Wollensky salad; split-pea soup; Maryland crab cakes; filet au poivre; sirloin steak.

OTHER RECOMMENDATIONS Caesar salad; Maine lobster, steamed or broiled; veal chop; lemon-pepper chicken; creamed spinach.

SUMMARY AND COMMENTS This pedigreed New York import gives great steak and great steak-house ambience, making it a great place to satisfy those carnivorous cravings. It has the feel of a classic, though it's been around only a few years.

Spacca Napoli ★★★★

PIZZA, ITALIAN	INEXPENSIVE	QUALITY ★★★★	VALUE ★★★★

1769 West Sunnyside Avenue, Ravenswood; ☎ 773-878-2420; www.spaccanapolipizzeria.com

Reservations Not accepted Friday or Saturday evenings. **When to go** Early weeknight dinner. **Entree range** $9.50–$16. **Payment** AE, D, DC, M, V. **Service rating** ★★★. **Friendliness rating** ★★★★. **Parking** Street. **Bar** Beer, wine, and Italian liqueurs. **Wine selection** Small but thoughtful all-Italian selection; $27–$95 bottle, $5.75–$8 glass. **Dress** Casual. **Disabled access** Yes. **Customers**

Locals, destination foodies. **Hours** Tuesday, 5–9 p.m.; Wednesday and Thursday, 11:30 a.m.–3 p.m. and 5–9 p.m.; Friday and Saturday, 11:30 a.m.–3 p.m. and 5–10 p.m.; Sunday, noon–9 p.m.; closed Monday.

SETTING AND ATMOSPHERE Lines form for the privilege of dining on some very serious handmade pizza created with avid attention to detail. The heart of the simply chic storefront is the showpiece wood-burning pizza oven (imported from Italy, along with the dough mixer). Indoors, expect modern lines, rustic natural elements, and interesting artwork—and noise at peak hours. Outdoors, there's seasonal sidewalk dining under umbrellas.

HOUSE SPECIALTIES Authentic Neapolitan pizza with thin, rustic, blistered crust is what Spacca Napoli is all about. Deceptively simple, ingredient-driven combinations begin with simple marinara (tomato, garlic, basil, oregano, olive oil) and build ingredient by ingredient (*fior de latte* mozzarella; mushrooms; Italian sausage; perhaps a change of cheese to *mozzarella di bufala*). Or you can go with white pizza (provolone, prosciutto, arugula) or white vegetarian variations, including basil-mozzarella-arugula and four-cheese.

OTHER RECOMMENDATIONS The menu is rounded out by simple salads and antipasti and such classic Italian desserts as tiramisù and zabaglione.

SUMMARY AND COMMENTS Part of a new wave of regional, artisanal pizza parlors, Spacca Napoli takes on the heart of deep-dish country with gusto and Southern (Italian) hospitality. As the Web site announces, " 'Spaccanapoli' is the old quarter and heart of Naples, Italy. Naples is famed as the birthplace of pizza."

Spiaggia ★★★★★

ITALIAN	VERY EXPENSIVE	QUALITY ★★★★★	VALUE ★★★

980 North Michigan Avenue, Gold Coast; ☎ 312-280-2750; www.spiaggiarestaurant.com

Reservations Required. **When to go** Big deals, special occasions. **Entree range** $19–$91. **Payment** AE, D, DC, JCB, MC, V. **Service rating** ★★★★½. **Friendliness rating** ★★★½. **Parking** Lot in building, $14 (validated). **Bar** Full service; numerous grappas, brandies, and *amari* (*digestivi*). **Wine selection** 600–700 Italian varietals and prestige cuvée Champagnes, $48–$1,850; more than 20 wines by the glass, $12–$28. **Dress** Jacket required; tie optional; no jeans or gym shoes. **Disabled access** Wheelchair-accessible. **Customers** Mature couples, international business types, upscale special-occasion celebrants such as Barack and Michelle Obama. **Hours** Monday–Thursday, 6–9:30 p.m.; Friday and Saturday, 5:30–10:30 p.m.; Sunday, 6–9 p.m.

SETTING AND ATMOSPHERE Spiaggia's ultrasophisticated ambience is dramatically enhanced by looming 40-foot windows overlooking the fashionable intersection of Oak Street and Michigan Avenue. The multitiered, architectural dining room is done in subtle neutrals with spectacular light fixtures, black-marble pillars, and topiary. Tables are sumptuously appointed. The cheese "cave" storage system harbors wonderful postprandial delights.

HOUSE SPECIALTIES The menu changes often but has included raw tuna and yellowtail with osetra caviar, citrus, and 2005 Cappezzana extra-virgin olive oil; veal-filled pasta with fennel pollen and braised veal breast; wood-roasted filet mignon with sunchoke puree–veal reduction, black trumpet mushrooms, and handcrafted black spaghetti with scungill, tomatoes, and basil.

OTHER RECOMMENDATIONS Examples from the changing menu: wood-roasted sea scallops with fennel puree, summer vegetables, and chef's garden micro rapini; fire-roasted summer eggplant with warm tomino cheese, wild arugula, and lemon *marmelatta*.

SUMMARY AND COMMENTS Spiaggia has long been known as Chicago's finest Italian restaurant. Chef Tony Mantuano has a deft hand with luxury ingredients and simply beautiful presentations, with fine wines and gracious service rounding out a superlative Italian dining experience.

Spring ★★★★½

SEAFOOD, NEW AMERICAN   EXPENSIVE   QUALITY ★★★★   VALUE ★★

2039 West North Avenue, Wicker Park; ☎ 773-395-7100; www.springrestaurant.net

Reservations Suggested. When to go Weekday dinner to avoid long waits. Entree range $22–$36. Payment AE, D, MC, V. Service rating ★★★★. Friendliness rating ★★. Parking Valet, $10. Bar Full service. Wine selection French, Californian, Italian, and Spanish; $39–$250 bottle, $27–$115 half bottles, $8–$16 glass. Dress Casual chic. Disabled access Yes. Customers Trendy young locals and suburbanites. Hours Tuesday–Thursday, 5:30–9:30 p.m.; Friday and Saturday, 5:30–10:30 p.m.; Sunday, 5:30–9 p.m.; closed Monday.

SETTING AND ATMOSPHERE In a former Roman bathhouse, the subterranean pool area is now the dining room with a Zen garden at the entrance and minimalist decor. The feng shui space has tables zigzagging down the center, separated by high banquettes for privacy. Pistachio-colored walls are illuminated by recessed lights, making the room glow.

HOUSE SPECIALTIES The menu changes frequently but has included fresh Hawaiian hearts of palm and green papaya salad with Maine lobster, shrimp, fresh mint, and a ginger dressing; lemongrass and coconut soup with Thai chili, Kaffir lime, and cellophane noodles; baramundi with grilled trumpet royale mushrooms, parsley-root purée, and white asparagus; poached pear strudel with walnuts, *cajeta* ice cream, and port-wine caramel.

OTHER RECOMMENDATIONS Maine lobster tempura with buckwheat soba noodles and apple-ginger broth; roasted red snapper with lobster and crabmeat risotto and lobster-vanilla reduction; sturgeon with roasted fingerling potatoes, horseradish sauce, and pickled beet relish; parsnip cake with cream-cheese ice cream.

SUMMARY AND COMMENTS Now a mainstay of Chicago's modern dining scene, Spring is revered for its serene space; exquisitely prepared and executed dishes with Asian accents and layers of ingredients in innovative combinations, fabulously broad wine list; and polished, professional servers.

kids Superdawg Drive-In ★★

| FAST FOOD | INEXPENSIVE | QUALITY ★★ | VALUE ★★ |

6363 North Milwaukee Avenue, North Central–O'Hare Airport;
☎ **773-763-0660; www.superdawg.com**

Reservations Not accepted. **When to go** For a junk food or nostalgia fix. **Entree range** $5–$10 (fries included). **Payment** Cash only. **Service rating** ★★. **Friendliness rating** ★★★★. **Parking** Lot. **Bar** None. **Wine selection** None. **Dress** Casual. **Disabled access** Yes. **Customers** Dawg lovers of all stripes. **Hours** Sunday–Thursday, 11 a.m.–1 a.m.; Friday and Saturday, 11 a.m.–2 a.m.

SETTING AND ATMOSPHERE The kitsch factor and old-timey, tray-on-the-window carhop service set this landmark hot-dog haven apart from the pack. That, and the adorable little boxes with fetching wienie graphics, and the hilarious he-man–cutie-pie costumed hot dogs on the roof.

HOUSE SPECIALTIES Superdawg (pure-beef hot dog with mustard, piccalilli—aka fluorescent relish, kosher dill pickle, chopped Spanish onions, and hot peppers); Whoopskidawg (Polish sausage with special sauce and grilled onions); Whoopercheesie (fresh-ground 100% beef double cheeseburger in a single bun); Superonionchips (chip-shaped chunks of battered onions); ice-cream sundaes and malts.

OTHER RECOMMENDATIONS Supershrimp (fried-shrimp boat with toasted bun); Superchickenmidgees (battered chicken strips); Superveggies (mixed battered vegetables); pineapple shakes.

SUMMARY AND COMMENTS Okay, it's junk food, and it's beyond out of the way. And there's—gasp!—no celery salt. And the fat crinkle fries are more limp than crispy. But somehow it all works. If you want a slice of vintage Americana with your Chicago dog, you can't beat this time-warped slice of the 1940s.

SUSHISAMBA rio ★★½

| NUEVO LATINO, SUSHI | EXPENSIVE | QUALITY ★★★ | VALUE ★★ |

504 North Wells Street, River North; ☎ **312-595-2300;**
www.sushisamba.com

Reservations Accepted. **When to go** Weekend evenings. **Entree range** $21–$44. **Payment** AE, MC, V. **Service rating** ★★. **Friendliness rating** ★★. **Parking** Valet, $12. **Bar** Full service with dozens of sake varieties, plus martinis, mojitos, and caipirinhas. **Wine selection** Californian, French, Austrian, German; $24–$325 bottle, $8–$14 glass. **Dress** Hip and modern. **Disabled access** Yes. **Customers** Trendy club-hoppers. **Hours** Sunday–Monday, 11:45 a.m.–11 p.m.; Tuesday, 11:45 a.m.–midnight; Wednesday–Friday, 11:45 a.m.–1 a.m.; Saturday, 11:45 a.m.–2 a.m.; Sunday brunch, 11:45 a.m.–3:30 p.m.

SETTING AND ATMOSPHERE The dizzying room, designed by David Rockwell, is like the Cirque du Soleil of restaurants, with glittering beads hanging, reflective light fixtures suspended from the ceiling, backlit panels on the walls, and raised seating areas along the perimeter. A 20-seat sushi bar centers the room, surrounded by wavy patterns of tables, all surrounded by thumping Latin tunes. The covered outdoor dining area is one of River North's hottest seats in warm weather.

HOUSE SPECIALTIES Raw regional oysters; a variety of seviches (which come on a tasting platter); Brazilian *churrascos* of pork tenderloin, chorizo, rib eye, linguiça sausage, and hanger steak; *moqueca mista* (a paella-like collection of nicely handled seafood with coconut milk and rice).

OTHER RECOMMENDATIONS Sushi and maki in dozens of varieties; shrimp tempura; *sawagani* (tiny Japanese river crabs flash-fried and salted); citrus-cured *anticuchos* (skewered meats), including cubes of grilled beef with mild red chile paste, or teriyaki-seasoned chicken livers, served on a bed of Peruvian white corn niblets.

SUMMARY AND COMMENTS The room and the music are quite loud at this branch of the chain (other incarnations are in New York, Miami, Las Vegas, and Tel Aviv, Israel). Japanese, Brazilian, and Peruvian food meet at a crossroads on the extraordinarily large menu. The food isn't fusion—rather, the menu is neatly separated into sections representing each cuisine. The front bar is frequently packed with those waiting, sometimes for up to an hour, for a coveted table in the main dining room, although the full menu can be had at the bar as well.

Three Happiness ★★½

| CHINESE | INEXPENSIVE | QUALITY ★★★ | VALUE ★★★★★ |

209 West Cermak Road, Chinatown; ☎ **312-842-1964**

Reservations Accepted. **When to go** Busy for lunch, crowds on weekend evenings. **Entree range** $8–$20. **Payment** AE, D, DC, MC, V. **Service rating** ★★★. **Friendliness rating** ★★★★. **Parking** Pay lot, $2 (will validate). **Bar** Beer and wine only. **Wine selection** Limited, but sake and plum wine also served. **Dress** Casual. **Disabled access** Yes. **Customers** Diverse crowd; university and Loop workers. **Hours** Daily, 24 hours.

SETTING AND ATMOSPHERE The simple, small room isn't fancy, but it's clean and efficient, and the friendly staff and owner help make it comfortable. Simple linoleum floors, a red Tsingtao paper dragon hanging from the ceiling, and booths lining the perimeter of the room complete the decor. The family-style dining with revolving lazy Susans at most tables makes for lively conversation at both lunch and dinner.

HOUSE SPECIALTIES Spare ribs with black-bean-and-garlic sauce; Szechuan diced chicken; shrimp lobster-style; pork chop Mandarin-style; seaweed soup; Buddhist delight (vegetarian medley of stir-fried vegetables).

OTHER RECOMMENDATIONS Pan-fried prawn in the shell; five-spice soy chicken; beef with ginger and scallion; various dim sum dishes served all day long, such as pan-fried taro root cake, rice in lotus leaf with pork and chicken, and *kow wong* (chicken and bean sprouts in rice pancake).

SUMMARY AND COMMENTS This small Chinatown storefront (easily confused with—but unrelated to—the prosaic, larger New Three Happiness on the corner) maintains high-quality fare. Lunch is a real bargain—$4.99 for a meal soup-to-nuts—but dinner or à la carte ordering allows for sampling of more interesting dishes from the incredibly broad menu. Dim sum, the array of small dishes normally served for a unique brunch, is available all day, every day. It's a midweek delight for adventurous nibblers.

Topolobampo ★★★★½

| REGIONAL MEXICAN | EXPENSIVE | QUALITY ★★★★★ | VALUE ★★★ |

445 North Clark Street, River North; ☎ 312-661-1434; www.rickbayless.com

Reservations Accepted for parties up to 8. **When to go** Weeknight dinner. **Entree range** Lunch, $14–$19; dinner, $25–$38; chef's 5-course tasting menu, $75, $115 with wine pairing. **Payment** All major credit cards. **Service rating** ★★★★. **Friendliness rating** ★★★½. **Parking** Valet, $12; public lots, street. **Bar** Extensive premium tequila list, margaritas, and beer. **Wine selection** Extensive global, 120 selections, $30–$260; 10 by the glass, $11. **Dress** Business casual. **Disabled access** Wheelchair-accessible. **Customers** Upscale locals and travelers, professionals, and couples. **Hours** Tuesday, 11:45 a.m.–2 p.m. and 5:30–9:30 p.m.; Wednesday–Thursday, 11:30 a.m.–2 p.m. and 5:30–9:30 p.m.; Friday, 11:30 a.m.–2 p.m. and 5:30–10:30 p.m.; Saturday, 5:30–10:30 p.m.; closed Sunday and Monday.

SETTING AND ATMOSPHERE Jeweled blues and sun-drenched hues of oranges and golds; colorful, evocative Mexican folk and fine art. Though more formal than the casual Frontera Grill adjacent, the Topolobampo dining room tempers its sophistication with a sense of fun.

HOUSE SPECIALTIES The menu of Mexican celebratory dishes, game, and little-known regional specialties changes every few weeks, and no single dish is considered a house specialty. Sample items might include *ensalada de chayote* (tender, delicate chayote salad dressed with Spanish sparkling-wine vinaigrette, house-made goat-milk queso fresco, Nueske's bacon, watercress, and pickled red onions); *langosta en crema de calabaza* (super-sweet roasted Maine lobster in ancho-tinged pumpkin cream with mushroom and chard–stuffed delicata); *cochinita adobada* (Maple Creek Farms pork slow-roasted in banana leaves with *guajillo* chile marinade, served with rich pan juices, grilled acorn squash, and braised greens).

OTHER RECOMMENDATIONS Again, menu choices change frequently but have included *pollito en mole verde* (roasted, marinated free-range baby chicken with classic green pumpkinseed mole, Mexican greens, and heirloom beans); *milanese de puerco* (crunchy-coated pork tenderloin, panfried in olive oil, with a spicy salsa of tomatoes, habaneros, onions, and sour orange with baby lettuces and pickled red onions); *chilaquiles verdes* (tangy tomatillo sauce simmered with crispy tortillas, topped with grilled chicken, thick cream, and jicama); *cuatro cositas* (a sampler plate of chicken enchilada in roasted tomatillo sauce; griddle-baked quesadilla of Jack cheese, duck, and peppers; tostada of marinated cactus salad; and black beans); lime tart.

SUMMARY AND COMMENTS Considered by many the nation's forerunner of fine Mexican dining, Topolobampo opens up a whole new world of soulful flavors from the regions of Mexico. Owner Rick Bayless is a true culinary artist and a dedicated scholar of Mexican cuisine (author of several cookbooks, he is also the host of *Mexico: One Plate at a Time* on PBS). The ever-changing menu creates a sense of unfolding seasonal pageantry that keeps loyalists returning frequently for another trip to Mexican culinary heaven. Make reservations well in advance. The adjacent sister restaurant, Frontera Grill (see page 229), offers a less formal (and less expensive) variation on Bayless's trailblazing regional-Mexican theme.

TRU ★★★★★

NEW AMERICAN	VERY EXPENSIVE	QUALITY ★★★★★	VALUE ★★★

676 North St. Clair Street, Streeterville; ☎ 312-202-0001; www.trurestaurant.com

Reservations Highly recommended. **When to go** Dinner. **Entree range** Prix-fixe "collection" tasting menus: 3 courses, $95; 7-course seasonal with wine, $350 (vegetarian available); 9-course chef's, $145. **Payment** All major credit cards. **Service rating** ★★★★½. **Friendliness rating** ★★★. **Parking** Valet, $14; nearby lots and garages. **Bar** Full service. **Wine selection** 1,700 wines, diverse with an emphasis on France and California, $32–$2,300; 17 wines and Champagnes by the glass, $7–$45. **Dress** Jackets required for men; ties optional. **Disabled access** Wheelchair-accessible. **Customers** Power money, Michigan Avenue denizens, creative professionals. **Hours** Monday–Thursday, 5:30–10 p.m.; Friday and Saturday, 5–11 p.m.; closed Sunday.

SETTING AND ATMOSPHERE   The dining room is ultracontemporary, stark, and simple with a few original artworks (Warhol, Mapplethorpe); the buzz of the patrons and the plushy, blue-velvet purse stools (for sale on the Web site) keep the space from feeling sterile. Don't miss the gravity-defying bathroom sinks.

HOUSE SPECIALTIES   With a constantly changing menu, regular items are few. Some mainstays include the caviar staircase, a sculptural glass spiral staircase dotted with various caviars and fixin's, and various foie gras preparations. Other items might run along the lines of Hawaiian hamachi with fennel, peach, and caraway; lobster soup with ground hominy, lobster emulsion, and spoonbread; Swan Creek Farm suckling pig with zucchini pavé, licorice, kumquat, and pig jus; or salt-crusted venison with cocoa, olive, and blood orange.

OTHER RECOMMENDATIONS   You can actually order any menu item à la carte if you prefer. Some extravagant luxury items are singled out on the menu, such as the caviar service, Kobe beef two ways, and a seasonal truffle dish. Desserts also rotate seasonally in the tradition of pastry chef Gale Gand, with examples including Champagne-poached peaches with pistachio blancmange, white-chocolate orb, and Bellini glacé; caramelized banana crepes with peanut butter–curry ice cream, peanut praline, and bittersweet chocolate sauce; and hot chocolate soufflé with cayenne-pistachio crumbs, Saigon cinnamon ice cream, vanilla marshmallow, and "5-alarm" chocolate sauce.

SUMMARY AND COMMENTS At TRU, originally a collaboration between Rich Melman's Lettuce Entertain You Enterprises and onetime couple Rick Tramonto and Gale Gand (also well known for their cookbooks), the latter pair, though still involved on a titular level, have turned the majority of their energies to their own restaurant development group. The high-concept fare is renowned for its contemporary creativity with touches of humor leavening the sophistication. This is *très* chic—and *très* lengthy—dining, so plan to make an evening of it, especially if you want to experience the full spectrum of the larger collection menus. European-style team service; no cell phones in the dining room.

 Twin Anchors ★★½

AMERICAN, RIBS **MODERATE** **QUALITY** ★★ **VALUE** ★★★

1655 North Sedgwick Street, Old Town; ☎ **312-266-1616;**
www.twinanchorsribs.com

Reservations Not accepted. **When to go** Weekend lunch, early dinner. **Entree range** $13–$26. **Payment** AE, D, DC, MC, V. **Service rating** ★★. **Friendliness rating** ★★★. **Parking** Street, valet $8. **Bar** Full service. **Wine selection** Extremely limited, generic; $25–$45 bottle, $6–$10 glass. **Dress** Casual. **Disabled access** Yes. **Customers** Locals, characters, rib lovers. **Hours** Monday–Thursday, 5–11 p.m.; Friday, 5 p.m.–midnight; Saturday, noon–midnight; Sunday, noon–10:30 p.m.

SETTING AND ATMOSPHERE Raucous, casual, and comfy, this Chicago neighborhood classic has the kind of history that restaurant developers are always trying to fake. A Frank Sinatra hangout in the old days and the setting for the film *Return to Me* (and, more recently, scenes from *The Dark Knight*), this divey, Wisconsin-esque saloon opened in 1932 (in an 1881 building). The mood is set by Old Town memorabilia, perpetual sports on TV, an eclectic jukebox heavy on the nostalgia, and, yes, two big anchors. The famous POSITIVELY NO DANCING sign was posted in the disco days, when Travolta wannabes were interfering with service. Nice patio, too.

> *unofficial* **TIP**
> Lots of celebs have visited Twin Anchors, with prime seats being Booth 7 (Frank Sinatra) and Booth 5 (John Belushi and Dan Aykroyd). Kids get their own menu items, games, and crayons.

HOUSE SPECIALTIES Barbecued baby-back ribs and chicken; chili; burgers; baked beans; onion rings; dark rye bread; cheesecake.

OTHER RECOMMENDATIONS Caesar salad; New York strip steak; fish fry; giant grilled shrimp; vegetarian sloppy joe.

SUMMARY AND COMMENTS While fanatics debate the relative merits of the original sweet sauce ("zesty" is available) and fall-off-the-bone texture, the long waits here speak for themselves. But, actually, the thing people seem to love most about this ribs-and-a-cold-one institution is that it stays the same. Service can be brusque. Carryout is a good option.

kids Wishbone ★★½

| CAJUN, SOUTHERN | INEXPENSIVE | QUALITY ★★★ | VALUE ★★★★★ |

3300 North Lincoln Avenue, Lakeview; ☎ 773-549-2663;
www.wishbonechicago.com
1001 West Washington Boulevard, West Loop; ☎ 312-850-2663

Reservations Suggested at lunch for parties of 6 or more. **When to go** Brunch, casual dinner. **Entree range** $6–$16. **Payment** AE, D, DC, MC, V. **Service rating** ★★. **Friendliness rating** ★★★. **Parking** *Lincoln:* public lot, street. *Washington:* valet, $8; street. **Bar** Full service. **Wine selection** Limited, $14–$21; 13 by the glass, $5–$6.50. **Dress** Casual. **Disabled access** Wheelchair-accessible. **Customers** Come-as-you-are locals, families. **Hours** *Lincoln:* Brunch, Saturday and Sunday, 8 a.m.–2:30 p.m.; breakfast, Monday–Friday, 7–11 a.m.; lunch, Monday–Friday, 11 a.m.–3 p.m.; dinner, Tuesday–Thursday and Sunday, 5–9 p.m.; Friday and Saturday, 5–10 p.m. *Washington:* Brunch, Saturday and Sunday, 8 a.m.–3 p.m.; breakfast, 7–11 a.m.; lunch, Monday–Friday, 11 a.m.–3 p.m.; dinner, Tuesday–Thursday, 5–9 p.m., Friday and Saturday, 5–10 p.m.

SETTING AND ATMOSPHERE The Washington Avenue location is funky-casual, warehouse-style: a big exposed-brick room with lots of windows and whimsical chicken-and-egg art. The Lincoln Avenue location has a darker, more neo-retro look.

HOUSE SPECIALTIES Menu specialties change daily. Possibilities include shrimp sautéed with bacon, mushrooms, and scallions, served over cheese grits; blackened chicken pan-seared in Cajun spices and served with coleslaw garnish; blackened catfish (fresh farm-raised catfish fillet, blackened with Cajun spices); red eggs (two eggs over corn tortillas with black beans, cheese, chile ancho sauce, scallions, sour cream, and salsa); and French toast dipped in cornflakes.

OTHER RECOMMENDATIONS Louisiana chicken salad (enormous salad with blackened chicken breast and corn muffin); North Carolina crab cakes; hoppin' John or hoppin' Jack (vegetarian black-eyed peas or black beans on rice with Cheddar cheese, scallions, and tomatoes).

SUMMARY AND COMMENTS The casual-dining and tousled brunch crowds head here for "Southern Reconstruction cooking" that's hearty and inexpensive, though hit-or-miss. There are numerous vegetarian options, as well as full-pint Bloody Marys. This is a prime destination for families with kids—there's a children's menu for breakfast, lunch, and dinner (till the 7 p.m. "adult swim"). On Thursday nights, the Lincoln Avenue location has music from 6:30 to 9 p.m.

PART NINE

SHOPPING *in* CHICAGO

By Laurie Levy

"NOTHING LIKE *It* BACK HOME"

SHOPPERS WHO COME TO CHICAGO expecting Second (or Third) City are overjoyed. Time was, fashion was the resultant mélange of trends that blew in from the Coast (either one). No more. Said mélange floated down "Boul Mich" (Michigan Avenue, that is), blew west across the Loop, fanned north and south, and became Chicago Style. Suddenly, the world sat up and took notice.

And it only gets better.

The City of the Big Shoulders still takes the best of the West, combines it with the best of the East, imports every possible plum from abroad, adds the dash that is all its own, and comes up with the formula that puts the *chic* in Chicago. As a clever copywriter for the erstwhile Marshall Field's said so succinctly long ago, "There's nothing like it back home." (Still true, though Field's is now Macy's.)

But where should you look in a city this size? There's always the obvious Michigan Avenue, but what about those neighborhood boutiques that are well-kept secrets? Sorry, natives, it's time to divulge the wheres and how-to-find-its.

THE WHERE OF IT

BORDERED BY THE CHICAGO RIVER on both the north and west is the **Loop,** a 35-block cornucopia of limited retail action circumscribed by elevated train tracks; it's the home of the giant aforementioned **Macy's.** The triumphant creation of gorgeous lakefront **Millennium Park** revitalized the Loop, including the fabled **Block 37.** The latter ceased being a winter skating rink and is being transformed into a five-story retail base next to an office media tower anchored by the new CBS studios facing Daley Plaza. Among the confirmed retailers are Zara, Puma, Ben Sherman, Club Monaco, and Aveda. The Lettuce Entertain You restaurant chain will have an eatery, or you can grab something from Au Bon Pain, Freshii, or Beard Papa's (Japanese cream puffs) on Block 37's transit level. Now in place is Block 37's green-minded **Sterling Business Center,** which has taken the 15th floor for suites of luxury offices. Tenants will have access to a spa, a graphic-design shop, concierge services, and more. The new **Joffrey Building,** at the corner of State and Randolph streets, houses the Joffrey Ballet but also contains retail at its base.

While you can still find **Carson Pirie Scott** stores in many suburban locations, the loss of the iconic retailer at its historic State Street location has opened has opened that site for other purposes. The famed Louis Sullivan building, designated as a landmark, underwent a $60 million restoration and now contains offices and some retail. A welcome addition on the seventh floor is the spacious Sullivan Galleries, an art space already drawing raves.

As Field's green awnings have transitioned to Macy's red and black, the look of State has changed. But as the *Chicago Tribune* has reported, "State Street is still standing, and very much open for business." Among the stores attracting shoppers are **Old Navy,** three stories high at 35 North State, along with discounters **Loehmann's,** at 151 North State, and the multistory **Nordstrom Rack,** at 24 North State.

Further shopping for the younger customer is assured at **H&M** (20 North State), **Forever 21** (34 South State), and **Charlotte Russe** (10 South State). Still more fashion has arrived with the Chicago-owned powerhouse **Akira,** (122 South State), which features boutique fashions at moderate prices.

It should be mentioned, additionally, that the area is a busy live-theater district. South of the river are several of the city's best museum stores (but more on those later).

Moving north of the river is the renowned **Magnificent Mile,** where grand malls and opulent boutiques flank both sides of Michigan Avenue. The **Near North Side**—known for streets that fan east and west of the Magnificent Mile, including the "tree" streets Maple, Chestnut, Oak, and so on—is home to small pockets of eclectic shopping pleasures. Off the north end of Michigan Avenue, heading west, **Oak Street** is a shopping venue in its own right. Ritzy, upscale, and generally expensive, Oak's single block is designer-fashion headquarters, with five of the city's top jewelers within steps of each other. **River North,** on the west side of Near North, is the epicenter of Chicago's art, antiques, and designer-furniture scenes.

Moving beyond Near North and River North and away from downtown are **Lincoln Park** and the ever-burgeoning **Bucktown–Wicker Park** area. The latter district, west of downtown, is filled with shopping, gallery hopping, and great dining, too, since some of the city's most interesting restaurants are nearby. Even farther west, more galleries, restaurants, and a few shops make up the area known as the **West Loop.**

Lincoln Park's parallel avenues of **Webster** and **Armitage** are such fun they warrant time of their own, though neither has shopping areas that are terribly large. Because many of these shops are mom-and-pop operations, they provide an antidote to any impersonality you might find on Boul Mich. In this same area, the north–south streets of **Halsted, Clark,** and **Southport** amble for miles, sometimes in drab fashion, occasionally glowing with a shop or two (especially Southport) and restaurants to rival top areas in the city. **Lincoln Avenue,** slanting northwest from Lincoln Park, is less likely to glow, but an occasional charmer can refute that theory.

Head north along the lake into **Evanston.** When you've finished trooping the Northwestern University campus, avail yourself of some of the town's fine shopping. North of Evanston are such affluent and shopping-rich communities as **Wilmette, Winnetka, Glencoe, North-brook, Highland Park,** and **Lake Forest.**

THE HOW OF IT

BECAUSE PEOPLE SHOP MICHIGAN AVENUE as if it's one huge consolidated shopping center, that is the way we've presented it. We describe the malls and the stores in and between them without attempting to organize what's available into specific categories of goods and services.

In discussing the other downtown and Greater Chicago shopping venues, however, the territory is immense and the stores geographically dispersed. Off Michigan Avenue it's more important, and sometimes necessary, to define what you're shopping for. When we talk about the myriad stores of the Loop, Oak Street, Near North, River North, and beyond, we organize our discussion around specific genres of merchandise. Some Michigan Avenue stores not incorporated in malls are also included in these categories.

MICHIGAN AVENUE:
The Magnificent Mile

FROM THE CHICAGO RIVER NORTH ALONG MICHIGAN AVENUE, the "Magnificent Mile" or "Miracle Mile" is home to what may be America's largest concentration of upscale shopping. Even chain habitués of suburban malls are enticingly packaged, and many stars in this shopping galaxy are tucked away inside huge buildings. To shopping junkies, the discovery of these merchandise cities is akin to passing, Alice-like, through the looking glass. And the malls are fairly gorgeous: **Water Tower Place** and **900 North Michigan,** just to name a couple.

Shopping: Magnificent Mile and the Loop

- **MAGNIFICENT MILE**
1. The Shops at North Bridge
2. Chicago Place
3. Neiman Marcus

4. Water Tower Place
5. 900 North Michigan
- **THE LOOP**
6. Macy's

Ⓜ Subway/El stop

It is no secret that Oprah loves Michigan Avenue, and tourists are dazzled by the proximity of so many great stores. "Everything in LA," one visitor laments, "is a car ride away." Still true. Add five B's (**Bloomingdale's, Barneys, Burberry, Brooks Brothers,** and **Bulgari**) to **Macy's, Saks Fifth Avenue, Neiman Marcus, Chanel, Ralph Lauren,** and dozens more, sometimes within a two-block area. We don't have the space to list every enticement, but what follows should whet your appetite.

MICHIGAN AVENUE'S GRAND EMPORIUMS

UNTIL SEPTEMBER 2000, while there was some shopping on Michigan Avenue between the river and Ohio Street, most of the primo shops were concentrated in the nine blocks from Ontario north to Oak. This changed when the "mall" at 520 North Michigan, known originally as North Bridge and housing the city's first **Nordstrom** (☎ 312-464-1515), opened (though suburban Nordstroms were already ensconced). The four-level, 271,000-square-foot fashion specialty store is strong on cosmetics, departments called "style stations," bath and spa shops, fitting rooms to accommodate persons with disabilities, outstanding kid stuff on level four, a concierge desk, and two restaurants.

THE SHOPS AT NORTH BRIDGE For general information, call the concierge desk at ☎ 312-327-2300 or visit **www.theshopsatnorthbridge .com.** In addition to Nordstrom, the shops include 50 top retailers, such as **Tommy Bahama** (sportswear), **Oilily** (vivid fashions for women and children), **A/X Armani, Vosges Haut-Chocolat, C.D. Peacock** (another big-name Chicago-area jeweler), and girlhood rave **Sanrio's Hello Kitty.** On the fourth level are such Chicago-style eateries as **Relish, Tuscany Café, Mezza, Max Orient,** and **Jaffa Bakery.**

CHICAGO PLACE This former eight-level mall at 700 North Michigan is converting to offices and will feature stores on the ground level only, including **Saks Fifth Avenue** (☎ 312-944-6500), one of the nation's prettiest. Saks has been on the avenue since 1929, and this is one of its showcase stores. Find traditional and cutting-edge clothing designers and a home section on the seventh floor.

NEIMAN MARCUS Just down the avenue from Chicago Place is this freestanding titan at 737 North Michigan (☎ 312-642-5900). Noteworthy at this Neiman's are the **Zodiac** restaurant, known for signature popovers, and unique home-decor items in the gift galleries.

WATER TOWER PLACE At 835 North Michigan is this seven-level marble palace, anchored by **Macy's.** One of the latest additions is **American Girl Place,** a hugely popular destination for girls and their moms (or dads or grandmas) featuring rooms full of the famed American Girl dolls and their accessories. American Girl Place Chicago calls itself an "experiential retail store" and packs its 52,000-square-foot space with Avenue AG specialty shops, a Celebration Screen photo studio, boutiques for doll necessities, a doll hair salon, and a cafe where girls, their family members, and their dolls (in special doll seats) can enjoy brunch, lunch, tea, or dinner. The number to call for reservations: ☎ 877-AG-PLACE.

Another new and huge **Forever 21** (☎ 312-202-9107) has arrived, and so have **Betsey Johnson** (☎ 312-280-6964), over from her former digs on Halsted; the teen rave **Aritzia** (☎ 312-867-9230); and **CUSP** (☎ 312-951-2299).

An interesting gallery here is **Chiaroscuro** (☎ 312-988-9253; **www .chiaroart.com**), where 300 artists and artisans show their wares, including jewelry, glass, furniture, and mixed media. (There's even a comic clock for a child's room.) And, on level four, a new destination for athletes is **Adidas Sports Performance** (☎ 312-867-1640). No standard racks or shoe cubbies here: clothes hang on weight-lifting equipment or locker-room hooks; sneakers are found in track starting blocks. And you can customize your high-tops.

Another of the more interesting aspects of this shopping center is the vast food court called **Foodlife** (☎ 312-335-3663; **www.foodlife chicago.com**) on the mezzanine, where you can dig in to (or take out) almost anything, from tacos to freshly baked pies. To see a list of all the stores and eateries here, visit **www.shopwatertower.com**.

900 NORTH MICHIGAN This formidable shopping venue houses beautiful **Bloomingdale's** (☎ 312-440-4460), gorgeous **Gucci** (☎ 312-664-5504), silvery **Pavillon Christofle** (☎ 312-664-9700), and a city mall of laid-back charm that makes it easy to shop. While on the first level, check out the china at **Bernardaud** (☎ 312-751-1700) and the watches, pens, and butter-soft leather goods at **Montblanc** (☎ 312-943-1200).

On 900's fifth floor, **Galt Toys + Galt Baby** (☎ 312-440-9550; **www .galttoysgaltbaby.com**) has items for kids; tiny **Glove Me Tender** (☎ 312-664-4022; **www.glovemetender.com**) is the place to buy gloves (natch) as well as hats. Other clothing stores include **Yolanda Lorente** (☎ 312-867-0900; **www.yolandalorente.com**), whose gowns have long adorned international fashionables, and **Club Monaco** (☎ 312-787-8757). At level four is a favorite at 900: **The Goldsmith Ltd.**, (☎ 312-751-1986; **www.thegoldsmithltd.com**), where Sherry Bender, one of the city's top gold artisans, works her magic with a variety of unusual stones and settings. This award-winning designer and her jewel-box setting are well worth a visit. For more on all the 900 shops, visit **www.shop900.com**.

The LOOP'S LANDMARK DEPARTMENT STORE

SOUTH OF THE CHICAGO RIVER and just west of Michigan Avenue is the Loop, circumscribed by elevated train tracks, and the aforementioned **Macy's** (111 North State Street; ☎ 312-781-1000). Either of the

71-ton clocks (at the Randolph and Washington street corners) that tower over this granddaddy of Chicago stores signals your arrival.

This is arguably the most beautiful department store in the country. Ongoing renovations include the ever-fabulous **beauty department,** under a Tiffany ceiling that arcs seven stories above the main-level floor. As Field's, this store was a source of firsts: first to establish a European buying office (in England, in 1871); first to open a dining room in a department store (in 1907); first to delight customers with lavish window displays; and first U.S. store to institute a bridal registry. Also notable is the Christmas season's **Great Tree,** which towers 45 feet and still delights patrons as much as they enjoy viewing the holiday windows.

Think of shopping here as not unlike exploring a small village. The **men's department** takes up part of Level One and a huge section on Two. Women enjoy designer wares on three, and on level four are the huge **women's shoe department** and the full-service **bridal salon.**

Five is for **petites, children's clothes,** and a big **FAO Schwarz toy shop.** The highlight of six is the **home section,** which offers more than 450 patterns of crystal and china, including **Waterford, Vera Wang,** and **Marc Jacobs.**

The seventh floor is for foodies, and the **Walnut Room** is legendary. It has a center fountain, and both natives and tourists like to come here at Christmas to gape at the Great Tree. A Wine Bar has been added to the Walnut Room, offering a selection of more than 100 wines, along with cheese assortments. The **Frango Café**—mostly likely named for the former Field's signature Frango Mint candies—is a 140-seat restaurant.

The eighth floor is earmarked for **furniture,** including such lines as **Martha Stewart** and **Baker,** plus the 2,000-square-foot **Trend House** rooms. On the ninth floor is more furniture and what is claimed to be (who knows?) the largest **Oriental-carpet collection** of any American department store.

WHERE *to* FIND . . .

ART AND FINE CRAFTS

ON NORTH MICHIGAN AVENUE When you say "art in Chicago," your number-one thought should be the **Art Institute of Chicago,** the magnificent institution south of the Chicago River (on Michigan Avenue at Adams; see profile, page 151) that consistently outpaces the finest museums in the world. Also extraordinary is the **Art Institute Museum Shop** (☎ 312-443-3583; www.artinstituteshop.org). Find art books, posters, scarves, unique Baltic amber jewelry, even umbrellas—such as a scenic one by "urban Impressionist" Gustave Caillebotte called *Paris Street, a Rainy Day* (in a collapsible size at $34, one of the most popular items ever carried in the store). Hours: Monday, Tuesday, and Wednesday, 10:30 a.m. to 5 p.m.; Thursday, 10:30 a.m. to 8 p.m. (summer, 10:30 a.m. to 9 p.m. from the first Thursday of June through Labor Day); Friday, 10:30 a.m. to 5 p.m. (summer, 10:30 a.m. to 9 p.m.); Saturday and Sunday, 10 a.m. to 5 p.m.; closed Thanksgiving, Christmas, and New Year's Day. (You need not be admitted to the museum to enter the shop.)

Another beauteous store, generously trimmed in oak, is a highlight of the **Museum of Contemporary Art** (220 East Chicago Avenue; ☎ 312-397-4000; **www.mcachicagostore.org**; see profile, page 178). Called **The MCA Store,** this light, bright, airy space comprises two levels connected by a sweeping two-story winding staircase under a skylight.

NEAR NORTH Joy-Us Jaunts (☎ 773-327-3366) also takes individuals and families on personalized artistic and cultural forays in Chicago (such as a trip to an auction house or an artist's studio) and around the world. The **Kamp Gallery,** an addition to the Drake Hotel (140 East Walton Place; ☎ 312-664-0090; **www.kampgallery.com**), shows fine historical and contemporary paintings.

Brightening Oak Street is **Aaron Galleries** (50 East Oak Street, second floor; ☎ 312-943-0660), where you'll find 19th- through 20th-century and contemporary American paintings, prints, and drawings. Another Oak Street gem is the **Colletti Gallery** (67 East Oak Street; ☎ 312-664-6767; **www.collettigallery.com**), which offers a primarily European collection of posters circa 1880–1940, fine-art ceramics, stunning furniture, wonderful glass pieces, and more. If you're in the market for a Mucha or Toulouse-Lautrec poster, this is certainly the place to find it.

RIVER NORTH Pearl Art & Craft Supply (225 West Chicago Avenue; ☎ 312-915-0200; **www.pearlpaint.com**) is a mostly discount store with a wide supply of artists' materials, from beads to brushes.

Don't miss **Robert Henry Adams Fine Art** (715 North Franklin Street; ☎ 312-642-8700; **www.adamsfineart.com**), featuring American modern art circa 1910–1970. The **Zolla/Lieberman Gallery** (325 West Huron Street; ☎ 312-944-1990; **www.zollaliebermangallery.com**) shows contemporary painting, sculpture, and works on paper. The popular **Aldo Castillo Gallery** (675 North Franklin Street; ☎ 312-337-2536; **www.artaldo.com**) specializes in Latin American art.

When you hit Superior Street, a good place to begin is **Ann Nathan Gallery** (212 West Superior Street; ☎ 312-664-6622; **www.annnathangallery.com**), a long-established yet edgy and right-now spot for paintings, sculpture, even unique furniture pieces. Move on, for fine contemporary art, to **Jean Albano** (215 West Superior Street; ☎ 312-440-0770; **www.jeanalbano-artgallery.com**). At the same address, and also specializing in fine art, is **Maya Polsky Gallery** (☎ 312-440-0055; **www.mayapolskygallery.com**). If you're looking for contemporary glass sculpture, note the **Marx-Saunders Gallery** (230 West Superior Street; ☎ 312-573-1400; **www.marxsaunders.com**). Also at 230 West Superior is **Schneider Gallery** (☎ 312-988-4033; **www.schneidergallery chicago.com**), a great source for contemporary photography by international artists. More fine glass can be found at **Habatat** (222 West Superior Street; ☎ 312-440-0288; **www.habatatchicago.com**). In the 300 Building are **Catherine Edelman** (☎ 312-266-2350; **www.edelman gallery.com**) for contemporary photography and the **Judy A. Saslow Gallery** (☎ 312-943-0530; **www.jsaslowgallery.com**) for contemporary artists and a mix of outsider, self-taught, and ethnographic works.

Another notable is **Stephen Daiter Gallery** (311 West Superior Street; ☎ 312-787-3350; **www.stephendaitergallery.com**); photography is special here, especially vintage black-and-white photos. **Printworks** (☎ 312-664-9407; **www.printworkschicago.com**), with contemporary prints, drawings, photographs, and artists' books, is also at 311 West Superior. A final rave at 311 West Superior is **Gallery KH** (☎ 312-642-0202; **www.gallerykh.com**), run by three young women who really know their contemporary (and some classic) art in multimedia. **Perimeter Gallery** (210 West Superior Street; ☎ 312-266-9473; **www.perimetergallery.com**) also specializes in contemporary fine art (and ceramics, works on paper, sculpture, fiber, and metalwork) by internationally recognized artists.

unofficial **TIP**
For the latest on the Chicago art scene, visit **www.chicagogallery news.com**, or ask a gallery you're visiting if you can get a Chicago gallery guide.

One of the best galleries in this area is **Roy Boyd** (739 North Wells Street; ☎ 312-642-1606; **www.royboydgallery.com**), featuring contemporary painting, sculpture, and works on paper; there are many abstractions but also some surprising exceptions. Nearby is **Carl Hammer Gallery** (740 North Wells Street; ☎ 312-266-8512), with an emphasis on contemporary artists whom some compare to a "punk rock" roster. **Primitive** (130 North Jefferson Street; ☎ 312-575-9600; **www.beprimitive.com**) features four floors of tribal and ethnic displays of authentic furniture, textiles, rugs, clothing, jewelry, and artifacts. Back on Wells is **Expression Galleries of Fine Art** (708 North Wells Street; ☎ 312-274-9848; **www.expressionfineart.com**), where you'll find a mix of master graphics by such stars as Pablo Picasso, Joan Miró, and James Whistler, as well as more-contemporary lesser-known artists.

Leaving Wells, you might want to stop at the famed **Tree Studios** for a look around **Hildt Galleries** (617 North State Street; ☎ 312-255-0005; **www.hildtgalleries.com**), which features paintings by British, American, and European artists of the 19th and early-20th centuries.

WEST (AND WEST LOOP GATE) Most of these galleries are of interest not so much to those looking for decorative mixed-use works as to fine-art collectors seeking the works of newer, younger, or more avant-garde artists. **Packer Schopf Gallery,** a merger of the former Aron Packer and Schopf galleries (942 West Lake Street; ☎ 312-226-8984; **www.packergallery.com**), offers contemporary and outsider art in all media.

Rhona Hoffman Gallery (118 North Peoria Street; ☎ 312-455-1990; **www.rhoffmangallery.com**) gets top reviews for the contemporary artists she features, and another hot gallery is **monique meloche** (118 North Peoria Street; ☎ 312-455-0299; **www.moniquemeloche.com**). At 119 North Peoria Street is **Tony Wight Gallery** (☎ 312-492-7261; **www .tonywightgallery.com**), which specializes in fine contemporary art by emerging and established nationally recognized artists. A Chicago favorite is **Douglas Dawson Gallery** (400 North Morgan Street; ☎ 312-226-7975; **www.douglasdawson.com**), known for ancient and historic ethnic art from Asia, Africa, and the Americas (textiles, furniture, sculpture, stone, and ceramics). Other suggestions in this area include **Thomas McCormick Gallery** (835 West Washington Boulevard; ☎ 312-226-6800; **www.thomasmccormick.com**) for modern and contemporary American painting; and more contemporary art at **Carrie Secrist Gallery** (835 West Washington Boulevard; ☎ 312-491-0917; **www .secristgallery.com**). Also purveying contemporary art at 835 West Washington is **Kavi Gupta** (☎ 312-432-0708; **www.kavigupta.com**). Finally, don't miss **Flatfile Galleries** (217 North Carpenter Street; ☎ 312-491-1190; **www.flatfilegalleries.com**) for fine photography and contemporary art.

LINCOLN PARK, CLYBOURN CORRIDOR, AND FARTHER NORTH   Art Effect (934 West Armitage Avenue; ☎ 773-929-3600; **www.shoparteffect.com**) was one of the first stores to feature wearable art, and that's still a strong point. National artists' works are displayed here, with attention paid to clothes, jewelry, and items for the home. Several interesting store-galleries can be found in Wicker Park–Bucktown. One of the most enticing is **Pagoda Red** (1714 North Damen Avenue; ☎ 773-235-1188; **www.pagodared.com**), an urban oasis with an Asian garden full of 18th- to 19th-century Chinese furniture and artifacts, as well as works by emerging Chinese artists. **Pavilion Antiques** (2055 North Damen Avenue; ☎ 773-645-0924; **www.pavilionantiques.com**) has mostly 20th-century French, Italian, and some American vintage pieces and antiques, with an emphasis on decorative arts.

BEAUTY

MICHIGAN AVENUE   A new Water Tower Place location is news for followers of the **Robert Lucas Studio** (at the Elizabeth Adam Salon & Day Spa, 845 North Michigan Avenue, Suite 908E, with elevator access from the ground level only; ☎ 312-642-6640; **www.robertlucas.com**).

NEAR NORTH   On Oak Street, the immaculate and sparkling jewel-box salon of international perfume and cosmetics creator **Marilyn Miglin**

(112 East Oak Street; ☎ 312-943-1120; **www.marilynmiglin.com**) offers Pheromone ("the world's most precious perfume"). Her salon is known for its exquisite, high-quality goods and services, including facials, manicures, massages, and makeup application.

The popular **Channing's Day Spa** (54 East Oak Street; ☎ 312-280-1994; **www.channings.com**), in contrast to the beauty palaces of chrome and glass, is housed in a vintage-y nook, with cozy niches upstairs and down for body treatments from a fantasy tan to a hot-glove manicure.

Face & Facial (104 East Oak Street; ☎ 312-951-5151; **www.mila bravifacials.com**) features internationally known facialist Mila Bravi. There are manicurists here, too, who are among the best (but not the most expensive) in the city. Another trained aesthetician with a soothing touch is **Kathleen Peara Studio,** a bit to the north at 534 West Eugenie Street in Old Town (by appointment only; ☎ 312-337-6734), where indulging in an aromatherapy facial, reflexology, or a massage (or all of the above) will have you purring.

Hair salons in the Near North aren't likely to indulge you with bargain prices, but they do deliver the goods. **Charles Ifergan** (106 East Oak Street; ☎ 312-642-4484; **www.charlesifergan.com**) is a trendsetting hair designer who wins national awards for his styles for men and women. The **Anita Russum Salon** (34 East Oak Street, sixth floor; ☎ 312-944-8533) is an oasis of tranquility where hair colorist Anita Russum works her magic. **Che Sguardo** (161 West Illinois Street; ☎ 312-464-1616) sells notable and unusual cosmetics, and they'll do your makeup and give makeup lessons for a big night out.

Spas are proliferating in Chicago, but followers of the **Elizabeth Arden Red Door Salon** (919 North Michigan Avenue, entrance on the Walton Street side; ☎ 312-988-9191; **www.reddoorspas.com**) remain pleased with the beautiful, large environs. The popular **Kiva** (196 East Pearson Street; ☎ 312-840-8120; **www.kivakiva.com**) is known for its "am I in Santa Fe?" ambience, but in actuality you're next door to the Ritz-Carlton hotel, enjoying an oasis for body, mind, and spirit, with every type of treatment—from aromatherapy and massages at the spa to pedicures and scalp analysis. The **Four Seasons Hotel** has an outstanding spa as well (120 East Delaware Place; ☎ 312-649-2340; **www.fourseasons.com/chicagofs**). Even if you're not a hotel guest, you can have a lovely Champagne-and-caviar facial. Speaking of hotel spas, a mighty one is **The Spa at Trump,** on the 14th floor of Trump International Hotel & Tower (401 North Wabash Avenue; ☎ 312-588-8020; **www.trumpchicagohotel.com**). Then there's **Dana Hotel & Spa** (660 North State Street; ☎ 312-202-6040; **www.danahoteland spa.com**), a green spa that backs up its concept with recycled-glass flooring and a "nourishing organics body scrub."

Another fine salon and spa is **Spa Emilia** (21 West Elm Street; ☎ 312-951-7415; **www.spaemilia.com**), a serene environment where

Grace, Elizabeth, and their staff offer manicures and pedicures that people rave about. And at 1401 West Hubbard Street, **Urban Spa Chic** (☎ 312-492-8050; **www.urbanspachic.com**) pays attention to the seasons; they do a fine pumpkin facial in the fall. One of the city's top makeup artists is definitely Diane Ayala at private makeup studio **Ayala Maquillage** (65 East Oak Street, third floor; ☎ 312-337-4233; **www.ayalamaquillage.com**). Finally, a welcome addition is **Beauty Overstock** (1230 West Washington Street; ☎ 312-943-2626), where you can pick up Marilyn Miglin products, fragrances, makeup, and skin-care products at great prices, all at less than retail.

Going north on Halsted Street, you'll find **Origins** (2130 North Halsted Street; ☎ 773-871-0702; **www.origins.com**), a crisp, luxe beauty boutique, charms with natural bath supplies and other products. For men and women, **GuiseChic** (2128 North Halsted Street; ☎ 773-929-6101; **www.guisechic.com**) combines a barbershop and salon with a clothing boutique.

On Armitage are three must-stops. **Kiehl's** (907 West Armitage Avenue; ☎ 773-665-2515; **www.kiehls.com**) is the famed purveyor of skin- and hair-care products' first freestanding store in Chicago. Then there's **L'Occitane** (846 West Armitage Avenue; ☎ 773-477-3900; **www .loccitane.com**). Whether you stop in here or at the 900 North Michigan location, the unique products fresh from Provence are winners (their hand cream is superb for Chicago winters). Don't miss **Lush Cosmetics** (859 West Armitage Avenue; ☎ 773-281-5874; **www .lushusa.com**). Here, all the products, from soaps to seaweed masks, not to mention foot lotions and dusting powders, are handmade and fresh, with minimal packaging to help the environment (no animal testing, either). **TRIM** (2503 North Lincoln Avenue, ☎ 773-525-8746; and 1629 North Milwaukee Avenue, ☎ 773-276-8746; **www.trimwax .com**) does custom waxing for men and women. They have a Boyfriend Package for $100, which includes a Brazilian for her and a back wax for him. Also on North Milwaukee Avenue, at 1468, is **Mojo Spa** (☎ 773-235-6656; **www.mojospa.com**), where one of the owners is a former chef and creates such amenities as a Chocolate Truffle body butter and Sugar Me Sweet cream and scrub. You can come for beauty and brunch on Sunday.

BOOKS

IN THE LOOP Adam Brent is the son of legendary bookseller Stuart Brent, whose store stood on Michigan Avenue for 50 years. **Brent Books & Cards, Ltd.,** in the Loop (309 West Washington Street; ☎ 312-364-0126), is where Adam has won success with his dedication to personal service. His well-read staff reveres books, and the store offers a huge selection of titles (including a wide selection of children's

unofficial **TIP**
Note: Because of the economy, stores in Chicago come and go, so call before you head out to shop.

books). Adam is out to "match and exceed discounts at the mega bookstores," with some of his own terrific discounts.

A bookshop that has scored high with literary Chicago is **Barbara's Bookstore** (with locations at Sears Tower, at Northwestern Hospital, at Macy's on State Street, at the corner of Roosevelt Road and Halsted Street, and in Oak Park; see **www.barbarasbookstore.com** for more info). In business since 1963, Barbara's often schedules author readings and pays attention to local writers.

OLD TOWN, LINCOLN PARK, CLARK, AND CLYBOURN CORRIDOR In Andersonville, is a terrific bookstore called **Women & Children First** (5233 North Clark Street; ☎ 773-769-9299; **www.womenandchildren first.com**), owned by knowledgeable women who care a lot about the books their customers like and buy accordingly. At the other end of town, out south, **Hyde Park 57th Street Books** (1301 East 57th Street; ☎ 773-684-1300) is also exemplary.

USED BOOKS At 2850 North Lincoln Avenue is **Powell's** (☎ 773-248-1444; **www.powellschicago.com**), which can also be found at 828 South Wabash (☎ 312-341-0748) and 1501 East 57th Street (the main store) in the Hyde Park neighborhood (☎ 773-955-7780). The South Wabash store is the only Powell's in the Loop, but we like the Lincoln Park location because it has the largest number of art books—and it's usually so quiet, the ghost of Hemingway could be lurking. In Hyde Park, a huge favorite (particularly for antiquarian books) is **O'Gara & Wilson** (1448 East 57th Street; ☎ 773-363-0993).

This is probably the place to mention a real find: **Yesterday** (1143 West Addison Street; ☎ 773-248-8087). It's a source for rare vintage and antique magazines, newspapers, and posters. And for more on comic books, two suggestions: **Dark Tower Comics** (4835 North Western Avenue; ☎ 773-733-4026; **www.darktowercomics.net**) has everything, including great service from owner Mark Beatty. An even older store, **Variety Comics** (4602 North Western Avenue; ☎ 773-334-2550), run by the very knowledgeable Rick Vitone, has towers of comics piled high to sell in the shop or to ship.

A final nod to rare books: two fine options are **Printers Row Fine & Rare Books** (715 South Dearborn Street; ☎ 312-583-1800; **www .printersrowbooks.com**), and, in the suburb of Highland Park, **Titles, Inc,** (1821 Saint Johns Avenue; ☎ 847-432-3690).

CLOTHING AND SHOES

A MULTITUDE OF DESIGNERS are lending excitement to Chicago. Elizabeth Mendenhall has opened her new custom-design boutique, **Elizabeth M,** at 100 East Walton Street (in the commercial section of the building; ☎ 312-255-1088; **www.elizabethmfashion.com**). Fabrics are available for selection.

A new young designer is **Anna Fong,** whose belts are already at Macy's. Her studio is at 1932 South Halsted in the Chicago Arts

District (☎ 312-952-0140; **www.anna-fong.com**). **Basia Frossard** designs fashions for both the body and home; she's working with exotic fabrics in her studio at 1101 West Fulton Market (☎ 312-226-5321; **www.basiafrossard.com**). If you don't see their pieces while browsing the stores, you may want to contact directly four designers featured in *Chicago Life* magazine: **Steven Rosengard Design** (☎ 773-327-9609; **www.stevenrosengard.com**) does elegant day and evening wear; **Elise Bergman** (☎ 312-952-7047; **www.elisebergman.com**) likes to work in vintage fabrics and sustainable materials; **Price Walton** (☎ 312-731-0156) does glam and hip designs using historical inspiration (such as Bob Mackie) as a guide; and **Joelle Nadine Designs** (☎ 312-951-9774; **www.joellenadine.com**) has stunning handmade handbags.

But number one of them all is (drumroll, please) **Maria Pinto,** with her beautiful new boutique at 135 North Jefferson Street at Randolph (☎ 312-648-1335; **www.mariapinto.com**). Its bamboo flooring and charcoal walls serve as a backdrop for Pinto's stunning fashions. A longtime local designer known for excellence, Pinto provides clothes for celebs and many of the city's best-dressed—among them, most obviously, Michelle Obama. The purple sleeveless dress she wore when her husband won the Democratic presidential nomination? The teal sheath she wore at the Democratic National Convention? The body-hugging red number she wore on her first visit to the White House post-election? All were Pinto's handiwork.

IN THE LOOP If you travel west on Lake Street, note a chic boutique called **Koros** (1039 West Lake Street; ☎ 312-738-0155; **www.korosartandstyle.com**), with some name brands and accessories along with labels you won't find anywhere else, plus art for sale on its brick walls. Also west is **Smitten Boutique** (1041 West Madison Street, ☎ 312-226-7777; **www.smittenboutique.net**), specializing in bridal accessories and consultation. **Strut** (1744 West Division Street; ☎ 773-227-2728) varies from chic Miss Sixty wares to button-down shirts for men. And at 1015 West Lake Street, **Bess & Loie** (☎ 312-226-2247; **www.bessandloie.com**) is the place for accessories; bags and jewelry are standouts here.

LaSalle Street houses several men's stores and emporiums dedicated to business accessories. The suits you buy at **Syd Jerome Men's Wear** (2 North LaSalle Street; ☎ 312-346-0333; **www.sydjerome.com**) will make you someone's best-dressed man, while menswear powerhouse **Brooks Brothers** (209 South LaSalle Street; ☎ 312-263-0100; **www.brooksbrothers.com**) is a traditional favorite. Many prefer the BB at 713 North Michigan Avenue (☎ 312-915-0060).

Another outfitter to try in this area is **Duru's,** known for its custom-tailored shirts and suits (221 North LaSalle Street; ☎ 312-782-4443; **www.duruscustomtailors.com**). Albert Karoll moved his **Richard Bennett Custom Tailors** to 175 West Jackson Boulevard (☎ 312-913-1100; **www.rbtailors.com**). Another custom clothier for men is **Nicholas Joseph,** with a Gold Coast location inside Halo for Men (21 West Elm Street; ☎ 312-895-1577; **www.nicholas-joseph.com;** by appointment).

One interesting new store west of the Loop is **Pivot** (1101 West Fulton Market; ☎ 312-243-4754; **www.pivotboutique.com**), which specializes in "eco-fashion"—created by designers who use organic and sustainable materials.

ON MICHIGAN AVENUE For men, let's begin with an old-time custom tailor recognized for expertise with hand-tailored suits: at **Lawrence Pucci** (333 North Michigan Avenue, second floor; ☎ 312-332-3759) they call themselves "architects of fashion for Chicago's living legends." Another word about **Nordstrom** (520 North Michigan Avenue): do note that the store has added the first Louis Vuitton–leased space within one of their department stores (large and on the first floor). And while you're cruising the Magnificent Mile, peruse the premises at **NikeTown** (669 North Michigan Avenue; ☎ 312-642-6363; **www.nike .com**); otherwise, people may not believe you've been to Chicago. This is a hotbed for sports enthusiasts—a veritable retail-sports arena of Nike footwear, apparel, accessories, and equipment. The third floor contains a wide-ranging selection of gear for active women.

Speaking of footwear, **Hanig's** shoes for men and women get around: in addition to the emporium at 875 North Michigan Avenue (main floor; ☎ 312-642-5330), there's a **Hanig's Footwear on Armitage** specializing in Birkenstocks and other comfort shoes (847 West Armitage Avenue; ☎ 773-929-5568; **www.hanigs.com.**), among other stores.

Fashion reigns at the beauteous **Burberry** (633 North Michigan Avenue; ☎ 312-787-2500; **www.burberry.com**), even as men and women seek the instantly recognizable camel-and-cream (with a touch of black) plaid that enhances so many raincoats, scarves, and other items. At 645 North Michigan is the local outpost of the great Italian menswear designer **Ermenegildo Zegna** (☎ 312-587-9660; **www.zegna.com**).

One of the chic names for men to hit the avenue is **Saks Fifth Avenue Men's Store** (717 North Michigan Avenue; ☎ 312-944-6500; **www.saksfifthavenue.com**), and another national classic is **Ralph Lauren** (750 North Michigan Avenue; ☎ 312-280-1655; **www.ralph lauren.com**). This 37,000-square-foot Chicago flagship is said to be the largest Ralph Lauren store in the United States. You'll find the designer's men's, women's, and children's clothing and accessories, plus home furnishings; there's even the chic **RL,** the first Ralph Lauren restaurant (115 East Chicago Avenue; ☎ 312-475-1100). Plus, there's a **Ralph Lauren Rugby** concept store at 1000 West Armitage Avenue (☎ 773-525-4627).

Banana Republic (744 North Michigan Avenue; ☎ 312-642-0020; and other locations; **www.bananarepublic.com**) started as a repository for clothes you wished you could afford to buy for camping expeditions; it's graduated to providing really nice sportswear and accessories, but you already knew that. What you may not know is that **Giorgio Armani** is holding court—and charging *molto* for its divine duds—at 800 North Michigan Avenue (☎ 312-573-4220). Also at 800 North Michigan, find the posh Park Hyatt Chicago Hotel; the address also houses **Marlowe** (☎ 312-988-9398; **www.marlowe.com**), a luxe store focusing on ultrachic Italian-made cashmere knitwear, handbags, and leathers. This is Marlowe's first flagship store in the United States.

Another titan, **Rochester Clothing** (840 North Michigan Avenue; ☎ 312-337-8877), offers top fashions for larger men (notable clients include many pro-basketball players). The emphasis is on fine Italian designers, from Zanella dress trousers to cashmere coats from Zegna, as well as Calvin Klein, Levi's, and a complete Polo casual line.

It took until the 1980s for the **Bloomingdale's** to reach Chicago, at 900 North Michigan Avenue (☎ 312-440-4460). Of all the national Bloomie's stores, this one is among the most beautiful. A source for menswear and women's wear is **Mark Shale** (☎ 312-440-0720), which has suburban stores as well. Stop at **Max Studio** (level four; ☎ 312-944-4445) for hot styles that won't decimate your wallet. Don't forget to check out the bras at **Intimacy** (third level; ☎ 312-337-8366); owner Susan Nethero has appeared on *Oprah* to talk about the importance of fitting bras properly.

Does anyone need a reminder that the north end of Michigan Avenue is Shoe Paradise? **Salvatore Ferragamo** has a sparkling store here (645 North Michigan Avenue; ☎ 312-397-0464; **www.ferragamo.com**)—the company's first in the Midwest. And don't forget to peruse the **Chanel** boutique (935 North Michigan Avenue; ☎ 312-787-5500; **www.chanel.com**), a lush store filled with internationally renowned clothes, jewelry, and accessories.

ON OAK STREET World-class shopping begins on Oak Street, Chicago's blockbuster block of fabulous fashion. The Oak Street Council carefully keeps the 38 Art Deco street lights new, the 33 trees replaced if winter has been particularly rough, and even its sidewalks colored a distinctive charcoal gray.

At the corner of Rush at 25 East Oak Street, you'll find **Barneys New York** (☎ 312-587-1700; **www.barneys.com**); keep an eye out, though, because the store is moving across the street to larger quarters. But one of Oak's secrets is that you can actually save money at the street's only drugstore: **Bravco Beauty Centre** (43 East Oak Street; ☎ 312-943-4305; **www.bravcobeauty.com**), where you can find anything from false eyelashes to toothpaste. The **Denim Lounge of Madison and Friends** (43 East Oak Street;

unofficial **TIP**
Because parking on Oak is such a nuisance, choose from two solutions: valet parking (an attendant is stationed midblock between 57 and 67 East Oak) or the 1 East Oak garage (at the corner of Oak and State streets).

☎ 312-642-6403; **www.madisonandfriends.com**) entices you to wade through the kiddie boutique before you take the stairs to find plentiful denim brands.

Oak's uniquely homegrown high-fashion treasure is **Ultimo** (116 East Oak Street; ☎ 312-787-1171; **www.ultimo.com**), known internationally for, as its name implies, the ultimate in high-end clothing for women as well as tomorrow-flavored accessories. Owner Sara Albrecht brings creations from some of the world's top designers here. You'll also find **Jil Sander** (48 East Oak Street; ☎ 312-335-0006; **www.jil sander.com**). A very special Oak Street treasure is the 35-year-old **Glasses Ltd.** (47 East Oak Street; ☎ 312-944-6876; **www.glasses limited.com**), a mom-and-pop business offering superb frames by designers such as Tom Ford, Gucci, Bulgari, and others. This is a full-service business: eyes are examined on-site, the frames have tomorrow's look (most don't come cheap), and the customer service is exemplary.

International flavor is ever-present on Oak. The French name of renown is **Yves St. Laurent Rive Gauche** (51 East Oak Street; ☎ 312-751-8995; **www.ysl.com**), with ready-to-wear for men and women, small leather goods, handbags, and the YSL *beauté* line. Begin your Italian fling at **Prada** (30 East Oak Street; ☎ 312-951-1113; **www .prada.com**). **Luca Luca** (59 East Oak Street; ☎ 312-664-1512; **www .lucaluca.com**) presents more Italian women's wear (the colors are lush); **Hermès of Paris** (110 East Oak Street; ☎ 312-787-8175; **www .hermes.com**) deals in exclusive scarves, ties, leather items, and other goodies *à la française;* and **The Wolford Boutique** (54 East Oak Street; ☎ 312-642-8787; **www.wolford.com**), part of an international chain originating in Austria, offers fun and fashionable imported hosiery, bodywear, and swimwear. Wolford's goods are worth the price because they fit, they last, and they're so luxe. Another favorite is **Kate Spade** (56 East Oak Street; ☎ 312-654-8853; **www.katespade.com**), packed with bags and shoes. In the former Kate Spade space is **Juicy Couture** (101 East Oak Street; ☎ 312-280-1637; **www.juicycouture .com**); you know the JC philosophy: lots of color, casual luxury, and hot but laid-back looks.

One of the most right-now bridal salons (specializing in couture gowns) is **Ultimate Bride** (106 East Oak Street; ☎ 312-337-6300; **www .ultimatebride.com**). Another gift to Oak Street is **Designs by Ming** (70 East Oak Street; ☎ 312-649-1510; **www.designsbyming.com**), a custom-clothing, alterations, and bridal store.

Of course, there's **Jimmy Choo** (63 East Oak Street; ☎ 312-255-1170; **www.jimmychoo.com**) for gorgeous shoes. Upstairs at **Scarlet Designs Studio** (65 East Oak Street, second floor; ☎ 312-421-9010; **www.scarlet designs.com** and **www.specialoccasionseparates.com**) is the creative studio's namesake Scarlet Designs as well as Special Occasion Separates.

The last word goes to **George Greene** (49 East Oak Street; ☎ 312-654-2490) for menswear that is truly exceptional.

NEAR NORTH High fashion knows fewer astute practitioners than Marilyn Blaszka and Dominic Marcheschi, whose **Blake** (212 West Chicago Avenue; ☎ 312-202-0047) lives in stunning quarters. The owners pay attention to knockout and tasteful European lines, such as Dries van Noten, Pierre Hardy, Balenciaga, Marni, Rick Owens, Martin Margiela, and others. Another of the important high-fashion emporiums is **Ikram** (873 North Rush Street; ☎ 312-587-1000; **www .ikram.com**), very special because of owner Ikram Goldman's exquisite taste in everything from shoes to vintage jewelry. A fashion spy reports that Ikram was the first in Chicago to carry Jimmy Choo shoes (and word has it she's a fashion adviser to Michelle Obama).

If you're jonesing for jeans, don't miss **AG Chicago** (48 East Walton Street; ☎ 312-787-7680; **www.agjeans.com**), which stocks more than 25 styles of denim under the AG label, plus belts. Styles range from flared to super-skinny, and they'll hem them for you free. Fans of that cute little penguin logo should head for **Original Penguin** (901 North Rush Street; ☎ 312-475-0792; **www.originalpenguin.com**), where men, women, boys, and girls (and golfers) will find polos, suits, tailored dresses, and more. And, while we're discussing Rush Street, we hear that a Marc Jacobs Collection boutique will open at the Elysian Hotel at Rush and Walton streets. It will carry even more top-tier Jacobs items than can be found at the Marc by MJ store in Bucktown.

Henry Beguelin (716 North Wabash Avenue; ☎ 312-335-1222; **www.henrybeguelin.it**) specializes in handmade leathers from Milan; these include handbags, shoes, furniture, and other home accessories. A lot of stunning women think **Mary Walter** (33 West Superior Street; ☎ 312-266-1094; **www.marywalter.net**) is their own best-kept secret, but of course they're not alone. In this attractive store, removed from hectic Avenue shoppers, you can browse among beautifully chosen suits, jackets, and other delectables such as hand-painted scarves and jewelry (note the one-of-a-kind pieces). There's also a full-time tailor here. A bit to the north is **Mary Mary** (706 North Dearborn Street; ☎ 312-654-8100; **www.marymarygifts.com**), a fabulous gift boutique where you'll find everything from shawls to chandeliers. Finally, before heading north, try a trip to North Avenue, also known as Akira Avenue because of the three **Akira** stores there: visit 1814 West North Avenue (☎ 773-489-0818) for women's clothing; find Akira shoes at 1849 West North (☎ 773-342-8684); and shop for Akira men's clothing at 1910 West North (☎ 312-423-6693; **www.akira chicago.com**).

WELLS STREET The address of 1350 North Wells is the spiffy home of **Haberdash** (☎ 312-440-1300; **www.haberdashmen.com**), a men's store that achieves a modern spin on a classic haberdashery. Shoppers find everything here from Theory to James Perse. At 1419 North Wells is the home of **Nicole Miller** (☎ 312-664-3532; **www.nicolemiller.com**). The New York designer is known for her often whimsical prints and her bridal collection. Bright-colored dresses shine at **Uri Boutique** (1445 North Wells Street; ☎ 312-475-9002; www.uriboutique.com), which also stocks great bags, blouses, and other accessories. At 1706 North Wells is **Handle with Care** (☎ 312-751-2929), famous for up-to-the-second women's fashions. **Fabrice** (1714 North Wells Street; ☎ 312-280-0011; www.fabricechicago.com) is a must-visit for faux and fab jewelry—the kind featured at the boutique's Paris branch, resin-based and painted.

LINCOLN PARK–CLYBOURN CORRIDOR One of Webster Avenue's outstanding shops is **Underthings** (804 West Webster Avenue; ☎ 773-472-9291), dedicated to lingerie, carrying everything from robes to bras. But let's back up a bit and go west to Kate Prange's **Shopgirl** (1206 West Webster Avenue; ☎ 773-935-7467), a sexy, sophisticated boutique with clothes by Trina Turk, Susana Monaco, and Michael Stars, and jewelry by mostly local designers such as Ulia Carrella.

The highly regarded Italian brand **Furla** has opened a store at 1211 West Webster (☎ 773-525-7420; www.furla.com) packed with gorgeous handbags (amazing leathers) and some accessories. Another smash hit is **Cotélac** (1159 West Webster Avenue; ☎ 773-281-2330; www.cotelac.fr), with an accent on superb, carefully edited clothing and shoes. Everything is washable and created by a French designer; this was the first Cotélac in the United States. Nearby is **The Left Bank** (1155 West Webster Avenue; ☎ 773-929-7422; www.leftbankjewelry.com), filled with yummy jewelry, great gifts, and candles, but the main stage is reserved for custom-made bridal wear.

Moving to West Armitage Avenue, you'll find clothes by inventive Chicago designer **Cynthia Rowley** at 810 (☎ 773-528-6160) and also at 1653 North Damen Avenue (☎ 773-276-9209; www.cynthiarowley.com). Handmade wearables by national artisans are for sale at **Isis on Armitage** (823 West Armitage Avenue; ☎ 773-665-7290); more of their glossy wearables can be found at **Isis on Melrose** (900 North Michigan Avenue; ☎ 312-664-7140). A fine place for lingerie is **Isabella** (840 West Armitage Avenue; ☎ 773-281-2352; www.shopisabella.com). Looking for unique goods by leading artists and craftspeople? **Art Effect** (934 West Armitage Avenue; ☎ 773-929-3600; www.shoparteffect.com) is chock-full of wearable art and jewelry. Celebrating its 25th anniversary in 2009, the Lincoln Park pioneer, owned by Esther Fishman, has jewelry from Jeanine Payer and Me&Ro; Orla Kiely bags; Michael Stars, Three Dots, and Billy Blues clothing; and Nigella Lawson, Michael Aram, and Cucina home products.

At **Mint Julep** (1013 West Armitage Avenue; ☎ 773-296-2997), Sarah Bruno has brought her great fashion sense to women's clothing with contemporary lines and affordable prices.

904 West Armitage is the latest location for **1154 Lill Studio** (☎ 773-477-5455; www.1154lill.com), where you can create your own handbag from their roster of fabrics and ideas. Very USA is **American**

Apparel (837 West Armitage Avenue; ☎ 773-880-9801; **www.american apparel.net**), where besides hoodies and tees you'll find an interesting tie-on dress; look also for their organic line. Before leaving Armitage, take a peek at the **Paul Frank Store** (851 West Armitage Avenue; ☎ 773-388-3122; **www.paulfrank.com**), purveyor of fun and funky women's and men's clothing, bikes, and home furnishings. Make a final stop at **She Boutique** (1024 West Armitage; ☎ 773-880-8061; **www.shopsheboutique.com**), blooming with everything from Zac Posen handbags to Ruthie Davis high heels.

WICKER PARK–BUCKTOWN This entire area is a booming source for boutiques, especially on Damen Avenue. Milwaukee Avenue has many boutiques, but one to love is **Eskell** At 1616 North Damen is **Shebang** (☎ 773-486-3800; **www.shopshebang.com**), for handbags and other accessories (including some great jewelry), many by emerging designers you won't see elsewhere. Interested in stylish athletic clothing? Don't miss the **lululemon athletica store** (1627 North Damen Avenue; ☎ 773-227-1869; **www.lululemon.com**) for workout clothes. If you're an expectant mother, you may want to stop at **Belly Dance Maternity** (1647 North Damen Avenue; ☎ 773-862-1133; **www.bellydancematernity.com**), which is filled to the brim with maternity fashions and skincare products. Don't miss **Riley** for more fashion delectables (1659 North Damen Avenue; ☎ 773-489-0101). **p.45** (1643 North Damen Avenue; ☎ 773-862-4523; **www.p45.com**) is another terrific (if a bit pricier than most boutiques around here) source for clothes, shoes, jewelry, and other accessories (including those by local talents). A step north, **Helen Yi** (1645 North Damen Avenue; ☎ 773-252-3838) offers some local designers and some national names, such as Derek Lam, Tracy Reese, and more; the goods include clothing, hats, shoes, and thoughtfully selected accessories.

Stop for a quick sandwich or salad at **The Goddess and Grocer** (1646 North Damen Avenue; ☎ 773-342-3200), and peek into **Cynthia Rowley,** at 1653 (see opposite page for contact info). Then amble into 1714 North Damen (just below Pagoda Red's Asian antiques) and you'll find **Marc by Marc Jacobs,** the designer's first freestanding Chicago boutique (☎ 773-276-2998). You'll also love the contemporary clothing and accessories at **Clothes Minded** (1735 North Damen Avenue; ☎ 773-227-3402; **www.clothesmindedchicago.com**). You absolutely must select a T-shirt or two from **The T-Shirt Deli,** where tees come packaged like sandwiches (1739 North Damen Avenue; ☎ 773-276-6266; **www.tshirtdeli.com**). Zip into **D Marie Handbags** (1867 North Damen Avenue; ☎ 773-489-3220; **www.dmariehandbags.com**) for high-quality bags, jewelry, and scarves, and stop at **Michelle Tan** (1872 North Damen Avenue; ☎ 773-252-1888; **www.michelletan.com**), featuring the Chicago designer's own fashions and her tasteful imported jewelry. This is Tan's first retail store, and she has some good-looking accessories.

Next, stop for shoes at **Grace** (1917 North Damen Avenue; ☎ 773-384-7223), and pop into **Hunny SheShe** (2027 North Damen Avenue; ☎ 773-292-1120) for both yummy jewelry and clothes. Then take a look at the superb fashions for the more voluptuous among us, and note the larger (but still stylish) sizes that have finally found a fashion home at **Vive La Femme** (2048 North Damen Avenue; ☎ 773-772-7429; **www.vivelafemme.com**). At **Saffron** (2064 North Damen Avenue; ☎ 773-486-7753; **www.saffronchicago.com**), owner Padmaja Manerikar Maryanski's displays her own elegant designs and ready-to-wear, plus the creations of others who love color and fine fabrics.

The next stop is **Robin Richman** (2108 North Damen Avenue; ☎ 773-278-6150; **www.robinrichman.com**), a visual treat rich with hot clothing, shoes, and accessories by small global designers such as Parisians Marc Le Bihan and Elsa Esturgie, New Yorker Gary Graham, Antipast from Tokyo, Maria Calderara from Italy, and more. Here too are unusual jewelry, the occasional vintage bag, and such treasures as Richman's own hand-knit sweaters.

Then peek into a little shop called **Soutache** (2125 North Damen Avenue; ☎ 773-292-9110; **www.soutacheribbons.com**), the place to find ribbons, braiding, every sort of embellishment. And, finally, an unusual find called **G Boutique** (2131 North Damen Avenue; ☎ 773-235-1234; **www.boutiqueg.com**) houses lingerie from lines such as Cosabella, Hanky Panky, and others, not to mention even-more-intimate wares (massage oils, sex toys).

Stores keep popping up on West Division, so if you explore the area, you'll probably find more shops that were still on the drawing board when we went to press. One of the most interesting is **Le Dress,** an experiment in selling dresses only, dreamed up by two clever sisters-in-law, Eva Anderson and Robyn Anderson, (1741 West Division Street; ☎ 773-697-9899; **www.ledresschicago.com**). If you can't find a frock here, there's no hope.

West Division is also home to an appealing boutique for shoes: **Pump** (1659 West Division Street; ☎ 773-384-6750; **www.pumpshoes chicago.com**) is owned by a true shoe-lover; you can tell because Maureen Bueltmann has found styles you don't see coming and going. Back on Milwaukee Avenue, male and female avant-garde–ists had better pick up their denims at the hot **G-Star** (1525 North Milwaukee Avenue; ☎ 773-342-2623), or skip to **The Levi's Store** at 1552 (☎ 773-486-3900). Another interesting boutique is **Hejfina** women's and men's fashions at 1529 North Milwaukee (☎ 773-772-0002; **www.hejfina .com**). **Saint Alfred** (1531 North Milwaukee Avenue; ☎ 773-486-7159; **www.stalfred.com**) specializes in apparel and affordable (and not-so) sneakers, including some limited-edition beauties. To the north is **Silver Moon** (1755 West North Avenue; ☎ 773-235-5797; **www.silver moonvintage.com**), which excels in vintage clothing, offers bridal-gown reconstruction, and designs gowns based on vintage styling.

ON HALSTED, CLARK, LINCOLN, SOUTHPORT Young women love to shop on North Halsted, thanks to standbys like **Nine West** for shoes and bags (2058 North Halsted Street; ☎ 773-871-4154; **www.nine west.com**). Note, too, **Lucky Brand** (2048 North Halsted Street; ☎ 773-975-8168; **www.luckybrand.com**), with clothing as well as jeans; and a don't-miss: **Calvin Tran** (2154 North Halsted Street; ☎ 773-529-4070; **www.calvintran.com**), maker of stunning clothes (dresses, gowns, and tops) that can change shape depending on how they're draped and fastened. Still looking for great jeans? The answer may be **DNA2050** (2122 North Halsted Street; ☎ 773-525-8004), where they promise to dig up your "jeanetic profile."

Farther north on Halsted is a collection of hot shops, some just doors from each other, so we'll take 'em as we see 'em. **Barneys New York CO-OP** (2209–11 North Halsted Street; ☎ 773-248-0426) offers fashion that's a bit more affordable than (but just as stylish as) the Barneys on Oak. Across the street is the **Blues Jean Bar** (2210 North Halsted Street; ☎ 773-248-5326; **www.bluesjeanbar.com**). And at **Club Monaco** (2206 North Halsted Street; ☎ 773-528-2031), find high style at good prices in women's wear.

Clark Street fashion stores include trendsetting sportswear and accessories (handbags and jewelry, especially) at **Panache** (2252 North Clark Street; ☎ 773-477-4537; **www.panachechicago.com**). There's also a large **Urban Outfitters** (2352 North Clark Street; ☎ 773-549-1711; **www.urbanoutfitters.com**), where some things are real finds and others real *junque,* both in clothes and home design.

We're going a few blocks west now to Southport Avenue, where you'll find the superb **Krista K** (3458 North Southport Avenue; ☎ 773-248-1967; **www.kristak.com**). Owner Krista Meyers carries only the most chic women's wear, accessories such as jewelry by local designer Sway, and handbag lines by Kooba and Luba J. A second location at 3530 North Southport (☎ 773-248-4477) carries maternity fashions, such as those by Olian and Ripe.

Southport is increasingly attracting young (and not so) shoppers for everything from plates to pleated skirts. **Perchance Boutique** (3512 North Southport Avenue; ☎ 773-244-1300; **www.perchanceboutique .com**) features stunning, oh-so-cool clothes, shoes, and accessories with a mod look that feels somewhat *Mad Men.* Another attractive boutique is **She One** (3402 North Southport Avenue; ☎ 773-549-9698), which offers clothing (including unique sweaters) and accessories at reasonable prices; we noticed pieces by several local designers. Little girls will love the tutus, costumes, and dolls at **The Princess Club** (3300 North Southport Avenue; ☎ 773-472-4733). Also for kids: **Chicago Kids Bookstore and More** at 3453 North Southport (☎ 773-472-6657; **www.chicagokidsbooks.com**). And at 3530, you'll find **Bourdage Pearls** (☎ 773-244-1126; **www.bourdagepearls.com**). A don't-miss is **Nuada** for creative, contemporary, and Celtic goods by

Irish artists (3727 North Southport Avenue; ☎ 773-525-4200; **www .nuada.com**), and you owe it to your stylish self to stop at **Trousseau** (3543 North Southport Avenue; ☎ 773-472-2727). Of course, they have a bridal section, but there's much more: bras by the dozens, swimsuits (ditto), candles, soaps, and more, all unusually tasteful in this fun-to-shop environment. Two final stops are **Cerulean One,** for men's and women's wear (3657 North Southport Avenue; ☎ 773-525-6869), and **Tula Boutique** (3738 North Southport Avenue, ☎ 773-549-2876), where among other accessories we noted great jewelry from Becky Kelso, Chan Luu, and Dana Kellin.

Back on Clark Street, head to **Hubba-Hubba** (3309 North Clark Street; ☎ 773-477-1414; **www.hubbahubbachicago.com**) for the best in vintage-inspired fashion (that means new and trendy clothes with a retro twist). The stores at **The Alley** are popular, too (one central number, ☎ 773-883-1800; **www.thealley.com**). The original store, **The Alley** (3228 North Clark Street), is trendy; one teen shopper told us, "They have really neat jewelry those hard-to-find Chicago-cop leather jackets, and T-shirts with the name of your favorite band." Other stores here include **Blue Havana** (856 West Belmont Avenue), a cigar and tobacco-accessory shop; **Taboo Tabou** (854 West Belmont Avenue), a source for adult novelties and lingerie; **Jive Monkey** (3224 North Clark Street), which offers some vintage wear but mostly custom T-shirts and accessories; and **Architectural Revolution** (3226 North Clark Street), dealing in home decor.

A trove of great vintage and thrift buys is at 812 West Belmont Avenue: **Hollywood Mirror** (☎ 773-404-2044; **www.hollywoodmirror .com**). In the same building, is **Ragstock** (☎ 773-868-9263; **www .ragstock.com**), purveying vintage buys; Ragstock is also at 1433 North Milwaukee Avenue (☎ 773-486-1783).

BEYOND WICKER PARK In Andersonville is **Turley Road** (5239 North Clark Street; ☎ 773-878-0097; **www.turleyroad.com**), owned by a designer sensitive to the clothing needs of fashionistas of all ages. The store offers its own line and clothing and accessories by other designers. **Trillium at the Landmark** (5245 North Clark Street; ☎ 773-728-5301) has great wearable art (and, in colder months, some toasty Icelandic sweaters), as well ageless styles. And while you're north, note that **Chicago Dance Supply** (5301 North Clark Street; ☎ 773-728-5344; **www.chicago dancesupply.com**) has ballroom-dancing shoes, jazz pants, children's ballet togs and shoes, clothing and shoes for belly dancing, and dance videos. At the opposite end of town, **Motion Unlimited** (218 South Wabash Avenue, second floor; ☎ 312-922-3330; **www.motionunlimited dancewear.com**) is a super supply store for dancers and wannabes. A great place to pick up new pointe shoes.

IN GLENCOE, WINNETKA, AND BEYOND When it comes to women's clothes, people from the city drive to **Shirise** in Glencoe (341 Park Avenue; ☎ 847-835-2595; **www.shirise.com**) for snazzy shoes, and while they're in that suburb they never miss **Nicchia** (688 Vernon; ☎ 847-835-2900; **www.shopnicchia.com**) for gorgeous sportswear (including great knits) for men and women. A favorite in Winnetka is **Neapolitan** (715 Elm Street; ☎ 847-441-7784; **www.neapolitanonline .com**), with an all-star roster of designer from Chloé to Carolina Herrera. Another favorite in the high-style category is Winnetka's **Frances Heffernan** (810 Elm Street; ☎ 847-446-2112; **www.frances heffernan.com**), sporting Bogner and Piazza Sempione; younger designers are the focus at Heffernan's adjacent **Frannie** (808 Elm Street; ☎ 847-446-5508; **www.frannieonline.com**).

Among Highland Park designers, **Sandra Joy, Inc.** (1760 Cloverdale Avenue; ☎ 847-831-2318; by appointment only) is hot for high-end, one-of-a-kind antique framed handbags and frames of sterling silver, bakelite, and the like, with fabrics such as beaded lace, silk, satin, and leathers; each is a collector's (read: expensive) item.

Finally, wardrobe consultant **Jane Miller,** who specializes in fashions for the over-40 set, works by appointment out of her women's clothing gallery in Evanston, where she specializes in independent designers; call ☎ 773-472-3027.

FOOD AND WINE

IN THE LOOP If you miss the Rue Cler in Paris, now is your moment. Just be in the Loop in the summer months, and shop at the **City of Chicago Farmer's Markets,** one of the biggest of which is held at Daley Plaza. The city sponsors these merry markets (overflowing with trucked-in *fleurs,* fruits, and vegetables) at more than 20 locations several times weekly. To check on the Loop market and other whens and wheres, call ☎ 312-744-3315 or visit **www.chicagofarmersmarkets.us.** Additionally, an independent organization sponsors what's known as the **Green City Market,** Wednesdays and Saturdays from mid-May through the end of October in Lincoln Park (between Clark Street and Cannon Drive), from 7 a.m. to 1:30 p.m. Green City Market moves to the Peggy Notebaert Nature Museum, 2430 North Cannon Drive (off Fullerton) in November and December; it's open on Wednesdays and Saturdays from 8 a.m. to 1 p.m., and there's talk of January through April openings on the first and third Saturday of the month. For exact Green City Market times and dates, call ☎ 773-880-1266 or visit **www .chicagogreencitymarket.org.** This is the only independent private market that supports local farmers who utilize sustainable and organic practices. Also showcasing sustainable food is the City of Chicago's new **Downtown Farmstand,** which sells fresh fruits and veggies in season, plus baked goods. Located at 66 East Randolph Street, it's closed from mid-December through early February. For more information, call ☎ 312-742-8419 or visit **www.chicagofarmstand.com.**

The object of hometown raves is the caramel-and-cheese popcorn made by **Garrett Popcorn** (26 West Randolph Street, 2 West Jackson

Boulevard, and 4 East Madison Street; ☎ 888-476-7267; **www.garrett popcorn.com**). The secret recipe assures hot-air-popped (no oils or fat) premium-quality popcorn; choose from plain, buttered, CheeseCorn, CaramelCrisp (with or without nuts), or the aforementioned caramel-cheese combo. A short cab ride from the Loop is **Greek Islands** (200 South Halsted Street; ☎ 312-782-9855; **www.greekislands.net**), which not only has top Greek dishes to enjoy there but sells its own fabulous honey, olive oil, and wines. In the West Loop, part personal wine-buying service, part specialty retail wine store, **Perman Wine Selections** is at 802 West Washington Street (☎ 312-666-4417; **www.permanwine .com**). Stop in and meet proprietor Craig Perman, sign up for his newsletter, and take home a bottle.

MICHIGAN AVENUE   To the east of the avenue is **Fox & Obel** (401 East Illinois Street; ☎ 312-379-0146; **www.fox-obel.com**), home of gourmet foods; the emphasis is on freshness, and chefs prepare an array of delectables (the breads and cheeses are among the best in town).

On South Michigan Avenue is **Caffé Baci** (332 South Michigan Avenue; ☎ 312-322-2109; **www.caffebaci.com**), an upscale yet moderately priced place to grab a quick lunch while shopping. The exotic-truffle emporium **Vosges Haut-Chocolat** (☎ 312-644-9450; **www.vosgeschocolate.com**) has joined the roster of **The Shops at North Bridge** (520 North Michigan Avenue). The knockout chocolates may contain flowers as well as rare spices; prices range from $2.25 to $10 for a multi-piece box, and up. *Yum.* Also at The Shops at North Bridge (third floor) is the new **TA-ZE** (☎ 312-527-2576), stocked with all things olive, including oils, from Turkey's famed olive-oil firm, Taris. A tiny chocolate shop called **Teuscher** (900 North Michigan Avenue, level five; ☎ 312-943-4400; **www.teuscher.com**) brings chocoholics happiness with yummy truffles, exquisitely packaged.

NEAR NORTH   The place to find fresh mozzarella is **L'Appetito** (30 East Huron Street; ☎ 312-787-9881; **www.lappetito.com**), along with many imported Italian goodies; there's a second location on the ground floor of the John Hancock Center (875 North Michigan Avenue; ☎ 312-337-0691). The divine breads from **Corner Bakery Cafe** (676 North St. Clair Street; ☎ 312-266-2570; **www.cornerbakerycafe .com**) are much praised.

A Gold Coast hot spot for foodies is **The Goddess & Grocer** (25 East Delaware; ☎ 312-896-2600; also at 1646 North Damen; ☎ 773-342-3200). Gourmet sandwiches, salads, and pastries add spice.

LINCOLN PARK–CLYBOURN CORRIDOR   At 2121 North Clybourn Avenue is Market Square. *Market* refers to a huge **Treasure Island** (☎ 773-880-8880; **www.tifoods.com**); some consider this location the chain's best. Others like the TIs at 1639 North Wells (☎ 312-642-1105) and 75 West Elm (☎ 312-440-1144). To the west, take Elston south till you reach North Avenue; you'll soon bump into **Stanley's** (1558 North Elston;

☎ 773-276-8050), notable for fruits and veggies. Some prefer **Whole Foods Market** (1000 West North Avenue; ☎ 312-587-0648; **www.whole foodsmarket.com**), which moves to a new location on adjacent Kingsbury Street in May 2009. The terrific **Trader Joe's** (1840 North Clybourn Avenue; ☎ 312-274-9733; **www.traderjoes.com**) is the place to pick up anything (at fair prices) from daisies to Pinot Gris.

On North Avenue, look for **Sam's Wines & Spirits** (1720 North Marcey Street; ☎ 312-664-4394; **www.samswine.com**). This is a place beloved by many Chicagoans, who know they can pick up the best wines for the best prices. Staffers here know how to advise you, so listen—you may come in for a California Cabernet and walk out with a Piemontese Barolo. Also check out the **House of Glunz** (1206 North Wells Street; ☎ 312-642-3000; **www.thehouseofglunz.com**), wine merchants with a very broad range thanks to their extensive cellar. Shoppers from certain (few) states may order their selections by mail and have them shipped sans Illinois sales tax. One of the best wine-tasting events is held the first Wednesday of the month at **Wine Discount Center** (1826 North Elston Avenue; ☎ 773-489-3454). In early 2009, the price was $10 to taste 30 wines—a good deal; you need to make reservations, usually about a week ahead. **The Chopping Block** (**www.thechoppingblock.net**), which also houses cooking schools at its Merchandise Mart Plaza (Suite 107; ☎ 312-644-6360) and Lincoln Square (4747 North Lincoln Avenue; ☎ 773-472-6700) locations, purveys appealing cookware and fine foodstuffs (such as a terrific walnut mustard from France).

Pastoral (2945 North Broadway Street; ☎ 773-472-4781; **www.pastoralartisan.com**) was named one of the top cheese shops in the United States by *Saveur* magazine. This gourmet retailer is a great stop for breads, condiments, and, of course, cheeses. They make up picnic packs, too.

Time for dessert? To the north, edging Lincoln Park, is a lovely pastry shop called **Bittersweet** (1114 West Belmont Avenue; ☎ 773-929-1100; **www.bittersweetpastry.com**). You can pick up yummies here from mini–fruit tarts to custom-ordered cakes, and if you need space in which to consume them, there's a cafe on the premises, too.

We've also entered cupcake territory: check out **Cupcakes** (613 West Briar Place; ☎ 773-525-0817; **www.chicagocupcakes.com**); Lincoln Park's **Mandy B's** (1208 West Webster Avenue; ☎ 773-244-1174); and the highly creative **Sensational Bites** (3751 North Southport Avenue; ☎ 773-248-2271; **www.sensationalbites.com**), where you can stop for coffee-and after a film at the Music Box Theater. Some people think **Twisted Sister Bakery** (1543 North Wells Street; ☎ 312-932-1128; **www.twistedsisterbakery.com**) has the best cupcakes, not to mention cookies, tarts, and other yummies. Other pastry lovers head for **Vanille** (2229 North Clybourn Avenue; ☎ 773-868-4574; **www.vanille patisserie.com**), where pastry chef Dimitri Fayard excels at chocolate pralines (and more). And speaking of more, **More** (1 East Delaware Place; ☎ 312-951-0001; **www.morecupcakes.com**) has a bacon, maple, and brown-sugar cupcake that people swoon for (they also love the Madras curry and crème brûlée cupcakes). *Wheee!*

Over at **iCream** (1537 North Milwaukee Avenue; ☎ 773-342-2834; **www.icreamcafe.com**), Cora Shaw and Jason McKinney offer customized ice cream and frozen yogurt, such as sugar-free green tea–soy ice cream topped with crushed Heath bars. Or investigate an organic dairy base, plus a pomegranate flavor extract, plus liquid nitrogen to help things along. In winter, try a great warm chocolate pudding.

How about a scoop of gelato (for one: goat cheese and caramel)? Created by Jessie Oloroso for her Black Dog gelato, it's sold at **Cippolina** (1543 North Damen Avenue; ☎ 773-227-6300) among other places. And you won't believe the fresh baguettes and croissants at **Cook au Vin** in Logan Square (2256 North Elston Avenue; ☎ 773-489-3141; **www.cook-au-vin.com**). Look for Pasta Puttana, the fresh pasta created by Jessica Volpe, found in such places as the seafood and gourmet market **Dirk's Fish** (2070 North Clybourn Avenue; ☎ 773-404-3475; **www.dirksfish.com**).

IN EVANSTON, WILMETTE, AND GLENVIEW Stop at **Foodstuffs** (2106 Central Street, Evanston; ☎ 847-328-7704) or farther north in Glencoe (338 Park Avenue; ☎ 847-835-5105; **www.foodstuffs.com**). Both stores have huge delis, bake their own pastries, feature fish (Glencoe) or meats and fish (Evanston), and offer gift baskets and catering (both are excellent). In Wilmette, the best take-out place is **A La Carte** (111 Green Bay Road; ☎ 847-256-4102; **www.alacarteinc .com**). You can also eat here, in the small lunchroom and, in summer, outdoors. More raves go to the seafood at **Burhop's** (1515 Sheridan Road, at Plaza del Lago, Wilmette; ☎ 847-256-6400; **www.burhops .com**), where everything from soups to crab cakes to smoked chub is terrific. Back in Evanston, additional treats include the coffees roasted on the premises at **Casteel Coffee** (2924 Central Street; ☎ 847-733-1187). Many prefer these to the (let's keep it nameless) chain stores' blends; a fave here is Decaf Sumatra. Another Evanston attraction is the **Spice House** (1941 Central Street; ☎ 847-328-3711; **www.thespice house.com**). This is the last word in everything from "Back of the Yards" garlic pepper to Saigon cinnamon. People came from miles around till they expanded to open a fragrant store in Chicago, too (1512 North Wells Street; ☎ 312-274-0378).

HOME, BED, AND BATH

Note: Many of the following stores may be affected by changes in the economy, so call or check online first to see if they're open.

ON MICHIGAN AVENUE *Major* is the word for **Crate & Barrel**'s flagship store (646 North Michigan Avenue; ☎ 312-787-5900; **www.crateand barrel.com**); it's as luminous at night as an ocean liner. Contemporary furniture and decorative items are provided at mostly moderate prices. Just off Michigan Avenue in the Gold Coast area at 17 East Pearson Street is **BRANCA**, the exquisite shop of Alessandra Branca (☎ 312-787-1017; **www.branca.com**). Her beautiful boutique is chock-full of items reflecting her taste: a $14,000 European oil painting or a stunning horn-and-bone votive for $35.

WEST OF THE LOOP   The West Loop is a growing source of furniture and home-furnishings sources; sometimes they run into each other in certain districts. Most of the West Loop stores are farther east than **Modern Times** (2100 West Grand Avenue; ☎ 312-243-5706), a fount of mid-20th-century modern furnishings, including the collectibles of Charles and Ray Eames. To look into more of their diverse items, consult **www.moderntimeschicago.com.** Nearby, **European Furniture Importers** (2145 West Grand Avenue; ☎ 312-243-1955; **www.eurofur niture.com**) is also worth the trek. They offer modern classics and contemporary furniture. Not as far west on Grand, at 1139–43, is **Design Inc.** (☎ 312-243-4333; **www.designinchicago.com**), founded by interior designer Bill Bruss, with a fine collection of offbeat artisan-made furniture and other goods he has found while roaming the world. On Kinzie, look into Asian-influenced furniture at **P.A. Larkin** (118 West Kinzie Street; ☎ 312-527-1217; **www.palarkin.com**). And if you want to decorate your walls with some good student art from the School of the Art Institute of Chicago (who says you always have to rely on posters?), look into the school's late-April or early-May Graduate Exhibition; inquire at the school by calling ☎ 312-899-5100 or visit **www.saic.edu.**

ON OAK STREET   Posh bed, bath, and table linens come with love (and great taste) from Italy at **Pratesi Linens** (67 East Oak Street; ☎ 312-943-8422). They're not inexpensive, but the quality is high. Another favorite is the fabled Italian linens emporium **Frette** (41 East Oak Street; ☎ 312-649-3744; **www.frette.com**), fresh from Milan with the company's signature linens, fragrances (scented candles and sachets), and an at-home clothing line lush with cashmeres. They're best known for their jacquard-print bedding of 300- to 600-thread-count Egyptian cotton and linen. Pricey, but you can always pop in for a divine sachet.

NEAR NORTH   One of the city's top home-furnishings emporiums is **Elements** (741 North Wells Street; ☎ 312-642-6574; **www.elements chicago.com**). Tabletop accessories can be found here, along with everything from picture frames to men's and women's jewelry and wedding gifts. Definitely a place to browse, **Cambium** (119 West Hubbard Street; ☎ 312-832-9920; **www.cambiumhome.com**) offers furniture, kitchen items, and some wonderful home and tabletop gifts. For contemporary lighting (and a huge showrooms), try **Light-ology** (215 West Chicago Avenue; ☎ 312-944-1000); they stock goods from 400 manufacturers.

At **Material Possessions** (704 North Wabash Avenue; ☎ 312-280-4885; **www.materialpossessions.com**), eclectic spirit is combined with a sense of humor in showcasing a unique selection of original home furnishings. Furniture includes custom tables starting at $1,200. Tabletop and custom-made dinnerware are specialties as well, plus linens and other one-of-a-kind decorative accessories from around the world. This is a must-see for the discerning shopper.

A bit west of Michigan Avenue, at Tree Studios, here's another must: **P.O.S.H.** (613 North State Street; ☎ 312-280-1602; **www.posh chicago.com**). Interesting items run rampant here—vintage hotel silver and commercial china (manufactured for hotels and country clubs but unused), Victorian ivory-handled fruit knives, coffee mugs with Chicago-skyline designs created for P.O.S.H., English guest towels, and more. Also at Tree Studios is the showroom of **Thos. Moser** (607 North State Street; ☎ 312-751-9684; **www.thosmoser.com**), a highly respected maker of handcrafted solid-wood furniture. Superlative craftsmanship is a trademark of these pieces known for graceful lines that echo the traditions of Shaker, Arts and Crafts, Mission, and other cultural influences in design.

RIVER NORTH One source for antiques is **Christa's Ltd.** (217 West Illinois Street; ☎ 312-222-2520; **www.christasltd.com**), with Continental antiques from furniture to andirons. Two more worthy antiques sources are **Jay Robert's Antique Warehouse** (149 West Kinzie Street; ☎ 312-222-0167; **www.jayroberts.com**) and **Thomas Jolly** (124 West Kinzie Street; ☎ 312-595-0018; **www.thomasjollyantiques.com**), a specialist in early-17th- through 19th-century European antiques, open Monday, Wednesday, and Friday. A new emporium, designed to be ultragreen, is **Florense** (300 West Ontario Street; ☎ 312-640-0066; **www.florense.com**). The appeal here is a showroom that features great-looking Brazilian contemporary furniture. Dazzling goods await at **Champagne Furniture Gallery** (65 West Illinois Street; ☎ 312-923-9800; **www.champagnefurniture.com**), and at the **Golden Triangle** (330 North Clark Street; ☎ 312-755-1266; **www.goldentriangle.biz**) you might find a teak-and-cane plantation chair from Thailand or Burmese wooden puppets. **Sawbridge Studios** (153 West Ohio Street; ☎ 312-828-0055) is a gallery of custom-made designs by craftspeople from across the United States. Furniture (from Shaker to traditional to Prairie) is predominant, and, considering the high cost for custom-made pieces, it's affordable.

Asian House (159 West Kinzie Street; ☎ 312-527-4848) boasts a complete line of Oriental furniture and accessories, such as cloisonné vases and animals, bronze statues, porcelain fishbowls, antique Chinese pieces, Coromandel screens, and more. On Hubbard Street, contemporary furniture by international designers reigns at **Roche Bobois** (222 West Hubbard Street; ☎ 312-951-9080; **www.roche-bobois .com**). And on LaSalle, at the **Kreiss Collection** showroom (415 North

LaSalle Street; ☎ 312-527-0907; **www.kreiss.com**), find the latest Kreiss family designs; the family manufactures its own elegant pieces, and you can pick out the finishes, fabrics, and accessories right here. Farther west, **Design Studio** (225 West Hubbard Street; ☎ 312-527-5272; **www .designstudiofurniture.com**) offers contemporary home furnishings.

The name **Rita Bucheit** (449 North Wells Street; ☎ 312-527-4080; **www.ritabucheit.com**) is synonymous with one of the finest collections of authentic Empire, Neoclassical, Biedermeier, Vienna Secession, and Art Deco antiques, fine art, and decorative arts in North America. Since 1988, the gallery has specialized in museum-quality European antiques from the 18th to 20th centuries.

Nearby is **Hästens** (430 North Wells Street; ☎ 312-527-5337; **www .passionforbeds.com**), the noted bed company that uses all-natural materials. Bargain shoppers, be forewarned: **Arrelle Fine Linens** (445 North Wells Street; ☎ 312-321-3696; **www.arrelle.com**) is not the place to come if you're looking for Fieldcrest on sale. Rather, you'll find a gorgeous Italian sheet, silky as gelato, that might set you back a bit. If that's a bit rich for your blood, at least have a look at the table linens and beautiful bed settings by Anichini, Sferra, Yves Delorme, Anali, and Graziano.

An extraordinarily artful collection of furniture and furnishings (half the pieces are Italian; some are designed by the owner-architect) is on offer at **Manifesto** (755 North Wells Street; ☎ 312-664-0733; **www.manifestofurniture.com**). If you peruse the three floors, you'll see dining tables, sofas, benches, lounge chairs, vases, lighting, and some accessories. **Luminaire** (301 West Superior Street; ☎ 312-664-9582) is a 30,000-square-foot showroom that began as a fine-lighting emporium and graduated into retail. Everything is top-flight here; find the very best international designers, including Philippe Starck. Luminaire sells the cutting-edge contemporary furniture from B&B Italia, but right next door more transitional pieces are on view at **Maxalto Chicago** (309 West Superior Street; ☎ 312-664-6190; **www .maxalto.it**).

The owners of **Orange Skin** (223 West Erie Street; ☎ 312-335-1033; **www.orangeskin.com**) work with the city's best designers. Represented in their showroom are top furniture manufacturers such as Minotti, Kartell, Magis, and Arper.

LINCOLN PARK–CLYBOURN CORRIDOR A new store featuring Scandinavian design (in this case, mainly Denmark-based) is **BoConcept** (1901 North Clybourn, Suite 100; ☎ 773-388-2900; **www.boconcept .us**). Bring your room measurements, and a helpful employee will walk you through a 3-D software program to see how the styles will look in your home. **Jayson Home & Garden** (1885 North Clybourn Avenue; ☎ 773-248-8180; **www.jaysonhomeandgarden.com**) has become one of the hottest retail stores in the Lincoln Park area (In vintage warehouses, you'll find treasures that interestingly combine old and new, domestic and imported. Unusual gifts include beautiful pillows; opulent sofas, chairs, and ottomans; and Euro bath luxuries. For the garden, there are plants and fresh flowers. An annex here is **Artists Frame Service** (1867 North Clybourn Avenue; ☎ 773-248-7713; **www.artistsframeservice.com**), and another annex is a gallery called **Chicago Art Source** (1871 North Clybourn Avenue; ☎ 773-248-3100; **www.chicagoartsource.com**).

A furnishings gallery called **Symmetry** (1925 West Division Street; ☎ 773-645-0502; **www.symmetryshowroom.com**) is the place to pick up a stunning Tibetan rug (they have quite a collection), or lamps from the Philippines, or a pedestal from Thailand.

You mustn't leave the area without a visit to **Verde** (2100 West Armitage Avenue; ☎ 773-486-7750; **www.verdedesignstudio.net**), where designer Michele Fitzpatrick offers high-quality custom furniture—pick a fabric and she'll design the piece you want. She also displays local artwork.

ON HALSTED, CLARK, AND LINCOLN Halsted has so much to offer, not the least of which are galleries full of decorative furnishings, but let's start with one on Lincoln. One of the best is way north: **Gallimaufry Gallery** (4712 North Lincoln Avenue; ☎ 773-728-3600; **www.gallimaufry.net**), where you'll find unique art glass, kaleidoscopes, perfume bottles, pottery, scarves, some great music boxes, jewelry boxes, and jewelry to put in them.

If contemporary furniture is your thing, head to **Pauline-Grace** (1414 North Kingsbury Street; ☎ 312-280-9880), a showroom that represents top lines such as Directional, Altura, and Della Robbia. It looks like a loft, and the stock is sleek. Back on North Halsted, a store that sets the style for sleepyheads is **Bedside Manor Ltd.** (2056 North Halsted Street; ☎ 773-404-2020; **www.bedsidemanorltd.com**), with beds, beautiful linens, and fluffy down comforters. They also have stores in several suburbs. At 3651 North Halsted is an excellent resale shop: **Brown Elephant** (☎ 773-549-5943); they also have another store at 5404 North Clark (☎ 773-271-9382). Another find is **Antique Resources** (1741 West Belmont Avenue; ☎ 773-871-4242; **www.antiqueresourcesinc.com**)—not your ordinary antiques store, because this two-story showroom excels in fine furniture, chandeliers (tons of them, from Art Nouveau to Victorian treasures), oil paintings, clocks, and accessories, all unearthed by owner Richard Weisz, and all at reasonable prices.

The **Broadway Antique Market** (6130 North Broadway; ☎ 773-743-5444; **www.bamchicago.com**) is an unlikely setting, but it's a good place to shop (though there are more vintage items—1930s to 1960s—than true antiques). Some furniture, some Russel Wright pottery, some vintage clothes and posters—it's all here.

I.D. (3337 North Halsted Street; ☎ 773-755-IDID) is a superb design emporium. Co-owned by Steven Burgert and Anthony

Almaguer, this contemporary-lifestyle store is a source for Blu Dot modern furniture, Ameico tabletops, titanium eyewear, and Santa & Cole lighting.

In Lincoln Square, **Griffins & Gargoyles Antiques** (2140 West Lawrence Avenue; ☎ 773-769-1255; **www.griffins-gargoyles.com**) is purveying such finds as an 1890 pine armoire from Germany, but you'll find many more treasures here.

Last—but certainly not least to the budget-conscious urban taste-makers who frequent it—let's add a few words about the 9,000-square-foot **CB2** (3757 North Lincoln Avenue; ☎ 773-755-3900; **www.cb2.com**), the cool design offspring of Crate & Barrel. The product mix is contemporary and full of priced-right furniture (futon sofas), hip accessories (Chinese wall clocks), home office gadgets, and storage objects.

IN BUCKTOWN AND WICKER PARK In Wicker Park, go see the French-flavored **Porte Rouge** with the red door at 1911 West Division Street (☎ 773-269-2800; **www.porterouge.biz**). There's antique furniture along with au courant housewares like Staub cast-iron cookware.

Many shoppers love the furniture (desks, coffee tables, and more) and leather goods at **Stitch** (1723 North Damen Avenue; ☎ 773-782-1570; **www.stitchchicago.com**); you'll find terrific leather handbags here, too. When it comes to antiques, put **Pagoda Red** (1714 North Damen Avenue; ☎ 773-235-1188; **www.pagodared.com**) high on your list. It's notable for unusual furniture and artifacts from China, Tibet, and Southeast Asia, and if you're looking for something as utilitarian as it is decorative, this is the place. Items range from fire-place mantels to 18th-century calligraphy brushes.

The new location of **Wow & Zen** is at 1912 North Damen (☎ 773-269-2600; **www.wowandzen.com**). You'll find Asian country antiques for a song; the owners travel a lot and pick up multiples of cultural objects like Chinese tea boxes and Mongolian toy chests. A tabletop and furniture shop you ought to investigate is **Crosell & Co.** (1922 North Damen Avenue; ☎ 773-252-9010; **www.crosellandco.com**); here's everything from Cisco furniture to stemware by Alan Lee, and even chandeliers. At **Kachi Bachi** (2041 North Damen Avenue; ☎ 773-645-8640; **www.kachibachi.com**), find pillows, duvet covers, and window treatments. At **Pavilion** (2055 North Damen Avenue; ☎ 773-645-0924; **www.pavilionantiques.com**), Deborah Colman and Neil Kraus specialize in all things French and Italian. How about lighting by Angelo Brotto, French ceramics by Georges Jouve, and French 1970s metal design?

Note the Victorian English and French antique tableware and fur-niture at **The Painted Lady** (2128 North Damen Avenue; ☎ 773-489-9145; **www.thepaintedladychicago.com**). The accent here is on hand-painted antique furniture, plus an array of bedding, linens, tabletops, rugs, lighting, and artwork. **Virtu** (2034 North Damen

Avenue; ☎ 773-235-3790; **www.virtuchicago.com**), probably one of the most interesting shops on Damen, offers a potpourri of wonderful handmade crafts, from teapots to sterling-silver rings. Nearby, **Jean Alan** (2134 North Damen Avenue; ☎ 773-278-2345; **www.jean alanchicago.com**) is a find: designer Alan reworks vintage furniture and custom-designs pillows, draperies, and much more. A little less esoteric, **Lubinski Furniture** is a source for major appliances and "quality furnishings for the home." It's at 1550 North Milwaukee Avenue, (☎ 773-276-2835). With so many stores in this area, it's fun to just take off and walk, walk, walk!

OFF THE BEATEN PATH Discover **Vintage Pine** (904 West Blackhawk Street; ☎ 312-943-9303; **www.vintagepine.com**), a 20,000-square-foot showroom overflowing with current custom, antique, and vintage looks in both furniture and accessories. The goods here range from shipments of English pine armoires, farm tables, chairs, and silver pieces to items sold by on-site galleries that deal in antiques and more-contemporary home furnishings. At 4727 North Damen is **Ravenswood Antique Mart** (☎ 773-271-3700; **www.ravenswood antiquemart.com**), a great source for mod midcentury finds. North and west, another don't-miss is the treasure trove to explore at family-owned, 50-year-old **B.J. Furniture & Antiques** (6901 North Western Avenue; ☎ 773-262-1000; **www.bjantiqueschicago.com**). Furnishings date from 1850 to 1960.

If you continue north, you'll arrive at **Architectural Artifacts** (4325 North Ravenswood Avenue; ☎ 773-348-0622; **www.architecturalarti facts.com**), an extraordinary outlet for furniture and decorative items from around the world. In this huge warehouse, find everything from garden furniture to old (and sometimes beautiful) fireplace mantels. There's even a big events space for weddings. Another sprawling warehouse stocked with retro and just plain old artifacts from long-ago buildings, **Salvage One** (1840 West Hubbard Street; ☎ 312-733-0098; **www.salvageone.com**) is reported to have some 250,000 items, including stained-glass windows, odd cornices, bathtubs, garden ornaments, hardware, and furniture. North on Lincoln, **Homey** (3656 North Lincoln Avenue; ☎ 773-248-0050; **www.ilovehomey.com**) is full of fine art, as well as art for the home. Also in the Ravenswood area is **Patina** (4907 North Damen Avenue; ☎ 773-334-0400; **www .patinachicago.com**), where Alan Shull purveys a delightfully tasteful roster of mostly 20th-century "farmhouse" vintage furnishings.

Seeking fabrics at deep discounts? **L.Z. Products** is the 75,000-square-foot warehouse to consult. It's at 2121 West 21st Street (☎ 773-847-0572). If you want to sew your own drapes and pillows, and you need fabric or lessons, go to **The Needle Shop** (2054 West Charleston Street; ☎ 773-489-4230; **www.theneedleshop.net**).

Finally, a green crusader named Elise Zelechowski has set up a program to reuse Chicago building materials; at the nonprofit

Community Rebuilding Exchange (3335 West 47th Street), you can find anything from lighting fixtures to reclaimed hardwood flooring at discount prices; see **chicagobmrc.blogspot.com** for more information.

JEWELRY

IN THE LOOP A big Loop attraction for those who must have baubles, bangles, and beads is a series of jewelers (both wholesale and retail) at the renovated **Jewelers Center** at the Mallers Building (5 South Wabash Avenue; ☎ 312-853-2057; **www.jewelerscenter.com**). It's worth a look just to see how beautifully one of the oldest buildings in the Loop was redesigned, and there are reputed to be more than 200 jewelers in the building to lure you. If you need an independent gemologist, call on Lorraine Oakes at the **Chicago Gem Lab** in room 1621. **Wabash Jewelers Mall** (21 North Wabash Avenue, street level; ☎ 312-263-1757) also entices with good values.

ON MICHIGAN AVENUE At 900 North Michigan Avenue glows **The Goldsmith Ltd.** (☎ 312-751-1986; **www.thegoldsmithltd.com**), where Sherry Bender does every kind of commission, from updating a fun heirloom to creating a spectacular diamond necklace. The Midwest's only **Bulgari** is a dazzling outpost of the Italian designer at 909 North Michigan (☎ 312-255-1313; **www.bulgari.com**). All of the contemporary classics are here, including Italian jewels and Swiss-made watches. Here, too, you'll find Bulgari fragrances for men and women (some made with green tea), scarves, handbags, and sunglasses. One of the most exclusive boutiques in the country is **Cartier** (630 North Michigan Avenue; ☎ 312-266-7440; **www.cartier.com**). At 636 North Michigan, **Van Cleef & Arpels** brings its posh baubles to your wondering eyes (☎ 312-944-8988; **www.vancleef-arpels.com**). And you mustn't slight **Tiffany & Co.** (730 North Michigan Avenue; ☎ 312-944-7500; **www .tiffany.com**), where you can find a crystal vase, stainless-steel flatware, picture frames, and all manner of gems to take home in that unmistakable blue box. In the John Hancock Center is the private jeweler **Manny B. & Co.** (875 North Michigan Avenue, suite 2644; ☎ 312-337-5275; by appointment only). This interesting gentleman manufactures his own very high-end pieces and deals primarily with clients by referral.

Just west of Michigan Avenue is **Sidney Garber** (118 East Delaware Street; ☎ 312-944-5225; **www.sidneygarber.com**), a creative jeweler here since 1945 that deals in fine watches as well as diamonds and pearls. Garber, who passed away recently, went directly to his sources all over the world for stones, and he designed his own pieces.

The Drake Hotel houses **Georg Jensen** (959 North Michigan Avenue; ☎ 312-642-9160; **www.georgjensen.com**), with a mélange of gorgeous jewelry and tabletop items. *Note:* A Swedish artist named Viviana Torun does superb silversmithing.

ON OAK STREET Jewelry is unbeatable here. A longtime Chicago standby is master designer **Lester Lampert** (57 East Oak Street;

☎ 312-944-6888; **www.lesterlampert.com**), offering three floors of custom-made contemporary and classic designs, estate jewelry, and a huge selection of fine watches. Another local star, **Trabert & Hoeffer** (111 East Oak Street; ☎ 312-787-1654), has operated since 1937, most of that time over on Michigan Avenue. Fine gemstones and custom designs are the rule here; you're not bombarded by lots of jewelry cases, and they bring items to you, somewhat in the style of an extra-haute fashion house. Don't be intimidated: the gems are expensive, but the staff here can make buying them pleasant. The fluid style of New York star **Judith Ripka** (129 East Oak Street; ☎ 312-642-1056; **www.judithripka.com**) incorporates interchangeable components (an earring can be a stud or evolve into a pendant drop on a French wire), and Hillary Clinton is among those who've been known to crave her creative work. The Chicago location of the international powerhouse **Graff** (103 East Oak Street; ☎ 312-604-1000; **www.graffdiamonds.com**) is striking enough to rival those in London, New York, Palm Beach, and Monte Carlo, among other Graff outposts, and this is probably one of the most impressive jewelry stores anywhere. They're known for such treasures as the Idol's Eye (70.21 carats), and they do it all themselves, from gathering rough gemstones to the finished jewelry. As if all this magnificence weren't enough, **Harry Winston** has become a part of this Diamond Row, too (55 East Oak Street; ☎ 312-705-1820; **www.harrywinston .com**). Yet another Oak Street jeweler is **Me&Ro** (61 East Oak Street; ☎ 312-957-8181; **www.meandrojewelry.com**), where a flower-filled pond, changed weekly, brightens the window. There are pieces for women, men, and babies, and the selections run from the affordable to the *très cher.*

Finally, watches take the starring role at **Geneva Seal,** just off Oak (1003 North Rush Street; ☎ 312-944-3100).

OFF THE BEATEN PATH In the Lincoln Park area, a boutique not to be missed is that of **Ani Afshar** (2009 North Sheffield Avenue; ☎ 773-477-6650; **www.aniafshar.net**). Nationally known as a jeweler who works exclusively with beads, Afshar creates stunning, mostly one-of-a-kind pieces. (For customizing, call her studio at ☎ 773-645-8922.) In Bucktown, find **Gem** (1710 North Damen Avenue; ☎ 773-384-7700; **www.gemjewelryboutique.com**), where owner-designer Laura Kitsos sells beautifully handcrafted one-of-a-kind pieces. You'll also find fun jewelry among the interesting accessories at **Robin Richman** (2108 North Damen Avenue; ☎ 773-278-6150) and pieces made by artisans at **p.45** (1643 North Damen Avenue; ☎ 773-862-4523). *Way* off the beaten path, in the suburb of Lincolnwood, is one of the prime showrooms in all of Chicagoland for fine watches and jewelry: **Smart Jewelers** (3350 West Devon Avenue; ☎ 847-673-6000; **www.smart jewelers.com**). They claim to have more watch lines than anyone, and the selection is *huge.* Farther north in the suburb of Highland Park, a jewelry designer of vintage looks with a modern flair is attracting notice (Sarah Jessica Parker has bought some pieces). **Jill Alberts Jewelry** is at 469 Roger Williams in Highland Park (☎ 847-681-1630; **www.jillalberts.com**).

TOYS, GAMES, CLOTHES, AND GIFTS FOR CHILDREN

ON MICHIGAN AVENUE A favorite is the **LEGO Store** (520 North Michigan; ☎ 312-494-0760; **www.lego.com**); there are additional stores with children's goods at the same address. One is the upscale **Oilily** (☎ 312-527-5747; **www.oilily-world.com**). Just off Michigan is **Madison and Friends** (43 East Oak Street; ☎ 312-642-6403; **www.madisonandfriends.com**), with adorable clothes for the kids whose moms shop Oak Street.

ON HALSTED, CLARK, AND LINCOLN Full of toys and clothes (for kids to age 6), **Psycho Baby** (1630 North Damen Avenue; ☎ 773-772-2815; **www.psychobabyonline.com**) is the choice of many moms. **The Red Balloon Co.** (2060 North Damen Avenue; ☎ 773-489-9800; **www.theredballoon.com**) has clothing for newborns through age 10, as well as wooden toys, children's books, and bedroom accessories. Also at 3224 North Damen is **Twinkle Twinkle Little One,** with furniture, bedding, and more (☎ 773-472-3000; **www.twinkletwinklelittleone.com**). A children's boutique specializing in organic and eco-friendly clothing, furniture, and gear is **Grow** (1943 West Division Street; ☎ 773-489-0009; **www.grow-kids.com**). And when it comes to kids' shoes for first walkers all the way up to juniors, note **Piggy Toes** (2205 North Halsted Street; ☎ 773-281-5583; **www.ptoes.com**). For children's clothes with oomph, try **Stinky Pants** (844 West Armitage Avenue; ☎ 773-281-4002; **www.stinky-pants.com**). Look for **The Children's Place** stores scattered throughout the city and suburbs; they often have hot looks and fair prices (**www.childrensplace.com**). **Uncle Fun** (1338 West Belmont Avenue; ☎ 773-477-8223; **www.unclefunchicago.com**) has everything from jelly beans to toys. Out south, the choice of thinking parents is **Toys Et Cetera** (1502 East 55th Street; ☎ 773-324-6039; **www.toysetcetera.com**), with fine educational toys. Out north and west, **Cut Rate Toys** (5409 West Devon Avenue; ☎ 773-763-5740; **www.cutratetoys.net**) has no frills but great prices for Brio, Playmobil, Webkinz, Little Tikes, and much more.

Ash's Magic Shop (4955 North Western Avenue; ☎ 773-271-4030; **www.ashs-magic.com**) is loads of fun. Magician Ash Baboorian and his wife, Bonnie, have clown shoes, rubber chickens, "Lithuanians for Nixon" buttons, and the main attraction: magic tricks.

And to all a good buy!

PART TEN

EXERCISE, RECREATION, *and* SPORTS

CHICAGOANS WORK HARD AND PLAY HARD. Their extreme ethic mirrors the weather. Chicago is a city of great contrasts when it comes to climate, and natives are willing to bring it on. In the summer, humidity is intense and temperatures often climb to about 90°F by midafternoon, making outdoor exercise and recreation problematic unless you plan to lounge on a Lake Michigan beach or go for a swim. Winter, on the other hand can be positively Arctic in intensity, especially in January and February, when cold temperatures and icy blasts off the lake plunge windchill factors to well below zero.

unofficial **TIP**
Regardless of the season, understand that Chicago's weather can change in minutes. Keep that in mind before setting out on an all-day outing, and take along appropriate raingear and/or warm clothing.

The idea in the summer is to exercise early, before the sun and humidity make conditions outdoors too hot and muggy. In the winter, only hardy outdoor types such as cross-country skiers will want to brave the cold and wind; everyone else should plan to exercise indoors. The rest of the story is that spring and fall are usually fine for enjoying the outdoors.

Chicago is one of America's best cities in terms of recreation and sports options. Local sports fans are loyal despite decades of being frustrated by mediocre product (with the exception of Michael Jordan's run with the Bulls). One of the reasons Theodore Thomas founded a symphony orchestra in Chicago was that "he understood the excitement and nervous strain that everyone, more or less, suffered from living there." So relax. And take a deep breath.

INDOOR ACTIVITIES

A QUINTESSENTIAL CHICAGO EXPERIENCE

BUILT IN 1906, the **Division Street Russian and Turkish Baths** (1916 West Division; ☎ 773-384-9671; **www.chicagorussiansauna.com**) is the only traditional bathhouse left in Chicago and one of only several that remain in the United States. Chicago authors Nelson Algren and Saul Bellow incorporated the baths into their writing, and John Belushi featured them in his hit film *The Blues Brothers*. Mobster Sam Giancana allegedly used to come here; these days you might run into the Reverend Jesse Jackson and/or assorted Chicago aldermen. (It's hard to define status when you're sitting in a sauna, wrapped in a hot sheet like a butt-naked burrito.) For $20, men and women visitors have access to a large whirlpool, cold pool, eucalyptus-scented steam bath, granite-stone heat room, and oak-leaf brooms. Invigorating Swedish massage is extra. A small lunch counter serves salads and soups. The baths are open weekdays from 8 a.m. to 8 p.m, Saturday from 7 a.m. to 8 p.m, and Sunday from 7 a.m. to 2 p.m. Don't miss this Chicago legend.

FREE WEIGHTS AND EXERCISE MACHINES

MOST OF CHICAGO'S MAJOR HOTELS have either spas or fitness rooms with weight-lifting equipment on-site or have arrangements with nearby health clubs that extend privileges to hotel guests. For an aerobic workout, most of the fitness rooms offer stationary bikes, stair-climbers, or rowing machines. Many clubs are also open to men and women and accept daily or short-term memberships. The **Chicago Fitness Center** (3131 North Lincoln Avenue at Belmont; ☎ 773-549-8181; **www.chicagofitnesscenter.com**) offers two weight rooms with equipment including free weights and Nautilus Universal fixed-weight machines. Aerobic equipment includes StairMasters, treadmills, and Cybex exercise bikes. The daily fee is $10; free day passes are available at the Web site. **Equinox** has three city locations: the Loop (200 West Monroe; ☎ 312-252-3100), the Gold Coast (900 North Michigan; ☎ 312-254-2500), and Lincoln Park (1750 North Clark Street; ☎ 312-254-4000). All offer studio cycling, yoga, Pilates, a spa, and a pool. The cost for guests is $25 a day, but you must find a member to bring you in. Just hang around the parking lot until you do.

EXERCISING IN YOUR HOTEL

YOU WORK OUT REGULARLY, but here you are, stuck on a rainy day in a hotel without an exercise room. Worse, your game is off from overeating, sitting in airplanes, and not being able to let off steam. Don't despair: unless your hotel is designed like a sprawling dude ranch, you can put on your workout clothes and find a nice interior stairwell, which all hotels are required to have in case of fire.

Because it's important for your step workout to be consistent with your fitness level, we've provided two different plans. Here's the first one, from Bob Sehlinger, creator of the *Unofficial Guide* series (for a ten-story hotel):

From your floor, descend to the very bottom of the stairwell. Walk up ten flights and down again to get warmed up. Then, taking the stairs two at a time, bound up two floors and return to the bottom quickly, but normally (that is, one step at a time). Next, bound up three floors and return. Add a floor after each circuit until you get to the top floor. Then reverse the process, ascending one less floor on each round-trip: nine, eight, seven—you get the idea. Tell somebody where you'll be in case you fall down the stairs. Listen to your body, and don't overdo it. If your hotel has 30 stories, don't feel compelled to make it all the way to the top.

Now here's coauthor Dave Hoekstra's plan:

Sit in the stairwell on the fourth-floor landing with a six-pack of Old Style and a slice of deep-dish pizza, and laugh at Bob every time he chugs past. Or just lie down on your hotel-room floor, hook your feet under some furniture, and knock out 50 sit-ups.

OUTDOOR ACTIVITIES

WALKING

CHICAGO IS A FANTASTIC TOWN for getting around by foot: as flat as an Illinois cornfield yet as ambitious as a shark at sea. If you mentally break up the city into discrete portions—the Loop, River North, the Magnificent Mile, and such—and you don't overextend yourself, walking is the best way to learn about Chicago. It keeps you on your toes. Every step requires a decision. Folks who are fit and enjoy using their own two feet should bring comfortable walking shoes and regularly give themselves a rest by occasionally taking a taxi, a bus, or the El.

unofficial **TIP**
The stretch of the Lakefront Trail from McCormick Place south to Hyde Park is tough turf; stay to the north in daylight hours and you'll be okay. Pedestrian tunnels under Lake Shore Drive make it possible to reach the trail without getting hit by a car on the busy drive.

Along the Lake

Serious walkers and people in search of great scenery and prime people-watching as they stretch their legs should head for Chicago's premier walking destination, the **Lakefront Trail** along Lake Michigan. The 20-mile paved path is flat, clean, well lit, and usually crowded with other people whose boots are made for walkin'. You really haven't done Chicago unless you've experienced the Lakefront Trail.

City Walks

Other good destinations for a scenic stroll include the **Gold Coast,** a neighborhood of sumptuous mansions and town houses located just above the Magnificent Mile; **Lincoln Park,** featuring 1,200 acres of greenery, three museums, and a free zoo; and **Oak Park,** a Near West suburb where strollers can explore a shady neighborhood full of homes designed by Frank Lloyd Wright. Ambitious walkers with the

Wright step will want to head to the South Side and take in the row houses at **3213–19 South Calumet Avenue.** These are the only Wright-designed row houses ever built.

In late 1996, the northbound lanes of Lake Shore Drive were relocated to the west of the Field Museum. Landscaping created a new traffic-free **Museum Campus** consisting of the Field Museum, the Shedd Aquarium, and the Adler Planetarium. Other pedestrian-friendly amenities at the ten-acre park include rows of elm trees; a large, sloping lawn in front of the Field Museum and to the west of the Shedd Aquarium; and a series of decorative plazas linked by walkways between the museums. A pedestrian concourse underneath Lake Shore Drive at Roosevelt Road serves as an entranceway to the Museum Campus, which hearty Chicagoans always come to by foot—it's more convenient than trying to find a parking place. The planetarium sits on a former island in Lake Michigan that's now linked to the shore by a half-mile peninsula. From this point—one of the city's most romantic spots—the view of the Chicago skyline is tremendous.

Another outstanding place to walk is the beautiful Gothic campus of the **University of Chicago** in Hyde Park, south of downtown. Don't miss the 12-ton abstract sculpture *Nuclear Energy* by Henry Moore; it's located on the spot where Enrico Fermi and other UC scientists split the atom and achieved the first self-sustained nuclear chain reaction in 1942. This may be one of the most important spots in America.

Farther afield, more great walking destinations include **Brookfield Zoo** (14 miles west of the city but easily accessible on the Metra train line), the **Morton Arboretum** (25 miles west of the Loop in Lisle, with 1,500 acres of native woodlands and 25 miles of trails), and the **Chicago Botanic Garden** (300 acres of landscaped gardens and island located 18 miles north of downtown).

RUNNING

NOT JUST CHICAGO'S FAVORITE WALKING PATH, the **Lakefront Trail** is also where the city's most serious runners come to work out. And runners, without handlebars sticking out or the need to weave like inline skaters, have it easier when it comes to penetrating the throngs who crowd the path when it's nice outside. The trail is most crowded between 6 a.m. and 10 a.m. in good weather. Folks looking for more elbowroom can head a little north of downtown and run on the section of trail between Belmont Harbor and the northern neighborhood of Edgewater. While the same holds true for the six-mile stretch starting south of McCormick Place, it's not nearly as safe.

Good news for runners who prefer training on a soft surface instead of asphalt: Chicago is surrounded by a network of forest preserves that are easy to reach by car. To run in a sylvan setting, head to **Palos Forest Preserve District** in southwest Cook County, about 20 miles from downtown. The nation's largest forest preserve (nearly 14,000 acres) features 80 miles of multipurpose trails, which are ten feet wide and covered with gravel or grass. For more information on Palos and other forest preserves, call ☎ 773-261-8400.

TENNIS

ONE HUNDRED THIRTY-FOUR PARKS in the **Chicago Park District** incorporate around 600 tennis courts. Some of them are convenient to visitors staying downtown; the better ones are along the lakefront. The nets go up in mid-April and usually stay up through October. Reservations aren't required for most courts—just put your racquet by the net, and the other players using the court will know you want to use it next. Other courts must be reserved by phone.

Daley Bicentennial Plaza, downtown at 337 East Randolph Street (between Columbus and Lake Shore drives), features 12 lighted courts. For reservations, call ☎ 312-742-7648 after 10 a.m. the day before you plan to play. Hours are 7 a.m. to 10 p.m. weekdays and 8 a.m. to 5 p.m. weekends; the fee is $7 an hour.

Six lighted courts are available in **Grant Park** (900 South Columbus Drive; ☎ 312-742-7648). Reservations aren't accepted; courts are free during the day, and there's a nominal charge after 5 p.m. Hours are 9 a.m. to 10 p.m. weekdays and 9 a.m. to 5 p.m. weekends. **Lake Shore Park** (808 North Lake Shore Drive, across from Northwestern University; ☎ 312-742-7891) has two lighted courts; no reservations are accepted. Hours are 7 a.m. to 11 p.m. daily, and there is no charge to use the courts.

Waveland, located in popular Lincoln Park (North Lake Shore Drive at Waveland Avenue; ☎ 312-742-8523), features 20 courts, 10 with lights. Reservations are required; cost is $7 an hour. Hours are 8 a.m. to 10 p.m. daily.

McFetridge Sports Center, on the Far Northwest Side (3843 North California Avenue), has six indoor tennis courts. Weekday rates are $17 per person per hour from 7 a.m. to 4 p.m., $26 from 4 to 10 p.m. Weekend rates are $26 from 7 a.m. to 7 p.m., $24 from 7 to 10 p.m. Call ☎ 773-478-2609 for reservations.

GOLF
Small Ball

Even most locals are unaware there's an 18-hole "putting" course tucked away in downtown Grant Park. The **Green at Grant Park** is strictly for putting on a true-to-form 18-hole putting course. The course looks like it's made from real grass; however, the grounds are filled with sand and made with synthetic material (real grass cannot be used because of heavy foot traffic). The Green at Grant Park is just west of Lake Shore Drive at 352 East Monroe Street (☎ 312-642-7888; **www.thegreenonline.com**). The fee (includes putters and balls) is $9 for an 18-hole round; kids pay $6. The Green also has a full-service restaurant and patio that are open from 10 a.m. to 10 p.m. daily.

Longer Shots

The **Chicago Park District** boasts six public courses managed by Billy Casper Golf. Affordable, accessible, and well maintained, they inspired *Golf Digest* magazine to call Chicago "a likely candidate for best golf city in America." The courses are open all year long from dawn to dusk, weather permitting. Make tee-time reservations at least a week in advance by phone or online (☎ 866-699-1910; **www .cpdgolf.com**).

The **Sydney R. Marovitz Golf Course** (usually called **Waveland,** the course's former name) is the crème de la crème of Chicago's public courses. Located near the ritzy Gold Coast and Lake Michigan, it offers great views and a design modeled on that of Pebble Beach. Not a lot of trees, but the fairways are fairly long (3,240 yards) compared with those of other municipal courses.

Waveland is the place to go to impress a client—and you won't be alone. The nine-hole golf course handles about 400 golfers a day, so figure on three hours to play a round. Hold your bets if you bump into noted golfer Michael Jordan. Fees are $15 for adults, $8 for juniors (age 17 and under) and seniors (age 62 and over) There's also a restaurant. The course is at Waveland Avenue and the lakefront in Lincoln Park. Call ☎ 312-742-7930 for more information.

South Shore Golf Course, at the South Shore Cultural Center (7059 Lake Shore Drive; ☎ 312-256-0986), is a public nine-holer that's fairly short (2,720 yards). The holes are well designed and moderately challenging, and South Shore is considered an undiscovered gem. The setting on the lake means that every hole is a visual feast, whether it's the waves off of Lake Michigan crashing along the fairway or spectacular views of the city. Fees are $10 for adults, $5 for juniors and seniors.

Robert A. Black Golf Course (2045 West Pratt Boulevard; ☎ 312-742-7931), near the lakefront and the city's northern boundary, is a good choice if you're staying in Evanston. It's a nine-hole, 2,339-yard course with no water hazards (it does have 21 bunkers, or sand traps, however). Fees are $10 for adults, $5 for juniors and seniors.

Chicago's only 18-hole municipal course is at **Jackson Park** (near the southern terminus of Lake Shore Drive at 63rd Street and Stony Island Avenue; ☎ 773-667-0524). It's a moderately difficult 5,463-yard course with lots of trees, but not much sand or water. Fees are $15 for adults, $8 for juniors and seniors.

Marquette Park Golf Course (6700 South Kedzie Avenue at 67th Street, near Midway Airport; ☎ 312-245-0909), a nine-holer, offers wide fairways and water on seven holes. The 3,187-yard course is rated as fairly easy. Fees are $10 for adults, $5 for juniors and seniors.

West of downtown near Oak Park, **Columbus Park Golf Course** (5700 West Jackson Boulevard at Central Avenue; ☎ 312-746-5573) is recommended for novices. The 2,753-yard course presents wide, open fairways and large greens. Fees are $10 for adults, $5 for juniors and seniors.

Golf for the Edgy

If you're in town on Memorial Day weekend, don't miss the annual **CUDGEL** (Chicago Urban Devils Golf Enthusiasts' League) urban-golf tournament in the Ukrainian Village and East Ukrainian Village neighborhoods, on the Near Northwest Side. Young hipsters chart their course by, say, shooting at an old dumpster or putting off a discarded mattress. Headquarters is **Tuman's Tavern** (2159 West Chicago Avenue; ☎ 773-782-1400), which in pre-gentrification days was known (in all seriousness) as Tuman's Alcohol Abuse Center. The tourney takes place rain or shine and is grittier in crummy weather. "Non-creative cheating will be punished," the official Web site advises. For more information, visit **www.cudgel.org** or **www.myspace.com/cudgel.**

ROAD BICYCLING AND INLINE SKATING

CHICAGO IS TO BIKES what Sturgis, South Dakota, is to bikers. Mayor Daley and community groups are driving to make Chicago a bike-friendly city. There's even a heated 300-space indoor bicycle-parking facility at the new Millennium Park. One downside of this biking-for-the-masses philosophy is the sense of entitlement many native bikers have developed. Along with bike messengers, most regular Chicago bicyclists ignore traffic signals and oncoming cars (though city streets have clearly marked bike lanes), zigging in and out of traffic like the late Bears running back Walter Payton.

unofficial **TIP**
If you're a recreational rider, stay off Chicago's mean streets. The same goes for inline skaters.

So where's the best place to ride a skinny-tire bike or skate the black ice? You guessed it—the **Lakefront Trail**—which is already chock-full of joggers (see the Running and Walking sections of this chapter). Any excursion on the paved path along Lake Michigan is an out-and-back endeavor, so try to figure out which way the wind blows before starting out. Then ride or skate into a headwind, which becomes a helpful tailwind on the return trip. If you want to avoid the worst of the crowds, try riding or blading north of downtown between Belmont Harbor and the Edgewater neighborhood. The six-mile stretch of trail south of McCormick Place is considered unsafe, in spite of beefed-up bike-mounted police patrols, but if you ride with a friend and go early, you should be okay.

Renting Bikes and Inline Skates

Bike Chicago rents bikes and gear at Millennium Park, Navy Pier, North Avenue Beach, and at far-north Foster Beach, and offers free maps, group guided tours, and delivery to your hotel. For more info, call ☎ 888-245-3929 or check out **www.bikechicago.com.** For inline skates, your best bet is the **Bike and Roll** at North Avenue Beach (☎ 866-736-8224; **www.bikeandroll.com**); rental fees are $8 per hour and $34 per day ($30 per day if you rent online). Closer to downtown, **Londo Mondo** (1100 North Dearborn Street; ☎ 312-751-2794; **www .londomondo.com**) is Chicago's oldest inline-skate shop.

Road Rides

Local roadies who like to go the distance say the best riding is out **Sheridan Road** and north along **Lake Michigan** to **Kenosha, Wisconsin,** a 115-mile round-trip, if you're up for it. A shorter option is to drive to Evanston, park at Northwestern University, and ride north to Sheridan Road and **Fort Sheridan,** about a 30-mile round-trip.

unofficial **TIP**
Although Sheridan Road is scenic and even has a couple of gentle hills, it's not very bicycle-friendly—there's no bike lane and often not much shoulder, and traffic is heavy—so it's a route best left to experienced road cyclists.

MOUNTAIN BIKING

EVEN THOUGH IT'S PAVED, THE **Lakefront Trail** is Chicago's top fat-tire route. But what if you want the feel of mud between your knobbies? Mountain biking has taken Chicago by storm (just as it has everywhere else), but, unfortunately, challenging single-track trails are scarce around the Chicago plains. Bicycles are restricted to designated single-track trails in the immensely popular 14,000-acre **Palos Forest Preserve,** a ravine-sliced forest 20 miles southwest of the city, and the best place around for dedicated fat-tire fanatics to get down in the dirt. Call ☎ 708-771-1330 for a free map showing trails that are okay to ride.

Easy Riding

Other off-road options close to Chicago are considerably tamer than the challenging trails in Palos. Forty miles west of the city, the beautiful **Fox River Trail** provides relative solitude and easy pedaling on a 37-mile stretch of asphalt and crushed limestone that follows the river between Aurora (near Naperville) and Elgin (Metra trains go to Aurora and Geneva along the Fox). **Mill Race Cyclery** in Geneva (11 East State Street; ☎ 630-232-2833; **www.millrace.com**) rents hybrid and mountain bikes for use on the trail. Rates are $6 an hour (two-hour minimum) and $25 a day on weekends. During good weather, stop in for a river-front drink and snack at the Mill Race Inn gazebo across the street.

The **Busse Woods Bicycle Trail** is an 11-mile scenic bike path weaving through the woods and meadows of the 3,700-acre **Ned Brown Preserve,** located in northwestern Cook County about 20 miles from the Loop. The **North Branch Bicycle Trail** starts at Caldwell and Devon avenues in Chicago and continues 20 miles along the North Branch of the Chicago River to the Chicago Botanic Garden. Pack a lunch and picnic in the gardens; freshwater wells can be found along the trail.

For the Hard-core

Local hammerheads say the most adventurous, varied, and accessible single-track action is found at **Kettle Moraine** in Wisconsin, about a 90-minute drive from Chicago. A system of trails originally designed for hikers (and now legal for mountain bikes) features some steep and narrow stuff that will thrill experienced mountain bikers, but might put off first-time riders. For up-to-date trail conditions, call ☎ 262-594-6202. To get there, take I-94 to Wisconsin Highway 50 to US 12. Park at the La Grange General Store, and pick up sandwiches and maps; then head down to County Road H one mile to the main parking area. The parking fee is $10, and there's a $4-per-person trail-use fee (bikers must be 16 or older).

SWIMMING

THE LAKE MICHIGAN SHORE IS LINED with 31 sand beaches for sunning and swimming. These free public beaches are manned with lifeguards daily from June to September, from 9 a.m. to 9 p.m. Lockers are available at the major beaches.

Oak Street Beach, the closest to downtown and only a credit card's throw away from Bloomingdale's, is known as the St. Tropez of the Midwest. It's also the most crowded of the lakefront beaches, as perfect-10 models, bodybuilders, jet-setting flight attendants, all-American Frisbee-tossing frat brothers and sorority sisters, Eurotrash, and ordinary folk blanket the sand on steamy summer weekends. Don't go if you're offended by skimpy clothing. Pedestrians can arrive safely via the underpass across from the Drake Hotel at Michigan Avenue and Oak Street.

unofficial **TIP**
Rule of thumb: the crowds at the popular beaches tend to thin out—and tummies tend to expand— the farther north you go.

In more family-oriented contrast to the nightclub-by-day vibe at Oak Street Beach, **North Avenue Beach** stretches north for a mile, from just above North Avenue to Fullerton Avenue. Farther north, **Montrose Avenue Beach** offers great views of the Chicago skyline.

Unabashed swimmers of all types flock to **Pratt Boulevard Beach** for illegal skinny-dipping in the wee hours. Separated by a seldom-used park, a wide beach, no spotlights, no high-rises, no searchlights, and even a little hill to block views, the dark, sandy beach near Morse Avenue is a good place to take it all off and dive into the surf.

Practical note: Lake Michigan water can be cold, even in August. So check out the Chicago Park District's 50 outdoor and 42 indoor pools. **Portage Park**'s Olympic-size outdoor pool, for example, was constructed for the 1954 Pan-American Games. For a complete list of pools, visit **www.chicagoparkdistrict.com.**

PADDLING

FOR FOLKS IN SEARCH OF WILDERNESS SOLITUDE, the best bet for achieving it in lakebound Chicago is by water. While powerboat traffic can make Lake Michigan a misery of chop, noise, and exhaust on summer afternoons, tranquility in a canoe or kayak can be found early in the morning or late at night. On the main branch of the Chicago River, canoeing is one of the most popular ways of enjoying the architectural delights of the city, while a canoe trek on the North Branch of the river reveals an astounding amount of wildlife for an urban stream. For background and seasonal trips (that include canoe rentals for $45), visit **Friends of the Chicago River** (☎ 312-939-0490; **www.chicagoriver.org**). Headquarters for paddling information and rentals in Chicago is **Chicagoland Canoe Base** (4019 North Narragansett Avenue; ☎ 773-777-1489; **www.chicagolandcanoebase.com**), one of the finest canoe shops in America. Owner Ralph Frese aims to please, sharing nature stories and pointing you to area secrets like the Skokie Lagoons, an urban jewel where boaters can eavesdrop on deer, coyote, fox, and blue heron. The Canoe Base schedules more than 100 organized free trips a year, including an annual New Year's Day paddle down the Chicago River, rain, shine, or snow. Canoe rentals are $45 the first day and $25 each additional day; kayak rentals are $55 the first day and $35 each additional day. Fees include a car-top carrier, paddles, and personal flotation devices, and Ralph and his staff will even load the boat onto your car for you.

WINDSURFING

THE WINDY CITY EARNS ITS EPITHET with nine-mile-an-hour average winds on Lake Michigan. Hey, it ain't Oregon's Columbia River Gorge, but Chicago's boardsailors aren't complaining. **Montrose Beach** is rated Chicago's safest point, with the **South Side Rainbow Beach** next in popularity. Never tried windsurfing? **Windward Sports** (3317 North Clark Street; ☎ 773-472-6868) offers a two-day certification course that will teach you all you need to know for $120. Lessons are given at Greenwood Beach in Evanston, just north of Chicago, where there's a good northeast wind, and sometimes at Wolf Lake, south of Chicago near the Indiana state line; the safe, controlled environment lets novices concentrate on learning skills. Board rentals, offered June through August by Windward Sports at Montrose Beach, are $35 a day. To get a marine weather forecast, call the National Weather Service at ☎ 815-834-0675. Keep in mind that Chicago's quick-change weather can leave novices stranded far from home.

ICE SKATING

Daley Bicentennial Plaza (337 East Randolph; ☎ 312-742-7648) features an outdoor 80-by-135-foot rink with superb views of Lake

Michigan and the Loop. The season starts in November and runs through mid-March. That's a long winter. Hours are 10 a.m. to 9:30 p.m. Monday through Friday and until 5 p.m. weekends. Admission is free; skate rental is $6.

The newest and most popular rink in Chicago is the **McCormick Tribune Ice Skating Rink** at Millennium Park (55 North Michigan Avenue; ☎ 312-742-5222), where scores of pedestrians catch a glimpse of the stars on ice. At this 16,000-square-foot outdoor rink, skaters waltz around to taped music. There's also a warming house and a nearby cafe. Hours are 10 a.m. to 8 p.m. from mid-November through mid-March. Admission is free; skate rental is $10.

DOWNHILL SKIING

THE CLOSEST SKI RESORT to Chicago is **Wilmot Mountain,** about an hour's drive north of O'Hare, just over the Wisconsin state line. The resort features 25 runs with a 230-foot vertical, snowmaking, night skiing until 11 p.m., a pro shop, rentals, instruction, a cafeteria, and a bar. Weather permitting. Wilmot is open from late November through late March; call its local snow-information line at ☎ 773-736-0787, or visit **www.wilmotmountain.net** and click on "Snow Report." For directions and a list of local motels, call ☎ 262-862-2301 or visit the Web site and click on "Directions" or "Motel Listing." To hook up with other downhill skiers on the Chicago prairie, visit the Chicago **Metropolitan Ski Council** at **www.skicmsc.com.**

CROSS-COUNTRY SKIING

WHEN MOTHER NATURE LAYS DOWN A BLANKET of the white stuff, a lot of Chicagoans strap on skinny skis and head for the nearest park or forest preserve or northwest Michigan (90 miles away) to enjoy a day of kicking and gliding. **Camp Sagawau,** about 20 miles southwest of the Loop in the Cook County Palos Forest Preserve District, features a system of groomed cross-country ski trails that traverse a scenic landscape of forest and prairie. The Sag Trail is gentle and ideal for novices, while rolling Ridge Run accommodates intermediate and advanced Nordic skiers. The trails are open whenever there's enough snow on the ground to ski; ski rentals and lessons are also available. Camp Sagawau is on Route 83 east of Archer Avenue at 12545 West 111th Street in Lemont. For more information, snow reports, and directions, call ☎ 630-257-2045.

SPECTATOR SPORTS

A SPORTS-CRAZY TOWN

CHICAGO IS THE MOST PASSIONATE SPORTS TOWN in the United States. Fans aren't as spoiled as New Yorkers, and they're not as rough as those in Boston or Philly. What's more, they're nowhere near as laid-back as fans on the West Coast—heck, Los Angeles doesn't even have an NFL team. Chicago sports fans are renowned for their tenacity, whether it's for the Bears (the most popular team in town), Bulls, White Sox, Cubs, or Blackhawks. The enthusiasm is stoked by a sports culture steeped in tradition and folklore. Consider this: in 1876, the same year General George Custer was shut out by Crazy Horse and Sitting Bull at Little Big Horn, the team that would evolve into today's Chicago Cubs won the National League Championship in its first season of baseball. Since then, Chicagoans have shown an unwavering passion for pro sports.

Other notable events and personalities from Chicago's sports past include the "Black Sox" betting scandal of 1919; Harry Caray, the late Hall of Fame TV and radio sports announcer, singing an off-key "Take Me Out to the Ballgame" during the seventh-inning stretch, first at Old Comiskey Park, then at Wrigley Field; the Bears' 1985 Super Bowl Championship; and Michael Jordan, the world's most famous athlete, leading the Chicago Bulls to consecutive NBA championships. Washington, D.C., has statues of war heroes. Chicago has statues of Michael Jordan, White Sox legend Minnie Minoso, and even Harry Caray (at Wrigley Field) and fellow announcer Jack Brickhouse (on North Michigan Avenue). That's a sports-crazy town.

For visitors, the quintessential Chicago sporting experience is an afternoon baseball game at **Wrigley Field,** home of the Cubs. It's a place where fans feel like they've stepped back in time. Spectators love the ivy-covered walls, the way errant breezes can turn pop-ups into home runs (usually for the opponent), and the opportunity for first-rate people-watching as all sizes, shapes, and classes of Chicagoans root for the Cubs.

The Chicago area has also become a nationally recognized mecca for minor-league baseball. The **Kane County Cougars** (an Oakland A's affiliate) of the Class A Midwest League play to huge crowds in west-suburban Geneva. Independent Northern League teams prosper in Joliet and northwest-suburban Schaumburg, both accessible by train. The Northern League even has a team in Gary, Indiana, just 35 miles south of Chicago.

The city is also blessed with many colleges and universities, which provide a wide array of spectator sports. For current listings and goings-on of both pro and amateur events, check out the daily sports sections of the *Chicago Sun-Times* (**www.suntimes.com/sports**) and the *Chicago Tribune* (**www.chicagotribune.com/sports**).

PRO TEAMS

Baseball

CHICAGO IS HOME to two professional baseball teams: the **Chicago Cubs** (National League), who play at venerable **Wrigley Field** on the North Side (1060 West Addison, in a neighborhood lined

unofficial **TIP**
Buyer beware: scalping is illegal in Chicago. The Web site **www.stubhub.com** is a safer and more reliable ticket source.

with restaurants and bars), and the **Chicago White Sox** (American League), who play at **U.S. Cellular Field** on the South Side (333 West 35th Street, in a mostly residential area). The season starts around the first week of April and continues through early October.

The Cubs, as most baseball fans know, are a testament to Chicagoans' unstoppable allegiance in the face of adversity: the team hasn't won a World Series since 1908. The odds of such a futile streak are off the table. No matter—like the Brooklyn Dodgers of yesteryear, the Cubs (never call them Cubbies) are affectionately embraced by Chicago fans, and picture-perfect Wrigley Field draws nearly 3 million fans each year for a taste of baseball history. Although lights were added to the stadium in 1988, a little less than half the games are still played during the day; aficionados insist it's still the only way to see a game at the park. For schedule information, call ☎ 773-404-2827 or go to **chicago.cubs.mlb.com** (click on "Schedule"); tickets can be ordered at the Web site (click on "Tickets") or by calling ☎ 800-843-2827 (in Illinois) or ☎ 866-652-2827 (outside Illinois). Get tickets as far in advance as possible, but you can try your luck at the ticket window or outside the gates before game time; some fans occasionally sell or give away extra tickets.

Street parking around Wrigley Field is restricted during day games—the city has even installed parking meters that must be fed on Sunday!—so public transportation is the best way for visitors to reach the original "house of blues." Take the Englewood-Howard El line to the Addison Street station.

Geography and family ties divide Cub fans and White Sox fans. Cub fans are considered more upscale and yuppie, while White Sox fans are more working-class and gritty. White Sox fans wear tattoos. Cub fans wear scars.

In 2005 the White Sox broke their own 88-year championship drought by winning the World Series, so tickets can also be hard to come by at U.S. Cellular Field. Unlike Wrigley Field, "the Cell," as Sox devotees proudly call it, features unobstructed views of the action. The upper-deck seats have been scaled down in recent years, but the radical vertical slope should be a point of caution for those scared of heights. Unlike the early-1990s ballparks of its era (Camden Yards in Baltimore, Coors Field in Denver, Miller Park in Milwaukee), U.S. Cellular was built on the cheap. Even the most stalwart White Sox supporter admits that.

To find out when the White Sox are playing at home or to buy tickets, call ☎ 866-769-4263 or go to **chicago.whitesox.mlb.com** (click on "Tickets"). Legal street parking begins around 29th Street; the walk several blocks south to the ballpark through old ethnic neighborhoods is safe and more authentically Chicago than anything near

Wrigley Field. If the Cell is crowded, the official lots are a nightmare to get in and out of. The El train runs along the Dan Ryan Expressway two blocks to the east; get off at 35th Street. Large crowds flocking to and from the game virtually eliminate the chance of getting mugged on the short walk, but watch out for pickpockets working the throngs. They may be Cub fans!

Football

Sports tradition in Chicago isn't restricted to baseball. The **Chicago Bears** point to a football history that goes back to the 1930s. They also have a bigger fan base than the Cubs or White Sox since they are the only National Football League team in town. The Bears won the NFL Championship in 1963 before 45,801 fans when they played at Wrigley Field. They also won the 1985 Super Bowl in New Orleans, and members of that team still maintain celebrity status in Chicago.

Pro gridiron action takes place at a renovated **Soldier Field,** where a colonnade of paired 100-foot concrete Doric columns rise majestically behind fans brave enough to endure icy blasts off Lake Michigan. The field is at 425 East McFetridge Drive (at Lake Shore Drive, just south of the Field Museum). For tickets and information on Bears games, call **Ticketmaster** at ☎ 312-559-1212, Monday through Friday, 9 a.m. to 4 p.m., or go to **www.chicagobears.com/tickets/ticketmaster.asp** and follow the link to the Ticketmaster site. Alas, subscription sales account for most tickets. Your best bet is to locate a subscriber trying to unload a ticket before the game or try the fan ticket site **www.stub hub.com.** Parking is relatively plentiful and nearby. To get to the game by public transportation, take the #146 State Street–North Michigan Avenue bus downtown or the Red or Orange Line El train to the Roosevelt Road station, and walk east.

Basketball

The National Basketball Association's **Chicago Bulls** almost always sell out. The team plays in the **United Center,** a $170-million arena that seats 21,500 and is outfitted with 217 luxury sky boxes. For game times, call ☎ 312-455-4000; to purchase tickets, call ☎ 800-462-2849; for online schedule and ticket info, go to **www.nba.com/bulls.** The season starts in October and runs through April—later when the Bulls make the playoffs. Tickets go on sale in September for the season, and some games sell out in a few weeks. You're more likely to get tickets when the Bulls play lower-tier teams. The United Center is located at 1901 West Madison Street, west of the Loop; take the #20 Madison Street bus.

A neat family option is the **Chicago Sky,** the city's entry in the Women's National Basketball Association. Fans can get up close and personal with the players, and they witness a style of team basketball you sometimes don't see in the NBA. The Sky plays from May to

August at the University of Illinois at Chicago (UIC) Pavilion (525 South Racine Avenue) on the Near West Side. For tickets, call ☎ 866-759-9622 or e-mail **tickets@chicagosky.net.**

Hockey

Loud, gregarious fans like to watch the **Chicago Blackhawks** of the National Hockey League mix it up on the ice just as much as they themselves like to mix it up in the stands. Longtime penny-pinching owner Bill Wirtz died in 2007, and the franchise was taken over by his son Rocky. There is rebirth in the air as Rocky has put the Hawks back on local television (his father thought televised audiences would detract from attendance) and hired front-office marketing staff from the megapopular Chicago Cubs. The Blackhawks have cross-promoted with both Chicago baseball teams, and it isn't uncommon to find an ex-Cub dropping the puck before the game. Blackhawks tickets used to be easy to get. No so anymore.

The Blackhawks own three NHL championships: 1924, 1938, and 1961. Yes, 1961 was a long time ago.

The team shares quarters with the Chicago Bulls in the United Center, at 1901 West Madison Street; take the #20 Madison Street bus. For schedules and game times, call ☎ 312-455-7000; for tickets, call ☎ 312-559-1212 or go to **blackhawks.nhl.com** and click on "Tickets." The season runs from October through April—unless the Hawks are fortunate enough to get in the playoffs.

Many Blackhawks fans love winning hockey so much that they've defected to the **Chicago Wolves,** a successful minor-league team that plays at the **Allstate Arena** (6920 North Mannheim Road in Rosemont, near O'Hare International Airport), sometimes outdrawing its major-league counterpart and usually making the American Hockey League playoffs. The Wolves' season runs from October to April. Tickets are cheaper than those for the Blackhawks; call Ticketmaster at ☎ 312-559-1212 or visit **www.chicagowolves.com/tickets.**

COLLEGE SPORTS

CHICAGO'S ONLY DIVISION I (Big Ten) football and basketball representatives are the **Northwestern University Wildcats,** who play in Evanston, just north of the Chicago border. Gridiron action takes place on Ryan Field (1501 Central Avenue). Basketball is played at McGaw Hall–Welsch-Ryan Arena (2705 Ashland Avenue). For tickets and schedules, call ☎ 847-491-2287 or visit **www.nusports.com.**

Other college basketball teams include the **DePaul Blue Demons,** who play at Allstate Arena (6920 North Mannheim Road in Rosemont; ☎ 773-325-7526; **www.depaulbluedemons.com**); the **Loyola Ramblers,** who provide on-the-court action at Loyola University Chicago, in the Rogers Park neighborhood (6511 North Winthrop Street; ☎ 773-508-9653; **www.loyolaramblers.com**); and the **University** of Illinois at Chicago Flames, who hold court at the UIC Pavilion (525 South Racine Avenue; ☎ 312-413-8421; www.uicflames.com).

HORSE RACING

FOR MORE THAN 80 YEARS, **Arlington Park** has been a Chicago thoroughbred-racing tradition. The horses run May through October; the track is located at Euclid Avenue and Wilkie Road in Arlington Heights (about 30 miles northwest of the Loop). For more information, call ☎ 847-385-7500 or visit www.arlingtonpark.com.

Hawthorne Race Course in Cicero features harness-racing excitement and thoroughbred racing. The track is at 3501 South Laramie Avenue, about five miles southwest of the Loop. For post times and more information, call ☎ 708-780-3700 or visit www.hawthorne racecourse.com.

OFF-TRACK BETTING AND RIVERBOAT CASINOS

CHICAGO'S DOWNTOWN OFF-TRACK-BETTING emporiums have closed—the real estate has become too valuable—but folks allergic to real horses and mud can still play the ponies at the excellent **Trackside Chicago** on the Near North Side (901 West Weed Street; ☎ 312-787-9600; www.arlingtonpark.com/trackside). Admission is $2. There are dining and beverage options, and the joint is jumping 364 days a year.

Riverboat gambling is as close as an hour away from downtown Chicago. **Hollywood Casino Aurora** features slots, table games, dining, Las Vegas–style entertainment (Frank Sinatra appeared for the last time in the Chicago area here), and movie memorabilia. Hollywood's boat (now permanently docked) is open from 9:30 a.m. to 4:30 a.m. on weekdays (until 5:30 a.m. weekends). Admission is free. Patrons must be age 21 and older; be prepared to show photo ID. For more information and directions, call ☎ 800-888-7777 or visit www.holly woodcasinoaurora.com.

The **Horseshoe Hammond** offers nearly 3,200 slots, a poker room, and nearly 100 table games in Hammond, Indiana, 30 miles southeast of downtown. A permanently docked barge, the casino is open 24 hours a day, seven days a week. Admission is free. Shuttle service to and from the casino is available from a number of locations throughout Chicago; call ☎ 866-711-7463 or visit www.horseshoehammond.com for more information.

Harrah's Joliet Casino, docked on the Des Plaines River (151 North Joliet Road, southwest of Chicago), operates daily from 8 a.m. to 6 a.m. Admission is free. Call ☎ 800-427-7247 or visit www.harrahs joliet.com for more information.

PART ELEVEN

ENTERTAINMENT
and
NIGHTLIFE

CHICAGO *after* DARK

CHICAGO NIGHTLIFE IS FULL OF POSSIBILITIES. You can be wicked or blue, mild or wild. You can laugh and dance and taste romance. The city has a defined work ethic and sports swagger, but when it comes to nightlife, try as it may, Chicago's just not glamorous enough to have attitude. (In Chicago, after all, TV anchors are regarded as celebrities.) So come as you are. You *will* fit in.

Chicago is a hands-on city. A true Chicagoan plays 16-inch softball—without the glove. A real Chicago woman drinks a 16-ounce beer—from the bottle. An authentic Chicago nightcrawler makes the rounds—without a doubt.

For the maximum Chicago experience, check out neighborhood bars, diners, music clubs, and theater groups. Stay away from chains like the Cheesecake Factory and T.G.I. Friday's. Skip any nightclub where people are waiting in long lines behind velvet ropes. Chicagoans only wait in line for smelt-fishing licenses and Cubs tickets.

Where New York and Los Angeles are about a "scene," Chicago is about a spirit. It's easy to get things done here. The late Irish bartender Butch McGuire redefined the Near North Side of Chicago by opening America's first true singles bar in 1961. Louisiana transplant and blues legend Buddy Guy was one of the first to put a nightclub in the once-seedy South Loop. In recent years, young Russian immigrant Jerry Kleiner regentrified the warehouse districts of the Near West Side and the South Loop with his bars and restaurants. His template? The Chicago speakeasies from 1880 to 1920.

You drink from that gritty spirit in Chicago.

As of January 2008, however, you can no longer smoke in Chicago's public places. The new law has odd repercussions that are, so, well, Chicago. For example, producers of the hit musical *Jersey Boys* had to eliminate smoking from their show when it played here. A Chicago alderman tried to float an exemption to the no-smoking city ordinance, reasoning that the smoke must go on.

Urban blues, soul, alternative country, and house music began as determined undercurrents of Chicago culture. Today, they are part of America's music lexicon. The **Second City** improvisational troupe, named because of the shadow cast by New York (for all their notorious toughness, Chicagoans still get squirrelly about the Big Apple), has become world famous, a direct influence on *Saturday Night Live*—in New York.

Architect Louis Sullivan's beautiful **Auditorium Theatre** tumbled into disrepair for more than 20 years, but in the mid-1960s Chicagoans came together to save the historic palace. In recent years, performers like Elvis Costello, Bob Dylan, and Radiohead have appeared at the Auditorium.

In the late 1990s, Chicago's downtown theater district was reborn with the renovation of classic movie palaces like the **Bank of America Theatre,** the **Oriental Theatre,** and the **Cadillac Palace**—all within walking distance of each other. The historic **Goodman Theatre** has opened an extravagant two-theater space downtown.

All the city's major sports teams carry storied legacies of coming back from one disaster or another. Even though the Chicago White Sox won the 2005 World Series, their fans still whine about being second fiddle to the Chicago Cubs. Chicagoans aren't shy about their opinions. It is that clarion that generations of them have followed through the night.

LIVE ENTERTAINMENT

THERE'S A FEISTY, ECLECTIC ETHIC AT THE HEART of Chicago's live-entertainment scene, which can be divided into seven categories: rock, jazz, country, blues, cabaret, theater, and classical music. According to the Chicago Music Commission, 250 venues in the city present live acts. The profiles of the clubs that follow focus on live music, dance clubs, and storied neighborhood taverns.

Nightly schedules of live-music clubs, comedy clubs, and theatrical productions, as well as comprehensive listings of movie show times and other events, are printed in the *Chicago Sun-Times*'s Friday "Weekend" section, the *Chicago Tribune*'s "Friday" section, the free *New City* and *Chicago Reader* alternative newspapers, *The Onion*, and *Chicago* and *Time Out Chicago* magazines. Among the best online resources are **Centerstage Chicago** (**www.centerstagechicago .com**), **Metromix** (**chicago.metromix.com**), and the *Time Out Chicago* Web site (**www.timeout.com/chicago**).

LIVE ROCK

CHICAGO IS THE INDEPENDENT-ROCK CAPITAL of America. A slew of critically acclaimed record labels such as Bloodshot, Touch and Go, Thrill Jockey, Minty Fresh, Drag City, Wax Trax, and others have created a scene that filters through the city's live-music clubs. Popular rock figures like Billy Corgan (Smashing Pumpkins), Jeff Tweedy (Wilco), and Jon Langford (Mekons, Waco Brothers) call Chicago home. Liz Phair's career tanked when she left her native Chicago for Los Angeles.

For the last four summers, Chicago's **Grant Park** has hosted the internationally acclaimed **Lollapalooza** festival, featuring international stars such as hometown rapper Kanye West, Chicago-based Wilco, Red Hot Chili Peppers, Gnarls Barkley, Rage Against the Machine, and many others. The 2008 festival raised an estimated $12.3 million for the Parkways Foundation, which benefits Chicago city parks.

Metro (3730 North Clark Street; ☎ 773-549-0203; **www.metro chicago.com**) is the mother lode for the indie-rock movement. Owner Joe Shanahan has consistently championed up-and-coming bands in his lovingly sleazy theater-cabaret in the shadows of Wrigley Field. Metro is heavily into alternative and grunge with a sprinkling of national acts such as Lucinda Williams and Tom Jones. Shanahan gave the Smashing Pumpkins their big break, allowing them to open for bands like Jane's Addiction. Demographics slide around as expected: young hipsters for alternative shows, old hippies for Dylan-esque gigs. Shanahan also owns the smaller **Double Door** (1572 North Milwaukee Avenue; ☎ 773-489-3160; **www.doubledoor.com**), which is a noisy dump. You're in luck if you go on a night when the young neighborhood crowd is actually listening to the music.

A more connective experience can be had down the street at **Phyllis' Musical Inn** (1800 West Division Street; ☎ 773-486-9862). Portions of the Michael J. Fox–Joan Jett film *Light of Day* were shot in this sweet, ramshackle, 100-seat family-run bar. After World War II and through the early 1960s, West Division Street was known as "Polish Broadway" because more than a dozen nightclubs on the strip featured live polka music. Open since 1954, Phyllis' is the last remnant of that era. The bar features alternative country and rock before an easygoing audience that generally falls into the 20-to-30-year-old age group.

One of the newer entries on the progressive-rock landscape is **The Abbey** (3420 West Grace at Elston; ☎ 773-478-4408; **www.abbeypub .com**). This old-school Irish pub's booking policy ranges from cutting-edge national acts like Pere Ubu and Mark Eitzel to Chicago-based alternative-country and rock bands. Sight lines can get a little fuzzy when the pub fills up, but a balcony affords a better view. The Abbey gets bonus points for live rugby matches broadcast via satellite on Sunday morning and a dinner and weekend breakfast menu. The event dictates the audience—young slackers come for the altrock shows; toothless beer-drinkers roll in for the Sunday-morning rugby sessions.

During the 1970s and 1980s, the Lincoln Park neighborhood was a focal point of live rock and blues, and the **Wise Fools Pub** was a smart player in that scene. The club has reopened in its original location at 2270 North Lincoln Avenue (☎ 773-929-1300; **www.wisefools.com**). You won't catch many big names playing the 250-seat listening room, but plenty of local pop and rock bands play for a crowd that includes students from nearby DePaul University. You can also catch a sense of history: George Thorogood made his Chicago debut in this room in 1979, and blues queen Koko Taylor used to hold court here.

The Wrigleyville neighborhood (near Wrigley Field, of course) is the home of one of America's oldest live-reggae clubs, **The Wild Hare** (3530 North Clark Street; ☎ 773-327-4273; **www.wildharereggae .com**). Co-owned by former members of the Ethiopian band Dallol, who toured behind reggae superstar Ziggy Marley, this cozy nightclub has presented live music and lots of dancing seven nights a week since 1979. It has evolved into a cultural mecca for transplanted Jamaicans and Africans. And the joint never runs short of Red Stripe and rum.

Just a few blocks south of Wrigleyville is **Schubas Tavern** (3159 North Southport Avenue; ☎ 773-525-2508; **www.schubas.com**), a very comfortable restaurant, bar, and music room that's heavy on acoustic acts and small jazz outfits. American roots artists such as Steve Earle, Steve Forbert, and Alex Chilton have performed for audiences of all ages in the pristine 100-seat club.

Other essential (and deeply intimate) rooms on the alternative rock–pop circuit include **Martyrs'** (3855 North Lincoln Avenue; ☎ 773-404-9494; **www.martyrslive.com**), the grungy **Empty Bottle** (1035 North Western Avenue; ☎ 773-276-3600; **www.emptybottle.com**), and **The California Clipper** (1002 North California Avenue; ☎ 773-384-2547; **www.californiaclipper.com**), a delightfully restored 1940s cocktail lounge that also sails off into live jazz and alternative country.

The Chicago area (don't call it Chicagoland) has several mega- and medium-sized rock-concert venues. Chicagoans love summer because of the temperamental nature of the other seasons, so the big outdoor sheds are very popular. The 28,000-seat **First Midwest Bank Amphitheatre** (formerly the Tweeter Center; 19100 South Ridgeland Avenue at Flossmoor Road in south suburban Tinley Park; ☎ 708-614-1616; **www.firstmidwestbankamphitheatre.com**) is one of the largest outdoor concert facilities in the country. Acts like Bruce Springsteen and John Mellencamp have played to full houses here even though the acoustics are below average. Bring binoculars—pavilion seats can be far away.

The **Ravinia Festival,** in the northern suburb of Highland Park (☎ 847-266-5000; **www.ravinia.org**), is older, prettier, and more inti-mate. The focus is generally on classical music, although light-rock and

88888

roots acts pop up. Ravinia has a capacity for 15,000 fans on lawn seating and 3,500 in a rustic pavilion. **Skyline Stage at Navy Pier** (☎ 312-595-7437; **www.navypier.com**) is east of downtown and just off Lake Michigan, which means it isn't a bad idea to bring a windbreaker.

In recent summers, some acts (like Jimmy Buffett and Eric Clapton's Crossroads Guitar Festival) have elected to play the three-year-old **Toyota Park** (7000 South Harlem Avenue at 71st Street, Bridgeview; ☎ 708-594-7200; **www.toyotapark.com**) over First Midwest Bank Amphitheatre. Also a world-class soccer stadium, the 28,000-seat venue has better acoustics than First Midwest and is closer to the city, in near-southwest suburban Bridgeview. A tip from the locals: Bridgeview is ten minutes from Midway Airport. For big concerts, fans in the city can take the CTA Orange Line to Midway and catch shuttle buses to Toyota Park.

unofficial **TIP**
Don't let the Allstate Arena's suburban location put you off: it's also accessible by the Chicago El.

The home of the Bulls and the Blackhawks, the 22,000-seat **United Center** (1901 West Madison Street; ☎ 312-455-4500; **www.unitedcenter.com**) also books major stadium-rock and pop acts. Although the arena only opened in 1995, Neil Diamond, Bob Dylan, and Barbra Streisand have already graced its stage.

Built in 1980, the **Allstate Arena** (6920 North Mannheim Road, in Rosemont, next to O'Hare Airport; ☎ 847-635-6601; **www.allstatearena.com**) also features superstar-caliber acts, including big names in country music. The arena holds up to 18,500 folks for music events.

Several miles west of the Allstate Arena, in Hoffman Estates, is the **Sears Centre Arena,** the Chicago area's newest venue. The 11,800-seat multipurpose arena hosts midsized concerts and is the home of the Chicago Hounds of the United Hockey League and the Chicago Shamrox of the National Lacrosse League. The Sears Centre is between the Illinois 59 and Beverly Road exits from the Northwest Tollway. It's not a Ticketmaster affiliate, so call ☎ 888-732-7784 or check out **www.searscentre.com** for ticket info.

Charter One Pavilion at Northerly Island (☎ 312-540-2667; or call Ticketmaster, ☎ 312-559-1212; **www.charteronepavilion.com**) is situated on a 90-acre peninsula along the shore of Lake Michigan. The four-year-old, 7,500-seat facility comes down during the winter (the site will eventually be developed for parkland). Featured acts have included the likes of Jack Johnson, Willie Nelson, and Tom Petty.

unofficial **TIP**
Getting to Charter One Pavilion at Northerly Island is almost as hard as remembering its name. There is no parking near the site—fans park by Soldier Field and take shuttle buses or grab a free trolley. But most folks walk from wherever they left their car.

Midrange rock venues include the **Park West** (322 West Armitage Avenue; ☎ 773-929-1322; **www.jamusa.com/venues/parkwest**), a former strip club turned elegant 800-seat music room; the 1,200-seat **Vic Theatre** (3145 North Sheffield Avenue; ☎ 773-472-0449; **www.victheatre.com**), a vaudeville house built in 1912; the cavernous **Riviera Theatre** (4746 North Racine Avenue at Lawrence and Broadway avenues; ☎ 773-275-1012; **www.jamusa.com/venues/riviera**), where the late Warren Zevon fell off the stage into the orchestra pit during his drinking days; and the crazy **Aragon Ballroom** (1106 West Lawrence Avenue; ☎ 773-561-9500; **www.aragon.com**). A popular spot for big-band dancing in the 1930s and 1940s, the Aragon has enjoyed a resurgence. During the 1990s it was best known for booking head-banging metal music, but the offerings have recently branched out to reggaetón, norteño music, and even live boxing in air-conditioned comfort. A $1-million renovation has made the 20,000-square-foot ballroom (capacity 5,500) sing again: the Spanish-Moorish stucco and gold-leaf columns have been repainted, and the terra-cotta arches have been repaired.

unofficial **TIP**
Tickets for shows at all these venues are usually available at **Ticketmaster** (☎ 312-559-1212; **www.ticketmaster.com**), but be on guard for service charges and handling fees.

JAZZ

Chicago's live-jazz scene has made a lively migration from downtown clubs and hotels into the neighborhoods. The first stop on any jazz lover's tour should be the historic **Green Mill Jazz Club** (4802 North Broadway Avenue; ☎ 773-878-5552; **www.greenmilljazz.com**), the anchor of the funky Uptown neighborhood (see profile, page 348). Al Capone hung out here; check out the hideaway trapdoor behind the bar. There's also a cemented underground tunnel between the Green Mill and the equally historic Aragon Ballroom. (Old-timers claim Capone's gang ran hooch through here.) Chicago's best-known jazz musicians—like Patricia Barber and Kurt Elling—have held court in this colorful club.

A fixture of the South Side, the **Velvet Lounge** has moved from its legendary location on South Indiana up to Chicago's old Motor Row district (67 East Cermak Road; ☎ 312-791-9050; **www.velvetlounge.net**). This is actually a better location for visitors, halfway between McCormick Place to the east and Chinatown to the west. Owner Fred Anderson, an influential jazz saxophonist, personally helped move artifacts from the old Velvet, such as the legendary chandeliers, Schlitz signs, and the "Velvet Lady" painting. Sight lines and acoustics in the new club are much better than those in the Velvet's previous century-old digs. Anderson knows what he is doing: he's a founding member of the South Side's respected Association for the Advancement of Creative Musicians.

The most dependable downtown jazz spot is **Andy's** (11 East Hubbard Street; ☎ 312-642-6805; **www.andysjazzclub.com**), a soulful bar and grill that's known for vibrant after-work sets featuring top local players. This is the only place in Chicago where you can hear traditional jazz. A little farther north, **Green Dolphin Street** (2200 North Ashland Avenue; ☎ 773-395-0066; **www.jazzitup.com**), named after the classic tune "On Green Dolphin Street," features straight-ahead local jazz with occasional salsa and blues. A cool decor is defined by a lofty ceiling, wood paneling, blinds, and white-clothed tables. The club seats around 120 guests and serves appetizer-type snacks and drinks; there is also an adjacent restaurant.

The legendary **Jazz Showcase** is back in the game in the historic Dearborn Station building in the South Loop (806 South Plymouth Court; ☎ 312-360-0234; **www.jazzshowcase.com**). This club opened in 1947 several blocks north at Clark Street and Grand Avenue. Dizzy Gillespie headlined the Showcase back in the day, and these days the 170-seat room features the likes of Ravi Coltrane, Larry Coryell, and McCoy Tyner. The sight lines are clear, and the sound is pristine.

For something completely different, catch the weekend jazz sets at the **Negro League Café** (301 East 43rd Street; ☎ 773-536-7000; **www.thenegroleaguecafe.info**), a South Side soul-food restaurant and lounge that honors black baseball players. The 5,000-square-foot cafe is on a dicey street corner in the Bronzeville neighborhood, so take a cab here instead of public transportation.

COUNTRY AND WESTERN

ALTHOUGH CHICAGO IS MOST CLOSELY IDENTIFIED with blues and jazz, it once was a mecca for country music. During the 1940s and 1950s, country artists from the South were drawn to Chicago since it was the home of WLS Radio's *National Barn Dance* (1924–1960). For its last 30 years, the live-music show was broadcast from the Eighth Street Theater (now the site of the Conrad Hilton International Ballroom). The hardscrabble aura of the big industrial city attracted a blue-collar population that worked hard and played hard. During the 1950s, the 3000 block of West Madison Street alone (not far from the current United Center) contained five live-country joints with evocative names such as the Casanova Club and the Wagon Wheel.

You can still feel this gritty spirit in the working-class Uptown neighborhood by visiting **Carol's Pub** (4659 North Clark Street; ☎ 773-334-2402; open until 4 a.m. Friday through Sunday). Once a late-1960s discotheque, Carol's has been a lovingly seedy honky-tonk since the early 1970s. For a quarter century it was a well-kept secret among Chicago's hard-core country-music community, but in the last couple of years Carol's has been discovered by everyone. The band Diamondback plays straight-ahead country on weekends (no cover). These days it's not uncommon to see a tourist trolley drop people off in front of Carol's. It's safer than it used to be, but the music is still dangerous.

For something a little slicker, the **Horseshoe** (4115 North Lincoln Avenue; ☎ 773-549-9292; **www.myspace.com/horseshoechicago**) books occasional bluegrass and rockabilly acts. The faux-cowboy atmosphere is accented by chicken wire, wood, and Western kitsch on the walls. Bathroom sinks are set on moonshine stills. There's pool and darts for restless hearts. Barbecue specials like baby-back ribs and smoked chicken are served, and there's a Sunday-morning bluegrass brunch. The club gets extra points for its popularity with Chicago's roller-derby queens.

It's inconveniently located in the Far North suburbs, but the **Sundance Saloon** (300 Lakehurst Road, Waukegan; ☎ 847-887-0858; **www.sundancesalooon.com**) isn't just another watering hole: it's reportedly the longest-running country-and-western bar in the state of Illinois. Opened in 1975 as Mickey's Honky Tonk, the club moved a few years ago from its longtime location in Mundelein to a bigger space in nearby Waukegan. The Sundance boasts 62,000 square feet on two levels, a huge stage, and a 4,000-square-foot dance floor, plus two restaurants and a gift shop. The saloon is a half mile off of Interstate 94, just south of Six Flags Great America amusement park; several hotels are nearby. The Sundance opens Tuesday through Friday at 5 p.m. and Saturday at 7 p.m.; no one under age 21 is allowed in the club area.

LIVE BLUES

CHICAGO BLUES ARE AT THE PROVERBIAL CROSSROADS. As young musicians continue to explore rap, hip-hop, and house, the traditional blues scene is faced with a talent void, and clubs have suffered. Among the ones that have closed in recent years is the legendary **Checkerboard Lounge** on East 43rd Street. Once the city's premier blues club for tourists, the Checkerboard was the home base for upstarts like Buddy Guy and Earl Hooker in the late 1950s and early 1960s when they arrived in Chicago. The **New Checkerboard Lounge** has opened in Hyde Park (5201 South Harper Avenue; ☎ 773-684-1472), but all it shares with its predecessor is the name. The room is bigger and cleaner, and live jazz and blues are featured. On the walls are pictures of the original Checkerboard, including a photo of the historic evening when the Rolling Stones dropped in to jam with their hero, Muddy Waters. Those days are gone. How do we know? As in the rest of Chicago's clubs, smoking isn't allowed at the New Checkerboard, which means Keith Richards would be denied admittance.

Any essential live-blues experience still reflects the city's segregated tradition: most whites and tourists go to North Side clubs, most African Americans to South Side clubs. It's been that way since the Hoochie Coochie Man was a kid.

unofficial **TIP**
South Side (and West Side) blues shows are casual—there is more sitting-in on sets, and the artists tend to hang out in the street with their friends. North Side shows are more structured, have better sound, and in general feature higher-quality musicianship because the artists are better paid.

Today, though, there aren't as many differences between North Side and South Side shows as there were in the 1960s and 1970s. These days, **Buddy Guy's Legends** is the city's leading blues club, not just because it's owned by the master bluesman, but because its South Loop location attracts fans from all walks of life (see full profile on page 342).

Here's the best of what's left:

Lee's Unleaded Blues (7401 South Chicago Avenue; ☎ 773-493-3477) has replaced the Checkerboard as the definitive South Side blues experience. Known as the Queen Bee until 1983, Lee's has a warm and outgoing crowd. Johnny Drummer and the Starlights, the weekend house band, stretch the definition of the blues by exploring soul, 1950s rock, and country idioms. The joint is small, which means it's always jumping. And the fact that Lee's looks like Christmas 365 days a year—with red carpeting and red tinsel around the 75-seat room—only adds to the merriment. There's ample street parking as well as valet, and while there's no cover, there is a two-drink minimum (the cocktails tend to be watered down, so stick to beer and shots).

Rosa's Lounge (3420 West Armitage Avenue; ☎ 773-342-0452; **www.rosaslounge.com**) celebrates traditional values in the middle of a transitional Hispanic neighborhood. The 150-person-capacity club is owned by Italian-born blues drummer Tony Manguilo and his mother, Rosa. Their passionate approach to American blues stretches from a tenderly refurbished mahogany bar to a spacious stage and impeccable sight lines. Shows start at 9:30 p.m. on weekdays and at 10 p.m. on weekends. Street parking all around.

B.L.U.E.S. (2519 North Halsted Street; ☎ 773-528-1012; **www .chicagobluesbar.com**) is the longest-running North Side club with the same location and ownership. You can arrive at any time of the night (or morning) and be assured a good shot at the stage, even though the room—which holds 100 people max—is usually crowded. B.L.U.E.S. features top-notch local bands every night of the year, attracting a throng of international and domestic tourists. Trying to find a place to park in this neighborhood might give you the blues, but valet parking is available on weekends. And don't fret: B.L.U.E.S. doesn't stand for anything in particular.

Finally, **Kingston Mines** (2548 North Halsted Street; ☎ 773-477-4646; **www.kingstonmines.com**) draws hard-core fans from B.L.U.E.S. across the street because it serves liquor later (until 5 a.m. Saturday and 4 a.m. Sunday). Local blues acts alternate on two stages, so there's rarely any dead time. This club has been around for more than 25 years in various North Side locations.

COMEDY AND INTERACTIVE THEATER

CHICAGO USED TO BE KNOWN JUST FOR ITS COMEDY CLUBS. But if you can't beat 'em with the shtick, join 'em: interactive theater has become popular in Chicago humor circles as well. Now in its 14th year at the **Pipers Alley Theater** (230 West North Avenue, directly behind The Second City), *Tony 'n' Tina's Wedding* (☎ 312-664-8844; **www.tonylovestina.com**) is a 2-hour-and-45-minute production with 32 cast members, a huge set, and an Italian buffet dinner. Audience members ("guests") enter a beautiful chapel for a wedding ceremony, followed by a dinner and dance reception (complete with a live band) that goes haywire. The wedding ceremony is scripted, but the rest of the show is improvised.

Tony 'n' Tina's Wedding features lots of hometown nuance. Many local media and sports figures—the biggest celebrities Chicago has to offer—have appeared in the show, and the occasional big name like Frankie Avalon drops in for a short residency. *Tony 'n' Tina's Wedding* does such a good job of meshing actors with the audience that you can't always tell who's who. Performances are Wednesday and Thursday at 7:30 p.m.; Friday at 8 p.m.; Saturday at 7 p.m.; and Sunday at 5 p.m.; matinees are the first Wednesday of the month at 12:30 p.m. Tickets are $55 to $65 per person.

For more improv, check out **iO** (formerly the ImprovOlympic), just down the street from Wrigley Field (3541 North Clark; ☎ 773-880-0199; **chicago.ioimprov.com**). Founded in 1981, iO has gained fame as a comedy training center and performance venue for long-form improvisation, including the house specialty, the "Harold." Attend a show and you just might see a star in the making; *Saturday Night Live* consistently hires comedians who have trained here, including Mike Myers, Tina Fey, Tim Meadows, Seth Meyers, and Rachel Dratch.

ComedySportz is known for its rat-a-tat-tat improv games performed by two teams in "heated" competition. Be forewarned: the pace can get as dizzy as a Cubs rebuilding plan. ComedySportz performs above Ann Sather's Restaurant (929 West Belmont Avenue; ☎ 773-549-8080; **www.comedysportzchicago.com**). Performances are Thursday at 8 p.m.; Friday at 8 and 10 p.m.; and Saturday at 6, 8, and 10 p.m. Tickets are $21.

Blue Man Group (Briar Street Theatre, 3133 North Halsted Street; ☎ 773-348-4000; **www.blueman.com**) is a popular roadside attraction of three cobalt-blue chrome-domed dudes who guide an audience of mostly tourists through a multisensory show of animation, percussive music, art, and vaudeville. Blue Man Group's 1999 debut album *Audio* was nominated for a Best Pop Instrumental Grammy. A must-see if you're into splattering paint, flying mushrooms, and progressive music. Main-floor seats are $64; balcony seats are $49 and $54. The gently interactive revue has been a local ritual since 1997. If you can't get a ticket here, other Blue Man groups perform in Boston, Las Vegas, New York, Orlando, Berlin, London, and Toronto.

DANCE CLUBS

CHICAGO HAS ALWAYS HAD A LEG UP on the rest of the country when it comes to dancing. Popular 1960s soul dances like the Monkey Time and Woodbine Twine came out of Chicago; in

unofficial **TIP**
Of the dance-oriented clubs mentioned here, some are new, others are standbys. But be aware that the scene is volatile—these clubs go in and out of style more than any other kind of Chicago nightspot, so be sure to call ahead.

the 1980s, spiky-haired punks were pogoing at rank, now long-gone, storefront clubs; and during the 1990s, industrial house music went worldwide after originating on the Near South and West sides.

Over the last few years, the gritty Lake Street corridor has been a breeding ground for cutting-edge dance clubs. Set under the noisy El tracks, this warehouse neighborhood is a cheap cab ride from downtown. That's the only thing you'll find cheap here.

Transit (1431 West Lake Street; ☎ 312-491-8600; **www.transit -usa.com**), an upscale dance club that is part of a 10,000-square-foot complex, features minimalist decor in a maximum setting. DJs deliver heavy doses of funk and R&B with no surrender, and the dense beats can boggle your mind after a few hours. With weekend covers as high as $20, Transit is not cheap—which, of course, keeps out the riffraff.

Several blocks north of Lake Street, **Ohm** (1958 West North Avenue; ☎ 773-954-4060; **www.ohmnightlife.com**) is the centerpiece of nightlife in Wicker Park. It offers progressive micro-house, techno, and drum-and-bass music in a traditional setting. A dark, mysterious mood is set by the clandestine entry from an alley behind the Tavern (formerly Border Line Tap). Ohm consists of three bars and three dance floors, which helps handle overflow weekend crowds. Be forewarned: it's tough to park in Wicker Park on weekends.

Dancing and punk-inspired DJs reign at **Angels & Kings** (710 North Clark Street; ☎ 312-482-8600, **www.angelsandkings.com/ chicago**), part-owned by Pete Wentz, bassist of the popular rock band Fall Out Boy. Bench seats line the dark bar, suggesting that everyone get in the game, and the walls are lined with celebrity mug shots of James Brown, Janis Joplin, and many others. There's also an Angels & Kings in New York City, also co-owned by Wentz.

Berlin (954 West Belmont Avenue; ☎ 773-348-4975; **www.berlin chicago.com**) is a beloved icon for the gay community, although everyone is welcome. The futuristic storefront dance club has been operating for 18 years in a convenient location just steps from the Belmont El stop (Red Line). Contemporary house, acid jazz, and neo-soul are accented by videos projected on big screens.

Le Passage (937 North Rush Street; ☎ 312-255-0022; **www.le passage.com**) harks back to the days when Rush Street was one of America's premier nightlife districts. The medium-sized club is located down a 1960s cobblestone alley, while the interior is peppered with *Playboy*-esque velvet couches and 14-karat-gold-leaf walls. Le Passage is a popular destination for touring rock stars staying along the Magnificent Mile.

Stepping

A tradition in Chicago's African American community, stepping is a stylized ballroom-dance form—with attitude. A smooth, clearly defined beat is what sets stepping apart from other dances. Classic steppers' songs include "Love's Gonna Last" by Jeffrey and "Windows" by The Whispers. Chicago steppers congregate at the legendary **Fifty Yard Line** (69 East 75th Street; ☎ 773-846-0005), an easy-to-find place (just east off the Dan Ryan Expressway) that mixes a sports theme with a dance theme. The club has 20 television sets and snacks like wings, popcorn shrimp, and perch. Jeans, sneakers, and toboggans aren't allowed after 9 p.m. And don't request any Jessica Simpson.

LIVE "GREENS"

CHICAGO WILL ALWAYS BE KNOWN FOR THE BLUES, but contemporary Chicago is the greenest urban center in America. In 2008, Chicago ranked first among U.S. and Canadian cities in terms of square green roof footage installed in one year, according to the nonprofit Green Roofs for Healthy Cities (**www.greenroofs.org**).

Uncommon Ground is on top of the green-nightclub movement with the original 18-year-old location at 3800 North Clark Street (a block north of Wrigley Field; ☎ 773-929-3680) and a newer venue at 1401 West Devon Avenue (two blocks west of Loyola University on the Far North Side; ☎ 773-465-9801; **www.uncommonground.com**). Both spots present national and local acoustic music, world and indie-pop music, generally without a cover. The clubs are adventurously booked by David Chavez, the respected former music director of HotHouse in Chicago. Uncommon Ground also includes showings from local artists in a rotation of two to three month residencies at each location.

The 1,500-square-foot performance space on Devon is larger and parking is much easier than at the location by Wrigley Field, even in the off-season (take a cab or the El if you want to check out the original Wrigleyville location). Breakfast, brunch, lunch, and dinner are served daily at each venue, with a strong emphasis on regional organic ingredients. The Uncommon Ground bars include house-infused cocktails, an international beer menu, and an eclectic wine list. Action at the Devon Uncommon Ground spins around a century-old Deco bar.

But the real hook at the Devon location is the city's first full-tilt 2,500-square-foot rooftop farm. Produce is raised here and brought downstairs to be deployed in food and cocktails. A pair of beehives produce fresh honey for the restaurant. Talk about growing local.

During the summer and early fall, the Uncommon Ground on Devon offers live music in the parking lot every Friday evening as part of its popular Farmer Friday series. Back in the day, such "happy hours" were good for picking up significant others. Now patrons pick up locally grown organic produce, fruit, and handmade goat-milk soap.

unofficial **TIP**
The economy being what it is, we'd be remiss if we didn't include at least a couple of nightlife options on the cheap. **Cleo's,** in the hip Ukrainian Village neighborhood (1935 West Chicago Avenue; ☎ 312-243-5600), is known for its free buffet from 11 p.m. Saturday to 1 a.m. Sunday (1-drink minimum). A few blocks away, the gritty **Empty Bottle** (1035 North Western Avenue; ☎ 773-276-3600) is one of the most authentic live-rock clubs in Chicago, and you can experience it gratis on Monday nights.

Weegee's Lounge is a superb drinking establishment at 3659 West Armitage Avenue (☎ 773-384-0707), on the western fringe of the Logan Square neighborhood. Take a cab or a car here—not the bus. The bar gets its name from famed 1930s New York photojournalist Arthur "Weegee" Fellig, but the goal of owners Alex Huebner and Lynn Marrs is to make the century-old building the greenest tavern in Chicago. They recycle nearly 90% of the bar waste and encourage staff and customers to ride bicycles to the lounge, which features small Weegee photographs and a vintage Brunswick bar.

Weegee's is one of the first corner taverns in Chicago with a green roof. Huebner and Marrs actively search out individual brewers and distillers with green practices and a minimal carbon footprint.

The **Butterfly Social Club** (722 West Grand Avenue; ☎ 312-666-1695) is the colorful Haight-Ashbury–esque building—with the big butterfly—directly west of the popular Funky Buddha Lounge (see page 347). Almost all the drinks are organic, and the club furniture was built with clay, sand, and straw salvaged from Chicago construction sites.

If you're near the historic Merchandise Mart, stop in for a drink at the new **Cityscape Bar,** on the 15th floor of the Holiday Inn Chicago Mart Plaza (350 Mart Center Drive; ☎ 312-836-5000; **www .martplaza.com**). Locals are digging the beautiful east and south views of downtown Chicago. The bar's drink stirrers are made from bamboo instead of plastic, and environmentally friendly paint was applied to the walls. The staff reports that the bar recycles grease, calculator tape, and even junk mail. Organic and biodynamic wines are offered. Appetizers include an artisanal-cheese-and-meat platter and shrimp-and-scallop seviche. The intimate room seats 99 people.

LOOKIN' FOR LOVE

BECAUSE CHICAGO IS A PREDOMINANTLY CATHOLIC CITY, attitudes toward sex can be ambivalent. And that means the singles scene can be unpredictable—sometimes friendly and relaxed, other times as uptight as Martha Stewart in a mosh pit. It was Chicago, after all, where Frank Sinatra sang that he actually "saw a man dancing with his own wife." That said, here's a rundown of what's out there.

From the 1950s through the 1980s, **Rush Street** was Chicago's answer to Bourbon Street, with its colorful assortment of jazz clubs, honky-tonks, and strip joints with names like the Candy Store. The city cleaned up the street, and in true Chicago fashion, Rush went south. Only recently has it staged a comeback through a combination of sleek retail and upscale nightclubs that are popular with the 35-to-60 age group.

Three clubs in particular make up what locals jokingly refer to as the "Viagra Triangle." The power player of the bunch is **Gibsons Bar & Steakhouse** (1028 North Rush Street; ☎ 312-266-8999; **www.gibsons steakhouse.com**). The dimly lit bar and restaurant opened in 1989 in what used to be Mister Kelly's nightclub. Known for its killer steaks and even-deadlier martinis (packing four to six ounces of vodka, the popular house martini is $13), Gibson's is a favorite of movie stars and athletes visiting Chicago. Jack Nicholson and Shaquille O'Neal do the hang here, and Dennis Rodman was a Gibson's regular when he played for the Bulls. That fact alone should tell you not to worry about a dress code.

The swingin' **Jilly's Piano Bar** (1007 North Rush Street; ☎ 312-664-1001; **www.jillyschicago.com**) is across the street from Gibson's. Named in honor of Jilly Rizzo, one of Sinatra's best pallies, the club is loosely modeled after the original Jilly's in New York City, where Sinatra, Johnny Carson, and others held court in the 1960s. This Jilly's has been around for more than a decade. It doesn't play up the Sinatra connection as much as it used to, but it still serves one of the best lemon-drop martinis in town. It's also a good place to watch the sidewalk traffic on Rush Street. No cover.

The third stop on the triangle is another steak house: **Tavern on Rush** (1031 North Rush Street; ☎ 312-664-9600; **www.tavernonrush .com**). Like Gibson's and Jilly's, it's a favorite of men with toupees and women with year-round tans, but it's so far beneath the other two spots on the buzz circuit that Michael Jordan can eat here with minimal hassle.

A few blocks north, a younger crowd descends on **Division Street.** Here you'll find one of the city's most legendary singles bars: **Butch McGuire's** (20 West Division Street; ☎ 312-337-9080; **www.butch mcguires.com**). Don't miss Butch's during the holiday season, when more than 200,000 Christmas lights twinkle in two rooms. Not far off Division, the bravest and boldest after-hours customers head to **Gamekeepers** (345 West Armitage Avenue; ☎ 773-549-0400; **www .gamekeeperschicago.com**), an *Animal House*–type establishment with lots of TV sets. If you were born before 1971, you don't belong here.

In **Wicker Park,** known for its live rock 'n' roll and slacker bars, the singles oasis is **Nick's Beergarden** (1516 North Milwaukee Avenue; ☎ 773-252-1155; **www.nicksbeergarden.com**). Formerly in the DePaul neighborhood, Nick's has found a niche in this part of town. It boasts one of the best jukeboxes in the city, with ample Memphis soul, Chicago blues, and Carolina beach music.

Just blocks north of Wicker Park is the trendy and less Bohemian neighborhood called **Bucktown.** It has several singles bars with singular names (just like Nick's). **Lottie's Pub** (1925 West Cortland Street; ☎ 773-489-0738; **www.lottiespub.com**) was originally called Busia's Polish Pub. As the neighborhood changed in the late 1980s, it was renamed in honor of the late Lottie Zagorski, who between 1934 and 1967 ran a combination grocery store and tavern at the same location. Lottie caused quite a stir in the working-class neighborhood because she was, in the parlance of the day, a "hermaphrodite." Look closely around the bar, and you'll find a black-and-white photograph of Lottie, built like a Bears linebacker but wearing a flower-print dress. Today, Lottie's causes quite a stir because of all the raging 20-something hormones bouncing around in a setting that includes sports on ten television sets and a crummy pool table in the back of the bar. A sedate sidewalk cafe is open in the summer.

A hipper Bucktown space is **Danny's Tavern** (1951 West Dickens Avenue; ☎ 773-489-6457), formerly a bookie joint called Art's Tap. Today, the walls are stark and the room is filled with progressive music by the likes of Magnetic Fields and Brand New Heavies. Other times, DJs spin old-school soul, funk, and reggae. The biggest night of the month is generally the first Wednesday, when "Sheer Magic" takes over, with DJs spinning some of the best funk and soul you will hear. The monthly set has even caught the attention of *Rolling Stone* magazine. Scenesters lounge around little tables and sit on high-backed chairs in cozy, dimly lit back rooms filled with candles; points for two bathrooms per gender.

Should you find yourself striking out around the University of Chicago on the South Side, check out **The Woodlawn Tap** (1172 East 55th Street; ☎ 773-643-5516). Since 1948, over 500 free-thinking UC students have tended bar at this funky working-class tavern. Notable drinkers have included the late bluesman Paul Butterfield, anthropologist Margaret Mead, and poet Dylan Thomas, who once stopped in three different times in one day.

For a late-night taste of the real Chicago, take in the twin spin of **Underbar** and **Bluelight,** adjacent bars underneath a grisly North Side overpass but across from a police station. Underbar (3243 North Western Avenue; ☎ 773-404-9363; **www.underbarchicago.com**) is the more popular joint. It's cleaner, there's an indie-rock soundtrack (played by hipster bartenders), and the room has intimate tables for smooching and arm wrestling. In the wee, wee hours, the Underbar fills with bar and restaurant workers, musicians, and actors from the nearby Viaduct Theater. It's open until 4 a.m. Sunday through Friday and until 5 a.m. Saturday; no cover. Bluelight (3251 North Western Avenue; ☎ 773-755-5875; **www.bluelightchicago.com**) is so named because it's popular with policemen. Under different ownership than Underbar, Bluelight resembles your uncle's rec room, filled with classic beer memorabilia and neon. The crowd looks rough, but hey, most of them are probably cops. Open nightly, 6 p.m. to 4 a.m.; no cover.

The city's grand piano bars (without restaurants) include the dark and tiny **Zebra Lounge** (1220 North State Street; ☎ 312-642-5140), done in enticing zebra decor, of course, and the subterranean **Redhead Piano Bar** (16 West Ontario Street; ☎ 312-640-1000; **www.thered headpianobar.com**), generally full of losers who've struck out in the Viagra Triangle.

Catering to single guys who've totally thrown in the towel, strip clubs have made a comeback in Chicago. This time around, however, they're called "gentlemen's clubs," following a nationwide trend toward nightspots where scantily clad or nude women are the attractions. The more mainstream gentlemen's clubs are **VIP's** (1531 North Kingsbury Street; ☎ 312-664-7400; **www.vipschicago.com**), which proudly touts itself as "Chicago's only full-liquor and topless bar," and **Heavenly Bodies** (1300 South Elmhurst Road; ☎ 847-806-1121) in Elk Grove Village, about ten miles from O'Hare International Airport. Collared shirts and/or nice sweaters are required at Heavenly Bodies after 7 p.m.—for customers, that is. Note that both clubs are topless-only (meaning there's no full nudity).

unofficial **TIP**
Chicago's ban on smoking in public places has been driving some locals to seek the pleasures of the night in neighboring Wisconsin. It's always easy to butt in at the **Brat Stop,** just five miles north of the Illinois border in Kenosha (12304 75th Street; ☎ 262-857-2011; **www.bratstop.com**). In business since 1961 and open 365 days a year, it has live rock 'n' roll and country, dozens of television sets, and (of course) excellent bratwurst and curd cheese. It's so popular, the Chicago Bulls team bus generally stops here on the way back from NBA games in Milwaukee.

LEGITIMATE THEATER

IN RECENT YEARS, Chicago theater has been a spawning ground of actors and directors for agents, producers, and casting directors from the East and West coasts. While the Loop (downtown) theaters enjoy success with safe, straight-from-Broadway touring companies—or, in some cases, workshop productions heading to Broadway (such as Mel Brooks's *The Producers* and Eric Idle's *Monty Python's Spamalot*)—a cutting-edge, off-Loop scene has flourished.

The Chicago area boasts more than 200 theater companies or producing organizations, ranging from established institutions to midlevel professional companies to smaller and younger troupes. The **Goodman Theatre** (170 North Dearborn; ☎ 312-443-3800; **www.goodman theatre.org**) is the oldest and largest resident theater in Chicago. Since its founding in 1925, the Goodman had worked out of the rear portion of the Art Institute but in the fall of 2000 moved to a glorious two-theater complex in the heart of Chicago's vibrant North Loop Theater District. The Goodman pioneered regional theater in America. Under artistic director Robert Falls, shows have ranged from experimental Shakespeare to Bertolt Brecht to James Baldwin.

On the Loop commercial front, a Broadway-in-Chicago texture colors the bookings at the **Bank of America Theatre** (formerly the Shubert; 40 West Monroe Street), the **Ford Center for the Performing Arts–Oriental Theatre** (24 West Randolph Street), and the **Cadillac Palace Theatre** (151 West Randolph Street). In recent years, Broadway producers have tried something new and used these theaters as a home for open-ended productions of musicals still playing in New York, most recently *Jersey Boys*. Tickets for all three venues should be ordered through **Ticketmaster** (☎ 312-902-1400; **www.broadwayinchicago.com**).

The Bank of America Theatre opened in 1906 as the Majestic Theatre and as the tallest building in Chicago. Its stature attracted vaudeville acts who performed from 1:30 to 10:30 p.m., six days a week; notable figures gracing the stage included Harry Houdini and Eddie Foy. The Palace and Oriental theaters opened in 1926; the Palace is worth a look-see even if the theater is dark. Designed by noted theater architects the Rapp Brothers, the interior features a spellbinding vision inspired by the palaces of Fontainebleau and Versailles. The lobby is accented with huge decorative mirrors and violet-and-white Breche marble, which sweeps through a succession of foyers. Chicago fun fact: during the mid-to-late 1980s, the Palace was used as a rock venue, and the pop group Frankie Goes to Hollywood had the stage collapse under them during a performance. No one was seriously injured.

All three beautifully restored theaters are owned by the Nederlander Organization, the largest commercial-theater producer in the United States. Call or check local listings for performance information. You can also visit **www.chicagoplays.com** for more information.

The **Steppenwolf Theatre** (1650 North Halsted; ☎ 312-335-1650; **www.steppenwolf.org**) is one of the pioneers in the Off-Loop movement. Steppenwolf is unique for the consistency of its ensemble; audiences have been able to watch a group of actors develop over the years. It's like a baseball farm system—which is why most Steppenwolf actors are devoted Cubs fans. The original 1976 ensemble included John Malkovich, Laurie Metcalf, and Gary Sinise. Steppenwolf has received international acclaim for its production of John Steinbeck's *The Grapes of Wrath* and, most recently, Tracy Letts's *August: Osage County*. It has also staged works by Sam Shepard, Tom Waits, and Tennessee Williams. The immaculate 500-seat main stage and 100-seat upstairs theater are a modest cab ride from downtown.

Some people perceive **The Second City** as simply a comedy club, but it is a legitimate local theatrical institution that started in 1959. Major talents like Ed Asner, John Belushi, Chris Farley, Bill Murray, and George Wendt cut their teeth here. The original founding format is still used. With minimal costuming and props, six or seven actors lampoon life in a torrid series of topical skits. Recent events have raised the bar for actors in critically acclaimed

productions like *Thank Heaven It Wasn't 7/11.*
Producer emeritus Joyce Sloane has always
pledged to keep the theater admission charge
($19 Tuesday through Thursday and Sunday,
$25 on Friday and Saturday) in the same ball-
park as a movie ticket—with popcorn. The
original 300-seat location at 1616 North Wells
Street (☎ 312-337-3992; **www.secondcity.com**)

also features a 180-seat back room for Second City E.T.C., which is
sometimes regarded as more rebellious than its big brother.

Donny's Skybox Studio Theater is a cabaret space on the fourth
floor of Piper's Alley, an entertainment complex adjacent to The
Second City. It's used as a classroom and performing venue for
Second City Training Center students and alumni. The studio presents various productions each term in the Skybox, including coached
ensembles, a Sunday doubleheader, and writing-program revues. The
space is named for Don DePollo, who joined the Second City cast in
1974 and went on to become one of the training center's most influential teachers (and biggest Cub fans) until his death in 1995. For
listings and tickets, call The Second City or check its Web site.

The **Court Theatre** (5535 South Ellis Avenue; ☎ 773-753-4472;
www.courttheatre.org) is the third-biggest theater in the city in terms
of annual operating budget. Established in 1955, the 251-seat theater
is just 12 minutes from the Loop on the University of Chicago campus. The critically acclaimed theater features classics such as Oscar
Wilde's *The Importance of Being Earnest*, Edward Albee's *Who's
Afraid of Virginia Woolf?*, and Samuel Beckett's *Endgame*.

Another long-established organization is the **Northlight Theatre,**
at the North Shore Center for the Performing Arts (☎ 847-673-6300;
www.northlight.org) in near-north suburban Skokie. For a little more
than 30 years, Northlight has been one of the largest and most innovative theaters in the Chicago area and is an artistic anchor of the
northern suburbs. Northlight has won critical acclaim for its production of a wide range of new and contemporary plays and original
chamber-sized musicals.

The **Chicago Shakespeare Theater** (800 East Grand Avenue; ☎ 312-
595-5600; **www.chicagoshakes.com**) resides in a seven-story glass-walled
structure on Navy Pier that affords a panoramic view of the lake and
the Chicago skyline. On its 500-seat main stage and 200-seat flexible
stage are offered cutting-edge productions of the Bard's greatest works,
as well as a menu of imported works from Europe and Canada.

The **Victory Gardens Theater** (2433 North Lincoln Avenue; ☎ 773-
871-3000; **www.victorygardens.org**), now in a 299-seat home in the
renovated Biograph Theater, stages mostly new works by its stable of
accomplished playwrights. Visitor bonus points: in 1934, bank rob-
ber and Public Enemy Number One John Dillinger was gunned down

in the alley adjacent to the Biograph. He had no encores. Victory Gardens' former home at 2257 North Lincoln Avenue is under new management but continues to book shows by the intimate, character-driven Shattered Globe Theatre, Eclipse Theatre Company, and Remy Bumppo Theatre Company.

High-quality midlevel theater includes the **Lookingglass Theatre Company,** in an immaculate 270-seat space at the downtown Water Tower Water Works (☎ 312-337-0665; **www.lookingglasstheatre.org**); the **Black Ensemble Theatre** (4520 North Beacon Street; ☎ 773-769-4451; **www.blackensembletheater.org**), which stages a lot of shows on dead rhythm-and-blues stars like Jackie Wilson and Howlin' Wolf; the **Mercury Theater** (3745 North Southport Avenue; ☎ 773-325-1700; **www.borealissystems.net/uat/mercury**); and the multistage **Royal George Theatre Center** (1641 North Halsted Street; ☎ 312-998-9000). The **Chicago Children's Theatre** (☎ 773-227-0180; **www.chicagochildrens theatre.org**) stages first-rate productions for the younger set.

One of the hottest midlevel theaters in town is the progressive **Redmoon Theater** (☎ 312-850-8440; **www.redmoon.org**), one of the only theaters in America that creates large outdoor public spectacles. These events deploy masks, puppets, irreverent mechanical devices, and live music. Redmoon's work can be seen in economically challenged neighborhoods, city parks, and landmarks. The theater group presents shows from its workshop space at 1463 West Hubbard Street, in an industrial neighborhood near downtown.

With the aim to give downtown theatergoers a glimpse of Off-Loop theater, a wide array of notable smaller theaters are invited to perform in two downtown venues sponsored by the Chicago Department of Cultural Affairs. The **Storefront Theater** (66 East Randolph Street) and the **Studio Theater** in the Chicago Cultural Center (77 East Randolph Street) have seen notable productions by 500 Clown, Seanachai Theatre, the House Theatre, and Plasticene. For more information on both theaters, call ☎ 312-742-8497 or visit **www.dcatheater.org**

unofficial **TIP**
The general dress code for Chicago theater is casual. Men need not wear ties, and women don't have to overdress. Jeans, slacks, and nice shirts are perfectly acceptable.

The days of Chicago dinner theater are long gone, but to immerse yourself in a total theatrical-tourist experience, check out **The Spirit of Chicago,** a floating dinner theater that cruises Lake Michigan with a mainstream song-and-dance revue. **The Spirit of Chicago** docks at Navy Pier (600 East Grand Avenue; ☎ 312-836-7899; **www.spiritcitycruises.com**). Advance reservations are recommended.

Apart from the young and experimental theater spaces, most of these shows can be expensive—and many often sell out. The League of Chicago Theatres offers a **Hot Tix** program that sells tickets at half price the day of the performance. Hot Tix booths are at 72 East Randolph Street in downtown Chicago; and at the Chicago Water Works Visitor Center, 163 East Pearson Street, near the Water Tower; for booth hours, call ☎ 312-554-9800 or check **www.hottix.org**. Many theaters also offer discounts for students, children, senior citizens, the disabled, and armed-forces personnel. Call ahead.

THE CLASSICS

THE WORLD-RENOWNED **Chicago Symphony Orchestra** (CSO; ☎ 312-294-3000; **www.cso .org**) is the touchstone of the Chicago classical-music landscape. Since 1960, the CSO has won 58 Grammy Awards, 23 of them between 1972 and 1991, when the great Georg Solti was music director. Overall, Solti won 31 Grammy Awards—more than any other musical artist, including Michael Jackson. Solti's tradition is consistently celebrated in the CSO's clarity and logic.

unofficial **TIP**
Book your Chicago Symphony tickets well in advance. Subscriptions account for roughly 75% of CSO tickets sold, and 2006–07 attendance filled more than 85% of Orchestra Hall's capacity. Sometimes tickets are available at the last minute, though, so try calling the box office (☎ 312-294-3000) on the day of the concert.

The 117-year-old orchestra is based in the 2,251-seat **Symphony Center** (220 South Michigan Avenue). Visiting domestic and international orchestras also appear at the complex's Orchestra Hall as part of the Symphony Center Presents series. In addition, the Symphony Center includes a beautiful gift shop and the **Club at Symphony Center** (☎ 312-294-3333), which features special events such as cabarets and a wine-tasting series.

The Symphony Center is also home to the **Chicago Sinfonietta** (☎ 312-236-3681; **www.chicagosinfonietta.org**), a chamber orchestra founded in 1986. The ensemble typically presents five programs a year, including collaborations with art rockers, international artists and an annual tribute to Martin Luther King Jr.

On a smaller scale, the **Newberry Consort** (☎ 312-255-3700; **www .newberry.org**) is the city's premier early-music ensemble. Its season begins in the fall at various locations in Chicago, Oak Park, and Evanston.

The **Lyric Opera of Chicago** (☎ 312-332-2244; **www.lyricopera .org**) presents the classics with an increased emphasis on progressive works to make opera relevant to younger audiences. Performances take place in the majestic **Civic Opera House** (20 North Wacker Drive), the second-largest opera auditorium in North America. The 45-story Art Deco limestone building was built in the 1920s to one-up the Auditorium Theatre. The entranceways' ornamental masks and musical instruments alone are covered with 2,000 gallons of gold paint.

NIGHTCLUB PROFILES

Bottom Lounge

LIVE-MUSIC VENUE, DANCE CLUB, AND TIKI LOUNGE

**1375 West Lake Street, Near North Side; ☎ 312-666-6775;
www.bottomlounge.com**

Cover $5–$30; age 21 and over only unless otherwise noted. **Minimum** None.
Mixed drinks $5–$15. **Wine** None. **Beer** $3–$40, including Pabst Blue Ribbon
tall boys. **Dress** Casual. **Food available** Lunch and nighttime dining Wednesday–
Sunday, including grilled Atlantic-salmon sandwich, curry-chicken lettuce wraps,
and weekly house specials. **Hours** Wednesday–Sunday, 11:30 a.m.–2 a.m.;
Saturday, 11:30 a.m.-2:30 a.m.

WHO GOES THERE Urban hipsters, hard-core music fans. But all locals talk
about the splendid rooftop view of the city skyline east of the club. A
huge deck replete with tall Red Bull tables can be accessed from the
upstairs Volcano Room Rum Bar.

WHAT GOES ON Live music from national touring bands such as the Dex
Romweber Duo, King Khan and the Shrines, and others; dancing to a
jukebox pumped up with steroidal sounds of punk, rock, and soul. A
late-night B-movie on the big screen generally closes the night.

SETTING AND ATMOSPHERE The main floor of this former auto-repair shop
(which holds 500) is geared for concerts and dancing in a loftlike setting. Industrially influenced decor includes low-slung tables, booths, silk
lighting fixtures, and loft-sized windows overlooking the gritty El tracks.
Rock 'n' roll memorabilia hangs on exposed-brick walls. The stairwell
leading to the second floor features a spray-painted mural from graffiti
artist Temper, made long before his work fetched upwards of $20,000.

   A dash of tiki culture is still afloat in the inner city: check out the
5,000-square-foot second-floor Volcano Room Rum Bar. The club-
within-a-club serves 20 specialty rums and includes a booming sound
system, a stage, and seating for up to 300. Selected Thursdays features
DJs spinning a mix of garage, punk, Vegas grind, and exotica.

IF YOU GO Give yourself time to absorb all the goings-on. Bottom Lounge
offers a free parking lot—unheard of at many Chicago clubs—on the east
side of the building, plus ample street parking and valet service. To get
there on public transportation, take the Ashland Green Line, which lets
you off a half block east of the lounge. We recommend bringing a car,
though, as the neighborhood can get sketchy late at night.

Buddy Guy's Legends

LIVE BLUES IN A DOWNBEAT, REC ROOM–TYPE SETTING

**754 South Wabash Avenue, South Loop; ☎ 312-427-0333;
www.buddyguys.com**

Cover $8–$15. **Minimum** None. **Mixed drinks** $4. **Wine** $4. **Beer** $3.50–$5. **Dress**
Everything from tees and sweats to after-work attire. **Specials** Local record-release

Chicago Nightclubs by Location

NAME	DESCRIPTION	COVER
NORTH SIDE		
The Closet	Classic gay-friendly bar	None
Club Lucky	A quintessential Chicago experience	None
Green Mill Jazz Club	Hepcat speakeasy with live jazz	$4–$12
The Hideout	Eclectic live music in the middle of nowhere	None–$15
Old Town School of Folk Music	Folk- and world-music mecca	Varies
Weeds	Retreat for Bohemian riffraff	None
NEAR NORTH SIDE		
Bottom Lounge	Live-music venue, dance club, and tiki bar	$5–$30
Davenport's Piano Bar and Cabaret	Find your inner Bobby Short	Varies
House of Blues	Juke-joint opera house	$10–$60
The Lodge	Neighborhood singles bar	None (usually)
The Matchbox	Tiny, intimate, friendly tavern	None
Old Town Ale House	Everything rom Bach to Bukowski	None
Sonotheque	Eclectic dance palace	Varies
Trader Vic's	Tiki bar *par excellence*	None
THE LOOP		
Funky Buddha Lounge	Urban-hip dance club and lounge	None–$20
SOUTH LOOP		
Buddy Guy's Legends	Home of the legendary bluesman	$8–$15
SOUTHERN SUBURBS		
FitzGerald's	Roots-music roadhouse	$5–$25

parties, spur-of-the-moment bookings such as Eric Clapton, and occasional live recordings, like owner Buddy Guy playing with G. E. Smith of the *Saturday Night Live* band. **Food available** Southern Louisiana cuisine: ribs, red beans and rice, and "Peanut Buddy Pie," a Buddy Guy–endorsed peanut butter pie. **Hours** Monday–Friday, 11 a.m.–2 a.m.; Saturday, 5 p.m.–3 a.m.; Sunday, 6 p.m.–2 a.m.

WHO GOES THERE International tourists, more of a racial mix than North Side blues clubs, and sometimes even Buddy Guy, the Chicago guitar great.

WHAT GOES ON A stately approach to booking live local, national, and international blues acts seven nights a week. From 1972 to 1986, local guitar hero Buddy Guy (who influenced Eric Clapton and Stevie Ray Vaughan) ran the Checkerboard Lounge, a South Side blues club that still stands today. In 1989, he reopened in a bigger and safer location as part of Chicago's developing South Loop. The sprawling storefront club is popular with tourists because of Guy's international reputation and its prime location.

SETTING AND ATMOSPHERE Urban roadhouse. Four pool tables are almost always occupied at stage left. Portraits of blues greats like Muddy Waters, Lightnin' Hopkins, and Howlin' Wolf hang throughout the museum-like space. Near the club entrance there's a display case featuring Guy's awards; guitars from the likes of Eric Clapton and Muddy Waters hang above the bar.

IF YOU GO Don't request Britney Spears. This is a blues sanctuary. It's also best to arrive early, as all shows are general admission and often sell out. The Southern Louisiana kitchen serves better-than-average bar food. And periodically check out the far west end of the bar. That's Guy's favorite spot.

The Closet

NEIGHBORHOOD BAR FOR AN ALWAYS-CHANGING NEIGHBORHOOD

3325 North Broadway Avenue, North Side; ☎ 773-477-8533

Cover None. **Minimum** None. **Mixed drinks** $3–$12. **Wine** $5. **Beer** $3–$6.50. **Dress** Casual. **Specials** Well drinks $3, Monday–Wednesday. **Food available** None. **Hours** Monday–Friday, 2 p.m.–4 a.m.; Saturday, noon–5 a.m.; Sunday, noon–4 a.m.

WHO GOES THERE Predominately lesbian crowd, although young, hipster gay men and straight couples are welcome and accepted.

WHAT GOES ON The Closet opened in 1978 and became a popular neighborhood bar for gay men. The Closet is still under its original ownership, a remarkable feat for Chicago nightlife. The bar is a staple of what real-estate developers used to call Newtown and is now known as Boystown. Expect music videos by the likes of Kelly Clarkson and Ne-Yo in constant rotation. Karaoke on Thursday.

SETTING AND ATMOSPHERE The Closet only holds about 70 people in a narrow space with a friendly U-shaped bar surrounded by burgundy walls. Lots of bump 'n' grind after 2 a.m. Just about anything goes where women are making out with women, guys making time, boys being boys, and somehow it all makes sense in a hassle-free environment. The Closet holds a late-night liquor license, which is becoming an endangered species in Chicago. There's a small dance floor, plus pinball and darts if you can find the space.

IF YOU GO Don't wear good clothes—when it's really crowded, odds are high that someone could spill a drink on you. Parking is tough, especially on weekends. Cabs and public transportation advised.

Club Lucky

1824 West Wabansia Avenue, North Side; ☎ 773-227-2300; www.clubluckychicago.com

Cover None. **Minimum** None. **Mixed drinks** $5.75–$7.75, martinis $6.50–$9.50, espresso and cappuccino are brewed to order. **Wine** More than 50 Italian wines are offered by the bottle ($27–$46) or glass ($6.50–$12); the reserve wine list focuses on Italy, Sicily, and the Americas. **Beer** $5–$8. **Dress** Casually hip; shorts OK in the summer. **Food available** House specialties include Chicken Vesuvio with roasted potatoes and peas and several pastas made on-site with homemade Club Lucky marinara sauce. **Hours** Food served Monday–Thursday, 11:30 a.m.–11 p.m.; Friday, 11:30 a.m.–midnight; Saturday, 5 p.m.–midnight; and Sunday, 4–10 p.m. Cocktail lounge open late during the week, until 2 a.m. Friday, and until 3 a.m. Saturday.

WHO GOES THERE Residents of the Bucktown neighborhood, downtowners on a ten-minute cab ride, and folks heading out to Chicago Bulls and Blackhawk games.

WHAT GOES ON No-nonsense drinking and eating. Subdued Dean Martin and Frank Sinatra play on a CD jukebox as people roll life's dice along the 35-seat black Formica–topped bar in the cocktail lounge. Feelin' lucky? "That's life," as the Chairman of the Board used to say. Club Lucky's Killer Martini (garnished with three blue-cheese olives) has been voted Chicago's best by the alternative newspaper *New City*.

SETTING AND ATMOSPHERE The corner building that houses the club was built in the 1920s as a hardware store. During Prohibition, it was remodeled to include a speakeasy with a basement entrance. Following Prohibition, the hardware store morphed into a Polish bar and banquet hall with a stage, also called Club Lucky (today's kitchen is where the old stage used to sit). Everyone enters through a 1950s-style cocktail-lounge area with rich red Naugahyde booths, a vintage Chicago back bar, and a barrel ceiling. During good weather, there is seating for 40 on a tree-lined street-side patio. The 135-seat dining room is accented by Art Deco chandeliers replicated from the Empire State Building. The red, black, and cream draperies were silk-screened with a neo-Constructivist design by a neighborhood artist.

IF YOU GO Even Chicagoans don't get jaded about Club Lucky. It's a throwback experience to find a establishment of this scope wedged in a residential neighborhood. You'll be lucky to feel the vibe of Chicago, and you'll take home a sense of local history.

Davenport's Piano Bar and Cabaret

1383 North Milwaukee Avenue, Near North Side; ☎ 773-278-1830; www.davenportspianobar.com

Cover Varies for cabaret shows, none for piano bar; reservations highly suggested for cabaret shows. **Minimum** 2 drinks for cabaret shows. **Mixed drinks** $7–$9, alcohol-free drinks $3.50–$5.25. **Wine** $6 (glass)–$38 (bottle). **Beer** $4.75–$6. **Dress** Anything but ratty T-shirts. **Specials** Don't walk away without trying Davenport's "Grown-Up Fountain Drinks" ($8 cocktails), including Cherry Coke (Effen Black Cherry Vodka and Coca-Cola), Chocolate Raspberry Coke (Stoli Razberi Vodka, Godiva Dark Chocolate, and Coca-Cola), Root Beer Float (Kahlúa, cream, IBC Root Beer), and Egg Cream Soda (Kahlúa, cream, and club soda). **Food available** None. **Hours** Monday, Wednesday, and Thursday, 7 p.m.–midnight; Friday and Saturday, 7 p.m.–2 a.m.; Sunday, 7–11 p.m.; closed Tuesday nights for private parties.

WHO GOES THERE Serious music fans, gays and straights, young and old.

WHAT GOES ON The cabaret is fashioned after Don't Tell Mama in New York City, where staff not only work but join in to perform. Vocalists such as Karen Mason, Debby Boone, and Julie Wilson have appeared in the cabaret room. Even Bea Arthur has stopped by just to sing at the piano bar. There are also occasional musical revues and comedy. Monday is open-mike night, and female Elvis impersonator Patty Elvis has been a popular Sunday-night booking.

SETTING AND ATMOSPHERE Davenport's opened in 1998 in a shuttered dry-goods store on the blue-collar strip of Milwaukee Avenue. The club consists of an informal piano bar and a cabaret space that seats about 75 people. (Sssssh!) Separated from the piano bar by a soundproof door, the cabaret room features cafe tables, velvet walls, and wood-veneer panels. It is one of the most intimate places in Chicago to hear live music. The piano bar is looser and louder; the bar itself is covered with boldly colored interpretations of cabaret music.

IF YOU GO Remember, this isn't Central Park. Davenport's is in the storied working-class neighborhood of Wicker Park (hardscrabble writer Nelson Algren only lived a few blocks away), but that incongruity only heightens its charm. Don't be shy—the staff won't let you be a wallflower. This is one of Chicago's most unique nightspots, especially in an era where sensationalism generally wins out over style.

FitzGerald's

LIVE AMERICAN ROOTS MUSIC IN A ROADHOUSE CLUB

6615 West Roosevelt Road, Berwyn, Southern Suburbs;
☎ **708-788-2118; www.fitzgeraldsnightclub.com**

Cover $5–$25. **Minimum** None. **Mixed drinks** $5–$8. **Wine** $5. **Beer** $3–$5 regionals, including Pabst Blue Ribbon and Bell's. **Dress** Casual. **Food available** Next door, the fantastic Wishbone (☎ 708-749-1295) serves "Southern Reconstruction" food Wednesday and Thursday, 11 a.m.–9 p.m.; Friday and Saturday until 10 p.m. **Hours** Tuesday–Thursday, 7 p.m.–1 a.m.; Friday and Saturday, 7 p.m.–3 a.m.; Sunday, 5 p.m.–1 a.m.; closed Monday.

WHO GOES THERE Music lovers of all ages, a hearty portion of Lake Wobegon characters, Near West suburban folks; slacker factor very low.

WHAT GOES ON   A family-run operation since it opened in 1980, FitzGerald's is one of the most passionately booked rooms in the Chicago area. Blues legend Stevie Ray Vaughan played the intimate 300-seat club in 1981, long before he hit it big. Other landmark shows that remain indicative of the club's musical mission include appearances from the late zydeco king Clifton Chenier and the Neville Brothers. Ample attention is also given to Chicago blues and folk, and Sunday-night sets are generally reserved for traditional and big-band jazz.

SETTING AND ATMOSPHERE   American roadhouse: The backwoods feel has even attracted Hollywood. The Madonna jitterbug scene from *A League of Their Own* was filmed here, as well as the pool-hall shots in the Paul Newman flick *The Color of Money*. Sound and sight lines are top-notch, and space for a dance floor is cleared when appropriate. In recent years the club has expanded to include the Sidebar, an intimate tavern equipped with television sets and a CD jukebox with thousands of selections. Chicago's popular Wishbone restaurant group (see profile, page 269) has also opened up shop directly east of FitzGerald's, serving blackened catfish, Louisiana chicken salad, cheese grits, and other Southern specialties. The Gulf Coast has never been this close to Chicago.

IF YOU GO   Respect the experience. Over the years, FitzGerald's has cultivated fans who love roots music as well as the roots texture of the room. Rarely do you hear an acoustic performance drowned out by audience chatter. And don't be intimidated by the suburban location. Berwyn is a ten-minute drive from the Loop, and the Congress El goes to Berwyn. Get off at Oak Park Avenue and walk three blocks south, then three blocks east. Or call co-owner Bill FitzGerald and ask him to pick you up. If he has time, he probably will.

Funky Buddha Lounge

URBAN-HIP DANCE CLUB AND LOUNGE THAT STANDS THE TEST OF TIME

728 West Grand Avenue, The Loop; ☎ 312-666-1695; www.funkybuddha.com

Cover None early in the week; $10–$20 Friday and Saturday. **Minimum** None. **Mixed drinks** $5–$8. **Wine** $5–$7. **Beer** $4–$8. **Dress** Casually hip—no shorts, no tank tops, no tennis shoes. **Specials** Occasional live Afro-Brazilian music early in the week. **Food available** None, but across-the-street La Scarola (721 West Grand Avenue; ☎ 312-243-1740) is one of the city's best Italian restaurants. **Hours** Sunday–Friday, 9 p.m.–2 a.m.; Saturday, 9 p.m.–3 a.m.

WHO GOES THERE   A unique group of African American, Asian, Indian, Latino, and white folks ages 21 to 30 that create a collective groove. David Schwimmer of *Friends* fame visits when in town, and it's a popular post-game hang for NBA stars (it's a cross-court pass away from the United Center, the home of the Chicago Bulls).

WHAT GOES ON   You can drink; dance to DJs spinning neo-soul, hip hop, and funk; then make out on exquisite leopard-print sofas.

SETTING AND ATMOSPHERE   Loungy Eurotrash. The Buddha has an up-front bar and lounge and a rear dance club. Decor is connected with (expensive)

antique-store ambience, and lighting is soft and dark. Murals are depictions of vintage mambo-record albums from the 1950s and 1960s. Bass-heavy hip hop can make conversation difficult on weekend nights.

IF YOU GO Make sure you're relatively young. The Buddha has been around for 13 years, which is a long time on the Chicago club scene. But the Buddha consistently reinvents itself and stays on top of music trends. Anyone over 35 could feel out of place here, with the possible exceptions of Charles Barkley or Keith Richards.

Green Mill Jazz Club

HEPCAT SPEAKEASY WITH GREAT LIVE JAZZ

4802 North Broadway Avenue, North Side; ☎ 773-878-5552; www.greenmilljazz.com

Cover $4–$12. **Minimum** None. **Mixed drinks** $3–$10. **Wine** $4–$7 **Beer** $3–$6, Schlitz $1.75–$4. **Dress** Casual and hip. **Specials** Uptown Poetry Slam, Sunday, 5–8 p.m. ($5 cover). **Food available** Bar snacks. **Hours** Monday–Friday, noon–4 a.m.; Saturday, noon–5 a.m.; Sunday 11 a.m.–4 a.m.—and those are vintage Chicago bar hours.

WHO GOES THERE Sincere jazz fans, local poets, romantic couples on the last stop before home, 25 to ageless.

WHAT GOES ON Top-notch local jazz artists such as Patricia Barber, Kurt Elling, and Von Freeman play here, as well as a steady influx of New York musicians who aren't heard anywhere else in town. The Green Mill is also the city's premiere joint for late-late jam sessions.

SETTING AND ATMOSPHERE Can't be beat. The dark, seductive Green Mill opened in 1907 as Pop Morse's Roadhouse, a joint where mourners often celebrated the departure of a friend before proceeding to a nearby cemetery. The club enjoyed its first run of popularity in the 1920s during the neighborhood's vaudeville heyday. Proprietor Dave Jemilo purchased the club in 1986, and instead of gutting it, he lovingly restored it to its earlier splendor. The only additions were a dance floor and a new stage. The piano behind the bar has always been there, and it's still used on Sunday nights. The Green Mill was featured in the films *High Fidelity,* starring John Cusack, and *Thief,* starring James Caan.

IF YOU GO Listen to the music. It's rare that high-quality jazz can be heard at affordable prices in a neighborhood setting.

The Hideout

AN URBAN ROADHOUSE IN THE MIDDLE OF NOWHERE, SURROUNDED BY EVERYTHING

1354 West Wabansia Avenue, North Side; ☎ 773-227-4433; www.hideoutchicago.com

Cover Free–$15, typically $8. **Minimum** None. **Mixed drinks** $3–$7. **Wine** $4. **Beer** $2 (Pabst Blue Ribbon, Goose Island depending on season)–$5. **Dress** Very casual. **Specials** Free bag of pretzels or a shot of Hot Damn! if you mention *The Unofficial Guide to Chicago.* **Food available** Chips and peanuts. **Hours**

Wednesday–Friday, 4 p.m.–2 a.m.; Tuesday, 7 p.m.–2 a.m.; Saturday, 7 p.m.–3 a.m.; closed Sunday and Monday.

WHO GOES THERE Local musicians and music-industry folks ages 25 to 35, older blue-collar workers, people trying to maintain a low profile.

WHAT GOES ON The uncanny ability of The Hideout to reinvent itself is what makes the eclectic live-music room a must-see. Although the tiny building's first deed dates back to 1890 and the club has been called The Hideout since 1934, only since the mid-1990s was the joint discovered by a young alt-country crowd. Popular "Americana" country singers such as Neko Case and Kelly Hogan not only perform at The Hideout, they've tended bar here. That vibe is what put The Hideout on the map and attracted the attention of national publications such as *Rolling Stone* magazine. National acts such as Wilco and the Mekons have been known to stop in The Hideout for impromptu sets; in the summer of 2008, Chicago soul legend Mavis Staples recorded a live album here. The club has branched out to feature harder live rock music, jazz, and art films, moving ever so slightly away from the country music that put The Hideout in the high life.

SETTING AND ATMOSPHERE Friendly. Live music is presented in a comfortable back room that resembles a Northern Wisconsin lodge. Adorned with Christmas lights and an efficient stage, the concert space seats about 100 people. The Devil in a Woodpile acoustic blues quartet performs free every Tuesday in the low-ceilinged front-bar space. Black-and-white pictures of the Chicago Cubs (circa 1969) hang behind the bar. Owners Tim and Katie Tuten found the pictures when they were cleaning up the place. Tim works for the Chicago public-school system, which accounts for The Hideout's social conscience. He can be heard quoting Margaret Mead: "Never doubt that a small group of thoughtful, committed people can change the world. Indeed, it is the only thing that ever has." So there's seating for about 18 people along the bar, and the staff is personal. No jukebox, just house tapes.

IF YOU GO Follow directions. The Hideout is in a hard-to-find industrial neighborhood. Known only by its crooked old-style sign out front, the club is directly west of the City of Chicago Fleet Management parking lot, two blocks north of North Avenue and a block east of Elston Avenue. There's ample free parking, and any decent cabdriver can find the place.

House of Blues

THE BLUES AS A TAPROOT FOR A COLORFUL MUSICAL TREE

329 North Dearborn Street, Near North Side; ☎ 312-923-2000; www.hob.com

Cover $10–$60, none in restaurant. **Minimum** None. **Mixed drinks** $5–$8. **Wine** $5–$7 by the glass. **Beer** $5–$6.50. **Dress** Anything from Bourbon Street to State Street. **Specials** The extremely popular Gospel Brunch ($15–$43)—seatings at 9:30 a.m. and noon every Sunday; "After 5 Live" concerts, held once a month inside the restaurant. **Food available** Back Porch restaurant serves Creole-Southern cuisine;

dinner until 10 p.m. daily, late-night menu until 2 a.m. weekdays, until 3 a.m. weekends. **Hours** Sunday–Friday, 8 p.m.–4 a.m.; Saturday, 8 p.m.–5 a.m.

WHO GOES THERE   Folks 21 and way over; very few blues fans; the audience demographic depends on the booking; always a smattering of tourists and a hard-core group of Chicago roots-music listeners.

WHAT GOES ON   Live music seven nights a week. Despite the 2006 purchase by Live Nation, House of Blues still gets booked with adventure and passion. The Chicago club opened Thanksgiving weekend 1996, and in the first three months of operation, acts as diverse as Soul Brother Number One James Brown, Johnny Cash, rocker-hunter Ted Nugent, and Cuban salsa singer Celia Cruz all graced the HOB (as locals call it) stage. In recent months the club has hosted everyone from Peter Frampton to world hip-hop star M.I.A.

SETTING AND ATMOSPHERE   House of Blues founder Isaac Tigrett called his Chicago music hall a "juke-joint opera house," and its design actually derives from that of the Tyl Theatre opera house in Prague, Czech Republic, where Mozart debuted *Don Giovanni* in 1787. The 1,465-capacity music room is the largest of the House of Blues chain. The four-tiered music hall is adorned with hundreds of pieces of eclectic Southern folk art and closed-circuit television monitors where fans can watch the live music while waiting for a drink. The music room is framed by 12 gold-plated private opera boxes that are sold to support House of Blues–related charities. Sound is impeccable, and sight lines are clear. If you want to sit down, arrive very early. There are a limited number of bar stools near serving areas. Otherwise, it truly is standing-room only.

IF YOU GO   It took a long time for musically provincial Chicagoans to get over the fact this is not a "blues" bar. *Hello?* Check your attitude at the door and you'll discover this club oozes with warmth and spirit.

The Lodge

IN-YOUR-FACE DRINKING AND SCHMOOZING IN A NEIGHBORHOOD TAVERN

21 West Division Street, Near North Side; ☎ 312-642-4406; www.rushanddivision.com/lodge.html

Cover Only for St. Patrick's Day and New Year's throngs. **Minimum** None. **Mixed drinks** $4–$5.50. **Wine** $6.50. **Beer** $3.75–$4.50. **Dress** Anything goes. **Specials** Stoli Sunday, Cuervo Monday, Ketel One Wednesday. **Food available** Shelled peanuts on the floor. **Hours** Sunday–Friday, noon–4 a.m.; Saturday, noon–5 a.m.

WHO GOES THERE   Jocks, aging jocks, wannabe jocks, real jocks like Charles Barkley, and conventioneers; curious suburban invasion on weekends.

WHAT GOES ON   Open since 1957, this is the longest-running act on Division Street, or what locals call "The Street of Dreams." One of the area's premier singles bars, The Lodge has held its own against evil influences such as disco, punk, and herpes. Its late-night license and 1:1 male-to-female ratio make it a popular stop for pro athletes winding down after a game. NBA superstar Charles Barkley and ex–Kansas City Royals infielder George Brett have made The Lodge a regular stop when they're in town.

SETTING AND ATMOSPHERE Less is more. The charm comes in a shoebox-sized room resplendent in refined cedar and pseudo-antique paintings, accented by three tottering chandeliers and one of the loudest oldies jukeboxes in Chicago. You can't help but meet someone in this setting.

IF YOU GO Stock up on breath mints, cologne, and perfume. On a busy night, it's like riding an El train at rush hour. And know all the words to Meat Loaf's "Paradise by the Dashboard Light"—it's a traditional Lodge sing-along.

The Matchbox

SPARKS FLY IN ONE OF THE CITY'S MOST INTIMATE TAVERNS

770 North Milwaukee Avenue, Near North Side; ☎ 312-666-9292

Cover None. **Minimum** None. **Mixed drinks** $5–$9; higher for single-malt Scotches, single-barrel Bourbons, aged rums, and ports. **Wine** $6.50–$11. **Beer** $4–$9; high end is Mad Bitch from Belgium, in a 750-mL bottle, and Fin du Monde ("the end of the earth") from Quebec. **Dress** Optional. **Specials** Manhattans, margaritas, vodka gimlets. **Food available** Chips, pretzels, nuts. **Hours** Sunday–Friday, 4 p.m.–2 a.m.; Saturday, 4 p.m.–3 a.m.

WHO GOES THERE A compelling group of characters, including cops, musicians, raconteurs, and folks visiting Intuit: The Center for Intuitive and Outsider Art next door (see profile, page 172). Chicago can be a segregated city, but you would never know it by spending time at The Matchbox.

WHAT GOES ON The mere size of The Matchbox dictates a sense of community: three feet wide at its narrowest, ten feet at its widest. The friendly bartenders will be the first to tell you that if you don't like being sociable, The Matchbox is not the place for you. The diversity of the crowd can also be attributed to the wide range of drinks, which go as low as a pint of Double Diamond for $3 to a $10 scotch. A high-end tequila selection includes Patrón, Porfidio, and Del Maguey Mezcal.

SETTING AND ATMOSPHERE Really friendly. The Matchbox opened in 1995 in a former shot-'n'-beer bar and package store of the same name. The back bar contains a collection of poster art, Matchbox toy cars, and a bouquet of flowers brought in every Thursday by a local florist.

IF YOU GO Arrive early so you can secure a barstool. During late spring and summer months, The Matchbox has sidewalk seating which offers a colorful view of a gentrified Near North neighborhood. No need to wear "Hello My Name Is . . ." tags in this joint, and no need to ask anyone for a light.

Old Town Ale House

EVERYTHING FROM BACH TO BUKOWSKI

219 West North Avenue, Near North Side; ☎ 312-944-7020; www.oldtownalehouse.net

Cover None. **Minimum** None, nor is there a maximum. **Mixed drinks** $5.25–$6. **Wine** $4–$5. **Beer** $3.75–$5. **Dress** Old-raincoated; funky; cigars are welcome. **Specials** None. **Food available** Snacks, but it's OK to bring in fast food. **Hours** Monday–Friday, 8–4 a.m.; Saturday, 8–5 a.m.; open 365 days a year.

WHO GOES THERE Whoever dares, ages 25 to 70, but a sanctuary for artists, journalists, Second City actors, and late-night waitresses and bartenders.

WHAT GOES ON Serious talking and serious drinking. Classic Chicago writers like Studs Terkel and the late Mike Royko used to pound 'em here. The original Ale House opened across the street in 1958. It burned down in 1970, maybe due to negative karma (it was run by a German who owned a pack of German shepherds named after Nazi generals). Only the long bar was salvaged from across the street. The Ale House's late-night license makes it a popular stop for nightcrawlers getting off work late.

SETTING AND ATMOSPHERE Sleazy, which is a word even the proprietors use. The jukebox is heavy on jazz, soul, classical, and opera. A cornucopia of crazy artifacts includes a gorilla bust that is decorated for appropriate seasons; a crooked JURASSIC PARK sign; strange newspaper clippings that bartenders cut and paste on the wall; and lots of colorful, primitive portraits of Chicago characters and, most recently, naked paintings of Sarah Palin and Rod Blagojevich (Blago is shown about to submit to a cavity search in the Big House). Chicago folk singer and humorist Larry Rand best summed up the Ale House as "a fern bar where the customers are often more potted than the plants."

IF YOU GO You won't be sorry. This is as authentic as a Near North Side drinking experience can get. Just don't cross the stray punch lines from the Second City folks, still winding down from their late-night sets across the street.

Old Town School of Folk Music

THE COUNTRY'S PREMIER RESOURCE CENTER FOR FOLK- AND WORLD-MUSIC IDIOMS

4544 North Lincoln Avenue, North Side; ☎ 773-728-6000; www.oldtownschool.org

Cover Varies. **Minimum** None. **Mixed drinks** None. **Wine** $3.50. **Beer** $3.50–$5. **Dress** No code. **Specials** 2-day outdoor roots-music festival during July; La Pena, free weekly showcase of Latin folk music and dance featuring the best in local and touring talent; World Music Wednesdays presents the music, dance, and cultures of Africa, Europe, Asia, and the Americas. **Food available** Sandwiches and snacks, $1–$5. **Hours** Monday–Thursday, 9 a.m.–10 p.m.; Friday and Saturday, 9 a.m.–5 p.m. (for concerts, the school closes at 1 a.m.); Sunday, 10 a.m.–5 p.m.

WHO GOES THERE Everyone between age 8 and 88; people who have either attended or taught here include John Prine, Roger McGuinn of the Byrds, Billy Corgan of Smashing Pumpkins, and Jeff Tweedy of Wilco.

WHAT GOES ON The Old Town School of Folk Music services more than 6,000 adult and youth students weekly in classes as eclectic as Bulgarian singing, flamenco-guitar playing, the songs of Bob Dylan, and Hawaiian hula dancing. Nearly 85,000 people attend Old Town School concerts annually. Singer-songwriter Joni Mitchell christened the current Old Town School in the fall of 1998. Other concert regulars include Guy Clark, Mavis Staples, bluegrass great Del McCoury, roots artist Taj Mahal, ironic rocker Robbie Fulks, and Hungarian folk legends Muzsikás. The Old Town School's previous home (909 West Armitage) remains open as the Old Town School of Folk Music's Children's Center. Some adult classes are offered at the old homestead.

SETTING AND ATMOSPHERE The Old Town School of Folk Music was restored from the 43,000-square-foot Hild Library, an Art Deco treasure built in 1929. The acoustically perfect $2-million concert hall is the crown jewel of the center. With 275 seats on the main floor and 150 in the balcony, no audience member is more than 45 feet from the proscenium stage. The $150,000 sound system features 38 speakers that ring throughout the intimate hall. Vintage acoustic instruments are hung on the hall's 14 pillars to absorb sound. The center also includes 31 teaching spaces. The Different Strummer music store sells instruments and rare recordings (instruments are also rented and repaired).

IF YOU GO This can be one of the most rewarding musical experiences in Chicago. During the day, the concert hall transforms into a cafe area where folk-music fans can relax, talk, and hear impromptu concerts by students. The Old Town School of Folk Music began in 1957 as an offshoot of the humanist movement in folk music—a notion of bringing people together under the belief that music belongs to the masses.

Sonotheque

DANCE CLUB AND DRINKING LOUNGE AS ECLECTIC AS THE CITY ITSELF

1444 West Chicago Avenue, Near North Side; ☎ 312-226-7600; www.sonotheque.net

Cover Varies depending on event; see Web site for details. **Minimum** None. **Mixed drinks** $5–$11 (topping off at premium Bourbon). **Wine** $7–$9; selections change seasonally. **Beer** Starts at $3. More than 40 brews available; selections change seasonally. **Dress** No code. **Food available** None, but plenty of restaurants nearby. **Hours** Sunday–Friday, 9 p.m.–2 a.m.; Saturday, 9 p.m.–3 a.m.

WHO GOES THERE Crowd depends on the genre of music—and what a crowd it can be. DJs spin electronica, Brazilian, hip-hop, African, reggae, old-school soul, and more. Live world music, hip-hop, and jazz are booked once or twice a month. But regardless of the music, dancing is the common denominator. No sports TVs at this place.

WHAT GOES ON Club owners include longtime Chicago impresarios Donnie Madia of the acclaimed Avec and Blackbird restaurants (see Part Eight) and Terry Alexander of the Violet Hour saloon. But co-owner Joe Bryl is a creative force, drawing on more than 25 years of spinning acid jazz, Brazilian, punk, rock, and soul at Chicago clubs. The sound system emphasizes tonality rather than the thumping bass of most dance clubs. The in-house sound library guarantees a year's worth of current experimental, vintage, and ethnic tunes before any one track is repeated.

SETTING AND ATMOSPHERE Sonotheque is a boutique dance venue with a modernistic design highlighted by an acoustically fashioned interior to enhance the sound. Cushionlike panels line the walls, creating a sleek European-airport-club atmosphere. Four projectors screen vintage film and videos. Minimal seating is first-come, first-available; free seating is reserved by contacting the club in advance.

IF YOU GO Sonically, be prepared for anything. On a weekend, take a cab—self-parking can be tough. There's a valet on weekends and some street parking early in the night.

Trader Vic's

TINY BUBBLES IN A BIG CITY; QUINTESSENTIAL TIKI EXPERIENCE

1030 North State Street (at Newberry Plaza), Near North Side;
☎ 312-642-6500; www.tradervicschicago.com

Cover None. Minimum None. Mixed drinks Of course; $5–$22 (Mai Tais, $8). Beer $5–$8. Dress Nice casual. Food available The traditional Trader Vic's sure bets are duck and lamb, both prepared in wood (applewood or oak) ovens. Hours Sunday–Thursday, 4 p.m.–midnight, until 2 a.m. Friday and Saturday; Sunday brunch, 10 a.m.–2 p.m.

WHO GOES THERE Chicago tiki aficionados and castaways from the adjacent "Viagra Triangle" on Rush Street (Gibson's, Jilly's, Lux Bar, etc.).

WHAT GOES ON Dining and drinking in a 1960s–70s ambience of bamboo, New Guinea planks, and 700-pound tiki totems. Don't miss the Mai Tai. In 1944, "Trader Vic" Bergeron created the sweet rum drink and served it to a Tahitian customer who had a sip and said, *"Mai tai roa ae"* (Tahitian for "Out of this world"). The Scorpion Bowl ($22.95 for four people) contains rums, fruit juices, and brandy.

SETTING AND ATMOSPHERE Chicago's original Trader Vic's, the first outside of California, closed on New Year's Eve 2005 after a 48-year run in the basement of the downtown Palmer House Hilton. The new incarnation, which opened December 1, 2008, doesn't have the nooks and crannies of the basement location, but a large enclosed atrium with palm trees in the center of the restaurant creates a year-round tropical feel. The 295-seat space is divided into three areas: a long bar with seating for 30, a large dining room adjacent to an open Chinese oven, and a separate private-events area.

IF YOU GO Don't drive for a couple of reasons: It's expensive and tough to park in this neighborhood (there is basement parking at Newberry Plaza); plus, the drinks can pack a punch: a Mai-Tai contains 2.75 ounces of alcohol.

Weeds

CULTURAL ANARCHY FOR A NEW BEAT GENERATION

1555 North Dayton Street, North Side; ☎ 312-943-7815

Cover None. Minimum None. Mixed drinks $3–$6. Wine $4. Beer $2–$4. Dress Grateful Dead–ish. Specials Free shot of tequila if it's late enough; a surreal beer garden in season. **Food available** Bar snacks, chips, peanuts, etc. **Hours** Monday–Friday, 4 p.m.–2 a.m.; Saturday, 4 p.m.–3 a.m.; Sunday, noon–9 p.m.

WHO GOES THERE Lovable riffraff between the ages of 21 and 65, artists and/or slackers, newspaper people, cab drivers, strippers.

WHAT GOES ON Just about anything. Monday is poetry night hosted by Gregorio Gomez, artistic director of the Chicago Latino Theater. Tuesday and Wednesday are "Comfort Nights," which means there are no scheduled activities. Some of the city's top jazz players jam on Thursday nights, featured rock bands play on Friday nights, and Saturday nights are reserved for open stage. Never a cover.

SETTING AND ATMOSPHERE Twisted Bohemian. Old bras and unused condoms hang from the ceiling along with the year-round-Christmas-lights thing. Sabbath candles and incense burn along the bar, and a funky beer garden is utilized in season. The bar gets its name from being at the corner of Dayton and Weed streets.

IF YOU GO Owner-proprietor-poet Sergio Mayora—who once ran for mayor of Chicago—wrote of his bar, "A place with a difference; where what you are or who you are is only as important as where you are." Be prepared to rub shoulders with all walks of life: hell-raisers and hillbillies, chicks and tricks. A once-in-a-lifetime experience.

ACCOMMODATIONS INDEX

RESTAURANT INDEX

Note: Page numbers in **boldface** type indicate restaurant profiles.

SUBJECT INDEX

Unofficial Guide Reader Survey

If you'd like to express your opinion about traveling in Chicago or this guidebook, complete the following survey and mail it to:

> *Unofficial Guide* Reader Survey
> P.O. Box 43673
> Birmingham, AL 35243

Inclusive dates of your visit:_____

Members of your party:

	Person 1	Person 2	Person 3	Person 4	Person 5
Gender:	M F	M F	M F	M F	M F

Age:_____

How many times have you been to Chicago?_____
On your most recent trip, where did you stay?_____

Concerning your accommodations, on a scale of 100 as best and 0 as worst, how would you rate:

The quality of your room? _____ The value of your room? _____
The quietness of your room? _____ Check-in/checkout efficiency? _____
Shuttle service to the airport?_____ Swimming pool facilities? _____

Did you rent a car?_____ From whom?_____

Concerning your rental car, on a scale of 100 as best and 0 as worst, how would you rate:

Pickup-processing efficiency?_____ Return-processing efficiency?___
Condition of the car?____ Cleanliness of the car?____
Airport-shuttle efficiency?_____

Concerning your dining experiences:

Estimate your meals in restaurants per day? _____

Approximately how much did your party spend on meals per day? ____

Favorite restaurants in Chicago: _____
_____

Did you buy this guide before leaving? _____ While on your trip?_____

How did you hear about this guide? (check all that apply)

☐ Loaned or recommended by a friend   ☐ Radio or TV
☐ Newspaper or magazine   ☐ Bookstore salesperson
☐ Just picked it out on my own   ☐ Library
☐ Internet

What other guidebooks did you use on this trip? _____
_____
_____
_____

On a scale of 100 as best and 0 as worst, how would you rate them?
_____
_____
_____

Using the same scale, how would you rate the *Unofficial Guide*(s)?
_____

Are *Unofficial Guides* readily available at bookstores in your area? _____

Have you used other *Unofficial Guides*? _____

Which one(s)? _____
_____
_____

Comments about your Chicago trip or the *Unofficial Guide*(s):
_____
_____
_____
_____
_____
_____
_____
_____
_____
_____
_____
_____
_____
_____
_____
_____
_____
_____